Lecture Notes in Computer Science 2841

Edited by G. Goos, J. Hartmanis, and J. van Leeuwen

T0226293

Springer
Berlin
Heidelberg
New York
Hong Kong
London
Milan
Paris
Tokyo

Carlo Blundo   Cosimo Laneve (Eds.)

Theoretical
Computer Science

8th Italian Conference, ICTCS 2003
Bertinoro, Italy, October 13-15, 2003
Proceedings

 Springer

Series Editors

Gerhard Goos, Karlsruhe University, Germany
Juris Hartmanis, Cornell University, NY, USA
Jan van Leeuwen, Utrecht University, The Netherlands

Volume Editors

Carlo Blundo
Università degli Studi di Salerno
Dipartimento di Informatica ed Applicazioni
Via. S. Allende, 43, 84081 Baronissi (SA), Italy
E-mail: carblu@unisa.it

Cosimo Laneve
Università degli Studi di Bologna
Dipartimento di Scienze dell'Informazione
Mura Anteo Zamboni 7, 40127 Bologna, Italy
E-mail: laneve@cs.unibo.it

Cataloging-in-Publication Data applied for

A catalog record for this book is available from the Library of Congress.

Bibliographic information published by Die Deutsche Bibliothek
Die Deutsche Bibliothek lists this publication in the Deutsche Nationalbibliografie;
detailed bibliographic data is available in the Internet at <http://dnb.ddb.de>.

CR Subject Classification (1998): F, E.1, G.1-2

ISSN 0302-9743
ISBN 3-540-20216-1 Springer-Verlag Berlin Heidelberg New York

Springer-Verlag Berlin Heidelberg New York
a member of BertelsmannSpringer Science+Business Media GmbH

http://www.springer.de

© Springer-Verlag Berlin Heidelberg 2003
Printed in Germany

Typesetting: Camera-ready by author, data conversion by Olgun Computergrafik
Printed on acid-free paper   SPIN: 10958179   06/3142   5 4 3 2 1 0

Preface

The Eighth Italian Conference on Theoretical Computer Science (ICTCS 2003) was held at the University Residential Center of Bertinoro, Italy, on October 13–15 2003. The center is composed of three large historical and monumental buildings not far from one another, forming a united complex on the top of the built up area of the ancient town of Bertinoro.

Previous conferences took place in Pisa (1972), Mantova (1974 and 1989), L'Aquila (1992), Ravello (1995), Prato (1998), and Torino (2001).

The conference aims at bringing together computer scientists, expecially young researchers, to foster cooperation and exchange ideas and results. Its main topics include: analysis and design of algorithms, data types and data structures, theory of logical design and layout, computability, complexity, automata, symbolic and algebraic computation, security, cryptography, specification and verification, formal languages, foundations of functional programming, foundations of logic programming, term-rewriting, semantics, type theory, new computing paradigms, parallel and distributed computation, theory of concurrency, theory of databases, theory of knowledge bases, theory of robotics.

The program committee, consisting of 14 members, considered 65 papers and selected 27 for presentation. These papers were selected on the basis of originality, quality, and relevance to theoretical computer science. These proceedings include the revised versions of the 27 accepted papers and the invited talks by Marios Mavronicolas (*Extreme Nash Equilibria*), Martin Hofmann (*Certification of Memory Usage*), and Gérard Boudol (*On Programming Models for Mobility*).

Paper selection was a difficult and challenging task, and many good submissions had to be rejected. Each submission was refereed by at least three reviewers and some had four reports or more. We are very grateful to all the program committee members, who devoted much effort and valuable time to reading and selecting the papers. In addition, we gratefully acknowledge the help of a large number of colleagues who reviewed submissions in their area of expertise. They are all listed on page VII. We apologize for any inadvertent omissions.

Following the example of ICTCS 2001, we encouraged authors to submit their contributions in electronic format. We handled the submissions with CyberChair (http://www.CyberChair.org) a free Web-based paper submission and reviewing system. With reference to this, we would like to thank Luca Padovani who helped us a lot at various stages of the whole process. His computer skills and the time and effort he invested were crucial ingredients of our ability to run the program committee.

Finally, we would like to thank all the authors that submitted their papers for making this conference possible, the program committee members, as well as all the conference participants.

October 2003

C. Blundo
C. Laneve

ICTCS 2003
October 13–15 2003, Bertinoro, Italy

Program Co-chairs

Carlo Blundo   Università di Salerno, Italy
Cosimo Laneve   Università di Bologna, Italy

General Chair

Roberto Gorrieri   Università di Bologna, Italy

Program Committee

Carlo Blundo   Università di Salerno (Co-chair)
Flavio Corradini   Università dell'Aquila
Mariangiola Dezani   Università di Torino
Raffaele Giancarlo   Università di Palermo
Cosimo Laneve   Università di Bologna (Co-chair)
Stefano Levialdi   Università di Roma
Fabrizio Luccio   Università di Pisa
Maurizio Martelli   Università di Genova
Simone Martini   Università di Bologna
Ugo Montanari   Università di Pisa
Andrea Pietracaprina   Università di Padova
Giovanni Pighizzini   Università di Milano
Roberto Segala   Università di Verona
Nicoletta Sabadini   Università di Milano

Organizing Committee

Andrea Asperti (Chair), Luca Padovani, Claudio Sacerdoti Coen, Lucian Wishick
Università di Bologna

Sponsoring Institutions

The European Association of Theoretical Computer Science (EATCS)
BICI: Bertinoro International Center for Informatics
Department of Computer Science, University of Bologna
Dipartimento di Informatica ed Applicazioni "R. M. Capocelli"
Facoltà di Scienze MM., FF. e NN. dell'Università di Salerno
Microsoft Research

Referees

Alessandro Aldini
Vincenzo Ambriola
Christoph Ambühl
Marcella Anselmo
Andrea Asperti
Paolo Baldan
Martin Berger
Anna Bernasconi
Elisa Bertino
Daniela Besozzi
Claudio Bettini
Gianfranco Bilardi
Chiara Bodei
Paolo Boldi
Diego Bonura
Pierre Boudes
Nadia Busi
Elena Camossi
Daniela Cancila
Felice Cardone
Walter Castelnovo
Barbara Catania
Franco Cazzaniga
Andrea Clementi
Gennaro Costagliola
Stefania Costantini
Rosario Culmone
Ugo Dal Lago
Ferruccio Damiani
Vincent Danos
Clelia De Felice
Pierpaolo Degano
Giuseppe della Penna
Giorgio Delzanno
Roberto De Prisco
Vincenzo Deufemia

Roberto Di Cosmo
Alessandra Di Pierro
Sophia Drossopoulou
Gianluigi Ferrari
Mauro Ferrari
Camillo Fiorentini
Riccardo Focardi
Maurizio Gabbrielli
Vincenzo Gervasi
Giorgio Ghelli
Roberto Gorrieri
Concettina Guerra
Stefano Guerrini
Min-Shiang Hwang
Bengt Jonsson
Dogan Kesdogan
Aggelos Kiayias
Kenji Kono
Lars Kristiansen
Sophie Laplante
Salvatore La Torre
Leonardo Lesmo
Luigi Liquori
Michele Loreti
Roberto Lucchi
Gerald Luettgen
Elena Machkasova
Fabio Mancinelli
Leonardo Mariano
Fabio Martinelli
Viviana Mascardi
Hernan Melgratti
Greg Meredieth
Carlo Mereghetti
Emanuela Merelli
G. Michele Pinna

Marino Miculan
Eugenio Moggi
Angelo Montanari
Karl-Heinz Niggl
Mario Ornaghi
Carles Padro
Elena Pagani
Linda Pagli
Beatrice Palano
Giuseppe Persiano
Alfonso Pierantonio
Lucia Pomello
Giuseppe Prencipe
Geppino Pucci
Gabriele Puppis
D. Romana Cacciagrano
Giuseppe Rosolini
Luca Roversi
Antonino Salibra
Davide Sangiorgi
Vladimir Sazonov
Ivan Scagnetto
Monica Sebillo
Matteo Slanina
Jeremy Sproston
Simone Tini
Paolo Torroni
Emilio Tuosto
Paola Velardi
Rorbert F.C. Walters
Herbert Wiklicky
Lucian Wishick
Gianluigi Zavattaro
Elena Zucca

Table of Contents

Invited Talks

Program Design, Models and Analysis

Algorithms and Complexity

Semantics and Formal Languages

Security and Cryptography

Extreme Nash Equilibria[*]

Martin Gairing[1], Thomas Lücking[1], Marios Mavronicolas[2],
Burkhard Monien[1], and Paul Spirakis[3]

[1] Faculty of Computer Science, Electrical Engineering and Mathematics,
University of Paderborn, Fürstenallee 11, 33102 Paderborn, Germany
{gairing,luck,bm}@uni-paderborn.de
[2] Department of Computer Science, University of Cyprus, 1678 Nicosia, Cyprus
mavronic@ucy.ac.cy
[3] Computer Technology Institute, P. O. Box 1122, 261 10 Patras, Greece, &
Department of Computer Engineering and Informatics, University of Patras,
Rion, 265 00 Patras, Greece
spirakis@cti.gr

Abstract. We study the combinatorial structure and computational
complexity of *extreme* Nash equilibria, ones that maximize or minimize
a certain objective function, in the context of a *selfish routing* game.
Specifically, we assume a collection of n *users,* each employing a *mixed
strategy,* which is a probability distribution over m parallel *links,* to control the routing of its own assigned *traffic.* In a *Nash equilibrium,* each
user routes its traffic on links that minimize its *expected latency cost.*
Our structural results provide substantial evidence for the *Fully Mixed
Nash Equilibrium Conjecture,* which states that the worst Nash equilibrium is the *fully mixed Nash equilibrium,* where each user chooses each
link with positive probability. Specifically, we prove that the Fully Mixed
Nash Equilibrium Conjecture is valid for pure Nash equilibria and that
under a certain condition, the social cost of any Nash equilibrium is
within a factor of $6 + \varepsilon$, of that of the fully mixed Nash equilibrium,
assuming that link *capacities* are identical.
Our complexity results include hardness, approximability and inapproximability ones. Here we show, that for identical link capacities and under
a certain condition, there is a randomized, polynomial-time algorithm to
approximate the worst social cost within a factor arbitrarily close to
$6 + \varepsilon$. Furthermore, we prove that for any arbitrary integer $k > 0$, it is
$\mathcal{NP}$-hard to decide whether or not any given allocation of users to links
can be transformed into a pure Nash equilibrium using at most k selfish
steps. Assuming identical link capacities, we give a polynomial-time approximation scheme (PTAS) to approximate the best social cost over all
pure Nash equilibria. Finally we prove, that it is $\mathcal{NP}$-hard to approximate the worst social cost within a multiplicative factor $2 - \dfrac{2}{m+1} - \varepsilon$.
The quantity $2 - \dfrac{2}{m+1}$ is the tight upper bound on the ratio of the worst
social cost and the optimal cost in the model of identical capacities.

---

[*] This work has been partially supported by the IST Program of the European Union
under contract numbers IST-1999-14186 (ALCOM-FT) and IST-2001-33116 (FLAGS),
by funds from the Joint Program of Scientific and Technological Collaboration between Greece and Cyprus, and by research funds from the University of Cyprus.

C. Blundo and C. Laneve (Eds.): ICTCS 2003, LNCS 2841, pp. 1–20, 2003.
© Springer-Verlag Berlin Heidelberg 2003

1 Introduction

Motivation and Framework. A *Nash equilibrium* [21,22] represents a stable state of the play of a *strategic game,* in which each player holds an accurate opinion about the (expected) behavior of other players and acts rationally. An issue that arises naturally in this context concerns the computational complexity of Nash equilibria of any given strategic game. Due to the ultimate significance of Nash equilibrium as a prime solution concept in contemporary *Game Theory* [23], this issue has become a fundamental algorithmic problem that is being intensively studied in the Theory of Computing community today (see, e.g., [3,6,29]); in fact, it is arguably one of the few, most important algorithmic problems for which no *general* polynomial-time algorithms are known today (cf. [24]).

The problem of computing arbitrary Nash equilibria becomes even more challenging when one considers *extreme* Nash equilibria, ones that maximize or minimize a certain *objective function.* So, understanding the combinatorial structure of extreme Nash equilibria is a necessary prerequisite to either designing efficient algorithms to compute them or establishing corresponding hardness and thereby designing efficient approximation algorithms. In this work, we embark on a systematic study of the combinatorial structure and the computational complexity of extreme Nash equilibria; our study is carried out within the context of a simple *selfish routing* game, originally introduced in a pioneering work by Koutsoupias and Papadimitriou [15], that we describe next.

We assume a collection of n users, each employing a *mixed strategy,* which is a probability distribution over m parallel *links,* to control the shipping of its own assigned *traffic.* For each link, a *capacity* specifies the rate at which the link processes traffic. In a Nash equilibrium, each user selfishly routes its traffic on those links that minimize its *expected latency cost,* given the network congestion caused by the other users. A user's *support* is the set of those links on which it may ship its traffic with non-zero probability. The *social cost* of a Nash equilibrium is the expectation, over all random choices of the users, of the maximum, over all links, *latency* through a link.

Our study distinguishes between *pure* Nash equilibria, where each user chooses exactly one link (with probability one), and *mixed* Nash equilibria, where the choices of each user are modeled by a probability distribution over links. We also distinguish in some cases between models of *identical capacities,* where all link capacities are equal, and of *arbitrary capacities.*

The Fully Mixed Nash Equilibrium Conjecture. In this work, we formulate and study a natural conjecture asserting that the fully mixed Nash equilibrium **F** is the *worst* Nash equilibrium with respect to social cost. Formally, we conjecture:

Conjecture 1 (Fully Mixed Nash Equilibrium Conjecture). For any traffic vector **w** such that the fully mixed Nash equilibrium **F** exists, and for any Nash equilibrium **P**, $\mathsf{SC}\,(\mathbf{w},\mathbf{P}) \leq \mathsf{SC}\,(\mathbf{w},\mathbf{F})$.

Clearly, the Fully Mixed Nash Equilibrium Conjecture is intuitive and natural: the fully mixed Nash equilibrium favors "collisions" between different users (since each user assigns its traffic with positive probability to *every* link); thus, this increased probability of "collisions" favors a corresponding increase to the (expected) maximum total traffic through a link, which is, precisely, the social cost. More importantly, the Fully Mixed Nash Equilibrium Conjecture is also significant since it precisely identifies the *worst* possible Nash equilibrium for the selfish routing game we consider; this will enable designers of Internet protocols not only to avoid choosing the worst-case Nash equilibrium, but also to calculate the worst-case loss to the system at *any* Nash equilibrium due to its deliberate lack of coordination, and to evaluate the Nash equilibrium of choice against the (provably) worst-case one.

Contribution and Significance. Our study provides quite strong evidence in support of the Fully Mixed Nash Equilibrium Conjecture by either establishing or near establishing the conjecture in a number of interesting instances of the problem.

We start with the model of arbitrary capacities, where traffics are allowed to vary arbitrarily. There we prove that the Fully Mixed Nash Equilibrium Conjecture holds for *pure* Nash equilibria. We next turn to the case of identical capacities. Through a delicate probabilistic analysis, we establish that in the special case, that the number of links is equal to the number of users and for a suitable large number of users, the social cost of *any* Nash equilibrium is less than $6 + \varepsilon$ (for any $\varepsilon > 0$) times the social cost of the fully mixed Nash equilibrium. Our proof employs concepts and techniques from *majorization theory* [17] and *stochastic orders* [28], such as comparing two random variables according to their *stochastic variability* (cf. [26, Section 9.5]).

For pure Nash equilibria we show that it is $\mathcal{NP}$-hard to decide whether or not any given allocation of users to links can be transformed into a pure Nash equilibrium using at most k *selfish steps,* even if the number of links is 2. Furthermore, we prove that there exists a polynomial-time approximation scheme (PTAS) to approximate the social cost of the best pure Nash equilibrium to any arbitrary accuracy. The proof involves an algorithm that transforms any pure strategy profile into a pure Nash equilibrium with at most the same social cost, using at most n reassignments of users. We call this technique *Nashification,* and it may apply to other instances of the problem as well.

Still for pure Nash equilibria, we give a tight upper bound on the ratio between $SC(\mathbf{w}, \mathbf{L})$ and $OPT(\mathbf{w})$ for any Nash equilibrium $\mathbf{L}$. Then we show that it is $\mathcal{NP}$-hard to approximate the worst-case Nash equilibrium with a ratio that is better than this upper bound. We close our section about pure Nash equilibria with a pseudopolynomial algorithm for computing the worst-case Nash equilibrium for any fixed number of links.

Related Work and Comparison. The selfish routing game considered in this paper was first introduced by Koutsoupias and Papadimitriou [15] as a vehicle for the study of the price of selfishness for routing over non-cooperative networks, like the Internet. This game was subsequently studied in the work of Mavronicolas and Spirakis [18], where fully mixed Nash equilibria were introduced and analyzed. In both works, the aim had been to quantify the amount of performance loss in routing due to selfish behavior of the users. (Later studies of the selfish routing game from the same point of view, that of performance, include the works by Koutsoupias *et al.* [14], and by Czumaj and Vöcking [2].)

The closest to our work is the one by Fotakis *et al.* [6], which focuses on the combinatorial structure and the computational complexity of Nash equilibria for the selfish routing game we consider. The Fully Mixed Nash Equilibrium Conjecture formulated and systematically studied in this paper has been inspired by two results due to Fotakis *et al.* [6] that confirm or support the conjecture. First, Fotakis *et al.* [6, Theorem 4.2] establish the Fully Mixed Nash Equilibrium Conjecture for the model of identical capacities and assuming that $n = 2$. Second, Fotakis *et al.* [6, Theorem 4.3] establish that, for the model of identical traffics and arbitrary capacities, the social cost of any Nash equilibrium is no more than 49.02 times the social cost of the (generalized) fully mixed Nash equilibrium; Note that Theorem 3 is incomparable to this result, since it assumes identical links and arbitrary traffics.

The routing problem considered in this paper is equivalent to the multiprocessor scheduling problem. Here, pure Nash equilibria and Nashification translate to local optima and sequences of local improvements. A schedule is said to be *jump optimal* if no job on a processor with maximum load can improve by moving to another processor [27].

Obviously, the set of pure Nash equilibria is a subset of the set of jump optimal schedules. Moreover, in the model of identical processors every jump optimal schedule can be transformed into a pure Nash equilibrium without altering the makespan. Thus, for this model the strict upper bound $2 - 2/(m + 1)$ on the ratio between best and worst makespan of jump optimal schedules [5,27] also holds for pure Nash equilibria.

Algorithms for computing a jump optimal schedule from any given schedule have been proposed in [1,5,27]. The fastest algorithm is given by Schuurman and Vredeveld [27]. It always moves the job with maximum weight from a makespan processor to a processor with minimum load, using $O(n)$ moves. However, in all algorithms the resulting jump optimal schedule is not necessarily a Nash equilibrium.

Road Map. The rest of this paper is organized as follows. Section 2 presents some preliminaries. Stochastic orders are treated in Section 3. Pure Nash equilibria are contrasted to the fully mixed Nash equilibrium in Section 4. Worst mixed Nash equilibria are contrasted to the fully mixed Nash equilibrium in Section 5. Sections 6 and 7 consider best and worst pure Nash equilibria, respectively. We conclude, in Section 8, with a discussion of our results and some open problems.

2   Framework

Most of our definitions are patterned after those in [18, Section 2] and [6, Section 2], which, in turn, were based on those in [15, Sections 1 & 2].

Mathematical Preliminaries and Notation. For any integer $m \geq 1$, denote $[m] = \{1, \ldots, m\}$. Denote Γ the *Gamma function*; that is, for any natural number N, $\Gamma(N + 1) = N!$, while for any arbitrary real number $x > 0$, $\Gamma(x) = \int_0^\infty t^{x-1}e^{-t}dt$. The Gamma function is invertible; both Γ and its inverse Γ^{-1} are increasing. It is well known that $\Gamma^{-1}(N) = \frac{\lg N}{\lg \lg N}(1 + o(1))$ (see, e.g., [9]). For our purposes, we shall use the fact that for any pair of an arbitrary real number α and an arbitrary natural number N, $\left(\frac{\alpha}{e}\right)^{\alpha} = N$ if and only if $\alpha = \Gamma^{-1}(N) + \Theta(1)$. For an event E in a sample space, denote $\mathbf{Pr}(E)$ the probability of event E happening.

For a random variable X, denote $\mathcal{E}(X)$ the *expectation* of X. In the *balls-and-bins* problem, m balls are thrown into m bins uniformly at random. (See [13] for a classical introduction to this problem.) It is known that the expected maximum number of balls thrown over a bin equals the quantity $R(m) = \Gamma^{-1}(m) - \frac{3}{2} + o(1)$ [9].

In the paper, we make use of the following Hoeffding inequality:

Theorem 1 ([19], Theorem 2.3.). *Let the random variables* $X_1, X_2, ..., X_n$ *be independent, with* $0 \leq X_k \leq 1$ *for each k and let* $S_n = \sum X_k$. *Then, for any* $\beta > 0$,
$$\mathbf{Pr}(S_n \geq (1+\beta)\mathcal{E}(S_n)) \leq e^{-((1+\beta)\ln(1+\beta)-\beta)\mathcal{E}(S_n)}.$$

Note that Theorem 1 also holds if $0 \leq X_k \leq \kappa$ for some constant $\kappa > 0$.

General. We consider a *network* consisting of a set of m parallel *links* $1, 2, \ldots, m$ from a *source* node to a *destination* node. Each of n *network users* $1, 2, \ldots, n$, or *users* for short, wishes to route a particular amount of traffic along a (non-fixed) link from source to destination. Denote w_i the *traffic* of user $i \in [n]$. Define the $n \times 1$ *traffic vector* $\mathbf{w}$ in the natural way. Assume throughout that $m > 1$ and $n > 1$. Assume also, without loss of generality, that $w_1 \geq w_2 \geq \ldots \geq w_n$. For a traffic vector $\mathbf{w}$, denote $W = \sum_1^n w_i$.

A *pure strategy* for user $i \in [n]$ is some specific link. A *mixed strategy* for user $i \in [n]$ is a probability distribution over pure strategies; thus, a mixed strategy is a probability distribution over the set of links. The *support* of the mixed strategy for user $i \in [n]$, denoted *support*(i), is the set of those pure strategies (links) to which i assigns positive probability.

A *pure strategy profile* is represented by an n-tuple $\langle \ell_1, \ell_2, \ldots, \ell_n \rangle \in [m]^n$; a *mixed strategy profile* is represented by an $n \times m$ *probability matrix* $\mathbf{P}$ of nm probabilities p_i^j, $i \in [n]$ and $j \in [m]$, where p_i^j is the probability that user i chooses link j. For a probability matrix $\mathbf{P}$, define *indicator variables* $I_i^\ell \in \{0, 1\}$, $i \in [n]$ and $\ell \in [m]$, such that $I_i^\ell = 1$ if and only if $p_i^\ell > 0$. Thus, the support of the mixed strategy for user $i \in [n]$ is the set $\{\ell \in [m] \mid I_i^\ell = 1\}$.

For each link $\ell \in [m]$, define the *view* of link ℓ, denoted *view*(ℓ), as the set of users $i \in [n]$ that may assign their traffics to link ℓ; so, *view*$(\ell) = \{i \in [n] \mid I_i^\ell = 1\}$. For each link $\ell \in [m]$, denote $V^\ell = |view(\ell)|$. A mixed strategy profile $\mathbf{P}$ is *fully mixed* [18, Section 2.2] if for all users $i \in [n]$ and links $j \in [m]$, $I_i^j = 1$ [1].

System, Models and Cost Measures. Denote $c^\ell > 0$ the *capacity* of link $\ell \in [m]$, representing the rate at which the link processes traffic. So, the *latency* for traffic w through link ℓ equals w/c^ℓ. In the model of *identical capacities*, all link capacities are equal to 1; link capacities may vary arbitrarily in the model of

---

[1] An earlier treatment of fully mixed strategies in the context of *bimatrix games* has been found in [25], called there *completely mixed strategies*. See also [20] for a subsequent treatment in the context of *strategically zero-sum games*.

arbitrary capacities. For a pure strategy profile $\langle \ell_1, \ell_2, \ldots, \ell_n \rangle$, the *latency cost for user* i, denoted λ_i, is $(\sum_{k:\ell_k=\ell_i} w_k)/c^{\ell_i}$; that is, the latency cost for user i is the latency of the link it chooses. For a mixed strategy profile $\mathbf{P}$, denote δ^ℓ the *actual traffic* on link $\ell \in [m]$; so, δ^ℓ is a random variable for each link $\ell \in [m]$, denote θ^ℓ the *expected traffic* on link $\ell \in [m]$; thus, $\theta^\ell = \mathcal{E}(\delta^\ell) = \sum_{i=1}^n p_i^\ell w_i$. Given $\mathbf{P}$, define the $m \times 1$ *expected traffic vector* $\mathbf{\Theta}$ induced by $\mathbf{P}$ in the natural way. Given $\mathbf{P}$, denote Λ^ℓ the *expected latency* on link $\ell \in [m]$; clearly, $\Lambda^\ell = \frac{\theta^\ell}{c^\ell}$. Define the $m \times 1$ *expected latency vector* $\mathbf{\Lambda}$ in the natural way. For a mixed strategy profile $\mathbf{P}$, the *expected latency cost* for user $i \in [n]$ on link $\ell \in [m]$, denoted λ_i^ℓ, is the expectation, over all random choices of the remaining users, of the latency cost for user i had its traffic been assigned to link ℓ; thus, $\lambda_i^\ell = \frac{w_i + \sum_{k=1, k \neq i} p_k^\ell w_k}{c^\ell} = \frac{(1-p_i^\ell)w_i + \theta^\ell}{c^\ell}$. For each user $i \in [n]$, the *minimum expected latency cost*, denoted λ_i, is the minimum, over all links $\ell \in [m]$, of the expected latency cost for user i on link ℓ; thus, $\lambda_i = \min_{\ell \in [m]} \lambda_i^\ell$. For a probability matrix $\mathbf{P}$, define the $n \times 1$ *minimum expected latency cost vector* λ induced by $\mathbf{P}$ in the natural way.

Associated with a traffic vector $\mathbf{w}$ and a mixed strategy profile $\mathbf{P}$ is the *social cost* [15, Section 2], denoted $\mathsf{SC}(\mathbf{w}, \mathbf{P})$, which is the expectation, over all random choices of the users, of the maximum (over all links) latency of traffic through a link; thus, $\mathsf{SC}(\mathbf{w}, \mathbf{P}) = \sum_{\langle \ell_1, \ell_2, \ldots, \ell_n \rangle \in [m]^n} \left(\prod_{k=1}^n p_k^{\ell_k} \cdot \max_{\ell \in [m]} \frac{\sum_{k:\ell_k=\ell} w_k}{c^\ell} \right)$.

Note that $\mathsf{SC}(\mathbf{w}, \mathbf{P})$ reduces to the maximum latency through a link in the case of pure strategies. On the other hand, the *social optimum* [15, Section 2] associated with a traffic vector $\mathbf{w}$, denoted $\mathsf{OPT}(\mathbf{w})$, is the *least possible* maximum (over all links) latency of traffic through a link; thus, $\mathsf{OPT}(\mathbf{w}) = \min_{\langle \ell_1, \ell_2, \ldots, \ell_n \rangle \in [m]^n} \max_{\ell \in [m]} \frac{\sum_{k:\ell_k=\ell} w_k}{c^\ell}$.

Nash Equilibria. We are interested in a special class of mixed strategies called Nash equilibria [21,22] that we describe below. Say that a user $i \in [n]$ is *satisfied for the probability matrix* $\mathbf{P}$ if for all links $\ell \in [m]$, $\lambda_i^\ell = \lambda_i$ if $I_i^\ell = 1$, and $\lambda_i^\ell > \lambda_i$ if $I_i^\ell = 0$; thus, a satisfied user has no incentive to unilaterally deviate from its mixed strategy. A user $i \in [n]$ is *unsatisfied for the probability matrix* $\mathbf{P}$ if i is not satisfied for the probability matrix $\mathbf{P}$. The probability matrix $\mathbf{P}$ is a *Nash equilibrium* [15, Section 2] if for all users $i \in [n]$ and links $\ell \in [m]$, $\lambda_i^\ell = \lambda_i$ if $I_i^\ell = 1$, and $\lambda_i^\ell > \lambda_i$ if $I_i^\ell = 0$. Thus, each user assigns its traffic with positive probability only on links (possibly more than one of them) for which its expected latency cost is minimized. The *fully mixed Nash equilibrium* [18], denoted $\mathbf{F}$, is a Nash equilibrium that is a fully mixed strategy. Mavronicolas and Spirakis [18, Lemma 15] show that all links are *equiprobable* in a fully mixed Nash equilibrium, which is unique (for the model of identical capacities).

Fix any traffic vector $\mathbf{w}$. The *worst Nash equilibrium* is the Nash equilibrium $\mathbf{P}$ that maximizes $\mathsf{SC}(\mathbf{w}, \mathbf{P})$; the *best Nash equilibrium* is the Nash equilibrium that minimizes $\mathsf{SC}(\mathbf{w}, \mathbf{P})$. The *worst social cost*, denoted $\mathsf{WC}(\mathbf{w})$, is the social cost of the worst Nash equilibrium; correspondingly, the *best social cost*, denoted $\mathsf{BC}(\mathbf{w})$, is the social cost of the best Nash equilibrium.

Fotakis *et al.* [6, Theorem 1] consider starting from any arbitrary pure strategy profile and following a particular sequence of selfish steps, where in a *selfish step*, exactly one unsatisfied user is allowed to change its pure strategy. A selfish step is a *greedy selfish step* if the unsatisfied user chooses its best link. A (greedy) selfish step does not increase the social cost of the initial pure strategy profile. Fotakis *et al.* [6, Theorem 1] show that this sequence of selfish steps eventually converges to a Nash equilibrium, which proves its existence; however, it may take a large number of steps. It follows that if the initial pure strategy profile has minimum social cost, then the resulting (pure) Nash equilibrium will have minimum social cost as well. This implies that there exists a pure Nash equilibrium with minimum social cost. Thus, we have $\mathsf{BC}(\mathbf{w}) = \mathsf{OPT}(\mathbf{w})$.

Algorithmic Problems. We list a few algorithmic problems related to Nash equilibria that will be considered in this work. The definitions are given in the style of Garey and Johnson [8]. A problem instance is a tuple (n, m, w, c) where n is the number of users, m is the number of links, $w = (w_i)$ is a vector of n user traffics and $c = (c^j)$ is a vector of m link capacities.

Π_1: NASH EQUILIBRIUM SUPPORTS
INSTANCE: A problem instance (n, m, w, c).
OUTPUT: Indicator variables $I_i^j \in \{0, 1\}$, where $i \in [n]$ and $j \in [m]$, that support a Nash equilibrium for the system of the users and the links.
Fotakis *et al.* [6, Theorem 2] establish that NASH EQUILIBRIUM SUPPORTS is in $\mathcal{P}$ when restricted to pure equilibria. We continue with two complementary to each other optimization problems (with respect to social cost).

Π_2: BEST NASH EQUILIBRIUM SUPPORTS
INSTANCE: A problem instance (n, m, w, c).
OUTPUT: Indicator variables $I_i^j \in \{0, 1\}$, where $i \in [n]$ and $j \in [m]$, that support the best Nash equilibrium for the system of the users and the links.

Π_3: WORST NASH EQUILIBRIUM SUPPORTS
INSTANCE: A problem instance (n, m, w, c).
OUTPUT: Indicator variables $I_i^j \in \{0, 1\}$, where $i \in [n]$ and $j \in [m]$, that support the worst Nash equilibrium for the system of the users and the links.
Fotakis *et al.* [6, Theorems 3 and 4] establish that both BEST NASH EQUILIBRIUM SUPPORTS and WORST NASH EQUILIBRIUM SUPPORTS are $\mathcal{NP}$-hard. Since both problems can be formulated as an integer program, it follows that they are $\mathcal{NP}$-complete.

Π_4: NASH EQUILIBRIUM SOCIAL COST
INSTANCE: A problem instance (n, m, w, c); a *Nash equilibrium* $\mathbf{P}$ for the system of the users and the links.
OUTPUT: The social cost of the Nash equilibrium $\mathbf{P}$.
Fotakis *et al.* [6, Theorem 8] establish that NASH EQUILIBRIUM SOCIAL COST is #$\mathcal{P}$-complete. Furthermore, Fotakis *et al.* [6, Theorem 9] show that there exists a fully polynomial, randomized approximation scheme for NASH EQUILIBRIUM SOCIAL COST.
The following two problems, inspired by NASH EQUILIBRIUM SOCIAL COST are introduced for the first time in this work.

Π_5: WORST NASH EQUILIBRIUM SOCIAL COST
INSTANCE: A problem instance (n, m, w, c).
OUTPUT: The worst social cost $WSC(\mathbf{w})$.

Π_6: BEST NASH EQUILIBRIUM SOCIAL COST
INSTANCE: A problem instance (n, m, w, c).
OUTPUT: The best social cost $BSC(\mathbf{w})$.

Π_7: k-NASHIFY
INSTANCE: A problem instance (n, m, w, c); a pure strategy profile $\mathbf{L}$ for the system of the users and the links.
QUESTION: Is there a sequence of at most k selfish steps that transform $\mathbf{L}$ to a (pure) Nash equilibrium?
The following problem is a variant of k-NASHIFY in which k is part of the input.

Π_8: NASHIFY
INSTANCE: A problem instance (n, m, w, c); a pure strategy profile $\mathbf{L}$ for the system of the users and the links; an integer $k > 0$.
QUESTION: Is there a sequence of at most k selfish steps that transform $\mathbf{L}$ to a (pure) Nash equilibrium?

In our hardness and completeness proofs, we will employ the following $\mathcal{NP}$-complete problems [12]:

Π_9: BIN PACKING
INSTANCE: A finite set $\mathcal{U}$ of items, a size $s(u) \in \mathbf{N}$ for each $u \in \mathcal{U}$, a positive integer bin capacity B, and a positive integer K.
QUESTION: Is there a partition of $\mathcal{U}$ into disjoint sets $\mathcal{U}_1, \ldots, \mathcal{U}_K$ such that for each set $\mathcal{U}_i$, $1 \leq i \leq K$, $\sum_{u \in \mathcal{U}_i} s(u) \leq B$?

Π_{10}: PARTITION
INSTANCE: A finite set $\mathcal{U}$ and a size $s(u) \in \mathbf{N}$ for each element $u \in \mathcal{U}$.
QUESTION: Is there a subset $\mathcal{U}' \subseteq \mathcal{U}$ such that $\sum_{u \in \mathcal{U}'} s(u) = \sum_{u \in \mathcal{U} \setminus \mathcal{U}'} s(u)$?

We note that BIN PACKING is *strongly $\mathcal{NP}$-complete* [7] [2].

3   Stochastic Order Relations

In this section, we treat stochastic order relations; we establish a certain stochastic order relation for the expected maxima of certain sums of Bernoulli random variables.

Recall that a function $f : \Re \to \Re$ is *convex* if for all numbers λ such that $0 < \lambda < 1$, $f(\lambda x_1 + (1 - \lambda)x_2) \leq \lambda f(x_1) + (1 - \lambda)f(x_2)$. We proceed to describe a stochastic order relation between two random variables.

Definition 1. *For any pair of arbitrary random variables X and Y, say that X is stochastically more variable than Y if for all increasing and convex functions $f : \Re \to \Re$, $\mathcal{E}(f(X)) \geq \mathcal{E}(f(Y))$.*

---

[2] A problem is *strongly $\mathcal{NP}$-complete* if it remains $\mathcal{NP}$-complete even if any instance of length n is restricted to contain integers of size polynomial in n. So, strongly $\mathcal{NP}$-complete problems admit no pseudopolynomial-time algorithms unless $\mathcal{P} = \mathcal{NP}$.

Call *stochastically more variability* the corresponding stochastic order relation on the set of random variables. (See [26, Section 9.5] for a more complete treatment of the notion of stochastically more variable and [17,28] for more on majorization theory and stochastic orders.) The following lemma [26, Proposition 9.5.1] provides an alternative, analytic characterization of stochastically more variability.

Lemma 1. *Consider any pair of non-negative random variables X and $\widehat{X}$. Then, X is stochastically more variable than $\widehat{X}$ if and only if for all numbers $\alpha \geq 0$, $\int_{x=\alpha}^{\infty} \mathbf{Pr}(X > x)dx \geq \int_{x=\alpha}^{\infty} \mathbf{Pr}(\widehat{X} > x)dx$.*

Consider now a setting of the balls-and-bins problem where n balls $1, \ldots, n$ with *traffics* $w_1, \ldots, w_n$ are allocated into m bins $1, \ldots, m$ uniformly at random. So, for each pair of a ball $i \in [n]$ and a link $j \in [m]$, define Bernoulli random variables $Y_i^j = w_i$ with probability $\frac{1}{m}$ and 0 with probability $1 - \frac{1}{m}$, and $\widetilde{Y_i^j} = \frac{W}{n}$ with probability $\frac{1}{m}$ and 0 with probability $1 - \frac{1}{m}$. For each link $j \in [m]$, define the random variables $\delta^j = \sum_{i \in [n]} Y_i^j$ and $\widetilde{\delta^j} = \sum_{i \in [n]} \widetilde{Y_i^j}$; thus, each of δ^j and $\widetilde{\delta^j}$, $j \in [m]$, is a sum of Bernoulli random variables; denote $\theta^j = \mathcal{E}(\delta^j)$ and $\widetilde{\theta^j} = \mathcal{E}(\widetilde{\delta^j})$ the expectations of δ^j and $\widetilde{\delta^j}$, respectively. Note that $\theta^j = \mathcal{E}\left(\sum_{i \in [n]} Y_i^j\right) = \sum_{i \in [n]} \mathcal{E}\left(Y_i^j\right) = \sum_{i \in [n]} \left(w_i \frac{1}{m} + 0\left(1 - \frac{1}{m}\right)\right) = \frac{W}{m}$, while $\widetilde{\theta^j} = \mathcal{E}(\widetilde{\delta^j}) = \mathcal{E}\left(\sum_{i \in [n]} \widetilde{Y_i^j}\right) = \sum_{i \in [n]} \mathcal{E}\left(\widetilde{Y_i^j}\right) = \sum_{i \in [n]} \left(\frac{W}{n} \frac{1}{m} + 0\left(1 - \frac{1}{m}\right)\right) = \frac{W}{m}$. So, $\theta^j = \widetilde{\theta^j}$ for each bin $j \in [m]$.

For two numbers $x, y \in \Re^+$ define $[x - y] = \begin{cases} x - y & : \text{ if } x > y \\ 0 & : \text{ else.} \end{cases}$

We can then show the following preliminary lemma:

Lemma 2. *Let $b_i \in \Re^+$ for $i \in [n]$ and let $d = \frac{1}{n} \sum_{i=1}^{n} b_i$. Then for all $x \geq 0$, $\sum_{i=1}^{n}[b_i - x] \geq n \cdot [d - x]$.*

Proof. Without loss of generality, assume that $b_1 \leq b_2 < \ldots \leq b_n$. The claim is true if $x > d$. If $x \leq b_1$, then $x \leq d$ and $\sum_{i=1}^{n}[b_i - x] = \sum_{i=1}^{n}(b_i - x) = n \cdot (d - x)$. Now let $b_j < x \leq b_{j+1}$ and $d > x$. It follows that $\sum_{i=1}^{n}[b_i - x] = \sum_{i=j+1}^{n}(b_i - x) = \sum_{i=j+1}^{n} b_i - (n - j)x = \sum_{i=j+1}^{n} b_i - n \cdot x + j \cdot x \geq \sum_{i=j+1}^{n} b_i - n \cdot x + \sum_{i=1}^{j} b_i = \sum_{i=1}^{n} b_i - n \cdot x = n \cdot (d - x)$ □

We finally prove:

Lemma 3 (Stochastically More Variability Lemma). *For any traffic vector $\mathbf{w}$, $\max\left\{\delta^1, \ldots, \delta^m\right\}$ is stochastically more variable than $\max\left\{\widetilde{\delta^1}, \ldots, \widetilde{\delta^m}\right\}$.*

Proof. Define the discrete random variables $X = \max\{\delta^1, \ldots, \delta^m\}$ and $\widetilde{X} = \max\{\widetilde{\delta^1}, \ldots, \widetilde{\delta^m}\}$. By Lemma 1, it suffices to show that $\int_{x=\alpha}^{\infty} \mathbf{Pr}(X > x)\, dx \geq \int_{x=\alpha}^{\infty} \mathbf{Pr}\left(\widetilde{X} > x\right)\, dx$ for all $\alpha \geq 0$. Let S_k be the collection of all pure strategy profiles, where the maximum number of traffics on any link $j \in [m]$ is exactly k. If $i \neq j$, then $S_i \cap S_j = \emptyset$. Furthermore $\bigcup_{i=\lceil \frac{n}{m} \rceil}^{n} S_i = [m]^n$. For any pure strategy profile $L \in S_k$, define $\mathrm{Link}(L)$ to be the smallest index of a link, holding k traffics. Furthermore, for any pure strategy profile L, let $I(L)$ be the collection of users that are assigned to $\mathrm{Link}(L)$. Every set of k traffics is equal to some $I(L), L \in S_k$ with the same probability, say p_k. Define the actual traffic on $\mathrm{Link}(L)$ as $b(L) = \sum_{i \in I(L)} w_i$. If all traffics are identical the actual traffic on $\mathrm{Link}(L)$ for a pure strategy profile $L \in S_k$ is simply $\widetilde{b}(L) = k \cdot \frac{W}{n}$.

Every pure strategy profile $L \in [m]^n$ occurs with the same probability $\frac{1}{m^n}$ and defines together with $b(L)$ a discrete random variable Z. Z is a discrete random variable that can take every possible value $b(L), L \in [m]^n$.

It is easy to see, that X is stochastically more variable than Z, since for any pure strategy profile L, Z refers to the actual traffic on $\mathrm{Link}(L)$, whereas X refers to the maximum actual traffic over all links. We will complete our proof by showing, that Z is stochastically more variable than $\widetilde{X}$. Since Z and $\widetilde{X}$ are discrete random variables $\int_{x=\alpha}^{\infty} \mathbf{Pr}(Z > x)dx = \sum_{k=\lceil \frac{n}{m} \rceil}^{n} (p_k \cdot A_k)$, where $A_k = \sum_{L \in S_k} [b(L) - \alpha]$ and $\int_{x=\alpha}^{\infty} \mathbf{Pr}(\widetilde{X} > x)dx = \sum_{k=\lceil \frac{n}{m} \rceil}^{n} \left(p_k \cdot \widetilde{A_k} \right)$, where $\widetilde{A_k} = |S_k| \cdot [k \cdot \frac{W}{n} - \alpha]$ Since for a fixed k each traffic contributes with the same probability to $b(L)$, $\sum_{L \in S_k} b(L) = |S_k| \cdot k \cdot \frac{W}{n}$. It follows from Lemma 2 that $A_k \geq \widetilde{A_k}$ for each k. Therefore Z is stochastically more variable than $\widetilde{X}$, which completes the proof of the lemma. □

By definition of stochastically more variability, Lemma 3 implies:

Corollary 1. *For any traffic vector* **w**,
$$\mathcal{E}\left(\max\left\{\delta^1, \ldots, \delta^m\right\}\right) \geq \mathcal{E}\left(\max\left\{\widetilde{\delta^1}, \ldots, \widetilde{\delta^m}\right\}\right).$$

In the balls-and-bins game in which m balls are thrown uniformly at random into m bins, Corollary 1 shows that, if the sum of the ball weights is the same, the expected maximum load over all bins is larger when the balls have different weights in comparison to all balls having the same weight.

4   Pure versus Fully Mixed Nash Equilibria

In this section, we establish the Fully Mixed Nash Equilibrium Conjecture for the case of pure Nash equilibria. This result holds also for the model of arbitrary capacities. We start by proving:

Lemma 4. *Fix any traffic vector* **w**, *mixed Nash equilibrium* **P** *and user i. Then,* $\lambda_i (\mathbf{w}, \mathbf{P}) \leq \lambda_i (\mathbf{w}, \mathbf{F})$.

Proof. Let $\mathbf{P} = \left(p_k^j\right), \mathbf{F} = \left(f_k^j\right)$ for $k \in [n]$ and $j \in [m]$. We can then state, that
$$\sum_{j \in [m]} \left(\sum_{k \in [n], k \neq i} p_k^j w_k\right) = \sum_{k \in [n], k \neq i} w_k \left(\sum_{j \in [m]} p_k^j\right) = \sum_{k \in [n], k \neq i} w_k \text{ , and}$$
$$\sum_{j \in [m]} \left(\sum_{k \in [n], k \neq i} f_k^j w_k\right) = \sum_{k \in [n], k \neq i} w_k \left(\sum_{j \in [m]} f_k^j\right) = \sum_{k \in [n], k \neq i} w_k. \text{ It}$$

follows that $\sum_{j\in[m]}\left(\sum_{k\in[n],k\neq i}p_k^j w_k\right) = \sum_{j\in[m]}\left(\sum_{k\in[n],k\neq i}f_k^j w_k\right)$. Therefore there exists some link $j_0 \in [m]$ such that $\sum_{k\in[n],k\neq i}p_k^{j_0} w_k \leq \sum_{k\in[n],k\neq i}f_k^{j_0} w_k$. Then, $\lambda_i(\mathbf{w},\mathbf{P}) \leq \lambda_i^{j_0}(\mathbf{w},\mathbf{P})$ (since λ_i is the minimum of all $\lambda_i^j, j \in [n])$ = $\frac{w_i+\sum_{k\in[n],k\neq i}p_k^{j_0} w_k}{c^{j_0}} \leq \frac{w_i+\sum_{k\in[n],k\neq i}f_k^{j_0} w_k}{c^{j_0}} = \lambda_i^{j_0}(\mathbf{w},\mathbf{F}) = \lambda_i(\mathbf{w},\mathbf{F})$ (since $f_i^{j_0} > 0$ and $\mathbf{F}$ is a Nash equilibrium). $\square$

We now prove:

Theorem 2. *Fix any traffic vector* $\mathbf{w}$ *and pure Nash equilibrium* $\mathbf{L}$. *Then,* $\mathsf{SC}(\mathbf{w},\mathbf{L}) \leq \mathsf{SC}(\mathbf{w},\mathbf{F})$.

Proof. For each user $i \in [n], \lambda_i(\mathbf{w},\mathbf{P})$ is the minimum, over all links $j \in [m]$, of the expected latency cost for user i on link j, and $\mathsf{SC}(\mathbf{w},\mathbf{P})$ is the expectation of the maximum (over all links) latency of traffic through a link. This implies that $\lambda_i(\mathbf{w},\mathbf{P}) \leq \mathsf{SC}(\mathbf{w},\mathbf{P})$ for every mixed Nash equilibrium $\mathbf{P}$. Hence, by Lemma 4: $\lambda_i(\mathbf{w},\mathbf{P}) \leq \lambda_i(\mathbf{w},\mathbf{F}) \leq \mathsf{SC}(\mathbf{w},\mathbf{F})$ The claim follows now since $\mathsf{SC}(\mathbf{w},\mathbf{L}) = \max_{i\in[n]}\lambda_i(\mathbf{w},\mathbf{L})$ holds for every pure Nash equilibrium $\mathbf{L}$. $\square$

5 Worst Mixed Nash Equilibria

In this section we show that if $n = m$ and m is suitable large then the social cost of any Nash equilibrium is at most $6 + \varepsilon$ times the social cost of the fully mixed Nash equilibrium.

Theorem 3. *Consider the model of identical capacities. Let* $n = m$, m *suitable large. Then, for any traffic vector* $\mathbf{w}$ *and Nash equilibrium* $\mathbf{P}$, $\mathsf{SC}(\mathbf{w},\mathbf{P}) < (6 + \varepsilon)\mathsf{SC}(\mathbf{w},\mathbf{F})$, *for any* $\varepsilon > 0$.

Proof. Fix any traffic vector $\mathbf{w}$ and Nash equilibrium $\mathbf{P}$. We start by showing a simple technical fact.

Lemma 5. *Fix any pair of a link* $\ell \in [m]$ *and a user* $i \in view(\ell)$. *Then,* $p_i^\ell w_i \geq \theta^\ell - \frac{W}{m}$.

Proof. Clearly, $\sum_{j\in[m]}\theta^j = \sum_{j\in[m]}\left(\sum_{i\in[n]}p_i^j w_i\right) = \sum_{i\in[n]}\left(\sum_{j\in[m]}p_i^j w_i\right) = \sum_{i\in[n]}\left(w_i\sum_{j\in[m]}p_i^j\right) = W$. This implies that there exists some link $\ell' \in [m]$ such that $\theta^{\ell'} \leq \frac{W}{m}$. Note that by definition of social cost, $\lambda_i^{\ell'} = (1 - p_i)w_i + \theta^{\ell'}$. It follows that $\lambda_i^{\ell'} \leq w_i + \frac{W}{m}$. On the other hand, $\lambda_i^\ell = (1 - p_i^\ell)w_i + \theta^\ell$.

Since $i \in view(\ell)$, we have, by definition of Nash equilibria, that $\lambda_i^\ell \leq \lambda_i^{\ell'}$ (with equality holding when $i \in view(\ell'))$. It follows that $(1-p_i^\ell)w_i+\theta^\ell \leq w_i+\frac{W}{m}$, or that $p_i^\ell w_i \geq \theta^\ell - \frac{W}{m}$, as needed. $\square$

As an immediate consequence of Lemma 5, we obtain:

Corollary 2. *Fix any link* $\ell \in [m]$. *Then,* $\theta^\ell \leq \frac{V^\ell}{V^\ell-1}\frac{W}{m}$.

Proof. Clearly, by Lemma 5 it follows, $\theta^\ell = \sum_{i\in[n]} p_i^\ell w_i = \sum_{i\in view(\ell)} p_i^\ell w_i \geq \sum_{i\in view(\ell)} \left(\theta^\ell - \frac{W}{m}\right) = V^\ell \left(\theta^\ell - \frac{W}{m}\right)$, or $\theta^\ell \leq \frac{V^\ell}{V^\ell-1}\frac{W}{m}$, as needed. $\qquad\square$

Since $V^\ell \geq 2$, $\frac{V^\ell}{V^\ell-1} \leq 2$. Thus, by Corollary 2:

Lemma 6. *Fix any link* $\ell \in [m]$ *with* $V^\ell \geq 2$. *Then,* $\theta^\ell \leq 2\frac{W}{m}$.

We now prove a complementary lemma. Fix any link $\ell \in [m]$ with $V^\ell = 1$. Let $view(l) = \{i\}$. Then $\theta^l = w_i \leq \max_i w_i \leq \mathsf{OPT}(\mathbf{w}) \leq \mathsf{SC}(\mathbf{w},\mathbf{F})$. Thus:

Lemma 7. *Fix any link* $\ell \in [m]$ *with* $V^\ell = 1$. *Then,* $\theta^\ell \leq \mathsf{SC}(\mathbf{w},\mathbf{F})$.

Use $\mathbf{w}$ to define the vector $\widetilde{\mathbf{w}}$ with all entries equal to $\frac{W}{n}$. By definition of social cost, $\mathsf{SC}(\widetilde{\mathbf{w}},\mathbf{F})$ is the load $\frac{W}{m}$ of each ball times the expected maximum number of balls thrown uniformly at random into m bins. Since $n = m$, we can state $\mathsf{SC}(\widetilde{\mathbf{w}},\mathbf{F}) = R(m) \cdot \frac{W}{m}$, or $\frac{W}{m} = \frac{\mathsf{SC}(\widetilde{\mathbf{w}},\mathbf{F})}{R(m)}$. Fix now any link $j \in [n]$ with $V^j \geq 2$. Then, $\theta^j \leq 2\frac{W}{m}$ (by Lemma 6) $= \frac{2}{R(m)}\mathsf{SC}(\widetilde{\mathbf{w}},\mathbf{F}) \leq \frac{2}{R(m)}\mathsf{SC}(\mathbf{w},\mathbf{F})$ (by Corollary 1).

Thus, for any constant $\varepsilon > 0$, $\mathbf{Pr}\left(\delta^j > 4(1+\varepsilon)\mathsf{SC}(\mathbf{w},\mathbf{F})\right)$
$\leq \mathbf{Pr}\left(\delta^j > 4(1+\varepsilon)\frac{R(m)}{2}\theta^j\right)$ (since $\theta^j \leq \frac{2}{R(m)}\mathsf{SC}(\mathbf{w},\mathbf{F})$)
$= \mathbf{Pr}\left(\delta^j > 2(1+\varepsilon)R(m)\theta^j\right) = \mathbf{Pr}\left(\delta^j > 2(1+\varepsilon)R(m)\mathcal{E}(\delta^j)\right)$.

¿From Theorem 1 it follows that for any $\beta > 0$, $\mathbf{Pr}\left(\delta^j \geq (1+\beta)\mathcal{E}(\delta^j)\right) \leq$
$e^{-((1+\beta)ln(1+\beta)-\beta)\mathcal{E}(\delta^j)} = \frac{e^{\beta\mathcal{E}(\delta^j)}}{(1+\beta)^{(1+\beta)\mathcal{E}(\delta^j)}} < \left(\frac{e}{1+\beta}\right)^{(1+\beta)\mathcal{E}(\delta^j)}$.

With $(1+\beta) = 2(1+\varepsilon)R(m)$ we get:
$$\mathbf{Pr}\left(\delta^j > 4(1+\varepsilon)\mathsf{SC}(\mathbf{w},\mathbf{F})\right) < \left(\frac{e}{2(1+\varepsilon)R(m)}\right)^{2(1+\varepsilon)R(m)\mathcal{E}(\delta^j)}.$$

Note that by definition of $R(m)$, $\frac{e}{2(1+\varepsilon)R(m)} < \frac{e}{2R(m)} = \frac{e}{2(\Gamma^{-1}(m)-\frac{3}{2}+o(1))} < \frac{e}{2\Gamma^{-1}(m)-3}$. Thus, $\frac{e}{2\Gamma^{-1}(m)-3} < 1$ if and only if $\Gamma^{-1}(m) > \frac{e+3}{2}$, which holds for all integers $m \geq 3$.

Thus, for all such integers $\frac{e}{2(1+\varepsilon)R(m)} < 1$ and $\left(\frac{e}{2(1+\varepsilon)R(m)}\right)^{2(1+\varepsilon)R(m)} < 1$ as well. Hence, $\left(\frac{e}{2(1+\varepsilon)R(m)}\right)^{2(1+\varepsilon)R(m)\mathcal{E}(\delta^j)} < \left(\frac{e}{2(1+\varepsilon)R(m)}\right)^{2(1+\varepsilon)R(m)}$. It follows that $\mathbf{Pr}\left(\delta^j > 4(1+\varepsilon)\mathsf{SC}(\mathbf{w},\mathbf{F})\right) < \left(\frac{e}{2(1+\varepsilon)R(m)}\right)^{2(1+\varepsilon)R(m)}$. Note, however, that $\left(\frac{e}{2(1+\varepsilon)R(m)}\right)^{2(1+\varepsilon)R(m)} = \left(\frac{1}{2}\right)^{2(1+\varepsilon)R(m)} \cdot \left(\left(\frac{e}{(1+\varepsilon)R(m)}\right)^{(1+\varepsilon)R(m)}\right)^2 < \left(\left(\frac{e}{(1+\varepsilon)R(m)}\right)^{(1+\varepsilon)R(m)}\right)^2$, since $\left(\frac{1}{2}\right)^{2(1+\varepsilon)R(m)} < 1$. Define now $\alpha > 0$ so that $\left(\frac{\alpha}{e}\right)^\alpha = m$. Then, clearly, $\alpha = \Gamma^{-1}(m) + \Theta(1)$. Note that $(1+\varepsilon)R(m) = (1+\varepsilon)\Gamma^{-1}(m) - (1+\varepsilon)\frac{3}{2} + o(1) = (1+\varepsilon)\Gamma^{-1}(m) + \Theta(1) > \alpha$, for suitable large m, since $\varepsilon > 0$. Since $\left(\frac{x}{e}\right)^x$ is an increasing function of x, this implies that

$$\left(\frac{(1+\varepsilon)R(m)}{e}\right)^{(1+\varepsilon)R(m)} > \left(\frac{\alpha}{e}\right)^{\alpha} = m. \text{ Thus } \left(\left(\frac{e}{(1+\varepsilon)R(m)}\right)^{(1+\varepsilon)R(m)}\right)^2 < \frac{1}{m^2}. \text{ It}$$

follows that $\mathbf{Pr}\left(\delta^j > 4(1+\varepsilon)\,\mathsf{SC}\,(\mathbf{w},\mathbf{F})\right) < \frac{1}{m^2}$. Hence

$\mathbf{Pr}\left(\max_{\ell\in[m]\ |\ |V^\ell|\geq 2}\delta^\ell > 4(1+\varepsilon)\mathsf{SC}\,(\mathbf{w},\mathbf{F})\right) =$

$\mathbf{Pr}\left(\bigvee_{\ell\in[m]\ |\ |V^\ell|\geq 2}\delta^\ell > 4(1+\varepsilon)\mathsf{SC}\,(\mathbf{w},\mathbf{F})\right) \leq$

$\sum_{\ell\in[m]\ |\ |V^\ell|\geq 2}\mathbf{Pr}\left(\delta^\ell > 4(1+\varepsilon)\mathsf{SC}\,(\mathbf{w},\mathbf{F})\right) < \sum_{\ell\in[m]\ |\ |V^\ell|\geq 2}\frac{1}{m^2} \leq m\cdot\frac{1}{m^2} =$
$\frac{1}{m}$. Now, clearly, $\max_{\ell\in[m]}\delta^\ell = \max\left\{\max_{\ell\in[m]\ |\ |V^\ell|\geq 2}\delta^\ell, \max_{\ell\in[m]\ |\ |V^\ell|=1}\delta^\ell\right\} \leq$
$\max_{\ell\in[m]\ |\ |V^\ell|\geq 2}\delta^\ell + \max_{\ell\in[m]\ |\ |V^\ell|=1}\delta^\ell \leq \max_{\ell\in[m]\ |\ |V^\ell|\geq 2}\delta^\ell + \max_{i\in[n]}w_i \leq$
$\max_{\ell\in[m]\ |\ |V^\ell|\geq 2}\delta^j + \mathsf{OPT}(\mathbf{w})$, so that

$\mathcal{E}\left(\max_{\ell\in[m]}\delta^\ell\right) \leq \mathcal{E}\left(\max_{\ell\in[m]\ |\ |V^\ell|\geq 2}\delta^j + \mathsf{OPT}(\mathbf{w})\right)$
$= \mathcal{E}\left(\max_{\ell\in[m]\ |\ |V^\ell|\geq 2}\delta^j\right) + \mathsf{OPT}(\mathbf{w})$. Note, however, that

$\mathcal{E}\left(\max_{\ell\in[m]\ |\ |V^\ell|=1}\delta^j\right) = \sum_{0\leq\delta\leq W}\delta\,\mathbf{Pr}\left(\max_{\ell\in[m]\ ||V^\ell|\geq 2}\delta^\ell = \delta\right)$
$= \sum_{0\leq\delta\leq 4(1+\varepsilon)\mathsf{SC}(\mathbf{w},\mathbf{F})}\delta\,\mathbf{Pr}\left(\max_{\ell\in[m]\ ||V^\ell|\geq 2}\delta^\ell = \delta\right)$
$+ \sum_{4(1+\varepsilon)\mathsf{SC}(\mathbf{w},\mathbf{F})<\delta\leq W}\delta\,\mathbf{Pr}\left(\max_{\ell\in[m]\ ||V^\ell|\geq 2}\delta^\ell = \delta\right)$
$\leq \sum_{0\leq\delta\leq 4(1+\varepsilon)\mathsf{SC}(\mathbf{w},\mathbf{F})}4(1+\varepsilon)\mathsf{SC}\,(\mathbf{w},\mathbf{F})\,\mathbf{Pr}\left(\max_{\ell\in[m]\ ||V^\ell|\geq 2}\delta^\ell = \delta\right)$
$+ \sum_{4(1+\varepsilon)\mathsf{SC}(\mathbf{w},\mathbf{F})<\delta\leq W}W\,\mathbf{Pr}\left(\max_{\ell\in[m]\ ||V^\ell|\geq 2}\delta^\ell = \delta\right)$
$= 4(1+\varepsilon)\mathsf{SC}\,(\mathbf{w},\mathbf{F})\sum_{0\leq\delta\leq 4(1+\varepsilon)\mathsf{SC}(\mathbf{w},\mathbf{F})}\mathbf{Pr}\left(\max_{\ell\in[m]\ ||V^\ell|\geq 2}\delta^\ell = \delta\right)$
$+ W\sum_{4(1+\varepsilon)\mathsf{SC}(\mathbf{w},\mathbf{F})<\delta\leq W}\mathbf{Pr}\left(\max_{\ell\in[m]\ ||V^\ell|\geq 2}\delta^\ell = \delta\right)$
$= 4(1+\varepsilon)\mathsf{SC}\,(\mathbf{w},\mathbf{F})\,\mathbf{Pr}\left(\max_{\ell\in[m]\ ||V^\ell|\geq 2}\delta^\ell \leq 4(1+\varepsilon)\mathsf{SC}\,(\mathbf{w},\mathbf{F})\right)$
$+ W\mathbf{Pr}\left(\max_{\ell\in[m]\ ||V^\ell|\geq 2}\delta^\ell > 4(1+\varepsilon)\mathsf{SC}\,(\mathbf{w},\mathbf{F})\right)$
$< 4(1+\varepsilon)\mathsf{SC}\,(\mathbf{w},\mathbf{F})\cdot 1 + W\cdot\frac{1}{m}$
(since $\mathbf{Pr}\left(\max_{\ell\in[m]\ |\ |V^\ell|\geq 2}\delta^\ell > 4(1+\varepsilon)\mathsf{SC}\,(\mathbf{w},\mathbf{F})\right) < \frac{1}{m}$). Hence,
$\mathsf{SC}\,(\mathbf{w},\mathbf{P}) = \mathcal{E}\left(\max_{\ell\in[m]}\delta^\ell\right) \leq \mathcal{E}\left(\max_{\ell\in[m]\ |\ |V^\ell|=1}\delta^j\right) + \mathsf{OPT}(\mathbf{w}) \leq 4(1+\varepsilon)\mathsf{SC}\,(\mathbf{w},\mathbf{F})+\frac{W}{m}+\mathsf{OPT}(\mathbf{w}) \leq 4(1+\varepsilon)\mathsf{SC}\,(\mathbf{w},\mathbf{F})+2\,\mathsf{OPT}(\mathbf{w}) \leq 4(1+\varepsilon)\mathsf{SC}\,(\mathbf{w},\mathbf{F})+$
$2\mathsf{SC}\,(\mathbf{w},\mathbf{F}) = (6 + \epsilon)\mathsf{SC}\,(\mathbf{w},\mathbf{F})$, for any ϵ, where $0 < \epsilon < 1$, as needed.   □

Recall that there is a randomized, polynomial-time approximation scheme (RPTAS) to approximate the social cost of any Nash equilibrium (in particular, the fully mixed) within any arbitrary $\varepsilon > 0$ [6, Theorem 9]. Thus, since, by Theorem 3, the worst social cost is bounded by $6 + \varepsilon$ times the social cost of the fully mixed Nash equilibrium, this yields:

Theorem 4. *Consider the model of identical capacities. Let $n = m$, m suitable large. Then, there exists a randomized, polynomial-time algorithm with approximation factor $6 + \varepsilon$, for any $\varepsilon > 0$, for* WORST NASH EQUILIBRIUM SOCIAL COST.

We significantly improve Theorem 3 under a certain assumption on the traffics.

Theorem 5. *Consider any traffic vector $\mathbf{w}$ such that $w_1 \geq w_2+\ldots+w_n$. Then, for any Nash equilibrium $\mathbf{P}$, $\mathsf{SC}\,(\mathbf{w},\mathbf{P}) \leq \mathsf{SC}\,(\mathbf{w},\mathbf{F})$.*

Proof. Since $w_1 \geq w_2 + \ldots + w_n$, it follows that the link with maximum latency has user 1 assigned to it in any pure strategy profile. Thus, in particular, $\mathsf{SC}\,(\mathbf{w},\mathbf{P}) = \lambda_1\,(\mathbf{w},\mathbf{P})$ and $\mathsf{SC}\,(\mathbf{w},\mathbf{F}) = \lambda_1\,(\mathbf{w},\mathbf{F})$. By Lemma 4, $\lambda_1\,(\mathbf{w},\mathbf{P}) \leq \lambda_1\,(\mathbf{w},\mathbf{F})$. It follows that $\mathsf{SC}\,(\mathbf{w},\mathbf{P}) \leq \mathsf{SC}\,(\mathbf{w},\mathbf{F})$, as needed.   □

6   Best Pure Nash Equilibria and Nashification

We start by establishing $\mathcal{NP}$-hardness for NASHIFY:

Theorem 6. NASHIFY *is $\mathcal{NP}$-hard, even if $m = 2$.*

Proof. By reduction from PARTITION. Consider any arbitrary instance of PARTITION consisting of a set A of k items $a_1, \ldots, a_k$ with sizes $s(a_1), \ldots, s(a_k) \in \mathbf{N}$, for any integer k. Construct from it an instance of NASHIFY as follows: Set $n = 3k$ and $m = 2$. Set $w_i = s(a_i)$ for $1 \le i \le k$, and $w_i = \frac{1}{2k}$ for $k+1 \le i \le 3k$. Take the pure strategy profile that assigns users $1, 2, \ldots, 2k$ to link 1 and users $2k + 1, \ldots, 3k$ to link 2.

We establish that this yields a reduction from PARTITION to NASHIFY. Assume first that the instance of PARTITION is positive; that is, there exists a subset $A' \subseteq A$ such that $\sum_{a \in A'} s(a) = \sum_{a \in A \setminus A'} s(a)$. Since either $|A'| \le \frac{k}{2}$ or $|A \setminus A'| \le \frac{k}{2}$, assume, without loss of generality, that $|A'| \le \frac{k}{2}$. Note that each user assigned to link 1 is unsatisfied in the constructed pure strategy profile since its latency cost on link 1 is $\sum_{a \in A} s(a) + k \cdot \frac{1}{2k} = \sum_{a \in A} s(a) + \frac{1}{2}$, while its latency cost on link 2 is $k \cdot \frac{1}{2k} = \frac{1}{2}$, which is less. Thus, each step that transfers an unsatisfied user that corresponds to an element $a \in A'$ from link 1 to link 2 is a selfish step, and the sequence of steps that transfer all users that correspond to elements of A' from link 1 to link 2 is a sequence of at most $\frac{k}{2} < k$ steps. As a result of this sequence of selfish steps, the latency of link 1 will be $\sum_{a \in A \setminus A'} s(a) + \frac{1}{2}$, while the latency of link 2 will be $\sum_{a \in A'} s(a) + \frac{1}{2}$. Since $\sum_{a \in A'} s(a) = \sum_{a \in A \setminus A'} s(a)$, these two latencies are equal and the resulting pure strategy profile is therefore a Nash equilibrium which implies that NASHIFY is positive.

Assume now that the instance of NASHIFY is positive; that is, there exists a sequence of at most k selfish steps that transforms the pure strategy profile in the constructed instance of NASHIFY to a Nash equilibrium. Assume that in the resulting pure strategy profile users corresponding to a subset $A' \subseteq A$ remain in link 1, users corresponding to the subset $A \setminus A' \subseteq A$ are transfered to link 2, while the sums of traffics of users with traffic $\frac{1}{2k}$ that reside in link 1 and link 2 are x and $1 - x$, respectively; thus, the latencies of links 1 and 2 are $\sum_{a \in A'} s(a) + x$ and $\sum_{a \in A \setminus A'} s(a) + 1 - x$, respectively. We consider two cases:

Assume first that $A' = A$. Then after at most k selfish steps the latency on link 2 is at most 1 whereas the latency on link 1 is at least $\sum_{a \in A} s(a) \ge k$. So there exists an unsatisfied user $a \in A$, a contradiction to the fact that NASHIFY is positive. So let $A' \ne A$. We show that this implies $\sum_{a \in A'} s(a) - \sum_{a \in A \setminus A'} s(a) = 0$. Assume $|\sum_{a \in A'} s(a) - \sum_{a \in A \setminus A'} s(a)| \ne 0$. Since the traffics of users in A are integer, this implies $|\sum_{a \in A'} s(a) - \sum_{a \in A \setminus A'} s(a)| \ge 1$. The fact that $A' \ne A$ shows that at least one user with large traffic was transformed to link 2. So we can make at most $k - 1$ selfish steps with the small traffics. However, transforming $k - 1$ small traffics to the link with smaller latency leaves one user with small traffic unsatisfied, a contradiction to the fact that NASHIFY is positive. So $|\sum_{a \in A'} s(a) - \sum_{a \in A \setminus A'} s(a)| = 0$ which implies that PARTITION is positive.   □

Algorithm $A_{nashify}$**:**

INPUT: A pure strategy profile **L** of n users with traffics $w_1, \ldots, w_n$.

OUTPUT: A pure strategy profile **L**$'$ that is a Nash equilibrium.

– Sort the user traffics in non-increasing order so that $w_1 \geq \ldots \geq w_n$.
– For each user $i := 1$ to n, **do**
    • remove user i from the link it is currently assigned;
    • find the link ℓ with the minimum latency;
    • reassign user i to the link ℓ.
od
– **Return** the resulting pure strategy profile **L**$'$.

Fig. 1. The algorithm $A_{nashify}$

We remark that NASHIFY is $\mathcal{NP}$-complete in the strong sense (cf. [8, Section 4.2]) if m is part of the input. Thus, there is no pseudopolynomial-time algorithm for NASHIFY (unless $\mathcal{P} = \mathcal{NP}$). In contrast, there is a natural pseudopolynomial-time algorithm $A_{k-nashify}$ for k-NASHIFY, which exhaustively searches all sequences of k selfish steps; since a selfish step involves a (unsatisfied) user and a link for a total of mn choices, the running time of $A_{k-nashify}$ is $\Theta((mn)^k)$. We continue to present an algorithm $A_{nashify}$ that solves NASHIFY when n selfish steps are allowed.

The algorithm $A_{nashify}$ sorts the user traffics in non-increasing order so that $w_1 \geq \ldots \geq w_n$. Then for each user $i := 1$ to n, it removes user i from the link it is currently assigned, it finds the link ℓ with the minimum latency, and it reassigns user i to the link ℓ. We prove:

Lemma 8. *A greedy selfish step of an unsatisfied user i with traffic w_i makes no user k with traffic $w_k \geq w_i$ unsatisfied.*

Proof. Let $\mathbf{L} = \langle l_1, \ldots, l_n \rangle$ be a pure strategy profile. Furthermore, let $p = l_i$, and let q be the link with minimum latency. Denote λ^j and $\widehat{\lambda}^j$ the latency of link $j \in [m]$ before and after user i changed its strategy, respectively. Assume that user k becomes unsatisfied due to the move of user i. Since only the latency on link p and q changed, we have to distinguish between two cases. Either $l_k \neq q$ and user k wants to change its strategy to p, or $l_k = q$ and user k becomes unsatisfied due to the additional traffic w_i on link q.

First, assume that $l_k \neq q$, and that user k wants to change its strategy to p. Since user i changed its strategy from p to q we know that $\lambda^q < \widehat{\lambda}^p$ and therefore $w_k + \lambda^q < w_k + \widehat{\lambda}^p$. So if user k wants to change its strategy to p, then user k was already unsatisfied before user i changed its strategy, a contradiction.

For the case that the strategy of user k is q we define $\widetilde{\lambda}_q = \lambda^q - w_k$. We have $\forall j \in [m] : \lambda^j + w_k \geq \lambda^j + w_i \geq \lambda^q + w_i = \widetilde{\lambda}_q + w_k + w_i$. Therefore k stays satisfied. $\square$

Theorem 7. *Let* $\mathbf{L} = \langle l_1, \ldots, l_n \rangle$ *be a pure strategy profile for* n *users with traffics* $w_1, \ldots, w_n$ *on* m *links with social cost* $\mathsf{SC}(\mathbf{w}, \mathbf{L})$. *Then algorithm* $\mathsf{A}_{nashify}$ *computes a Nash equilibrium from* $\mathbf{L}$ *with social cost* $\leq \mathsf{SC}(\mathbf{w}, \mathbf{L})$ *using* $O(n \lg n)$ *time.*

Proof. In order to complete the proof of Theorem 7, we have to show that algorithm $\mathsf{A}_{nashify}$ returns a pure strategy profile $\mathbf{L}'$ that is a Nash equilibrium and has social cost $\mathsf{SC}(\mathbf{w}, \mathbf{L}') \leq \mathsf{SC}(\mathbf{w}, \mathbf{L})$. It is easy to see that $\mathsf{SC}(\mathbf{w}, \mathbf{L}') \leq \mathsf{SC}(\mathbf{w}, \mathbf{L})$, since for user j we always choose the link with lowest latency as its strategy. After every iteration the user that changed its strategy is satisfied. Since we go through the list of users in descending order of their traffic and because of Lemma 8, all users that changed their strategy in earlier iterations stay satisfied. Therefore after we went through the complete list of users, all users are satisfied and thus $\mathbf{L}'$ is a Nash equilibrium.

The running time of algorithm $\mathsf{A}_{nashify}$ is $O(n \lg n)$ for sorting the n user traffics, $O(m \lg m)$ for constructing a heap with all latencies in the input pure strategy profile $\mathbf{L}$, and $O(n \lg m)$ for finding the minimum element of the heap in each of the n iterations of the algorithm. Thus, the total running time is $O(n \lg n + m \lg m + n \lg m)$. The interesting case is when $m \leq n$ (since otherwise, a single user can be assigned to each link, achieving an optimal Nash equilibrium). Thus, in the interesting case, the total running time of $\mathsf{A}_{nashify}$ is $O(n \lg n)$. $\square$

Running the PTAS of Hochbaum and Shmoys [10] for scheduling n *jobs* on m identical *machines* yields a pure strategy profile $\mathbf{L}$ such that $\mathsf{SC}(\mathbf{w}, \mathbf{L}) \leq (1 + \varepsilon)\, \mathsf{OPT}(\mathbf{w})$. On the other hand, applying the algorithm $\mathsf{A}_{nashify}$ on $\mathbf{L}$ yields a Nash equilibrium $\mathbf{L}'$ such that $\mathsf{SC}(\mathbf{w}, \mathbf{L}') \leq \mathsf{SC}(\mathbf{w}, \mathbf{L})$. Thus, $\mathsf{SC}(\mathbf{w}, \mathbf{L}') \leq (1 + \varepsilon)\mathsf{OPT}(\mathbf{w})$. Since also $\mathsf{OPT}(\mathbf{w}) \leq \mathsf{SC}(\mathbf{w}, \mathbf{L}')$, it follows that:

Theorem 8. *There exists a* PTAS *for* BEST PURE NASH EQUILIBRIUM, *for the model of identical capacities.*

7   Worst Pure Nash Equilibria

Denote with m-WCpNE the decision problem corresponding to the problem to compute the worst-case pure Nash equilibrium for n users with traffics $w_1, \ldots, w_n$ on m links. If m is part of the input, then we call the problem WCpNE. We first show:

Theorem 9. *Fix any traffic vector* $\mathbf{w}$ *and pure Nash equilibrium* $\mathbf{L}$. *Then,* $\frac{\mathsf{SC}(\mathbf{w}, \mathbf{L})}{\mathsf{OPT}(\mathbf{w})} \leq 2 - \frac{2}{m+1}$. *Furthermore, this upper bound is tight.*

Proof. Schuurman and Vredeveld [27] showed the tightness of the upper bound for jump optimal schedules proved by Finn and Horowitz [5]. Since every pure Nash equilibrium is also jump optimal, the upper bound follows directly. Greedy selfish steps on identical links can only increase the minimum load over all links. Thus, we can transform every jump optimal schedule into a Nash equilibrium without altering the makespan, proving tightness. $\square$

Theorem 10. *It is $\mathcal{NP}$-hard to find a pure Nash equilibrium L with $\frac{WC(\mathbf{w})}{SC(\mathbf{w},L)} <$ $2 - \frac{2}{m+1} - \varepsilon,$ for any $\varepsilon > 0$. It is $\mathcal{NP}$-hard in the strong sense if the number of links m is part of the input.*

Proof. We show that for a certain class of instances we have to solve BIN PACK-ING in order to find a Nash equilibrium with desired property. BIN PACKING is $\mathcal{NP}$-complete in the strong sense [8]. Consider an arbitrary instance of BIN PACKING consisting of a set of items $\mathcal{U} = \{u_1, \ldots, u_{|\mathcal{U}|}\}$ with sizes $s(u_j) \leq \delta$, $\sum_{u_j \in \mathcal{U}} = m - 1$, and $K = m - 1$ bins of capacity $B = 1$. From this in-stance we construct an instance for the stated problem as follows: Set $\varepsilon = 2\delta$. There are $n - 2 = |\mathcal{U}|$ users with traffic $w_i = s(u_i)$ and two users with traffic $w_{n-1} = w_n = 1$. Note that the social cost of a Nash Equilibrium is either 2 when the users with traffic 1 are on the same link, or at most $\frac{m+1}{m} + \delta$ otherwise.

If BIN PACKING is negative, then there exists no Nash equilibrium with both users with traffic 1 on the same link. Thus every Nash equilibrium has the desired property. If BIN PACKING is positive, then there exists a Nash equilibrium with both users with traffic 1 on the same link. The social cost of this Nash equilibrium is $WC(\mathbf{w}) = 2$. For any other Nash Equilibrium $\mathbf{L}$ where the users with traffic 1 use different links, $SC(\mathbf{w}, \mathbf{L}) \leq \frac{m+1}{m} + \delta$. This yields

$$\frac{WC(\mathbf{w})}{SC(\mathbf{w}, \mathbf{L})} \geq \frac{2}{\frac{m+1}{m} + \delta} = \frac{2}{\frac{m+1}{m} + \frac{\varepsilon}{2}} = \frac{2m}{m + 1 + \frac{\varepsilon m}{2}}$$

$$= 2 - \frac{2}{m + 1 + \frac{\varepsilon m}{2}} - \frac{\varepsilon m}{m + 1 + \frac{\varepsilon m}{2}} > 2 - \frac{2}{m+1} - \varepsilon.$$

So, to find a Nash equilibrium with desired property, we have to find a distribu-tion of the small traffics $w_1, \ldots, w_{n-2}$ to $m - 1$ links which solves BIN PACKING.

Since BIN PACKING is $\mathcal{NP}$-hard in the strong sense, if the number of bins is part of the input, it follows that computing a pure Nash equilibrium L with $\frac{WC(\mathbf{w})}{SC(\mathbf{w},L)} < 2 - \frac{2}{m+1} - \varepsilon$ is also $\mathcal{NP}$-hard in the strong sense, if m is part of the input. $\square$

Since WCpNE is $\mathcal{NP}$-hard in the strong sense [6], there exists no pseudopoly-nomial algorithm to solve WCpNE. However, we can give such an algorithm for m-WCpNE.

Theorem 11. *There exists a pseudopolynomial-time algorithm for m-WCpNE.*

Proof. We start with the state set S_0 in which all links are empty. After inserting the first i traffics the state set S_i consists of all $(2m)$-tuples $(\lambda_1, \tilde{w}_1, \ldots, \lambda_m, \tilde{w}_m)$ describing a possible placement of the largest i traffics with λ_j being the latency on link j and $\tilde{w}_j$ the smallest traffic placed on link j. We need at most $m \cdot |S_i|$ steps to create S_{i+1} from S_i, and $|S_i| \leq (W_i)^m \cdot (w_1)^m$, where $W_i = \sum_{j=1}^{i} w_j$. Therefore the overall computation time is bounded by $O(n \cdot m \cdot W^m \cdot (w_1)^m)$. The best-case Nash equilibrium and the worst-case Nash equilibrium can be found by exhaustive search over the state set S_n using $O(n \cdot m \cdot W^m \cdot (w_1)^m)$ time. $\square$

Remark 1. Theorem 11 also holds for the case of arbitrary link capacities.

8   Conclusions and Discussion

In this work, we have studied the combinatorial structure and the computational complexity of the extreme (either *worst* or *best*) Nash equilibria for the selfish routing game introduced in the pioneering work of Koutsoupias and Papadimitriou [15].

Our study of the combinatorial structure has revealed an interesting, highly non-trivial, combinatorial conjecture about the worst such Nash equilibrium, namely the *Fully Mixed Nash Equilibrium Conjecture,* abbreviated as FMNE Conjecture; the conjecture states that the fully mixed Nash equilibrium [18] is the worst Nash equilibrium in the setting we consider. We have established that the FMNE Conjecture is valid when restricted to pure Nash equilibria. Furthermore, we have come close to establishing the FMNE Conjecture in its full generality by proving that the social cost of any (pure or mixed) Nash equilibrium is within a factor of $6 + \varepsilon$, for any $\varepsilon > 0$, of that of the fully mixed Nash equilibrium, under the assumptions that all link capacities are identical, the number of users is equal to the number of links and the number of links is suitable large. The proof of this result has relied very heavily on applying and extending techniques from the theory of *stochastic orders* and *majorization* [17,28]; such techniques are imported for the *first* time into the context of selfish routing, and their application and extension are both of independent interest. We hope that the application and extension of techniques from the theory of stochastic orders and majorization will be valuable to further studies of the selfish routing game considered in this paper and for the analysis and evaluation of mixed Nash equilibria for other games as well.

Our study of the computational complexity of extreme Nash equilibria has resulted in both positive and negative results. On the positive side, we have devised, for the case of identical link capacities, equal number of users and links and a suitable large number of links, a randomized, polynomial-time algorithm to approximate the worst social cost within a factor arbitrarily close to $6 + \varepsilon$, for any $\varepsilon > 0$. The approximation factor $6 + \varepsilon$ of this randomized algorithm will immediately improve upon reducing 6 further down in our combinatorial result described above, relating the social cost of any Nash equilibrium to that of the fully mixed. We have also introduced the technique of *Nashification* as a tool for converging to a Nash equilibrium starting with any assignment of users to links in a way that does not increase the social cost; coupling this technique with a polynomial-time approximation scheme for the optimal assignment of users to links [10] has yielded a polynomial-time approximation scheme for the social cost of the *best* Nash equilibrium. In sharp contrast, we have established a *tight* limit on the approximation factor of any polynomial-time algorithm that approximates the social cost of the *worst* Nash equilibrium (assuming $\mathcal{P} \neq \mathcal{NP}$). Our approximability and inapproximability results for the best and worst Nash equilibria, respectively, establish an essential difference between the approximation properties of the two types of extreme Nash equilibria.

The most obvious problem left open by our work is to establish the FMNE Conjecture. Some progress on this problem has been already reported by Lücking *et al.* [16], where the conjecture is proved in various special cases of the model of selfish routing introduced by Koutsoupias and Papadimitriou [15] and considered in this work; furthermore, Lücking *et al.* disprove the FMNE Conjecture in a different model for selfish routing that borrows from the model of *unrelated machines* [11] studied in the scheduling literature.

The technique of *Nashification,* as an algorithmic tool for the computation of Nash equilibria, deserves also further study. Some steps in this direction have been taken already by Feldmann *et al.* [4].

Acknowledgments

We would like to thank Rainer Feldmann and Manuel Rode for many fruitful discussions. We are also very grateful to Petra Berenbrink and Tasos Christophides for many helpful discussions on stochastic orders.

References

1. P. Brucker, J. Hurink and F. Werner, "Improving Local Search Heuristics for Some Scheduling Problems. Part II," *Discrete Applied Mathematics,* Vol. 72, No.1-2, pp. 47–69, 1997.
2. A. Czumaj and B. Vöcking, "Tight Bounds for Worst-Case Equilibria," *Proceedings of the 13th Annual ACM Symposium on Discrete Algorithms,* pp. 413–420, January 2002.
3. X. Deng, C. Papadimitriou and S. Safra, "On the Complexity of Equilibria," *Proceedings of the 34th Annual ACM Symposium on Theory of Computing,* pp. 67–71, May 2002.
4. R. Feldmann, M. Gairing, T. Lücking, B. Monien and M. Rode, "Nashification and the Coordination Ratio for a Selfish Routing Game," *Proceedings of the 30th International Colloquium on Automata, Languages and Programming,* pp. 514–526, Vol. 2719, Lecture Notes in Computer Science, Springer-Verlag, Eindhoven, The Netherlands, June/July 2003.
5. G. Finn and E. Horowitz, "A linear time approximation algorithm for multiprocessor scheduling," *BIT,* Vol. 19, pp. 312–320, 1979.
6. D. Fotakis, S. Kontogiannis, E. Koutsoupias, M. Mavronicolas and P. Spirakis, "The Structure and Complexity of Nash Equilibria for a Selfish Routing Game,' *Proceedings of the 29th International Colloquium on Automata, Languages and Programming,* pp. 123–134, Vol. 2380, Lecture Notes in Computer Science, Springer-Verlag, Málaga, Spain, July 2002.
7. M. R. Garey and D. S. Johnson, "Complexity Results for Multiprocessor Scheduling Under Resoiurce Constraints," *SIAM Journal on Computing,* Vol. 4, pp. 397–411, 1975.
8. M. R. Garey and D. S. Johnson, *Computers and intractability: A Guide to the Theory of NP-Completeness,* W. H. Freeman and Company, 1979.
9. G. H. Gonnet, "Expected Length of the Longest Probe Sequence in Hash Code Soarching," *Journal of the ACM,* Vol. 28, No. 2, pp. 289–304, April 1981.
10. D. S. Hochbaum and D. Shmoys, "Using Dual Approximation Algorithms for Scheduling Problems: Theoretical and Practical Results," *Journal of the ACM,* Vol. 34, No. 1, pp. 144–162, 1987.

11. E. Horowitz and S. Sahni, "Exact and Approximate Algorithms for Scheduling Non-Identical Processors," *Journal of the ACM,* Vol. 23, No. 2, pp. 317–327, 1976.
12. R. M. Karp, "Reducibility among Combinatorial Problems," in R. E. Miller and J. W. Thatcher eds., *Complexity of Computer Computations,* pp. 85–103, Plenum Press, New York, 1972.
13. V. F. Kolchin, V. P. Chistiakov and B. A. Sevastianov, *Random Allocations,* V. H. Winston, New York, 1978.
14. E. Koutsoupias, M. Mavronicolas and P. Spirakis, "Approximate Equilibria and Ball Fusion," *Proceedings of the 9th International Colloquium on Structural Information and Communication Complexity,* Andros, Greece, June 2002. Accepted to *Theory of Computing Systems.*
    Earlier version appeared as "A Tight Bound on Coordination Ratio," Technical Report 0100229, Department of Computer Science, University of California at Los Angeles, April 2001.
15. E. Koutsoupias and C. H. Papadimitriou, "Worst-case Equilibria," *Proceedings of the 16th Annual Symposium on Theoretical Aspects of Computer Science,* G. Meinel and S. Tison eds., pp. 404–413, Vol. 1563, Lecture Notes in Computer Science, Springer-Verlag, Trier, Germany, March 1999.
16. T. Lücking, M. Mavronicolas, B. Monien, M. Rode, P. Spirakis and I. Vrto, "Which is the Worst-case Nash Equilibrium?" *26th International Symposium on Mathematical Foundations of Computer Science,* August 2003, to appear.
17. A. Marshall and I. Olkin, *Theory of Majorization and Its Applications,* Academic Press, Orlando, FL, 1979.
18. M. Mavronicolas and P. Spirakis, "The Price of Selfish Routing," *Proceedings of the 33rd Annual ACM Symposium on Theory of Computing,* pp. 510–519, July 2001.
19. C. McDiarmid, "Concentration," Chapter 9 in *Probabilistic Methods for Algorithmic Discrete Mathematics,* M. Habib, C. McDiarmidt, J. Ramires-Alfonsin and B. Reed eds., Springer, 1998.
20. H. Moulin and L. Vial, "Strategically Zero-Sum Games: The Class of Games whose Completely Mixed Equilibria Cannot be Improved Upon," *International Journal of Game Theory,* Vol. 7, Nos. 3/4, pp. 201–221, 1978.
21. J. F. Nash, "Equilibrium Points in N-Person Games," *Proceedings of the National Academy of Sciences,* Vol. 36, pp. 48–49, 1950.
22. J. F. Nash, "Non-cooperative Games," *Annals of Mathematics,* Vol. 54, No. 2, pp. 286–295, 1951.
23. M. J. Osborne and A. Rubinstein, *A Course in Game Theory,* The MIT Press, 1994.
24. C. H. Papadimitriou, "Algorithms, Games and the Internet," *Proceedings of the 33rd Annual ACM Symposium on Theory of Computing,* pp. 749–753, July 2001.
25. T. E. S. Raghavan, "Completely Mixed Strategies in Bimatrix Games," *Journal of London Mathematical Society,* Vol. 2, No. 2, pp. 709–712, 1970.
26. S. M. Ross, *Stochastic Processes,* Second Edition, John Wiley & Sons, Inc., 1996.
27. P. Schuurman and T. Vredeveld, "Performance Guarantees of Load Search for Multiprocessor Scheduling," *Proceedings of the 8th Conference on Integer Programming and Combinatorial Optimization,* pp. 370–382, June 2001.
28. M. Shaked and J. G. Shanthikumar, *Stochastic Orders and Their Applications,* Academic Press, San Diego, CA, 1994.
29. A. Vetta, "Nash Equilibria in Competitive Societies, with Applications to Facility Location, Traffic Routing and Auctions," *Proceedings of the 43rd Annual IEEE Symposium on Foundations of Computer Science,* October 2002, pp. 416–425.

Certification of Memory Usage

Martin Hofmann

Institut für Informatik
Ludwig-Maximilians-Universität München
Oettingenstrasse 67
D-80538 München, Germany

Abstract. We describe a type-based approach for inferring heap space usage of certain functional programs and a mechanism for generating certificates as to the thus inferred memory consumption in the form of proofs in a VDM-style program logic fore Java bytecode (Java bytecode being the target of compilation). This gives a current snapshot of our work in the EU-funded project 'Mobile Resource Guarantees' http://www.dcs.ed.ac.uk/home/mrg/ between LMU-Munich and LFCS Edinburgh.

C. Blundo and C. Laneve (Eds.): ICTCS 2003, LNCS 2841, p. 21, 2003.
© Springer-Verlag Berlin Heidelberg 2003

On Programming Models for Mobility

Gérard Boudol

INRIA
2004, Route des Lucioles
B.P. 93
06902 Sophia Antipolis Cedex, France

Abstract. In this talk I will discuss some models for mobile code from a programming perspective. I will first present some requirements for this style of programming, arising from the features of the "global computing" context. Then I will discuss some of the models and programming languages that have been proposed - Obliq, pi-based and Linda-based models, Ambients. I will then present a model based on the ideas of "synchronous" programming, that is based on suspension and preemption primitives associated with locally broadcast events.

C. Blundo and C. Laneve (Eds.): ICTCS 2003, LNCS 2841, p. 22, 2003.
© Springer-Verlag Berlin Heidelberg 2003

On the Computational Complexity
of Cut-Elimination in Linear Logic

Harry G. Mairson[1] and Kazushige Terui[2,*]

[1] Computer Science Department, Brandeis University,
Waltham, Massachusetts 02454, USA
mairson@cs.brandeis.edu
[2] National Institute of Informatics, 2-1-2 Hitotsubashi, Chiyoda-ku,
101-8430 Tokyo, Japan
terui@nii.ac.jp

Abstract. Given two proofs in a logical system with a confluent cut-elimination procedure, the *cut-elimination problem* (CEP) is to decide whether these proofs reduce to the same normal form. This decision problem has been shown to be PTIME-complete for Multiplicative Linear Logic (Mairson 2003). The latter result depends upon a restricted simulation of weakening and contraction for boolean values in **MLL**; in this paper, we analyze how and when this technique can be generalized to other **MLL** formulas, and then consider CEP for other subsystems of Linear Logic. We also show that while additives play the role of *nondeterminism* in cut-elimination, they are not needed to express *deterministic* PTIME computation. As a consequence, affine features are irrelevant to expressing PTIME computation. In particular, Multiplicative Light Linear Logic (**MLLL**) and Multiplicative Soft Linear Logic (**MSLL**) capture PTIME even without additives nor unrestricted weakening. We establish hierarchical results on the cut-elimination problem for **MLL** (PTIME-complete), **MALL** (coNP-complete), **MLLL** (EXPTIME-complete), and for **MLLL** (2EXPTIME-complete).

1 Introduction

Cut-elimination is naturally seen as a *function* from proofs to their normal form, and we can derive from it an equally natural *decision problem:* if L is a logical system with a confluent cut-elimination procedure, and we are given two proofs in L, do they reduce to the same normal form? Call this the *cut elimination problem (CEP)*. When L has reasonable representations of boolean values as proofs, an even simpler decision problem is to ask: given a proof, does it reduce to the representation for "true"?

Through the Curry-Howard correspondence, we know that proofs in linear logics represent programs, typically in a functional programming language with

* Supported by "Software Evolution for Declarative Programming" project in Grant-in-Aid of Scientific Research on Priority Area "Informatics Studies for the Foundation of IT Evolution," MEXT, JAPAN.

C. Blundo and C. Laneve (Eds.): ICTCS 2003, LNCS 2841, pp. 23–36, 2003.

highly specified forms of copying, where cut-elimination serves as an interpreter: normalization is evaluation. The cut-elimination problem is then a fundamental question about program equivalence, and how hard it is to decide. Moreover, the correspondence facilitates our identification of particular logics with associated complexity classes, where our goal is to link the expressive power of proofs with a suitably powerful interpreter that can "run" representations of programs in that complexity class.

The cut-elimination problem is known to be non-elementary for simply typed λ-calculus [Sta79], and hence for linear logic. Several low order fragments of simply typed λ-calculus are investigated in [Sch01]. In this paper, we consider the decision problem for various weak subsystems of linear logic that have no exponentials, or have very weak forms of them (i.e., the so-called "light" linear logics). Such an investigation suggests another way to characterize the complexity of linear logics: not only by the complexity of theorem proving (proof search)—see, for example, [Lin95]—but also by the complexity of theorem simplification (proof normalization).

Even in intuitionistic multiplicative linear logic (**IMLL**), which has no exponentials, it is possible to simulate weakening and contraction for a restricted set of formulas, including a formula whose proofs code boolean values. As a consequence, we derive PTIME-completeness for CEP in **IMLL**; see Section 2. This result contradicts folkloric intuitions that **MLL** proofnets could be normalized in logarithmic space—that is, with only a finite number of pointers into the proofnet, presumably following paths in the style of the geometry of interaction. Similar to the results for **IMLL**, in Section 3 we derive coNP-completeness results for **IMALL**, where we also have additives.

An alternative way to represent a complexity class by some logic is to consider the functions realizable (say, by a Turing machine) in the class, and show how each can be coded as a *fixed* proof (program) in the logic. For example, Light Linear Logic has been shown to so represent PTIME computations [Gir98], and the use of additives in that proof was replaced by unrestricted weakening in Light Affine Logic [Asp98,AR02]. We improve these results to show that such weakening is also unnecessary: Multiplicative Light Linear Logic is sufficient to capture PTIME (see Section 4), where we also prove that deciding CEP is complete for doubly-exponential time. Finally, in Section 5 we show similar characterizations of exponential time in Multiplicative Soft Linear Logic [Laf01].

2   Expressivity of Multiplicatives

2.1   Weakening in MLL

We restrict our attention to the intuitionistic $(-\circ, \forall)$ fragment **IMLL** of **MLL**, although all the results in this section carry over to the full classical **MLL** with no difficulty. Moreover, we omit type annotation from the proof syntax, and identify proofs of **IMLL** with type-free terms of linear λ-calculus.

A *term* (*proof*) of **IMLL** is either a variable x, or an application (tu) where t and u are terms such that $FV(t) \cap FV(u) = \emptyset$, or an abstraction $(\lambda x.t)$ where

t is a term and $x \in FV(t)$. Terms are considered up to α-equivalence, and the variable convention is adopted. The substitution operation $t[u/x]$ and the β reduction relation are defined as usual. The *size* $|t|$ of a term t is the number of nodes in its syntax tree. The *type assignment rules* are as follows[1]:

$$\frac{}{x:A \vdash x:A} \qquad \frac{\Gamma \vdash u:A \quad x:A, \Delta \vdash t:C}{\Gamma, \Delta \vdash t[u/x]:C} \qquad \frac{x:A, \Gamma \vdash t:B}{\Gamma \vdash \lambda x.t:A \multimap B}$$

$$\frac{\Gamma \vdash u:A \quad x:B, \Delta \vdash t:C}{\Gamma, y:A \multimap B, \Delta \vdash t[yu/x]:C} \qquad \frac{\Gamma \vdash t:A}{\Gamma \vdash t:\forall \alpha.A} \; \alpha \notin FV(\Gamma) \qquad \frac{x:A[B/\alpha], \Gamma \vdash t:C}{x:\forall \alpha.A, \Gamma \vdash t:C}$$

Here, $\Gamma, \Delta \ldots$ stand for finite multisets of *declarations* $x:A$ and $FV(\Gamma)$ denotes the set of all free type variables in Γ. We say that a term t is *of type A* (or t *is a proof of A*) if $\vdash t:A$ is derivable by the above rules. A type A is *inhabited* if there is a term of type A.

Unit **1** and tensor product $\otimes$ are introduced by means of the second order definitions:

$$\mathbf{1} \equiv \forall \alpha.\alpha \multimap \alpha \qquad\qquad A \otimes B \equiv \forall \alpha.(A \multimap B \multimap \alpha) \multimap \alpha$$

$$\mathsf{I} \equiv \lambda x.x \qquad\qquad t \otimes u \equiv \lambda x.xtu$$

$$\text{let } t \text{ be } \mathsf{I} \text{ in } u \equiv tu \qquad\qquad \text{let } t \text{ be } x \otimes y \text{ in } u \equiv t(\lambda xy.u)$$

Tensor product is naturally extended to n-ary ones: $t_1 \otimes \ldots \otimes t_n$ and let u be $x_1 \otimes \cdots \otimes x_n$ in t. The expression $\lambda x_1 \otimes \cdots \otimes x_n.t$ stands for $\lambda z.\text{let } z$ be $x_1 \otimes \cdots \otimes x_n$ in t. We also use shorthand notations such as $id \equiv \lambda x.x$, $t \circ u \equiv \lambda x.t(u(x))$, $A^n \equiv \underbrace{A \otimes \cdots \otimes A}_{n \text{ times}}$, $A^{(n)} \multimap B \equiv \underbrace{A \multimap \cdots A}_{n \text{ times}} \multimap B$.

Our first observation is that a version of weakening rule can be constructed for a certain restricted class of **IMLL** formulas.

Definition 1 (Π_1, Σ_1, $e\Pi_1$, $e\Sigma_1$). *A type A is Π_1 (Σ_1) if it is built from type variables by $\multimap$, $\mathbf{1}$, $\otimes$ and positive (negative) occurrences of $\forall$. An $e\Pi_1$ ($e\Sigma_1$) type is like a Π_1 (Σ_1) type, but it may additionally contain negative (positive) occurrences of inhabited $\forall$-types.*

The above definition of Π_1 and $e\Pi_1$ involves **1** and $\otimes$ as primitives, but we may ignore them in practice, because negative occurrences of $\otimes$ and **1** can be removed by isomorphisms $((A \otimes B) \multimap C) \multimap\circ (A \multimap B \multimap C)$ and $(\mathbf{1} \multimap C) \multimap\circ C$, while positive occurrences can be replaced with their Π_1 definitions.

Finite data types are naturally represented by closed inhabited Π_1 types. A typical example is the boolean type: $\mathbf{B} \equiv \forall \alpha.\alpha \multimap \alpha \multimap \alpha \otimes \alpha$. Meanwhile, functional types over those finite data types, such as $(\mathbf{B} \multimap \mathbf{B}) \multimap \mathbf{B}$, are all included in the class $e\Pi_1$.

---

[1] Note that *any* term of linear λ calculus has a propositional type [Hin89]; the role of second order quantifiers here is not to increase the number of typable terms, but to classify them by assigning a uniform type to structurally related terms.

Theorem 1 ($e\Pi_1$-Weakening). *For any closed $e\Pi_1$ type A, there is a term* w_A *of type* $A \multimap \mathbf{1}$.

Proof. Without loss of generality, we may assume that A does not contain $\otimes$ and $\mathbf{1}$. Let $B[\mathbf{1}]$ be the type B with all free variables replaced with $\mathbf{1}$. By simultaneous induction, we prove: (i) for any $e\Pi_1$ type B, $B[\mathbf{1}] \vdash \mathbf{1}$ is provable; and (ii) for any $e\Sigma_1$ type B, $\vdash B[\mathbf{1}]$ is provable. When B is a variable, the claims are obvious. When B is $C \multimap D$, for (i) we derive $(C \multimap D)[\mathbf{1}] \vdash \mathbf{1}$ from $\vdash C[\mathbf{1}]$ and $D[\mathbf{1}] \vdash \mathbf{1}$, and for (ii) we derive $\vdash (C \multimap D)[\mathbf{1}]$ from $C[\mathbf{1}] \vdash \mathbf{1}$ and $\vdash D[\mathbf{1}]$. Let B be $\forall \alpha.C$. If B is $e\Pi_1$, we derive $(\forall \alpha.C)[\mathbf{1}] \vdash \mathbf{1}$ from $C[\mathbf{1}] \vdash \mathbf{1}$. If B is $e\Sigma_1$, $\vdash B$ is provable by definition, and so is $\vdash B[\mathbf{1}]$. ∎

2.2   Encoding Boolean Circuits

Let A be an arbitrary type, and B be a type that supports weakening in the sense we have just described; we can then define a projection function fst_B : $A \otimes B \multimap A$, given by $\mathsf{fst}_B \equiv \lambda x.\mathsf{let}\ x$ be $y \otimes z$ in (let $\mathsf{w}_B(z)$ be I in y). By using this coding, we can then specify boolean values, weakening, and operations (including duplication) as:

$$
\begin{array}{lll}
\mathsf{true} \equiv \lambda xy.x \otimes y & & :\mathbf{B} \\
\mathsf{false} \equiv \lambda xy.y \otimes x & & :\mathbf{B} \\
\mathsf{w}_\mathbf{B} \equiv \lambda z.\mathsf{let}\ z\mathsf{II}\ \text{be}\ x \otimes y\ \text{in (let}\ y\ \text{be}\ \mathsf{I}\ \text{in}\ x) & :\mathbf{B} \multimap \mathbf{1} \\
\mathsf{not} \equiv \lambda Pxy.Pyx & :\mathbf{B} \multimap \mathbf{B} \\
\mathsf{or} \equiv \lambda PQ.\mathsf{fst}_\mathbf{B}(P\,\mathsf{true}\,Q) & :\mathbf{B} \multimap \mathbf{B} \multimap \mathbf{B} \\
\mathsf{cntr} \equiv \lambda P.\mathsf{fst}_{\mathbf{B} \otimes \mathbf{B}}(P(\mathsf{true} \otimes \mathsf{true})(\mathsf{false} \otimes \mathsf{false})):\mathbf{B} \multimap \mathbf{B} \otimes \mathbf{B}
\end{array}
$$

Recall that a language $X \subseteq \{0,1\}^*$ is *logspace reducible* to $Y \subseteq \{0,1\}^*$ if there exists a logspace function $f : \{0,1\}^* \longrightarrow \{0,1\}^*$ such that $w \in X$ iff $f(w) \in Y$. Language X is PTIME-*complete* if $X \in$ PTIME and each language $L \in$ PTIME is logspace reducible to X; a decision problem is said to be PTIME-complete when the language defined by that problem is PTIME-complete. The canonical PTIME-complete decision problem is the following:

Circuit Value Problem: Given a boolean circuit C with n inputs and 1 output, and truth values $\boldsymbol{x} = x_1, \ldots, x_n$, is $\boldsymbol{x}$ accepted by C? [Lad75]

Using the above coding of boolean operations, the problem is logspace reducible to CEP for **IMLL**:

Theorem 2 (PTIME-completeness of IMLL, [Mai03]). *There is a logspace algorithm which transforms a boolean circuit C with n inputs and m outputs into a term t_C of type $\mathbf{B}^n \multimap \mathbf{B}^m$, where the size of t_C is $O(|C|)$. As a consequence, the cut-elimination problem for* **IMLL** *is* PTIME-*complete.*

Since binary words of length n can be represented by $\mathbf{B}^n$, the theorem implies that any finite function $f : \{0,1\}^n \longrightarrow \{0,1\}^m$ can be represented by a term $t_f : \mathbf{B}^n \multimap \mathbf{B}^m$. In this sense, **MLL** captures all the finite functions.

2.3   Contraction in MLL

One of the key observations in proving Theorem 2 is that contraction is available for **B**. We now generalize this observation, and show that the same holds for all closed inhabited Π_1 types (i.e. finite data types). First we show that conditional is available in **IMLL**:

Lemma 1 (Conditional). *Let t_1 and t_2 be terms such that $x_1 : C_1, \ldots, x_n : C_n \vdash t_i : D$ for $i = 1, 2$, and the type $A \equiv C_1 \multimap \cdots C_n \multimap D$ is $e\Pi_1$ (not necessarily closed). Then there is a term if b then t_1 else t_2 such that*

$$b : \mathbf{B}, x_1 : C_1, \ldots, x_n : C_n \vdash \text{if } b \text{ then } t_1 \text{ else } t_2 : D,$$

where (if true then t_1 else t_2) $\longrightarrow t_1$ *and* (if false then t_1 else t_2) $\longrightarrow t_2$.

Proof. Define if b then t else $u \equiv \text{fst}_{\forall \alpha. A}(b(\lambda \boldsymbol{x}.t)(\lambda \boldsymbol{x}.u))\boldsymbol{x}$, where $\boldsymbol{x}$ abbreviates $x_1, \ldots, x_n$ and $\forall \alpha. A$ is the universal closure of A. This term can be typed as required; $\lambda \boldsymbol{x}.t$ and $\lambda \boldsymbol{x}.u$ have type $\forall \alpha. A$, thus $b(\lambda \boldsymbol{x}.t)(\lambda \boldsymbol{x}.u)$ has type $\forall \alpha. A \otimes \forall \alpha. A$, to which the projection $\text{fst}_{\forall \alpha. A}$ applies. The rest is obvious. ∎

Fix a quantifier-free type A of size k, built from a single type variable α. A *long normal form* of type A is a term t in β-normal form such that $\vdash t : A$ has a derivation in which all identity axioms are *atomic*, i.e., of the form $x : \alpha \vdash x : \alpha$. It is clear that every long normal form t of type A has size bounded by k, and we may assume that all variables occurring in it are from a fixed set of variables $\{x_1, \ldots, x_k\}$ (due to α-equivalence). Therefore, t can be written as a word in $\{0, 1\}^n$, where $n = O(k \log k)$. Since $\{0, 1\}^n$ can in turn be represented by $\mathbf{B}^n$, there must be a function $\lceil \ \rceil$ which maps a given term u of size bounded by k into a term $\lceil u \rceil$ of type $\mathbf{B}^n$. Furthermore, as a consequence of Theorem 2, we can associate to this coding two terms $\text{abs}, \text{app} : \mathbf{B}^n \multimap \mathbf{B}^n \multimap \mathbf{B}^n$ which satisfy

$$\text{abs} \lceil y \rceil \lceil t \rceil \longrightarrow^* \lceil \lambda y.t \rceil, \quad \text{if } |\lambda y.t| \le k \text{ and } y \in \{x_1, \ldots, x_k\};$$
$$\text{app} \lceil t \rceil \lceil u \rceil \longrightarrow^* \lceil tu \rceil, \quad \text{if } |tu| \le k.$$

We now show that the coding function $\lceil \ \rceil$ can be internalized in **IMLL**, as far as the long normal forms of a fixed type A is concerned. For each subtype B of A, define $\sigma_B(t)$ and $\tau_B(t)$ as follows:

$$\sigma_\alpha(t) \equiv t \qquad\qquad \sigma_{B \multimap C}(t) \equiv \text{abs} \lceil y \rceil \sigma_C(t \, \tau_B(\lceil y \rceil))$$
$$\tau_\alpha(t) \equiv t \qquad\qquad \tau_{B \multimap C}(t) \equiv \lambda z. \tau_C(\text{app} \, t \, \sigma_B(z))$$

Here y is from $\{x_1, \ldots, x_k\}$ and $\lceil fresh \rceil$, in the sense that $\lceil y \rceil$ does not occur in t. The term $\sigma_B(t)$ has type $\mathbf{B}^n$ whenever t has type $B[\mathbf{B}^n/\alpha]$, and $\tau_B(t)$ has type $B[\mathbf{B}^n/\alpha]$ whenever t has type $\mathbf{B}^n$. Finally, let $\text{code}_A \equiv \lambda x.\sigma_A(x) : A[\mathbf{B}^n/\alpha] \multimap \mathbf{B}^n$.

Lemma 2 (Internal Coding). *Let A be as above. For each closed long normal form t of type A, $\text{code}_A(t) \longrightarrow^* \lceil t \rceil$.*

For example, let A_1 be $((\alpha \multimap \alpha) \multimap \alpha) \multimap (\alpha \multimap \alpha) \multimap \alpha$, which has two long normal forms $t_1 \equiv \lambda F f.f(F(\lambda y.y))$ and $t_2 \equiv \lambda F f.F(\lambda y.fy)$. The term code_{A_1} is defined as follows:

$$\tau_{\alpha \multimap \alpha}(\lceil f \rceil) \equiv \lambda x.\mathsf{app}\lceil f \rceil x$$
$$\tau_{(\alpha \multimap \alpha) \multimap \alpha}(\lceil F \rceil) \equiv \lambda g.\mathsf{app}\lceil F \rceil(\mathsf{abs}\lceil y \rceil(g\lceil y \rceil))$$
$$\mathsf{code}_{A_1} \equiv \lambda z.\mathsf{abs}\lceil F \rceil(\mathsf{abs}\lceil f \rceil(z\tau_{(\alpha \multimap \alpha) \multimap \alpha}(\lceil F \rceil)\tau_{\alpha \multimap \alpha}(\lceil f \rceil)))$$

It is then easy to check that $\mathsf{code}_F(t_i)$ reduces to $\lceil t_i \rceil$ for $i = 1, 2$.

Theorem 3 (Π_1-Contraction). *Let A be a closed Π_1 type which is inhabited. Then there is a contraction map $\mathsf{cntr}_A : A \multimap A \otimes A$ such that for any normal form t of type A, $\mathsf{cntr}_A(t)$ reduces to $t' \otimes t'$, where t' is a long normal form η-equivalent to t.*

Proof. Without loss of generality, we may assume that A is free from $\otimes$ and $\mathbf{1}$. Let A^- be obtained from A by replacing all subtypes $\forall \beta.C$ by $C[\alpha/\beta]$ for a fixed variable α. Then, there is a canonical map $\mathsf{iso}_A : A \multimap A^-[D/\alpha]$ for any D which preserves the structure of terms up to η-equivalence. By applying Lemma 2 to the type A^- we obtain a coding map $\mathsf{code}_{A^-} : A^-[\mathbf{B}^n/\alpha] \multimap \mathbf{B}^n$.

Let $t_1, \ldots, t_l$ be the long normal forms of type A. By using the conditional in Lemma 1 several times, we can build a term $\mathsf{copy}_A : \mathbf{B}^n \multimap A \otimes A$ which satisfies

$$\begin{aligned}\mathsf{copy}_A(u) &\longrightarrow^* t_i \otimes t_i, \quad \text{if } u \equiv \lceil t_i \rceil; \\ &\longrightarrow^* t_1 \otimes t_1, \quad \text{otherwise.}\end{aligned}$$

Finally, define $\mathsf{cntr}_A \equiv \mathsf{copy}_A \circ \mathsf{code}_{A^-} \circ \mathsf{iso}_A$.   ∎

3   Additives as Nondeterminism

3.1   Additive Slices and Nondeterministic Cut-Elimination

We now move on to the multiplicative additive fragment of Linear Logic. We again confine ourselves to the intuitionistic fragment **IMALL**, and furthermore, we only consider & as the additive connective, although $\oplus$ could be added harmlessly[2].

The *terms of* **IMALL** are defined analogously to the terms of **IMLL**, but we have in addition: (i) if t and u are terms and $FV(t) = FV(u)$, then so is $\langle t, u \rangle$; (ii) if t is a term, then so are $\pi_1(t)$ and $\pi_2(t)$. The type assignment rules are extended with

$$\frac{\Gamma \vdash t_1 : A_1 \quad \Gamma \vdash t_2 : A_2}{\Gamma \vdash \langle t_1, t_2 \rangle : A_1 \,\&\, A_2} \qquad \frac{x : A_i, \Gamma \vdash t : C}{y : A_1 \,\&\, A_2, \Gamma \vdash t[\pi_i(y)/x] : C} \, i = 1, 2$$

---

[2] However, we have to be careful when considering the classical system, which is *not* confluent as it stands [Gir87]. It could be overcome by adopting Tortora's proofnet syntax with generalized & boxes, which enjoys confluence [dF03]; see also [MR02].

and the reduction rules are extended with $\pi_i\langle t_1, t_2\rangle \longrightarrow t_i$, for $i = 1, 2$.

Note that some reductions such as $(\lambda x.\langle x, x\rangle)t \longrightarrow \langle t, t\rangle$ cause duplication, hence the straightforward cut-elimination procedure costs exponential time in general[3]. Our idea is to avoid duplication by computing each component of $\langle t_1, t_2\rangle$ separately. To formalize this idea, we recall the notion of *slice* [Gir87].

Definition 2 (Slices). *A slice of a term t is obtained by applying the following operation to t as much as possible: $\langle u, v\rangle \mapsto \langle u\rangle_1$, or $\langle u, v\rangle \mapsto \langle v\rangle_2$.*

We say that two slices t and u (of possibly different terms) are *compatible* if there is no context (i.e. a term with a hole) Φ such that $t \equiv \Phi[\langle t'\rangle_i]$, $u \equiv \Phi[\langle u'\rangle_j]$, and $i \neq j$.

Lemma 3 (Slicewise checking). *Two terms t and u are equivalent if and only if for every compatible pair (t', u') of slices of t and u, we have $t' \equiv u'$.*

The reduction rules are naturally adapted for slices:

$$(\lambda x.t)u \xrightarrow{sl} t[u/x] \qquad \pi_i\langle t\rangle_i \xrightarrow{sl} t \qquad \pi_i\langle t\rangle_j \xrightarrow{sl} \text{fail, if } i \neq j.$$

Lemma 4 (Pullback). *Let $t \longrightarrow^* u$ and u' be a slice of u. Then there is a unique slice t' of t such that $t' \xrightarrow{sl}{}^* u'$.*

Proof. See the following diagrams:

Note that there are exponentially many slices for a given term, but once a slice has been chosen, the computation afterwards can be done in linear steps, thus in quadratic time, since each slice is entirely a linear term. We therefore have a nondeterministic polynomial time cut-elimination procedure, viewing the slicing operation in Definition 2 as a nondeterministic reduction rule. Lemma 3 states that the equivalence of two normal forms can be checked slicewise, and Lemma 4 assures that every slice of a normal form can be obtained by the above nondeterministic procedure. Hence we may conclude that the cut-elimination problem for **IMALL** is in coNP.

3.2 Encoding a coNP-Complete Problem

Now we show that the following coNP-complete problem is logspace reducible to CEP for **IMALL**:

---

[3] There is, however, a linear step cut-elimination procedure for terms (proofnets) of *lazy* types, i.e., those which do not contain positive occurrences of & and negative occurrences of ∀.

Logical Equivalence Problem: Given two boolean formulas, are they logically equivalent? (cf. [GJ78])

By Theorem 2, every boolean formula C with n variables can be translated into a term t_C of type $\mathbf{B}^{(n)} \multimap \mathbf{B}$ in $O(\log |C|)$ space. For each $1 \leq k \leq n$, let

$$\mathsf{ta}_k \equiv \lambda f.\lambda x_1 \cdots x_{k-1}.\langle f \text{ true } x_1 \cdots x_{k-1}, f \text{ false } x_1 \cdots x_{k-1}\rangle,$$

which is of type $\forall \alpha.(\mathbf{B}^{(k)} \multimap \alpha) \multimap (\mathbf{B}^{(k-1)} \multimap \alpha \& \alpha)$, and define $\mathsf{ta}(t_C)$ by

$$\mathsf{ta}(t_C) \equiv \mathsf{ta}_1(\cdots(\mathsf{ta}_n t_C)\cdots) : \underbrace{\mathbf{B} \& \cdots \& \mathbf{B}}_{2^n \ times}.$$

It is clear that the term $\mathsf{ta}(t_C)$ can be built from t_C with the help of a counter of size $O(\log n)$.

The normal form of $\mathsf{ta}(t_C)$ consists of 2^n boolean values, each of which corresponds to a "truth assignment" to the formula C. For example, $\mathsf{ta}(\mathsf{or})$ reduces to $\langle\langle\mathsf{or}\ \mathsf{true}\ \mathsf{true}, \mathsf{or}\ \mathsf{true}\ \mathsf{false}\rangle, \langle\mathsf{or}\ \mathsf{false}\ \mathsf{true}, \mathsf{or}\ \mathsf{false}\ \mathsf{false}\rangle\rangle$, and thus to $\langle\langle\mathsf{true}, \mathsf{true}\rangle, \langle\mathsf{true}, \mathsf{false}\rangle\rangle$.

Therefore, two formulas C and D with n variables are logically equivalent if and only if $\mathsf{ta}(t_C)$ and $\mathsf{ta}(t_D)$ reduce to the same normal form.

Theorem 4 (coNP-completeness of IMALL). *The cut-elimination problem for* **IMALL** *is coNP-complete.*

Remark 1. We do not claim that *the* complexity of **MALL** is coNP. What we have shown is that a specific problem, CEP for **MALL**, is complete for coNP. If we had considered the complement of CEP, then the result would have been NP-completeness. Likewise, we could obtain a $\mathcal{C}$-completeness result for any class $\mathcal{C}$ in the polynomial time hierarchy by complicating the problem more and more.

However, we do claim that additives have something to do with *nondeterminism*, as they provide a notion of nondeterministic cut-elimination, as well as a very natural coding of nondeterministic Turing machine computation.

4   Multiplicative Light Linear Logic and 2EXPTIME

In this section, we show that the intuitionistic multiplicative fragment **IMLLL** of Light Linear Logic is already expressive enough to represent all polynomial time functions; it needs neither additives (as in [Gir98]) nor unrestricted weakening (as in [Asp98]).

Since our concern is not normalization but representation, we do not need to introduce a proper term calculus with the polynomial time normalization property (see [Asp98] and [Ter01] for such term calculi). We rather use the standard λ-calculus and think of **IMLLL** as a typing system for it.

The type assignment rules of **IMLLL** are those of **IMLL** with the following:

$$\frac{x:B \vdash t:A}{x:!B \vdash t:!A} \qquad \frac{\Gamma \vdash t:C}{x:!B,\Gamma \vdash t:C} \qquad \frac{x:!A,y:!A,\Gamma \vdash t:C}{z:!A,\Gamma \vdash t[z/x,z/y]:C} \qquad \frac{\overline{x}:\overline{A},\overline{y}:\overline{B} \vdash t:C}{\overline{x}:\overline{!A},\overline{y}:\overline{\S B} \vdash t:\S C}$$

where $x:B$ may be absent in the first rule. Define $\mathbf{W}$ to be $\forall \alpha.!(\mathbf{B} \multimap \alpha \multimap \alpha) \multimap \S(\alpha \multimap \alpha)$. Then each word $w = i_1 \cdots i_n$, where $n \geq 0$ and $i_k \in \{0,1\}$, is represented by $\underline{w} \equiv \lambda c x. c i_1 \circ \cdots \circ c i_n(x) : \mathbf{W}$, where $\underline{i_k}$ is false if $i_k = 0$, and is true if $i_k = 1$. A function $f : \{0,1\}^* \longrightarrow \{0,1\}^*$ is *represented* by a term t if $f(w) = v \iff t\underline{w} \longrightarrow^* \underline{v}$ for every $w \in \{0,1\}^*$.

Simulation of polynomial time Turing machines in Light Linear Logic (see [Gir98,AR02]) consists of two parts; one for coding of polynomials and the other for simulation of one-step transition (as well as initialization and output extraction). Since the former is already additive-free in [Gir98], we focus on the latter here.

Let M be a Turing machine with two symbols[4] and 2^n states, and let

$$\delta : Symbols \times States \longrightarrow Symbols \times States \times \{left, right\}$$

be the associated instruction function. A *configuration* of M can be specified by a triple $\langle w_1, w_2, q \rangle$, where the stack $w_1 \in \{0,1\}^*$ describes the non-blank part of the tape to the left of the head, the stack $w_2 \in \{0,1\}^*$ describes the non-blank part of the tape to the right of the head, and $q \in States$ denotes the current state. By convention, w_1 is written in the reverse order, and w_1 includes the content of the cell currently scanned.

The configurations are represented by terms of type $ID[\mathbf{B}^n]$, where $ID[A]$ is defined by $ID[A] \equiv \forall \alpha.!(\mathbf{B} \multimap \alpha \multimap \alpha) \multimap \S(\alpha \multimap \alpha \multimap (\alpha \otimes \alpha \otimes A))$. Note that $ID[A]$ is a generalization of $\mathbf{W}$, which allows to encode two words and an additional datum of type A into one term. For example, the configuration $\langle 010, 11, q \rangle$ is represented by

$$\underline{\langle 010, 11, q \rangle} \equiv \lambda c. \lambda x_1 x_2. (c\underline{0} \circ c\underline{1} \circ c\underline{0}(x_1)) \otimes (c\underline{1} \circ c\underline{1}(x_2)) \otimes \underline{q},$$

where $\underline{q}$ is a term of type $\mathbf{B}^n$ coding $q \in States$.

To simulate one-step transition, it is convenient to divide it into two parts: the decomposition part and the combination part.

Lemma 5 (Decomposition). *There is a term* $\mathsf{dec} : ID[\mathbf{B}^n] \multimap ID[\mathbf{B} \otimes \mathbf{B} \otimes \mathbf{B}^n]$ *such that for any configuration* $\langle i_1 \cdots i_n, j_1 \cdots j_m, q \rangle$,

$$\mathsf{dec}\underline{\langle i_1 \cdots i_n, j_1 \cdots j_m, q \rangle} \longrightarrow^* \underline{\langle i_2 \cdots i_n 0, j_2 \cdots j_m 0, i_1, j_1, q \rangle}.$$

---

[4] Although more than two symbols are required in general, we describe the two symbols version here for simplicity. The extension is straightforward.

Proof. We largely follow [NM02]. Define dec to be $\lambda z.\lambda c.G(z\,F(c))$, where the "step" function F and the "basis" function G are defined as follows:

$$F(c) \equiv \lambda b_1.\lambda b_2 \otimes w.(b_1 \otimes (cb_2w))$$

$$G(y) \equiv \lambda x_1 x_2.\text{let } (y(\underline{0} \otimes x_1)(\underline{0} \otimes x_2)) \text{ be } (i_1 \otimes w_1) \otimes (j_1 \otimes w_2) \otimes q \text{ in}$$

$$(w_1 \otimes w_2 \otimes i_1 \otimes j_1 \otimes q)$$

$$c\!:\!B \multimap \alpha \multimap \alpha \vdash F(c)\!:\!\mathbf{B} \multimap D \multimap D$$

$$y\!:\!D \multimap D \multimap D \otimes D \otimes \mathbf{B}^n \vdash G(y)\!:\!\alpha \multimap \alpha \multimap (\alpha \otimes \alpha \otimes \mathbf{B} \otimes \mathbf{B} \otimes \mathbf{B}^n)$$

Here, D stands for $\mathbf{B} \otimes \alpha$. The behavior of F may be illustrated by

$$(F(c)\underline{i_1}) \circ \cdots \circ (F(c)\underline{i_n})(\underline{0} \otimes x) \longrightarrow^* \underline{i_1} \otimes (c\underline{i_2} \circ \cdots \circ c\underline{i_n} \circ c\underline{0}(x))\!:\!D,$$

while G plays the roles of initialization and rearrangement of the output.   ∎

Lemma 6 (Combination). *There is a term* com $: ID[\mathbf{B} \otimes \mathbf{B} \otimes \mathbf{B}^n] \multimap ID[\mathbf{B}^n]$ *such that for any* $\langle w_1, w_2, i_1, i_2, q \rangle$ *with* $\delta(i_1, q) = (s, q', m)$,

$$\text{com}\underline{\langle w_1, w_2, i_1, i_2, q \rangle} \longrightarrow^* \underline{\langle w_1,\ si_2 w_2, q' \rangle},\ \ \textit{if } m = \textit{left;}$$
$$\longrightarrow^* \underline{\langle i_2 s w_1,\ w_2, q' \rangle},\ \ \textit{if } m = \textit{right.}$$

Proof. Let $\underline{left} \equiv$ true and $\underline{right} \equiv$ false. By Theorem 2, there is a term delta such that delta $\underline{i_1 q}$ reduces to $\underline{s} \otimes \underline{q'} \otimes \underline{m}$ when $\delta(i_1, q) = (s, q', m)$. Now the key trick is to use the boolean value $\underline{m}$ as "switcher." Observe that $\underline{m s i_2}$ reduces to $\underline{s} \otimes i_2$ ($i_2 \otimes \underline{s}$) and $\underline{m} w_1 w_2$ reduces to $w_1 \otimes w_2$ ($w_2 \otimes w_1$) when $\underline{m}$ is $\underline{left}$ ($\underline{right}$)—thus $\underline{m}$ can be used to determine on which side of the tape we push symbols, and in what order they are pushed.

Formally, let $\text{cntr}^3 : \mathbf{B} \multimap \mathbf{B}^3$ be a generalized contraction which produces three copies of a given boolean value, and define $G(m, w_1, w_2, i_2, s, c_1, c_2)$ to be

$$\text{let cntr}^3(m) \text{ be } m_1 \otimes m_2 \otimes m_3 \text{ in } (\text{let } m_1 s i_2 \text{ be } j_1 \otimes j_2 \text{ in}$$

$$(\text{let } m_2 w_1 w_2 \text{ be } v_1 \otimes v_2 \text{ in } m_3 v_1(c_1 j_1 \circ c_2 j_2(v_2)))),$$

which is of type $m\!:\!\mathbf{B}, w_1\!:\!\alpha, w_2\!:\!\alpha, i_2\!:\!\mathbf{B}, s\!:\!\mathbf{B}, c_1\!:\!\mathbf{B} \multimap \alpha \multimap \alpha, c_2\!:\!\mathbf{B} \multimap \alpha \multimap \alpha \vdash$ $G(m, w_1, w_2, i_2, s, c_1, c_2)\!:\!\alpha \otimes \alpha$. Then, depending on the value of m, we have

$$G(\text{true}, w_1, w_2, i_2, s, c, c) \longrightarrow^* w_1 \otimes (cs \circ ci_2(w_2));$$
$$G(\text{false}, w_1, w_2, i_2, s, c, c) \longrightarrow^* (ci_2 \circ cs(w_1)) \otimes w_2.$$

Finally, the term com is defined to be

$$\lambda z.\lambda c x_1 x_2.\text{let } z c x_1 x_2 \text{ be } w_1 \otimes w_2 \otimes i_1 \otimes i_2 \otimes q \text{ in}$$

$$(\text{let delta } i_1 q \text{ be } s \otimes q' \otimes m \text{ in } G(m, w_1, w_2, i_2, s, c, c) \otimes q').$$

Although the "cons" variable c is used three times in com, it does not matter since it is assigned a type $!(\mathbf{B} \multimap \alpha \multimap \alpha)$.   ∎

The desired one-step transition function is obtained by composing dec and com.

Theorem 5 (IMLLL represents PTIME functions). *A function* $f: \{0,1\}^* \longrightarrow$ $\{0,1\}^*$ *is computable in* DTIME$[n^k]$ *if and only if it is represented by an* **IMLLL** *term t of type* $\mathbf{W} \multimap \S^d \mathbf{W}$, *where* $d = O(\log k)$.

In general, cut-elimination in Light Affine Logic, hence in **IMLLL**, requires of time $O(s^{2^{d+1}})$, where s is the size of a proof and d is its *depth*, which counts the nesting of ! and § inferences. The reason why we have a characterization of PTIME above is that we consider a fixed program t, so all the terms $t\underline{w}$ to be evaluated have a fixed depth. On the other hand, CEP allows the depth to vary, thus it results in a characterization of doubly-exponential time as in [NM02].

Theorem 6 (2EXPTIME-completeness of IMLLL). *The cut-elimination problem for* **IMLLL** *is complete for* 2EXPTIME $= \bigcup_k$ DTIME$[2^{2^{n^k}}]$.

5 Multiplicative Soft Linear Logic and EXPTIME

In this section, we show that the intuitionistic multiplicative fragment **IMSLL** of Soft Linear Logic is expressive enough to represent all polynomial time functions, as conjectured by Lafont [Laf01]. As before, we do not introduce a term calculus for **IMSLL**, thinking of it as a type assignment system for the standard λ-calculus.

The type assignment rules of **IMSLL** are those of **IMLL** with the following:

$$\frac{x_1 : B_1, \ldots, x_m : B_m \vdash t : A}{x_1 : !B_1, \ldots, x_m : !B_m \vdash t : !A} \ m \geq 0 \qquad \frac{x_1 : A, \ldots, x_n : A, \Gamma \vdash t : C}{z : !A, \Gamma \vdash t[z/x_1, \ldots, z/x_n] : C} \ n \geq 0$$

The former is called *soft promotion* and the latter is called *multiplexing*. A term which can be typed without multiplexing is called *generic*. Note that every generic term is a linear λ-term.

The policy of **MSLL** programming is to write each program in a generic way; multiplexing (i.e. duplication) is used only in data. Due to this restriction, simulation of Turing machines is more sophisticated than before. Let M and δ be as before. Define $ID_k[A]$ to be $\forall \alpha.!(\mathbf{B} \multimap \alpha \multimap \alpha) \multimap ((\alpha \multimap \alpha)^k \otimes A)$. Then each term of type $ID_k[A]$ encodes k words as well as an element of type A. For instance, the configuration $\langle 010, 11, q \rangle$ is represented by

$$\langle 010, 11, q \rangle \equiv \lambda c.(c\underline{0} \circ c\underline{1} \circ c\underline{0}) \otimes (c\underline{1} \circ c\underline{1}) \otimes \underline{q} : ID_2[\mathbf{B}^n].$$

Lemma 7 (Decomposition). *For every $k \geq 1$, there exists a generic term* dec *of type* $ID_k[\mathbf{B}^n] \multimap ID_{2k}[\mathbf{B} \otimes \mathbf{B}^n]$ *such that for any* $\langle i_1 w_1, \ldots, i_k w_k, q \rangle \in (\{0,1\}^+)^k \times States$,

$$\mathsf{dec}\langle i_1 w_1, \ldots, i_k w_k, q \rangle \longrightarrow^* \langle w_1, \ldots, w_k, i_1, \ldots, i_k, i_1, q \rangle.$$

Note that the output contains two occurrences of i_1; the first is a word of length 1 which will be thrown away, while the second is a boolean value which will be used as input to the δ function in the next combination part.

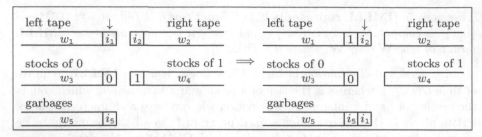

Fig. 1. "Write 1 and move right" ($\downarrow$ indicates the head position)

Proof. The idea is essentially the same as the ψ function of [Laf01]. Consider the case $k = 1$. The term dec is defined to be $\lambda z.\lambda c.\lambda z \otimes q.(zF(c)(id \otimes id \otimes \underline{0})) \otimes q$, where the step function F is defined by

$$F(c) \equiv \lambda b.\mathsf{let}\ \mathsf{cntr}(b)\ \mathsf{be}\ b_1 \otimes b_2\ \mathsf{in}\ (\lambda g \otimes h \otimes e.\mathsf{fst}(((h \circ g) \otimes cb_1 \otimes b_2) \otimes e))$$
$$c:\mathbf{B} \multimap \alpha \multimap \alpha \vdash F(c):\mathbf{B} \multimap ((\alpha \multimap \alpha)^2 \otimes \mathbf{B}) \multimap ((\alpha \multimap \alpha)^2 \otimes \mathbf{B}).$$

The behavior of F is illustrated as follows;

$$(F(c)\underline{i_1}) \circ \cdots \circ (F(c)\underline{i_n})(id \otimes id \otimes \underline{0}) \longrightarrow^* (c\underline{i_2} \circ \cdots \circ c\underline{i_n}) \otimes c\underline{i_1} \otimes \underline{i_1}.$$

The case $k \geq 2$ is similar, except that we remove all redundant boolean values $i_2, \ldots, i_k$ by weakening for $\mathbf{B}$. ∎

Now let us move on to the combination part. Due to the genericity restriction, we face two difficulties: (i) we cannot create a new tape cell, since the "cons" variable c of type $!(\mathbf{B} \multimap \alpha \multimap \alpha)$ cannot be used twice; (ii) we cannot simply remove an unnecessary tape cell of type $\alpha \multimap \alpha$, since we do not have weakening for the open type $\alpha \multimap \alpha$. To resolve the first difficulty, we prepare two additional stacks which are filled with $\underline{0}$'s and $\underline{1}$'s respectively, and instead of creating a new cell, we pick one from these two stacks according to the instruction δ. To resolve the second difficulty, we further prepare a 'garbage' stack where unnecessary tape cells are collected. Thus we associate five stacks in total with a configuration. The transition corresponding to "write 1 and move right" is illustrated in Figure 1.

Lemma 8 (Combination). *There is a generic term* com *of type* $ID_{10}[\mathbf{B} \otimes \mathbf{B}^n] \multimap ID_5[\mathbf{B}^n]$ *such that for any* $\langle w_1, \ldots, w_5, i_1, \ldots, i_5, b, q \rangle \in (\{0,1\}^+)^5 \times \{0,1\}^5 \times \{0,1\} \times States$ *with* $\delta(b, q) = (s, q', m)$,

$$\begin{array}{ll} \mathsf{com}\langle w_1, \ldots, w_5, i_1, i_2, 0, 1, i_5, b, q \rangle & \\ \longrightarrow^* \langle w_1,\ 0i_2w_2,\ w_3,\ 1w_4,\ i_1i_5w_5, q' \rangle & \textit{if } s = 0 \textit{ and } m = \textit{left;} \\ \longrightarrow^* \langle w_1,\ 1i_2w_2,\ 0w_3,\ w_4,\ i_1i_5w_5, q' \rangle & \textit{if } s = 1 \textit{ and } m = \textit{left;} \\ \longrightarrow^* \langle i_20w_1,\ w_2,\ w_3,\ 1w_4,\ i_1i_5w_5, q' \rangle & \textit{if } s = 0 \textit{ and } m = \textit{right;} \\ \longrightarrow^* \langle i_21w_1,\ w_2,\ 0w_3,\ w_4,\ i_1i_5w_5, q' \rangle & \textit{if } s = 1 \textit{ and } m = \textit{right.} \end{array}$$

Keep in mind that the third and the fourth stacks are to be filled with $\underline{0}$'s and $\underline{1}$'s, so that we always find $\underline{0}$ and $\underline{1}$ at positions i_3 and i_4, respectively.

Proof. As before, there is a term delta such that delta $\underline{bq}$ reduces to $\underline{s} \otimes \underline{q'} \otimes \underline{m}$ when $\delta(b, q) = (s, q', m)$. Define 1Right by

$$\text{1Right} \equiv (i_2 \circ i_4 \circ w_1) \otimes w_2 \otimes (i_3 \circ w_3) \otimes w_4 \otimes (i_1 \circ i_5 \circ w_5)$$

$$w_1 : \alpha \multimap \alpha, \ldots, w_5 : \alpha \multimap \alpha, i_1 : \alpha \multimap \alpha, \ldots, i_5 : \alpha \multimap \alpha \vdash \text{1Right} : (\alpha \multimap \alpha)^5,$$

which corresponds to the case $s = 1$ and $m = right$ (see Figure 1) and gives five stacks as output. 0Left, 1Left and 0Right are defined analogously. By using conditionals in Lemma 1 three times, we obtain

$$G(m, s, w_1, \ldots, w_5, i_1, \ldots, i_5) \equiv \left(\begin{array}{l} \text{if } m \text{ then if } s \text{ then 0Left } \text{ else 1Left} \\ \text{else if } s \text{ then 0Right else 1Right} \end{array} \right)$$

$$\text{com} \equiv \lambda z.\lambda c.\text{let } zc \text{ be } w_1 \otimes \cdots \otimes w_5 \otimes i_1 \otimes \cdots \otimes i_5 \otimes b \otimes q \text{ in}$$

$$(\text{let delta } bq \text{ be } s \otimes q' \otimes m \text{ in } G(m, s, w_1, \ldots, w_5, i_1, \ldots, i_5) \otimes q').$$

∎

The rest of coding is basically the same as in [Laf01] except the initialization part, where we need to fill two stacks with $\underline{0}$'s and $\underline{1}$'s. As in [Laf01], we have no idea how to extract a single word as output from the final configuration consisting of five stacks. Instead, we can extract the boolean value which tells us whether the final configuration is accepting or not. Thus the representation theorem below is stated in terms of languages rather than functions in general. Furthermore, due to the genericity restriction, we need to relax the definition of representation slightly. Define $\mathbf{W}_S$ to be $\forall \alpha.!(\mathbf{B} \multimap \alpha \multimap \alpha) \multimap \alpha \multimap \alpha$. We say that a language $X \subseteq \{0, 1\}^*$ is *represented by* a term $t : \mathbf{W}_S^l \multimap \mathbf{B}$ if $w \in X \iff t \underbrace{w \cdots w}_{l \; times} \longrightarrow^* \text{true}$
for every $w \in \{0, 1\}^*$.

Theorem 7 (IMSLL captures PTIME). *A language $X \subseteq \{0, 1\}^*$ is accepted in* DTIME$[n^k]$ *if and only if it is represented by a generic term t of type $\mathbf{W}_S^l \multimap \mathbf{B}$, where $l = O(k)$.*

As in the case of **IMLLL**, the complexity of CEP exceeds polynomial time. A difference is that cut-elimination in **IMSLL** only requires exponential time $O(s^{d+2})$ [Laf01]. Hence we have:

Theorem 8 (EXPTIME-completeness of IMSLL). *The cut-elimination problem for* **IMSLL** *is complete for* EXPTIME *under logspace reducibility.*

Proof (sketch). Suppose that a language X be accepted by a Turing machine M in time $O(2^{n^k})$. For each word w of length n, the following terms (of suitable types) can be constructed in $O(k \log n)$ space: (1) the Church representation $\underline{w}$ of w; (2) the term $\exp(n^k)$ of size and depth $O(n^k)$, which reduces to the tally integer $\underline{2^{n^k}}$; (3) the term $M_{n,k}(w, x)$ with two variables w and x, which outputs the result of x-steps computation on the input w, when w is of length n and x is of the same type as $\exp(n^k)$. By putting them together, we obtain a term $M_{n,k}(\underline{w}, \exp(n^k))$ which normalizes to true if and only if $w \in X$.   ∎

Acknowledgments

We wish to thank Patrick Baillot and Marco Pedicini for very stimulating discussions, and Jean-Yves Girard, Stefano Guerrini, Yves Lafont, Satoshi Matsuoka, Peter Neergaard, Peter Selinger, Izumi Takeuti, Rene Vestergaard and the anonymous referees for a lot of useful comments.

References

Asp98.   A. Asperti. Light affine logic. In *Proceedings of the Thirteenth Annual IEEE Symposium on Logic in Computer Science*, pages 300–308, 1998.

AR02.   A. Asperti and L. Roversi. Intuitionistic light affine logic (proof-nets, normalization complexity, expressive power, programming notation). *ACM Transactions on Computational Logic*, 3(1):1–39, 2002.

dF03.   L. Tortora de Falco. The additive multiboxes. *Annals of Pure and Applied Logic*, 120(1):65–102, 2003.

Gir87.   J.-Y. Girard. Linear logic. *Theoretical Computer Science*, 50:1–102, 1987.

Gir98.   J.-Y. Girard. Light linear logic. *Information and Computation*, 14(3):175–204, 1998.

GJ78.   M. Garey and D. Johnson. *Computers and Intractability: A Guide to the Theory of NP-completeness*. Freeman, San Francisco, 1978.

Hin89.   J. R. Hindley. BCK-combinators and linear λ-terms have types. *Theoretical Computer Science*, 64:97–105, 1989.

Lad75.   R. E. Ladner. The circuit value problem is logspace complete for P. *SIGACT News*, 7(1):18–20, 1975.

Laf01.   Y. Lafont. Soft linear logic and polynomial time. *Theoretical Computer Science*, to appear.

Lin95.   P. D. Lincoln. Deciding provability of linear logic formulas. In *Advances in Linear Logic*, London Mathematical Society Lecture Notes Series, Volume 222, Cambridge University Press, 1995, 109–122.

MR02.   H. G. Mairson and X. Rival. Proofnets and context semantics for the additives. *Computer Science Logic (CSL) 2002*, 151–166.

Mai03.   H. G. Mairson. Linear lambda calculus and polynomial time. *Journal of Functional Programming*, to appear.

NM02.   P. M. Neergaard and H. G. Mairson. LAL is square: representation and expressiveness in light affine logic. Presented at the Fourth International Workshop on Implicit Computational Complexity, 2002.

Sch01.   A. Schubert. The Complexity of β-Reduction in Low Orders. *Typed Lambda Calculi and Applications (TLCA) 2001*, 400–414.

Sta79.   R. Statman. The typed λ-calculus is not elementary recursive. *Theoretical Computer Science*, 9:73–81, 1979.

Ter01.   K. Terui. Light affine lambda calculus and polytime strong normalization. In *Proceedings of the sixteenth annual IEEE symposium on Logic in Computer Science*, pages 209–220, 2001. The full version is available at http://research.nii.ac.jp/~terui.

A Constructive Proof of the Soundness of the Encoding of Random Access Machines in a Linda Calculus with Ordered Semantics

Claudio Sacerdoti Coen*

Department of Computer Science
Via di Mura Anteo Zamboni 7, 40127 Bologna, ITALY.
sacerdot@cs.unibo.it

Abstract. Random Access Machines (RAMs) are a deterministic Turing-complete formalism especially well suited for being encoded in other formalisms. This is due to the fact that RAMs can be defined starting from very primitive concepts and operations, which are unbounded natural numbers, tuples, successor, predecessor and test for equality to zero. Since these concepts are easily available also in theorem-provers and proof-assistants, RAMs are good candidates for proving Turing-completeness of formalisms using a proof-assistant. In this paper we describe an encoding in Coq of RAMs into a Linda Calculus endowed with the Ordered Semantics. We discuss the main difficulties that must be faced and the techniques we adopted to solve them.

1 Introduction

A Random Access Machine (RAM) [12] is a computational model composed of a finite set of registers and of a program, that is a sequence of simple numbered instructions, like arithmetical operations (on the content of registers) or conditional jumps. A register holds an unbounded natural number. The state of a RAM is the set of values stored in each register plus the program counter (PC), which is the address of the next instruction to execute. The computation starts from an initial state and proceeds iterating the two operations of fetching and executing the next instruction (determined by the PC). The computation ends as soon as the value of the PC is greater than the index of the last instruction.

The RAMs formalism is Turing complete and has several characteristics that make it particularly appealing for being encoded into other formalisms to show their Turing completeness. First of all a RAM can be defined using only very primitive concepts and operations, which are unbounded natural numbers, tuples, successor, predecessor and test for equality to zero. These concepts are likely to be already provided in any formalism which we want to show Turing complete. Moreover it is possible to reduce the set of instructions to only two elements, Succ (which increments a register) and DecJump which decrements a

---

* Work partially supported by the European Project IST-33562 MoWGLI

C. Blundo and C. Laneve (Eds.): ICTCS 2003, LNCS 2841, pp. 37–57, 2003.
© Springer-Verlag Berlin Heidelberg 2003

register if it is not zero or jumps to a given address otherwise. As a consequence the proofs of completeness of the encodings are very small, having to address only a couple of cases and only three possible transitions. Finally, RAMs are completely deterministic, which prevents the usual difficulties given by the simulation of non-deterministic systems into deterministic ones.

Just to mention a couple of examples, RAMs have been successfully encoded into several process algebras, such as asynchronous CCS [13] and the ambient calculus [14]. Even if providing the encoding can be challenging, the soundness and completeness proofs are usually given in just a few lines, and heavily rely on the reader intuition to figure out the details by case reasoning.

In the last few years, several process calculi have been formalized, using proof-assistants, in both constructive and classical logics. Surprisingly, to our knowledge nobody tried to reproduce a proof of Turing-completeness of those calculi. Nevertheless, when we started this work, we used to think that giving one of those proofs by means of a sound and complete encoding of RAMs into the calculus would have been completely trivial. The reason of our belief was that the same characteristics that make RAMs so well suited for their encoding in other formalisms also make their definition in a logical framework quite straightforward. Moreover the soundness proof would just be a laborious induction on the derivation.

In this paper we present our experience in using the proof-assistant Coq [2] to provide an encoding of RAM into a Turing complete process algebra. We also give a constructive proof of the soundness property of the encoding. As usual, the soundness proof exploits the completeness property. However, we axiomatically assume the completeness of the calculus, that can be proved by induction over the structure of RAMs and that of their derivations. Since the RAM formalism is deterministic, the required induction is almost straightforward and presents no major challenge, even if it is extremely laborious and time consuming. The soundness proof quickly turned out to require a major effort and its proof-script is currently more than 10.000 lines long and it is still under development, since we plan to provide soon also the proof of completeness. The up-to-date set of Coq files are available for download at the following address: http://www.cs.unibo.it/RAMs_to_Linda.tgz.

In section 2 we briefly introduce the Coq proof-assistant and the main features of its expressive logic. In section 3 we review the usual definition of RAMs and we present its formal definition in the Coq system. In section 4 we introduce a minimal process algebra built around the Linda primitives [5], originally proposed in [1]. The formal definition in Coq is also provided. In section 5 we present the encoding of RAMs into the Linda Calculus of section 4 and we outline the formal proof of soundness. Finally, in section 6 we present our conclusions and future work proposal.

2   The Coq Proof Assistant

Coq [2] is one of the most advanced proof-assistants, used in Europe both in academical and industrial settings. It is based on an expressive logical framework, the Calculus of (Co)Inductive Constructions (CIC), which allows both constructive and classical proofs and that is particularly suitable for proving the correctness of programs with respect to their specifications, with the additional possibility of automatically extracting a certified program from a constructive proof of the existence of a function that satisfies a given specification.

Briefly, a Coq development is made of a list of definitions, inductive definitions and theorems whose correctness is checked by the system. Inductive definitions, which are one of the main features of CIC, can be used to define both inductive data types (lists, trees, natural numbers) and inductive properties (by giving the set of inference rules that define the property). It is possible to define by structural recursion total functions over an inductive data-type (in the style of the system T); in the same way it is also possible to prove by structural induction properties over an inductive data-type. A primitive notion of case analysis over inductive defined terms is also provided.

Since the main topic of the paper is the technique used for the encoding of the soundness proof in Coq, the interested reader needs a general expertise in the world of proof-assistants and in the Coq system in particular. Due to lack of space, the required knowledge can not be provided in this paper.

3 Random Access Machines

The following is the usual presentation of a particular class of RAMs with only two-instructions. The proof of their Turing completeness was given in [11].

Definition 1. *A Random Access Machine (RAM) is a pair $(\boldsymbol{r}, \boldsymbol{p})$ where $\boldsymbol{r} = (r_1, \ldots, r_n)$ is the set of registers and the program $\boldsymbol{p} = (i_1, \ldots, i_m)$ is a finite list of instructions. Each instruction can have one of the following two forms:*

- *$Succ(r_j)$: adds 1 to the content of register r_j*
- *$DecJump(r_j, s)$: if the content of register r_j is not zero, then decreases it by 1 and go to the next instruction; otherwise jumps to instruction s*

Definition 2. *Let R be a RAM whose registers are $(r_1, \ldots, r_n)$. A configuration of R is a tuple $(p, c_1, \ldots, c_n)$ where the program counter (PC) p is the index of the next instruction to be executed and c_l is the content of the register r_l.*

Definition 3. *Let R be a RAM whose registers are $(r_1, \ldots, r_n)$ and whose program is $(i_1, \ldots, i_m)$. A configuration $(p, c_1, \ldots, c_n)$ moves into a configuration $(q, c'_1, \ldots, c'_n)$ (notation: $(p, c_1, \ldots, c_n) \longrightarrow_R (q, c'_1, \ldots, c'_n)$) iff:*

- *$i_p = Succ(r_j)$ and $c'_j = c_j + 1$ and $\forall l \neq j.\ c'_n = c_n$ and $q = p + 1$*
- *$i_p = DecJump(r_j, s)$ and $c_j > 0$ and $c'_j = c_j - 1$ and $\forall l \neq j.\ c'_n = c_n$ and $q = p + 1$*
- *$i_p = DecJump(r_j, s)$ and $c_j = 0$ and $\forall l.\ c'_n = c_n$ and $q = s$*

Definition 4. *A configuration $(p, c_1, \ldots, c_n)$ is stuck or final when it cannot move. This happens only when $p > m$, where m is the length of the program.*

As usual, given a RAM R and an initial configuration C, we say that C reduces to C' when $C \longrightarrow_R^* C'$ and C' is final, where $\longrightarrow_R^*$ is the reflexive and transitive closure of $\longrightarrow_R$.

3.1   RAMs in Coq

The only non-trivial issue on the formalization of RAMs in Coq is the way registers are encoded. In fact the tuple $(r_1, \ldots, r_n)$ of registers just plays the role of a finite set of indexes such that no instruction refers to a non-existent index. The only additional constraint we need to impose on the set is that there exists a decidable equality relation over its elements.

Since the list of instructions is finite and since registers not referred by any instruction play no role during the reduction, we could have used just the type of natural numbers for register indexes (with no concern about the fact that the set of indexes is actually infinite). In this case it would have been possible in Coq to define a function to compute the greatest used register index. Instead we preferred to stick ourselves to this alternative definition:

```
Definition register := nat.
```

```
Inductive instruction : Set :=
   Succ : register→instruction
 | DecJump : register→nat→instruction.
```

```
Inductive uses_at_most [r:register] : instruction→Prop :=
   okSucc : ∀r':register.(r'<r)→(uses_at_most r (Succ r'))
 | okDecJump :
      ∀r':register.∀n:nat.(r'<r)→(uses_at_most r (DecJump r' n)).
```

```
Record RAM : Set :=
 { registers_number : nat ;
   program : (list instruction) ;
   program_ok : (AllS (uses_at_most registers_number) program)
 }.
```

i.e. a RAM is a record where the number of available registers is made explicit and a proof is provided of the fact that each instruction in the program does not refer to any unavailable register. We prefer this formalization for several reasons:

- This formalization is closer to the traditional one and does not identify two RAMs with the same program, but a different set of available registers. Unused but still available registers play a role in the traditional proofs of some operations used to combine or derive RAMs from other RAMs.
- The fact that the number of available registers is invariant during the reduction holds trivially for RAMs, but can be much more difficult to prove when RAMs are encoded into other calculi. That invariant plays an important role in the soundness and completeness proofs. For example, in section 5 we will see that we need to encode in the same data-type (i.e. natural numbers) both the indexes of registers and the value of the program counter (which is an unbounded natural number). The easiest way to do that is to encode each program counter value p as $M + p$ where M is the number of available registers. The decoding function relies on the fact that M does not change during the reduction.

We must now formalize configurations. In particular we must choose a representation of the state of the registers. The choice has a great impact on the way two configurations are checked for equality: we may choose an encoding where two configurations are equal iff they are equal using Leibniz equality; or we can provide an ad-hoc equality predicate. The first scenario seems at first more appealing, since Leibniz equality is better handled by Coq's tactics with respect to a user-provided one. Moreover, a possible implementation could be using ordered lists of natural numbers of length n. Unfortunately, reasoning on ordered lists of fixed length may complicate some proofs and introduce the usual problems related to the fact that every operation working on them (and, in particular, the state update function) must be proof-irrelevant on the proof argument. Proof-irrelevance and dependent types do not combine easily in intensional proof theories as the one of Coq [3,4].

A good compromise is using functions from natural numbers to natural numbers, using extensional equality to compare the content *of available registers only*:

```
Record configuration : Set :=
{ program_counter : nat ;
  registers : register→nat
}.

Definition RAM_configuration_equality :
nat→configuration→configuration→Prop
:=
λregisters_no:nat.λH,H':configuration.
  Cases H of
  (Build_configuration program_counter registers)⇒
  Cases H' of
  (Build_configuration program_counter' registers')⇒
   program_counter=program_counter'∧
   ∀r:register.
    (r<registers_no)→
    (registers r)=(registers' r)
  end
 end.
```

The relation $\longrightarrow_R$ is given as an inductive predicate step. Its definition and some of its properties (determinism, decidability of being stuck, non modification of unavailable registers) as well as the definition of $\longrightarrow_R^3$ and its basic properties are straightforward.

Since we have just defined an encoding of RAMs into CIC, we should prove the adequacy of the encoding; a detailed proof would be quite complex since it heavily relies on the metatheory of CIC. Nevertheless, the usual sources of complexity that are involved in the encodings of calculi — as the handling of bound variables and α-conversion — are not raised by RAMs, due to the simplicity of the formalism. As a consequence, the adequacy property is not much interesting and it is essentially pretty obviously granted by construction. The same remark holds also for the Linda calculus that we are going to present in the next section.

The whole definition of RAMs, their operational semantics and the proof of these basic properties are provided in the file RAMs.v which is just 366 lines long.

4   The Linda Calculus

Linda [5] is the most prominent representative of the family of coordination languages based on the principle of *generative communication* [5,6]: a sender communicates with a receiver through a shared data space (called *tuple space* TS) where emitted messages are collected; the receiver can read the message or even remove it from the TS; a message generated by a process has an independent existence in the TS and can be concurrently manipulated by any process.

The Linda coordination primitives are meant to be embedded into an already existent programming language. Moreover their semantics is not specified formally and there are several reasonable interpretations for the semantics of some operations. In particular, it is unclear if a sender who is emitting a message should block until the message actually appears in the tuple space (*ordered semantics*) or is free to continue immediately its execution (*unordered semantics*).

Busi, Gorrieri and Zavattaro defined in [1] a minimal process algebra containing the coordination primitives of Linda together with parallel composition and a limited form of recursion (the replication operator [10] guarded on inputs). The algebra is named *Linda Calculus*. In the same paper they proved that the Linda Calculus is Turing complete only when the ordered semantics is assumed. The first part of the proof is made showing a sound and complete embedding of RAMs in the Linda Calculus with ordered semantics. The proof of soundness and completeness is just three lines long in the full version of the paper.

In this section we present a formalization in Coq of the Linda Calculus presented in [1]. The next section is devoted to the formalization of the encoding.

Let *Messages* be a denumerable set of message names, ranged over by $a, b, \ldots$ The syntax of the Linda Calculus is defined by the following grammar:

$$P ::= <a> \mid C \mid P|P$$

$$C ::= 0 \mid \eta.C \mid \mu?C\_C \mid C||C$$

where:

$$\eta ::= in(a) \mid rd(a) \mid out(a) \mid !in(a) \tag{1}$$

$$\mu ::= inp(a) \mid rdp(a) \tag{2}$$

Agents, ranged over by $P, Q, \ldots$, consist of the parallel composition of the messages already in the TS (each one denoted by one agent $<a>$) and the concurrent programs denoted by $C, D, \ldots$, that share the tuples. A program can be a terminated program 0, a prefix form $\eta.P$, an *if-then-else* form $\mu?P\_Q$, or the parallel composition of programs. A prefix η can be one of the Linda primitives $in(a)$, $rd(a)$ or $out(a)$ indicating the withdrawing, the reading (without

Table 1. Operational semantics (symmetric rules omitted).

(1)	$<a> \xrightarrow{\overline{a}} 0$		(2)	$in(a).P \xrightarrow{a} P$
(3)	$rd(a).P \xrightarrow{a} P$		(4)	$!in(a).P \xrightarrow{a} P\|!in(a).P$
(5)	$inp(a)?P\_Q \xrightarrow{a} P$		(6)	$rdp(a)?P\_Q \xrightarrow{a} P$
(7)	$inp(a)?P\_Q \xrightarrow{\neg a} Q$		(8)	$rdp(a)?P\_Q \xrightarrow{\neg a} Q$
(9)	$P\|Q \xrightarrow{\tau} P|Q$		(10)	$out(a).P \xrightarrow{\tau} <a> |P$

$$(11) \quad \frac{P \xrightarrow{\alpha} P'}{P|Q \xrightarrow{\alpha} P'|Q} \quad \alpha \neq \neg a \qquad\qquad (12) \quad \frac{P \xrightarrow{\neg a} P' \quad Q \not\xrightarrow{\overline{a}}}{P|Q \xrightarrow{\neg a} P'|Q}$$

$$(13) \quad \frac{P \xrightarrow{a} P' \quad Q \xrightarrow{\overline{a}} Q'}{P|Q \xrightarrow{\tau} P'|Q'} \qquad\qquad (14) \quad \frac{P \xrightarrow{a} P' \quad Q \xrightarrow{\overline{a}} Q'}{P|Q \xrightarrow{\tau} P'|Q}$$

consumption) or the emission of message a, respectively. We also consider the bang operator $!in(a)$ which is a form of replication guarded on input operations. The if-then-else forms are used to model the $inp(a)$ and $rdp(a)$ Linda primitives: $inp(a)?P\_Q$ ($rdp(a)?P\_Q$) is a program which requires the message a to be consumed (or simply read); if a is present, the program P is executed, otherwise Q is chosen. In the following, *Agent* denotes the set containing all possible agents.

To give the Ordered Semantics, we use the labeled transition system (*Agent*, *Label*, $\longrightarrow$) where $Label = \{\tau\} \cup \{a, \underline{a}, \overline{a}, \neg a \mid a \in Messages\}$ (ranged over by α, β, ...) is the set of possible labels. The labeled transition relation $\longrightarrow$ is the smallest one satisfying all the axioms and rules in Table 1 plus the symmetric rules of (11) - (14). Due to lack of space, we can not explain here every rule. The interested reader can find the description of all the rules but (9) in [1]. Rule (9) is missing in the original paper since in it no syntactic distinction is made between the inactive parallel composition $\_\|\_$ and the active parallel composition $\_|\_$.

Particular attention should be given to rule (10), which is the one that characterizes the Ordered Semantics: the continuation P and the message $<a>$ reach the tuple space at the same time.

Note that rule (12) uses a negative premise. The authors of [1] claim their operational semantics to be well defined since they can prove that the transition system is strictly stratifiable. To formalize rule (12) in Coq we prefer to substitute the negative premise with an equivalent decidable auxiliary predicate $NoMessage_a$, which is the smallest predicate such that:

(A)	$NoMessage_a(<b>)$ if $a \neq b$
(B)	$NoMessage_a(C)$
(C)	$\dfrac{NoMessage(P) \quad NoMessage(Q)}{NoMessage(P|Q)}$

In what follows we are interested only in computations consisting of reduction steps, i.e. the internal derivations that a *stand-alone* agent is able to perform independently of the context. In the Linda Calculus reductions are not only the usual derivations labeled with τ, but also those labeled with $\neg a$. In fact, a derivation $P \xrightarrow{\neg a} P'$ indicates that P can become P' if no tuples $<a>$ are avail-

able in the external environment, which is always true for stand-alone processes.
Formally we define a new transition $\longrightarrow$ (called *step*) in the following way:

Definition 5. $\longrightarrow = (\bigcup_a \xrightarrow{\neg a}) \cup \xrightarrow{\tau}$

Since in process algebras there is no explicit notion of state, the only reasonable form of termination of an agent is the absence of outgoing transitions. Because of the presence of the bang operator, it is senseless to distinguish between properly terminated (i.e. consisting of the parallel composition of agents 0) and deadlocked agents. Thus we say that an agent Q is *stuck* if $Q \not\longrightarrow$ and we say that an agent P terminates if there exist a computation leading to a deadlock, i.e. there exists a stuck agent Q such that $P \longrightarrow^* Q$.

No structural congruence relation is defined in [1] on the agents. Nevertheless many statements given in the paper are true only assuming that processes are identified up to commutativity and associativity of parallel composition and neutrality of 0 with respect to parallel composition. Here we prefer to avoid the definition of a structural congruence relation. Instead in section 5 we will state the soundness theorem using the congruence relation induced by the equivalence relation on RAMs[1].

4.1   The Linda Calculus in Coq

The formalization in Coq of the Linda Calculus syntax and its transition system (where rule (12) is modified as already described) is straightforward. Due to lack of space we do not show here all the constructors of the inductive predicate OStep which formalizes the labeled transition:

```
Definition message := nat.
```

```
Inductive action : Set :=
   In : message→action
| Rd : message→action
| Out : message→action
| BangIn : message→action.
```

```
Inductive program : Set :=
   Dead : program
| Action : action→program→program
| IfThenElseAction : action→program→program→program
| Parallel : program→program→program.
```

```
Inductive agent : Set :=
   Message : message→agent
| Program : program→agent
| AParallel : agent→agent→agent.
```

---

[1] The two congruence relations are provably equal, but we do not provide the formal proof neither here nor in Coq.

```
Inductive label : Set :=
   Tau : label
 | LIn : message→label
 | LRead : message→label
 | LOut : message→label
 | LNot : message→label.

(* A step in the ORDERED semantics. *)
Inductive OStep : agent→label→agent→Prop :=
   SMessage :
     ∀m:message.(OStep (Message m) (LOut m) (Program Dead))
 | SOut :
     (* This is the transition that makes the semantics ORDERED *)
     ∀m:message.∀P:program.
     (OStep
      (Program (Action (Out m) P))
      Tau
      (AParallel (Message m) (Program P)))
 | ...
```

The formalization of the Linda Calculus can be found in the Linda.v file, which is about 130 lines long.

5   The Encoding

We start by reviewing the encoding of RAMs into Linda Calculus agents given in [1].

To model a RAM in the Linda Calculus we need both an encoding for the configurations and one for the programs. The program counter in the configuration $(p, c_1, \ldots, c_n)$ is represented by the *program counter tuple* $< p >$ while the contents of registers r_l is modeled by c_l occurrences of the tuple $< r_l >$ (for $l = 1 \ldots n$):

$$\|(p, c_1, \ldots, c_n)\| \stackrel{\text{def}}{=} < p > | \underbrace{< r_1 > | \ldots | < r_1 >}_{c_1 \text{ times}} | \ldots | \underbrace{< r_n > | \ldots | < r_n >}_{c_n \text{ times}}$$

To model the program R composed of the sequence of instructions $i_1 \ldots i_m$ we consider the parallel composition of m agents, each one modeling an instruction:

$$
\begin{aligned}
\|R\| &\stackrel{\text{def}}{=} \|i_1\|^1 | \ldots | \|i_m\|^m \\
\|\text{Succ}(r_j)\|^i &\stackrel{\text{def}}{=} !in(p_i).out(r_j).out(p_{i+1}) \\
\|\text{DecJump}(r_j, s)\|^i &\stackrel{\text{def}}{=} !in(p_i).inp(r_j)?out(p_{i+1}) \_out(p_s)
\end{aligned}
$$

Each RAM instruction is realized by means of three internal steps: the first one $(!in(p_i))$ consumes the program counter; the second update/tests the contents of the register; the third one introduces the new program counter. The instruction is never consumed because of the replication operator.

Finally, the agent modeling the program R that starts its computation from the configuration $(1, c_1, \ldots, c_n)$ is $\|R\| \| (1, c_1, \ldots, c_n)\|$.

The part of [1] that describes the encoding ends with the following theorem:

Theorem 1. *Let R be a RAM program, then:*

- Soundness: *if* $\|R\| \| (p, c_1, \ldots, c_n)\| \longrightarrow^3 Q$ *then there exists a unique configuration* $(p', c'_1 \ldots, c'_n)$ *such that:*
  $$Q = \|R\| \| (p', c'_1, \ldots, c'_n)\| \quad and \quad (p, c_1, \ldots, c_n) \longrightarrow_R (p', c'_1, \ldots, c'_n)$$
- Completeness: *if* $(p, c_1, \ldots, c_n) \longrightarrow_R (p', c'_1, \ldots, c'_n)$ *then also*
  $$\|R\| \| (p, c_1, \ldots, c_n)\| \longrightarrow^3 \|R\| \| (p', c'_1, \ldots, c'_n)\|$$

Proof. By cases on the possible instructions that can be activated. In the proof of soundness we use the fact that the program counter tuple $< p_i >$ in the term $\|R\| \| (p_i, c_1, \ldots, c_n)\|$ ensures that only the agent corresponding to the ith instruction can move. ∎

Note in the soundness statement the usage of the equality $=$ between agents. That equality should be intended up to the undefined structural congruence rule.

5.1 The Encoding in Coq

As already suggested in Sect. 3, we decide to encode both register indexes (i.e. numbers in the interval $[0 \ldots n)$) and program counter values (i.e. unbounded integers) as natural numbers: a register index i is mapped to i; a program counter value p is mapped to $n + p$.

The encoding relation $\|\_\|$ is straightforwardly formalized in Coq as a set of (recursive) definitions. As an example, we show here only the two functions that map the RAM registers into the corresponding agent:

```
Fixpoint agent_of_register [r: register ; v:nat] : agent :=
Cases v of
   0 ⇒ (Program Dead)
 | (S n) ⇒ (AParallel (Message r) (agent_of_register r n))
end.


Fixpoint agent_of_registers [f:register→nat ; n:nat] : agent :=
Cases n of
   0 ⇒ (Program Dead)
 | (S m) ⇒
   (AParallel
     (agent_of_register m (f m))
     (agent_of_registers f m))
end.
```

Technical induction/recursion principles in the spirit of [7] are sometimes provided to reason on the recursive definitions. Example:

```
Theorem agent_of_registers_ind :
∀f:(register→nat).∀registers_no:nat.∀P: agent→Prop.
 (P (Program Dead))→
 (∀r:nat.
  (r<registers_no)→
  (P (agent_of_registers f r))→
  (P (AParallel
       (agent_of_register r (f r)) (agent_of_registers f r))))→
 (P (agent_of_registers f registers_no)).
```

The functions that define the encoding can be found in the file RAMs_to_Linda.v, which is only 84 lines long.

We are now left with the formalization of the soundness and completeness statements and their proof.

5.2 The Soundness Proof in Coq

Coq is based on a constructive logic and allows automatic code extraction from constructive proofs. In particular, since we decide to stick ourselves to constructive rules only, we can try to automatically obtain code for:

- Mapping RAMs into Linda agents.
- Recognizing Linda agents that are encoding of a RAM.
- Mapping Linda agents to the RAMs they encode.
- Executing RAMs and Linda agents.

Of course, as we will see later, the price to pay is not neglectable.

Before addressing soundness, we need to characterize Linda agents that are encodings of RAMs. Let's fix two positive integer numbers N and M. A Linda agent is the encoding of a RAM with N available registers and whose program has length M iff:

- the agent is made of parallel compositions of messages $< m >$ (representing either registers or program counters), dead processes 0 and processes which are images of a Succ or a DecJump instruction (i.e. have either the shape $!in(p_1).out(r).out(p_2)$ or the shape $!in(p_1).?inp(r).out(p_2)\_out(p_3)$ where $r \in [0, M)$ and $p_i \geq M$ for each i
- there is exactly one message $< m >$ such that $m \geq N$ (which is the encoding of the PC $m - N$)
- for every $m \in [M, \ldots, M + N)$ there is exactly one sub-process which is the image of an instruction and that is guarded by $!in(m)$. The process is the encoding of the $(m - M)$-th instruction
- for every $m \geq M + N$ there is no sub-process which is the image of an instruction and that is guarded by $!in(m)$

Formally, we define in Coq the following (decidable) inductive predicates in Prop:

```
Inductive is_RAM_instruction [registers_no : nat ; pc : nat] :
  program→Prop

Inductive is_RAM_image_no_pc [registers_no : nat] : agent→Prop

Inductive is_RAM_image_pc [registers_no : nat] : agent→Prop

Inductive instruction_does_not_occur [registers_no:nat; n:nat] :
  agent→Prop

Inductive instruction_occurs_once [registers_no:nat ; n:nat] :
  agent→Prop

Inductive is_RAM_image
  [registers_no : nat ; program_length : nat ; P:agent] : Prop
:=
Build_is_RAM_image:
 (is_RAM_image_pc registers_no P)→
  (∀n:nat.(n<program_length)→
    (instruction_occurs_once registers_no (plus registers_no n) P))→
  (∀n:nat.(n≥program_length)→
    (instruction_does_not_occur registers_no (plus registers_no n) P))→
  (is_RAM_image registers_no program_length P).
```

Note that several of these predicates are used to characterize only sub-processes of RAM images: for example is_RAM_image_no_pc is satisfied by RAM image fragments where all the messages are in the $[0, n)$ interval (i.e. are registers).

We also need to provide some more predicates to identify the transient states that are assumed by the Linda agent during the two intermediate steps of the $\longrightarrow^3$ transition:

```
Inductive is_RAM_image_succ [registers_no:nat ; r:register ; pc:nat]:
  agent→Prop

Inductive is_RAM_image_decjump
  [registers_no:nat ; r:register ; pc':nat ; pc:nat] : agent→Prop

Inductive is_RAM_image_out_pc [registers_no:nat ; pc:nat] :
  agent→Prop

Inductive instruction_does_not_occur2 [registers_no:nat; n:nat] :
  agent→Prop

Inductive instruction_does_not_occur3 [registers_no:nat; n:nat] :
  agent→Prop
```

The first predicate is used to check that no PC message appears in the agent and that the "body" of the Succ instruction does (i.e. there is exactly one sub-process $out(r).out(pc)$); the second predicate does the same for the DecJump instruction; the third predicate checks that no PC message appears in the agent and that there is exactly one sub-process $out(pc)$; the last two predicates are almost equivalent to the instruction_does_not_occur predicate, but are used to state that no instruction guarded by $!in(n)$ is present in agents satisfying respectively the is_RAM_image_succ/is_RAM_image_decjump predicates or the is_RAM_image_out_pc predicate.

Since all the preceding predicates are given in Prop[2], the Coq system is able to automatically generate only the corresponding induction and inversion principles over Prop (i.e. those where the property P to prove is not computationally relevant and lives in Prop). Nevertheless, since all of them are decidable, it is possible to manually define also the corresponding recursion principles (which are extremely useful when proving constructive existential quantifications). In particular, for each inductive predicate we prove a subset of the following lemmas:

1. The decidability proof
2. The corresponding recursion principles (which are proved by induction on the object of the property and using its decidability lemma and the decidability property of all the other properties used in the type of the constructors)
3. An inversion principle in Set (i.e. over computational properties)
4. A dependent version of the induction principle

The defined induction/recursion principles can be easily exploited to prove by induction static properties of RAM images. For example, we use them to prove that no agent satisfies both is_RAM_image_no_pc and is_RAM_image_pc.

The predicate is_RAM_image_pc is particularly important, since it guarantees the existence of just one program counter message in the agent. Later on we will have to prove that an agent satisfying this predicate can make a τ move unless the corresponding RAM is stuck. The τ move will be obtained when the program counter message will be consumed by the program that encodes the corresponding instruction, i.e. the program counter message will perform a $\xrightarrow{\overline{p}}$ move and the instruction program a $\xrightarrow{p}$ move where p is the value of the program counter message. To be able to give a constructive proof of this fact, we need to provide a computable function (in Set) that, given a process that satisfies is_RAM_image_pc, gives back its program counter:

---

[2] Prop is the sort of all the types whose terms have no computational content; subterms of sort Prop are removed during code extraction. The propositions whose type is Prop can also be proved classically without interfering with the extraction machinery. Set, instead, is the sort of the types whose terms have computational content; subterms of sort Set are kept during code extraction. Thus any subterm of sort Set can not perform any elimination step over a term of sort Prop, since that term will not be available in the extracted code.

```
Definition pc_of_RAM_image_pc :
 Πregisters_no:nat. ΠP:agent.
 (is_RAM_image_pc registers_no P) → message.
```

The definition must be given carefully to ensure its proof-irrelevance in the third argument:

```
Lemma pc_of_RAM_image_pc_proof_irrelevant :
 ∀registers_no:nat. ∀P:agent.
  ∀P0,P1:(is_RAM_image_pc registers_no P).
   (pc_of_RAM_image_pc registers_no P P0) =
   (pc_of_RAM_image_pc registers_no P P1).
```

We must also prove several technical lemmas ensuring that the definition is compositional, i.e. that the value of the program counter of an agent which is a parallel composition is the same value computed on the branch which actually holds the program counter. E.g.:

```
Lemma pc_of_AParallel_equal_pc1 :
 ∀registers_no:nat. ∀P,Q:agent.
  ∀HPQ:(is_RAM_image_pc registers_no (AParallel P Q)).
   ∀HP:(is_RAM_image_pc registers_no P).
    (pc_of_RAM_image_pc ? ? HPQ) = (pc_of_RAM_image_pc ? ? HP).
```

Once we have characterized all the possible states a RAM image can assume, we need to start describing the dynamic properties of the system. In particular, for every possible label and for every possible RAM image state, we need to study which are the possible moves and their outcome. As an example, we show here a very small subset of the main lemmas we need to prove[3]:

an agent P that satisfies is_RAM_image_no_pc

1. does not perform any $\xrightarrow{\neg a}$ move
2. does not perform any $\xrightarrow{a}$ move
3. can perform a $\xrightarrow{a}$ move only if a is a program counter (i.e. $a \geq n$)
4. can perform a $\xrightarrow{\overline{a}}$ move only if a is a register (i.e. $a < n$)
5. if $P \xrightarrow{\overline{a}} P'$ then P' satisfies is_RAM_image_no_pc

an agent P that satisfies is_RAM_image_pc

1. does not perform any $\xrightarrow{\neg a}$ move
2. does not perform any $\xrightarrow{a}$ move
3. can perform a $\xrightarrow{a}$ move only if a is a program counter (i.e. $a \geq n$)
4. * $P \xrightarrow{\overline{p}} P'$ where p is the PC computed by pc_of_RAM_image_pc
5. if $P \xrightarrow{\overline{a}} P'$ then P' satisfies is_RAM_image_no_pc
6. the $\xrightarrow{\overline{a}}$ move is deterministic both in a and in the produced agent

---

[3] The lemmas marked with a * are the one with a computational content.

an agent P that satisfies `instruction_does_not_occur`

1. can not perform a $\xrightarrow{a}$ move on the instruction that does not occur

an agent P that satisfies `instruction_occurs_once`

1. $*$ performs a $\xrightarrow{r}$ move on the instruction guarded by $!in(r)$ that occurs just once
2. the $\xrightarrow{a}$ move is deterministic

an agent P that satisfies `is_RAM_decjump`

1. does not perform any $\xrightarrow{a}$ move
2. can perform a $\xrightarrow{a}$ move only if a is a program counter (i.e. $a \geq n$) or if a is the register to be decremented
3. can perform a $\xrightarrow{\overline{a}}$ move only if a is a register (i.e. $a < n$)

...

Proving all these statements without any form of automation turned out to be extremely annoying, since for each proof we need to consider many cases, most of them absurd. Moreover many of the proofs are very similar, since (1) the different predicates just state slightly different properties over similar classes of processes and (2) many cases are due to Linda process constructors or to Linda transitions that are symmetric cases of already considered situations. For example, let's consider a typical proof fragment:

Proof. Given two agents Q and Q' such that `is_RAM_image_pc`(Q) and $Q \xrightarrow{\tau} Q'$, we need to prove a certain property $\mathbf{P}(Q)$. We proceed by induction on the proof of the hypothesis `is_RAM_image_pc`(Q). The two inductive cases are symmetric. The first one is:

Case AParallel1: let Q_1, Q_2 be two agents such that `is_RAM_image_pc`(Q_1), `is_RAM_image_no_pc`(Q_2) and $Q_1|Q_2 \xrightarrow{\tau} Q'$. We need to prove $\mathbf{P}(Q)$. We proceed by cases on the definition of $\xrightarrow{\tau}$. Four out of six cases are absurd:

Case Tau-Right: $Q_2 \xrightarrow{\tau} Q_2'$. Absurd because every process P such that `is_RAM_image_no_pc`(P) is stuck.

Case In-Out: $Q_1 \xrightarrow{r} Q_1'$ and $Q_2 \xrightarrow{\overline{r}} Q_2'$. Absurd since $r < n$ (because Q_2 has no program counter) and $r \geq n$ since Q_1 is a RAM image and the only sub-processes that starts with an $rd(\_)$ guard are the instructions which expect to read a program counter message.

Case Read-Out: $Q_1 \xrightarrow{r} Q_1'$ and $Q_2 \xrightarrow{\overline{r}} Q_2'$. Absurd since a RAM image can not move with a $\xrightarrow{r}$ move.

Case Out-Read: Dual of the previous case.

There are several alternative ways to reduce the size of the proofs and the time spent to develop them:

- Register all the lemmas in the database used by the Auto tactic of Coq to try to automatically prove the theorems.
- Develop ad-hoc tactics able to prune out all the typical absurd cases.

– Develop a whole library of elimination principles used to reason on the *dynamic* properties of processes.

The first solution is not very effective and leads to very poor performances during the proof-searching/compilation phase. In fact, just expanding the few Auto tactics we were using to the script they were producing, we cut down the overall compilation time from 2m30s to less than 2m. Moreover, as for the second solution, only the size of the script is reduced, and not the size of the generated proof-object (lambda-term). Big proof-objects make type-checking slow, are unmanageable when exported to libraries of mathematical knowledge [8], are difficult to data-mine and to render [9]. Moreover, ad-hoc tactics are a form of *implicit* knowledge that can not be easily shared with other proof assistants, nor presented to the users.

The third solution is the one we tried to pursue[4]. The idea is to introduce one elimination principle à la McBride [4] for each combination of moves and preconditions on the agents that perform the move. In appendix A we show the thesis of the elimination principle over the dynamic behavior of a process P such that is_RAM_image_pc(P), instruction_occurs_once$_{pc}(P)$ and $P \xrightarrow{\tau} P'$. The elimination principle can be exploited to enormously reduce the size of both the scripts and the proof-objects of, for example, proof of reduction invariants.

A typical case of a statement whose proof is a simple application of one of these elimination principles[5] is:

```
Lemma is_RAM_image_decjump_Tau_message_multiplicity_eq:
 ∀registers_no:nat. ∀r,m:register. ∀pc,pc':nat. ∀P,P':agent.
  r≠m→
   (is_RAM_image_decjump registers_no r pc' pc P)→
    (OStep P Tau P')→
     (message_multiplicity m P)=(message_multiplicity m P').
```

Once that we have characterized all the possible transitions that RAM images are subject to in each of their states, we can state the completeness axiom and put our attention on the soundness proofs:

```
Axiom RAMs_to_Linda_completeness:
 (r:RAM ; c,c':configuration)
 (RAMs.step r c c')→
  (step3
   (agent_of_RAM_and_configuration r c)
   (agent_of_RAM_and_configuration r c')).
```

---

[4] So far only a few elimination principles have been introduced. We plan to give all the needed principles and re-prove all the theorems using them.

[5] The one describing the dynamic behavior of RAM images where a DecJump instruction is under execution.

```
Theorem RAMs_to_Linda_soundness:
∀r:RAM. ∀c:configuration. ∀P':agent.
 ∀H:(step3 (agent_of_RAM_and_configuration r c) P').
  (Σc':configuration |
  (ΣHO:(RAMs.step r c c')
   let Hc be (agent_of_RAM_and_configuration_is_RAM_image r c) in
   let Hc' be (is_RAM_image_step3_is_RAM_image ? ? ? ? Hc H) in
    let Hc'' be (agent_of_RAM_and_configuration_is_RAM_image r c') in
     (RAM_image_equivalence' ? ? P'
      (agent_of_RAM_and_configuration r c') Hc' Hc'')));.
```

Note that, to state the soundness theorem, we need to provide another set of lemmas that grants that

- the encoding of a RAM satisfies the predicate is_RAM_image (Lemma agent_of_RAM_and_configuration_is_RAM_image). The proof is quite straightforward.
- after three steps a RAM image becomes again a RAM image (Lemma is_RAM_image_step3_is_RAM_image). The proof is very complex and relies on all the previous lemmas.

Many of the difficulties met in the second proof derive from the combination of dependent types (used all over the theory) with proof-irrelevant definitions (the function to extract the program counter from a RAM image). In particular we were forced to introduce the following axiom[6].

```
Axiom pc_of_RAM_image_pc_dependent_proof_irrelevant:
∀registers_no:nat. ∀P,P':agent.
 ∀H:(is_RAM_image_pc registers_no P).
  ∀H':(is_RAM_image_pc registers_no P').
   P=P'→
    (pc_of_RAM_image_pc registers_no P H) =
    (pc_of_RAM_image_pc registers_no P' H').
```

Notice that both the compleness axiom and the axiom we have just introduced are non-informative (i.e. they are of sort Prop). As a consequence, they do not inhibit code extraction, even if inconsistent axioms can destroy the strong normalization property of the extracted code. Indeed, Coq 7.2 successfully extracts code from all the modules that make up our development.

The proof of the soundness theorem is obtained by the completeness axiom and by two further lemmas which state that:

---

[6] The axiom is surely related to the axiom used to derive Leibniz equality from John-Major equality [4]. As a future work, it should be possible to show the consistency of our axiom by adapting one of the modes that validates the John-Major equality axiom.

1. A RAM is stuck iff its RAM image is:
2. The $\longrightarrow^3$ relation is deterministic up to the congruence induced by the equality on RAMs:

```
Theorem step3_almost_deterministic:
∀registers_no:nat. ∀program_length:nat. ∀P,P',P'':agent.
 (is_RAM_image registers_no program_length P)→
  (step3 P P')→(step3 P P'')→
   ∀H:(is_RAM_image registers_no program_length P').
    ∀H':(is_RAM_image registers_no program_length P'').
     (RAM_image_equivalence' registers_no program_length P' P'' H H').
```

The two lemmas are proved combining all the previously proved lemmas. A key observation to prove the second lemma is that the transition relation of RAM images is *almost* deterministic: the only situation where more than one transition is possible is the execution of the DecJump(r, s) instruction, that can remove from the tuple space any instance of the $< r >$ message in case the value of the register r (in the corresponding RAM) is greater than 1.

Once the lemmas have been proved, the proof becomes almost straightforward. Informally, if the agent that encodes the RAM r and the configuraiont c can move in a new agent P', than the couple (r, c) must move in a new state (r, c') (because of the first lemmas); the completeness property grants that the image P of (r, c) moves into a new agent P''; since the second lemma states that the reduction $\longrightarrow^3$ is deterministic (up to the congruence induced by the equality on RAMs), we must conclude that $P' = P''$, ending the proof.

All the lemmas and proof can be found into the two files RAMs_to_ Linda_proofs.v and RAMs_to_Linda_proofs1.v, which are currently about 8700 lines long and require some minutes to be compiled.

6   Conclusions

In this paper we present the formalizations in Coq of both Random Access Machines (RAMs) and a Turing complete version of a process algebra built around the Linda coordination primitives. We also give an encoding of RAMs into the process algebra and a constructive proof of the soundness of the encoding.

The formalizations of the two calculi as well as the formalization of the encoding are almost straightforward. The soundness proof, instead, turned out to be extremely long and complex. The deep reasons of the complexity of some parts of the proof can be traced back to the constructive nature of the proof and the heavy usage of functions having both a computational content and proof-irrelevant arguments (i.e. functions of the form $\Pi x : A.(P \ x) \to B \ : \ Set$). More concretely, though, the proof required so much work because of lack of automation in the Coq system: in particular Coq provides only a very limited support for the generation of inversion/induction principles over *decidable* predicates and no automation at all for the handling of "similar" or "symmetric" cases.

Finally, we strongly believe that both the size of the proof script and of the proof-objects can be highly reduced introducing many more elimination and inversion principles to characterize the dynamic behavior of the processes. The generation of these principles, though, should be automatized, since even guessing their precise statement is a non-trivial task.

The difficulties we have met and the solutions proposed seem to be unrelated from the particular proof we are examining. Thus further work could be spent in trying to generalize the technique and apply it to other proofs about the mutual encoding of formalisms. Automatizing part of the proofs would be very promising. As a matter of facts, though, it is evident that without any additional automation, the Coq system is not very effective in dealing with this kind of proofs: even for relatively trivial facts, the time spent in the development of the boring details of a constructive and fully formalized proof largely overcomes the time required by the interesting steps.

In the next few months we are going to finish the whole development giving also the completeness proof and extracting the code to read-back a RAM from its Linda encoding.

A long term goal would be to define inside the RAM formalism its own interpreter and then proving the undecidability of the halting problem. This would really pave the way to far more interesting results, as the proof that the two versions of the Linda Calculus (with Ordered and Unordered Semantics) are not equivalent.

References

1. N. Busi, R. Gorrieri and G. Zavattaro. On the Expressiveness of Linda Coordination Primitives. *Information and Computation*, 156(1/2):90-121, 2000.
2. The Coq proof-assistant: http://coq.inria.fr/
3. M. Hofmann. *Extensional concepts in intensional type theory.* Ph.D. thesis, University of Edinburgh, July 1995.
4. C. McBride. *Dependently Typed Functional Programs and their Proofs.* Ph.D. thesis, University of Edinburgh, 2000.
5. D. Gelernter. Generative Communication in Linda. *ACM Transactions on Programming Languages and Systems*, 7(1):80-112, 1985.
6. D. Gelernter and N. Carriero. Coordination Languages and their Significance. *Communications of the ACM*, 35(2):97-102, 1992.
7. G. Barthe and P. Courtieu. Efficient Reasoning about executable specifications in Coq. In V. Carreño, C. Munõz and S. Tahar editors, *Theorem Proving in Higher Order Logics (TPHOLS)*, volume 2410 of *LNCS*, pages 31-46, Springer Verlag, 2001.
8. A. Asperti, F. Guidi, L.Padovani, C. Sacerdoti Coen and I. Schena. Mathematical Knowledge Management in HELM. In *On-Line Proceedings of the First International Workshop on Mathematical Knowledge Management (MKM2001)*, RISC-Linz, Austria, September 2001.
9. A. Asperti, F. Guidi, L.Padovani, C. Sacerdoti Coen and I. Schena. XML, Stylesheets and the re-mathematization of Formal Content. In *On-Line Proceedings of EXTREME 2001*.

10. R. Milner. The Polyadic π-Calculus: A Tutorial Technical Report, Department of Computer Science, University of Edinburgh, ECS-LFCS-91-180, October 1991.
11. M. L. Minsky. *Computation: finite and infinite machines*. Prentice-Hall, Englewood Cliffs, 1967.
12. J. C. Shepherdson and J. E. Sturgis. Computability of recursive functions. *Journal of the ACM*, 10:217-255, 1963.
13. N. Busi, R. Gorrieri and G. Zavattaro. A Process Algebraic View of Linda Coordination Primitives. Theoretical Computer Science, 192(2):167-199, 1998.
14. N. Busi and G. Zavattaro. On the Expressiveness of Movement in Pure Mobile Ambients. In *Prof. of Workshop on Peer-to-Peer Computing*, LNCS 2376, Springer-Verlag, 2002.

A   One Example of Elimination Principle Characterizing a Dynamic Behaviour

```
Lemma is_RAM_image_pc_instruction_occurs_once_Tau_ind:
∀registers_no:nat. ∀P:(agent→agent→Prop).
 (∀P0,P',Q:agent.
  ∀H:(is_RAM_image_pc registers_no P0).
  (is_RAM_image_no_pc registers_no Q)→
   let pc be (pc_of_RAM_image_pc ? ? H) in
    (* This hypothesis can be strengthened *)
    (instruction_occurs_once registers_no pc (AParallel P0 Q))→
    (P P0 P')→(P (AParallel P0 Q) (AParallel P' Q)))→
 (∀P0,Q,Q':agent.
  (is_RAM_image_no_pc registers_no P0)→
  (is_RAM_image_pc registers_no Q)→
   let pc be (pc_of_RAM_image_pc ? ? H) in
    (* This hypothesis can be strengthened *)
    (instruction_occurs_once registers_no pc (AParallel P0 Q))→
    (P Q Q')→(P (AParallel P0 Q) (AParallel P0 Q')))→
 (∀P0,P',Q,Q':agent. ∀r:register.
  ∀H:(is_RAM_image_pc registers_no P0).
  (is_RAM_image_no_pc registers_no Q)→
   let pc be (pc_of_RAM_image_pc ? ? H) in
    (* This hypothesis can be strengthened *)
    (instruction_occurs_once registers_no pc (AParallel P0 Q))→
    (OStep P0 (LOut r) P')→
    (OStep Q (LIn r) Q')→
    (P (AParallel P0 Q) (AParallel P' Q')))→
 (∀P0,P',Q,Q':agent. ∀r:register.
  (is_RAM_image_no_pc registers_no P0)→
  ∀H:(is_RAM_image_pc registers_no Q).
   let pc be (pc_of_RAM_image_pc ? ? H) in
    (* This hypothesis can be strengthened *)
```

```
  (instruction_occurs_once registers_no pc (AParallel P0 Q))→
    (OStep P0 (LIn r) P')→
    (OStep Q (LOut r) Q')→
    (P (AParallel P0 Q) (AParallel P' Q')))→
∀a,a':agent.
∀H:(is_RAM_image_pc registers_no a).
 let pc be (pc_of_RAM_image_pc ? ? H) in
  (instruction_occurs_once registers_no pc a)→
    (OStep a Tau a')→
    (P a a').
```

Finite Horizon Analysis of Stochastic Systems with the Murφ Verifier*

Giuseppe Della Penna[1], Benedetto Intrigila[1,**], Igor Melatti[1],
Enrico Tronci[2], and Marisa Venturini Zilli[2]

[1] Dip. di Informatica, Università di L'Aquila, Coppito 67100, L'Aquila, Italy
{dellapenna,intrigila,melatti}@di.univaq.it
[2] Dip. di Informatica Università di Roma "La Sapienza",
Via Salaria 113, 00198 Roma, Italy
{tronci,zilli}@dsi.uniroma1.it

Abstract. Many reactive systems are actually *Stochastic Processes*. Automatic analysis of such systems is usually very difficult thus typically one simplifies the analysis task by using simulation or by working on a simplified model (e.g. a *Markov Chain*).

We present a *Finite Horizon Probabilistic Model Checking* approach which essentially can handle the same class of stochastic processes of a typical simulator. This yields easy modeling of the system to be analysed together with formal verification capabilities. Our approach is based on a suitable *disk based* extension of the Murφ verifier.

Moreover we present experimental results showing effectiveness of our approach.

1   Introduction

Correctness of digital hardware, embedded software and protocols can often be verified with *Model Checking* techniques [5,9,14,13,18,26] by modeling such systems as *Nondeterministic Finite State Systems* (NFSS).

However, there are many reactive systems that exhibit uncertainty in their behavior, i.e. which are stochastic systems. Examples of such systems are: fault tolerant systems, randomized distributed protocols and communication protocols. Typically stochastic systems cannot be conveniently modeled using NFSS. However they can often be modeled as *Stochastic Processes* [19].

Unfortunately, automatic analysis of stochastic processes is quite hard, apart from some noticeable special classes of stochastic processes. For this reason typically approximated approaches are used. Namely: *simulation* or *model approximation*. *Simulation* carries out an approximate analysis on the given stochastic

---

* This research has been partially supported by MURST projects: MEFISTO and SAHARA
** Corresponding Author: Benedetto Intrigila. Tel: +39 0862 43 31 32. Fax: +39 0862 43 31 80

C. Blundo and C. Laneve (Eds.): ICTCS 2003, LNCS 2841, pp. 58–71, 2003.
© Springer-Verlag Berlin Heidelberg 2003

process. *Model approximation* carries out an exact analysis on a simplified (approximated) model of the given stochastic process. For example, *Markov Chains* [3,11] can be used to approximate a given stochastic process.

Automatic analysis of *Markov Chains* can be effectively performed by using *Probabilistic Model Checkers* [28,6,17,23,12,25,4,7,8,2,15,27].

Probabilistic Model Checkers have been developed also for some particular class of *Stochastic Processes* [10], namely those in which the probability of an outgoing transition from state *s* is a function of the sojourn time in state *s* (semi-Markov Processes).

Stochastic Simulators [19] typically can handle fairly general *stochastic systems*. However, from a simulator we can only get information about the *average behavior* of the system at hand, whereas from a model checker we also get information about *low probability* events.

In this paper we focus on *Discrete Time Stochastic Processes* (SP). Our goal is to compute the probability that a given SP reaches an *error state* in at most *k* steps starting from a given *initial state* (*Finite Horizon Verification*).

We will present an approach and a tool to carry out *Finite Horizon Verification* of a class of SP that is essentially as large as the class of SP that can be handled by many simulators (e.g. [27,19]). To the best of our knowledge, this is the first time that such an approach is presented. Our results can be summarized as follows.

1. We present (Section 3) *Probabilistic Rule Based Transition Systems*(PRBTS) and show (Section 4) how PRBTS can be used to model a fairly large class of *Finite State* SP (*Discrete Time Stochastic Processes*). By using *finite precision real numbers* as in [21] (and as in any simulator) we can also handle *Discrete Time Hybrid Stochastic Processes*, i.e. stochastic processes which have continuous (i.e. finite precision real) as well as discrete state variables.
2. PRBTS can be used as a *low level* language to define stochastic systems. This is useful to separate the task of designing high level languages for system descriptions from the task of designing *Verification Engines*. As an example, we show (Section 5) how a *high level Communicating Processes* definition of a stochastic system can be translated, in linear time, into a *low level* PRBTS definition of the same system.
3. We show (Section 7) how FHP-Murφ [22], a suitable *disk based* extension of the Murφ verifier [18], can be used for automatic *Finite Horizon Verification* of PRBTS.
   Indeed, using FHP-Murφ, PRBTS can be used as a *low level* language to define stochastic systems whereas FHP-Murφ can be used as a low level *Verification Engine* for *Finite Horizon Verification* of stochastic systems.
4. We show (Section 7) effectiveness of our approach by presenting experimental results on automatic analysis of two nontrivial stochastic systems using with FHP-Murφ.
   Our experimental results show that FHP-Murφ can handle more general models than state-of-the-art *Probabilistic Model Checkers* like PRISM [24,2,16] or TwoTowers [27].

On the other hand PRISM as well as TwoTowers can verify more general properties (e.g. all PCTL [12] properties for PRISM) than FHP-Murφ. In fact FHP-Murφ can only handle *Finite Horizon Verification*.

2   Basic Notation

We give some basic definitions on Finite State/Discrete Time General Stochastic Processes. For more details on stochastic processes see, e.g., [20].

Definition 1.

1. *A* Finite State/Discrete Time Stochastic Process *(shortened* SP *in the following) is a triple* $\mathcal{X} = (S, \mathbf{P}, q)$ *where* S *is a finite set (of states),* $q \in S$ *is the initial state,* $Seq(S)$ *is the set of all finite sequences of elements of* S, *and* $\mathbf{P} : S \times Seq(S) \times S \to [0, 1]$ *is a transition probability function, i.e. for all* $s \in S$, $\pi \in Seq(S)$, $\sum_{t \in S} \mathbf{P}(s, \pi, t) = 1$. *(We included the* initial state q *in the SP definition to simplify our exposition.)*
2. *An execution sequence (or path) in the SP* $\mathcal{X} = (S, \mathbf{P}, q)$ *is a nonempty (finite or infinite) sequence* $\pi = s_0 s_1 s_2 \ldots$ *where* s_i *are states and*

$$\mathbf{P}(s_i, s_0 \ldots s_{i-1}, s_{i+1}) > 0$$

   for $i = 0, 1, \ldots$. *If* $\pi = s_0 s_1 s_2 \ldots$ *we write* $\pi(k)$ *for* s_k, *and we write* $\pi|k$ *for the sequence* $s_0 s_1 s_2 \ldots s_{k-1}$. *The* length *of a finite path* $\pi = s_0 s_1 s_2 \ldots s_k$ *is* k *(number of transitions), whereas the length of an infinite path is* ∞. *We denote with* $|\pi|$ *the length of* π. *We denote with* $Path(\mathcal{X}, s)$ *the set of infinite paths* π *in* $\mathcal{X}$ *s.t.* $\pi(0) = s$. *If* $\mathcal{X} = (S, \mathbf{P}, q)$ *we write also* $Path(\mathcal{X})$ *for* $Path(\mathcal{X}, q)$.
3. *For* $s \in S$ *we denote with* $\sum(s)$ *the smallest* σ-*algebra on* $Path(\mathcal{X}, s)$ *which, for any finite path* ρ *starting at* s, *contains the basic cylinders* { $\pi \in Path(\mathcal{X}, s)$ | ρ *is a prefix of* π }. *The probability measure* Pr *on* $\sum(s)$ *is the unique measure with* $Pr\{ \pi \in Path(\mathcal{X}, s) \mid \rho$ *is a prefix of* π } $= \mathbf{P}(\rho) = \prod_{i=0}^{k-1} \mathbf{P}(\rho(i),$ $\rho|i, \rho(i+1)) = \mathbf{P}(\rho(0), \epsilon, \rho(1)) \, \mathbf{P}(\rho(1), \rho|1, \rho(2)) \cdots \mathbf{P}(\rho(k-1), \rho|(k-1), \rho(k))$, *where* $k = |\rho|$ *and* ϵ *is the empty sequence.*

We recall that a *Markov Chain* is a particular SP, such that the probability transition function $\mathbf{P}(s, \pi, t)$ actually does not depend on π ("lack of memory") and therefore reduces to a *Stochastic Matrix* (see [3]).

Given a SP, we want to compute the probability that a path of length k starting from the initial state q reaches a state s satisfying a given boolean formula ϕ. If ϕ models an *error condition*, this computation allows us to compute the probability of reaching an error condition in at most k transitions.

Problem 1. Let $\mathcal{X} = (S, \mathbf{P}, q)$ be a SP, $k \in \mathbb{N}$, and ϕ be a boolean function on S. We want to compute: $P(\mathcal{X}, k, \phi) = Pr((\exists i \leq k \; \phi(\pi(i))) \mid \pi \in Path(\mathcal{X}))$. That is, we want to compute the probability of reaching a state satisfying ϕ in *at most* k steps in the SP $\mathcal{X}$ (starting from the initial state q).

Problem 1 can be very difficult both from a computational and from an analytical point of view [4,6,7]. So, the first task is to single out a (large enough) class of *tractable* SP. Moreover, we need to better specify the computational model we want to use. We introduce this model in Section 3. Then, in Section 4 we will show how we intend to cope with our verification problem.

3   Probabilistic Rule Based Transition Systems

Definition 2. *A Probabilistic Rule Based Transition System (PRBTS) S is a 3-tuple (S, Rules, q), where: S is a finite set (of states), $q \in S$ and Rules is a finite set of pairs (p, f), with p being a function from S to $[0, 1]$ and f being a function from S to S and $\forall s \in S \sum_{(p,f) \in \text{Rules}} p(s) = 1$.*

Definition 3. *Let $S = (S, \text{Rules}, q)$ be a PRBTS. An execution sequence in S is a nonempty (finite or infinite) sequence $\pi = s_0 s_1 s_2 \ldots$ where s_i are states and for every $i = 0, 1, \ldots$ there exists a pair $(p, f) \in \text{Rules}$, such that $f(s_i) = s_{i+1}$ and $p(s_i) > 0$.*

As expected, to a PRBTS we can univocally associate a Markov Chain. This can be done as follows.

Definition 4. *Let $S = (S, \text{Rules}, q)$ be a PRBTS. The Markov Chain $S^{mc} = (S, \mathbf{P}, q)$ associated to S is defined as follows: $\mathbf{P}(s, t) = \sum_{(p,f) \in \text{Rules } s.t. f(s) = t} p(s)$ (taking as 0 summation on an empty set).*

Proposition 1. *Let $S = (S, \text{Rules}, q)$ be a PRBTS. Then, the Markov Chain S^{mc} associated to S is well defined.*

4   From Stochastic Processes to PRBTS

As we discussed in Section 1, we cannot hope to analyze all possible SP. So, we restrict our analysis to SP such that their transition probabilities depend only on some fixed characteristics of the process history. We formalize this as follows.

Definition 5. *Let the SP $\mathcal{X} = (S, \mathbf{P}, q)$ be given. We say that $\mathcal{X}$ has finite character n iff there exists an equivalence relation R on $Seq(S)$ of finite index n (that is with n equivalence classes) such that for every $\pi_1, \pi_2 \in Seq(S)$*

$$\text{if } R(\pi_1, \pi_2) \text{ then } \forall s, t \in S. \, \mathbf{P}(s, \pi_1, t) = \mathbf{P}(s, \pi_2, t)$$

Now we show that to a finite character SP $\mathcal{X}$ we can associate a PRBTS S, in such a way that the verification Problem 1 for $\mathcal{X}$ can be reduced to that for S.

Proposition 2. *Let the SP $\mathcal{X} = (S, \mathbf{P}, q)$ be of finite character n w.r.t. an equivalence relation R. Let moreover $Q_0, \ldots, Q_{n-1}$ be an enumeration of the equivalence classes of R. Then there exists a PRBTS $\mathcal{S} = (S_1, \mathtt{Rules}, q_1)$, such that:*

1. *$S_1 = S \times \mathbf{n}$, where $\mathbf{n}$ denotes the set $\{0, \ldots, n-1\}$;*
2. *if π is any sequence in $Path(\mathcal{X})$, such that $\pi \in Q_i$ and $\pi_1 = \pi s$ is in Q_j, where by πs we denote the concatenation of s to the sequence π, and $\mathbf{P}(s, \pi, t) > 0$, then*
   - *there exists at least one pair (p, f) in $\mathtt{Rules}$ such that $f((s, i)) = (t, j)$ and $p((s, i)) > 0$,*
   - *$\sum_{(p,f) \in \mathtt{Rules} \ s.t. f((s,i))=(t,j)} p(s) = \mathbf{P}(s, \pi, t)$;*
3. *$q_1 = (q, i_0)$, where $q \in Q_{i_0}$;*
4. *Problem 1 on $\mathcal{X}$ with respect to ϕ can be reduced to compute: $P(\mathcal{S}^{mc}, k, \phi_1) = Pr_{\mathcal{S}^{mc}}((\exists i \leq k \ \phi_1(\pi(i))) \mid \pi \in Path(\mathcal{S}^{mc}))$ where $\forall j \in \mathbf{n}$, $\phi_1((s, j)) = \phi(s)$, that is $P(\mathcal{X}, k, \phi) = P(\mathcal{S}^{mc}, k, \phi_1)$.*

Proof. (Sketch) It is easy to see that a PRBTS $\mathcal{S}$, verifying the required conditions, can be specified from $\mathcal{X}$: simply insert in $\mathtt{Rules}$ a suitable pair (p, f) of functions, for every transition $\mathbf{P}(s, \pi, t) > 0$, taking into account to choose one representative for each equivalence class. As an example, given $\mathbf{P}(s, \pi, t) > 0$ with $\pi \in Q_i$ and $\pi s \in Q_j$, set f as the constant function on S_1 returning always (t, j), and set p as the function that returns $\mathbf{P}(s, \pi, t)$ for input (s, i) and 0 otherwise. For the last point, observe that for every such $\mathcal{S}$, the associated Markov Chain $\mathcal{S}^{mc}$ gives rise to essentially the same probability measure of $\mathcal{X}$ on cylinders and therefore on every set. Indeed, given a path $\pi \in Path(\mathcal{S}^{mc})$ the indexes in π give no information, since they are univocally determined by the path π itself.

We stress that a PRBTS is *always defined by a program* of a suitable (e.g. C-like) programming language. This allows us to specify functions $(p, f) \in \mathtt{Rules}$ inside the program as *procedures*. This makes their formulation parametric and concise. On the basis of such considerations, we state the following claim:

Claim. A *rule based (i.e. PRBTS oriented)* approach to SP specification is *in many cases* exponentially shorter than a *Markov Chain based* specification approach. By a *Markov Chain based* specification approach we mean any language requiring *in many cases* an explicit (i.e. tabular) definition of the stochastic matrix of the input Markov Chain.

In fact, by comparing the protocol LQS modeled in Section 7.1 (with FHP-Murφ, so with PRBTS) with the model of the same protocol in PRISM (that it is not included here, for space reasons: see [29]), we can see that the former is much shorter than the latter, since it does not grow with the parameter ITEM_Q.

One may wonder whether this is only a problem of language expressiveness. In a sense, this is not the case, since PRISM needs to store in memory the *complete* Markov Chain stochastic matrix. On the opposite, FHP-Murφ treats the Markov Chain exactly with the transition rules given in the model and it does not need to generate all the transition matrix.

5 From Communicating Stochastic Processes to PRBTS

As an example of usage of PRBTS as a low level definition language for SP, in this Section we show how the definition of an SP S specified by *Communicating Stochastic Processes* can be translated into a suitable PRBTS.

Definition 6. *A System of Communicating Stochastic Processes (SCSP) S is a 4-tuple $(n, S, \mathbf{q}, \mathcal{R})$, where:*
n is an integer (denoting the number of processes in our system);
$S = S_1 \times \ldots \times S_n$ is the Cartesian product of finite sets (of states) S_i, $i = 1, \ldots, n$;
$\mathbf{q} = (q_1, \ldots, q_n) \in S$;
$\mathcal{R} = \langle \mathcal{R}_1, \ldots, \mathcal{R}_n \rangle$ is a n-tuple of sets $\mathcal{R}_i$ $i = 1, \ldots, n$ s.t. $\mathcal{R}_i$ is a finite set of pairs (p, f) where p is a function from S to $[0, 1]$, f is a function from S to S_i, and $\forall i \in \{1, \ldots, n\}$ $\forall s \in S$ $\sum_{(p,f) \in \mathcal{R}_i} p(s) = 1$.

In the following we denote with boldface letters (e.g. $\mathbf{x}$) elements of $S = S_1 \times \ldots \times S_n$ and with x_i the i-th component of $\mathbf{x}$. We can define the transition relation of a SCSP assuming that processes are scheduled with uniform probability ($1/n$ if we have n processes).

Definition 7. *Let $S = (n, S, \mathbf{q}, \mathcal{R})$ be a SCSP. The Markov Chain $S^{mc} = (S, \mathbf{P}, \mathbf{q})$ associated to S is defined as follows:*
$$\mathbf{P}(\mathbf{s}, \mathbf{t}) = \sum_{i=1}^{i=n} \sum_{(p,f) \in \mathcal{R}_i \ s.t. \ (s_1, \ldots, s_{i-1}, f(\mathbf{s}), s_{i+1}, \ldots, s_n) = \mathbf{t}} (\tfrac{1}{n} \cdot p(\mathbf{s}))$$
(taking as 0 summations on empty sets).

Essentially PRBTS are (probabilistic) *shared variable* concurrent programs. Thus it is not surprising [1] that a SCSP can be transformed into a PRBTS using a suitable uniform probability *scheduler*. The following definition shows how this can be done (e.g. along the lines in PRISM [24]).

Definition 8. *Let $S = (n, S, \mathbf{q}, \mathcal{R})$ be a SCSP. We denote with $\Gamma(S)$ the PRBTS $(S, \mathbf{q}, \texttt{Rules})$ defined as follows:* $\texttt{Rules} = \cup_{i=1}^{i=n} \cup_{(p,f) \in \mathcal{R}_i} \{(\lambda\mathbf{x}.(\tfrac{1}{n} \cdot p(\mathbf{x})), f)\}$

The following proposition follows immediately from the construction in Definition 8.

Proposition 3. *Let S be a SCSP. Then $S^{mc} = \Gamma(S)^{mc}$*

Remark 1. Note that the PRBTS transformation of a SCSP is not limited to the case in which the processes are scheduled with a uniform probability. In fact, it is sufficient to modify Definition 8 in this way: $\texttt{Rules} = \cup_{i=1}^{i=n} \cup_{(p,f) \in \mathcal{R}_i} \{(\lambda\mathbf{x}.(s(i) \cdot p(\mathbf{x})), f)\}$, where s is a function from $\{1, \ldots, n\}$ to $[0, 1]$ denoting the scheduling probability of the process $i \in \{1, \ldots, n\}$ (obviously, s must be such that $\sum_{i=1}^{n} s(i) = 1$).

6   Defining Probabilistic Systems with the Murφ Verifier

We want to extend the input language of the Murφ verifier to allow definition
of SP using PRBTS. Since Murφ input language defines NFSS, our main modification to Murφ input language consists of adding transition probabilities to
transition rules.

In this Section we show how we modified Murφ input language to achieve the
above goal thus defining FHP-Murφ input language. The length of FHP-Murφ
finite horizon is passed on the command line to FHP-Murφ.

6.1   FHP-Murφ Input Language

We modify Murφ input language in the following parts: 1. We add a probability
specification to each start state; 2. We change the semantics of rules; 3. We only
allow one invariant to which we add a probability bound.

To handle *Discrete Time Hybrid Stochastic Processes* it is useful to have
state variables ranging on real numbers. For this reason in the following we
will consider the Murφ version enhanced with *finite precision real numbers*, as
described in [21].

To add probabilities in definitions of startstates, we modify the `startstate`
nonterminal production of the Murφ language grammar (Chapter 7 of the documentation [18]) as follows: `<startstate> ::=`
`startstate [<string>] [<realexpr>] [{<decl>} begin] [<stmts>] end`
where the expression `realexpr` must evaluate to a real number in $[0, 1]$, and de-
faults to 1 when it is not specified. If we are given h startstates with probabilities
$p_1, \ldots, p_h$, then $\sum_{i=1}^{h} p_i$ has to be 1, or FHP-Murφ will return an error.

To add probabilities on rules, we modify the semantics of the `simplerule`
nonterminal production of the Murφ language grammar (Chapter 7 of the documentation [18]) as follows. The original production, without priority and fairness
(not modified in our work), was
`<simplerule> ::= rule [ <expr> ] ==> [ <decl> begin ] [ stmts ] end`.
In FHP-Murφ, we simply require the expression after the keyword `rule` (i.e.
`expr`) to be a real expression valued in $[0, 1]$, instead of a boolean as it is for
Murφ. FHP-Murφ does not allow simultaneous use of both boolean and probability based rules.

The above modification to `<simplerule>` has a deep impact on Murφ semantics. In fact, with boolean rules, each state has a set of enabled transitions,
leading to other states; the activation of a rule only depends on its condition
being true or false. In our probabilistic setting, each Murφ rule defines a pair
(p, f) of the PRBTS being defined.

Finally, we modify the `invariant` nonterminal production of the Murφ language grammar (Chapter 7 of the documentation [18]) as follows:
`<invariant> ::= invariant [ <string> ] <realexpr> <booleanexpr>`
where `<realexpr>` has to be a real valued expression in $[0, 1]$, while
`<booleanexpr>` has to be a boolean valued expression.

```
type real_type : real(4, 10);
var x : real_type;

startstate "init" begin x := 1.0; end;

rule "reset" (x = 0.0? 1.0 : 0.0) ==> begin x := 1.0; end;
rule "beetwen 0 and x" (x > 0.0? x : 0.0) ==> begin x := x/10; end;
rule "beetwen x and 1" (x > 0.0? 1.0 - x : 0.0) ==> begin x := (1.0 + x)/2.0; end;

invariant "never reaches 0.0" 0.0 (x != 0.0)
```

Fig. 1. An example of FHP-Murφ input file

In FHP-Murφ the invariant statement **invariant** p γ requires that with probability at least p the following holds: "all states reachable in at most k steps from an initial state satisfy γ" (k is FHP-Murφ horizon).

This is equivalent to say that the probability of reaching in at most k steps from an initial state a state not satisfying γ is less than $(1 - p)$.

6.2   A Toy Example

Consider the SP S defined as follows. Initially S is in state 1. If S is in a state $x > 0$, then with probability x S moves to state $x/10$, and with probability $(1 - x)$ S moves to state $(1 + x)/2$. If S is in state 0 then S deterministically moves to state 1. In Fig. 1 we give the FHP-Murφ definition for S.

The FHP-Murφ invariant in Fig. 1 requires that, with probability at least 0.0 (i.e. always), in all the states, that are reachable in at most k transitions (horizon), $x \neq 0$ holds. That is, the probability that we reach, within horizon k, state 0, is less than 0. That is, state 0 is not reachable in S.

From definition of S should be quite clear that indeed state 0 is not a reachable state for S. However, since we are using finite precision real numbers, state 0 may be reached because of numerical approximations.

In Fig. 1, since the precision of x is 10^{-9} (with this precision, we have $10^{-10} = 0$), we will reach the state 0 if the horizon is a $k \geq 10$. For example, if $k = 10$, then the probability to reach state 0 is 10^{-45}.

7   Two Protocols in FHP-Murφ

In this Section we show how FHP-Murφ (*Finite Horizon Probabilistic* Murφ) [22], a suitable *disk based* extension of the Murφ verifier [18], can be used for automatic *Finite Horizon Verification* of PRBTS.

More specifically, we give two examples of our approach describing the behavior of two different queueing systems, showing their implementation in FHP-Murφ and sketching why they are more naturally described in FHP-Murφ than in PRISM.

Both examples describe queue systems with a certain probability that an element in the queue decides to leave its slot without having being served. This results in an error state.

7.1   A Length-Based Queue System

The first system models a "Length-Based" Queue System (LQS in the following), and it has the dynamics described below. In a generic state s, the following moves are allowed:

1. An enqueue operation. This operation is possible only if the queue is not full;
2. A dequeue operation. This operation is possible only if the queue is not empty;
3. Each element in the queue can leave its slot (this results in an error state);
4. The system may remain in the same state s.

The probabilities of the preceding moves are as follows. Let n be the number of queue slots. Suppose that, in state s, h operations are allowed. We have that $1 \leq h \leq 3 + n$, since each of the at most n elements in the queue can go in an error state. Then the probability of the first two moves (if they are allowed) is $\frac{1}{h}$. The probability that a queue element i enters an error state is $\frac{1-e^{-j}}{h}$, where j is the number of elements preceding i in the queue (i.e. the number of dequeue operations that i must wait for before it is its turn). This means that the more elements preceding i, the higher the probability that i leaves the queue. Finally, the probability that no operation is performed is the complement to 1 of the sum of the other defined probabilities.

The implementation of such a system in FHP-Murφ is quite simple. The queue is modeled with a circular array managed by two pointers, **head** and **tail**. For each slot in the queue, we memorize if it is in a correct state or in an error state (i.e. the element has left).

In Figure 2 we show the two main functions, **prob_trans** and **make_trans**, and how they are called by the **rule ''main''**.

Function **prob_trans** returns the outgoing probabilities from the current state s. The parameter i is needed to identify which of the moves allowed in s is the one to be calculated. Note that the function $\frac{1-e^{-j}}{h}$, where j is the number of elements preceding an element in the queue, is calculated by the function **prob_err**.

Function **make_trans** changes state s so as to generate a next state. It uses the parameter i in the same manner as **prob_trans**.

The **ruleset** in Figure 2 calls the **rule ''main''** with the different values for the variable i which are needed in functions **prob_trans** and **make_trans**.

Finally, the invariant to be checked states that the probability of the event "for all states s that are reachable in a finite number of steps k, s is not an error state" must be at least 0, where k is a parameter of the verification. Having set the probability to be $p \geq 0$ (which is always true) forces FHP-Murφ to always reach the horizon k (if we had set it to be $p \geq \gamma$, with $0 < \gamma \leq 1$, the visit would have stopped when p had become less than γ).

```
function prob_trans(i : trans_possib_type) : real_type; begin
  tmp := 0; /* number of moves except enqueue and dequeue */
  trans_possib := 1; /* total number of possible moves */
  calc_trans_possib(trans_possib, tmp);
  if (i >= trans_possib) then return 0.0;
/* i ranges on the max transitions number,
whilest they are not always all possible */
  else
    if (i < tmp) then return 1.0/trans_possib;
    else if (i = trans_possib - 1) then return 1.0/trans_possib - sum_prob_prec();
    else return prob_err(i - tmp)/trans_possib;
    endif; endif; endif; end;

procedure make_trans(i : trans_possib_type); begin
  /* the first part is the same as prob_trans */
  tmp := 0; trans_possib := 1; calc_trans_possib(trans_possib, tmp);
  if (i<trans_possib) then /* now, instead of giving probabilities, moves are done */
    if (!queue_empty() & i = 0) then /* dequeue */
      q[head] := noerr;
      if (head = ITEM_Q - 1) then head := 0;
      else head := head + 1; endif;
    else if (!queue_full() & (tmp = 1 ? i = 0 : i = 1)) then /* enqueue */
      q[tail] := noerr;
      if (tail = ITEM_Q - 1) then tail := 0;
      else tail := tail + 1; endif;
    else if (i != trans_possib - 1) then /* gone away */
      q[i - tmp] := err;
    endif; endif; endif; endif; end; /* if i = trans_possib - 1 no action is done */

ruleset i : trans_possib_type do /* general rule for the whole system */
  rule "main" prob_trans(i) ==> begin make_trans(i); end; end;

invariant "queue ok" 0.0 forall i : queue_range do q[i] != err endforall);
```

Fig. 2. FHP-Murφ implementation sketch for LQS

7.2   A Time-Based Server-Queue System

The second system models a "Time-Based" Server-Queue System (TSQS in the following), and it has the sequent behavior. In a generic state s, there are two different set of allowed moves. The first set just consists of the enqueue, the dequeue, the server status change and the null operations, with uniform probability.

The server status is given by a counter ranging from 0 to MAX_COUNT_S, modeling the time of service. If the server counter is 0, the server is free, then a dequeue (on a nonempty queue) can be made. In this case, the server counter is set to MAX_COUNT_S. If the server counter is greater than 0, then it is reset to 0 with probability proportional to the current server counter, and it is simply decremented with a complementary probability.

This models the fact that the higher the time of service, the higher the probability of returning free.

The second set of moves consists in updating a counter associated to each element in the queue, modeling the time spent by the element in the queue. When this counter reaches a given maximum value (MAX_COUNT_Q), we are in an error state. The updating phase consist in $n + 1$ possible transitions, where n is the number of elements currently in the queue: each of the element counters can immediately reach MAX_COUNT_Q with probability directly proportional to

```
function prob_trans(i : trans_possib) : real_type;
begin
  num_trans_possib := 1; calc_trans_possib(trans_possib);
  if (i >= num_trans_possib) then return 0.0;
  else /* mod_glob distinguish the two set of moves */
    if (mod_glob = 0) then
      if (s > 0 & i < 2) then
        if (i = 1) then return (s/MAX_COUNT_S)/(num_trans_possib - 1);
        else return (1.0 - s/MAX_COUNT_S)/(num_trans_possib - 1);
        endif;
      else return 1.0/(s > 0? num_trans_possib - 1 : num_trans_possib);
      endif;
    else
      if (i!=num_trans_possib-1) then return (q[slot(i)]/MAX_COUNT)/num_trans_possib;
      else return 1.0/trans_possib - sum_prob_prec();
      endif; endif; endif;
end;

procedure make_trans(i : trans_possib);
begin
  num_trans_possib := 1; calc_trans_possib(trans_possib);
  if (i < num_trans_possib) then
    if (mod_glob = 0) then
      if (s > 0 & i < 2) then s := (i = 1? s - 1 : 0);
      else if (!queue_empty() & s = 0 & i < 1) then
        .   .   .     /* dequeue operation */
        s := MAX_COUNT_S;
      else
        if (!queue_full()&(s>0?i<3:(!queue_empty()?i<2:i<1))) then
        .   .   .     /* enqueue operation */
        endif; endif; endif;
    else
      if (i != num_trans_possib - 1) then
        /* function slot(i) return the i-th element in the queue */
        q[slot(i)] := MAX_COUNT;
      endif;
      for k : queue_range do
        if (in_queue(k) & q[k] != MAX_COUNT) then q[k] := q[k] + 1;
        endif; endfor;
      /* if i = trans_possib - 1 no action is done */
    endif; endif;
  mod_glob := (mod_glob + 1)%2; /* switch between the two set of moves */
end;

invariant "queue ok" 1.0
(forall i : queue_range do q[i] != MAX_COUNT endforall);
```

Fig. 3. FHP-Murφ implementation sketch for TSQS

the current counter value, while all the other counters are simply incremented. Moreover, the last possibility is that all counters are simply incremented.

This models the fact that the higher the time spent in queue, the higher the probability to go away without being served.

Also the FHP-Murφ implementation of TSQS is simple, and it is sketched in Figure 3. The data structures are essentially the same as in LQS: the only modification consists in maintaining a counter (and not a boolean) for each slot, and in adding a counter to model the server. The structure of the code is the same as in Figure 2, so we only give functions prob_trans and make_trans.

Note that both these protocols are more difficult to write in PRISM input language. In fact, PRISM only allows constant probabilities to be defined on

ITEM_Q	Horizon	Memory (disk)	Visited	Time	Probability
4	10	0	104	3.900	0.2843699449
4	20	0	264	6.450	0.6043041472
5	10	0	126	3.930	0.3189541147
5	20	0	375	6.790	0.6333385081

Fig. 4. Results for LQS on a INTEL Pentium III 750Mhz with 128MB of RAM. Murφ options: -b (bit compression), -c (40 bit hash compaction), -m80 (use 80 MB of RAM). Memory occupations are in MB, time is in seconds.

ITEM_Q	MAX_COUNT_Q	MAX_COUNT_S	Horizon	Memory (disk)	Visited	Time	Probability
5	3	3	10	0	114	13.090	0.595936214
5	3	3	20	0	518	20.850	0.9432926435
10	20	20	30	0	705081	2243.830	0.7360071576
10	20	20	40	139.810176	20072051	65949.160	0.885392219
>10						> 1 day	

Fig. 5. Results for TSCS on a INTEL Pentium III 750Mhz with 128MB of RAM. Murφ options: -b (bit compression), -c (40 bit hash compaction), -m200 (use 200 MB of RAM). Memory occupations are in MB, time is in seconds.

transitions. On the other hand, here we have that the transition probabilities depends on the current state. Hence, to implement these protocols in PRISM, we are forced to list the values of the parameters from which they depend (e.g., in LQS, we have to list all the possible values representing the number of elements preceding the current one, asking for each of them if it is the correct value [29]), and then to tabulate, for each of them, the transition probability values. On the opposite, in FHP-Murφ we have been able to describe the transition probabilities in a uniform way.

7.3 Experimental Results

In Figures 4 and 5 we report the results obtained verifying, respectively, LQS and TSCS with FHP-Murφ. For each verification we report the values of the parameters from which the protocol depends (i.e. ITEM_Q for LQS, indicating the number of available slots in the queue, ITEM_Q, MAX_COUNT_Q and MAX_COUNT_S for TSCS), the finite horizon of the verification, the memory (on disk), the visited states, the time required by the verification and the final probability (of violating the invariant). Observe that, in TSCS, we were able to cope with quite large numbers of visited states. In fact, being the FHP-Murφ verification algorithm disk-based, almost any verification can be performed, if one waits for a suitable amount of time. This is symbolized by the last row of Figure 5.

8 Conclusions

We presented (Section 3) *Probabilistic Rule Based Transition Systems* (PRBTS) and showed (Section 4) how PRBTS can be used to model a fairly large class of *Finite State Discrete Time Stochastic Processes* as well as *Discrete Time Hybrid Stochastic Processes* (by approximating reals with *finite precision real numbers*).

PRBTS can be used as a *low level* language for *Stochastic Verification Engines*. As an example (Section 5) we showed how a high level definition of a stochastic system based on *Systems of Communicating Stochastic Processes* can be translated into a PRBTS definition.

We showed (Section 7) how FHP-Murφ [22], a suitable *disk based* extension of the Murφ verifier [18] can be used for automatic *Finite Horizon Verification* of PRBTS.

We showed (Section 7) effectiveness of our approach by presenting experimental results on automatic analysis with FHP-Murφ of two nontrivial stochastic systems. Our experimental results show that FHP-Murφ can handle more general models than state-of-the-art *Probabilistic Model Checkers* like PRISM [24,2,16] or TwoTowers [27]. On the other hand PRISM as well as TwoTowers can verify more general properties (e.g. all PCTL [12] properties for PRISM) than FHP-Murφ.

Future works include extending our approach to more general properties than *Finite Horizon Verification*, e.g. PCTL formulas with unbounded until. Moreover, it would be interesting to compare our approach with the discounting theory in [30]. In fact, this approach, where the future becomes less and less relevant, seems to fit well with a finite horizon point of view.

Acknowledgments

We are grateful to the anonymous referees for their help in improving a previous version of this paper.

References

1. Krzysztof R. Apt and Ernst-Rudinger Olderog. *Verification of Sequential and Concurrent Programs*. Text and Monographs in Computer Science. Springer–Verlag, 1991.
2. C. Baier, E. M. Clarke, V. Hartonas-Garmhausen, M. Kwiatkowska, and M. Ryan. Symbolic model checking for probabilistic processes. *Automata, Languages and Programming*, pages 430–440, 1997.
3. E. Behrends. *Introduction to Markov Chains*. Vieweg, 2000.
4. A. Bianco and L. de Alfaro. Model checking of probabilistic and nondeterministic systems. In *Proc. Foundations of Software Technology and Theoretical Computer Science*, volume 1026 of *LNCS*, pages 499–513. Springer, 1995.
5. J. R. Burch, E. M. Clarke, K. L. McMillan, D. L. Dill, and L. J. Hwang. Symbolic model checking: 10^{20} states and beyond. *Information and Computation*, 98, 1992.
6. C. Courcoubetis and M. Yannakakis. Verifying temporal properties of finite-state probabilistic programs. In *Proc. of FOCS'88*, pages 338–345. IEEE CS Press, 1988.
7. C. Courcoubetis and M. Yannakakis. The complexity of probabilistic verification. *J. ACM*, 42(4):857–907, 1995.
8. L. de Alfaro. Formal verification of performance and reliability of real-time systems. Technical report, Stanford University, 1996.

9. D. L. Dill, A. J. Drexler, A. J. Hu, and C. H. Yang. Protocol verification as a hardware design aid. In *IEEE International Conference on Computer Design: VLSI in Computers and Processors*, pages 522–5, 1992.

10. H. Hermanns G.G. Infante Lopez and J. Katoen. Beyond memoryless distribution: Model checking semi-markov chains. In *Proc. of PAPM-PROBMIV*, number 2165 in LNCS, pages 57–70. Springer, 2001.

11. H. Hansson. *Time and Probability in Formal Design of Distributed Systems*. Elsevier, 1994.

12. H. Hansson and B. Jonsson. A logic for reasoning about time and probability. *Formal Aspects of Computing*, 6:512–535, 1994.

13. G. J. Holzmann. *Design and Validation of Computer Protocols*. Prentice Hall, New Jersey, 1991.

14. G. J. Holzmann. The spin model checker. *IEEE Trans. on Software Engineering*, 23(5):279–295, May 1997.

15. M. Kwiatkowska, G. Norman, and D. Parker. PRISM: Probabilistic symbolic model checker. In P. Kemper, editor, *Proc. Tools Session of Aachen 2001 International Multiconference on Measurement, Modelling and Evaluation of Computer-Communication Systems*, pages 7–12, September 2001. Available as Technical Report 760/2001, University of Dortmund.

16. M. Kwiatkowska, G. Norman, and D. Parker. Probabilistic symbolic model checking with prism: A hybrid approach. In *Proc. TACAS'02*, volume 2280. LNCS, Springer Verlag, April 2002.

17. K. Larsen and A. Skou. Bisimulation through probabilistic testing. *Information and Computation*, 94:1–28, 1991.

18. url: http://sprout.stanford.edu/dill/murphi.html.

19. Barry L. Nelson. *Stochastic Modeling: Analysis And Simulation*. Dover Publications, 1995.

20. A. Papoulis. *Probability, Random Variables and Stochastic Processes*. McGraw-Hill Series in System Sciences, 1965.

21. G. Della Penna, B. Intrigila, I. Melatti, M. Minichino, E. Ciancamerla, A. Parisse, E. Tronci, and M. V. Zilli. Automatic verification of a turbogas control system with the murphi verifier. In *Proc. of 6th International Workshop on: Hybrid Systems: Computation and Control (HSCC)*, LNCS, Prague, Czech Republic, April 2003. Springer.

22. G. Della Penna, B. Intrigila, I. Melatti, E. Tronci, and M. V. Zilli. Finite horizon analysis of markov chains with the murphi verifier. *Submitted for publication*, 2003.

23. A. Pnueli and L. Zuck. Probabilistic verification. *Information and Computation*, 103:1–29, 1993.

24. url: http://www.cs.bham.ac.uk/~dxp/prism/.

25. R. Segala and N. Lynch. Probabilistic simulations for probabilistic processes. In *Proc. of CONCUR*, number 836 in LNCS, pages 381–496. Springer, 1994.

26. url: http://netlib.bell-labs.com/netlib/spin/whatispin.html.

27. url: http://www.sti.uniurb.it/bernardo/twotowers/.

28. M. Vardi. Automatic verification of probabilistic concurrent finite-state programs. In *Proc. of FOCS'85*, pages 327–338. IEEE CS Press, 1985.

29. url: http://www.di.univaq.it/melatti/ICTCS03/.

30. L. de Alfaro and T. A. Henzinger and R. Majumdar. Discounting the Future in Systems Theory. ICALP 2003: 1022–1037

Towards Compact and Tractable Automaton-Based Representations of Time Granularities

Ugo Dal Lago[1], Angelo Montanari[2], and Gabriele Puppis[2]

[1] Dipartimento di Scienze dell'Informazione
Università di Bologna
Mura Anteo Zamboni 7, 40127 Bologna, Italy
dallago@cs.unibo.it

[2] Dipartimento di Matematica e Informatica
Università di Udine
via delle Scienze 206, 33100 Udine, Italy
{montana,puppis}@dimi.uniud.it

Abstract. Different approaches to time granularity have been proposed in the database literature to formalize the notion of calendar, based on algebraic, logical, and string-based formalisms. In this paper, we further develop an alternative approach based on automata, originally proposed in [4], which makes it possible to deal with infinite time granularities in an effective (and efficient) way. In particular, such an approach provides an effective solution to fundamental problems such as equivalence and conversion of time granularities. We focus our attention on two kinds of optimization problems for automaton-based representations, namely, computing the smallest representation and computing the most tractable representation, that is, the one on which crucial algorithms (e.g., granule conversion algorithms) run fastest. We first introduce and compare these two minimization problems; then, we give a polynomial time algorithm that solves the latter.

1 Introduction

The notion of time granularity comes into play in a variety of problems involving time representation and management in database applications, including temporal database design, temporal data conversion, temporal database interoperability, temporal constraint reasoning, data mining, and time management in workflow systems. Different approaches to time granularity have been proposed in the database literature, based on algebraic [1,9], logical [3], and string-based [11] formalisms. We restrict our attention to the latter.

The string-based formalism eases access to and manipulation of data associated with different granularities, making it possible to solve some basic problems about time granularities, such as the equivalence problem, in an effective way. String-based algorithms, however, may potentially process every element (symbol) of representations, independently from their redundancy, thus requiring a large amount of computational time. This efficiency problem is dealt with by

C. Blundo and C. Laneve (Eds.): ICTCS 2003, LNCS 2841, pp. 72–85, 2003.

the automaton-based approach to time granularity, that revises and extends the string-based one.

According to such an approach, granularities are viewed as strings generated by a specific class of automata, called Simple Single-String Automata (Simple SSA for short), thus making it possible to (re)use well-known results from automata theory. Simple SSA were originally proposed by Dal Lago and Montanari to model infinite periodical granularities [4]. Furthermore, they showed that regularities of modeled granularities can be naturally expressed by extending Simple SSA with counters (let us call SSA the resulting class of automata). This extension makes the structure of the automata more compact, and it allows one to efficiently deal with those granularities which have a quasi-periodic structure.

In [5], we proved that SSA provide an efficient solution to the fundamental problems of equivalence, namely, the problem of establishing whether two different representations define the same granularity, and granule conversion, namely, the problem of relating granules of a given granularity to those of another one. To this end, we introduced a suitable variant of SSA, called Restricted Labeled Single-String Automata (RLA for short), and we showed that these automata are at least as expressive as the string-based formalism, better fitting for direct algorithmic manipulation. As an example, granule conversion problems can be solved in polynomial time with respect to the size of the involved RLA.

The algorithmic flavor of automaton-based representations of time granularity suggests an alternative point of view on their role: RLA can be used not only as a formalism for the direct specification of time granularities, but also as a low-level formalism into which high-level time granularity specifications can be mapped. From this point of view, the problem of reducing as much as possible the complexity of basic algorithms becomes even more crucial. In [5], we defined a suitable set of algorithms mapping expressions of Calendar Algebra (the high-level formalism for modeling time granularities developed by Ning et al. in [9]) to equivalent RLA-based representations. In this paper, we focus our attention on minimization problems for RLA.

There exist at least two possible notions of minimization. According to the first one, minimizing means computing the smallest representation of a given time granularity; according to the second one, minimizing means computing the most tractable representation of a given granularity, that is, the one on which crucial algorithms run fastest. The former kind of automaton-based representation is called a *size-optimal* representation, while the latter is called a *complexity-optimal* representation. These two criteria are clearly not equivalent, since the smallest representation is not necessarily the most tractable one, and vice versa. Furthermore we claim that both problems yield non-unique solutions. In the following, we tackle the complexity-minimization problem by using dynamic programming: we state some closure properties of RLA with respect to concatenation, iteration, and repetition of words, and we show how to compute complexity-optimal automata from smaller (optimal) ones in a bottom-up fashion. The resulting algorithm runs in polynomial time with respect to the size of the string-based description of the involved granularity.

The rest of the paper is organized as follows. In Section 2, we give a definition of time granularity and we briefly describe the main features of Wijsen's string-based formalism, which represents regular granularities by means of (encodings of) ultimately periodic words. In Section 3 we focus our attention on the automaton-based approach to time granularity. We define RLA and we state some basic properties of them. In Section 4 we briefly describe some polynomial algorithms which can be used to efficiently solve the equivalence and granule conversion problems for RLA-based representations of time granularies. In Section 5 we introduce the size-minimization and complexity-minimization problems, we point out important aspects about their solutions, and we give an intuitive explanation of the computation of complexity-optimal automata. In Section 6, we discuss the details of the proposed solution; in particular, we show how a complexity-optimal automaton recognizing a given ultimately periodic word can be effectively built up from a suitable representation of the repetitions of the word. In Section 7 we outline future research directions, with a special emphasis on possible improvements on the proposed complexity-minimization algorithm and on promising strategies to efficiently solve the size-minimization problem. (Reference [6] is an extended version of this work, including all proof details.)

2   The String-Based Model of Time Granularities

Since in many applications different time granularities can be used to specify the validity intervals of different facts [1], database systems need the ability of properly relating granules belonging to different time granularities. Such an ability presupposes the formalization of the notion of granularity. In this section, we first give a formal definition of time granularity, which captures a reasonably large class of temporal structures; then, we specialize such a definition in order to allow a finite representation and an efficient manipulation of the associated data.

Definition 1. *Given a set T of temporal instants and a total order $<$ on T, a time granularity on the temporal domain $(T, <)$ is a total function $G : \mathbb{Z} \to 2^T$ such that, for every pair of integers x and y, $x < y$ implies*

$$\forall\, t_x \in G(x).\; \forall\, t_y \in G(y).\; t_x < t_y.$$

Each non-empty set $G(x)$, with $x \in \mathbb{Z}$, is called a *granule* and each integer in the set $\{x \in \mathbb{Z} \;:\; G(x) \neq \emptyset\}$ is called a *label*. Note that Definition 1 captures both time granularities that cover the entire temporal domain, such as Day, Week, and Month, and time granularities with gaps within and between granules, like, for instance, BusinessDay, BusinessWeek, and BusinessMonth. Figure 1 depicts some of these granularities.

In the following, we assume granularity labels to belong to the set $\mathbb{N}^+$ (as a matter of fact, most applications assume the existence of a first granule). It is immediate to see that the set of all functions satisfying Definition 1 becomes uncountable as soon as the underlying temporal domain becomes infinite. As

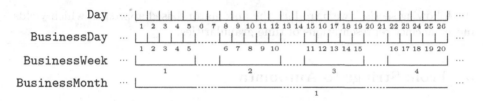

Fig. 1. Some examples of time granularities.

a consequence, it is not possible to deal with all of them by means of a fini-
tary formalism. However, the problem of mastering temporal structures for time
granularity can be tackled in an effective way by restricting to periodical granularities. In [11], Wijsen shows that such granularities can be naturally expressed
in terms of ultimately periodic words over an alphabet of three symbols, namely,
■ (filler), □ (gap), and ≀ (separator), which are respectively used to denote time
points covered by some granule, to denote time points not covered by any granule, and to delimit granules. In the following, we assume the reader to be familiar
with basic terminology and notation on finite and infinite strings [10]. In particular, we will often write a generic string u as $u[1]u[2]u[3]\ldots$, where $u[i]$ denotes
the i-th element of the string, and we will use the notation $u[i, j]$ to denote the
substring $u[i]u[i+1]\ldots u[j]$ of u. Furthermore, given a finite set S, we will denote
by S^∞ the set $S^\omega \cup S^*$, where S^ω (respectively, S^*) stands for the set of all and
only the infinite (respectively, finite) strings over S.

Definition 2. *Given a word $u \in \{■, □, ≀\}^\omega$ containing infinitely many occurrences of non-separator symbols, we say that u represents G if, for every pair
of positive integers x and y, $x \in G(y)$ if and only if $u[x + y - 1] = ■$ and
$u[1, x + y - 2]$ contains exactly $y - 1$ occurrences of $≀$.*

As an example, the infinite word ■■■■■□□≀■■■■■□□≀... represents the
granularity BusinessWeek over the temporal domain of days.

In order to *finitely* model time granularities, Wijsen introduces the notion
of *granspec*. A granspec is an ordered pair (u, v) of finite strings such that
$u, v \in \{■, □, ≀\}^*$ and v contains at least one occurrence of a non-separator symbol. Strings u and v are respectively called the *prefix* and the *repeating pattern* of
the ultimately periodic string $u \cdot v^\omega$ representing the (periodical) time granularity.
For instance, the granularity BusinessWeek ■■■■■□□≀■■■■■□□≀... can
be encoded by the granspec $(\varepsilon, ■■■■■□□≀)$. Furthermore, to solve the equivalence problem for (representations of) time granularities, Wijsen proposed a
suitable *canonical form* of granspecs, which turns out to be a sort of minimum
representation of periodical granularities. However, it is worth mentioning that,
whenever the granularity to be represented has a long period and/or a long
prefix, the granspec formalism produces lengthy canonical granspecs. As a consequence, computations on time granularities represented by granspecs may take
a great deal of time. For example, if (u, v) is a granspec representing months of
the Gregorian Calendar in terms of days, we have that $|u| + |v| \geq 146097$. In

the following section, we introduce the automaton-based approach, which yields more succinct representations of time granularities.

3   From Strings to Automata

The idea of viewing granularities as ultimately periodic strings naturally connects time granularity to the fields of formal languages and automata, because any ω-regular language is uniquely determined by its ultimately periodic words [2]. The basic idea underlying the automaton-based approach to time granularity is simple: we take an automaton M recognizing a *single* word $u \in \{\blacksquare, \square, \wr\}^{\omega}$ and we say that M represents granularity G if and only if u represents G. In the following, we introduce Restricted Labeled Single-String Automata (RLA for short), which differ from finite automata and Büchi automata as they accept single words instead of sets of words. As a matter of fact, RLA can also be viewed as a variant of SSA [4], in which counters over discrete domains are exploited to obtain succinct representations of time granularities.

Before formalizing the notion of RLA, we give an intuitive explanation of the structure and behavior of automata belonging to this class. In order to simplify the notation and the formalization of useful properties, RLA label states instead of transitions. The set of states of an RLA, denoted by S, is partitioned into two groups, respectively denoted by S_Σ and S_ε. S_Σ is the set of states where the labeling function is defined, while S_ε is the set of states where it is not defined. Furthermore, there are two kinds of transitions, respectively called *primary* and *secondary* transitions. Intuitively, primary transitions are defined in the standard way, while secondary transitions have been introduced to succinctly represent repetitions. At any point of the computation, at most one (primary or secondary) transition is taken according to an appropriate rule envisaging the state at which the automaton lies and the value of a *counter*.

Figure 2 depicts two RLA, that respectively recognize the words $(\blacksquare\square^6\wr)^{\omega}$ and $(\blacksquare\wr(\square\wr)^6)^{\omega}$, both representing mondays in terms of days (the former associates the labels $1, 2, 3, \ldots$ with the granules, while the latter associates the labels $1, 8, 15, \ldots$ with them). States in S_Σ are represented by labeled circles, while states in S_ε are represented by triangles. Primary and secondary transitions are represented by continuous and dashed arrows, respectively. The initial state is identified by a little triangular tip. The (initial values of) counters are associated with states in S_ε. This simple example provides an intuitive idea of how RLA allow one to compactly encode repeating patterns in granularities by means of counters and transitions.

Definition 3. *A* Restricted Labeled Single-String Automaton *is an 8-tuple* $M = (S_\Sigma, S_\varepsilon, \Sigma, \Omega, \delta, \gamma, s_0, C_0)$, *where*
- *S_Σ and S_ε are disjoint finite sets of* states *(let $S = S_\Sigma \cup S_\varepsilon$);*
- *Σ is a finite* alphabet*;*
- *$\Omega : S_\Sigma \to \Sigma$ is the* labeling function*;*
- *$\delta : S \rightharpoonup S$, is a partial function, called* primary transition function*;*

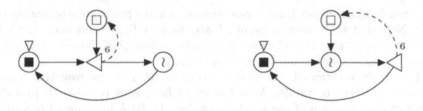

Fig. 2. Two RLA that represent mondays in terms of days.

- $\gamma : S_\varepsilon \to S$ *is a total function, called* secondary transition function, *such that:*
  - i) *for every* $s \in S_\varepsilon$, $(\gamma(s), s)$ *belongs to the reflexive and transitive closure* δ^* *of* δ; *the least* $n \in \mathbb{N}$ *such that* $(\gamma(s), s) \in \delta^n$ *is called the* γ-degree *of* s *and* $\Gamma_M \subseteq S_\varepsilon \times S$ *is a relation such that* $(s, r) \in \Gamma_M$ *iff* $r = \delta^i(\gamma(s))$ *with* i *less than or equal to the* γ-degree *of* s;
  - ii) *the reflexive and transitive closure* Γ_M^* *of* Γ_M *must be antisymmetric;*
- $s_0 \in S$ *is the* initial state;
- $C_0 : S_\varepsilon \to \mathbb{N}$ *is the* initial valuation.

Conditions i) and ii) on the secondary transition function enforce the existence of a partial order Γ_M^* on states of M. Such an order immediately suggests an induction principle, called γ-*induction*, which may be used in both formal definitions and proofs.

The definition of the computation of an RLA is based on the notion of configuration. For any finite set S of states, a *valuation* C on S is any function $C : S \to \mathbb{N}$. In the following, we denote as $\mathcal{C}_M$ the class $\mathbb{N}^{S_\varepsilon}$ of all the valuations for the counters of an RLA $M = (S_\Sigma, S_\varepsilon, \Sigma, \Omega, \delta, \gamma, s_0, C_0)$. A *configuration* is a pair (s, C), with $s \in S$ and $C \in \mathcal{C}_M$. The transitions of M are taken according to a partial function $\Delta_M : S \times \mathcal{C}_M \rightharpoonup S \times \mathcal{C}_M$ such that $\Delta_M(s, C) = (t, D)$ if and only if one of the following three conditions holds:

- $s \in S_\Sigma \wedge t = \delta(s) \wedge \forall r.\ D(r) = C(r)$ (namely, whenever the automaton lies in a labeled state, then it always makes a primary transition);
- $s \in S_\varepsilon \wedge C(s) \neq 0 \wedge t = \gamma(s) \wedge D(s) = C(s) - 1 \wedge \forall r \neq s.\ (D(r) = C(r))$ (namely, whenever the automaton lies in a non-labeled state and the corresponding counter is positive, then it makes a secondary transition);
- $s \in S_\varepsilon \wedge C(s) = 0 \wedge t = \delta(s) \wedge D(s) = C_0(s) \wedge \forall r \neq s.\ (D(r) = C(r))$ (namely, whenever the automaton lies in a non-labeled state and the corresponding counter is 0, then it makes a primary transition and it re-initializes the counter).

The *computation* of M is the maximum (possibly infinite) sequence $\rho \in (S \times \mathcal{C}_M)^\infty$ such that $\rho[1] = (s_0, C_0)$ and $\Delta_M(\rho[i]) = \rho[i + 1]$ for every $i \geq 1$. From the computation ρ of M, it is easy to extract a sequence of states $\rho_\Sigma \in S_\Sigma^\infty$ by discarding states belonging to S_ε and valuations. We say that M *recognizes* the word u if and only if $u = \Omega(\rho_\Sigma)$, where $\Omega(\rho_\Sigma)$ is the sequence obtained by applying the labeling function Ω to (each element of) the sequence of states ρ_Σ. Thus, RLA recognize either finite words or ultimately periodic words (namely, those words which result from concatenating a finite prefix to a repeating pattern). Note that the computation of M may be an infinite sequence, even if the recognized word is finite. However we can overcome this clumsy situation by discarding useless states and transitions of RLA.

As already mentioned, the main feature of RLA is the way they encode repeating patterns of words. As a matter of fact, it is possible to provide a formal characterization of the words recognized by RLA in terms of repetitions of smaller substrings. Precisely, given a RLA $M = (S_\Sigma, S_\varepsilon, \Sigma, \Omega, \delta, \gamma, s_0, C_0)$, one can show that it recognizes the word

$$u = \Omega \left(\rho_{s_0} \cdot \rho_{\delta(s_0)} \cdot \rho_{\delta^2(s_0)} \cdot \dots \right)$$

where each ρ_s is defined to be
- s, whenever $s \in S_\Sigma$;
- $\left(\rho_{\gamma(s)} \cdot \rho_{\delta(\gamma(s))} \cdot \rho_{\delta^2(\gamma(s))} \cdot \dots \cdot \rho_{\delta^{n-1}(\gamma(s))} \right)^{C_0(s)}$, where n is the γ-degree of s, whenever $s \in S_\varepsilon$.

As a consequence, any word recognized by an RLA can be represented using expressions as $(\blacksquare^5 \square^2 \wr)^\omega$, $((\blacksquare^2 \square)^2 \square \wr)^\omega$, ... denoting nested repetitions.

4   Granularity Equivalence and Granule Conversions

In this section, we briefly discuss the equivalence and the granule conversion problems. The decidability of the former problem implies the possibility of effectively testing the semantic equivalence of two descriptions, making it possible to use smaller, or more tractable, representations in place of bigger, or less tractable, ones. The relevance of the granule conversion problem has been advocated by several authors, e.g., [1], even though in most solutions it has been only partially worked out in a rather complex way.

To explain our solutions, we first address a simpler problem, which arises very often when dealing with representation of time granularities as well as with infinite strings in general, namely, the problem of finding the n-th occurrence of a given symbol in a string. From the point of view of the theory of automata, this problem can obviously be solved in linear time *with respect to the number of transitions* needed to reach the n-th occurrence of the symbol: it suffices to follow the transitions of the automaton (of the RLA in our case) until the n-th occurrence of the symbol is recognized. Nevertheless, we can improve this straightforward solution by taking advantage of the definition of RLA. For instance, if we are searching for an occurrence of a symbol $a \in \Sigma$ in the word u recognized by the RLA $M = (S_\Sigma, S_\varepsilon, \Sigma, \Omega, \delta, \gamma, s_0, C_0)$ and $\Omega(\rho_{s_0})$ contains no occurrences of symbol a, then we can avoid processing the first $|\rho_{s_0}|$ symbols in u. Similarly, if $s_0 \in S_\varepsilon$ and $\Omega(\rho_{s_0})$ contains at least an occurrence of a, but $\Omega(\rho_{\gamma(s_0)})$ does not, then we can start searching for an occurrence of a in u from the position $(1 + |\rho_{\gamma(s_0)}|)$. For every state $s \in S$ and every symbol $a \in \Sigma$, the length of ρ_s and the number of occurrences of a in $\Omega(\rho_s)$ can be computed in polynomial time *with respect to the number of states* by exploiting the definition of ρ_s. Furthermore, such values can be pre-computed and stored into appropriate data structures for M. On the grounds of the above observations, we can define an algorithm, called *SeekAtOccurrence*, which returns the configuration reached by simulating transitions of M from a given configuration (s, C) until the n-th occurrence of a symbol in a distinguished set $A \subseteq \Sigma$ has been read. As a side effect, *SeekAtOccurrence*$(M, s, C, A, n, counter)$ returns in $counter[a]$ the number of processed occurrences for each symbol $a \in \Sigma$.

In spite of the simplicity of this idea, *SeekAtOccurrence* turns out to be rather complex and the formal analysis of its complexity is even more involved [5]. However, it is not difficult to show that the worst-case time for *SeekAtOccurrence*$(M, s, C, A, n, counter)$ is asymptotically equivalent to a suitable *complexity measure*, defined in terms of the nesting structure of the transition functions of M. We use $\|M\|$ to denote such a measure, which is defined, according to the principle of γ-induction, as follows:

$$\|M\| = max\{\mathbf{C}^M_{s_0,t} \ : \ (s_0, t) \in \delta^*\},$$

where, for each pair of states $(s, t) \in \delta^*$, $\mathbf{C}^M_{s,t}$ is defined to be
- 1, if $s = t$;
- $1 + \mathbf{C}^M_{\delta(s),t}$, if $s \in S_\Sigma$ and $s \neq t$;
- $max\{1 + \mathbf{C}^M_{\delta(s),t}, \mathbf{C}^M_{\gamma(s),s}\}$, if $s \in S_\varepsilon$ and $s \neq t$.

As for relationships between the complexities of automaton-based and string-based representations, there exist a number of cases that account for the compactness and tractableness of RLA with respect to granspecs. As an example, it is not difficult to provide an RLA representing the granularity Month in terms of days and having complexity 520, which is significantly less than the size of any equivalent granspec.

We now give an intuitive account of how to decide whether or not two given RLA represent the same granularity. Details of the algorithm, which exploits noticeable properties of equivalent representations and extensively uses *SeekAtOccurrence*, are given in [5]. The basic ingredients are the following ones. First, it holds that two RLA M and N represent the same granularity if and only if ultimately periodic words u and v, recognized respectively by M and N and having prefix lengths p_u and p_v and period lengths q_u and q_v, are *G-aligned*. Two ultimately periodic words u and v are said to be G-aligned if and only if all occurrences of the filler symbol in u and v lie at the same positions and are interleaved by the same number of occurrences of the separator symbol. Such a characterization of equivalent representations can be exploited by showing that a sufficient condition for u and v to be G-aligned is that two prefixes of u and v (not shorter than $max(p_u + q_u, p_v + q_v) + lcm(q_u, q_v)$) are G-aligned. Algorithm *SeekAtOccurrence* can be used to check the G-alignment property on words recognized by two RLA M and N in time $O((\|M\| + \|N\|)n)$, where n bounds the number of occurrences of ■ in the prefix and period of u and v.

Consider now the problem of converting temporal intervals from a given granularity to a coarser or finer one. RLA can be exploited to solve many conversion problems in polynomial time with respect to the number of states of the involved automata. In particular, we can define two functions mapping intervals of temporal points to intervals of labels of a given granularity covering the input interval, and vice versa. It is worth pointing out that such functions are similar to the conversion operators introduced by Snodgrass et al. [7] and that they can be computed on RLA by exploiting the algorithm *SeekAtOccurrence*. As an example, the following two algorithms solve conversion problems by requiring only a finite number of calls to *SeekAtOccurrence*. It is not difficult to show that such algorithms, as well as many others which compute similar functions, can be executed in time $O(\|M\|)$, where M is the RLA representing the involved granularity.

$UpConversion(M, t_1, t_2)$

1: **let** $M = (S_\Sigma, S_\varepsilon, \Sigma, \Omega, \delta, \gamma, s_0, C_0)$
2: $(s, C) \leftarrow (s_0, C_0)$
3: $SeekAtOccurrence(M, s, C, \{\blacksquare, \square\}, t_1 - 1, counter_1)$
4: $SeekAtOccurrence(M, s, C, \{\blacksquare\}, 1, counter_2)$
5: $x_1 \leftarrow counter_1[\wr] + counter_2[\wr] + 1$
6: $(s, C) \leftarrow (s_0, C_0)$
7: $SeekAtOccurrence(M, s, C, \{\blacksquare, \square\}, t_2, counter_3)$
8: $(s, C) \leftarrow (s_0, C_0)$
9: $SeekAtOccurrence(M, s, C, \{\blacksquare\}, counter_3[\blacksquare], counter_4)$
10: $x_2 \leftarrow counter_4[\wr]$
11: **return** (x_1, x_2)

$DownConversion(M, x_1, x_2)$

1: **let** $M = (S_\Sigma, S_\varepsilon, \Sigma, \Omega, \delta, \gamma, s_0, C_0)$
2: $(s, C) \leftarrow (s_0, C_0)$
3: $SeekAtOccurrence(M, s, C, \{\wr\}, x_1 - 1, counter_1)$
4: $SeekAtOccurrence(M, s, C, \{\blacksquare\}, 1, counter_2)$
5: $t_1 \leftarrow counter_1[\blacksquare] + counter_2[\blacksquare] + counter_1[\square] + counter_2[\square]$
6: $(s, C) \leftarrow (s_0, C_0)$
7: $SeekAtOccurrence(M, s, C, \{\wr\}, x_2, counter_3)$
8: $(s, C) \leftarrow (s_0, C_0)$
9: $SeekAtOccurrence(M, s, C, \{\blacksquare\}, counter_3[\blacksquare], counter_4)$
10: $t_2 \leftarrow counter_4[\blacksquare] + counter_4[\square]$
11: **return** (t_1, t_2)

---

5   Optimality of Automaton-Based Representations

In the previous section we briefly summarized the main features of two basic algorithms working on RLA M, whose worst-case time complexity linearly depends on $\|M\|$. It immediately follows that it is worth to minimize $\|M\|$. Furthermore, there exists a widespread recognition of the fact that state minimization is a crucial problem in classical automata theory as well as in the theory of reactive systems. Another goal of practical interest is thus the minimization of the

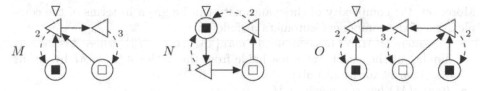

Fig. 3. Size-optimal and complexity-optimal automata.

number of states of M (let us denote it by $|M|$), so that smaller representations, in place of bigger ones, can be used. The former problem is called complexity-minimization problem, while the latter is called size-minimization problem.

Size and complexity of an RLA are obviously related one to the other; however, corresponding problems are not equivalent at all. In particular, the size-minimization problem seems to be harder than the complexity-minimization problem and it will not be discussed in detail in this paper. Furthermore, optimal automata are not guaranteed to be unique (up to isomorphisms) as it happens, for instance, for Deterministic Finite Automata. As an example, Figure 3 depicts two size-optimal automata (M and N) and two complexity-optimal automata (M and O) recognizing the finite word ■■□■■□■■□.

Automata minimization problems can be addressed in many different ways, e.g., by partitioning the state space or by exploiting noticeable relations between automata and expressions encoding recognized words. In this paper, we cope with the minimization problem for RLA by using dynamic programming, that is, by computing an optimal automaton starting from smaller (optimal) automata in a bottom-up fashion. The key point of such a solution is the proof that the problem enjoys an optimal-substructure property. In the following we describe three operations on RLA, and we prove closure properties for them; then, we compare the complexity of compound automata with that of their components. In the next section we will take advantage of these results to give an optimal substructure property for RLA.

The class of RLA is closed with respect to the operations of concatenation, repetition, and iteration of words. Given two RLA M and N, which respectively recognize a (finite) word u and a (not necessarily finite) word v, let $Concatenate(M, N)$, $Iterate(M)$, and $Repeat(M, k)$ respectively be the *concatenation of M and N*, which recognizes the word $u \cdot v$, the *iteration of M*, which recognizes the word u^ω, and the *k-repetition of M*, which recognizes the word u^k. The resulting automata can be computed as follows:

- the automaton $Concatenate(M, N)$ can be obtained in the usual way by linking the final state of M, namely, the state reached at the end of the computation of M, to the initial state of N by means of a primary transition;
- the automaton $Iterate(M)$ can be obtained by linking the final state of M to the initial state of M by means of a primary transition;
- the automaton $Repeat(M, k)$ can be obtained by introducing a new non-labeled state s_{loop} and by adding (i) a primary transition from the final state of M to s_{loop}, (ii) a secondary transition from s_{loop} to the initial state of M, and (iii) a counter on s_{loop}, with initial valuation equal to k.

Moreover, the complexity of these automata can be given in terms of the complexities of the component automata as follows:

- $Concatenate(M, N)$ has complexity $max\{\|M\|, n + \|N\|\}$, where n is the cardinality of the set of states reachable from the initial state of M by means of primary transitions only;
- $Iterate(M)$ has complexity $\|M\|$;
- $Repeat(M, k)$ has complexity $\|M\| + 1$.

As a matter of fact, we can actually give the status of algorithms running in linear time to $Concatenate$, $Iterate$, and $Repeat$, as it can be easily checked.

Finally, let Σ be a finite alphabet and let $\mathcal{B}_\Sigma$ be the set $\{M_a : a \in \Sigma\}$, where M_a is the single-state RLA recognizing $a \in \Sigma$. We denote by $\mathcal{C}_\Sigma$ the class of all the RLA which can be obtained from $\mathcal{B}_\Sigma$ by applying the operations of $Concatenate$, $Iterate$, and $Repeat$. $\mathcal{C}_\Sigma$ is *properly* included in the class of all the RLA, that is, there exist some RLA, including size-optimal and complexity-optimal ones (e.g., the automaton M in Figure 3), which cannot be generated from automata in $\mathcal{B}_\Sigma$ by applying the operations of concatenation, iteration, and k-repetition. Nevertheless, it turns out that, for every RLA M, $\mathcal{C}_\Sigma$ always contains at least one RLA which is equivalent to M and has the same complexity. This property can be used to prove that a complexity-optimal automaton for a given string can be generated by appropriately composing smaller (complexity-optimal) automata using the operators $Concatenate$, $Iterate$, and $Repeat$. Unfortunately, similar properties do not hold for the size of RLA.

6   Computing Complexity-Optimal Automata

6.1   Sharing Free Automata

For every RLA $M = (S_\Sigma, S_\varepsilon, \Sigma, \Omega, \delta, \gamma, s_0, C_0)$ and for every pair of states r, s such that $(r, s) \in \delta^*$, let $\Delta_{r,s}^M$ denote the set $\{\delta^i(r) : 0 \le i \le n\}$, where n is the least natural number such that $s = \delta^n(r)$.

Definition 4. *Given an RLA $M = (S_\Sigma, S_\varepsilon, \Sigma, \Omega, \delta, \gamma, s_0, C_0)$ and a state $s \in S_\varepsilon$, s is said to be* sharing *if there is a state $t \notin \Delta_{\gamma(s),s}^M \setminus \{s_0\}$ such that the set $\Delta_{t,s}^M \cap \Delta_{\gamma(s),s}^M$ contains states other than s itself. M is* sharing-free *if S_ε does not contain sharing states.*

As a matter of fact, any automaton in $\mathcal{C}_\Sigma$ is sharing free. The following lemma shows that sharing states can be eliminated by replicating states, without increasing complexity.

Lemma 1. *For every RLA M, there exists an equivalent sharing-free RLA, denoted $SharingFree(M)$, such that $\|M\| = \|SharingFree(M)\|$.*

6.2   An Optimal Substructure Property

In this section, we prove that RLA satisfy the optimal substructure property. Lemma 1 implies that for any (finite or ultimately periodic) word $u \in \Sigma^\infty$, there

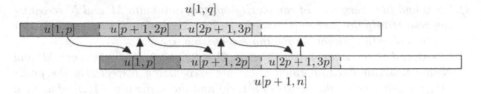

Fig. 4. Relationship between partial periods and borders.

is at least one sharing free complexity-optimal automaton M which recognizes u. In fact, we are going to show that we can choose M in such a way that it belongs to $\mathcal{C}_\Sigma$ and it is decomposable into complexity-optimal automata.

As a preliminary step, we characterize repeating patterns of words through the notions of period, partial period, and border.

Definition 5. *A word u has* period *p if there is a positive integer k such that $u = u[1,p]^k$. The* period *of u is the minimum period of u. By analogy we define the* prefix length *and the* period *of an ultimately periodic word u to be the integers l and q such that $u = u[1,l] \cdot u[l+1, l+q]^\omega$ and $l+q$ is minimum. Furthermore, p is said to be a* partial period *of u provided u is a prefix of $u[1,p]^\omega$. Finally a* border *of a finite word u is a non-empty string v different from u such that v is both a prefix and a suffix of u.*

It is worth noticing that $u[1,q]$ is a (maximum) border of u if and only if $p = |u| - q$ is a (minimum) partial period of u (see Figure 4).

The following two theorems state optimal substructure properties for finite and ultimately periodic words, respectively. Notice that both theorems provide only a *finite* number of ways to build a complexity-optimal automaton for u from (optimal) automata for substrings of u.

Theorem 1. *Given a finite word u such that $|u| > 1$, one of the following conditions holds:*

  i) for every pair of complexity-optimal automata M and N recognizing respectively the prefix $u[1]$ and the suffix $u[2,n]$ of u, Concatenate(M,N) is a complexity-optimal automaton recognizing u;

  ii) there exists an integer $r \in [1, |u| - 1]$ such that whenever M and N are two complexity-optimal automata recognizing respectively the prefix $u[1,p]$ (with p being the period of $u[1,r]$) and the suffix $u[r+1, |u|]$ of u, then Concatenate$(Repeat(M, \frac{r}{p}), N)$ is a complexity-optimal automaton recognizing u.

  iii) for every complexity-optimal automaton M recognizing $u[1,p]$, with $p < |u|$ being the period of u, Repeat$(M, \frac{n}{p})$ is a complexity-optimal automaton recognizing u;

Theorem 2. *Given an ultimately periodic word u with minimum prefix length l and minimum period q, one of the following conditions holds:*

i) $l > 0$ and for every pair of complexity-optimal automata M and N recognizing respectively the prefix $u[1]$ and the suffix $u[2, \omega]$ of u, Concatenate(M, N) is a complexity-optimal automaton recognizing u;

ii) $l > 0$ and there is an integer $r \in [1, 2l + 2q]$ such that whenever M and N are two complexity-optimal automata recognizing respectively the prefix $u[1, p]$ (with p being the period of $u[1, r]$) and the suffix $u[r + 1, \omega[$ of u, then Concatenate$(Repeat(M, \frac{r}{p}), N)$ is a complexity-optimal automaton recognizing u.

iii) $l = 0$ and for every complexity-optimal automaton M recognizing $u[1, q]$, Iterate(M) is a complexity-optimal automaton recognizing u;

Theorems 1 and 2 suggest a simple dynamic programming algorithm which, given a finite string u or a string-based representation of an ultimately periodic word u, computes in polynomial time a complexity-optimal RLA recognizing u. This algorithm heavily uses information on periods of all the substrings of u. For any finite string v (or any finite prefix v of a given ultimately periodical word), the periods of all the substrings of v can be efficiently computed in time $\Theta(|v|^2)$ by exploiting noticeable properties of periods and borders (the approach is somehow similar to the one used by Knuth, Morris, and Pratt in order to compute the prefix function of a pattern in the context of string-matching problems [8]). In particular, it turns out that the length $q(j)$ of the maximum border of $v[1, j]$ satisfies the equations $q(1) = 0$ and, for every $j > 1$, $q(j) = max(\{0\} \cup \{l \ : \ v[l] = v[j] \ \wedge \ l - 1 \in q^+(j - 1)\})$, where q^+ denotes the transitive closure of the function q. Since to each maximum border corresponds a minimum partial period, it turns out that the minimum partial periods of all the prefixes of v can be computed in linear time. The above mentioned bound easily follows.

7   Further Work

In this paper we gave a polynomial time algorithm that determines a complexity-optimal representation for RLA. We believe that such an algorithm can actually be improved, by exploiting subtle relationships between repeating patterns of strings and secondary transition functions of complexity-optimal RLA. As a matter of fact, we conjecture that loops of primary and secondary transition functions of a complexity-optimal RLA can be related to *maximal repetitions* in the recognized word (a maximal repetition of u is a periodical substring $u[i, j]$ whose minimum period increases as soon as $u[i, j]$ is prolonged to the right, e.g., $u[i, j + 1]$, or to the left, e.g., $u[i - 1, j]$.

Another interesting research direction is the development of an algorithm that efficiently solves the size-minimization problem. To this end, we conjecture that size-optimal automata can be built up from smaller components, as we did for complexity-optimal ones, via concatenation, repetition, iteration, and a new operator which collapses "non-distinguishable" states of RLA (at the moment, the major stumbling block is the problem of finding an appropriate definition of RLA distinguishable states).

References

1. C. Bettini, S. Jajodia, and X.S. Wang. *Time Granularities in Databases, Data Mining, and Temporal Reasoning.* Springer, July 2000.
2. H. Calbrix, M. Nivat, and A. Podelski. Ultimately periodic words of rational ω-languages. In *Proceedings of the 9th International Conference on Mathematical Foundations of Programming Semantics,* volume 802 of *Lecture Notes in Computer Science,* pages 554–566. Springer, 1994.
3. C. Combi, M. Franceschet, and A. Peron. A logical approach to represent and reason about calendars. In *Proceedings of the 9th International Symposium on Temporal Representation and Reasoning,* pages 134–140. IEEE Computer Society Press, 2002.
4. U. Dal Lago and A. Montanari. Calendars, time granularities, and automata. In *Proceedings of the 7th International Symposium on Spatial and Temporal Databases (SSTD),* volume 2121 of *Lecture Notes in Computer Science,* pages 279–298. Springer, July 2001.
5. U. Dal Lago, A. Montanari, and G. Puppis. Time granularities, calendar algebra, and automata. Technical Report 4, Dipartimento di Matematica e Informatica, Università degli Studi di Udine, Italy, February 2003.
6. U. Dal Lago, A. Montanari, and G. Puppis. Towards compact and tractable automaton-based representations of time granularities. Technical Report 17, Dipartimento di Matematica e Informatica, Università degli Studi di Udine, Italy, July 2003.
7. C.E. Dyreson, W.S. Evans, H. Lin, and R.T. Snodgrass. Efficiently supporting temporal granularities. *IEEE Transactions on Knowledge and Data Engineering,* 12(4):568–587, July/August 2000.
8. D.E. Knuth, J.H. Morris, and V.R. Pratt. Fast pattern matching in strings. *SIAM Journal on Computing,* 6:323–350, 1977.
9. P. Ning, S. Jajodia, and X.S. Wang. An algebraic representation of calendars. *Annals of Mathematics and Artificial Intelligence,* 36:5–38, 2002.
10. W. Thomas. Languages, automata, and logic. In G. Rozemberg and A. Salomaa, editors, *Handbook of Formal Languages,* volume 3, pages 389–455. Springer, 1997.
11. J. Wijsen. A string-based model for infinite granularities. In C. Bettini and A. Montanari, editors, *Proceedings of the AAAI Workshop on Spatial and Temporal Granularities,* pages 9–16. AAAI Press, 2000.

Lower Bounds on the Size of Quantum Automata Accepting Unary Languages*

Alberto Bertoni, Carlo Mereghetti, and Beatrice Palano

Dipartimento di Scienze dell'Informazione
Università degli Studi di Milano
via Comelico 39/41, 20135 Milano, Italy
{bertoni,mereghetti,palano}@dsi.unimi.it

Abstract. In this paper, we study *measure-once 1-way quantum automata* accepting *unary languages*, i.e., of type $L \subset \{a\}^*$. We give two *lower bounds on the number of states* of such automata accepting certain languages.

1. We prove the existence of n-periodic languages requiring $\Omega(\sqrt{\frac{n}{\log n}})$ states to be recognized. This should be compared with results in the literature stating that every n-periodic language can be recognized with $O(\sqrt{n})$ states.
2. We give a lower bound on the number of states of automata accepting the finite language $L^{<n} = \{a^k \in L \mid k < n\}$, for a given L. This bound is obtained by using quantum information theory arguments.

Keywords: quantum automata, quantum information theory

1 Introduction

Quantum computing is a research area, halfway between computer science and physics [14]. In the early 1980's, Feynman suggests that the computational power of quantum mechanical processes might be beyond that of traditional computation models [11]. Almost at the same time, Benioff already determines that such processes are at least as powerful as Turing machines [2]. Discussing the notion of "quantum computer", Deutsch [10] develops the model of quantum Turing machine as a physically realizable model for a quantum computer. From the point of view of structural complexity, in [9], the class **BQP** of problems solvable in polynomial time on quantum Turing machines is introduced and compared with the corresponding deterministic class **P** or probabilistic class **BPP**.

A well known result witnessing quantum power is Shor's algorithm for integer factorization which runs in polynomial time on a quantum computer [23]. Another relevant progress is made by Grover [13], who proposes a quantum algorithm for searching an item in an unsorted database containing n items in time $O(\sqrt{n})$.

---

* Partially supported by MURST, under the project "Linguaggi formali: teoria ed applicazioni".

C. Blundo and C. Laneve (Eds.): ICTCS 2003, LNCS 2841, pp. 86–96, 2003.

Some efforts have been made for constructing quantum devices, and their realizations seems to be a difficult task. For this reason, it might be useful to study the computational characteristics of simple devices such as *quantum finite automata*. Some models have been introduced: measure-once [3,7,21], measure-many [1,17], enhanced [22], reversible [12], with control language [5].

In this paper, we consider *measure-once 1-way quantum automata* (1qfa's, for short) accepting *unary languages*, i.e., languages of type $L \subset \{a\}^*$. Our main contributions are the following.

- First of all, we consider *n-periodic languages*. In [20], it has been proved that every n-periodic language can be recognized by a 1qfa with $O(\sqrt{n})$ states. In Section 3, we prove that certain n-periodic languages require $\Omega(\sqrt{n/\log n})$ states to be accepted by 1qfa's.
- Next, we consider *unary finite languages* of type $L^{<n} = \{a^k \in L \mid k < n\}$. For $0 \leq s < j < n$, let $\#_L(s,j) = \{a^k \in L \mid s \leq k < j\}$ and, for $1 \leq t < n/2$, let $\gamma_L(t,n) = \max_{t \leq k \leq n-t} \left\{ \frac{|\#_L(k-t,k) - \#_L(k,k+t)|}{t} \right\}$.
  Fixed $\varepsilon > 0$, we give a lower bound on the number q of states of 1qfa's accepting $L^{<n}$ in terms of numbers $\tau_L(t,n,\varepsilon)$, where

$$\tau_L(t,n,\varepsilon) = \begin{cases} 0 & \text{if } \gamma_L(t,n) < \varepsilon/(1-\varepsilon) \\ (1-\varepsilon)\,\gamma_L(t,n) - \varepsilon & \text{otherwise.} \end{cases}$$

Precisely, in Section 4 we state, and prove in Section 5, that

$$\log q \geq \sum_{k=0}^{\log n - 1} \left(1 - H\left(\frac{1}{2} + \frac{1}{2}\,\tau_L(2^k, n, \varepsilon) \right) \right),$$

where $H(X) = -x \log x - (1-x) \log(1-x)$ is the entropy function. For instance, any quantum automaton accepting the language $\{a^k \mid n/2 \leq k < n\}$ with probability $1 - \varepsilon$ must have at least $n^{1-H(1-\varepsilon)}$ states.

Since the latter result requires quantum information theory arguments, in Section 2, among basics on quantum computing, we briefly recall the notion of Von Neumann's entropy and Holevo's theorem.

2   Preliminaries

2.1   Linear Algebra

We quickly recall some notations of linear algebra. For more details, we refer the reader to, e.g., [18,19].

We denote by $\mathbf{C}$ the field of complex numbers and by $\mathbf{C}^{n \times m}$ the set of $n \times m$ matrices having entries in $\mathbf{C}$. Given a complex number $z \in \mathbf{C}$, its *conjugate* is denoted by $\bar{z}$, and its *modulus* is $|z| = \sqrt{z\bar{z}}$. The *adjoint* of a matrix $M \in \mathbf{C}^{n \times m}$ is the matrix $M^\dagger \in \mathbf{C}^{m \times n}$, where $M_{ij}^\dagger = \overline{M_{ji}}$. For matrices $A, B \in \mathbf{C}^{n \times m}$, their sum is the matrix $(A + B)_{ij} = A_{ij} + B_{ij}$. For matrices $C \in \mathbf{C}^{n \times m}$ and

$D \in \mathbf{C}^{m \times r}$, their product is the matrix $(CD)_{ij} = \sum_{k=1}^{m} C_{ik} D_{kj}$ in $\mathbf{C}^{n \times r}$. The *trace* of a matrix $M \in \mathbf{C}^{n \times n}$ is $\mathrm{Tr}(M) = \sum_{i=1}^{n} M_{ii}$.

An Hilbert space of dimension n is the linear space $\mathbf{C}^{1 \times n}$ equipped with sum and product by elements in $\mathbf{C}$, in which the *inner product* $(\pi, \xi) = \pi \xi^{\dagger}$ is defined. If $(\pi, \xi) = 0$ we say that π is *orthogonal* to ξ. The *norm* of vector π, is defined as $\| \pi \| = \sqrt{(\pi, \pi)}$. Two subspaces X, Y are orthogonal if each vector in X is orthogonal to any vector in Y; in this case, the linear space generated by $X \cup Y$ is denoted by $X \oplus Y$.

A matrix $M \in \mathbf{C}^{n \times n}$ can be view as the automorphism $\pi \mapsto \pi M$ of the Hilbert space $\mathbf{C}^{1 \times n}$ in itself. M is said to be *unitary* whenever $MM^{\dagger} = I = M^{\dagger}M$, where I is the identity matrix; moreover, a matrix is unitary if and only if it preserves the norm, i.e., $\| \pi M \| = \| \pi \|$ for each vector $\pi \in \mathbf{C}^{1 \times n}$. The eigenvalues of unitary matrices are complex numbers of modulus 1, i.e., they are in the form $e^{i\vartheta}$, for some real ϑ. M is said to be *Hermitian* whenever $M = M^{\dagger}$. Given an Hermitian matrix $\mathcal{O}$, let $c_1, \ldots, c_s$ be its eigenvalues and $E_1, \ldots E_s$ the corresponding eigenspaces. It is well known that each eigenvalue c_k is real, that E_i is orthogonal to E_j, for any $i \neq j$, and that $E_1 \oplus \cdots \oplus E_s = \mathbf{C}^{1 \times n}$. Each vector $\pi \in \mathbf{C}^{1 \times n}$ can be uniquely decomposed as $\pi = \pi_1 + \cdots + \pi_s$, where $\pi_j \in E_j$. The linear transformation $\pi \mapsto \pi_j$ is the *projector* P_j on the subspace E_j. It is easy to see that $\sum_{j=1}^{s} P_j = I$. An Hermitian matrix $\mathcal{O}$ is biunivocally determined by its eigenvalues and its eigenspaces (or, equivalently, by its projectors); it holds that $\mathcal{O} = c_1 P_1 + \cdots + c_s P_s$. If $c_1, \ldots, c_s \geq 0$ then $\mathcal{O}$ is called *positive semidefinite*.

2.2   Axiomatic for Quantum Mechanics in Short

Here, we use the previous formalism to describe quantum systems.

Given a set $Q = \{q_1, \ldots, q_m\}$, every q_i can be represented by its characteristic vector $e_i \in \{0, 1\}^m$ having 1 at the i-th position and 0 elsewhere. A *quantum state* on Q is a superposition $\pi = \sum_{k=1}^{m} \alpha_k e_k$, where the coefficients α_k are complex *amplitudes* and $\| \pi \| = 1$. Every e_k is called *pure state*. Given an alphabet $\Sigma = \{a_1, \ldots, a_l\}$, with every symbol a_i we associate a unitary transformation $U(a_k) : \mathbf{C}^{1 \times m} \to \mathbf{C}^{1 \times m}$. An *observable* is described by an Hermitian matrix $\mathcal{O} = c_1 P_1 + \cdots + c_s P_s$. Suppose that a quantum system is described by the quantum state π. Then, we can operate:

1. *Evolution* $U(a_j)$. The new state $\xi = \pi U(a_j)$ is reached; this dynamics is *reversible*, since $\pi = \xi U^{\dagger}(a_j)$.
2. *Measurement of* $\mathcal{O}$. Every result in $\{c_1, \ldots, c_s\}$ can be obtained; c_j is obtained with probability $\| \pi P_j \|^2$ and the state after such a measurement is $\pi P_j / \| \pi P_j \|$. The state transformation induced by a measurement is typically *irreversible*.

2.3   Von Neumann's Entropy

We briefly recall elements of quantum information theory. For more details, we refer the reader to, e.g., [14].

Consider the quantum system $\langle \{\pi_1, \ldots, \pi_m\}, p\rangle$, where $\pi_1, \ldots, \pi_m \in \mathbf{C}^{1 \times q}$ are quantum states and p a probability distribution on $\{\pi_1, \ldots, \pi_m\}$, so that p_k is the probability of π_k. Such a system is described by the so called *density matrix* $\sigma \in \mathbf{C}^{q \times q}$, where

$$\sigma = \sum_{k=1}^{m} p_k \, \pi_k^\dagger \pi_k$$

It is not difficult prove that:

- σ is Hermitian, positive semidefinite.
- Let $\lambda_1, \ldots, \lambda_q$ be the eigenvalues of σ. Then $\sum_{k=1}^{q} \lambda_i = 1$.

Since σ is positive semidefinite, we have that $\lambda_1, \ldots, \lambda_q \geq 0$. Therefore, $\lambda_1, \ldots, \lambda_q$ can be viewed as a distribution probability. *Von Neumann's entropy* $S(\sigma)$ of σ is Shannon's entropy of $\lambda_1, \ldots, \lambda_q$, i.e.:

$$S(\sigma) = -\sum_{k=1}^{q} \lambda_k \log \lambda_k.$$

We observe that, given a unitary matrix U, the density matrix of the system $\langle \{\pi_1 U, \ldots, \pi_m U\}, p\rangle$ is $U^\dagger \sigma U$. Since $U^\dagger \sigma U$ has the same eigenvalues of σ, then $S(U^\dagger \sigma U) = S(\sigma)$.

Given an observable $\mathcal{O} = 1 \cdot P_1 + 0 \cdot P_0$, where $P_0 + P_1 = I$, the probability that a measurement of $\mathcal{O}$ on σ gives 1 as result is $\sum_{k=1}^{m} p_k \parallel \pi_k P_1 \parallel^2$ or, equivalently, $\mathrm{Tr}(P_1 \sigma P_1)$.

An important tool in this theory is Holevo's Theorem [16]:

Theorem 1. *Given density matrices $\sigma_1, \ldots, \sigma_m$, consider their convex linear combination $\sigma = \sum_{k=1}^{m} p_k \sigma_k$, for $p_1, \ldots, p_m \geq 0$ and $\sum_{i=1}^{m} p_i = 1$. Given an observable $\mathcal{O} = 1 \cdot P_1 + 0 \cdot P_2$, consider the random variables X and Y, with values in $\{1, \ldots, m\}$ and $\{0, 1\}$ respectively, such that*

$$\mathrm{Prob}\{X = k, Y = b\} = p_k \, \mathrm{Prob}\{measurement \ of \ \mathcal{O} \ on \ \sigma_k \ gives \ b\}.$$

Then

$$S(\sigma) \geq \sum_{k=1}^{m} p_k S(\sigma_k) + I(X, Y).$$

Recall that the *mutual information* $I(X, Y)$ is defined as

$$I(X, Y) = H(\mathrm{Prob}\{X\}) + H(\mathrm{Prob}\{Y\}) - H(\mathrm{Prob}\{X, Y\}),$$

where H is the entropy.

To obtain lower bound on the number of states of quantum automata by using quantum information arguments, it is fundamental to observe that the entropy $S(\sigma)$ of a density matrix σ attains its maximum whenever the eigenvalues of σ are all equal [22]. This yields

Theorem 2. *If σ is a $q \times q$ density matrix, then $S(\sigma) \leq \log q$.*

2.4 1-Way Unary Quantum Automata

1-way quantum finite automata (1qfa, for short) are computational devices particularly interesting because of their simplicity. Moreover, their analysis provides a good insight into the nature of quantum computation, since 1qfa's are a theoretical model for a quantum computer with finite memory.

From the point of view of computational capabilities, quantum models of 1-way finite automata present both advantages and disadvantages with respect to their classical (deterministic or probabilistic) counterpart. Essentially, quantum superposition offers some computational advantages on probabilistic superposition. On the other hand, quantum dynamics are reversible: because of limitation of memory, it is generally impossible to simulate classical automata by quantum automata. Limitations due to reversibility can be partially attenuated by systematically introducing measurements of suitable observables as computational steps.

Several models of quantum automata have been proposed in the literature. Basically, they differ in measurement policy [5,15]. In this paper we consider only the *measure-once model in the simple unary case*. The measure-once model is the simplest 1qfa [3,7,21]. In this case, the transformation on a symbol of the input alphabet is realized by a unitary operator. A *unique* measurement is performed at the end of computation.

More formally, a *measure-once 1qfa* with q control states on the unary alphabet $\{a\}$ is a system $A = \langle \pi, U, P \rangle$, where $\pi \in \mathbf{C}^{1 \times q}$, $U \in \mathbf{C}^{q \times q}$ is a unitary matrix and $P \in \mathbf{C}^{q \times q}$ is a projector that biunivocally individuate the observable $\mathcal{O} = 1 \cdot P + 0 \cdot (I - P)$. The behavior of A is the stochastic event $p_A : a^* \to [0, 1]$ defined by

$$p_A(a^k) = \| \pi U^k P \|^2 .$$

In general, we say that a stochastic event $p : \{a\}^* \to [0, 1]$ is *n-periodic* if $p(a^k) = p(a^{k+n})$, for every $k \geq 0$.

In what follows, we will simply write 1qfa, understanding the designation "measure-once".

3 Lower Bound for Unary Periodic Languages

In this section, we prove a lower bound on the number of states of 1qfa's recognizing certain unary *periodic* languages.

Definition 1. *A language $L \subset \{a\}^*$ is n-periodic if and only if $a^k \in L$ implies $a^{k+n} \in L$, for every $k \geq 0$.*

For a given $\varepsilon \in (0, 1/2)$, a unary language $L \subset \{a\}^*$ is recognized by a 1qfa $A = \langle \pi, U, P \rangle$ with probability $1 - \varepsilon$ if and only if the following holds for any $k \geq 0$:

- $a^k \in L$ implies $p_A(a^k) \geq 1 - \varepsilon$,
- $a^k \notin L$ implies $p_A(a^k) \leq \varepsilon$.

In [20], it is proved that

Theorem 3. *Every n-periodic language can be accepted with probability $1 - \varepsilon$ greater than $1/2$ by 1qfa's with $O(\sqrt{n})$ states.*

Here, we prove an $\Omega(\sqrt{n/\log n})$ bound for certain languages.

Theorem 4. *There exist n-periodic languages that cannot be accepted by 1qfa's inducing n-periodic events with less than $\sqrt{n/(3\log n)}$ states.*

Proof. Let p be an n-periodic event induced by a unary 1qfa with q states. In [6, Lemma 3], it is proved that there exists $\Delta = \{a_1, a_2, \ldots, a_q\} \subseteq \mathbf{Z}_n$ and a matrix $C \in \mathbf{C}^{q \times q}$ such that:

$$p(a^k) = \sum_{1 \leq s,t \leq q} e^{i\frac{2\pi}{n}(a_s - a_t)k} C_{st}.$$

We can set $1/2$ as cut point. Moreover, we can choose Δ in $\binom{n}{q}$ different ways, each one yielding n hyperplanes of the form

$$\sum_{1 \leq s,t \leq q} D_{st} \cos(\frac{2\pi}{n}k(a_s - a_t)) + E_{st} \sin(\frac{2\pi}{n}k(a_s - a_t)) = \frac{1}{2},$$

for $0 \leq k < n$ and reals D_{st}, E_{st}. These n hyperplanes lay in a $2q^2$ dimensional space S and can divide S in at most n^{2q^2} different regions [8]. The event induced by coefficients D_{st} and E_{st} in the same region define the same language. This implies that the number of n-periodic languages accepted by q-state 1qfa's is bounded above by $\binom{n}{q}n^{2q^2} < n^{3q^2}$.

By noticing that the number of distinct n-periodic languages is 2^n, we must require that $n^{3q^2} \geq 2^n$, in order to accept every n-periodic languages by using q-state 1qfa's. Such an inequality is easily seen to yield $q \geq \sqrt{n/(3\log n)}$.

4   Lower Bound for Finite Unary Languages

In this section, we state a lower bound on the number of states of 1qfa's which "recognize" *finite* unary languages. Since 1qfa's cannot accept finite languages [4] (except, of course, the empty set), we need to introduce a different notion of acceptance:

Definition 2. *Given a unary language $L \subset \{a\}^*$, a 1qfa $A = (\pi, U, P)$ accepts $L^{<n} = \{a^k \in L \mid k < n\}$ with probability $1 - \varepsilon$, for a given $\varepsilon \in (0, 1/2)$, if and only if the following holds for any $k < n$:*

- *$a^k \in L^{<n}$ implies $p_A(a^k) \geq 1 - \varepsilon$,*
- *$a^k \notin L^{<n}$ implies $p_A(a^k) \leq \varepsilon$.*

We are now going to prove a lower bound on the number of states of a 1qfa accepting $L^{<n}$ with probability $1 - \varepsilon$. First, we introduce some notations. For any $0 \leq s < j < n$, we let $\#_L(s,j) = |\{a^k \in L \mid s \leq k < j\}|$. Moreover, for every $1 \leq t < n/2$, we write

$$\gamma_L(t,n) = \max_{t \leq k \leq n-t} \left\{ \frac{|\#_L(k-t,k) - \#_L(k,k+t)|}{t} \right\},$$

and

$$\tau_L(t,n,\varepsilon) = \begin{cases} 0 & \text{if } \gamma_L(t,n) < \varepsilon/(1-\varepsilon) \\ (1-\varepsilon)\,\gamma_L(t,n) - \varepsilon & \text{otherwise.} \end{cases}$$

Example 1. Consider the language $E^{<n} = \{a^{2k} \mid k < n/2\}$. In this case, we get

$$\tau_{E^{<n}}(t,n,\varepsilon) = \begin{cases} 0 & \text{for even } t \\ (1-\varepsilon)/(t-\varepsilon) & \text{for odd } t. \end{cases}$$

Example 2. Consider the language $F^{<n} = \{a^k \mid n/2 \leq k < n\}$. In this case, for any $t \geq 1$, we get

$$\tau_{F^{<n}}(t,n,\varepsilon) = 1 - 2\varepsilon.$$

We are ready to state our main result which will be proved in Section 5 by using quantum information theory arguments.

Theorem 5. *If $L^{<n}$ is accepted by a q-state 1qfa, then*

$$\log q \geq \sum_{k=0}^{\log n - 1} \left(1 - H\left(\frac{1}{2} + \frac{1}{2}\tau_L(2^k, n, \varepsilon) \right) \right).$$

Example 3. By Theorem 5, we get that a q-state 1qfa accepting the language $E^{<n} = \{a^{2k} \mid k < n/2\}$ at Example 1 must satisfy the trivial lower bound $\log q \geq (1 - 2\varepsilon)^2$ yielding $q \geq 2$. Actually, $E^{<n}$ can be recognized with probability 1 by the following 2-state automaton

$$A = \left((1,0), \begin{pmatrix} 0 & 1 \\ 1 & 0 \end{pmatrix}, \begin{pmatrix} 1 & 0 \\ 0 & 0 \end{pmatrix} \right).$$

Example 4. By Theorem 5, any q-state 1qfa accepting with probability $1 - \varepsilon$ the language $F^{<n} = \{a^k \mid n/2 \leq k < n\}$ at Example 2 must satisfy $\log q \geq (1 - H(1 - \varepsilon)) \log n$, i.e., $q \geq n^{1 - H(1-\varepsilon)}$.

5   The Proof of the Main Result

Let us consider two density matrices σ_a and σ_b, and an observable $\mathcal{O} = 1 \cdot P + 0 \cdot (I - P)$ such that

- Prob{measurement of $\mathcal{O}$ on σ_a gives 1} $\geq p$,
- Prob{measurement of $\mathcal{O}$ on σ_b gives 1} $\leq q$,

The following lemma is an extension of Lemma 3.2 in [22]:

Lemma 1. *If $p > q$, then*

$$S\left(\frac{1}{2}\sigma_a + \frac{1}{2}\sigma_b\right) \geq \frac{1}{2}S(\sigma_a) + \frac{1}{2}S(\sigma_b) + 1 - H\left(\frac{1}{2} + \frac{1}{2}(p - q)\right).$$

Proof. (Outline.) By Holevo's Theorem (see Section 2.3), we have

$$S\left(\frac{1}{2}\sigma_a + \frac{1}{2}\sigma_b\right) \geq \frac{1}{2}S(\sigma_a) + \frac{1}{2}S(\sigma_b) + I(X, Y),$$

where X and Y are random variables with values in $\{a, b\}$ and $\{0, 1\}$, respectively, such that

$$\text{Prob}\{X = a, Y = 1\} \geq \tfrac{1}{2}p \qquad \text{Prob}\{X = a, Y = 0\} \leq \tfrac{1}{2}(1 - p)$$

$$\text{Prob}\{X = b, Y = 1\} \leq \tfrac{1}{2}q \qquad \text{Prob}\{X = b, Y = 0\} \geq \tfrac{1}{2}(1 - q).$$

Easy calculations shows that

$$I(X, Y) = H(\text{Prob}\{X\}) + H(\text{Prob}\{Y\}) - H(\text{Prob}\{X, Y\})$$
$$\geq H\left(\frac{1}{2}p + \frac{1}{2}q\right) - \frac{1}{2}H(p) - \frac{1}{2}H(q) \geq 1 - H\left(\frac{1}{2} + \frac{1}{2}(p - q)\right).$$

$\square$

Consider now a 1qfa $A = (\pi, U, P)$ and the observable $\mathcal{O} = 1 \cdot P + 0 \cdot (I - P)$. Let $\pi_k = \pi U^k$ be the superposition reached by A after reading a^k, and let $\sigma_k = \pi_k^\dagger \pi_k$ be the corresponding density matrix. For $s < j$, define $\sigma_{s,j} = \frac{1}{j-s}\sum_{k=s}^{j-1}\sigma_k$, and let $p_{s,j}$ be the probability that measuring $\mathcal{O}$ on $\sigma_{s,j}$ yields 1. It is easy to verify that

$$p_{s,j} = \frac{1}{j - s}\sum_{k=s}^{j-1} p_A(a^k).$$

We can show that the entropy of $\sigma_{s,j}$ is invariant under translation.

Theorem 6. *For any k, $S(\sigma_{s,j}) = S(\sigma_{s+k,j+k})$.*

Proof. By definition, we have $S(\sigma_{s+k,j+k}) = (U^\dagger)^k \sigma_{s,j} U^k$. Since U is unitary, the claimed result follows. $\square$

The following lemma is crucial in the proof of our main result:

Lemma 2. *For every $1 \leq t \leq s$,*

$$S(\sigma_{0,2t}) = S(\sigma_{s-t,s+t}) \geq S(\sigma_{0,t}) + 1 - H\left(\frac{1}{2} + \frac{1}{2}(p_{s-t,s} - p_{s,s+t})\right).$$

Proof. In fact:

$$\mathcal{S}(\sigma_{0,2t}) = \mathcal{S}(\sigma_{s-t,s+t}) \quad \text{(by Theorem 6)}$$

$$\geq \frac{1}{2}\mathcal{S}(\sigma_{s-t,s}) + \frac{1}{2}\mathcal{S}(\sigma_{s,s+t}) + 1 - H\left(\frac{1}{2} + \frac{1}{2}(p_{s-t,s} - p_{s,s+t})\right)$$

(by Lemma 1)

$$= \mathcal{S}(\sigma_{0,t}) + 1 - H\left(\frac{1}{2} + \frac{1}{2}(p_{s-t,s} - p_{s,s+t})\right) \quad \text{(by Theorem 6)}.$$

□

Suppose now that the 1qfa $A = (\pi, U, P)$ accepts $L^{<n}$ with probability $1-\varepsilon$. Recall that, for $0 \leq s < j < n$, we write $\#_L(s,j) = |\{a^k \in L \mid s \leq k < j\}|$. The following lemma relates the probability $p_{s,j}$ to the number $\#_L(s,j)$.

Lemma 3. *For $0 \leq s < j < n$,*

$$(1-\varepsilon)\frac{\#_L(s,j)}{j-s} \leq p_{s,j} \leq (1-\varepsilon)\frac{\#_L(s,j)}{j-s} + \varepsilon.$$

Proof. By recalling that $p_{s,j} = \frac{1}{j-s}\sum_{k=s}^{j-1} p_A(a^k)$, and by observing that $a^k \in L$ implies $p_A(a^k) \geq 1 - \varepsilon$ and $a^k \notin L$ implies $p_A(a^k) \leq \varepsilon$, we get the result.   □

We are now ready to prove our main result.

Theorem 7. *If $L^{<n}$ is accepted by a q-state 1qfa, then*

$$\log q \geq \sum_{k=0}^{\log n - 1}\left(1 - H\left(\frac{1}{2} + \frac{1}{2}\tau_L(2^k, n, \varepsilon)\right)\right).$$

Proof. (Outline.) Recall, from the previous section, the notation

$$\gamma_L(t,n) = \max_{t \leq k \leq n-t}\left\{\frac{|\#_L(k-t,k) - \#_L(k,k+t)|}{t}\right\},$$

for $1 \leq t < n/2$. Our proof consider two distinct cases, for every $0 \leq j < \log n$:

- $\gamma_L(2^j, n) \leq \varepsilon/(1-\varepsilon)$: In this case, we have $\tau_L(2^j, n, \varepsilon) = 0$. Thus, we can write

$$\mathcal{S}(\sigma_{0,2^{j+1}}) \geq \mathcal{S}(\sigma_{0,2^j}) \quad \text{(by Lemma 2)}$$

$$= \mathcal{S}(\sigma_{0,2^j}) + 1 - H\left(\frac{1}{2} + \frac{1}{2}\tau_L(2^j, n, \varepsilon)\right) \quad \text{(since } \tau_L(2^j, n, \varepsilon) = 0\text{)}.$$

- $\gamma_L(2^j, n) > \varepsilon/(1-\varepsilon)$: Let

$$k' = \operatorname*{argmax}_{2^j \leq k \leq n-2^j}\left\{\frac{|\#_L(k-2^j, k) - \#_L(k, k+2^j)|}{2^j}\right\}.$$

Without loss of generality, we can assume (the opposite case follows by the same reasoning) that

$$(1 - \varepsilon) \frac{\#_L(k' - 2^j, k') - \#_L(k', k' + 2^j)}{2^j} > \varepsilon.$$

By Lemma 3, we get

$$(1 - \varepsilon) \frac{\#_L(k' - 2^j, k')}{2^j} \leq p_{k' - 2^j, k'} \quad \text{and} \quad p_{k', k' + 2^j} \leq (1 - \varepsilon) \frac{\#_L(k', k' + 2^j)}{2^j} + \varepsilon.$$

As a consequence, we get

$$p_{k' - 2^j, k'} - p_{k', k' + 2^j} \geq (1 - \varepsilon) \frac{\#_L(k' - 2^j, k') - \#_L(k', k' + 2^j)}{2^j} - \varepsilon$$

$$= \tau_L(2^j, n, \varepsilon). \tag{1}$$

By Lemma 2 and inequality (1), we obtain

$$S(\sigma_{0,2^{k+1}}) \geq S(\sigma_{0,2^k}) + 1 - H \left(\frac{1}{2} + \frac{1}{2} \left(p_{k' - 2^j, k'} - p_{k', k' + 2^j} \right) \right)$$

$$\geq S(\sigma_{0,2^k}) + 1 - H \left(\frac{1}{2} + \frac{1}{2} \tau_L(2^j, n, \varepsilon) \right).$$

Hence, for any $0 \leq k \leq \log n - 1$, we have

$$S(\sigma_{0,2^{k+1}}) \geq S(\sigma_{0,2^k}) + 1 - H \left(\frac{1}{2} + \frac{1}{2} \tau_L(2^j, n, \varepsilon) \right).$$

By solving this system of inequalities and by Theorem 2, we conclude that

$$\log q \geq S(\sigma_{0,n}) \geq \sum_{j=0}^{\log n - 1} \left(1 - H \left(\frac{1}{2} + \frac{1}{2} \tau_L(2^j, n, \varepsilon) \right) \right).$$

$\square$

References

1. A. Ambainis and R. Freivalds. 1-way quantum finite automata: strengths, weaknesses and generalizations. In *Proc. 39th Symposium on Foundations of Computer Science*, pp. 332–342, 1998.
2. P. Benioff. Quantum mechanical Hamiltonian models of Turing machines. *J. Stat. Phys.*, 29:515–546, 1982.
3. A. Bertoni and M. Carpentieri. Regular languages accepted by quantum automata. *Information and Computation*, 165:174–182, 2001.
4. A. Bertoni and M. Carpentieri. Analogies and differences between quantum and stochastic automata. *Theoretical Computer Science*, 262.69–81, 2001.
5. A. Bertoni, C. Mereghetti and B. Palano. Quantum computing: 1-way quantum automata. In *Proc. 7th Conf. Develop. Lang. Th.*, LNCS, Springer, 2003. To be published.

6. A. Bertoni, C. Mereghetti and B. Palano. Golomb rulers and difference sets for succinct quantum automata. *Int. J. Found. Comp. Sci.*, 2003. To be published.
7. A. Brodsky and N. Pippenger. Characterizations of 1-way quantum finite automata. Technical Report TR-99-03, Department of Computer Science, University of British Columbia, 2000.
8. A. Bertoni and M. Torelli. *Elementi di matematica combinatoria.* ISEDI, 1977. In Italian.
9. E. Bernstein and U. Vazirani. Quantum complexity theory. *SIAM J. Comput.*, 26:1411–1473, 1997. A preliminary version appeared in *Proc. 25th ACM Symp. on Theory of Computation*, pp. 11–20, 1993.
10. D. Deutsch. Quantum theory, the Church-Turing principle and the universal quantum computer. *Proc. Roy. Soc. London Ser. A*, 400:97–117, 1985.
11. R. Feynman. Simulating physics with computers. *Int. J. Theoretical Physics*, 21:467–488, 1982.
12. M. Golovkins and M. Kravtsev. Probabilistic Reversible Automata and Quantum Automata. In *Proc. 8th International Computing and Combinatorics Conference*, LNCS 2387, Springer, pp. 574-583, 2002
13. L. Grover. A fast quantum mechanical algorithm for database search. In *Proc. 28th ACM Symposium on Theory of Computing*, pp. 212–219, 1996.
14. J. Gruska. *Quantum Computing.* McGraw-Hill, 1999.
15. J. Gruska. Descriptional complexity issues in quantum computing. *J. Automata, Languages and Combinatorics*, 5:191–218, 2000.
16. A.S. Holevo. Some estimates of the information transmitted by quantum communication channels. *Problemy Peredachi Informatsii*, 9:3–11, 1973. English translation in *Problems of Information Transmission*, 9:177–183, 1973.
17. A. Kondacs and J. Watrous. On the power of quantum finite state automata. In *38th Symposium on Foundations of Computer Science*, pp. 66–75, 1997.
18. M. Marcus and H. Minc. *Introduction to Linear Algebra.* The Macmillan Company, 1965. Reprinted by Dover, 1988.
19. M. Marcus and H. Minc. *A Survey of Matrix Theory and Matrix Inequalities.* Prindle, Weber & Schmidt, 1964. Reprinted by Dover, 1992.
20. C. Mereghetti and B. Palano. On the size of one-way quantum finite automata with periodic behaviors. *Theoretical Informatics and Applications*, 36:277-291, 2002.
21. C. Moore and J. Crutchfield. Quantum automata and quantum grammars. *Theoretical Computer Science*, 237:275–306, 2000. A preliminary version of this work appears as Technical Report in 1997.
22. A. Nayak. Optimal lower bounds for quantum automata and random access codes. In *Proc. 40th Symposium on Foundations of Computer Science*. pp. 369–376, 1999.
23. P. Shor. Polynomial-time algorithms for prime factorization and discrete logarithms on a quantum computer. *SIAM Journal on Computing*, 26:1484–1509, 1997. A preliminary version appeared in *Proc. 35th IEEE Symp. on Foundations of Computer Science*, pp. 20–22, 1994.

Refined Effects for Unanticipated Object Re-classification: $\mathcal{F}ickle_3$[*]

(Extended Abstract)

Ferruccio Damiani[1], Sophia Drossopoulou[2], and Paola Giannini[3]

[1] Dipartimento di Informatica, Università di Torino
[2] Department of Computing, Imperial College
[3] Dipartimento di Informatica
Università del Piemonte Orientale

Abstract. In previous work on the language $\mathcal{F}ickle$ and its extension $\mathcal{F}ickle_{II}$ Dezani and us introduced language features for object re-classification for imperative, typed, class-based, object-oriented languages. In this paper we present the language $\mathcal{F}ickle_3$, which on one side refines $\mathcal{F}ickle_{II}$ with more expressive effect annotations, and on the other eliminates the need to declare explicitly which are the classes of the objects that may be re-classified. Therefore, $\mathcal{F}ickle_3$ allows to correctly type meaningful programs which $\mathcal{F}ickle_{II}$ rejects. Moreover, re-classification may be decided by the client of a class, allowing *unanticipated object re-classification*. As for $\mathcal{F}ickle_{II}$, also the type and effect system for $\mathcal{F}ickle_3$ guarantees that, even though objects may be re-classified across classes with different members, they will never attempt to access non existing members.

The type and effect system of $\mathcal{F}ickle_3$ has some significant differences from the one of $\mathcal{F}ickle_{II}$. In particular, besides the fact that intra-class type checking has to track the more refined effects, when a class is combined with other classes some additional inter-class checking is introduced.

1 Introduction

Re-classifiable objects support the changing of an object's behaviour by changing its class membership at runtime, see e.g. [2,10,8,11]. In previous work on the language $\mathcal{F}ickle$ [5] and its extension $\mathcal{F}ickle_{II}$ [6] Dezani and us introduced language features which allow objects to change class membership dynamically and showed how to combine these features with a strong type system. We based our approach on an imperative, class-based language, where classes are types and subclasses are subtypes, and where methods are defined inside classes and selected depending on the class of the object on which the method is invoked.

[*] Work partially supported by IST-2001-33477 DART, MIUR Cofin '01 NAPOLI, and MIUR Cofin'02 McTati projects. The founding bodies are not responsible for any use that might be made of the results presented here.

C. Blundo and C. Laneve (Eds.): ICTCS 2003, LNCS 2841, pp. 97–110, 2003.
© Springer-Verlag Berlin Heidelberg 2003

In this paper we present the language $\mathcal{F}ickle_3$, which on one side refines $\mathcal{F}ickle_{II}$ with more expressive effect annotations, and on the other eliminates the need to declare explicitly which are the classes of the objects that may be re-classified. We focus on the differences of the new proposal over $\mathcal{F}ickle_{II}$. For comparison with other proposals in the literature we refer to [6].

$\mathcal{F}ickle_3$ is a Java-like language with a *re-classification* operation that changes the class membership of an object while preserving its identity. The basic problem in the design of the language is to have a sound type system, that is, a type system that, even in the presence of object re-classification, insures that no attempt is made at accessing non existing members. This is obtained by changing the type of this and of local identifiers that might point at a re-classified object in a method body. An object o of class c could also be pointed at by a field f of type d (of some other object o'), where d is a superclass of c. Therefore, to achieve type soundness, we must forbid re-classification from (a subclass of) d to a class which is not a subclass of d (otherwise subsequent accesses to members of o'.f existing in class d could fail). Classes for which this does not happen are said to be "respected" by re-classification and can be safely used as types for fields.

- In $\mathcal{F}ickle_{II}$, this was guaranteed by explicitly marking classes which had to be respected by re-classification with the keywords **state** and **root**. *State* classes are the possible sources and targets of re-classifications, and *root* classes are the superclasses of state classes and declare all the members common to them.
- In $\mathcal{F}ickle_3$ the set of classes that are respected by re-classification is inferred by tracing all possible re-classifications in the program.

Re-classifications are traced by *effects*, see [9,12], and methods are annotated with the effects that may be caused by the execution of their body.

- In $\mathcal{F}ickle_{II}$ effects are just sets of root classes, $\{c_1, ..., c_n\}$, meaning that the method may perform any re-classification between two subclasses of a class in the set.
- In $\mathcal{F}ickle_3$ effects are sets of pairs, $\{c_1 \Downarrow c_1', ..., c_n \Downarrow c_n'\}$, meaning that the method may perform any re-classification from a subclass of c_i to a subclass c_i'.

$\mathcal{F}ickle_{II}$-style effect annotations can be coded into $\mathcal{F}ickle_3$-style effect annotations, but not vice versa, and $\mathcal{F}ickle_3$ allows to correctly type meaningful programs which $\mathcal{F}ickle_{II}$ rejects. Moreover, by eliminating the explicit marking of classes that must be respected by re-classification, we obtain a language that is syntactically simpler, and allows *unanticipated dynamic object replacement* (see e.g. [3]). However, this has a drawback: when linking a class c with an existing set of classes we have to check on one side that the effects of the methods of c respect the classes used as types of fields of the preexisting classes, and on the other that the effects of the methods of the preexisting classes respect the classes used as types of fields of c.

The operational semantics (which ignores effect annotations and types) of $\mathcal{F}ickle_3$ is essentially unchanged w.r.t. $\mathcal{F}ickle_{II}$[1], whereas in the type and effect system there are some significant differences. In particular, as previously mentioned, along with the intra-class checking we also need some inter-class checking.

This paper is organized as follows: In Section 2 we introduce $\mathcal{F}ickle_3$ informally using an example. In Section 3 we give syntax and operational semantics. In Section 4 we present the typing rules and state type soundness. Some technical definitions are listed in the appendix.

2   The Example of the **Frog** and of the **Prince**

In Figure 1 we give, by using a syntax similar to Java's, an example inspired by adventure games. The example is essentially the same example illustrated in Section 2 of [6]. Besides the differences in the syntax of the language, the only difference is that, in class Princess, we have replaced the method walk2 with the method walk3.

We define a class Player with subclasses Frog and Prince. When woken up, a frog inflates its pouch, while a prince swings his sword. When kissed, a frog turns into a prince; when cursed, a prince turns into a frog.

Annotations like { }, { Frog⇓Prince} , and { Prince⇓Frog} before method bodies are called *effects*; expressions like Prince⇓Frog and Frog⇓Prince are called *atomic effects*. Effects list potential re-classifications that may be caused by the invocation of that method (each atomic effect represents a potential re-classification). Methods with the empty effect { }, *e.g.* wake, may not cause any re-classification. Methods with non-empty effects, *e.g.* kissed with effect { Frog⇓Prince} , may re-classify objects from a subclass of the left-hand side of one of their atomic effects to a subclass of the right-hand side of that atomic effect; in our case from Frog to Prince. Such re-classifications may be caused by *re-classification expressions* (*e.g.* this⇓Prince in method kissed of class Frog, or mate2⇓Prince in method walk3 of class Princess), or by further method calls (*e.g.* mate.kissed () in method walk1 of class Princess).

The classes c such that an object belonging to some subclass of c may be re-classified to a class that is not a subclass of c *cannot* be used as type for fields; in our example Frog and Prince.

The method body of kissed in class Frog contains the re-classification expression this⇓Prince. At the beginning of the method the receiver is an object of class Frog, therefore it contains the fields brave and pouch, but not the field sword. After execution of this⇓Prince the receiver is of class Prince, and therefore sword can be selected, while pouch can not, and brave retains its value. This mechanism supports the transmission of some information from the object before the re-classification to the object after the re-classification.

---

[1] The only difference is that, in $\mathcal{F}ickle_3$, object re-classification preserves the fields of the least common superclass of the source and target of re-classification while, in $\mathcal{F}ickle_{II}$, the field preserved are those of the root class.

```
abstract class Player extends Object{
    bool brave;
    abstract bool wake() { } ;
    abstract Weapon kissed() { Frog⇓Prince } ;
}
class Frog extends Player{
    Vocal pouch;
    bool wake() { } {pouch.blow() ; brave}
    Weapon kissed() { Frog⇓Prince } {this⇓Prince; sword:= new Weapon}
}
class Prince extends Player{
    Weapon sword;
    bool wake() { } {sword.swing(); brave}
    Weapon kissed() { } {sword}
    Frog cursed() { Prince⇓Frog } {this⇓Frog; pouch:= new Vocal; this}
}
class Princess extends Object{
    bool walk1(Frog mate) { Frog⇓Prince } {mate.wake();
 mate.kissed();  mate.wake()}
    Weapon walk3(Prince mate1, Frog mate2) { Frog⇓Prince }
        {mate2⇓Prince;  mate2.sword:= mate1.sword}
}
```

Fig. 1. Program P_{pl}- players with re-classifications in $\mathcal{F}ickle_3$.

Consider the instructions in the method body of walk1 in class Princess:

$$
\begin{array}{lll}
1. & \text{mate.wake();} & \text{// inflates pouch} \\
2. & \text{mate.kissed();} & \\
3. & \text{mate.wake()} & \text{// swings sword}
\end{array}
\tag{1}
$$

Suppose that the parameter mate is bound to a Frog object with field brave containing true. After line 2., the object is re-classified to Prince with the same value for brave. Therefore, the call of wake in line 1. selects the method from Frog, and inflates the pouch, while the call of wake in line 3. selects the method from Prince, and swings the sword.

Re-classification from class c_1 to class c_2 removes from the object all fields that are not defined in the least common superclass of c_1 and c_2, and adds the remaining fields of the target class. *E.g.* after line 2. in example (1) the object denoted by mate has a sword but not a pouch.

Consider now the instructions in the method body of walk3 in class Princess:

$$
\begin{array}{ll}
1. & \text{mate2⇓Prince;} \\
2. & \text{mate2.sword:= mate1.sword}
\end{array}
\tag{2}
$$

Let the parameters mate1 and mate2 be bound to a Prince and to a Frog object, respectively. After line 1., the object pointed at by mate2 is re-classified to Prince and, in the left-hand side of line 2., field sword can be selected. Moreover, the object pointed at by mate1 is unchanged and, in the right-hand side of line 2, field sword can be selected. So the execution of this method is safe.

As a matter of fact in $\mathcal{F}ickle_{II}$ [6] walk3 does not type-check because the effect inferred for the re-classification mate2⇓Prince, in line 1, is {Player }, meaning that the type of all the local identifiers having as type a subclass of Player is changed to Player (except for mate2, whose type is changed to Prince). So in line 2 the variable mate1 is of class Player and mate1.sword gives type error. Note that mate2.sword type-checks both in $\mathcal{F}ickle_{II}$ and $\mathcal{F}ickle_3$.

3   Syntax and Operational Semantics

The syntax of $\mathcal{F}ickle_3$ is given in Fig. 2^2. We use standard extended BNF, where a [-] pair means optional, and A^* means zero or more repetitions of A. We follow the convention that non terminals appear as *nonTerm*, keywords appear as **keyword**, literals appear as `literal` and identifiers appear as identifier. We omit separators like "; " or "," where they are obvious. Expressions are usually called e, e', e_1 *etc.*, and values are usually called v, v', v_1 *etc.*. By id, id',*etc.*we will denote either this or a parameter name (x, x',*etc.*). A program is a sequence of class definitions. Method declarations have the shape:

$$t\ m\ (t_1\ x_1, ..., t_q\ x_q)\ \{\ c_1{\Downarrow}c_1', ..., c_n{\Downarrow}c_n'\ \}\ \{\ e\ \}$$

where t is the result type, $t_1, ..., t_q$ are the types of the formal parameters $x_1, ..., x_q$, and e is the body[3]. The effect consists of atomic effects $c_1{\Downarrow}c_1', ..., c_n{\Downarrow}c_n'$, with $n \geq 0$. Each atomic effect $c_i{\Downarrow}c_i'$ means that any object of a subclass of c_i may be re-classified to any subclass of c_i'.

The operational semantics of $\mathcal{F}ickle_3$ (which ignores effects annotations) differs from that of $\mathcal{F}ickle_{II}$ [6] only in the evaluation of re-classification expressions, id⇓c. Here we briefly present the signature of the rewriting relation, $\leadsto$, and the semantics of re-classification expressions, id⇓d. A detailed description of the other rules of the operational semantics is given in Section 4 of [6]. The signature of the rewriting relation $\leadsto$ is:

$$\leadsto\ :\ progr \longrightarrow e \times store \longrightarrow (val \cup dev) \times store$$

The operational semantics rewrites pairs of expressions and stores into pairs of values, exceptions, or errors, and stores in the context of a program P. The store maps this to an address, parameters to values, and addresses to objects. Values are addresses, or the source language values as in Section 3. Addresses may point to objects, but *not* to other addresses, primitive values, or null. Thus, in $\mathcal{F}ickle_3$,

---

[2] The syntax of $\mathcal{F}ickle_3$ differs from the syntax of $\mathcal{F}ickle_{II}$ [6] only in the keywords **root** and **state** (that are not present in $\mathcal{F}ickle_3$) and in the effect annotations occurring in methods' signatures. Section 2 follows a slightly more liberal syntax, with abstract classes, abstract methods, and the implicit use of this to access fields and methods from the current class.

[3] Extending $\mathcal{F}ickle_3$ to allow methods to have local variables would be straightforward. The typing rules for local variables would be the same as for parameters.

$$
\begin{array}{lll}
progr & ::= & class^* \\
class & ::= & \textbf{class } c \textbf{ extends } c \ \{ \ field^* \ meth^* \ \} \\
field & ::= & type \ f \\
meth & ::= & type \ m \ (par^*) \ eff \ \{ \ e \ \} \\
type & ::= & \textbf{bool} \mid c \\
par & ::= & type \ x \\
a & ::= & c{\Downarrow}c \\
eff & ::= & \{ \ a^* \ \} \\
e & ::= & \textbf{if } e \textbf{ then } e \textbf{ else } e \mid var := e \mid e \ ; \ e \mid sVal \mid \\
& & \textbf{this} \mid var \mid \textbf{new } c \mid e.m(e^*) \mid id{\Downarrow}c \\
var & ::= & x \mid e.f \\
sVal & ::= & \textbf{true} \mid \textbf{false} \mid \textbf{null} \\
id & ::= & \textbf{this} \mid x \\
\end{array}
$$

with the following conventions

$$
\begin{array}{llll}
c & ::= \textsf{c} \mid \textsf{c}' \mid \textsf{c}_i \mid \textsf{d} \mid \ ... & \text{for class names} \\
f & ::= \textsf{f} \mid \textsf{f}' \mid \textsf{f}_i \mid \ ... & \text{for field names} \\
m & ::= \textsf{m} \mid \textsf{m}' \mid \textsf{m}_i \mid \ ... & \text{for method names} \\
x & ::= \textsf{x} \mid \textsf{x}' \mid \textsf{x}_i \mid \ ... & \text{for parameter names}
\end{array}
$$

Fig. 2. Syntax of $\mathcal{F}ickle_3$.

as in Java, pointers are implicit, and there are no pointers to pointers. As we will show, execution of well-typed expressions never produces an error, although it may throw a null pointer exception. Stores are denoted with σ, addresses with ι, exceptions and errors with dv.

$$
\begin{array}{lll}
store & = & (\{\textbf{this}\} \longrightarrow addr) \ \cup \ (x \longrightarrow val) \ \cup \ (addr \longrightarrow object) \\
val & = & sVal \cup addr \\
dev & = & \{\textbf{nullPntrExc}, \textbf{Err}\} \\
object & = & \{ \ [\![f_1 : v_1, ..., f_r : v_r]\!]^c \ \mid \ f_1, ..., f_r \ \text{are fields names}, \\
& & \qquad\qquad v_1, ..., v_r \in val, \ \text{and} \ \textsf{c} \ \text{is a class name} \ \}
\end{array}
$$

To evaluate a re-classification expressions, $id{\Downarrow}\textsf{d}$, we find the address of id, which points to an object of class c. We replace the original object by a new object of class d. We preserve the fields belonging to least common superclass of c and d, and initialize the other fields of d according to their types. For example, for store σ_1, with $\sigma_1(\textsf{x}_1) = \iota$, and $\sigma_1(\iota) = [\![\textsf{brave} : \textbf{true}, \textsf{sword} : \iota']\!]^{\textsf{Prince}}$, $\sigma_1(\iota') = [\![...]\!]^{\textsf{Weapon}}$, we have $\textsf{x}_1{\Downarrow}\textsf{Frog}, \sigma_1 \leadsto_{\text{pl}}^? \iota, \sigma_2$ where $\sigma_2 = \sigma_1[\iota \mapsto [\![\textsf{brave} : \textbf{true}, \textsf{pouch} : \textbf{null}]\!]^{\textsf{Frog}}]$. *I.e.* we obtain an object of class Frog with unmodified field brave.

4   Typing

The following assertions, defined in Fig. 3 (where $\mathcal{C}(\textsf{P},\textsf{c})$, formally defined in Appendix A, returns the definition of class c in program P), describe classes, types, the subclassing relationship, and the widening relationship between types:

$$\frac{\text{The definitions in P are unique}}{\vdash P \diamond_u} \qquad \frac{\vdash P \diamond_u \text{ and the class hierarchy of P is acyclic}}{\vdash P \diamond_h}$$

$$\frac{\vdash P \diamond_u}{\text{Object} \sqsubseteq_P \text{Object}} \qquad \frac{\vdash P \diamond_u \quad P = \dots \text{ class } c \text{ extends } c' \{ \dots \} \dots}{c \sqsubseteq_P c \qquad c \sqsubseteq_P c'} \qquad \frac{c \sqsubseteq_P c' \quad c' \sqsubseteq_P c''}{c \sqsubseteq_P c''}$$

$$\frac{\vdash P \diamond_h \quad \mathcal{C}(P, c) = \text{ class } c \dots}{P \vdash c \diamond_{ct}} \qquad \frac{P \vdash c \diamond_{ct}}{P \vdash c \diamond_t} \qquad P \vdash \text{bool } \diamond_t \qquad \text{bool} \leq_P \text{bool} \qquad \frac{c \sqsubseteq_P c'}{c \leq_P c'}$$

$$t_1 \sqcup_P t_2 = \begin{cases} t & \text{if } t_1 \leq_P t \quad t_2 \leq_P t \quad \forall t'.(t_1 \leq_P t' \text{ and } t_2 \leq_P t') \Rightarrow t \leq_P t' \\ \mathcal{U}df & \text{otherwise} \end{cases}$$

Fig. 3. Programs with unique definitions, well-formed inheritance hierarchy, subclasses, types, widening, and lub on types.

$$\frac{\Gamma = \{x_1 : t_1, \dots, x_n : t_n, \text{this} : c\}}{\Gamma(id) = \begin{cases} t_i & \text{if } id = x_i \\ c & \text{if } id = \text{this} \\ \mathcal{U}df & \text{otherwise} \end{cases}} \qquad \Gamma[id \mapsto t](id') = \begin{cases} t & \text{if } id' = id \\ \Gamma(id') & \text{otherwise} \end{cases}$$

Fig. 4. Environment lookup and update.

$P \vdash c \diamond_{ct}$ means "c is a class in P",
$P \vdash t \diamond_t$ means "t is a type in P" (*i.e.* either a class or **bool**),
$c \sqsubseteq_P c'$ means "class c is a subclass of c' in P", and
$t \leq_P t'$ means "type t' widens type t in P" (*i.e.* t subclass of, or identical to, t').

Environments, Γ, map parameter names to types, and the receiver this to a class. They have the form $\{x_1 : t_1, \dots x_n : t_n, \text{this} : c\}$. Lookup, $\Gamma(id)$, and update, $\Gamma[id \mapsto t]$, are defined in Fig. 4.

An atomic effect is a pair of classes, $c \Downarrow c'$, meaning that any object of a subclass of c may be re-classified to any subclass of c'. An effect, ϕ, is a set $\{c_1 \Downarrow c'_1, \dots, c_n \Downarrow c'_n\}$ of atomic effects; it means that any object of a subclass of c_i may be re-classified to any subclass of c'_i. The empty effect, $\{\ \}$, guarantees that no object is re-classified. We say that the effect $\{c_1 \Downarrow c'_1, \dots, c_n \Downarrow c'_n\}$ is well formed in P, and write $P \vdash \{c_1 \Downarrow c'_1, \dots, c_n \Downarrow c'_n\} \diamond$, to mean that

1. $c_1, \dots, c_n$ are not subclasses of each other in P, and
2. for all $i, j \in \{1, \dots, n\}$, if (c'_i is a subclass of c_j) or (c_j is subclass of c'_i), then c'_j is a subclass of c'_i.

These two requirements simplify the definition of the operation of application of an effect to a type (that will be defined in Section 4.1). The first requirement assures that, for any class c, there is at most one atomic effect saying that objects belonging to class c might be re-classified. The second requirement assures that there is no atomic effect saying that objects belonging to a subclass of the target class c' of another atomic effect might be re-classified to a class that is not a subclass of c'. For instance, { Prince⇓Frog, Frog⇓Prince} is not a well-formed effect, since it does not satisfy the second requirement. The effect { Prince⇓Player, Frog⇓Player} is, instead, well-formed.

4.1   Typing Rules for Expessions

Typing an expression e in the context of program P and environment Γ involves three components, namely

$$P, \Gamma \vdash e : t \parallel \Gamma' \parallel \phi$$

where t conservatively estimates the type of e after its evaluation, the environment Γ' contains conservative estimations of the types of this and of the parameters after evaluation of e, and ϕ conservatively estimates the re-classification effect of the evaluation of e on objects[4].

The typing rules for expressions are given in Fig. 5[5]. We use the lookup functions $\mathcal{F}(P, c, f)$ and $\mathcal{M}(P, c, m)$ which return, respectively, the definition of the field f and of the method m in the class c, going through through the class hierarchy, if necessary (see Appendix A). We follow the convention that rules can be applied only if the types in the conclusion are defined. This is useful in rules (*cond*) and (*id*).

Consider the rule (*cond*) for conditionals. The branches of the conditional, e_1 and e_2, are typed in the environment Γ_0, *i.e.* the environment updated by typing the first expression, e. Rule (*cond*) uses least upper bounds on types, environments, and effects to determine a conservative approximation of the type, of the resulting environment, and of the effect of the conditional expression. With $t \sqcup_P t'$ we denote the *least upper bound of* t *and* t' with respect to $\leq_P$, when it exists[6] (see Fig. 3). With $\Gamma \sqcup_P \Gamma'$ we denote the *least upper bound operation on environments in* P, defined by:

$$\Gamma \sqcup_P \Gamma' = \{id : (t \sqcup_P t') \mid \Gamma(id) = t \text{ and } \Gamma'(id) = t'\}.$$

The *subeffecting relation,* $\sqsubseteq_P$, defined by:

$$\phi \sqsubseteq_P \phi' \text{ iff }, \text{ for all } c \Downarrow c' \in \phi, \text{ there exists } d \Downarrow d' \in \phi' \text{such that } c \sqsubseteq_P d \text{ and } c' \sqsubseteq_P d',$$

---

[4] In $\mathcal{F}ickle_{II}$ [6], where *effect annotations are set of root classes*, typing has the format $P, \Gamma \vdash e : t \parallel \Gamma' \parallel \{c_1, ..., c_n\}$, where the $\mathcal{F}ickle_{II}$-style effect annotation $\{c_1, ..., c_n\}$ is equivalent to the $\mathcal{F}ickle_3$-style effect annotation $\{c_1 \Downarrow c_1, ..., c_n \Downarrow c_n\}$, meaning that any object of a subclass of the root class c_i may be re-classified to any subclass of the root class c_i.

[5] Besides the fact that the typing rules of $\mathcal{F}ickle_3$ use the least upper bound operator on effects ($\sqcup_P$) instead of the set-theoretic union ($\cup$), the only difference between the typing rules for expressions of $\mathcal{F}ickle_3$ (in Fig. 5) and the typing rules for expressions of $\mathcal{F}ickle_{II}$ (in Fig. 6 of [6]) is in rule (*recl*).

[6] Note that for any class c the least upper bound c $\sqcup_P$**bool** does not exist.

$$\frac{P,\Gamma \vdash e : \text{bool} \parallel \Gamma_0 \parallel \phi \qquad P,\Gamma_0 \vdash e_1 : t_1 \parallel \Gamma_1 \parallel \phi_1 \qquad P,\Gamma_0 \vdash e_2 : t_2 \parallel \Gamma_2 \parallel \phi_2}{P,\Gamma \vdash \text{if } e \text{ then } e_1 \text{ else } e_2 : t_1 \sqcup_{\text{Pt}}2 \parallel \Gamma_1 \sqcup_P \Gamma_2 \parallel \phi \sqcup_P \phi_1 \sqcup_P \phi_2} \quad (cond)$$

$$\frac{\begin{array}{l} P,\Gamma \vdash e : c \parallel \Gamma_0 \parallel \phi \\ P,\Gamma_0 \vdash e' : t \parallel \Gamma' \parallel \phi' \\ \mathcal{F}(P,\phi'@_{\text{PC}},f) = t' \qquad t \leq_P t' \end{array}}{P,\Gamma \vdash e.f:=e' : t \parallel \Gamma' \parallel \phi \sqcup_P \phi'} \quad (a\text{-}field) \qquad \frac{\begin{array}{l} P,\Gamma \vdash e : t' \parallel \Gamma' \parallel \phi \\ \Gamma'(x) = t \qquad t' \leq_P t \end{array}}{P,\Gamma \vdash x:=e : t' \parallel \Gamma' \parallel \phi} \quad (a\text{-}var)$$

$$\frac{\begin{array}{l} P,\Gamma \vdash e : c \parallel \Gamma' \parallel \phi \\ \mathcal{F}(P,c,f) = t \end{array}}{P,\Gamma \vdash e.f : t \parallel \Gamma' \parallel \phi} \quad (field) \qquad \frac{\begin{array}{l} P,\Gamma \vdash e : t \parallel \Gamma_0 \parallel \phi \\ P,\Gamma_0 \vdash e' : t' \parallel \Gamma' \parallel \phi' \end{array}}{P,\Gamma \vdash e; e' : t' \parallel \Gamma' \parallel \phi \sqcup_P \phi'} \quad (seq)$$

$$\frac{}{\begin{array}{l} P,\Gamma \vdash \text{true} : \text{bool} \parallel \Gamma \parallel \{\,\} \\ P,\Gamma \vdash \text{false} : \text{bool} \parallel \Gamma \parallel \{\,\} \end{array}} \quad (bool) \qquad \frac{P \vdash c \diamond_{ct}}{P,\Gamma \vdash \text{null} : c \parallel \Gamma \parallel \{\,\}} \quad (null)$$

$$\frac{}{P,\Gamma \vdash id : \Gamma(id) \parallel \Gamma \parallel \{\,\}} \quad (id) \qquad \frac{P \vdash c \diamond_{ct}}{P,\Gamma \vdash \text{new } c : c \parallel \Gamma \parallel \{\,\}} \quad (new)$$

$$\frac{\begin{array}{l} P,\Gamma \vdash e_0 : c \parallel \Gamma_0 \parallel \phi_0 \\ P,\Gamma_{i-1} \vdash e_i : t'_i \parallel \Gamma_i \parallel \phi_i \quad (\forall i \in \{1,...,n\}) \\ \mathcal{M}(P,(\phi_1 \sqcup_P \cdots \sqcup_P \phi_n)@_{\text{PC}},m) = t\ m(t_1\ x_1,...,t_n\ x_n)\ \phi\ \{\ ...\ \} \\ (\phi_{i+1} \sqcup_P \cdots \sqcup_P \phi_n)@_{\text{Pt}'_i} \leq_P t_i \quad (\forall i \in \{1,...,n\}) \end{array}}{P,\Gamma \vdash e_0.m(e_1,...,e_n) : t \parallel \phi@_P\Gamma_n \parallel \phi \sqcup_P \phi_0 \sqcup_P \cdots \sqcup_P \phi_n} \quad (meth)$$

$$\frac{P \vdash \Gamma(id) \diamond_{ct}}{P,\Gamma \vdash id \Downarrow c : c \parallel (\{\,\Gamma(id) \Downarrow c\,\}@_P\Gamma)[id \mapsto c] \parallel \{\,\Gamma(id) \Downarrow c\,\}} \quad (recl)$$

Fig. 5. Typing rules for expressions.

formalizes the fact that the effect ϕ is a conservative approximation of the effect ϕ'. The effect $\phi \sqcup_P \phi'$, defined by:

$$\phi \sqcup_P \phi' = \textbf{let}$$
$$\phi_0 = \{c \Downarrow (c' \sqcup_P (\sqcup_P \{d' \mid d \Downarrow d' \in \phi' \text{ and } d \sqsubseteq_P c\})) \mid c \Downarrow c' \in \phi\}$$
$$\qquad \cup \ \{d \Downarrow (d' \sqcup_P (\sqcup_P \{c' \mid c \Downarrow c' \in \phi \text{ and } c \sqsubseteq_P d\})) \mid d \Downarrow d' \in \phi'\}$$
$$\textbf{in}$$
$$\{c_0 \Downarrow (c'_0 \sqcup_P (\sqcup_P \{d'_0 \mid d_0 \Downarrow d'_0 \in \phi_0 \text{ and } (c'_0 \sqsubseteq_P d_0 \text{ or } d_0 \sqsubseteq_P c'_0)\})) \mid c_0 \Downarrow c'_0 \in \phi_0\}$$

is the *least upper bound of the effects ϕ and ϕ'* with respect to $\sqsubseteq_P$. Note that the least upper bound of well-formed effects is always defined and it is a well-formed effect. The two branches of a conditional may cause different re-classifications for this and the parameters. So, after the evaluation we can only assert that this and the parameters belong to the least upper bound of their relative classes in Γ_1 and Γ_2. We can prove that for this rule $\Gamma_1 \sqcup_P \Gamma_2$ is defined. On the other hand, the least upper bound of the types of the branches, $t_1 \sqcup_P t_2$, may not be defined, in which case the rule cannot be applied.

Consider now the typing of assignments, *i.e.* rules (*a-field*) and (*a-var*). Evaluation of the right hand side may modify the type of the left hand side. In particular, in (*a-var*) evaluation of e can modify the type of x. This is taken into account by looking up x in the environment Γ'. Also, in rule (*a-field*) evaluation of e' may modify the class of the object e. For this purpose, we define the application of effects to types:

$$\{c_1 \Downarrow c_1', ..., c_n \Downarrow c_n'\} @_P t = \begin{cases} c_i' \sqcup_P t & \text{if } t \sqsubseteq_P c_i \text{ for some } i \in 1, ..., n \\ c_{i_1}' \sqcup_P ... \sqcup_P c_{i_m}' \sqcup_P t & \text{if } i_j \in 1, ..., n \ (j \in 1, ..., m \text{ and } m \geq 1) \\ & \text{are all the indexes such that } c_{i_j} \sqsubseteq_P t \\ t & \text{otherwise} \end{cases}$$

For example, $\{\text{Frog} \Downarrow \text{Prince}\} @_{P_{pl}} \text{Frog} = \text{Player}$, $\{\text{Frog} \Downarrow \text{Prince}\} @_{P_{pl}} \text{Prince} = \text{Prince}$, and $\{\text{Frog} \Downarrow \text{Prince}\} @_{P_{pl}} \text{Princess} = \text{Princess}$.

In rule (a-$field$), by applying ϕ' to c before looking up f, we provide for the case where evaluation of e' might re-classify e and remove f in the process.

We say that *an effect ϕ respects a set of classes C in P* to mean that, for all $c \in C$, $\phi @_P c = c$.

Note that the field type cannot be changed since classes not respected by the effects listed in the program are not allowed to be used as types for fields. The effect of field assignment is the least upper bound of the effects of the left-hand side and of the right-hand side of the assignment, which conservatively approximates the application of the effect of the left-hand side followed by the application of the effect of the right-hand side. (This is due to the fact that: if $P \vdash \phi \diamond$, $P \vdash \phi' \diamond$, and $P \vdash c \diamond_{ct}$, then $\phi' @_P(\phi @_P c) \sqsubseteq_P (\phi \sqcup_P \phi') @_P c$).

Consider now ($recl$): $\text{id} \Downarrow c$ is type correct if $\Gamma(\text{id})$ (the type of id before the re-classification) is a class; note that, since the class hierarchy is a tree, this implies that c (the target of the re-classification) and $\Gamma(\text{id})$ have a common superclass. The typing rule for re-classification updates the environment by changing the class of the identifier id. Moreover, since there could be aliasing with identifiers of classes that are subclasses or superclasses of the class of id, the static type of all such variables is set to the least upper bound of the current type and of the target of the re-classification. For this reason, we define the application of effects to environments:

$$\phi @_P \Gamma = \{\text{id} : \phi @_P t \mid \Gamma(\text{id}) = t\}$$

For example, for an environment Γ_1, with $\Gamma_1(x_1) = \Gamma_1(x_2) = \text{Frog}$, $\Gamma_1(x_3) = \text{Prince}$, we have $\{\text{Frog} \Downarrow \text{Prince}\} @_{P_{pl}} \Gamma_1 = \Gamma_2$, where $\Gamma_2(x_1) = \Gamma_2(x_2) = \text{Player}$ and $\Gamma_2(x_3) = \text{Prince}$. Therefore, the following typing judgement can be derived:

$$P_{pl}, \Gamma_1 \vdash x_2 \Downarrow \text{Prince} : \text{Prince} \parallel \Gamma_3 \parallel \{\text{Frog} \Downarrow \text{Prince}\}$$

where $\Gamma_3(x_1) = \text{Player}$, but $\Gamma_3(x_2) = \Gamma_3(x_3) = \text{Prince}$.

Consider rule ($meth$) for method calls, $e_0.m(e_1, ..., e_n)$. The evaluation of the arguments $e_{i+1}, ..., e_n$ may modify the types of the arguments $e_1, ..., e_i$ and of the object e_0. This could happen if the original type of e_j ($0 \leq j \leq i$) is a subclass or superclass of the left-hand side of an atomic effect among the effects of $e_{i+1}, ..., e_n$. The definition of m has to be found in the new class of the object e_0, and the types of the formal parameters must be compared with the new types of $e_1, ..., e_{n-1}$. In ($meth$) we look up the definition of m in the class obtained by applying the effect of the arguments to the class of the receiver and we compare the types of formal and actual parameters by keeping into account the effects of the actual parameters.

$\mathcal{C}(\mathsf{P},\mathsf{c}) = \textbf{class } \mathsf{c} \textbf{ extends } \mathsf{c}' \ \{...\}$
$\forall \mathsf{f}: \ \mathcal{FD}(\mathsf{P},\mathsf{c},\mathsf{f}) = \mathsf{t}_0 \ \implies \ \ \ \ \ \mathsf{P} \vdash \mathsf{t}_0 \ \Diamond_t \ \ \ \ \text{and} \ \ \ \ \mathcal{F}(\mathsf{P},\mathsf{c}',\mathsf{f}) = \mathcal{U}df$
$\forall \mathsf{m}: \ \mathcal{MD}(\mathsf{P},\mathsf{c},\mathsf{m}) = \mathsf{t} \ \mathsf{m}(\mathsf{t}_1 \ \mathsf{x}_1, ..., \mathsf{t}_n \ \mathsf{x}_n) \ \phi \ \{ \ \mathsf{e} \ \} \ \implies$
$\ \ \ \ \ \ \mathsf{P} \vdash \phi \ \Diamond$
$\ \ \ \ \ \ \mathsf{P}, \{\mathsf{x}_1 : \mathsf{t}_1, ..., \mathsf{x}_n : \mathsf{t}_n, \mathsf{this} : \mathsf{c}\} \ \vdash \ \mathsf{e} \ : \ \mathsf{t}' \ \| \ \Gamma' \ \| \ \phi'$
$\ \ \ \ \ \ \mathsf{t}' \leq_\mathsf{P} \mathsf{t}$
$\ \ \ \ \ \ \phi' \sqsubseteq_\mathsf{P} \phi$

$$\frac{\ \ \ \ \ \ \mathcal{M}(\mathsf{P},\mathsf{c}',\mathsf{m}) = \mathcal{U}df \ \text{ or } \ (\mathcal{M}(\mathsf{P},\mathsf{c}',\mathsf{m}) = \mathsf{t} \ \mathsf{m}(\mathsf{t}_1 \ \mathsf{x}_1, ..., \mathsf{t}_n \ \mathsf{x}_n) \ \phi'' \ \{ \ ... \ \} \ \text{ and } \ \phi \sqsubseteq_\mathsf{P} \phi'')}{\mathsf{P} \vdash \mathsf{c} \ \Diamond} \ \ (wfc)$$

$$\frac{\vdash \ \mathsf{P} \ \Diamond_h \ \ \ \ \ \ \forall \mathsf{c}: \ \ \mathcal{C}(\mathsf{P},\mathsf{c}) \neq \mathcal{U}df \ \implies \ \ \mathsf{P} \vdash \mathsf{c} \ \Diamond \ \ \ \ \ \ \textbf{Effect}(\mathsf{P}) \text{ respects } \textbf{ClassesFT}(\mathsf{P})}{\vdash \mathsf{P} \ \Diamond} \ \ (wfp)$$

Fig. 6. Rules for well-formed classes and programs.

4.2 Rules for Well-Formed Classes and Programs

The rules for checking that a program is well-formed are listed in Fig. 6[7]. With **Effect**(P) we denote the effect

$$\sqcup_\mathsf{P} \{\phi \mid \phi \text{ occurs in the signature of a method defined in a class of } \mathsf{P}\}$$

and with **ClassesFT**(P) we denote the set of classes

$$\{\mathsf{c} \mid \mathsf{c} \text{ is used as type for a field defined in a class of } \mathsf{P}\}.$$

A program is well formed (*i.e.* $\vdash \mathsf{P} \ \Diamond$) if the inheritance hierarchy is well-formed (*i.e.* $\vdash \ \mathsf{P} \ \Diamond_h$), all its classes c are well-formed (*i.e.* $\mathsf{P} \vdash \mathsf{c} \ \Diamond$), and the effects respect the classes used as types for fields (*i.e.* **Effect**(P) respects **ClassesFT**(P)). Fields may not redefine fields from superclasses, and methods may redefine superclass methods only if they have the same name, arguments, and result type, and their effect is a subeffect of that of the overridden method[8]. Method bodies must be well formed, must return a value appropriate for the method signature, and their effect must be a subeffect of that in the signature. See Fig. 6, where $\mathcal{C}(\mathsf{P},\mathsf{c})$ returns the definition of class c in program P, and the lookup functions $\mathcal{FD}(\mathsf{P},\mathsf{c},\mathsf{f})$, $\mathcal{MD}(\mathsf{P},\mathsf{c},\mathsf{m})$ return, respectively, the definition of field f and method m in class c (the formal definitions are given in Appendix A).

---

[7] The only differences between the rules for well-formed classes and programs of $\mathcal{F}ickle_3$ (in Fig. 6) and those of $\mathcal{F}ickle_{\mathrm{II}}$ (in Fig. 7 of [6]) are the following. In rule (*wfc*), the rule for $\mathcal{F}ickle_3$ uses a different notion of well-formed effect and uses the subeffecting relation instead of the set-theoretic inclusion. In rule (*wfp*), the rule for $\mathcal{F}ickle_3$ has the additional requirement that the effects must respect the classes used as types for fields.

[8] Thus, in contrast to Java and C++, $\mathcal{F}ickle_3$ does not allow field shadowing, nor method overloading. These features can be included into $\mathcal{F}ickle_3$ adopting the approach from [7]. However, this would complicate the presentation unnecessarily.

$$\frac{v = \text{true or } v = \text{false}}{P, \sigma \vdash v \prec \text{bool}} \quad (\text{bool} \prec) \qquad \frac{P \vdash t \; \Diamond_{ct}}{P, \sigma \vdash \text{null} \prec t} \quad (\text{null} \prec)$$

$$\frac{\sigma(\iota) = [\![...]\!]^c \quad c \leq_P t}{P, \sigma \vdash \iota \prec t} \quad (\iota \prec)$$

$$\frac{P, \sigma \vdash v \prec t \quad v \in sVal}{P, \sigma \vdash v \lhd t} \quad (sVal \lhd) \qquad \frac{\sigma(\iota) = [\![...]\!]^c \quad P, \sigma \vdash \iota \prec t}{\forall f \in \mathcal{F}s(P, c) : \; P, \sigma \vdash \sigma(\iota)(f) \prec \mathcal{F}(P, c, f)}{P, \sigma \vdash \iota \lhd t} \quad (\iota \lhd)$$

$$\frac{\sigma(\text{this}) = \sigma'(\text{this})}{\sigma(\iota) = [\![...]\!]^c \implies \sigma'(\iota) = [\![...]\!]^{c'} \text{ and } \begin{cases} c' \sqsubseteq_P c \sqcup_P d' & \text{if } c \sqsubseteq_P d \text{ for some } d \Downarrow d' \in \phi \\ c' = c & \text{otherwise} \end{cases}}{P, \phi \vdash \sigma \lhd \sigma'} \quad (\sigma \lhd)$$

$$\frac{\sigma(\iota) = [\![...]\!]^c \implies P, \sigma \vdash \iota \lhd c \quad \text{(for all addresses } \iota)}{\Gamma(\text{id}) \neq \mathcal{U}df \implies P, \sigma \vdash \sigma(\text{id}) \lhd \Gamma(\text{id}) \quad \text{(for all identifiers id)}}{P, \Gamma \vdash \sigma \Diamond} \quad (\Diamond)$$

Fig. 7. Agreement between programs, stores, and values.

4.3   Soundness

Figure 7 introduces agreement notions between programs, stores, and values[9]. The judgement $P, \sigma \vdash v \prec t$ is instrumental to the definition of $P, \sigma \vdash v \lhd t$: it avoids the use of coinduction. The judgement $P, \phi \vdash \sigma \lhd \sigma'$ guarantees that the differences from σ to σ' are "small"; in particular, only objects of a subclass of a class occurring in the left-hand side of an atomic effect in ϕ may be reclassified. The judgement $P, \sigma \vdash v \lhd t$, guarantees that value v conforms to type t. In particular, it requires that when v is an address it corresponds to an object of some class c subclass of t, that the object contains all fields required in the description of c, and that the fields contain values which conform to their type in c. The judgement $P, \Gamma \vdash \sigma \Diamond$ guarantees that all object fields contain values which conform to their types in the class of the objects, and that all parameters and the receiver are mapped to values which conform to their types in Γ.

The type system is sound in the sense that a converging well-typed expression returns a value which agrees with the expression's type, or `nullPntrExc`.

Theorem 1 (Type Soundness). *For a well-formed program* P, *environment* Γ, *and expression* e, *such that* $P, \Gamma \vdash e : t \parallel \Gamma' \parallel \phi$ *if* $P, \Gamma \vdash \sigma \Diamond$, *and* e, σ *converges then*

- *either* $e, \sigma \rightsquigarrow v, \sigma'$, $P, \sigma' \vdash v \lhd t$, $P, \Gamma' \vdash \sigma' \Diamond$,
- *or* $e, \sigma \rightsquigarrow$ `nullPntrExc`, σ'.

---

[9] The definitions in Fig. 7 differs from the analogous definition introduced in [6] for $\mathcal{F}ickle_{II}$ in the rule for the judgment $P, \phi \vdash \sigma \lhd \sigma'$ (which is crucial to prove Theorem 1).

5   Conclusions

In this paper we have proposed the language $\mathcal{F}ickle_3$ which improves $\mathcal{F}ickle_{II}$ [6] by providing a more expressive type and effect system, and removing the need for the qualifiers **root** and **state** for classes. This makes possible uses of classes that were not anticipated at their definition time, so that a same class can be used for re-classifiable objects in certain contexts and for non re-classifiable objects in others.

Keeping the **root** and **state** qualifiers results in the language $\mathcal{F}ickle_{III}$, an extension of $\mathcal{F}ickle_{II}$, described in [4].

More experimentation with $\mathcal{F}ickle_3$ and $\mathcal{F}ickle_{III}$ is needed in order to assess the "real usefulness" of their features and to compare the two languages from the "software engineering point of view".

The paper [1] provides a translation of $\mathcal{F}ickle$ into Java. The same translation scheme could be used for $\mathcal{F}ickle_3$ and $\mathcal{F}ickle_{III}$.

Acknowledgements

We would like to thank Mariangiola Dezani and the anonymous ICTCS'03 referees for useful comments and suggestions.

References

1. D. Ancona, C. Anderson, F. Damiani, S. Drossopoulou, P. Giannini, and E. Zucca. An Effective Translation of Fickle into Java. In *ICTCS'01*, volume 2002 of *LNCS*, pages 215–234, Berlin, 2001. Springer.
2. C. Chambers. Predicate Classes. In *ECOOP'93*, volume 707 of *LNCS*, pages 268–296, Berlin, 1993. Springer.
3. P. Costanza. Dynamic Object Replacement and Implementation-Only Classes. In *WCOP'01 (at ECOOP'01)*, 2001. Available from http://www.cs.uni-bonn.de/~costanza/implementationonly.pdf.
4. F. Damiani, M. Dezani-Ciancaglini, S. Drossopoulou, and P. Giannini. Refined Effects for Re-classification: Fickle$_{III}$. Report for the IST-2001-33477 DART project - available at the url http://www.cee.hw.ac.uk/DART/reports/D3.1/DDDG02b.pdf, 2002.
5. S. Drossopoulou, F. Damiani, M. Dezani-Ciancaglini, and P. Giannini. Fickle: Dynamic Object Re-classification. In *ECOOP'01*, volume 2072 of *LNCS*, pages 130–149, Berlin, 2001. Springer. A shorter version is available in: Electronic proceedings of FOOL8 (http://www.cs.williams.edu/~kim/FOOL/).
6. S. Drossopoulou, F. Damiani, M. Dezani-Ciancaglini, and P. Giannini. More Dynamic Object Re-classification: Fickle$_{II}$. *ACM Transactions On Programming Languages and Systems*, 24(2):153–191, 2002.
7. Sophia Drossopoulou, Susan Eisenbach, and Sarfraz Khurshid. Is the Java Type System Sound? *Theory and Practice of Object Systems*, 5(1).3–24, 1999.
8. G. Ghelli and D. Palmerini. Foundations of Extended Objets with Roles (*extended abstract*). In *FOOL6*, 1999. Available from http://www.cs.williams.edu/~kim/FOOL/FOOL6.html.

9. M. Lucassen and D. K. Gifford. Polymorphic Effect Systems. In *POPL'88*, pages 47–57, New York, 1988. ACM Press.
10. M. Serrano. Wide Classes. In *ECOOP'99*, volume 1628 of *LNCS*, pages 391–415, Berlin, 1999. Springer.
11. A. Tailvasaari. Object Oriented Programming with Modes. *Journal of Object Oriented Programming*, 6(3):27–32, 1993.
12. J.-P. Talpin and P. Jouvelot. Polymorphic Type, Region and Effect Inference. *Journal of Functional Programming*, 2(3):245–271, 1992.

A   Definitions Concerning Lookup

For program P with $\vdash P \diamond_u$ (see Fig. 3) and identifier $c \neq \mathsf{Object}$, we define the lookup of the class declaration for c:

$$\mathcal{C}(\mathsf{P}, \mathsf{c}) = \begin{cases} \textbf{class } \mathsf{c} \textbf{ extends } \mathsf{c}'\{\mathsf{cBody}\} & \textit{if } \mathsf{P} = \mathsf{P}' \textbf{ class } \mathsf{c} \textbf{ extends } \mathsf{c}'\{\mathsf{cBody}\} \; \mathsf{P}'', \\ \mathcal{U}df & \textit{otherwise} \end{cases}$$

For program P with $\vdash P \diamond_h$ (see Fig. 3), identifier c such that

$$\mathcal{C}(\mathsf{P}, \mathsf{c}) = \textbf{class } \mathsf{c} \textbf{ extends } \mathsf{c}'\{\mathsf{cBody}\},$$

and identifiers f and m we define:

$$\mathcal{FD}(\mathsf{P}, \mathsf{c}, \mathsf{f}) = \begin{cases} \mathsf{t} & \textit{if } \mathsf{cBody} = \ldots \mathsf{t} \; \mathsf{f} \ldots \\ \mathcal{U}df & \textit{otherwise} \end{cases}$$

$$\mathcal{F}(\mathsf{P}, \mathsf{c}, \mathsf{f}) = \begin{cases} \mathcal{FD}(\mathsf{P}, \mathsf{c}, \mathsf{f}) & \textit{if } \mathcal{FD}(\mathsf{P}, \mathsf{c}, \mathsf{f}) \neq \mathcal{U}df, \\ \mathcal{F}(\mathsf{P}, \mathsf{c}', \mathsf{f}) & \textit{otherwise} \end{cases}$$

$$\mathcal{F}(\mathsf{P}, \mathsf{Object}, \mathsf{f}) = \mathcal{U}df$$

$$\mathcal{F}s(\mathsf{P}, \mathsf{c}) = \{\mathsf{f} \mid \mathcal{F}(\mathsf{P}, \mathsf{c}, \mathsf{f}) \neq \mathcal{U}df\}$$

$$\mathcal{MD}(\mathsf{P}, \mathsf{c}, \mathsf{m}) = \begin{cases} \mathsf{t} \; \mathsf{m}(\mathsf{t}_1 \; \mathsf{x}_1, \ldots, \mathsf{t}_n \; \mathsf{x}_n) \, \phi \, \{ \, \mathsf{e} \, \} & \textit{if } \mathsf{cBody} = \ldots \mathsf{t} \; \mathsf{m} \, (\mathsf{t}_1 \; \mathsf{x}_1 \ldots \mathsf{t}_n \; \mathsf{x}_n) \phi \{\mathsf{e}\} \ldots \\ \mathcal{U}df & \textit{otherwise} \end{cases}$$

$$\mathcal{M}(\mathsf{P}, \mathsf{c}, \mathsf{m}) = \begin{cases} \mathcal{MD}(\mathsf{P}, \mathsf{c}, \mathsf{m}) & \textit{if } \mathcal{MD}(\mathsf{P}, \mathsf{c}, \mathsf{m}) \neq \mathcal{U}df, \\ \mathcal{M}(\mathsf{P}, \mathsf{c}', \mathsf{m}) & \textit{otherwise} \end{cases}$$

$$\mathcal{M}(\mathsf{P}, \mathsf{Object}, \mathsf{m}) = \mathcal{U}df$$

Cost Constrained Fixed Job Scheduling

Qiwei Huang[1] and Errol Lloyd[2]

[1] UTStarcom Inc.
33 Wood Ave. South, Iselin, NJ 08830, USA
qhuang@utstar.com
[2] Dept. of Computer and Information Sciences
University of Delaware, Newark, DE 19716, USA
elloyd@cis.udel.edu

Abstract. In this paper, we study the problem of cost constrained fixed job scheduling (*CCFJS*). In this problem, there are a number of processors, each of which belongs to one of several classes. The unit time processing cost for a processor varies with the class to which the processor belongs. There are N jobs, each of which must be processed from a given start time to a given finish time without preemption. A job can be processed by any processor, and the cost of that processing is the product of the processing time and the processor's unit time processing cost. The problem is to find a feasible scheduling of the jobs such that the total processing cost is within a given cost bound. This problem (*CCFJS*) arises in several applications, including off-line multimedia gateway call routing. We show that *CCFJS* can be solved by a network flow based algorithm when there are only two classes of processors. For more than two classes of processors, we prove that *CCFJS* is not only *NP-Complete*, but also that there is no constant ratio approximation algorithm. Finally, we present an approximation algorithm, derive its worst-case performance ratio (non constant), and show that it has a constant approximation ratio in several special cases.

1 Introduction

Fixed job scheduling (sometimes called *interval scheduling*) has been studied extensively. In fixed job scheduling, we need to process without preemption a given set of jobs on several processors, such that a job starts at a given time and finishes at a given time. Many variations of *fixed job scheduling* have been considered in the literature (cf. Fischetti, Martello & Toth [1,2], Kolen & Kroon [3,4,5,6], Kroon, Sen, & Deng [7], and Jansen [8]), and the computational complexity of those variants has been established. In particular, Kroon, Sen, & Deng [7] studied the optimal cost chromatic partition problem (*OCCP*), one variation of *fixed job scheduling* with processor-dependent processing cost. In that problem, a sufficient number of processors are available. A job can be processed by any one processor during a fixed time interval, and if job j is carried out by processor p, then the associated processing cost is k_p.

The objective is to find a feasible non-preemptive schedule to achieve the minimum total processing cost.

In this paper, we study cost constrained fixed job scheduling (*CCFJS*), which is similar to [7]. In *CCFJS*, there are a number of processors, each of which belongs to

C. Blundo and C. Laneve (Eds.): ICTCS 2003, LNCS 2841, pp. 111–124, 2003.

one of several classes. The unit time processing cost for a processor varies with the class to which the processor belongs. Each job requires processing by one and only one processor without preemption. The cost of processing a job is the unit time processing cost of the processor times the job's processing time. The problem is to find a feasible scheduling of the jobs within a given cost bound, or equivalently, to find a feasible scheduling of minimum cost. The difference between *CCFJS* and *OCCP* is that, in *OCCP*, the processing cost of a job depends only on the processor: if a number of jobs are processed by the same processor, they have the same processing costs; In *CCFJS*, the processing cost of a job depends not only on the processor, but also on the processing time (the processing cost is equal to the product of the unit time processing cost of that processor and the processing time).

CCFJS arises in off-line multimedia gateway call routing. Multimedia gateways interconnect different media networks (circuit-switched PSTN, packet-switched IP, ATM, wireless). A multimedia gateway routes each incoming call to one of its media networks. Media networks differ in the unit time media cost for calls routed to the network, and each media network has a bandwidth capacity on the number of simultaneous calls. The media cost of a call is equal to the call duration times the unit time media cost of the network to which the call is routed. The goal of call routing is to minimize the media cost (or equivalently within its cost bound) taken over all calls.

In section 2, we formally define *CCFJS* and provide relevant terminology. In section 3, we show that *CCFJS* can be solved by a network flow based algorithm (i.e. in polynomial time) when there are only two classes of processors. In section 4, we show that for more than two classes of processors, *CCFJS* is not only *NP-Complete*, but also that there is no constant ratio approximation algorithm. In section 5, we present an approximation algorithm, derive its worst-case performance ratio (non constant), and show that it has a constant approximation ratio in several special cases.

2   Problem Descriptions and Terminology

In this section, we formally define *CCFJS* as a decision problem. The optimization version of the problem should be clear.

Instance of *CCFJS*: A cost bound $C_B > 0$; Jobs $J_1,...J_N$, and for each job J_i, a start time s_i and a finish time f_i ($0 \le s_i < f_i$); K classes of processors, and for each class $j = 1,...K$, the number B_j of processors, and the unit time processing cost C_j for processors in this class. Let $B = \sum_{i=1}^{K} B_i$ be the total number of processors. We assume that $0 < C_1 < C_2 < ... < C_K$.

Question: Does there exist a feasible schedule for the N jobs, such that the cost $C_T = \sum_{i=1}^{N} C_{j_i}(f_i - s_i) \le C_B$? Here, C_{j_i} is the unit time processing cost of the processor on which job J_i is processed.

Relative to the specification of *CCFJS*, a feasible schedule is an assignment of each job to a processor such that each job must be processed by one processor from its given start time to its given finish time without preemption, and each processor can process at most one job at a time.

Throughout this paper, we make use of the following terminology: Jobs J_i and J_j $(i \neq j)$ are *compatible* if the time intervals $[s_i, f_i)$ and $[s_j, f_j)$ do not overlap. Job J_i is *active* at time t if $t \in [s_i, f_i)$. *Rank(t)* is the number of *active* jobs at time t. Further, *Rank*(J_i) is the maximum number of active jobs (including J_i itself) at any point of time $t \in [s_i, f_i)$. To avoid trivial infeasible instances, we assume throughout the paper that:

$$\max \left(Rank(J_i)(i = 1, 2, ...N) \right) \leq B \qquad (2.1)$$

A *null job* has zero processing time with start time equal to finish time. Adding *null jobs* to an instance of *CCFJS* doesn't affect the feasibility of the problem since *null jobs* introduce no cost. A feasible schedule has the following fundamental property:

Partition Property: n of the total N jobs ($n<N$) can be processed by P processors ($P<B$) if and only if the remaining $N - n$ jobs can be processed by $B - P$ processors.

3   A Polynomial Time Algorithm for Two Classes of Processors

In this section, we show that when there are two classes of processors (i.e. $K=2$), *CCFJS* can be solved in polynomial time. The algorithm we give has two steps: (1) Build a flow network based on each job's start time and finish time along with the total number of processors; (2) Apply a minimum cost network flow algorithm [9] to obtain a minimum total cost for the constructed flow network. It will follow that if the minimum total cost is greater than C_B, then *CCFJS* has no feasible solution; otherwise *CCFJS* has a feasible solution.

3.1   Construct a Flow Network

The algorithm that we give constructs a flow network in the form of a layered directed acyclic graph (*DAG*). Each layer has exactly B vertices and each edge connects two vertices from two adjacent layers. Each vertex represents a job, and will be assigned a weight equal to the job's processing time. A path represents a sequence of jobs that can be processed by the same processor. Clearly, any two jobs on the same path must be compatible. Further, if any P vertex-disjoint paths ($0 < P < B$) are removed from the flow network, then in the remaining flow network, there will exist $B - P$ vertex-disjoint paths, such that each remaining vertex belongs to exactly one of the $B - P$ vertex-disjoint paths (i.e. the **Partition Property** holds). In section 3.2, we will let P be equal to B_2, and the jobs on the resulting B_2 vertex-disjoint paths will be assigned to processors of class 2. Likewise, the jobs on the remaining B_1 vertex-disjoint paths will be assigned to the processors of class 1.

3.1.1 Building a Layered DAG

The algorithm ***Build_Layered_DAG*** described below has two inputs: the total number of processors B and an array of N jobs stored in $J[1..N]$. The output is a layered DAG in which each layer contains exactly B vertices, and each edge is directed from a vertex in one layer to a vertex in the next higher layer.

Algorithm Build_Layered_DAG(Input J[1..N], B; Output G=(V,E))
Sort and store the 2N values of J[k].start_time and J[k].finish_time (k=1..N) into ascending order in A[1..2N];
V ← {s, t}; L ← 1; F ← 0;
weight(s) ←0; weight(t) ← 0; Layer[0] ←{s};
for i ← 1 to N+1 do Layer[i] ←NULL;
for i ← 1 to 2N do
     j←A[i].index;
     if A[i].type = start_time
         Layer[L] ← Layer[L] ∪ vertex(J[j]); // Add job J[j] into Layer L
         weight(vertex(J[j]))←J[j].proc_time; // Set job J[j]'s weight to its length
         F ← 0;
     else / A[i].type = finish_time */*
         if (F =0)
             F ← 1;
             //Duplicate vertices of layer L into layer L+1
             Layer[L+1] ← Layer[L];
             //Set duplicated vertices' weight to zero
             weight(v) ← 0 for each v ∈ Layer[L+1];
                Add an adequate number of vertices with weight zero (null jobs) into layer L, such that laye L has exactly B number of vertices;
             L←L+1; //Advance the current layer L to L+1
         //Remove job J[j] from the current layer L
         Layer[L] ← Layer[L] - vertex(J[j]);
Layer[L] ←{t};
for i ← 1 to L-1 do V←V ∪ Layer[i];
for every vertex v ∈ Layer[i]
     if v has a duplicated vertex u ∈ Layer[i+1] then E ← E ∪ (v,u);
     else for each non-duplicated vertex u ∈ Layer[i+1], E ← E ∪ (v,u) ;
Assign capacity one and weight zero to each edge;

The data structures used in the algorithm are: Each element of $J[1..N]$ has three fields: $J[k].start\_time$ is job J_k's start time, $J[k].finish\_time$ is job J_k's finish time and $J[k].proc\_time$ is job J_k's processing time. Clearly, $J[k].start\_time+$ $J[k].proc\_time= J[k].finish\_time$. Array $A[1..2N]$ stores the sorted start and finish times of all the jobs. Each element of A has three fields: $A[i].type$ (*start_time* or *finish_time*) indicates whether it is a start time or a finish time; $A[i].value$ is either the start or the finish time depending on the $A[i].type$; $A[i].index$ is the job's index in $J[1..N]$. Each element of array $Layer[1..N+2]$ is used to store the vertices of a given layer.

Build_Layered_DAG works as follows: The algorithm first sorts the $2N$ time values into ascending order, and stores them in array $A[1..2N]$. If the finish time of a job is the same as the start time of other jobs, the finishing times are placed before the starting times in $A[1..2N]$.

Then, the algorithm processes $A[i]$ with index i increasing from 1 to $2N$. If $A[i].type$ is *start_time*, then a vertex representing job $J[A[i].index]$ is added to layer L, and the weight of the vertex is set to $J[A[i].index].proc\_time$. If $A[i].type$ is *finish_time*, then each vertex of layer L is duplicated and placed in a new layer $(L+1)$. The weight of each duplicated vertex in this new layer is set to zero, and the vertex of job $J[A[i].index]$ is removed from the new layer. Note that if there are contiguous elements of $A[i].type$ equal to *finish_time*, then the algorithm keeps on removing the vertex of job $J[A[i].index]$ from the new layer until encountering the first $A[i].type$ equal to *start_time*. (i.e. a new layer is constructed only for the first of a series of *finish_times*). Note that the number of vertices in the new layer is at most B from the assumption (2.1). If the old layer has fewer than B vertices, the algorithm adds enough vertices with weight zero into the old layer to ensure that it has exactly B vertices (vertices with weight zero represent *null jobs*).

After building the final layer, the algorithm adds edges: for each vertex v in layer k (not the final layer), if v has a duplicated vertex u in layer $k+1$, add edge (v,u); otherwise add edge (v,u) for each non-duplicated vertex u in the layer $k+1$. The running time of **Build_Layered_DAG** is $O(N \log N + NB^2)$.

3.1.2 An Example
Figure 1 shows seven jobs with start times and finish times in sorted order. Each job's processing time is shown in parentheses. Figure 2 is the layered DAG produced by **Build_Layered_DAG**. Each vertex's weight is indicated in the parentheses.

3.1.3 Properties of the Layered DAG
In this section we prove the following theorem about the properties of the layered DAG. These properties are clearly illustrated in the example above.

Theorem (3.1) The graph $G = (V, E)$ generated by **Build_Layered_DAG** has the following properties: 1. $G = (V, E)$ is a DAG in which each layer (except the first and the last) has exactly B vertices, and any two vertices (except for the *null jobs* vertices) in that layer are not compatible. 2. Each vertex in a layer can have at most one duplicated vertex in the next layer. 3. Each edge connects two vertices from two adjacent layers. 4. Each vertex u is located on at least one path from s to t (an s-t path). 5. There exist exactly B vertex disjoint s-t paths in the graph, such that each vertex (except s and t) belongs to exactly one of those B paths. Note that the selection of those B paths may not be unique. 6. If any P vertex-disjoint paths ($0 < P < B$) are removed (except s and t) from $G = (V, E)$, then the remaining flow network has the above 1-5 properties with B replaced by $B - P$. 7. A set of m jobs can be processed by P processors subject to the **Partition Property** if and only if there exist P ($0 < P < B$) vertex-disjoint s-t paths in $G = (V, E)$ containing all non-duplicated and duplicated vertices of those m jobs. These P vertex-disjoint paths may not be unique.

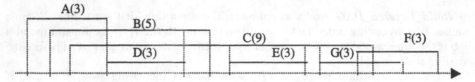

Fig. 1. Job Sequence Input for *Build_Layered_DAG*, *B=3*

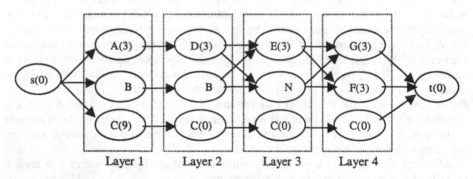

Fig. 2. Output Layered DAG from Fig. 1

The first 4 properties and property 6 follow easily from the algorithm. Property 5 can be proved by using induction on the number of layers constructed. In property 7, the "if" part is straightforward and the "only if" part can be proved by using induction on the number of processors P. The details of the proofs are omitted here due to space limitation.

3.2 The Algorithm and Its Correctness

Algorithm Two_Class_Scheduling(*Input J[1..N]*, B_1, B_2, C_1, C_2 ; *Output* C_T^*)

    Build_Layered_DAG(*Input J[1..N]*, $B_1 + B_2$; *Output G'=(V',E'))*;

    Convert G'=(V',E') into an edge capacitated flow network G=(V,E) using the standard techniques (i.e. split each vertex $u \in V'-\{s,t\}$ into two vertices u' and u" and add an directed edge (u',u") with direction the same as $s \rightarrow t$ direction, capacity equal to one and weight equal to vertex u's weight).

Compute a minimum cost flow in $G=(V,E)$ with flow value of B_2 [9];

Assign the jobs that are on the minimum cost flow to class 2 processors, and let L_2^* be the total processing time of such jobs; Assign the jobs that are not on the minimum cost flow to class 1 processors and let L_1^* be the total processing time of such jobs.

Calculate the total cost $C_T^* \leftarrow L_1^* * C_1 + L_2^* * C_2$.

Having constructed a flow network, we use a minimum cost network flow algorithm [9] to find B_2 vertex-disjoint paths with minimum total weight. Clearly, all vertices not on those B_2 vertex-disjoint paths can fit into $B - B_2 = B_1$ vertex-disjoint paths. In **Two_Class_Scheduling** described below, input *J[1..N]* is the same as the input for **Build_Layered_DAG**, B_1 and B_2 are the numbers of processors of the two processor classes, and C_1 and C_2 are the unit time processing costs of those classes. We assume $C_1 < C_2$. The algorithm returns the minimum cost C_T^*. Note that $C_T^* \leq C_B$ (C_B is the cost bound) decides the feasibility of the scheduling.

The following theorem establishes the correctness of the algorithm:

Theorem (3.2): **Two_Class_Scheduling** correctly computes the minimum cost and the feasibility of *CCFJS* when there are only two classes of processors.

Proof: For given *N* jobs, let *L* be the total processing time. Given a scheduling, let L_1 be the total processing time on class 1 processors and L_2 be the total processing time on class 2 processors. Thus $L = L_1 + L_2$. Since $C_1 < C_2$, the cost $L_1 * C_1 + L_2 * C_2$ of processing all of the jobs is minimized if L_2 is minimized. From property 7 of theorem (3.1), L_2 is minimized if and only if all the jobs contributing to L_2 are on the minimum cost flow with flow value B_2. Thus, the theorem is established. ∎

For the flow network $G=(V,E)$ where all capacities are one, the running time of the best minimum cost flow algorithm is $O(|VE| + |V|^2 \log |V|)$ ([9]), which is also the running time of **Two_Class_Scheduling**.

4   Complexity for More Than Two Classes of Processors

In this section, we show that *CCFJS* is not only *NP-Complete*, but also that there is no constant ratio approximation algorithm for *CCFJS* when the number of classes of processors is more than two.

Theorem (3.3): If $P \neq NP$ and $r \geq 1(r$ is a constant$)$, then there is no polynomial time approximation algorithm with ratio bound r for *CCFJS* when the number of classes of processors is at least 3.

Proof: The proof is by contradiction. Suppose that for some $r \geq 1$, there is a polynomial time approximation algorithm A for *CCFJS* with ratio bound r, i.e. $C_A / C_T^* \leq r$ where C_A is the cost returned by the algorithm A and C_T^* is the optimal solution. We will show how to use A to solve instances of *Numerical 3-Dimensional Matching* (*N3DM*) in polynomial time. Since *N3DM* problem is *NP-Complete* [10], our theorem follows. Recall the definition of *N3DM* [10]:

INSTANCE of N3DM: Integers t, d and a_i, b_i, c_i for $i = 1, 2, ...t$, satisfying the following relations: $\sum_{i=1}^{t} (a_i + b_i + c_i) = td$ and $0 < a_i, b_i, c_i < d$ for $i = 1, 2, ...t$.

QUESTION: Are there permutations ρ and σ of $\{1, 2, ..., t\}$, such that: $a_i + b_{\rho(i)} + c_{\sigma(i)} = d$ $(i = 1, ..., t)$?

Consider a particular instance of *N3DM*. We construct an instance of *CCFJS* instance (inspired in part from [7]) as follows. Define

$$U = 49dt^4 r^2 \tag{3.4}$$

$$V = U - 7dt^2 r = 49dt^4 r^2 - 7dt^2 r \tag{3.5}$$

$$W = U + 7dt^2 r + 3d = 49dt^4 r^2 + 7dt^2 r + 3d \tag{3.6}$$

$$Z = W + U + d = 98dt^4 r^2 + 7dt^2 r + 4d \tag{3.7}$$

Define $K=3$, $C_1 = \left(14dt^3 + 14dt^2 - 5dt/r + 5d/r\right)/Z$, $C_2 = 1/r$ and $C_3 = 7t^2$. It can be easily verified that $0 < C_1 < C_2 < C_3$. Define $C_B = 49dt^4$, $B_1 = t$, $B_2 = t^2 - t$ and $B_3 = t^2$. In this instance of *CCJFS*, the total number of processors is $B = B_1 + B_2 + B_3 = 2t^2$. Next, we choose $t^2 + 2t$ distinct rational numbers (see figure 3) E_i, F_j and $X_{i,j}$ with $i, j = 1, 2, ..., t$ such that:

$$U < F_j < U + d < E_i < U + 2d < X_{i,j} < U + 3d \tag{3.8}$$

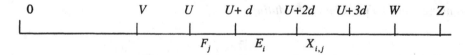

Fig. 3. Job instance construction relationship

Then, we define $N = 6t^2 + t$ jobs. We will identify these jobs by their start time and finish time pairs, rather then by separate names. In that context, these jobs are as follows:

$[0, E_i)$ $(i = 1, 2, ..., t)$ $\qquad\qquad$ $[E_i, X_{i,j})$ $(i, j = 1, 2, ..., t)$

$(t-1)$ times $[V, F_j)$ $(j = 1, 2, ..., t)$ $\qquad$ $[F_j, X_{i,j})$ $(i, j = 1, 2, ..., t)$

$[X_{i,j}, W + a_i + b_j)$ $(i, j = 1, 2, ..., t)$ $\qquad$ $[W + d - c_k, Z)$ $(k = 1, 2, ..., t)$

$(t-1)$ times $[U, E_i)$ $(i = 1, 2, ..., t)$ $\qquad\qquad$ $[U, F_j)$ $(j = 1, 2, ..., t)$

$[X_{i,j}, U + 3d)$ $(i, j = 1, 2, ...t)$

This completes the construction of the instance of *CCFJS*. Clearly, this construction requires polynomial time, and it is easy to verify that the instance satisfies (2.1). Assume algorithm *A* is applied to the above instance of *CCFJS*. We show that $C_A \leq r * C_B$ if and only if the instance of *N3DM* has a solution, thus algorithm *A* can solve the instance of *N3DM* in polynomial time.

To show that the instance of *N3DM* has a solution when $C_A \leq r * C_B$, we prove the following lemmas:

Lemma (3.9): Jobs $[0, E_i)$ $(i = 1, 2, ..., t)$ can only be assigned to class 1 processors.

Proof: Suppose a job $[0, E_i)$ is assigned to a non class 1 processor. Thus the unit time processing cost for this job is at least $1/r$. From (3.8) and (3.4), the processing time of this job is $E_i > U + d > U = 49dt^4r^2$. Thus $C_A > 49dt^4r = r * C_B$, a contradiction. ∎

Lemma (3.10): Jobs $(t-1)$ times $[V, F_j)$ $(j = 1, 2, ..., t)$ can only be assigned to class 2 processors.

Proof: Jobs $(t-1)$ times $[V, F_j)$ $(j = 1, 2, ..., t)$ can't be assigned to class 1 processors due to lemma (3.9). The rest of proof is similar to the proofs of lemma (3.9). ∎

Lemma (3.11): Jobs $(t-1)$ times $[U, E_i)$ $(i = 1, 2, ..., t)$ and $[U, F_j)$ for $j = 1, 2, ..., t$ can only be assigned to class 3 processors.

Proof: Immediate result of lemmas (3.9) and (3.10). ∎

Lemmas (3.12): Jobs $[W + d - c_k, Z)$ $(k = 1, 2, ..., t)$ can only be assigned to class 1 processors.

Proof: Similar to the proofs of lemma (3.9). ∎

Lemma (3.13): Jobs $[X_{i,j}, W + a_i + b_j)$ $(i, j = 1, 2, ..., t)$ can't be assigned to class 3 processors, and there is no idle time for each of the class 1 and class 2 processors during $[U + 3d, W)$.

Proof: Similar to the proofs of lemma (3.9). ∎

Lemma (3.14): Jobs $[X_{i,j}, U + 3d)$ for $i, j = 1, 2, ...t$ can only be assigned to class 3 processors.

Proof: Immediate result of lemma (3.13) ∎

Lemma (3.15): There is no idle time for each of the $2t^2$ processors during time $[U, U + 3d)$.

Proof: Obvious from the definition of the jobs.   ∎

After proving the above lemmas, now we show that there is no idle time for each of the class 1 processors during time interval $[W, W + d]$ and the instance of *N3DM* has a solution. From lemmas (3.9), (3.12), (3.13) and (3.15), it follows that jobs $[0, E_i)$, $[E_i, X_{i,j})$, $[X_{i,j}, W + a_i + b_j)$ and $[W + d - c_k, Z)$ $(i, k = 1, 2, ..., t)$ must be assigned to class 1 processors. Each i and k occur exactly once. From lemmas (3.10), (3.13) and (3.15), it follows that jobs $(t-1)$ times $[V, F_j)$, $[F_j, X_{i,j})$, $[X_{i,j}, W + a_i + b_j)$ must be assigned to class 2 processors, where each j $(j = 1, 2, ..., t)$ occurs exactly $(t-1)$ times. Thus from lemma (3.13), for the jobs $[X_{i,j}, W + a_i + b_j)$ assigned to class 1 processors, each j $(j = 1, 2, ..., t)$ occurs exactly once. From lemmas (3.11), (3.14) and (3.15), it follows that jobs $(t-1)$ times $[U, E_i)$, $[E_i, X_{i,j})$ and $[X_{i,j}, U + 3d)$ must be assigned to class 3 processors, where each i $(i = 1, 2, ..., t)$ occurs $(t-1)$ times, and that jobs $[U, F_j)$ and $[F_j, X_{i,j})$ $(j = 1, 2, ..., t)$ must be assigned to class 3 processors. Finally, from the fact that $\sum_{i=1}^{t} (a_i + b_i + c_i) = td$ and the conclusions that each i, j and k occurs exactly once for jobs $[X_{i,j}, W + a_i + b_j)$ and $[W + d - c_k, Z)$ assigned to class 1 processors, it follows that there is no idle time for each of the class 1 processors during time interval $[W, W + d]$. Thus $W + a_i + b_j = W + d - c_k$. If we define $\rho(i) = j$ and $\sigma(i) = k$, then $a_i + b_{\rho(i)} + c_{\sigma(i)} = d$ for $i = 1, 2, ..., t$ and the instance of *N3DM* has a solution.

Now suppose the instance of *N3DM* has a solution, the jobs assignment can follow the above proof (see figure 4). The total processing cost

$$C_A = tZ * \left(14dt^3 + 14dt^2 - 5dt / r + 5d / r\right) / Z + (t^2 - t) * (W + 2d - V) / r + t^2 * 3d * 7t^2$$

$$= 49dt^4 = C_B \le r * C_B$$

Thus algorithm A can solve *N3DM* in polynomial time, which contradicts the assumption that $P \ne NP$.   ∎

From theorem (3.3), we can easily prove the following corollary by letting $r=1$ and $C_A = C_T$:

Corollary (3.16) *CCFJS* is *NP-Complete*.

Class 1 processors: $B_1 = t$, $C_1 = (14dt^3 + 14dt^2 - 5dt/r + 5d/r)/Z$

0	E_1	X_{11}	$W + a_1 + b_1$	$W + d - c_3$	Z
0	E_2	X_{23}	$W + a_2 + b_3$	$W + d - c_1$	Z
0	E_3	X_{32}	$W + a_3 + b_2$	$W + d - c_2$	Z

Class 2 processors: $B_2 = t^2 - t$, $C_2 = 1/r$

0	V	F_1	X_{21}	$W + a_2 + b_1$		Z
0	V	F_1	X_{31}	$W + a_3 + b_1$		Z
0	V	F_2	X_{12}	$W + a_1 + b_2$		Z
0	V	F_2	X_{22}	$W + a_2 + b_2$		Z
0	V	F_3	X_{13}	$W + a_1 + b_3$		Z
0	V	F_3	X_{33}	$W + a_3 + b_3$		Z

Class 3 processors: $B_3 = t^2$, $C_3 = 7t^2$

0	U	E_1	X_{12}	$U + 3d$	Z
0	U	E_1	X_{13}	$U + 3d$	Z
0	U	E_2	X_{21}	$U + 3d$	Z
0	U	E_2	X_{22}	$U + 3d$	Z
0	U	E_3	X_{31}	$U + 3d$	Z
0	U	E_3	X_{33}	$U + 3d$	Z
0	U	F_1	X_{11}	$U + 3d$	Z
0	U	F_2	X_{32}	$U + 3d$	Z
0	U	F_3	X_{23}	$U + 3d$	Z

Fig. 4. An *CCFJS* Instance when $t=3$

5   An Approximation Algorithm

In this section, we present an approximation algorithm based on network flows, derive its worst-case performance ratio (non constant), and show that it has a constant approximation ratio in some special cases.

5.1   The Algorithm *Approximate_Cost*

Recall in section 3 for the two classes of processors case, the minimum cost flow is computed with flow value equal to the number of processors of the most expensive class of processors. The jobs that are on the minimum cost flow are assigned to the processors of the expensive class, and the remaining jobs are assigned to the processors of the cheap class. Adapting this method to three or more classes of processors, in the algorithm *Approximate_Cost*, we consider partitioning the classes of processors into an expensive set and a cheap set. We then compute the minimum cost flow with flow value equal to the sum of the number of processorss of the expensive set of processors. Each job that is on that minimum cost flow will be assigned to one of the processors in the expensive set, and each job that is not on that minimum cost flow will be assigned to one of the processors in the cheap set. In order to assign each job in the two sets to a particular class of processor, we use a greedy approach: specifically, we compute the minimum cost flow with flow value equal to the number of processors of the most expensive class and assign the jobs that are on that minimum cost flow to processors of that most expensive class. We then remove those jobs and the processors of that class and iterate until every job is assigned to a processor of a particular class. Since we don't know in advance how to partition the processors into an expensive set and a cheap set, we perform the above computation for each possible partition (for K classes of processors, there are K-1 partitions), and retain the partition and the associated assignment of jobs to the processors that yield the smallest cost.

5.2 Algorithm Complexity and Performance Ratio

Similarly to section 3.2, the running time of *Approximate_Cost* is

$$O(K^2 \mid VE \mid + K^2 \mid V \mid^2 \log \mid V \mid).$$

Note that we are not partitioning the expensive set and the cheap set recursively (instead, we use the greedy approach described above). Recursive partitioning will lead to exponential complexity in terms of K. Before we analyze the performance ratio of the algorithm, we first provide the following theorem and corollary (recall that we assume $0 < C_1 < C_2 < ... < C_K$):

Theorem (3.17) In *Approximate_Cost*, for $i = 1,...,K$, let X_i be the total processing time assigned to class i processors, let y_i be the minimum total processing time assigned to a single class i processor, and let Y_i be the maximum total processing time assigned to a single class i processor. Then

$$Y_1 \geq X_1 / B_1 \geq y_1 \geq Y_2 \geq X_2 / B_2 \geq y_2 ... \geq Y_K \geq X_K / B_K \geq y_K \qquad (3.18)$$

Corollary (3.19) Let $X = \sum_{i=1}^{K} X_i$ be the total processing time, and *approx_cost* be

the cost returned. Then $approx\_cost = \sum_{i=1}^{K} C_i X_i \leq x \sum_{i=1}^{K} C_i B_i / \sum_{i=1}^{K} B_i \qquad (3.20)$

In *Approximate_Cost*, a minimum cost network flow algorithm is applied between each pair $(i, i+1)(i < K)$ classes of processors, such that the flow value includes B_{i+1} without B_i. Thus theorem (3.17) can be proved by using minimum cost network flow property. Corollary (3.19) can be proved by showing that when

$$X_1 / B_1 = X_2 / B_2 = \ldots = X_K / B_K,$$

approx_cost reaches its upper bound $x \sum_{i=1}^{K} C_i B_i / \sum_{i=1}^{K} B_i$.

Consider a particular partition in **Approximate_Cost** where the cheap set includes processors from class 1 to class j ($j=1\ldots K-1$) and the expensive set includes processors from class $j+1$ to K. After the minimum cost flow is computed, let $X_{1..j}$ be the total processing times and c_{j_1} be the cost of jobs that are assigned to the cheap set, and let $X_{j+1..K}$ be the total processing times and c_{j_2} be the cost of jobs that are assigned to the expensive set. Let c_j be the final cost as calculated in that partition. Analogous to corollary (3.19), we have:

$$c_{j\_1} \le X_{1..j} \sum_{i=1}^{j} C_i B_i / \sum_{i=1}^{j} B_i, \quad c_{j\_2} \le X_{j+1..K} \sum_{i=j+1}^{K} C_i B_i / \sum_{i=j+1}^{K} B_i,$$

$$c_j = c_{j\_1} + c_{j\_2} \le X_{1..j} \sum_{i=1}^{j} C_i B_i / \sum_{i=1}^{j} B_i + X_{j+1..K} \sum_{i=j+1}^{K} C_i B_i / \sum_{i=j+1}^{K} B_i \tag{3.21}$$

Let c_{opt} be the optimal processing cost. Since $0 < C_1 < \ldots < C_K$, the optimal value c_{opt} will not decrease if $C_2, \ldots C_j$ decreases to C_1 and $C_{j+2}, \ldots C_K$ decrease to C_{j+1}. Thus,

$$c_{opt} \ge X_{1..j} C_1 + X_{j+1..K} C_{j+1} \tag{3.22}$$

$$\frac{c_j}{c_{opt}} \le \frac{X_{1..j} \dfrac{\sum_{i=1}^{j} C_i B_i}{\sum_{i=1}^{j} B_i} + X_{j+1..K} \dfrac{\sum_{i=j+1}^{K} C_i B_i}{\sum_{i=j+1}^{K} B_i}}{X_{1..j} C_1 + X_{j+1..K} C_{j+1}} \le \max \left(\frac{\sum_{i=1}^{j} C_i B_i}{C_1 \sum_{i=1}^{j} B_i}, \frac{\sum_{i=j+1}^{K} C_i B_i}{C_{j+1} \sum_{i=j+1}^{K} B_i} \right) \tag{3.23}$$

Since the algorithm returns the smallest cost for each j,

$$\rho = \min\{c_j \mid j = 1, 2, \ldots, K-1\} / c_{opt} \tag{3.24}$$

Finally from (3.23) and (3.24),

$$\rho \le \min \left(\max \left(\frac{\sum_{i=1}^{j} C_i B_i}{C_1 \sum_{i=1}^{j} B_i}, \frac{\sum_{i=j+1}^{K} C_i B_i}{C_{j+1} \sum_{i=j+1}^{K} B_i} \right), j = 1, 2, \ldots, K-1 \right) \tag{3.25}$$

Example $K = 3, C_1 = 3, B_1 = 100, C_2 = 6, B_2 = 50, C_3 = 12, B_3 = 25$.

By applying (3.25), we have $\rho \le 4/3$. In practical situations (for example in the off-line multimedia gateway call routing), the more expensive the processors, the less the number of processors. In this example, $C_1 B_1 = C_2 B_2 = C_3 B_3$. In general, if $K>2$ is a constant and $C_1 B_1 = C_2 B_2 = ... = C_K B_K$, then from (3.25), $\rho \le K/2$, i.e. ρ is bounded by a constant.

Example $K = 4, C_1 = 1, B_1 = 100, C_2 = 2, B_2 = 100, C_3 = 4, B_3 = 100, C_4 = 8, B_4 = 100$

By applying (3.25), we have $\rho \le 3/2$. In this example, $B_1 = B_2 = B_3 = B_4$, $C_{i+1} / C_i = 2$ $(i = 1, 2, 3)$. In general, if $K>2$ is a constant, $B_1 = B_2 = ... = B_K$, and

$C_{i+1} / C_i = q$ $(i = 1, ..., K-1)$ is a constant, then from (3.25), $\rho \le 2 \sum_{j=0}^{K/2-1} q^j / K$, i.e. ρ

is also bounded by a constant.

6 Summary

In this paper, we have studied the problem of *CCFJS* and we present a complete classification of its computational complexity. We show that *CCFJS* is polynomial solvable when there are only two classes of processors. We prove that the general *CCFJS* is *NP-Complete* and that there is no constant ratio approximation algorithm. We further present an approximation algorithm and analyze its worse case performance ratio.

References

1. Matteo Fischetti, Silvano Martello, Paolo Toth, *The Fixed Job Schedule Problem with Spread-Time Constraints,* Operations Research. 35(6), 849-858, 1987.
2. Matteo Fischetti, Silvano Martello, Paolo Toth, *The Fixed Job Schedule Problem with Working-Time Constraints,* Operations Research. 37(3), 395-403, 1989.
3. Antoon W.J. Kolen, Leo G. Kroon, *On the Computational Complexity of (Maximum) Class Scheduling*, European Journal of Operational Research, 54, 23-38, 1991.
4. Antoon W.J. Kolen, Leo G. Kroon, *License Class Design: Complexity and Algorithms*, European Journal of Operational Research, 63, 432-444, 1992
5. Antoon W.J. Kolen, Leo G. Kroon, *On the Computational Complexity of (Maximum) Shift Class Scheduling*, European Journal of Operational Research, 64, 138-151, 1993.
6. Antoon W.J. Kolen, Leo G. Kroon, *An Analysis of Shift Class Design Problems*, European Journal of Operational Research, 79, 417-430, 1994.
7. Leo G. Kroon, Arunabha Sen, Haiyong Deng, Asim Roy, *The optimal cost chromatic partition problem for trees and interval graphs*, Graph Theoretical Concepts in Computer Science, LNCS, vol. 1197, Springer-Verlag, New York/Berlin, 1996.
8. Klaus Jansen, *Approximation Results for the Optimal Cost Chromatic Partition Problem*, Journal of Algorithms, 34, 54-89, 2000.
9. Ravindra K.Ahuja, Thomas L.Magnanti, James B.Orlin, *Network Flows.* Prentice Hall, 1993
10. Michael R.Garey, David S.Johnson, *Computer and Intractability, A Guide to the Theory of NP-Completeness.* Twenty-second printing, 2000.

A Work-Optimal Coarse-Grained PRAM Algorithm for Lexicographically First Maximal Independent Set[*]

Jens Gustedt[1] and Jan Arne Telle[2]

[1] LORIA & INRIA Lorraine, France
Jens.Gustedt@loria.fr
[2] University of Bergen, Bergen, Norway
telle@ii.uib.no

Abstract. The *Lexicographically First Maximal Independent Set Problem* on graphs with bounded degree 3 is at most $\sqrt{n}$-complete, and thus very likely not parallelizable in a fine-grained setting. On the other hand, we show that in a coarse-grained setting (few processors and a lot of data) the situation is different, by giving a work-optimal algorithm on a shared memory machine for n and p such that $p \cdot \log p \in O(\log n)$.

1 Motivation and Background

It is commonly believed that not all problems are parallelizable, but what parallelizable means in practice and what theoretical models are able to capture differs somewhat. If $T^*(n)$ is the best sequential runtime on an input of size n, then with p processors the best parallel runtime we can hope for is $\Theta(T^*(n)/p)$, yielding a work-optimal algorithm. Most actual parallel computers are *coarse-grained*, having p orders of magnitude smaller than n for practical problems. However, the well-known parallel complexity class NC requires a parallel runtime polylogarithmic in n, implying $p = \Omega(T^*(n)/polylog(n))$, and this we call *fine-grained*. Showing that a problem is P-complete, meaning that it is not in NC unless P=NC, is therefore an argument for non-parallelizability only on a fine-grained computer, and may not have practical implications.

To remedy this situation Kruskal et al[10] studied parallel complexity classes EP, AP and SP that require only parallel runtime $O(T^*(n)^{1-\epsilon})$ for some $\epsilon > 0$. EP implies work-optimality, whereas AP (and SP) allows a factor polylogarithmic (and polynomial) in n away from work-optimality. Vitter et al showed that some P-complete problems indeed are parallelizable in this sense [14]. Condon[2] extended this work also with non-parallelizability results by showing, roughly, problems that could not have $O(\sqrt{n}^{1-\epsilon})$ parallel runtime unless all problems in P had a similar parallel speedup over its best sequential runtime. She showed this for the Lexicographically First Maximal Independent Set (LFMIS) problem, among others.

In the current paper, we look for a positive parallel result for the LFMIS problem, for which Condon gave only the negative result. The requirement that a lexicographic

---

[*] Research partially supported by the "Pôle rgional lorrain *Intelligence Logicielle*" and a visiting grant by *Région Lorraine* for Jan Arne Telle.

ordering of vertices must be respected gives the problem an inherently sequential flavor. Hardly any results are known on parallel algorithms for LFMIS, whereas efficient parallel solutions exist if the ordering requirements are dropped, see e.g Ferreira and Schabanel [5] and Gebremedhin et al. [6]. Uehara [12] gave an NC algorithm for LFMIS restricted to graphs with a $polylog(n)$ bound on the length of the longest path respecting the lexicographic order given in the input.

We instead focus on a variant of LFMIS that is known to remain P-complete [11], that we call LFMIS3, where input graphs have bounded degree 3. We first extend Condon's result on the hardness of LFMIS to LFMIS3. Then, our main result is stated as follows:

Theorem 1. *There is a parallel algorithm for LFMIS3 that is work-optimal for all n and p such that $p \cdot \log p \in O(\log n)$.*

The paper is organized as follows. In the following section, we will introduce the models of parallel computation that will be used throughout the paper. We also provide a brief discussion about the complexity issues involved. Then Section 3 will introduce the problem and our main technique to handle it which we call *block graph*. The parallel algorithm itself is described in Section 3, followed by two sections that discuss the two different phases of preprocessing that this parallel algorithm needs. The main part of the paper being presented for a PRAM, in Section 7 we find it convenient to outline how the assumption of using a shared random access memory might be relaxed. This is done by specifying a concrete communication pattern between different processors.

2   Parallel Machine Models and Performance Measures

Although our research was guided by the more practical and realistic coarse grained machine models for parallel computation, see [13, 3, 4, 7], we will for this paper use simply the PRAM while taking the granularity restriction into account. This is done to make the approach as transparent as possible and not get lost behind certain (practically motivated) constraints of the coarse-grained models. At the end of this paper we will indicate how our results can be extended to a distributed coarse-grained setting.

We use a convenient modification of the classical CREW-PRAM[1], see [9] for an overview. The algorithm that we give will use bit-parallelism so we have to be more precise about the "RAM" part of the machine description. We will assume that each processor is a word-RAM with word size w and that it supports all conventional operations (*e.g* memory access, addition, subtraction, bitwise and and or) on machine words *in constant time.*

The choice of a word-RAM as a base for the machine model is in contrast to some of the complexity theoretic work cited above, e.g [2]. The difference in the performance measures as presented hereafter when using a more restricted RAM (so mainly considering *bit complexity*) would be a w-factor on time and cost. To allow for a fair comparison, that factor would have to be taken into account for both sequential and parallel algorithms. So, as long as we handle such a factor consistently when measuring

---

[1] Concurrent Read Exclusive Write - Parallel Random Access Machine

the speed up of a parallel algorithm over a sequential one this effect would cancel out. Thus we may choose this variant of the PRAM for convenience.

We will assume that the word-size of our machine is at least logarithmic in the input size (here the number of vertices of a graph G) since otherwise our input could not be randomly addressed in its entirety, *i.e.*

$$\log n \leq w. \tag{1}$$

The main performance measures of a PRAM algorithm $\mathcal{A}$ are its parallel *running time* $T_{\mathcal{A}}(n)$ and its *overall work* or *cost* $C_{\mathcal{A}}(n) = T_{\mathcal{A}}(n)p_{\mathcal{A}}(n)$, where $p_{\mathcal{A}}(n)$ denotes the number of processors used by $\mathcal{A}$. Unless such PRAM algorithms are *work-optimal*, i.e. $C_{\mathcal{A}}(n) = O(T_{\mathcal{A}^*}(n))$, they will show poor performance when scaled down, using Brent's principle, see [1], to fewer processors.

An inconvenience of requiring work-optimality is the fact that the definition depends on $\mathcal{A}^*$, an optimal sequential algorithm that for a specific problem may not be known. But for this paper we luckily avoid this since the problem we will consider has a linear-time sequential algorithm. So for work-optimality it will be sufficient to prove a linear upper bound on $C_{\mathcal{A}}(n)$.

When we want algorithms that are scalable for a range of processors their running time $T_{\mathcal{A}}(p, n)$ and cost $C_{\mathcal{A}}(p, n)$ become also functions of p, the number of processors. In this paper we aim for an algorithm $\mathcal{A}$ that will be work-optimal for n and p such that $p \cdot \log p \in O(\log n)$. To be more precise on the quantifications there are constants $1 \geq \delta, e > 0$ and p_0 (all independent from n and p) such that for all n and p that fulfill $p \geq p_0$ and

$$p \log p \leq \delta \log n. \tag{2}$$

we have

$$C_{\mathcal{A}}(p, n) \leq e T_{\mathcal{A}^*}(n) \tag{3}$$

or equivalently

$$T_{\mathcal{A}}(p, n) \leq e \frac{T_{\mathcal{A}^*}(n)}{p}. \tag{4}$$

To ease the design and presentation of our algorithm $\mathcal{A}$ we will consider p as being determined by n, namely maximal p such that it fulfills (2). The full algorithm $\mathcal{A}'$ with input of size n and p' processors would then consist of computing the right value of p as imposed by maximizing for (2) and then simulating $\mathcal{A}$ (with n and p) via Brent's principle on p' processors. The only obstacle for the design of $\mathcal{A}'$ is the computation of p on p' processors in time $O(n/p')$ which can be done easily for what is needed here.

3 LFMIS and the Block Graph

Given a linear ordering on the vertices of a graph, the lexicographically first maximal independent set is the subset of vertices built starting from the empty set by considering vertices in the order given, and adding the considered vertex to the set if it does not have a neighbor already in the set. The problem that is treated in Theorem 1 is the following, see the book [8] for an overview.

Problem 1 (Lexicographically First Maximal Independent Set-3 (LFMIS3)).
Input: An undirected graph $G = (V, E)$ of maximum degree 3 with an ordering $v_1, \ldots, v_n$ on V such that the edges are lexicographically sorted, and a designated vertex v.
Output: Is vertex v in the lexicographically first maximal independent set?

The assumption on the ordering of the edges which is a bit more than is usually required for LFMIS has no impact on parallel complexity of the problem: because of the bounded degree of the graph it can be achieved efficiently if necessary by a linear-work algorithm: in $O(\log n)$ time on a PRAM, or in $O(n/p)$ time in a conventional coarse grained setting.

The LFMIS3 problem is P-complete even if the input graph is restricted to be planar and have maximum degree 3, see [11]. From now on we consider only graphs of maximum degree 3. We first note that the P-completeness proof given for LFMIS3 by Miyano in [11] in fact also shows that LFMIS3 is hard in the sense defined by Condon in [2].

Corollary 1. *The LFMIS3 problem is at most $\sqrt{n}$-complete for P.*

Proof. In the paper [11] LFMIS3 is shown to be P-complete by a reduction from the circuit value problem CVP, which itself was shown in the paper [2] to be at most $\sqrt{n}$-complete for P. Since the given reduction preserves the input size, i.e. the graph is linear in the circuit given as input, it follows from the results of [2] that also LFMIS3 is at most $\sqrt{n}$-complete for P.   □

This corollary means, roughly, that if anyone would give a parallel algorithm for LFMIS3 with a parallel runtime $O(n^\epsilon)$ for $\epsilon < \frac{1}{2}$ then all problems in P would have a parallel algorithm with polynomial speedup over their best sequential algorithm.

We now turn to our parallel algorithm for LFMIS3. In the following we will in fact not solve the decision problem as given by the definition, but give an algorithm that produces the corresponding independent set. We will derive our algorithm from a straightforward linear-time sequential algorithm, see Algorithm 1.

Algorithm 1 Sequential LFMIS3.

Input: A graph $G = (V, E)$ of max degree 3 with an ordering $v_1, \ldots, v_n$ on V.
Output: The lexicographically first maximal independent set S.
Data Str.: Boolean vector $\mathrm{S}[v_1 \ldots v_n]$ with $\mathrm{S}[v_i] = 0$ only if $v_i \notin S$.
begin
    for $i = 0$ **to** n **do** $\mathrm{S}[v_i] = 1$
    for $i = 0$ **to** n **do**
        for all edges $v_i v_j \in E$ with $i < j$ **do**
            if $\mathrm{S}[v_i] == 1$ **then** $\mathrm{S}[v_j] = 0$
        output $\{v : \mathrm{S}[v] == 1\}$
end;

The idea presented in this paper to obtain a parallel algorithm is to alter the conventional data structure for the input graph so that several processors will be able to handle a set of different edges concurrently. Therefore we will need to compress information concerning certain vertex and edge sets into machine words. To obtain such a "*compressed*" representation of the input graph, we partition it into vertex blocks of fixed size B, and consider the representation of intra-block and inter-block edges.

Definition 1. *Given an undirected graph $G = (V, E)$ of max degree 3 with an ordering of vertices $v_1, \ldots, v_n$ and an integer $1 \le B \le n$, we define the B-block graph of G by the following:*

vertex partition *We partition V into $\lceil n/B \rceil$ blocks $V_0, \ldots, V_{\lfloor n/B \rfloor}$ following the given vertex ordering, i.e. with $V_i = \{v_{iB+1}, \ldots, v_{iB+B}\}$ for $0 \le i \le \lfloor n/B \rfloor - 1$ and $V_{\lfloor n/B \rfloor}$ the remaining vertices. For simplicity we may assume w.l.o.g. that B divides n. A vertex $v = v_i$ of G is thus given a a block number $b_B(v) = \lfloor i/B \rfloor$ and a relative number $r_B(v) = (i \bmod B) + 1$ between 1 and B within its block.*

inter-block edges *The vertices of block V_i have neighbors in at most $3B$ other vertex blocks V_j with $i < j$. Each such pair i, j constitutes an inter-block edge $E_{i,j}$. For each of these inter-block edges we store a vector $E_{i,j}[1 \ldots 3B]$ that encodes the induced subgraph between vertices of blocks V_i and V_j. It has entries $3k - 2, 3k - 1, 3k$, for $1 \le k \le B$, containing the relative number of the 3 possible neighbors that the kth relative vertex in V_i has in V_j.*

intra-block edges *Intra-block edges inside a vertex block V_i are represented by a similar vector $V_i[1 \ldots 3B]$.*

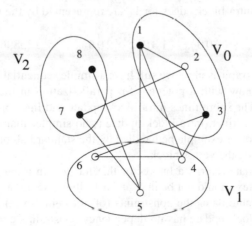

Fig. 1. The B-block of a graph with max degree 3 and vertices ordered $1 \ldots 8$ for $B = 3$, i.e. 3 vertices per block. Black vertices are in the LFMIS.

See Figure 1 for an example. A relative vertex number $r_B(v)$ requires $\lceil \log B \rceil$ bits of storage. Total storage *in bits* for the block graph is therefore at most

$$(\underbrace{(n/B)3B}_{\text{\# inter edges}} + \underbrace{n/B}_{\text{\# intra edges}}) \underbrace{3B \log B}_{\text{vector encoding}} = O(nB \log B). \tag{5}$$

So this encoding of our graph is in fact not compressed in the sense that it occupies less space than a conventional one. If we assume in addition that

$$2B \log B < \log n \tag{6}$$

by our bound for the word size (1) we obtain

$$2B \log B < w. \tag{7}$$

So the number of machine words needed for this new encoding is still linear in the number of vertices (and edges).

To discuss the example of Figure 1 we will write machine words as a vector of (small) numbers. We note such words as $\langle a\, b \ldots \rangle_\ell$ where $a, b, \ldots$ are numbers that are written with ℓ bits and that are concatenated in the machine word. E.g

$$\left\langle \langle 1\,2\,0 \rangle_2 \cdot \langle 0\,0\,0 \rangle_2 \cdot \langle 1\,3\,0 \rangle_2 \right\rangle_6 = \langle 24 \cdot 0 \cdot 28 \rangle_6$$

$$= \langle 0\,1\,1\,0\,0\,0\,0\,0\,0\,0\,0\,0\,1\,1\,1\,0\,0 \rangle_1 \tag{8}$$

which represents the decimal number 98332.

Inter-block edges between V_0 and V_1 are represented by a vector of $3B$ numbers in the range $0 \ldots B$, namely $\left\langle \langle 1\,2\,0 \rangle_2 \cdot \langle 0\,0\,0 \rangle_2 \cdot \langle 1\,3\,0 \rangle_2 \right\rangle_6$, with $\langle 1\,2\,0 \rangle_2 \approx 24$ denoting that vertex 1 is adjacent to 4 and 5 (which have relative numbers 1 and 2 in V_1), $\langle 0\,0\,0 \rangle_2 \approx 0$ denoting that vertex 2 has no adjacencies, and $\langle 1\,3\,0 \rangle_2 \approx 28$ denoting that vertex 3 is adjacent to vertices 4 and 6 (which have relative numbers 1 and 3). Likewise, intra-block edges for V_0 are represented by the vector

$$\left\langle \langle 2\,0\,0 \rangle_2 \cdot \langle 1\,3\,0 \rangle_2 \cdot \langle 2\,0\,0 \rangle_2 \right\rangle_6 \approx 132896. \tag{9}$$

Taking a B-block graph as input we still have a simple sequential linear-time algorithm for LFMIS3, but now with a potential for parallelization in the innermost **for**-loop, see Algorithm 2. The subroutines Intra-block-update and Inter-block-update in that algorithm are quite distinct. Intra-block-update is no simpler than the original LFMIS3 problem, and could for example be handled by the standard algorithm restricted to the subgraph induced by the vertex block.

Inter-block-update returns a bit-vector that has a 0 in a particular position if the corresponding vertex should not be in S and a 1 otherwise. So anding the bits of $\text{s}[V_j]$ with this value accumulates the constraints (of not being in S) imposed by different neighbors. Inter-block-update has no dependency constraints coming from the vertex ordering, as we simply have to find the vertices of block V_j that have a neighbor in $V_i \cap S$.

Algorithm 2 Sequential Block-LFMIS3.

Input: The B-block graph of some G with max degree 3, with an ordering
$V_0, \ldots, V_{n/B}$ on vertex blocks, intra-block edges $V_i[1 \ldots 3B]$ and inter-block
edges $E_{i,j}[1 \ldots 3B]$ (if non-empty) for $0 \le i < j \le n/B$.
Output: The lexicographically first maximal independent set S of G.
Data Str.: Boolean matrix $S[V_0 \ldots V_{n/B}][1 \ldots B]$
Invariant: $S[V_i][k] == 0$ only if the kth vertex of V_i (*i.e.* the vertex
number $iB + k - 1$) is known not to be in S.
begin
    for $i = 0$ **to** n/B **do** $S[V_i] = \langle 1 \cdot 1 \cdots 1 \rangle_1$
    for $i = 0$ **to** n/B **do**
        $S[V_i] = $ Intra-block-update$(V_i[1 \ldots 3B], S[V_i])$
        for all $j > i$ with $E_{i,j}[1 \ldots 3B]$ non-empty **do**
            $S[V_j] = S[V_j]$ **bit-and** Inter-block-update$(E_{i,j}[1 \ldots 3B], S[V_i])$
    output $\{v : S[b_B(v)][r_B(v)] == 1\}$
end;

---

4   The Parallel Algorithm

We now consider a CREW PRAM implementation of Algorithm 2, see Algorithm 3.
The representation of the block graph will be computed in a pre-processing step that
we discuss in Section 4. Moreover, the subroutine calls Intra-block-update and Inter-
block-update will be handled by simple table lookups, and these two tables will also be
computed in a pre-processing step discussed in Section 5. The index to the tables will
be the parameters for the subroutine calls, namely: $V_i[1 \ldots 3B]$ (where each entry has
$\log B$ bits) plus $S[V_i][1 \ldots B]$ (with boolean entries) for Intra-Block and $E_{i,j}[1 \ldots 3B]$
plus $S[V_i][1 \ldots B]$ for Inter-Block. These indices consist of $3B \log B + B$ bits which
by (7) fit into one word of our machine.

We choose the block-size equal to the number of processors, $p = B$. To ensure that
we can compute the lookup tables in $O(n/p)$ time, we must constrain the table size to
n/p, thus

$$(2p + 1) \log p \le \log n \tag{10}$$

Constraints (7) and (10) are both met with the granularity condition (2).

Thus the $Intra$ and $Inter$ tables will have about n/p entries each. Using table
lookup, the initialization of all n/p entries of the S vector and all n/p intra-block updates are done in $O(n/p)$ time by a single processor. For the inter-block edges, there are
at most $3p$ such edges out of block V_i, going to at most $3p$ distinct blocks in increasing
order $V_{i_0}, V_{i_1}, \ldots, V_{i_{3p-1}}$ and processor P_k, $0 \le k < p$ will be responsible for those
going to $V_{i_k}, V_{i_{p+k}}, V_{i_{2p+k}}$.

For the example graph in Figure 1, when handling inter-block edges from V_0, processor P_0 will first update $S[V_1]$, since $V_{i_0} = V_1$, by setting

$$S[V_1] = S[V_1] \textbf{ bit-and } Inter \left[\left\langle \langle 1\,2\,0 \rangle_2 \cdot \langle 0\,0\,0 \rangle_2 \cdot \langle 1\,3\,0 \rangle_2 \right\rangle_6, \langle 1\,0\,1 \rangle_2 \right] \tag{11}$$

Algorithm 3 Parallel LFMIS3 with processors P_i, $i = 0, \ldots p - 1$ such that $p\lceil \log p \rceil \leq \lfloor \delta \log n \rfloor$ and $B = p$.

Input: A graph $G = (V, E)$ of max degree 3 with an ordering $v_1, \ldots, v_n$ on V.
Output: The lexicographically first maximal independent set S.
Data Str.: Boolean matrix $\mathrm{S}[V_0 \ldots V_{n/B}][1 \ldots B]$ with $\mathrm{S}[V_i][k] == 0$ only if kth
  vertex of $V_i \notin S$.
Vectors for intra-block edges $V_i[1 \ldots 3p]$ and inter-block edges $E_{i,j}[1 \ldots 3p]$ (if
  non-empty) for $0 \leq i < j \leq n/p$.
Tables $Intra[1 \ldots n/p]$ and $Inter[1 \ldots n/p]$ giving instructions for
  Intra-block-update and Inter-block-update.
begin
  Compute the p-block graph of G, see Section 4.
  Compute lookup tables $Intra$ and $Inter$, see Section 5.
  for $i = 0$ **to** n/p **do** P_0: $\mathrm{S}[V_i][k] = \langle 1 \cdot 1 \cdots 1 \rangle_1$
  for $i = 0$ **to** n/p **do**
    P_0: $\mathrm{S}[V_i] = Intra[V_i[1 \ldots 3B], \mathrm{S}[V_i]]$
    foreach P_k **in-parallel do**
      for $x = 0$ **to** 2 **do**
        $\mathrm{S}[V_{i_{xp+k}}] = \mathrm{S}[V_{i_{xp+k}}]$ **bit-and** $Inter[E_{i,i_{xp+k}}[1 \ldots 3B], \mathrm{S}[V_i]]$ (*)
    foreach P_k **in-parallel do**
      for $x = 0$ **to** $n/p^2 - 1$ **do**
        for $j = 1$ **to** p **do**
          if $\mathrm{S}[V_{xp+k}][j] == 1$ **then output** $v_{(xp+k)p+j}$
end;

(since $E_{0,1} = \left\langle \langle 1\,2\,0 \rangle_2 \cdot \langle 0\,0\,0 \rangle_2 \cdot \langle 1\,3\,0 \rangle_2 \right\rangle_6$ and $\mathrm{S}[V_0] = \langle 1\,0\,1 \rangle_2$) while P_1 will update $\mathrm{S}[V_2]$ since $V_{2_0} = V_2$ (there are not enough vertex blocks in the example to see the parallel scheme in full effect). The processors will lookup the inter-block update action in parallel, thus possibly reading concurrently, and then write the new information to distinct blocks.

Apart from the pre-processing involved in computing the representation of the block graph and the tables, discussed in the next section, we see that this algorithm takes time $O(n/p)$ using p processors on a CREW PRAM.

5   Pre-processing: The p-Block Graph

We indicate how to compute the representation of the p-block graph of G using p processors on a CREW PRAM in time $O(n/p)$, see Algorithm 4. Processor $P_k, 0 \leq k \leq n/p$ will be uniquely responsible for the n/p^2 blocks with contiguous indices $kn/p^2, kn/p^2 + 1, \ldots, kn/p^2 + n/p^2 - 1$ thus avoiding any write conflicts. A single processor will go through all the at most $3p$ edges out of a block and will spend constant time per edge for total time $O(n/p)$. When processing edges out of a block V_i, say an edge $v_a v_b$ with $a < b$, the processor must first find the block number and relative

---

Algorithm 4 Compute p-block graph with processors P_i, $i = 0, \ldots p - 1$ such that $p\lceil \log p \rceil \leq \lfloor \delta \log n \rfloor$

Input: A graph $G = (V, E)$ of max degree 3 with an ordering $v_1, \ldots, v_n$ on V.
Data Str.: Vectors for intra-block edges $V_i[1 \ldots 3p]$,
and inter-block edges $E_{i,j}[1 \ldots 3p]$ (if non-empty) for $0 \leq i < j \leq n/p$.
begin
    foreach P_k **in-parallel do**
        for $i = 0$ **to** $n/p^2 - 1$ **do**
            foreach edge $e = v_a v_b$ with $a < b$ and $a \in V_{kn/p^2+i}$ **do**
                compute block number j of v_b and relative numbers of v_a and v_b
                if $j = kn/p^2 + i$, i.e. e is an intra-block edge **do**
                    update $V_{kn/p^2+i}[1 \ldots 3p]$
                else do
                    if e is the first inter-block edge $V_{kn/p^2+i}, V_j$ **do**
                        initialize $E_{kn/p^2+i,j}$ to 0-vector
                    update $E_{kn/p^2+i,j}$ in correct position by e
end;

---

number of v_a and v_b, and based on this information it can write to the appropriate word in memory. If this is the first edge between these two blocks initialize $E_{i,j}[1 \ldots 3p]$ to the 0-vector, otherwise update $E_{i,j}[1 \ldots 3p]$ in the correct bit positions using an OR-operation with the old $E_{i,j}[1 \ldots 3p]$ and an appropriate mask. Consider an example: For the graph in Figure 1 when computing the intra-block edge between V_0 and V_1 a single processor will go through the edges in order $(1, 4), (1, 5), (3, 4), (3, 6)$ and for each of these (say $(1, 5)$) the processor merely computes the low-endpoint block-number, 0, and high-endpoint block-number, 1, and low-endpoint relative number, 1, and high-endpoint relative number, 2, and this allows it to find the correct $\langle x_1 x_2 x_3 \rangle_6$ slot in the $E_{0,1}$ intra-block edge, and within this slot it first checks if x_1 is 0 (assume no) then sees if x_2 is 0 (assume yes) so it now has the appropriate mask to update $E_{0,1}[1 \ldots 3p]$ in the correct bit positions using an OR-operation with the old $E_{0,1}[1 \ldots 3p]$, thereby inserting the correct relative number, 2, at x_2.

6   Pre-processing: The Lookup Tables

Now we consider the computation of the lookup tables for block-size p, see Algorithm 5. Note that this is independent of the input graph G, except for the fact that p is chosen as a function of n such that the tables will have n/p entries. The table $Inter$ has indices of the form $E_{i,j}[1 \ldots 3p]$ (where each entry has $\log p$ bits) plus $S[V_i][1 \ldots p]$ (with boolean entries) thus consisting of $3p \log p + p$ bits total. For each boolean index of this length, we must compute the corresponding update word. The processors will each be responsible for n/p^2 entries, and can spend $O(p)$ time per entry.

For the example of Figure 1, $S[V_1]$ is updated by inter block edges from V_0 to V_1 by setting

$$S[V_1] = Inter\left[\left\langle \langle 1\,2\,0 \rangle_2 \cdot \langle 0\,0\,0 \rangle_2 \cdot \langle 1\,3\,0 \rangle_2 \right\rangle_6, \langle 1\,0\,1 \rangle_2\right] \qquad (12)$$

Algorithm 5 Compute lookup tables with processors P_i, $i = 0, \ldots p - 1$ **such that** $p\lceil \log p \rceil \leq \lfloor \delta \log n \rfloor$.

Data Str.: Tables $Intra[1 \ldots 2^{3p \log p}, 1 \ldots 2^p]$ and $Inter[1 \ldots 2^{3p \log p}, 1 \ldots 2^p]$
begin
    foreach P_k **in-parallel do**
        for $i = 0$ **to** $n/p^2 - 1$ **do** update $Intra[kn/p^2 + i]$ and $Inter[kn/p^2 + i]$
end;

(since $E_{0,1} = \left\langle \langle 1\,2\,0 \rangle_2 \cdot \langle 0\,0\,0 \rangle_2 \cdot \langle 1\,3\,0 \rangle_2 \right\rangle_6$ and $\mathrm{S}[V_0] = \langle 1\,0\,1 \rangle_2$). This data forces all vertices of V_1 to be not in S, thus the lookup table must be set

$$Inter\left[\left\langle \langle 1\,2\,0 \rangle_2 \cdot \langle 0\,0\,0 \rangle_2 \cdot \langle 1\,3\,0 \rangle_2 \right\rangle_6 , \langle 1\,0\,1 \rangle_2 \right] = \langle 0\,0\,0 \rangle_2. \tag{13}$$

As mentioned earlier the crucial point is to find the vertices of block V_j that have a neighbor in $V_i \cap S$. In the index $\left\langle \langle 1\,2\,0 \rangle_2 \cdot \langle 0\,0\,0 \rangle_2 \cdot \langle 1\,3\,0 \rangle_2 \right\rangle_6 , \langle 1\,0\,1 \rangle_2$ the second component $\langle 1\,0\,1 \rangle_2$ tells us that only the first and third parts of the first component, *i.e.* $\langle 1\,2\,0 \rangle_2$ and $\langle 1\,3\,0 \rangle_2$ are of interest. From these we must union all numbers mentioned, and those bit positions in the output word should be set to 0. All this can be done, for each index, by $O(p)$ word operations.

For the intra-block table $Intra$ the procedure is slightly more complicated, as the vertex ordering is important. Thus, for the graph in the example, the update operation

$$\mathrm{S}[V_0] = Intra\left[\left\langle \langle 2\,0\,0 \rangle_2 \cdot \langle 1\,3\,0 \rangle_2 \cdot \langle 2\,0\,0 \rangle_2 \right\rangle_6 , \langle 1\,1\,1 \rangle_2 \right] \tag{14}$$

accounts for edges inside block V_0. This data forces the second vertex of V_0 to be not in S, thus the lookup table must be set

$$Intra\left[\left\langle \langle 2\,0\,0 \rangle_2 \cdot \langle 1\,3\,0 \rangle_2 \cdot \langle 2\,0\,0 \rangle_2 \right\rangle_6 , \langle 1\,1\,1 \rangle_2 \right] = \langle 1\,0\,1 \rangle_2. \tag{15}$$

Here we need a sequential traversal through the p parts of the first and second index components simultaneously. Again, this can be done using $O(p)$ word operations.

7 Organizing the Communication

The force of the recent coarse grained parallel models (*e.g* BSP [13], CGM [4] and PRO [7]) is that they are able to account for communication more realistically than the PRAM. They assume that each processor has its private share of memory and that all information needed by more than one processor has to be communicated explicitly between the processors via messages. When doing so, they account for the sending *and* receiving of message. So to be efficient, in general an algorithm has to ensure that at any moment every processor sends out and also receives about the same amount of data. Otherwise the running time on the different processors would desequilibrate.

To fit into such a setting we have to replace the random access to memory by communication between processors. Therefore we have to design a communication pattern that is able to fulfill these constraints of sending and receiving the same amount of data at any processor and time. In fact, for most of what was described above this is easy to do: *e.g* in Algorithm 4 the processors mainly do all computation by their own. They only have to communicate the tables that they computed at the very end.

The memory access that is difficult to handle is the line (*) in Algorithm 3. We will assume that each processor P_k will assemble the values $\mathsf{S}[V_i]$ for all k such that $i = j \cdot p + k$ for some j.

The algorithm performs in steps where each processor P_k performs the following:

1. Receive a previously computed value $\mathsf{S}[V_{i'}]$ for some i' from P_{k-1}.
2. Perform the line (*) for at most three block-edges, namely such that the source block-vertex of the edge is before $V_{i''}$ and the target block-vertex is V_i.
3. Send a value $\mathsf{S}[V_{i''}]$ for some i'' to processor P_{k+1}.

Some tedious choice of the indices i', i'' and for the block-edges and some computation shows that the number of steps can be bounded to $O(n/p)$. We postpone the detailed arguments and proofs to the journal version of this paper.

8   Conclusion

We have shown that the behavior of a problem that is notoriously hard in a fine grained PRAM setting may be solved *work-optimally* compared to a sequential algorithm, if the number of processors p is restricted to some (slowly) growing function in n. This result is first of all a theoretical, we would not expect it to be efficiently implemented in a realistic setting. Nevertheless, it proves the potential of such a setting and shows that the complexity of problems can be quite different in fine grained and coarse grained settings.

Perhaps more subproblems or algorithms known from sequential algorithmics could in principle be used for the design of parallel (coarse grained) algorithms than what is commonly thought. A prominent example would be the computation of a DFS-tree in a coarse grained setting.

For each problem $\mathcal{P}$ it might also be interesting to look at the borderline for what function of p in n such work-optimal parallel algorithms exist, see *e.g* [7] for such an approach.

References

1. BRENT, R. P. The parallel evaluation of generic arithmetic expressions. *Journal of the ACM 21*, 2 (1974), 201–206.
2. CONDON, A. A theory of strict P-completeness. *Computational Complexity 4* (1994), 220–241.

3. CULLER, D., KARP, R., PATTERSON, D., SAHAY, A., SCHAUSER, K., SANTOS, E., SUB-RAMONIAN, R., AND VON EICKEN, T. LogP: Towards a Realistic Model of Parallel Computation. In *Proceeding of 4-th ACM SIGPLAN Symp. on Principles and Practises of Parallel Programming* (1993), pp. 1–12.

4. DEHNE, F., FABRI, A., AND RAU-CHAPLIN, A. Scalable parallel computational geometry for coarse grained multicomputers. *International Journal on Computational Geometry 6*, 3 (1996), 379–400.

5. FERREIRA, A., AND SCHABANEL, N. A randomized BSP/CGM algorithm for the maximal independent set. *Parallel Processing Letters 9*, 3 (2000), 411–422.

6. GEBREMEDHIN, A. H., GUÉRIN LASSOUS, I., GUSTEDT, J., AND TELLE, J. A. Graph coloring on a coarse grained multiprocessor. In *WG 2000* (2000), U. Brandes and D. Wagner, Eds., vol. 1928 of *LNCS*, Springer-Verlag, pp. 184–195.

7. GEBREMEDHIN, A. H., GUÉRIN LASSOUS, I., GUSTEDT, J., AND TELLE, J. A. PRO: a model for parallel resource-optimal computation. In *16th Annual International Symposium on High Performance Computing Systems and Applications* (2002), IEEE, The Institute of Electrical and Electronics Engineers, pp. 106–113.

8. GREENLAW, R., HOOVER, J., AND RUZZO, W. *Limits to parallel computation: P-completeness theory*. Oxford University Press, 1995.

9. KARP, R. M., AND RAMACHANDRAN, V. Parallel Algorithms for Shared-Memory Machines. In *Handbook of Theoretical Computer Science* (1990), J. van Leeuwen, Ed., vol. A, Algorithms and Complexity, Elsevier Science Publishers B.V., Amsterdam, pp. 869–941.

10. KRUSKAL, C. P., RUDOLPH, L., AND SNIR, M. A complexity theory of efficient parallel algorithms. *Theoretical Computer Science 71*, 1 (march 1990), 95–132.

11. MIYANO, S. The lexicographically first maximal subgraph problems: P-completeness and NC-algorithms. *Mathematical Systems Theory 22*, 1 (1989), 47–73.

12. UEHARA, R. A measure for the lexicographically first maximal independent set problem and its limits. *International Journal of Foundations of Computer Science 10*, 4 (1999), 473–482.

13. VALIANT, L. G. A bridging model for parallel computation. *Communications of the ACM 33*, 8 (1990), 103–111.

14. VITTER, J. S., AND SIMONS, R. A. New classes for parallel comlexity. *IEEE Trans. Comput. 35* (1986), 403–418.

An Approximation Algorithm
for the Minimum Weight Vertex-Connectivity
Problem in Complete Graphs
with Sharpened Triangle Inequality*

Alessandro Ferrante and Mimmo Parente

Dipartimento di Informatica ed Applicazioni
Università degli Studi di Salerno
Baronissi, Italia
{ferrante,parente}@dia.unisa.it

Abstract. Consider a complete graph G with the edge weights satisfying the β-sharpened triangle inequality: $weight(u,v) \leq \beta(weight(u,x) + weight(x,v))$, for $1/2 \leq \beta < 1$. We study the NP-hard problem of finding a minimum weight spanning subgraph of G which is k-vertex-connected, $k \geq 2$, and give a detailed analysis of an approximation quadratic-time algorithm whose performance ratio is $\frac{\beta}{1-\beta}$.
The algorithm is derived from the one presented by Böckenhauer et al. in [3] for the k-edge connectivity problem on graphs satisfying the β-sharpened triangle inequality.

1 Introduction

Graph connectivity problems are of fundamental importance in network design and fault-tolerance problems hence many efforts have always been devoted towards a better comprehension of their various aspects. A graph is k-vertex connected if the deletion of up to $k-1$ vertices leaves the graph still connected (the deletion of the vertices can be seen as occurrences of arbitrary failures). Given a k-vertex connected weighted graph G, the *k-vertex connectivity problem* is the problem of finding a minimum-weight spanning subgraph of G which is still k-vertex connected. Similar definitions can be given for the *edge* connectivity by substituting edges for vertices in the definitions. In what follows when we speak generally of connectivity without specifying edges or vertices, we refer to both the problems. The connectivity problem, for $k > 1$, is well known to be NP-hard [8], thus it is natural to study its particular instances: for small values of k, efficient ad-hoc approximation algorithms with very small performance ratio have been proposed see e.g. [1,10]; for $k = 2$ in [6,7] its APX-hardness has been proved (even in the case of bounded degree and identical weights).

---

* Work partially supported by funds for the research from MIUR, grant ex-60% 2002 Università di Salerno.

C. Blundo and C. Laneve (Eds.): ICTCS 2003, LNCS 2841, pp. 137–149, 2003.

Recently in a series of papers [5,4,2,3] it has been proposed to study the connectivity problem when the graph G is *complete* and the weights of the edges satisfy the *β-sharpened triangle inequality*: $w(u,v) \leq \beta(w(u,x)+w(x,v))$, $1/2 \leq \beta < 1$. The motivation for the study of this particular case of edge weights is well described in those papers, here let us simply recall that in this way one can characterize and hence classify hard instances of the problem using the achievable performance ratio of an approximation algorithm as parameter. Moreover the existing PTAS for the Euclidean Travelling Salesman Problem (TSP) are rather impractical due to their worst case running time, thus often one uses Christofides algorithm for the metric TSP, getting an approximation ratio of $3/2$. Hence it is desirable to characterize significative subclasses of the problem which have a better performance ratio.

In [2] the 2-connectivity problem is considered (both for edges and vertices) and the authors prove its APX-hardness even if the edge weights belong to an interval $[1, 1 + \epsilon]$, for an arbitrary small ϵ. In [2] a $(2/3 + 1/3\beta/(1 - \beta))$-approximation algorithm for both the edge and vertex connectivity problems, when $k = 2$, is given. In [3] a $\beta/(1 - \beta)$-approximation algorithm is given only for the edge-connectivity, anyway the result holds for all $k > 1$.

In this paper we provide an approximation algorithm with the same performance ratio of $\beta/(1-\beta)$ for the case of *k-vertex-connectivity problem*, $k > 1$. The algorithm we show is derived from the one given in [3], anyway here we present a detailed and non trivial analysis of the graph in order to show its k-vertex connectivity. To this aim let us recall that an equivalent definition of k-vertex connectivity is that in such graphs for each pair of vertices i and j there exist k internal-vertex disjoint paths, that is paths that have only the end-point vertices i and j in common.

In [5,4,3] a lemma relating the weights of two edges incident to the same vertex in a complete graph, where the β-sharpened triangle inequality holds, was given. The lemma states that these two weights cannot differ too much, in particular for all adjacent edges e_1, e_2 the inequality $w(e_1)/w(e_2) \leq \beta/(1 - \beta)$ holds.

Let us recall that a graph is k-regular if all its vertices have degree k. From the above lemma and a very simple combinatorial argument we informally observe that the weight of an optimal k-vertex-connected spanning subgraph cannot differ too much from the weight of any k-regular subgraph. This observation generalizes theorem 1 of [3], as a k-vertex-connected subgraph is k-edge-connected as well. (Note that when $k \cdot n$ is odd the definition of k-regular does not apply, does to cover this case too, we call *almost-k-regular* a graph which is either k-regular if $k \cdot n$ is even or it is such that all its vertices but one have degree k and one vertex has degree $k + 1$, for our purposes suppose also that this vertex has a minimum-weight edge incident in it.) More formally, we have the following theorem.

Theorem 1. *Let $1/2 \leq \beta < 1$ and let G be a complete graph with n vertices, whose edges are weighted with a cost function $w(\cdot)$ satisfying the β-sharpened triangle inequality and let $2 \leq k \leq n - 1$ be a constant. Let G' be an almost-k-*

regular spanning subgraph of G and let G'' be a spanning subgraph of G whose vertices have degree greater than or equal to k. Then $\frac{w(G')}{w(G'')} \leq \frac{\beta}{1-\beta}$.

From this, it immediately follows that the weight of an arbitrary almost-k-regular spanning subgraph that is also k-vertex-connected is at most $\beta/(1-\beta)$ times worse than the weight of a minimal k-vertex-connected spanning subgraph.

The algorithm VCONN(k, G), we give in section 3, returns a k-vertex-connected spanning subgraph H which is almost-k-regular. It is similar to the algorithm given in [3], for the edge-connectivity problem, thus we obtain their same approximation ratio of $\beta/(1-\beta)$. The rest of the paper is devoted to the non trivial proof that H is k-vertex-connected.

Organization of the paper. In the next section we give some definitions used in the paper. In section 3 we show the algorithm and give some invariant properties on the returned graph. In section 4 we show how to find the k internal vertex disjoint paths between any two vertices, through a series of technical lemma. Finally in section 5 we put together the pieces to get the main result of the k-vertex connectivity problem.

2   Definitions and Notations

Consider a complete and weighted graph $G = (V, E, w)$ where $V = \{0, 1, \cdots, n-1\}$ and $w(\cdot)$ is an edge weight function satisfying the sharpened triangle inequality $w(i, j) \leq \beta(w(i, l) + w(l, j))$, for $1/2 \leq \beta < 1$.

Define the **distance** between two vertices i and j as the value $dist(i, j) = j - i$, where the subtraction is in $\mathbb{Z}_n$ [1]. From this, it is obvious that $dist(i, j) = n - dist(j, i)$.

The edge $\left(i, i + \lfloor \frac{n}{2} \rfloor\right)$ for $0 \leq i \leq \lfloor \frac{n}{2} \rfloor$ and the edge $\left(i, i + \lceil \frac{n}{2} \rceil\right)$ for $\lfloor \frac{n}{2} \rfloor \leq i \leq n-1$ are called **diameter-edges of vertex** i (note that the vertex $\lfloor \frac{n}{2} \rfloor$ is the only vertex which has two distinct diameter-edges, when n is odd). We will denote (i, u_i) the diameter edge of i, if $i = \lfloor \frac{n}{2} \rfloor$ and n is odd then $(i, u_i) = \left(\lfloor \frac{n}{2} \rfloor, 0\right)$ and $(i, u_i') = \left(\lfloor \frac{n}{2} \rfloor, n-1\right)$.

Given vertices i, j, we define **IVDP(i,j)** as an abbreviation for *internal vertex disjoint path* constituted only by vertices in $\{(i+1), (i+2), \cdots (j-1)\}$. For a vertex i, $NBH^+(i)$ denotes the set of vertices $\left\{i+1, i+2, \cdots, i + \lfloor \frac{n}{2} \rfloor\right\}$ and $NBH^-(i)$ denotes the set $\left\{i-1, i-2, \cdots, i - \lfloor \frac{n}{2} \rfloor\right\}$. Moreover $NBH(i) = NBH^+(i) \cup NBH^-(i)$, (the neighborhood of i).

Finally, we will use a specific notation to describe paths:

- $i \xrightarrow{NBH^+} j$ is the edge (i, j) with $j \in NBH^+(i)$. We extend this notation to use $i \xrightarrow{NBH^+} i$ to denote no edge;
- $i \xrightarrow{NBH^-} j$ is the edge (i, j) with $j \subset NBH^-(i)$. We extend this notation to use $i \xrightarrow{NBH^-} i$ to denote no edge;

---

[1] Throughout all the paper the operations on the vertices are in $\mathbb{Z}_n$.

Algorithm **VCONN**(k, G)
INPUT: A complete undirected weighted graph $G = (V, E, w)$ where w is the weight function and an integer $2 \leq k \leq (n - 1)$.
OUTPUT: A k-vertex-connected spanning subgraph $H = (V, E_H)$ of G.

$E_H \leftarrow \emptyset$
if k odd **then**
    if n odd **then**
        Let (u, v) be an edge with minimum weight.
        Rename vertex $\lfloor \frac{n}{2} \rfloor$ as u and vice-versa.
        Rename vertex $n - 1$ as v and vice-versa.
    endif
    for $i \leftarrow 0$ **to** $\lfloor \frac{n}{2} \rfloor$ **do**
        $E_H \leftarrow E_H \cup \left(i, i + \lfloor \frac{n}{2} \rfloor\right)$ /* diameter-edge of vertex i */
    endfor
endif
for $i \leftarrow 0$ **to** $n - 1$ **do**
    for $j = 1$ **to** $\lfloor \frac{k}{2} \rfloor$ **do**
        $E_H \leftarrow E_H \cup (i, i + j)$ /* set NBH(i) */
    endfor
endfor
return $H \leftarrow (V, E_H)$

Fig. 1. Algorithm VCONN.

- $i \xrightarrow{JMP} j$ is the edge (i, j) where $j = i + \lfloor \frac{k}{2} \rfloor$ (called *jump-edge*). We extend this notation as follows: $i \xrightarrow{JMP^k} j$ stands for the path $i \xrightarrow{JMP} j_1 \xrightarrow{JMP} j_2 \xrightarrow{JMP} \cdots \xrightarrow{JMP} j_k$ where $j_k = j$.
- $i \xrightarrow{DMT} j$ is the diameter-edge (i, j) of vertex i.

3   Algorithm VCONN

In this section we show a quadratic-time approximation algorithm VCONN for the k-vertex-connected problem (see fig. 1). As said in section 1, the algorithm strongly resembles the one given in [3] (although there the case when $k \times n$ is odd was not explicitly mentioned), thus its performance ratio is the same.

Theorem 2. *Given a constant $1 < k < n$ and a complete graph G with the edge weight function obeying the β-sharpened triangle inequality, the algorithm $VCONN(k, G)$ is an approximation algorithm for the k-vertex-connectivity problem with performance ratio $\frac{\beta}{1-\beta}$.*

Proof. The approximation ratio derives from theorem 2 of [3], while the k-vertex-connectivity of the returned graph is given in theorem 3. $\qquad \square$

It is easy to see that the graph $H = (V, E_H, w)$ returned by the algorithm has the following properties.

Property 1. If $i \notin NBH(j)$ then $\lfloor \frac{k}{2} \rfloor < dist(i,j) < n - \lfloor \frac{k}{2} \rfloor$.

Property 2. If k is odd, $j = i + \lfloor \frac{n}{2} \rfloor$ and $i \leq \lfloor \frac{n}{2} \rfloor$ then $(i,j) \in E_H$.

Property 3. If k is odd, $j = i + \lceil \frac{n}{2} \rceil$ and $i \geq \lfloor \frac{n}{2} \rfloor$ then $(i,j) \in E_H$.

When n is odd, from the last two properties, the vertices 0 and $n-1$ share one endpoint of their own diameter edge.

Let us abuse in the notation and use in the rest of the paper the set $NBH^+(i)$ as the vertex set of the complete graph induced by its vertices (analogously for $NBH^-(i)$).

4 Internal Vertex Disjoint Paths

In this section we give some results on the existence of internal vertex disjoint paths between two vertices in a graph returned by VCONN. We will use these results in the next section to prove the k-vertex-connectivity of the graph returned by VCONN. All these results are constructive (we prove not only their existence, but we show also the edges constituting the paths).

The next lemma gives a result on the existence of $\lfloor \frac{k}{2} \rfloor$ paths between two vertices i, j such that either $(i,j) \notin E_H$ or (i,j) is a diameter-edge.

Lemma 1. *Let $H = (V, E_H, w)$ be the graph returned by $VCONN(k, G)$. Given $i, j \in V$ s.t. $j \notin NBH(i)$, then there exist $\lfloor \frac{k}{2} \rfloor$ IVDP(i,j) of length greater than 1.*

Proof. Suppose w.l.o.g. $i < j$ and let $d = dist(i,j)$. Let $d = q \lfloor \frac{k}{2} \rfloor + r$ with $0 \leq r < \lfloor \frac{k}{2} \rfloor$. By property 1, $q \geq 1$. We will show that for all $1 \leq t \leq \lfloor \frac{k}{2} \rfloor$, there exist the following IVDP(i,j)

$$p(t) = i \xrightarrow{NBH^+} i+t \xrightarrow{JMP^{s(t)}} i+t+s(t) \left\lfloor \frac{k}{2} \right\rfloor \xrightarrow{NBH^+} j$$

where

$$s(t) = \begin{cases} q & \text{if } 1 \leq t < r \\ q-1 & \text{if } r \leq t \leq \lfloor \frac{k}{2} \rfloor \end{cases}$$

These paths have length $s(t) + 2$. The first edge $(i, i+t)$ exists as $i+t \in NBH^+(i)$ and the next $s(t)$ ones exist as well, as they are *jump-edges*. Since $d = j - i = q \lfloor \frac{k}{2} \rfloor + r$, then

$$dist\left(i + t + s(t) \left\lfloor \frac{k}{2} \right\rfloor, j\right) - j - i - t - s(t) \left\lfloor \frac{k}{2} \right\rfloor \leq$$

$$\leq \begin{cases} j - i - 1 - q \lfloor \frac{k}{2} \rfloor = r - 1 < \lfloor \frac{k}{2} \rfloor & \text{if } 1 \leq t \leq r-1 \\ j - i - r - (q-1) \lfloor \frac{k}{2} \rfloor = \lfloor \frac{k}{2} \rfloor & \text{if } r \leq t \leq \lfloor \frac{k}{2} \rfloor \end{cases}$$

Now, we prove that these paths only use the vertices $(i+1), \cdots, (j-1)$. Let $(i+t+a \lfloor \frac{k}{2} \rfloor)$ be the vertices of the paths then:

- for $0 \le a \le q$ and $1 \le t \le r-1$

$$i+t+a \left\lfloor \frac{k}{2} \right\rfloor < i+r+q \left\lfloor \frac{k}{2} \right\rfloor = i+d = j$$

- for $0 \le a \le (q-1)$ and $r \le t \le \lfloor \frac{k}{2} \rfloor$

$$i+t+a \left\lfloor \frac{k}{2} \right\rfloor \le i+q \left\lfloor \frac{k}{2} \right\rfloor < i+d = j$$

Finally, we show that these paths have all disjoint vertices. In fact, suppose by way of contradiction that there exists a vertex $i+t+a \lfloor \frac{k}{2} \rfloor$ that belongs to the paths $p(t)$ and $p(t_1) \ne p(t)$ ($1 \le t, t_1 \le \lfloor \frac{k}{2} \rfloor$). Then $i+t+a \lfloor \frac{k}{2} \rfloor = i+t_1+a_1 \lfloor \frac{k}{2} \rfloor$ for $0 \le a_1 \le r$. Now, if $a_1 = a$ then $t_1 = t$, which is a contradiction as we assumed that $t_1 \ne t$, whereas, if $a_1 \ne a$ then $|t - t_1| = |a_1 - a| \lfloor \frac{k}{2} \rfloor$ which is impossible because $1 \le t, t_1 \le \lfloor \frac{k}{2} \rfloor$. This completes the proof of theorem. □

The next lemma shows the existence of internal vertex disjoint paths when $(i,j) \in E_H$ and $j \in NBH(i)$. In particular, the lemma returns a different number of paths if $j \in NBH^+(i)$ and if $j \in NBH^-(i)$.

Lemma 2. *Let $H = (V, E_H, w)$ be the graph returned by $VCONN(k,G)$ for $k \ne 3$. Given $i, j \in V$ s.t. $j \in NBH(i)$, there exist*

1. *$dist(i,j) - 1$ IVDP(i,j) of length greater than 1 if $j \in NBH^+(i)$*
2. *$k - dist(j,i)$ IVDP(i,j) of length greater than 1 if $j \in NBH^-(i)$*

Proof. Let $d = dist(i,j)$ and $d' = n - d$. Consider first the case $j \in NBH^+(i)$. By property 1, $d \le \lfloor \frac{k}{2} \rfloor$, then the following $d - 1$ paths

$$p(t) = i \xrightarrow{NBH^+} i+t \xrightarrow{NBH^+} j$$

for $1 \le t \le d' - 1$ are all IVDP(i,j) and this completes the first case of lemma.

Now, let $j \in NBH^-(i)$, i.e. $d' \le \lfloor \frac{k}{2} \rfloor$ and by property 1 $d \ge n - \lfloor \frac{k}{2} \rfloor$. Let $|NBH^+(i) \cap NBH^-(j)| = x$, if $x \ge d'$ than $d = 2 \lfloor \frac{k}{2} \rfloor - x \le 2 \lfloor \frac{k}{2} \rfloor - n + d$, i.e. $n \le k$ which is impossible. Therefore let $x < d'$. First we will prove that for $1 \le t \le \lfloor \frac{k}{2} \rfloor - d'$ the following IVDP(i,j) exist:

$$p(t) = i \xrightarrow{NBH^+} i+t \xrightarrow{NBH^-} j.$$

Clearly all these paths are internal vertex disjoint and it is also clear that $(i+t) \in NBH^+(i)$. Now to show that $j \in NBH^-(i+t)$ note that $dist(j, i+t) = d'+t \le d' + \lfloor \frac{k}{2} \rfloor - d' = \lfloor \frac{k}{2} \rfloor$.

Symmetrically we can prove that for $1 \le t \le \lfloor \frac{k}{2} \rfloor - d'$ the following IVDP(i,j) exist:

$$p(t) = i \xrightarrow{NBH^-} j - t \xrightarrow{NBH^+} j.$$

Now observe that $(j - \lfloor \frac{k}{2} \rfloor + d' - i - \lfloor \frac{k}{2} \rfloor + d') > 0$, thus all the $2\lfloor \frac{k}{2} \rfloor - 2d'$ paths we have found until now are vertex disjoint. Moreover, none of them uses the vertices $i + \lfloor \frac{k}{2} \rfloor - d' + 1, \cdots, j - \lfloor \frac{k}{2} \rfloor + d' - 1$: therefore the remaining d' paths (or $d' + 1$ if k odd) will use only these vertices. We distinguish the case k even and k odd.

CASE 1 [k even]: In this case we have to distinguish two subcases:
CASE 1a [$x = 0$]: let $dist(i + \frac{k}{2} - d' + 1, j - \frac{k}{2} + d' - 1) = q\frac{k}{2} + r$ with $0 \le r < \frac{k}{2}$ and $y = |d' - r|$. It is easy to see that for $\frac{k}{2} - d' + 1 \le t \le \frac{k}{2}$ the following IVDP(i,j) exist: if $r \ge d'$ then

$$p(t) = i \xrightarrow{NBH^+} i+t \xrightarrow{JMP^q} i+t+q\frac{k}{2} \xrightarrow{NBH^+} i+t+q\frac{k}{2}+I(t)d' \xrightarrow{NBH^+} j$$

where

$$I(t) = \begin{cases} 1 \text{ if } t \le \frac{k}{2} - d' + 1 + y \\ 0 \text{ if } t > \frac{k}{2} - d' + 1 + y \end{cases}$$

whereas if $r < d'$ then

$$p(t) = i \xrightarrow{NBH^+} i+t \xrightarrow{JMP^{s(t)}} i+t+s(t)\frac{k}{2} \xrightarrow{NBH^+} j$$

where

$$s(t) = \begin{cases} q & \text{if } \frac{k}{2} - d' + 1 \le t \le \frac{k}{2} - d' + 1 + r \\ q - 1 & \text{otherwise} \end{cases}$$

CASE 1b [$1 \le x < d'$]: In this case, we have that $i + \frac{k}{2} \ge j - \frac{k}{2}$. Therefore, it is clear that for $\frac{k}{2} - x \le t \le \frac{k}{2}$ the following IVDP(i,j) exist (see figure 2a)

$$p(t) = i \xrightarrow{NBH^+} i+t \xrightarrow{NBH^+} j.$$

Moreover, since for $\frac{k}{2} - d' + 1 \le t \le \frac{k}{2} - x - 1$ it holds $dist(i+t, i+t+d') = d'$, it is easy to see that the following IVDP(i,j) exist (see figure 2b)

$$p(t) = i \xrightarrow{NBH^+} i+t \xrightarrow{NBH^+} i+t+d' \xrightarrow{NBH^+} j.$$

CASE 2 [k odd]: Let (i, u_i) be the diameter-edge of i and (j, u_j) the diameter-edge of j. If $i = \lfloor \frac{k}{2} \rfloor$ then $u_i - n - 1$ and if $j = \lfloor \frac{k}{2} \rfloor$ then $u_j = 0$. We now distinguish between two subcases.

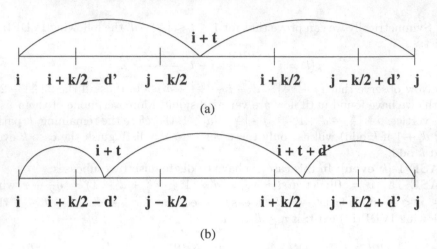

Fig. 2. Paths for case 2.

CASE 2a $[x = 0]$**:** We have two cases:

- if $i + \lfloor \frac{k}{2} \rfloor - d' + 1 \leq u_j \leq i + \lfloor \frac{k}{2} \rfloor$ (which implies $j - \lfloor \frac{k}{2} \rfloor \leq u_i \leq j - \lfloor \frac{k}{2} \rfloor + d' - 1$), $(d' - 1)$ IVDP(i,j) are constituted by connecting a vertex of $[i + \lfloor \frac{k}{2} \rfloor - d' + 1, u_j - 1] \cup [u_j + 1, i + \lfloor \frac{k}{2} \rfloor]$ to a vertex in $[j - \lfloor \frac{k}{2} \rfloor, u_i - 1] \cup [u_i + 1, j - \lfloor \frac{k}{2} \rfloor + d' - 1]$ through a series of jump-edges, but possibly the last. Then this path continues directly to j as the last vertex considered is in $NBH^-(j)$. More specifically, let $dist(i + \lfloor \frac{k}{2} \rfloor - d', j - \lfloor \frac{k}{2} \rfloor) = q \lfloor \frac{k}{2} \rfloor + r$ with $0 \leq r < \lfloor \frac{k}{2} \rfloor$. Then these IVDP(i,j) are given by

$$i \xrightarrow{NBH^+} i+t \xrightarrow{JMP^{s(t)}} i+t+s(t)\left\lfloor \frac{k}{2} \right\rfloor \xrightarrow{NBH^+}$$

$$i+t+s(t)\left\lfloor \frac{k}{2} \right\rfloor + I(t)d' \xrightarrow{NBH^+} j$$

for $\lfloor \frac{k}{2} \rfloor - d' < t \leq \lfloor \frac{k}{2} \rfloor$, where

$$s(t) = \begin{cases} q & \text{if } 1 \leq t \leq r-1 \\ q-1 & \text{otherwise} \end{cases} \quad I(t) = \begin{cases} 0 \text{ if } 1 \leq t \leq r-1 \\ 1 \text{ otherwise} \end{cases}$$

The others two IVDP(i,j) are

$$i \xrightarrow{NBH^+} u_j \xrightarrow{DMT} j \text{ and}$$

$$i \xrightarrow{DMT} u_i \xrightarrow{NBH^+} j$$

which give the desired $(d' + 1)$ IVDP(i,j).

- if $u_j > i + \lfloor \frac{k}{2} \rfloor$ (which implies $u_i < j - \lfloor \frac{k}{2} \rfloor$) and whenever n is odd, $(i,j) \neq (0, n-1)$ results, then d' IVDP(i,j) are constituted by connecting a vertex in $[i + \lfloor \frac{k}{2} \rfloor - d' + 1, i + \lfloor \frac{k}{2} \rfloor]$ to a vertex in $[u_j, u_i - 1]$ through a series of jump-edges, but possibly the last. Then one path continues from u_j to j through the diameter-edge of j, the others $d' - 1$ paths continues from a vertex in $[u_j + 1, u_i - 1]$ to a vertex in $[j - \lfloor \frac{k}{2} \rfloor, j - \lfloor \frac{k}{2} \rfloor + d' - 1]$ (note that this interval contains d' vertices and we use only $d' - 1$ of them). Finally, the last $(d' + 1)$-th path is constituted by the diameter edge of i and a series of jump-edges, but possibly the last, ending in the unused vertex of $[j - \lfloor \frac{k}{2} \rfloor, j - \lfloor \frac{k}{2} \rfloor + d' - 1]$. More precisely let $dist(i + \lfloor k/2 \rfloor - d', u_i) = q_1 \lfloor k/2 \rfloor + r_1$ with $0 \le r_1 < \lfloor k/2 \rfloor$ and $dist(u_j, j - \lfloor k/2 \rfloor + d') = q_2 \lfloor k/2 \rfloor + r_2$ with $0 \le r_2 < \lfloor k/2 \rfloor$ (note that $u_j < u_i$) and proceed in the following way:

1. get the following d' internal vertex disjoint paths:

$$p_2(t) = i \xrightarrow{NBH^+} i + t \xrightarrow{JMP^{s_1(t)}} i + t + s_1(t) \left\lfloor \frac{k}{2} \right\rfloor \xrightarrow{NBH^+}$$

$$i + t + s_1(t) \left\lfloor \frac{k}{2} \right\rfloor + I_1(t) d'$$

for $\lfloor k/2 \rfloor - d' + 1 \le t \le \lfloor k/2 \rfloor$, where

$$s_1(t) = \begin{cases} q_1 & \text{if } 1 \le t \le r_1 - 1 \\ q_1 - 1 & \text{otherwise} \end{cases} \quad I_1(t) = \begin{cases} 0 \text{ if } 1 \le t \le r_1 - 1 \\ 1 \text{ otherwise} \end{cases}$$

Note that these paths end in the vertices of the interval $[u_j, u_i - 1]$.

2. get the following d' internal vertex disjoint paths:

$$p_2(t) = u_j + t \xrightarrow{JMP^{s_2(t)}} u_j + t + s_2(t) \left\lfloor \frac{k}{2} \right\rfloor \xrightarrow{NBH^+}$$

$$u_j + t + s_2(t) \left\lfloor \frac{k}{2} \right\rfloor + I_2(t) d' \xrightarrow{NBH^+} j$$

for $1 \le t \le d'$, where

$$s_2(t) = \begin{cases} q_2 & \text{if } 1 \le t \le r_2 - 1 \\ q_2 - 1 & \text{otherwise} \end{cases} \quad I_2(t) = \begin{cases} 0 \text{ if } 1 \le t \le r_2 - 1 \\ 1 \text{ otherwise} \end{cases}$$

3. For a vertex $u_j \le v \le u_i - 1$, let p_1^v be the path $p_1(t)$ which ends in the vertex v and for a vertex $u_j + 1 \le v \le u_i$, let p_2^v be the path $p_2(t)$ which ends in the vertex v.

4. Get the following $(d' - 1)$ IVDP(i,j) (as sequences of subpaths):

$$< p_1^v, p_2^v >$$

for $u_j + 1 \le v \le u_i - 1$.

5. Get the following 2 IVDP(i,j) (as sequences of subpaths and edges):

$$< p_1^{u_j}, (u_j, j) >$$
$$< (i, u_i), p_2^{u_i} >$$

- if n is odd and $(i,j) = (0, n-1)$, then $d' = 1$, therefore we need only to show the existence of two IVDP(i,j). Let $dist(i, \frac{n-1}{2} - 1) = q_1 \frac{k-1}{2} + r_1$ with $0 \le r_1 < \frac{k-1}{2}$ and $dist(\frac{n-1}{2} + 1, j - \frac{k-1}{2}) = q_2 \frac{k-1}{2} + r_2$ with $0 \le r_2 < \frac{k-1}{2}$. It is easy to see that the following two IVDP(i,j) exist:

$$i \xrightarrow{DMT} \frac{n-1}{2} \xrightarrow{DMT} j$$

and

$$i \xrightarrow{JMP^{q_1}} q_1 \frac{k-1}{2} \xrightarrow{NBH^+} \frac{n-3}{2} \xrightarrow{NBH^+} \frac{n+1}{2} \xrightarrow{JMP^{q_2}}$$
$$\frac{n+1}{2} + q_2 \frac{k-1}{2} \xrightarrow{NBH^+} j - \frac{k-1}{2} \xrightarrow{NBH^+} j$$

Let us note that if $k = 3$ this last path cannot exist, as the edge $\left(\frac{n-3}{2}, \frac{n-1}{2}\right)$ does not exist.

CASE 2b $[1 \le x < d']$: In this case, as seen in the CASE 1b, for $\lfloor \frac{k}{2} \rfloor - x \le t \le \lfloor \frac{k}{2} \rfloor$ the following IVDP(i,j) exist (see figure 2a)

$$p(t) = i \xrightarrow{NBH^+} i+t \xrightarrow{NBH^+} j.$$

Moreover, since for $\lfloor \frac{k}{2} \rfloor - d' + 1 \le t \le \lfloor \frac{k}{2} \rfloor - x - 1$ s.t. $i + t \ne u_j$ it holds $d(i+t, i+t+d') = d'$, it is easy to see that the following IVDP(i,j) exist (see figure 2b)

$$p(t) = i \xrightarrow{NBH^+} i+t \xrightarrow{NBH^+} i+t+d' \xrightarrow{NBH^+} j.$$

Finally let us note that, as $u_j + d' = u_i$, the vertices u_i and u_j have not been used. Therefore, we can consider the IVDP(i,j)

$$i \xrightarrow{NBH^+} u_j \xrightarrow{DMT} j \text{ and}$$

$$i \xrightarrow{DMT} u_i \xrightarrow{NBH^+} j.$$

In this way we have $d' + 1$ IVDP(i,j) which completes the proof of this lemma.
□

Finally, the following lemma shows the existence of internal vertex disjoint paths when k is odd.

Lemma 3. Let $H = (V, E_H, w)$ the graph returned by $VCONN(k, G)$ when k is odd and $k > 3$. Given $i, j \in V$ s.t. $(i, j) \notin E_H$ and $dist(i, j) \ge \lceil \frac{n}{2} \rceil$, then there exist $\lceil \frac{k}{2} \rceil$ IVDP(i,j).

Proof. W.l.o.g suppose $i < j$. Note that $dist(i, u_j) < dist(i, u_i)$. Let $d = dist(i,j) = q\lfloor k/2 \rfloor + r$ with $0 \le r < \lfloor k/2 \rfloor$, let $d_1 = dist(i, u_j) = q_1\lfloor k/2 \rfloor + r_1$ with $0 < leqr_1 < \lfloor k/2 \rfloor$ and let $d_2 = dist(i, u_i) = q_2\lfloor k/2 \rfloor + r_2$ with $0 \le r_2 < \lfloor k/2 \rfloor$. Then we can get the following IVDP(i,j):

$$p(t) = i \xrightarrow{NBH^+} i+t \xrightarrow{JMP^{s(t)}} i+t+s(t)\left\lfloor\frac{k}{2}\right\rfloor \xrightarrow{NBH^+} j$$

for $0 \le t < \lfloor k/2 \rfloor$ and $t \ne r_1, r_2$, where

$$s(t) = \begin{cases} q & \text{if } 0 \le t < r \\ q-1 & \text{if } r \le t < \lfloor\frac{k}{2}\rfloor \end{cases}$$

These are respectively $\lfloor k/2 \rfloor - 1$ IVDP(i,j) if $r_1 = r_2$ and $\lfloor k/2 \rfloor - 2$ IVDP(i,j) if $r_1 \ne r_2$. To get the last 2 paths in the former case or 3 paths in the latter, we proceed in the following way:

- if $r_1 = r_2$ we get the following two paths:

$$p_1(r_1) = i \xrightarrow{NBH^+} i+r_1 \xrightarrow{JMP^{q_1}} u_j \xrightarrow{DMT} j$$

and

$$p_2(r_1) = i \xrightarrow{DMT} u_i \xrightarrow{JMP^{s-q_2}} i+r_1+s\left\lfloor\frac{k}{2}\right\rfloor \xrightarrow{NBH^+} j$$

where

$$s = \begin{cases} q & \text{if } 0 \le r_1 < r \\ q-1 & \text{if } r \le r_1 < \lfloor\frac{k}{2}\rfloor \end{cases}$$

- if $r_1 \ne r_2$, let x be the maximum vertex such that $x < u_i$ and $x \equiv u_i \bmod \lfloor k/2 \rfloor$ and let y be the maximum vertex such that $y < u_i$ and $y \equiv u_j \bmod \lfloor k/2 \rfloor$. Since $dist(x, u_i) \le \lfloor k/2 \rfloor$ and $dist(y, u_i) \le \lfloor k/2 \rfloor$ then either $y \in NBH^+(x)$ or $y \in NBH^-(x)$. Hence we get the following two paths:

$$p(r_1) = i \xrightarrow{NBH^+} i+r_1 \xrightarrow{JMP^{q_1}} u_j \xrightarrow{DMT} j$$

and

$$p(r_2) = i \xrightarrow{DMT} u_i \xrightarrow{JMP^{s-q_2}} i+r_2+s\left\lfloor\frac{k}{2}\right\rfloor \xrightarrow{NBH^+} j$$

where

$$s = \begin{cases} q & \text{if } 0 \le r_1 < r \\ q-1 & \text{if } r \le r_1 < \lfloor\frac{k}{2}\rfloor \end{cases}$$

Finally, if $y \in NBH^+(x)$ we get the following path:

$$p = i \xrightarrow{NBH^+} i + r_2 \xrightarrow{JMP^{q_2-1}} x \xrightarrow{NBH^+} y \xrightarrow{JMP^{s-(q_2-1)}} i + r_2 + s \left\lfloor \frac{k}{2} \right\rfloor \xrightarrow{NBH^+} j$$

else we get the following path:

$$p = i \xrightarrow{NBH^+} i + r_2 \xrightarrow{JMP^{q_2-1}} x \xrightarrow{NBH^-} y \xrightarrow{JMP^{s-(q_2-1)}} i + r_2 + s \left\lfloor \frac{k}{2} \right\rfloor \xrightarrow{NBH^+} j$$

This completes the proof of the lemma. □

5 k-Vertex-Connectivity

In this section we give the main result of the paper by showing that the graph returned by the algorithm is k-vertex-connected.

Theorem 3. *The graph* $H = (V, E_H, w)$ *returned from algorithm* $VCONN$ (k, G, w) *is* k-*vertex-connected.*

Proof. For $k = 3$, H is constituted by an external cycle $< 0, 1, \cdots, n-1, 0 >$ and by the set of diameter-edges. Deleting two vertices i and j we split the external cycle into the two sequences of vertices $S_1 =< i+1, i+2, \cdots, j-1 >$ and $S_2 =< j+1, j+2, \cdots, i-1 >$. W.l.o.g. suppose $|S_1| \le |S_2|$. Since $dmt(j-1) \in S_2$, then the graph is still connected.

Let $k \ne 3$. We have to show that, given two vertices $i, j \in V$, k internal vertex disjoint paths exist that connect the vertex i to the vertex j. If $i \in NBH(j)$ then w.l.o.g. let $dist(i, j) < dist(j, i)$. Then, from the first item of lemma 2, $(dist(i, j) - 1)$ IVDP(i,j) exist with length greater than 1 and from the second item $(k - dist(i, j))$ IVDP(j,i) exist with length greater than 1. Therefore, $(k-1)$ internal vertex disjoint paths exist with length greater than 1 connecting i to j. Then, considering the path constituted by the edge (i, j) we have the k desired paths.

Now, let $i \notin NBH(j)$. If k is even, then applying two times lemma 1, there exist $\frac{k}{2}$ IVDP(i,j) (from i to j) and $\frac{k}{2}$ IVDP(j,i) (from j to i), which proves that k internal vertex disjoint paths exist in this case.

If k is odd and $(i, j) \notin E_H$ then from lemma 1, $\lfloor \frac{k}{2} \rfloor$ IVDP(i,j) exist and from lemma 3, $\lceil \frac{k}{2} \rceil$ IVDP(j,i) exist, which gives k internal vertex disjoint paths for this case. If k is odd and (i, j) is a diameter-edge then by applying two times lemma 1, there exist $\lfloor \frac{k}{2} \rfloor$ IVDP(i,j) with length greater than one (from i to j) and $\lfloor \frac{k}{2} \rfloor$ IVDP(j,i) with length greater than one (from j to i). Now, considering the path constituted by the diameter-edge (i, j) we have the k desired paths. This completes the proof of theorem. □

References

1. V. Auletta, Y. Dinitz, Z. Nutov, M. Parente, *A 2 Approximation Algorithms for Finding an Optimum 3 Vertex Connected Spanning Subgraph* J. of Algorithms 32 (1999), 21-30.

2. H.-J. Böckenauer, D. Bongartz, J. Hromkovič, R. Klasing, G. Proietti, S. Seibert, W. Unger *On the hardness of constructing minimal 2-connected spanning subgraphs in complete graphs with sharpened triangle inequality* in Proc. of FST-TCS '02, L.N.C.S. series 2556, 59–70, 2002.
3. H.-J. Böckenauer, D. Bongartz, J. Hromkovič, R. Klasing, G. Proietti, S. Seibert, W. Unger *On k-Edge-Connectivity Problems with Sharpened Triangle Inequality* to appear in Proc. of CIAC '03, L.N.C.S. series (2003).
4. H.-J. Böckenauer, J. Hromkovič, R. Klasing, S. Seibert, W. Unger *Approximation Algorithms for the TSP with Sharpened Triangle Inequality*, Information Processing Letters 75 (2000), 133–138.
5. H.-J. Böckenauer, J. Hromkovič, R. Klasing, S. Seibert, W. Unger *An Improved Lower Bound on the Approximability Algorithms for the TSP with Sharpened Triangle Inequality*, in Proc. of STACS '00, L.N.C.S. series 1770, 382–394, 2000.
6. A. Czumaj, A. Lingas, *On Approximability of the minimum-cost k-connected spanning subgraph problem*, in Proc. of SODA '99, 281–290, 1999.
7. C.G. Fernandes *A Better Approximation Ratio for the Minimum Size k-Edge-Connected Spanning Subgraph Problem*, J. of Algorithms, 28(1) (1998), 105–124.
8. M.R. Garey, D.S. Johnson, *Computers and Intractability*, W.H. Freeman and Company, New York, 1979.
9. S. Khuller, U. Vishkin, *Biconnectivity approximation and graph carvings*. Journal of the ACM 41 (1994), 214–235.
10. M. Penn, H. Shasha-Krupnik, *Improved approximation Algorithms for weighted 2 and 3-vertex connectivity augmentation* J. of Algorithms 22 (1997), 187–196.

Channel Assignment in Honeycomb Networks

Alan A. Bertossi[1], Cristina M. Pinotti[2,*], Romea Rizzi[2], and Anil M. Shende[3]

[1] Department of Computer Science
University of Bologna
40127 Bologna, Italy
[2] Dept. of Computer Science and Telecom.
University of Trento
38050 Trento, Italy
pinotti@science.unitn.it
[3] Department of Computer Science
Roanoke College, Salem, VA, USA

Abstract. The honeycomb grid is a network topology based on the hexagonal plane tessellation, which is convenient to model the regular placement on the plane of the base stations of wireless networks. For an efficient use of the radio spectrum in such networks, channels have to be assigned to the base stations so as to avoid interferences. Such a problem can be modeled as a suitable coloring problem. Precisely, given an integer t and a honeycomb grid $G = (V, E)$, an $L(1^t)$-coloring of G is a function f from the vertex set V to a set of nonnegative integers such that $|f(u) - f(v)| \geq 1$, if the distance between the vertices u and v is at most t. This paper presents efficient algorithms for finding optimal $L(1^t)$-colorings of honeycomb grids.

1 Introduction

In the 4th generation of wireless access systems, due to the decreasing cost of infrastructures and to the need of wider bandwidth, a large number of small cells, each with significant power, is expected to cover a huge communication region [16]. Such a covering can be achieved by placing the base stations according to a regular plane tessellation. It is well-known that only three different regular tessellations of the plane exist, depending on the kind of regular polygons used. Specifically, the honeycomb, square and hexagonal tesselations cover the plane, respectively, by regular hexagons, squares, and triangles. Such tessellations can be used to place at the polygon vertices the base stations of the wireless communication networks, leading to three well-known topologies: *honeycomb*, *square* and *hexagonal* grids, depicted in Fig. 1 for 16 vertices.

So far, the most studied topology for wireless communication networks has been the hexagonal grid [3,9,12]. However, the performance of a topology can be evaluated with respect to several parameters, such as *degree* and *diameter*. As proved in [14], defined the network *cost* as the product of the degree and diameter, the honeycomb grid beats both the hexagonal and square grids, as

---

* Corresponding author

C. Blundo and C. Laneve (Eds.): ICTCS 2003, LNCS 2841, pp. 150–162, 2003.

Table 1. [14] Comparison of networks, each with n vertices (data are approximated).

network	degree	diameter	cost
honeycomb grid	3	$1.63\sqrt{n}$	$4.9\sqrt{n}$
square grid	4	$2\sqrt{n}$	$8\sqrt{n}$
hexagonal grid	6	$1.16\sqrt{n}$	$6.93\sqrt{n}$

(a)   (b)   (c)

Fig. 1. The possible grids of 16 vertices: (a) honeycomb, (b) square, and (c) hexagonal.

summarized in Table 1 for grids with n vertices (in such a table, coefficients are rounded and additive constants are neglected). Therefore, the honeycomb grid appears more convenient than the hexagonal and square grids to model the placement of the base stations.

In a wireless network, the main difficulty against an efficient use of the radio spectrum is given by *interferences*, which result in damaged communications. Interferences can be eliminated by means of suitable *channel assignment* techniques, which partition the given radio spectrum into a set of disjoint channels. The same channel can be reused by two stations at the same time provided that no interference arises. To avoid interference, a *separation vector* $(\delta_1, \delta_2, \ldots, \delta_t)$ of non increasing positive integers is introduced in such a way that channels assigned to interfering stations at distance i be at least δ_i apart, with $1 \leq i \leq t$, while the same channel can be reused only at stations whose distance is larger than t [8,9]. Since only a continuous interval of the radio spectrum can be acquired, the objective is to minimize its width (or span), namely the difference between the highest and lowest channels assigned. In case of separation vectors containing repeated integer values, a more compact notation will be convenient and so, as an example, $(\delta_1, 1^q)$ is a shorthand for $(\delta_1, \underbrace{1, 1, \ldots, 1}_{q})$.

Formally, given $(\delta_1, \delta_2, \ldots, \delta_t)$ and an undirected graph $G = (V, E)$, an $L(\delta_1, \delta_2, \ldots, \delta_t)$-coloring of G is a function f from the vertex set V to the set of nonnegative integers $\{0, \ldots, \lambda\}$ such that $|f(u) - f(v)| \geq \delta_i$, if $d(u, v) = i$, $1 \leq i \leq t$, where $d(u, v)$ is the distance between vertices u and v. An *optimal* $L(\delta_1, \delta_2, \ldots, \delta_t)$-coloring for G is one minimizing λ over all such colorings. Thus, the channel assignment problem consists of finding an optimal $L(\delta_1, \delta_2, \ldots, \delta_t)$-coloring for G.

The $L(1^t)$-coloring problem has been widely studied in the past [1,6,10,12]. In particular, its intractability has been proved by McCormick [10], while optimal $L(1^t)$-colorings have been proposed in [1,2] for rings, trees, and square grids. Moreover, optimal $L(\delta_1, 1^{t-1})$-colorings have been proposed in [3,13] for rings, square grids and hexagonal grids. Optimal $L(\delta_1, \delta_2)$-colorings on square grids and hexagonal grids have been given by Van Den Heuvel et al. [15], who provided also an optimal $L(2, 1^2)$-coloring for square grids. The $L(2, 1^2)$-coloring problem has been also optimally solved for hexagonal grids and rings in [3]. Finally, the $L(2, 1)$-coloring problem has been studied also in [4,5,7,11].

This paper provides, for the first time, optimal $L(1^t)$-colorings on honeycomb grids. Such colorings use less colors than those needed by the hexagonal and square grids. Therefore, honeycomb grids beat the hexagonal and square grids in terms of both the network cost and channel requirement. The proposed algorithms allow any vertex to self-assign its proper channel in constant time, provided that it knows its relative position within the network. If this is not the case, such relative positions can be computed for all the vertices using simple distributed algorithms requiring optimal time and optimal number of messages, as explained in [3].

2   Preliminaries

The $L(1)$-coloring problem on a graph G is exactly the classical vertex coloring problem on G, where the minimum number of colors needed is $\lambda + 1 = \chi(G)$, the *chromatic number* of G. In the case of $L(1^t)$-colorings, the term *t-chromatic number* of G, denoted by $\chi_t(G)$, will be used. A lower bound for $\chi_t(G)$ is the size $\omega(A_{G,t})$ of the *maximum clique* of the *augmented* graph $A_{G,t}$, which has the same vertex set as G and the edge $[r, s]$ iff $d(r, s) \leq t$ in G.

A *t-independent set* is a subset S_t of vertices of G whose pairwise distance is at least $t + 1$. If the size of S_t is the largest possible, then S_t is a *maximum t-independent set*, and is denoted by S_t^*. Assigning different colors to different t-independent sets one obtains a feasible $L(1^t)$-coloring. Conversely, given a feasible $L(1^t)$-coloring, all the vertices with the same color form a t-independent set. Any feasible $L(1^t)$-coloring uses at least as many colors as the minimum number $\mu_t(G)$ of maximum t-independent sets that cover all the vertices, that is $\chi_t(G) \geq \mu_t(G)$.

Let G_1 and G_2 be any two graphs, and let $V(G)$ denote the vertex set of a graph G. A *t-homomorphism* from G_1 to G_2 is a total function $\phi : V(G_1) \mapsto V(G_2)$ such that: (i) $\phi(u) = \phi(v)$ only if $u = v$ or $d(u, v) > t$, and (ii) $d(\phi(u), \phi(v)) \leq d(u, v)$ for all nodes u, v of G_1. Now, if g is an $L(\delta_1, \ldots, \delta_t)$-coloring of G_2, and ϕ is a t-homomorphism from G_1 to G_2, then the composition $g \circ \phi$ is an $L(\delta_1, \ldots, \delta_t)$-coloring of G_1.

In this paper, *brick* representations of honeycomb grids are adopted where each hexagon is represented by a rectangle spanning 3 rows and 2 columns. In this way, a honeycomb grid H of size $n = rc$ is represented by r rows and c columns, indexed respectively from 0 to $r - 1$ (from top to bottom) and from 0 to $c - 1$ (from left to right), with $r \geq 3$ and $c \geq 2$. A generic vertex u of H is denoted by $u = (i, j)$, where i is its row index and j is its column index. Note that each vertex (i, j), which does not belong to the grid borders, has degree 3 and is adjacent to the following 3 vertices: $(i - 1, j)$, $(i + 1, j)$, and $(i, j + 1)$ if $i + j$ is even, or $(i, j - 1)$ if $i + j$ is odd.

3   Optimal $L(1^t)$-Coloring

In this section, optimal $L(1^t)$-colorings of sufficiently large honeycomb grids will be presented, which depend on the parity of t. In particular, when t is odd the lower bound on $\chi_t(H)$ is given by $\omega(A_{H,t})$ and this bound is achievable. When t is even, such a lower bound is not achievable, and a stronger lower bound is needed which depends on $\mu_t(H)$. In both cases, the optimal colorings are based on a grid tessellation.

3.1 $L(1^t)$-Coloring with t Odd

Lemma 1. *Let $t = 8p + q$, with $p \geq 0$ and $q = 1, 3, 5, 7$. There is an $L(1^t)$-coloring of a honeycomb grid H of size $r \times c$, with $r \geq t + 1$ and $c \geq \lceil \frac{t-3}{4} \rceil + \lfloor \frac{t+1}{4} \rfloor + 1$, only if*

$$\chi_t(H) \geq \omega(A_{H,t}) = \begin{cases} 24p^2 + 12p + 2 & \text{if } q = 1 \\ 24p^2 + 24p + 6 & \text{if } q = 3 \\ 24p^2 + 36p + 14 & \text{if } q = 5 \\ 24p^2 + 48p + 24 & \text{if } q = 7 \end{cases}$$

Proof. The maximum clique of $A_{H,t}$ is a *diamond* with $\lceil \frac{t-3}{4} \rceil + \lfloor \frac{t+1}{4} \rfloor + 1$ columns. The leftmost column has $(t+1) - 2 \lceil \frac{t-3}{4} \rceil$ vertices, and each subsequent column has two extra vertices up to the central column which counts $t+1$ vertices. Each of the remaining $\lfloor \frac{t+1}{4} \rfloor$ columns, on the right of the central one, decreases its size by two. In particular, the rightmost column has $(t+1) - 2 \lfloor \frac{t+1}{4} \rfloor$ vertices. Depending on the value of q, the number of left and right columns is, respectively:

$$\left\lceil \frac{t-3}{4} \right\rceil = \begin{cases} 2p & \text{if } q = 1, 3 \\ 2p+1 & \text{if } q = 5, 7 \end{cases} \qquad \left\lfloor \frac{t+1}{4} \right\rfloor = \begin{cases} 2p & \text{if } q = 1 \\ 2p+1 & \text{if } q = 3, 5 \\ 2p+2 & \text{if } q = 7 \end{cases}$$

Note that the shape of the maximum clique varies with q. For instance, Fig. 2 shows the maximum cliques when $q = 1, 3, 5$ and 7 and $t = 17, 19, 21$ and 23, respectively. Then,

$$\omega(A_{H,t}) = (t+1) + \sum_{i=1}^{\lfloor \frac{t+1}{4} \rfloor} (t + 1 - 2i) + \sum_{i=1}^{\lceil \frac{t-3}{4} \rceil} (t + 1 - 2i)$$

Solving the above formula with $t = 8p + q$, the proof follows. ∇

By the above lemma, all the vertices of each diamond must get a different color. An optimal $L(1^t)$-coloring, with t odd, can be easily achieved tessellating the honeycomb grid by means of diamonds, all colored in the same way. Observing Fig. 2, one notes that diamonds have the same number of left and right columns, i.e. they are symmetric, for $q = 1, 5$; while they have one more right column, i.e., they are asymmetric, for $q = 3, 7$. Therefore, there are two possible tessellations depending on the symmetry of the diamonds, which are illustrated in Figure 3 (where $t = 13$ and $t = 15$ are assumed).

In the following, it is shown how a color can be assigned in constant time to any vertex u of the grid. The coloring depends on the symmetry of the diamond.

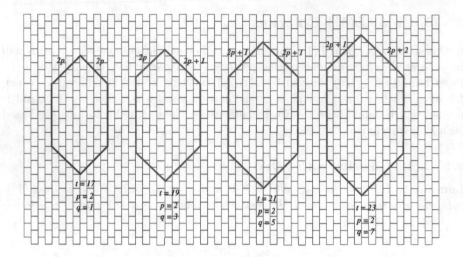

Fig. 2. The maximum cliques (diamonds) for $t = 17, 19, 21$ and 23.

Table 2. The order in which diamond columns are encountered.

order	0	1	2	3	4	...	$4p-1$	$4p$
column	0	$2p$	$4p$	$2p-1$	$4p-1$	...	1	$2p+1$

Coloring with Symmetric Diamonds in $O(1)$ Time. Consider the case with $t = 8p + 1$ (the other case with $t = 8p + 5$ can be dealt with similarly). The diamond has as many right columns as its left columns, namely $2p$ (see the leftmost diamond in Fig. 2).

Observe the honeycomb tessellation by the symmetric diamonds, and restrict the attention to the rectangle $\mathcal{R}$, consisting of the leftmost $4p + 1$ columns and the uppermost $\omega(A_{H,8p+1}) = 24p^2 + 12p + 1$ rows of the grid, as depicted in Fig. 4 (left) for $t = 9$, namely $p = 1$. Clearly, the top left corner of $\mathcal{R}$ has coordinates $(0, 0)$. Sequentially scanning top-down the vertices in column 0 of $\mathcal{R}$, $4p + 1$ different diamonds are encountered. Moreover, for each traversed diamond, a different column is encountered and overall all the $4p + 1$ diamond columns, and hence all the diamond vertices, are met. By the above property, assigning a different color to each vertex in column 0 of $\mathcal{R}$ allows each diamond within the tessellation to be colored the same using the minimum number of colors.

To achieve such a goal, let the diamond columns be numbered from left to right, starting from 0 and ending at $4p$. The diamond columns met along column 0 of $\mathcal{R}$ follow the order shown in Table 2. Formally, denoted by $x(j)$ the order in which the diamond column j is encountered, $x(j) = j(4p - 1) \bmod (4p + 1)$. Conversely, given the order x in which a column is encountered, the column index $col(x) = 2px \bmod (4p + 1)$.

Moreover, the size, i.e. the number of vertices, of the diamond column j is:

$$size(j) = \begin{cases} 4p + 2 + 2j & \text{if } 0 \le j \le 2p \\ 12p + 2 - 2j & \text{if } 2p \le j \le 4p \end{cases}$$

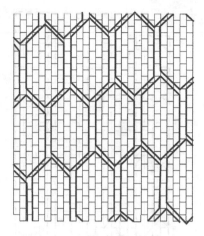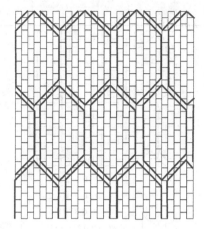

Fig. 3. The honeycomb tessellation: on the left, by the symmetric diamonds ($t = 13$); on the right, by the asymmetric diamonds ($t = 15$).

Finally, the number of vertices of a diamond that have been encountered before the topmost vertex of column j is:

$$pred(j) = \sum_{k=0}^{x(j)-1} size(col(k)).$$

As an example, $x(j), size(j)$ and $pred(j)$ are also shown in Fig. 4 for $t = 9$ (i.e. $p = 1$).

Now, in order to assign different colors to all the vertices in column 0 of $\mathcal{R}$, let the color of vertex $(i, 0)$ be simply $g(i, 0) = i$. The coloring of the entire rectangle $\mathcal{R}$ is obtained assigning to the remaining columns a suitable cyclic shift of the coloring of column 0. Such a cyclic shift is chosen so that all the diamond columns with the same number are colored the same in all diamonds. To do this, let the shift for column j be denoted by $\Delta(j)$. Given the above coloring for column 0 of $\mathcal{R}$, it is easy to see that $\Delta(j)$, where $0 \leq j \leq 4p$, must be:

$$\Delta(j) = \begin{cases} (pred(j) + 2p) - (2p - j) & \text{if } 0 \leq j \leq 2p \\ (pred(j) + 2p) - (j - 2p) & \text{if } 2p \leq j \leq 4p \end{cases}$$

In conclusion, given any vertex $(i, j) \in \mathcal{R}$, its color is defined as

$$g(i, j) = (\Delta(j) + i) \bmod (24p^2 + 12p + 1).$$

The coloring of the entire grid H is obtained by defining a t-homomorphism $\phi : V(H) \mapsto V(\mathcal{R})$, which can be viewed as a covering of H with colored copies of $\mathcal{R}$. Such copies are shifted up by one row, to reproduce, within each rectangle, the same diamond pattern as in $\mathcal{R}$, as shown in Fig. 4 (right). Hence, for any vertex $(i, j) \in H$, its color $f(i, j)$ is given by $g(\phi(i, j))$, where

$$\phi(i, j) = \left(\left(i + \left\lfloor \frac{j}{4p + 1} \right\rfloor \right) \bmod (24p^2 + 12p + 1), j \bmod (4p + 1) \right).$$

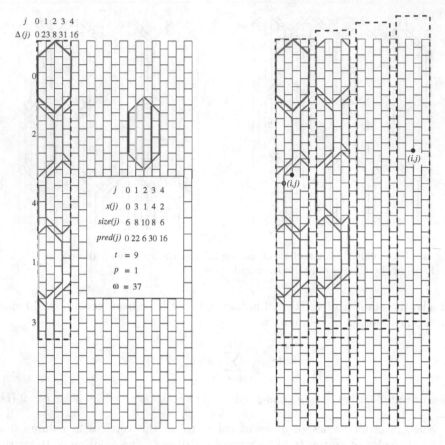

Fig. 4. The diamond columns encountered by scanning column 0 of $\mathcal{R}$ (left). The coloring of H by copies of $\mathcal{R}$ (right).

Observe that $\left\lfloor \frac{j}{4p+1} \right\rfloor$ counts how many rows the rectangle to which (i,j) belongs is shifted up with respect to the leftmost rectangle containing row i. Clearly, if $(i,j) \in \mathcal{R}$ then $\phi(i,j) = (i,j)$ and thus $f(i,j) = g(i,j)$. The correctness easily follows since all diamonds are colored the same, while the t-homomorphism provides a constant time coloring of each vertex which depends only on the vertex indices. Observe also that $\mathcal{R}$ contains $O(p^3)$ vertices, and that the computation of each $\Delta(j)$ requires $O(p)$ time. Since t (and hence p) is a costant, the coloring of vertex (i,j) takes $O(1)$ time.

Coloring with Asymmetric Diamonds in $O(1)$ Time. Consider now the case with $t = 8p+q$, where $q = 3, 7$. The diamond has one more right column than its left columns (see Fig. 2). Due to the fact that the diamonds are horizontally aligned in the tessellation (see Fig. 3), the coloring is much simpler than in the symmetric case. Let *left* and *right* denote the number of left and right columns, respectively. As one can check in the proof of Lemma 1:

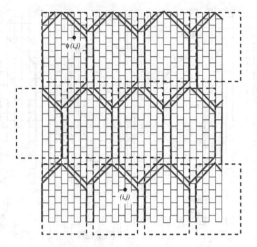

Fig. 5. The coloring of H by copies of $\mathcal{R}$ in the asymmetric case.

$$left = \begin{cases} 2p & \text{if } q = 3 \\ 2p+1 & \text{if } q = 7 \end{cases} \qquad right = \begin{cases} 2p+1 & \text{if } q = 3 \\ 2p+2 & \text{if } q = 7 \end{cases}$$

Observe the honeycomb tessellation by the asymmetric diamonds, and restrict the attention to the rectangle $\mathcal{R}$, consisting of the leftmost $left+right+1$ columns and the uppermost $t - left - 1$ rows of the grid. As before, the top left corner of $\mathcal{R}$ is vertex $(0,0)$. The number of vertices in $\mathcal{R}$ is exactly $\omega(A_{H,t})$, where

$$\omega(A_{H,t}) = \begin{cases} 24p^2 + 24p + 5 & \text{if } q = 3 \\ 24p^2 + 48p + 23 & \text{if } q = 7 \end{cases}$$

Any coloring of the grid H obtained by covering H by colored copies of $\mathcal{R}$ leads to a feasible and optimal coloring (see Fig. 5). Let $\mathcal{R}$ be colored in row-major order. In details, given any vertex $(i,j) \in \mathcal{R}$, let its color be

$$g(i,j) = (i(left + right + 1) + j) \bmod \omega(A_{H,t}).$$

The coloring of the entire grid H is obtained by defining a t-homomorphism $\phi : V(H) \mapsto V(\mathcal{R})$. For any vertex $(i,j) \in H$, $f(i,j) = g(\phi(i,j))$ where

$$\phi(i,j) = \left(i \bmod (t - left), \left(j - right \left\lfloor \frac{i}{t - left} \right\rfloor \right) \bmod (left + right + 1) \right)$$

3.2 $L(1^t)$-Coloring with t Even

Lemma 2. *Let $t = 8p + q$, with $p \geq 0$ and $q = 0, 2, 4, 6$. There is an $L(1^t)$-coloring of a honeycomb grid H of size $r \times c$, with $r \geq t+1$ and $c \geq \lfloor \frac{t}{4} \rfloor + \lceil \frac{t}{4} \rceil + 1$, only if*

$$\chi_t(H) \geq \omega(A_{H,t}) = \begin{cases} 24p^2 + 6p + 1 & \text{if } q = 0 \\ 24p^2 + 18p + 4 & \text{if } q = 2 \\ 24p^2 + 30p + 10 & \text{if } q = 4 \\ 24p^2 + 42p + 19 & \text{if } q = 6 \end{cases}$$

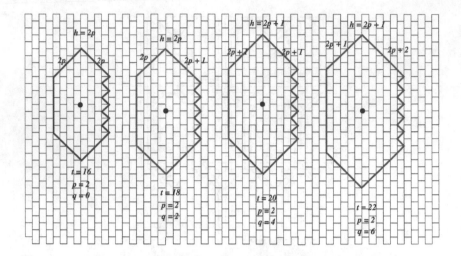

Fig. 6. The maximum cliques (diamonds) for $t = 16, 18, 20$ and 22. The number of holes is denoted by h.

Proof. As in Lemma 1, the maximum clique of $A_{H,t}$ is again a diamond, which can be symmetric or asymmetric. However, there are some *holes* (i.e., vertices not included in the clique) on a single border column of the diamond. The holes are located according to the *center* of the diamond. The center is the middle vertex (i, j) of the central column, which can be termed either *left center* or *right center* depending on whether it is horizontally connected either to vertex $(i, j - 1)$ or $(i, j+1)$, respectively. In the symmetric case, the holes are located in the furthest column on the opposite side with respect to the horizontal connection of the center. Instead, in the asymmetric case, the holes are located on the same side as the center connection.

To compute the clique size $\omega(A_{H,t})$, a reasoning similar to that in the proof of Lemma 1 is followed. As an example, Fig. 6 shows the maximum cliques when $q = 0, 2, 4$ and 6 and $t = 16, 18, 20$ and 22, respectively (in such a figure, the clique centers are depicted by black dots). $\qquad\qquad \nabla$

A Stronger Lower Bound Based on t-Independent Sets. In contrast to the case t odd, when t is even the lower bound on the number of colors given by $\omega(A_{H,t})$ is no more reachable by an $L(1^t)$-coloring. Indeed it is possible to derive a stronger lower bound by considering how a maximum t-independent set S_t^* can be built.

Lemma 3. *When t is even, the minimum distances among three closest vertices belonging to S_t^* are $t + 1, t + 1$ and $t + 2$.*

Proof. Let a vertex $u = (i, j)$ of H be a *left vertex*, if it is horizontally connected to vertex $s = (i, j - 1)$, or a *right vertex* if it is connected to $d = (i, j+1)$. By contradiction, assume there are 3 vertices u, v and w such that $d(u, v) = d(v, w) = d(w, u) = t + 1$. W.l.o.g., let u be a left vertex. Since $t + 1$ is odd, then both v and w must be right vertices. This implies that $d(v,w)$ must be even and greater than t. But this is a contradiction, and $d(v,w) = t + 2$. ∇

Given a vertex v, let $B_t(v)$ be the set of vertices at distance exactly $t + 1$ from v. One can show that $|B_t(v)| = 3t + 3$ for any t even. To build a maximum t-independent set that contains v, let select as many vertices as possible among those in $B_t(v)$. By Lemma 3, since those vertices are all at distance $t + 1$ from v, they must be at distance at least $t + 2$ among them.

Lemma 4. *When t is even, there is no way to select 6 vertices $u_0, u_1, \ldots, u_5$ of $B_t(v)$ such that $d(u_i, u_{(i+1) \bmod 6}) = t + 2$.*

Proof. Since any two consecutive vertices of $B_t(v)$ are at distance 2, no more than one out of $\frac{t+2}{2}$ consecutive vertices of $B_t(v)$ can be selected. Therefore at most $\left\lfloor \frac{3t+3}{\frac{t+2}{2}} \right\rfloor = 5$ vertices can be selected. ∇

Lemma 5. *When t is even, there is no way to select 6 vertices $u_0, u_1, \ldots, u_5$ such that: (1) u_i belongs to $B_t(v)$ for $i = 1, \ldots, 5$; (2) $d(u_i, u_{i+1}) = t + 2$, for $i = 1, \ldots, 4$; and (3) $d(u_0, u_1) = d(u_0, u_5) = t + 1$.*

Proof. After selecting $u_1, \ldots, u_5$ on $B_t(v)$ such that $d(u_i, u_{i+1}) = t + 2$ for $i = 1, \ldots, 4$, there are $t - 2$ vertices of $B_t(v)$ left out between u_5 and u_1. Then, there are t vertices at distance $t + 2$ from v between u_5 and u_1. Moreover, the shortest path from u_5 to u_1, which does not include any other vertex of $B_t(v)$, has length $2t$. Therefore, there is no way to choose on such a path any vertex u_0 at distance $t + 1$ from both u_0 and u_5. ∇

By the previous lemmas, to build a maximum t-independent set including a given vertex v, one should choose the six vertices closest to v such that at most four of them are at distance $t + 1$ from v, and at least two of them are at distance $t + 2$. Moreover, in a maximum t-independent set such a property should hold for any of its vertices, and in particular for the 6 vertices closest to v.

Lemma 6. *Let $t = 8p + q$, with $p \geq 0$ and $q = 0, 2, 4, 6$. The minimum number of maximum t-independent sets that cover a sufficiently large honeycomb grid H is:*

$$\mu_t(H) \geq \begin{cases} 24p^2 + 8p + 1 & \text{if } q = 0 \\ 24p^2 + 20p + 4 & \text{if } q = 2 \\ 24p^2 + 32p + 11 & \text{if } q = 4 \\ 24p^2 + 44p + 20 & \text{if } q = 6 \end{cases}$$

Proof. Choose a vertex v of S_t^* and its 6 closest vertices such that 4 of them are at distance $t + 1$ and the remaining 2 are at distance $t + 2$. By Lemma 2, each of these vertices can be perceived as a center of a diamond. The vertices of each diamond must belong all to different independent sets because they are pairwise at distance at most t. Building such a diamond around each vertex of S_t^*, one obtains a tessellation of H with some *uncovered* vertices between any two diamonds whose centers are at distance $t + 2$. A possible placement of the

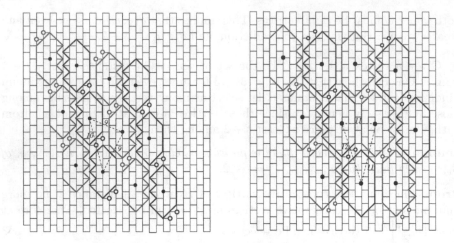

Fig. 7. The maximum 8-independent set (left) and 10-independent set (right) consisting of the diamond centers (depicted by black dots). The uncovered vertices are shown by white circles.

vertices of the maximum t-independent set is depicted in Figure 7 for $t = 8$ (on the left) and $t = 10$ (on the right). Note that there is no way to decrease the number of uncovered vertices because, by Lemmas 4 and 5, v and its 6 closest vertices are as dense as possible. Clearly, these uncovered vertices cannot belong to S_t^*.

Since every center has two closest vertices at distance $t + 2$, by observing Figure 7, one notes that there are two groups of uncovered vertices adjacent to any diamond: one group is above the diamond left columns and the other group is below the diamond right columns. Now, a mapping can be defined between each diamond center and the uncovered vertices by assigning to a diamond with a left center the uncovered vertices above its left columns, and assigning to a diamond with a right center the uncovered vertices above its right columns. Note that if the two diamond centers are at distance $t + 2$, they are both either left or right centers. Hence, the mapping assigns the uncovered vertices between the two diamonds to one and only one of them.

Finally, the number of uncovered vertices associated to each diamond is the minimum between the number of left and right columns of the diamond, which in turn is exactly equal to the number h of holes of the diamond, that is: $h = 2p$ if $q = 0, 2$, or $h = 2p + 1$ if $q = 4, 6$. Hence, only one vertex out of the diamond vertices and its holes, that is one out of $\omega(A_{H,t}) + h$ vertices, can belong to S_t^*. Therefore, $\mu_t(H) \geq \omega(A_{H,t}) + h$, and by Lemma 2 the proof follows.   ▽

Optimal Coloring. By Lemma 6, to derive optimal colorings when t is even, one only needs to consider a diamond enlarged in such a way that it includes also all its h holes. Then one tessellates the grid by means of the enlarged diamonds, using exactly the same techniques already seen in the case that t is odd.

Table 3. Minimum number χ_t of channels used for a sufficiently large network G (for honeycomb grids, $t = 8p + q$, with $p \geq 0$ and $0 \leq q \leq 7$).

Network G	$L(1^t)$
honeycomb grid	$\chi_t = \begin{cases} 24p^2 + 8p + 1 & \text{if } q = 0 \\ 24p^2 + 12p + 2 & \text{if } q = 1 \\ 24p^2 + 20p + 4 & \text{if } q = 2 \\ 24p^2 + 24p + 6 & \text{if } q = 3 \\ 24p^2 + 32p + 11 & \text{if } q = 4 \\ 24p^2 + 36p + 14 & \text{if } q = 5 \\ 24p^2 + 44p + 20 & \text{if } q = 6 \\ 24p^2 + 48p + 24 & \text{if } q = 7 \end{cases}$
square grid	$\chi_t = \lceil \frac{(t+1)^2}{2} \rceil$
hexagonal grid	$\lceil \frac{3}{4}(t+1)^2 \rceil \leq \chi_t \leq (t+1)^2 - t$
References	[1,12,13]

4 Conclusion

Table 3 summarizes the results for optimal $L(1^t)$-coloring for the three grids based on regular tessellations. By observing Table 3, one notes that the proposed colorings for honeycomb grids use less colors than those required by the hexagonal and square grids for any $t > 1$. Therefore, honeycomb grids beat the hexagonal and square grids in terms of both network cost and channel requirement. However further work has still to be done on honeycomb grids. For instance, one could study the $L(\delta_1, \delta_2)$- and $L(\delta_1, 1^{t-1})$-coloring problems with arbitrary δ_1, δ_2 or t.

References

1. A.A. Bertossi and M.C. Pinotti, "Mappings for Conflict-Free Access of Paths in Bidimensional Arrays, Circular Lists, and Complete Trees", *Journal of Parallel and Distributed Computing*, Vol. 62, 2002, pp. 1314-1333.
2. A.A. Bertossi, M.C. Pinotti, and R. Rizzi, "Channel Assignment on Strongly-Simplicial Graphs", *3rd Int'l Workshop on Wireless, Mobile and Ad Hoc Networks*, Nice, April, 2003.
3. A.A. Bertossi, M.C. Pinotti, and R.B. Tan, "Channel Assignment with Separation for Interference Avoidance in Wireless Networks", *IEEE Transactions on Parallel and Distributed Systems*, to appear February 2003.
4. H.L. Bodlaender, T. Kloks, R.B. Tan, and J. van Leeuwen, "Approximation λ-Coloring on Graphs", *STACS*, 2000.
5. G. J. Chang and D. Kuo, "The $L(2,1)$-Labeling Problem on Graphs", *SIAM Journal on Discrete Mathematics*, Vol. 9, 1996, pp. 309-316.
6. I. Chlamtac and S.S. Pinter, "Distributed Nodes Organizations Algorithm for Channel Access in a Multihop Dynamic Radio Network", *IEEE Transactions on Computers*, Vol. 36, 1987, pp. 728-737.
7. J. R. Griggs and R.K. Yeh, "Labelling Graphs with a Condition at Distance 2", *SIAM Journal on Discrete Mathematics*, Vol. 5, 1992, pp. 586-595.

8. W.K. Hale, "Frequency Assignment: Theory and Application", *Proceedings of the IEEE*, Vol. 68, 1980, pp. 1497-1514.
9. I. Katzela and M. Naghshineh, "Channel Assignment Schemes for Cellular Mobile Telecommunication Systems: A Comprehensive Survey", *IEEE Personal Communications*, June 1996, pp. 10-31.
10. S.T. McCormick, "Optimal Approximation of Sparse Hessians and its Equivalence to a Graph Coloring Problem", *Mathematical Programming*, Vol. 26, 1983, pp. 153–171.
11. D. Sakai, "Labeling Chordal Graphs: Distance Two Condition", *SIAM Journal on Discrete Mathematics*, Vol. 7, 1994, pp. 133-140.
12. A. Sen, T. Roxborough, and S. Medidi, "Upper and Lower Bounds of a Class of Channel Assignment Problems in Cellular Networks", Technical Report, Arizona State University, 1997.
13. A.M. Shende et al., "A Characterisation of Optimal Channel Assignments for Wireless Networks Modelled as Cellular and Square Grids", *3rd Int'l IEEE Workshop on Wireless, Mobile and Ad Hoc Networks*, Nice, April 2003.
14. I. Stojmenovic, "Honeycomb Networks: Topological Properties and Communication Algorithms", *IEEE Transactions on Parallel and Distributed Systems*, Vol. 8, 1997, pp. 1036-1042.
15. J. Van den Heuvel, R. A. Leese, and M.A. Shepherd, "Graph Labelling and Radio Channel Assignment", *Journal of Graph Theory*, Vol. 29, 1998, pp. 263-283.
16. J. Zander, "Trends and Challenges in Resource Management Future Wireless Networks", *IEEE Wireless Communications & Networks Conference*, 2000.

Exact Solution of a Class of Frequency Assignment Problems in Cellular Networks

(Extended Abstract)

Tiziana Calamoneri

Department of Computer Science
University of Rome "La Sapienza" – Italy
via Salaria 113, 00198 Roma, Italy
calamo@dsi.uniroma1.it

Abstract. The $L(h, k)$-labeling is an assignment of frequencies to the transmitters/receivers of a multihop radio network such that 'close' transmitters must have frequencies which differ by at least k, and 'very close' transmitters must have frequencies which differ by at least h. The span of an $L(h, k)$-labeling is the difference between the largest and the smallest assigned frequency. In this paper we study the $L(h, k)$-labeling problem of cellular graphs, seeking those with minimum span for each value of k and $h \geq k$.

Keywords: $L(h, k)$-labeling, multihop radio networks, frequency assignment problem, cellular graphs.

1 Introduction

The huge class of *frequency assignment* problems play a very important role in wireless networking, due to the rapid growth of wireless networks and to the relatively scarce radio spectrum. The importance of these problems is even bigger for mobile cellular communication networks as the demand for communication services is significantly going to grow in the future. Many variants of the frequency assignment problem have been defined and studied in many fields such as graph theory, simulated annealing, genetic algorithms, tabu search and neural networks (e.g. see [1,16,19,22]), but the task of all of them is to assign radio frequencies to transmitters at different locations using minimum *span* and without causing *interference*. In a *mobile cellular network* the service area is divided into a number of cells, each one in charge of a transmitter/receiver; a frequency is assigned to each cell to satisfy the local traffic demand. The same frequency can be used in two different cells if there is no perceptible interference.

In this paper, we study the $L(h, k)$-*labeling problem*. It refers to the frequency assignment problem where two kinds of interferences are avoided: *direct collisions* (neighboring cells must have far frequencies, so their signals will not interfere) and *hidden collisions* (a cell must not receive signals of the same frequency from any of its adjacent neighbors, so cells distant two hops must use far frequencies). More precisely, neighbor cells must use frequencies at least h apart, and cells

C. Blundo and C. Laneve (Eds.): ICTCS 2003, LNCS 2841, pp. 163–173, 2003.
© Springer-Verlag Berlin Heidelberg 2003

that are neighbors of the same cell (two hops far) must use frequencies at least k apart. The nature of the environment and the geographical distance are the major factors determining parameters h and k; we can assume $h \geq k$ from the definitions of direct and hidden collisions. The *span* of an $L(h, k)$-labeling is the difference between the largest and the smallest assigned frequency. The aim of the $L(h, k)$-problem is to satisfy the distance constraints using the minimum span.

Since its formal definition as a specialization of the frequency assignment problem [14] the $L(h, k)$-labeling problem has been widely studied by means of techniques from disparate research areas and receiving many names (an absolutely non exhaustive list of related references is [4,5,6,7,10,9,11,17,18,20]). However, almost all the literature concerns the special case of $k = 1$ and $h = 2$, and very few papers [8,12,13,15] investigate on the more general problem. Nevertheless, the solution of the problem for any h and k is worthy since it allows one to handle more realistic scenarios.

The $L(h, k)$-labeling problem can be formulated as a coloring problem and, hence, its decisional version is NP-complete [2]. This motivates seeking optimal solutions on particular classes of graphs.

In this paper we completely solve the frequency assignment problem with $L(h, k)$ constraints on cellular networks covering full range of frequencies expressed in terms of $k > 0$ and $h \geq k$. The proposed labelings are optimal, except a very small range, where we give a good approximation as we provide close upper and lower bounds. For theoretical completeness we study the same problem also on hexagonal and squared grids, although we do not include the proofs of these latter results in this extended abstract.

Exploiting the upper bounds presented in this paper, a frequency can be assigned to any node in a distributed fashion in constant time in all considered grids, provided that the relative position of the node in the graph is locally known. To avoid heaviness in notation we do not express explicitly each label as function of the coordinates of any node in the grid.

2   Preliminaries and Discussion of the Results

A *mobile cellular network* is usually represented as a tassellation of hexagonal cells. We do not care about the dimension of the network, so we consider it as an infinite graph.

From now on, we study the cellular network by means of its *interference graph*: each cell of the network is represented as a node and two nodes have an edge in between if the corresponding cells are subject to direct collisions, i.e. they are adjacent. This graph is a triangular grid and we call it *cellular graph*, according to the notation introduced in [21].

In this context, the $L(h, k)$-*labeling problem* can be formulated as a graph coloring problem, where colors represent possible frequencies. More precisely, given real positive k and $h \geq k$, an $L(h, k)$-*labeling* of a graph $G = (V, E)$ is a function $L : V \to \mathbb{R}$ such that

- $|L(u) - L(v)| \geq h$ if $(u, v) \in E$ and
- $|L(u) - L(v)| \geq k$ if there exists $w \in V$ such that $(u, w) \in E$ and $(w, v) \in E$.

The *span* of an $L(h, k)$-labeling is the difference between the largest and the smallest value of L, so it is not restrictive to assume 0 as the smallest value of L. For any positive reals k and $h \geq k$, we denote by $\lambda_{h,k}(G)$ the smallest integer λ such that graph G has an $L(h, k)$-labeling of span λ.

In this paper, we study the $L(h, k)$-labeling problem on cellular graph C, proving that:

$$\lambda_{h,k}(C) = 6h \text{ if } k \leq h \leq \tfrac{4}{3}k;$$
$$\lambda_{h,k}(C) = 8k \text{ if } \tfrac{4}{3}k \leq h \leq 2k;$$
$$3h + 2k \leq \lambda_{h,k}(C) \leq \min(4h, 11k) \text{ if } 2k \leq h \leq 3k;$$
$$\lambda_{h,k}(C) = 3h + 2k \text{ if } 3k \leq h < 4k;$$
$$\lambda_{h,k}(C) = 2h + 6k \text{ if } h \geq 4k;$$

For theoretical completeness we have considered also the other regular tassellations of the plane, i.e. hexagonal and squared grids, but we omit these study in this extended abstract.

A graphical summary of results is depicted in Fig. 1.

The $L(h, k)$-labeling problem on regular grids has already been studied in [3] for $h = 2$ and $k = 1$, and in [5] for $h = 0, 1, 2$ and $k = 1$. Of course, the results obtained in this paper include as special case the previous ones.

In [15] the distance between two labels $i, j \in \{0, 1, \ldots, n - 1\}$ is defined as $min\{|i - j|, n - |i - j|\}$. Using this definition and restricting h and k to be integer, the authors study a variant of $L(h, k)$-labeling on triangular and squared grids (for a summary of their results see Fig. 2). They approach this different problem from a purely combinatorial point of view, with completely different techniques, for each integer h and k. Furthermore, observe that – despite the similarity of the $L(h, k)$-labeling problem and the variant introduced in [15] – it does not seem possible to shift from results in [15] to ours (compare Fig. 1 and Fig. 2).

Before proving one by one all bounds listed above, we state some general results that will be useful in the following.

Observation 1 *Any two neighboring nodes have different labels, so given any regular grid of the plane G with degree Δ ($\Delta = 3, 4$ or 6) with an optimal $L(h, k)$-labeling, there always exists a node x and one of its neighbors y such that $L(y) < L(x)$. If, in addition, G is a cellular graph, then any three nodes x, y and z, forming a triangle can be choosen in such a way that $L(y) < L(x) < L(z)$.*

Observe that, in any $L(h, k)$-labeling, if $L(x) > L(y)$ and x and y are neighbors in the grid, then it must be $L(x) \geq L(y) + h \geq h$. Analogously, if $L(z) > L(w)$ and z and w are at distance two in the grid, then $L(z) \geq L(w) + k \geq k$.

Theorem 2. *Given any regular grid of the plane G with degree Δ ($\Delta = 3, 4$ or 6), the following conditions for $\lambda_{h,k}(G)$ hold:*
a. $\lambda_{h,k}(G) \geq \Delta h$ for any $k \leq h \leq (\tfrac{\Delta+2}{\Delta})k$;

166   Tiziana Calamoneri

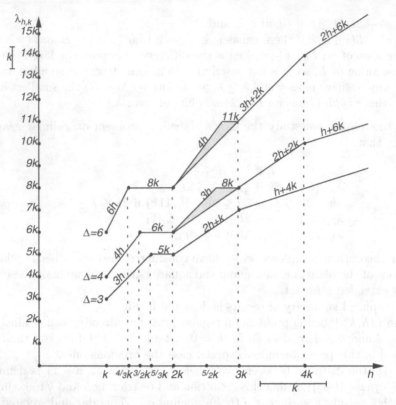

Fig. 1. Summary of the results. Lines labeled by $\Delta = 6, \Delta = 4$ and $\Delta = 3$ summarize the results on cellular graphs, squared and hexagonal grids, respectively. Value h is considered as a function of k.

b. $\lambda_{h,k}(G) \geq (\Delta + 2)k$ for any $(\frac{\Delta+2}{\Delta})k \leq h \leq 2k$;

Sketch of Proof. Let be given any optimal $L(h,k)$-labeling of G, and let us consider a node x according to Obs. 1. Node x has degree Δ and, in view of the definition of $L(h,k)$-labeling, its label $L(x)$ must be at least h apart from the label of each one of its neighbors. On the other hand, all Δ neighbors of x are at distance 2 in the graph via x, so their labels must differ by at least k.

Let us prove bounds a. and b. together.

Let $k \leq h \leq 2k$. Consider set U of distinct used labels in the $L(h,k)$-labeling. $|U|$ must be at least $\Delta + 1$. Furthermore, since each label can assume the role of $L(x)$, we have to impose that the $L(h,k)$-constraints hold for each element of U. We can focus on two special cases:

1. Let us consider the distance-1 constraint of the $L(h,k)$-labeling, first: since $L(x)$ must differ by at least h from the labels of all its neighbors, we can assume that all used values are positioned at distance h from each other. In this way, we need a span of $\Delta h, \forall h \geq k$.

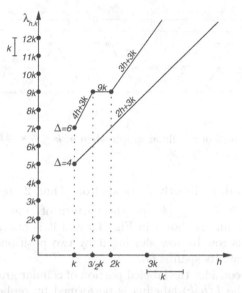

Fig. 2. Summary of the results presented in [15] translated in our nomenclature. Observe that here $\lambda_{h,k}$ refers to 'cyclic' $L(h,k)$-labeling, with h and k integer values. Lines labeled by $\Delta = 6$ and $\Delta = 4$ summarize the results on cellular graphs and squared grids, respectively. Value h is considered as a function of k.

2. Now, let us add the distance-2 constraint: since all neighbors of x must differ at least by k from each other, we can assume that all used labels are positioned at distance k from each other. As $h \leq 2k$, it is enough to have only $\Delta + 3$ different values (i.e. one used for x, Δ used for its neighbors and at most two – too close to $L(x)$ – not used). In this case the span is $(\Delta + 2)k$.

The previously defined $L(h,k)$-labelings are both feasible. Furthermore, any other $L(h,k)$-labeling cannot use span smaller than the minimum of the previously found values because it has to join the distance-1 and distance-2 constraints. The claim follows.   □

3   Cellular Graphs

Given a cellular graph with an optimal $L(h,k)$-labeling, for any node x we call $a_1, a_2, \ldots a_6$ its neighbors arranged in clockwise order around x. It is not restrictive to assume that a_1 has the smallest label, and that $L(a_2) < L(a_6)$.

In this section, we derive exact values of $\lambda_{h,k}(C)$ by proving coinciding upper and lower bounds, except for interval $2k \leq h \leq 3k$, where bounds are slightly different.

3.1 $k \leq h \leq 2k$

Theorem 3. If $k \leq h \leq \frac{4}{3}k$, then $\lambda_{h,k}(C) = 6h$; if $\frac{4}{3}k \leq h \leq 2k$, then $\lambda_{h,k}(C) = 8k$.

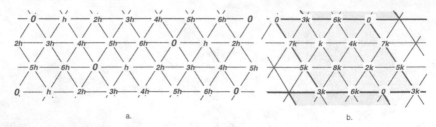

Fig. 3. Optimal labelings of a cellular graph when a. $k \leq h \leq \frac{4}{3}k$ and when b. $\frac{4}{3}k \leq h \leq 2k$.

Proof. **Lower bound.** It directly descends from Thm. 2, items a. and b.

Upper bound. If $k \leq h \leq \frac{4}{3}k$, use the pattern of labels $0, h, 2h, \ldots, 6h$. A possible feasible labeling is shown in Fig. 3.a and it is obtained by replicating the pattern of labels row by row shifting it by two positions on the left when going to the next row. Its span is $6h$.

If $\frac{4}{3}k \leq h \leq 2k$, consider the labeled portion of cellular graph limited by bold lines in Fig. 3.b. The $L(h, k)$-labeling is performed by replicating this pattern of labels. This is possible because nodes on both horizontal and vertical sides of the labeled portion are colored with the same ordered set of labels ($0\ 3k\ 6k$ and $0\ 7k\ 5k\ 3k$, respectively). In view of the distances between the used labels, it is straightforward to see that the produced coloring is a feasible $L(h, k)$-labeling and its span is $8k$. Observe that this labeling is exactly the same as a $L(2, 1)$-labeling, where each value has been multiplied by k. □

3.2 $2k \leq h < 4k$

Theorem 4. *If $3k \leq h < 4k$, then $\lambda_{h,k}(C) = 3h + 2k$; if $2k \leq h \leq 3k$ then $3h + 2k \leq \lambda_{h,k}(C) \leq min(4h, 11k)$.*

Proof. **Upper bound.** If $2k \leq h \leq 3k$, the $L(h, k)$-labelings derived by replicating the labeled portions of cellular grid limited by bold lines in Fig. 4.a and 4.b are both feasible and their span is $4h$ and $11k$, respectively. It follows that $\lambda_{h,k}(C) \leq \min(4h, 11k)$. The threshold value of h changing the result of min function is $\frac{11}{4}k$.

If $3k \leq h < 4k$, consider the labeled portion of cellular graph limited by bold lines in Fig. 5.a, and replicate this pattern. The produced coloring is a feasible $L(h, k)$-labeling and its span is $3h + 2k$.

Lower bound. Let be given a cellular graph with any optimal $L(h, k)$-labeling, $2k \leq h < 4k$. We consider a node x according to Obs. 1 (i.e. having two neighbors y and z such that $L(y) < L(x) < L(z)$) and all possible relative orders of the labels of x and its neighbors. We prove – by contradiction – that $\lambda_{h,k}(C) \geq 3h + 2k$ if $2k \leq h < 4k$. So, assume $\lambda_{h,k}(C) < 3h + 2k$. For the nomenclature, we refer to Fig. 6.

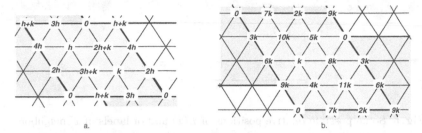

Fig. 4. Two feasible labelings of a cellular graph when $2k \leq h \leq 3k$. Their span is a. $4h$ and b. $11k$.

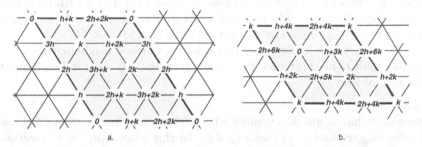

Fig. 5. Two optimally labeled portions of cellular graph when a. $3k \leq h < 4k$ and b. $h \geq 4k$.

Case $5 - x - 1$:

Suppose first that x has 5 neighbors whose labels are smaller than $L(x)$ and only one with label bigger than $L(x)$ (see Fig. 6.a). Hence, in all this item, $L(x)$ is in position F while $L(a_1)$ is in position A.

First of all, observe that two adjacent nodes a_i and a_{i+1} cannot have their labels in consecutive positions (e.g. $L(a_i)$ in C and $L(a_{i+1})$ in D), otherwise the span would become too large, against the hypothesis $\lambda_{h,k}(C) < 3h + 2k$. In the same way, two adjacent nodes a_i and a_{i+1} cannot have their labels separated by only one label (e.g. $L(a_i)$ in C and $L(a_{i+1})$ in E) otherwise the span would be $\geq 3h + 2k$. Therefore, $L(a_2)$ cannot be in position B, or in C. $L(a_2)$ cannot be in G because we know that $L(a_2) < L(a_6)$.

It follows that $L(a_2)$ lies either in D or in E.

If $L(a_2)$ in D – for the previous considerations – $L(a_3)$ must be in G and hence $L(a_6)$ must be in E. In this way, $L(a_4)$ and $L(a_5)$ would be in B and C, in some order, achieving in any case a too large span.

Finally, if $L(a_2)$ is in E, then $L(a_6)$ must necessarily be in F and $L(a_3), L(a_4)$ and $L(a_5)$ occupy positions B, C and D in some order, leading again to a too large span.

We deduce that – under the hypothesis $\lambda_{h,k}(C) < 3h + 2k$ – this configuration never occurs.

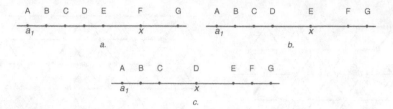

Fig. 6. Some possible relative positions of $L(x)$ and of labels of x' neighbors.

Cases $4 - x - 2$, $2 - x - 4$ and $1 - x - 5$:
If x has 4 neighbors whose labels are smaller than $L(x)$ and 2 with label bigger than $L(x)$ (see Fig. 6.b), with considerations similar to the previous ones, it is possible to prove that this case never occurs when $\lambda_{h,k}(C) < 3h + 2k$.

The cases in which x has either two neighbors or one neighbor whose labels are smaller than $L(x)$ are symmetrical to the previous two cases and then omitted for the sake of brevity.

Case $3 - x - 3$:
Suppose now that x has 3 neighbors whose labels are smaller than $L(x)$ and 3 with label bigger than $L(x)$ (see Fig. 6.c). In this case, $L(a_1)$ is in position A and $L(x)$ is in position D.

Since this case does not lead to any contradiction, it can occur when $\lambda_{h,k}(C) < 3h + 2k$.

We have proven that, in the hypothesis $\lambda_{h,k}(C) < 3h + 2k$, only three cases can occur; namely, it can happens that the six labels of x's neighbors are either all smaller than $L(x)$, or all bigger than $L(x)$ or three smaller and three bigger than $L(x)$. Now we want to study which values $L(x)$ can assume and prove that no value is feasible, i.e. our hypothesis $\lambda_{h,k}(C) < 3h + 2k$ is false.

$0 \leq L(x) < 2h - 3k$
In this interval $L(x)$ would have all six labels of x's neighbors to its right. If $L(x)$ was $\geq 2h - 3k$ then the space to its right would be not sufficient to keep the span $< 3h + 2k$ and, at the same time, to fit six labels at mutual distance k and at distance $\geq h$ from $L(x)$.

$2h - 3k \leq L(x) < h + 2k$
$L(x)$ never lies inside this interval because there is not enough room to fit six label to the right of $L(x)$ and not enough room to fit three labels to the left of $L(x)$. From the previous part of the proof, we know that other configurations are not possible.

$h + 2k \leq L(x) < 2h$
If $L(x)$ lies in this interval, three labels must be smaller than $L(x)$ and three labels must be bigger than it.

$2h \leq L(x) < h + 5k$
$L(x)$ never lies here, for analogous reasons with respect to the second interval.

$h + 5k \leq L(x) < 3h + 2k$
This interval is analogous to the first one.

So, only three intervals are feasible for $L(x)$. Now observe that the second one, $[h + 2k, 2h)$, is $h - 2k$ wide; since $h - 2k < 2k$ when $h < 4k$, we deduce that inside this interval we can fit at most two labels at mutual distance k. It follows that the other two intervals must contain at least four labels each and hence they must be at least $3k$ wide. This is absurd if $2k \leq h < 3k$ and the proof is concluded in this case. If $3k \leq h < 4k$ let us consider the general $L(x)$ in the first (third) feasible interval. All six x's neighbors must have label bigger (smaller) than $L(x)$, and only two can be in the second feasible interval while four are in the third (first) one. Let us focus on the labels $L(a_i)$ and $L(a_j)$ lying inside the second feasible interval. If a_i and a_j are neighbors, then the second interval must be at least h wide, and this is absurd. If a_i and a_j have distance two in the cycle induced by x's neighbors, then consider the three nodes different from a_i, a_j and their common neighbor; they must all lie in the third (first) interval. If a_i and a_j have distance three in the cycle induced by x's neighbors, then there exist two pairs of neighbors whose labels all lie in the third (first) interval. Both configurations imply that the third (first) feasible interval is at least $h + k$ wide, possible if and only if $h \geq 4k$, i.e. an absurd.

The contradictions raised from the hypothesis $\lambda_{h,k}(C) < 3h + 2k$.   □

In the interval $2k \leq h \leq 3k$, the achieved upper and lower bounds for $\lambda_{h,k}(C)$ are not coinciding. The following result, whose proof is omitted in this extended abstract, ensures us that the lower bound is not tight, at least in a subinterval:

Theorem 5. *If $2k < h < \frac{5}{2}k$, then $\lambda_{h,k}(C) > 3h + 2k$.*

On the base of the previous theorem and of the continuity of function $\lambda_{h,k}(C)$ we conjecture that $\lambda_{h,k}(C) = 4h$ if $2k \leq h \leq \frac{5}{2}k$ and $\lambda_{h,k}(C) = 2h + 5k$ if $\frac{5}{2}k \leq h \leq 3k$.

3.3 $h \geq 4k$

Theorem 6. *If $h \geq 4k$, then $\lambda_{h,k}(C) = 2h + 6k$.*

Sketch of Proof. **Upper bound.** Consider the labeled portion of cellular graph limited by bold lines in Fig. 5.b and replicate it in all directions.

The produced coloring is a feasible $L(h, k)$-labeling and its span is $2h + 6k$.

Lower bound. Let be given a cellular graph with an optimal $L(h, k)$-labeling. Let x be any node in the grid such that $L(x) \geq h$ according to Obs. 1. By contradiction, let us assume $\lambda_{h,k}(C) < 2h + 6k$. By considering all different cases and, very similarly to the proof of Thm 4, it is possible to prove that either all labels of x's neighbors lie to the same side with respect to $L(x)$ or they are three to the left and three to the right of $L(x)$. By examining which values $L(x)$ can assume, we can show that the assumption $\lambda_{h,k}(C) < 2h + 6k$ is absurd.   □

4   Conclusions and Open Problems

In this paper we have studied the $L(h, k)$-labeling problem on cellular networks. For each value of k and $h \geq k$ we have obtained exact values of the span, except in a small interval, where we provide slightly different upper and lower bounds for $\lambda_{h,k}(C)$. It is easy to see that the replication schemes presented for the upper bounds lead to simple distributed algorithms to label the whole grid in constant time, provided that each node knows its coordinates in the grid.

Three open problems arise from this work.

The first one is to prove (or disprove) our conjecture and close the gap between upper and lower bound when $2k \leq h \leq 3k$.

The second one is to understand if there exists some shifting method to go from the results collected in the present paper and those presented in [15] (see Fig. 2) and vice-versa. Indeed, it is not surprising that the values of $\lambda_{h,k}$ under the 'cyclicity' assumption are bigger than ours, but it is not clear the reason why our $\lambda_{h,k}$ function is fragmented in a bigger number of segments.

Finally, it would be interesting to study the $L(h, k)$-labeling problem for other (not regular) tilings, built with different shaped tiles (i.e. the edge-clique graph of the cellular graph, having degree 4, constituted by triangular and hexagonal tiles).

References

1. K.I. Aardal, S.P.M. van Hoesel, A.M.C.A. Koster, C. Mannino and A. Sassano. Models and Solution Techniques for Frequency Assignment Problems. *ZIB-Report 01-40, Konrad-Zuse-Zentrum fur Informationstechnik Berlin*, 2001.
2. A.A. Bertossi and M.A. Bonuccelli. Code Assignment for Hidden Terminal Interference Avoidance in Multihop Packet Radio Networks. *IEEE/ACM Trans. on Networking*, 3:441–449, 1995.
3. A.A. Bertossi, C.M. Pinotti and R.B. Tan: Channel assignment with separation for interference avoidance in wireless networks. *IEEE Transactions on Parallel and Distributed Systems* (in press). Preliminary version in *ACM Workshop DIAL M 2000*, 2000.
4. H.L. Bodlaender, T. Kloks, R.B. Tan and J. van Leeuwen. λ-Coloring of Graphs. In *Proc. of STACS 2000*, pages 395–406. Lectures Notes in Computer Science 1770, 2000.
5. T. Calamoneri and R. Petreschi: $L(2, 1)$-Labeling of Planar Graphs (Extended Abstract). In Proceedings of *5th ACM Int. Workshop on Discrete Algorithms and Methods for Mobile Computing and Communications (DIAL M)*, 2001, pages 28-33.
6. T. Calamoneri and R. Petreschi: On the Radiocoloring Problem. In Proceedings of *4th Int.l Workshop on Distributed Computing (IWDC*, Lecture Notes in Computer Science 2571, 2002, pages 118–127.
7. T. Calamoneri and R. Petreschi: λ-*Coloring Unigraphs*. In Proceedings of *LATIN 2002*. Lectures Notes in Computer Science Science 2286, pp. 236-247, 2002.
8. T. Calamoneri, A. Pelc and R. Petreschi. Labeling trees with a condition at distance two. In Proceedings of *R.C. Bose Centenary Symp. on Discr. Math. and Applications*; electronic notes in discrete mathemathics, 2002.

9. T. Calamoneri and P. Vocca: On the Approximability of the $L(h,k)$-Labelling Problem. Manuscript, 2003.

10. G.J. Chang and D. Kuo. The $L(2,1)$-labeling Problem on Graphs. *SIAM J. Disc. Math.*, 9:309–316, 1996.

11. D.A. Fotakis, S.E. Nikoletseas, V.G. Papadoulou and P.G. Spirakis: NP-completeness Results and Efficient Approximations for Radiocoloring in Planar Graphs. In Proceedings of *25th Int.l Symp. on Math. Foundations of Compu. Sci. (MFCS 2000)*, 2000.

12. J.P. Georges and D.W. Mauro, Some results on λ_k^j-numbers of the products of complete graphs, *Congr. Numer.* 140 (1999), 141-160.

13. J.P. Georges, D.W. Mauro and M.I. Stein, Labeling products of complete graphs with a condition at distance two, *SIAM J. Discr. Math.* 14 (2000), 28-35.

14. J.R. Griggs and R.K. Yeh. Labeling graphs with a Condition at Distance 2. *SIAM J. Disc. Math*, 5:586–595, 1992.

15. J. van den Heuvel, R.A. Leese and M.A. Shepherd: Graph Labelling and Radio Channel Assignment. *Journal of Graph Theory* 29 (1998): 263–283.

16. A.M.C.A. Koster. *Frequency Assignment*. Ph.D. thesis, Universiteit Maastricht, 1999.

17. D. Liu and R.K.Yeh, On distance two labelings of graphs, *Ars Combinatoria* 47 (1997), 13-22.

18. M.Molloy and M.R. Salavatipour. Frequency channel assignment on planar networks. In Proceedings of *10th Annual European Symposium on Algorithms (ESA)* 2002, pp 736–747.

19. R.A. Murphey, P.M. Pardalos and M.G.C. Resende. Frequency Assignment Problems. In *Handbook of Combinatorial Optimization*, D.-Z. Du and P.M. Pardalos (Eds.) :295–377, 1999. Kluweker Academic Publishers.

20. D. Sakai. Labeling Chordal Graphs: Distance Two Condition. *SIAM J. Disc. Math*, 7:133–140, 1994.

21. A. Sen, T. Roxborough and S. Medidi: Upper and Lower Bounds of a Class of Channel Assignmet Problems in Cellular Networks. *IEEE INFOCOM 1998*, 1998.

22. M. Shepherd: *Radio Channel Assignment*. Ph.D. thesis, Merton College, Oxford, 1998.

The Complexity of Checking Consistency
of Pedigree Information and Related Problems

Luca Aceto[1], Jens A. Hansen[1], Anna Ingólfsdóttir[1,2],
Jacob Johnsen[1], and John Knudsen[1]

[1] **BRICS** (Basic Research in Computer Science),
Centre of the Danish National Research Foundation, Department of Computer Science,
Aalborg University, Fr. Bajersvej 7E, 9220 Aalborg Ø, Denmark
{luca,alsted,annai,johnsen,johnk}@cs.auc.dk
[2] deCODE Genetics, Sturlugata 8, 101 Reykjavík, Iceland
annai@decode.is

Abstract. Consistency checking is a fundamental computational problem in genetics. Given a pedigree and information on the genotypes (of some) of the individuals in it, the aim of consistency checking is to determine whether these data are consistent with the classic Mendelian laws of inheritance. This problem arose originally from the geneticists' need to filter their input data from erroneous information, and is well motivated from both a biological and a sociological viewpoint. This paper shows that consistency checking is NP-complete, even with focus on a single gene and in the presence of three alleles. Several other results on the computational complexity of problems from genetics that are related to consistency checking are also offered. In particular, it is shown that checking the consistency of pedigrees over two alleles, and of pedigrees without loops, can be done in polynomial time.

1 Introduction

A paradigmatic problem from the field of genetics in which the use of algorithmic techniques is by now widespread, and is embodied in software tools like Allegro [6], Genehunter [8], Merlin [1] and Pedcheck [11], is that of linkage analysis. *Linkage analysis* is a well established, statistical method used to relate genes in the human genome to some biological trait that an individual possesses. Example traits that may be investigated range from simple ones like blood type and eye colour to those that may predispose an individual for a disease. Genes causing major diseases (e.g., Parkinson's disease, obesity and anxiety) have already been discovered using this technique [4].

In order to track the inheritance of genetic traits, geneticists use structures called pedigrees. A *pedigree* describes the family relations amongst a collection of individuals, and usually comes equipped with (possibly partial) information on their genotypes – i.e., on the pairs of alleles at a locus in their genome. (An *allele* is one of the possible forms a gene may have.) Pedigrees are the subject of algorithmic analysis via methods like linkage analysis.

A computational problem that is closely related to that of linkage analysis is *consistency checking*. Given a pedigree and information on the genotypes (of some) of the

C. Blundo and C. Laneve (Eds.): ICTCS 2003, LNCS 2841, pp. 174–187, 2003.
© Springer-Verlag Berlin Heidelberg 2003

individuals in it, the aim of consistency checking is to determine whether these data are consistent with the classic Mendelian laws of inheritance (see, e.g., the reference [7]). If it turns out that the inheritance of the genotypes in the pedigree is in conflict with the Mendelian laws of inheritance, then the pedigree and the information on the genotypes are *inconsistent*. If no such conflict arises, then the data are *consistent*.

The problem of consistency checking arose originally from the geneticists' need to filter their input data from erroneous information, because inconsistent data are undesirable. According to [15, p. 496], it is essential that all Mendelian inconsistencies be eliminated prior to linkage analysis as "a few inopportunely placed errors, if ignored, can tremendously affect evidence for linkage." Furthermore, as reported in [11], in many real-life cases the manual identification of inconsistencies can be very difficult, time consuming, and sometimes unsuccessful. It would therefore be most helpful to have automatic tool support for this task.

Hence, consistency checking is a well motivated problem from a biological viewpoint. Another issue is whether it is computationally feasible. The aim of this paper is to show that consistency checking is NP-complete *even if we focus on genotype information for a single gene*, and thus that the existence of consistency checking algorithms that have polynomial worst case complexity is unlikely – cf., e.g., the claim by O'Connell and Weeks that their "new genotype-elimination algorithm is guaranteed to detect every Mendelian inconsistency efficiently and quickly" [12, pp. 1739–1740]. To the best of our knowledge, this is a new result in both computer science and genetics.

After discussing a simple formal model for pedigrees and associated genotype information, we use it to formalize the consistency checking problem with focus on a single gene (Sect. 2). The consistency checking problem is shown to be NP-complete in Sect. 3, even in the presence of *three* alleles. Our proof of NP-hardness for this problem is based on a reduction from 3SAT (a classic NP-complete problem – see, e.g., [13, Propn. 9.2, p. 183]), and uses pedigrees with loops. As stated in [12, p. 1733], likelihood computations on, and consistency checking of, pedigrees with loops continue to pose daunting computational challenges. This is confirmed by the use of looping pedigrees in our NP-completeness proof, and by the fact that pedigrees without loops can be checked for consistency in polynomial time (Thm. 2). (Note, however, that the loops that arise in our constructions are of the kind geneticists call "marriage loops" [14], and not loops arising from inbreeding.) Sect. 4 presents results on the computational complexity of three problems from the genetics literature that are closely related to consistency checking. In particular, we show that checking consistency of pedigrees over *two* alleles is in P (Thm. 4). On the other hand, checking consistency of phase known genotype information, and deciding whether a pedigree has k critical genotypes (with $k \geq 0$) are both NP-complete (Thms. 3 and 5). The paper concludes with a brief mention of avenues to future work (Sect. 5).

A full account of the work presented in this extended abstract may be found in [2], to which the reader is referred for the technical details.

Related Work. As previously mentioned, linkage analysis is a statistical method used to relate genes in the human genome to some biological trait that an individual possesses. Like this method, other pedigree analysis techniques involve calculations with probability distributions describing, e.g., the likelihood of gene transmission from one generation to the next. The study [14] investigates the structural complexity of two problems whose solution is part and parcel of many statistical pedigree analysis methods, viz. the calculation of the so-called *marginal probability*, and that of computing the so-called *maximum likelihood*. The decision problems associated with both of these computational tasks are shown NP-hard in *op. cit.* even for pedigrees without inbreeding loops, and with focus on a single gene. There is a close connection between our NP-completeness result for the consistency checking problem and the NP-hardness results from [14], but neither set of results implies the other. For instance, a pedigree with genotype information is consistent if, and only if, the maximum likelihood for that pedigree is positive. The consistency checking problem can therefore be reduced to an instance of the decision version of the maximum likelihood problem. However, this does not yield our NP-completeness result as a corollary. Moreover, we focus on consistency checking, an apparently very basic problem in genetics, with a purely combinatorial flavour, that does not involve any likelihood computations. It is also interesting to look at similarities and differences in the proofs of the NP-completeness result for consistency checking we offer here (see Thm. 1), and of Thms. 5 and 9 in [14]. Both sets of results use reductions from 3SAT. The reductions are, however, very different, and, at first sight, somewhat at odds with one another. In our proof of Thm. 1, we focus on a single gene with three alleles. The use of three alleles in this proof of NP-hardness of the consistency checking problem is most likely necessary because, as stated in Thm. 4, checking consistency of pedigrees over *two* alleles is in P. The reduction employed in [14] instead uses only two alleles, and the threshold value on, e.g., the maximum likelihood plays a crucial role in the proofs of the NP-hardness results offered *ibidem*. Indeed, the pedigrees over two alleles generated by the reductions employed there are *always* consistent, as would be detected by the algorithm on which the proof of our Thm. 4 is based.

In an effort to accelerate likelihood calculations, geneticists have proposed genotype elimination algorithms. The aim of these algorithms is to identify, and eliminate, those genotypes that are not consistent with the observed phenotype information in the pedigree. The first algorithm for genotype elimination was proposed by Lange and Goradia in [9], where it was shown that the algorithm is correct for genotype elimination over non-looping pedigrees, but fails to detect all superfluous genotypes for inbred pedigrees. An algorithm for genotype elimination that is correct also in the presence of loops in pedigrees has been offered by O'Connell and Weeks in [12]. Genotype elimination algorithms may be used to detect Mendelian inconsistencies and critical genotypes in pedigrees – see, e.g., the proof of Thm. 2, detailed in [2], where we make use of the aforementioned algorithm by Lange and Goradia to argue that pedigrees without loops can be checked for consistency in polynomial time. This makes them suitable as preprocessing steps in algorithms that assume that the input genotype data be consistent. An example of such a use of genotype elimination algorithms is presented in [10], where the authors propose a rule-based, iterative, heuristic algorithm, the *block extension algorithm*, for the so-called *Minimum-Recombinant Haplotype Configuration Problem*. Although this problem is shown to be NP-hard in *op. cit.*, the encouraging preliminary experimental results given in that reference seem to indicate that the block extension algorithm performs rather well in practice under the assumption that its input data are consistent. As we show in this paper, however, checking the consistency of the input data is itself computationally hard. The reference [10] also offers a polynomial time algorithm for haplotype reconstruction *without recombination*; this algorithm assumes input data with no missing genotypes, whose consistency can be checked in linear time in the number of non-founders of the input pedigree. (See the proof of Thm. 1 in this extended abstract.)

2 Formalizing Gene Inheritance and Mendelian Consistency

As already mentioned in Sect. 1, a pedigree is a fundamental structure used in genetics. In order to reason about pedigrees and the genotype information that they contain, we need a formal model for them. Several formalizations of the notion of pedigree have been presented in the literature on computational genetics. (See, e.g., [10, 14].) We now proceed to present the models for pedigrees and their associated genotype information adopted in this study, and then use these models to formalize the consistency checking problem.

Definition 1 (Pedigree). *A pedigree consists of a 4-tuple $P = \langle V, F, \mathbf{p}, \mathbf{m} \rangle$ where:*

- *V is a finite, non-empty set of members of the pedigree (ranged over by u, v),*
- *$F \subseteq V$ is the set of founders,*
- *$\mathbf{p}, \mathbf{m} : V \setminus F \longrightarrow V$ are the paternal and maternal functions, respectively, where*

$$\mathbf{p}(V \setminus F) \cap \mathbf{m}(V \setminus F) = \emptyset$$

(that is, nobody can be both a mother and a father), and
- *the transitive closure of the binary relation obtained as the union of the graphs of $\mathbf{p}$ and $\mathbf{m}$ is irreflexive (that is, a member of the pedigree is never its own ancestor).*

The set $N = V \setminus F$ is usually referred to as the set of non-founders of the pedigree.

Note that the set of founders in a pedigree is always non-empty. Moreover, since the model specifies the sex of an individual only implicitly via the paternal and maternal functions, the sex of a "leaf" in a pedigree (i.e., of an individual without offspring) is not specified. In our examples and constructions, the sex of individuals in a pedigree without offspring will be chosen arbitrarily, as it is immaterial in consistency checking. Our pictorial representation of pedigrees (with associated genotype information) is borrowed from the genetics literature, and is introduced in Fig. 1. That figure represents a pedigree whose founders are individuals 1 and 2, who are respectively the father and the mother of individual 3.

For the sake of precision, we now offer a formal definition of loop in a pedigree. The following definition is based on that in [12].

Definition 2 (Looping Pedigree). *Let $P = \langle V, F, \mathbf{p}, \mathbf{m} \rangle$ be a pedigree. Two distinct members u and v of the pedigree are said to* mate *if they have an offspring in common – that is, if there is a non-founder v' of P such that $\{\mathbf{p}(v'), \mathbf{m}(v')\} = \{u, v\}$. Such a v' is a* child *of u and v.*

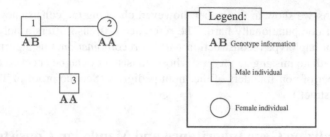

Fig. 1. Example of a pedigree.

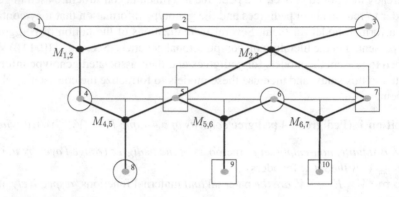

Fig. 2. A pedigree illustrated as done throughout this paper, and its associated mating graph as defined in Def. 2. The black dots are the mating nodes and the grey dots are "person nodes".

The mating graph *associated with P is the undirected graph G_P whose set of nodes includes V, and contains* mating nodes *$M_{u,v}$ for every pair (u, v) of members of P that mate. The edges in such a graph are those that connect members u and v that mate to the mating node $M_{u,v}$, and those that connect such a mating node to the common children of u and v.*

A loop *in G_P is a non-empty path consisting of* distinct *edges that starts and ends in the same node.*

Finally, we say that a pedigree P is looping *(or has a loop) if its associated mating graph G_P contains a loop.*

An example of a looping pedigree is given in Fig. 2, together with its associated mating graph. One of the loops in that pedigree is due to inbreeding, and arises because individuals 4 and 5 mate, and have a common ancestor. Another is a so-called marriage loop, and stems from the matings between individual 6 and the two brothers 5 and 7.

Consistency checking of a pedigree is based on its associated genotype information; intuitively, the pedigree defines the structure of the family relationships that are being modelled, and the genotype information is the data which must be consistent with the structure. We now present a formal genotype model. In what follows, it is always assumed that instances of this genotype model are in the context of a specific gene and pedigree. We also assume a fixed, finite and non-empty set $\mathcal{A}$ of *alleles* ranged over by **A, B**, etc.

In what follows, $\mathrm{Two}(\mathcal{A})$ denotes the family of non-empty subsets of $\mathcal{A}$ that contain no more than two alleles. As described below, an element of $\mathrm{Two}(\mathcal{A})$ will be used to represent a genotype over the set of alleles $\mathcal{A}$.

Definition 3 (Genotype Information). *Let* $P = \langle V, F, \mathbf{p}, \mathbf{m} \rangle$ *be a pedigree. A geno-type information for P is a partial function* $\mathcal{G} : V \hookrightarrow \mathrm{Two}(\mathcal{A})$ *that associates a geno-type to (some of) the members of the pedigree. The domain,* $\mathrm{dom}(\mathcal{G})$, *of the function is referred to as the set of genotyped members of the pedigree. The genotype information* $\mathcal{G}$ *is* complete *if* $\mathrm{dom}(\mathcal{G}) = V$.

Let $\mathcal{G}$ *and* $\mathcal{G}'$ *be two genotype information. We say that* $\mathcal{G}'$ *extends* $\mathcal{G}$ *if* $\mathrm{dom}(\mathcal{G})$ *is included in* $\mathrm{dom}(\mathcal{G}')$, *and* $\mathcal{G}$ *and* $\mathcal{G}'$ *coincide over* $\mathrm{dom}(\mathcal{G})$.

In the above definition, a genotype information may be seen as assigning an *unordered* pair of alleles to members of the pedigree. This indicates that the phase of the alleles is unknown. If a pedigree member is *homozygous* at a given locus in its genome, i.e., the two alleles at that locus coincide, the function $\mathcal{G}$ returns a singleton set. In the literature on genetics, and in our pictorial representation of pedigrees, the genotype $\{$**A,B**$\}$ is given as the string **AB** (or **BA**). In particular, the genotype $\{$**A**$\}$ is given as **AA**. In the remainder of this paper, we shall use these notations interchangeably without further explanations.

Considering consistency for a specific gene amounts to checking whether the pedi-gree and the genotype information are consistent according to the Mendelian law of segregation (see [7]). The law of segregation implicitly defines the following constraint on consistent genotype assignments: *Each individual must inherit precisely one allele from each of its parents.*

Our order of business will now be to formalize this constraint, and what it means that a genotype information is consistent with respect to a pedigree.

Definition 4 (Consistent Genotype Information). *Let* $P = \langle V, F, \mathbf{p}, \mathbf{m} \rangle$ *be a pedi-gree.*

1. *A complete genotype information* $\mathcal{G}$ *for P is consistent with P if, whenever* $v \in N$:
   (a) *if* $\mathcal{G}(v) = \{$**A,B**$\}$, *then either* **A**$\in \mathcal{G}(\mathbf{p}(v))$ *and* **B**$\in \mathcal{G}(\mathbf{m}(v))$, *or* **B**$\in \mathcal{G}(\mathbf{p}(v))$ *and* **A**$\in \mathcal{G}(\mathbf{m}(v))$;
   (b) *if* $\mathcal{G}(v) = \{$**A**$\}$, *then* **A** *is contained in both* $\mathcal{G}(\mathbf{p}(v))$ *and* $\mathcal{G}(\mathbf{m}(v))$.
2. *A genotype information for P is consistent with P if it can be extended to a com-plete, consistent genotype information for P.*

3 Consistency Checking Is NP-Complete

In what follows, CONS will denote the consistency checking problem for genes with an arbitrary number of alleles. We shall use nCONS to refer to the consistency checking problem for a gene with n possible alleles, for some positive integer n. Our aim in the remainder of this section will be to show the following result:

Theorem 1. *The problems nCONS ($n \geq 3$) and CONS are NP-complete.*

Remark 1. The proviso in the statement of the above theorem that the number of alleles n be larger than, or equal to, three is most likely necessary. In fact, in the presence of a single allele, there is only one complete genotype information, viz. that which assigns the only allele to each member of the pedigree, and that is consistent. Hence, in that case, each genotype information is consistent with respect to every pedigree. Moreover, as will be shown in Thm. 4, the problem 2CONS is decidable in polynomial time.

To prove Thm. 1, we shall first show that CONS, and thus nCONS for every n, is in NP. We then show that 3CONS, and therefore CONS and nCONS for every $n \geq 3$, is NP-hard.

It is not too hard to see that CONS is in NP. To this end, given any pedigree P with genotype information $\mathcal{G}$, it is sufficient to exhibit a certificate that is verifiable in polynomial time. The certificate for an instance of problem CONS is a complete and consistent genotype information $\mathcal{G}^c$ that extends $\mathcal{G}$ in the sense of Def. 3. To check the consistency of $\mathcal{G}^c$ we only have to make sure that the conditions in Def. 4(1) are satisfied for each non-founder of the pedigree. This only takes constant time for each non-founder, and thus the whole consistency check takes linear time in the number of non-founders of the pedigree. Note that the complexity of this consistency check is independent of the number of possible alleles, which shows that nCONS is in NP for every n.

Our order of business will now be to show that 3CONS, and thus CONS, is NP-hard. Note that this is a strong indication that the structural complexity of consistency checking does *not* depend on the number of alleles for a gene, if that number is at least three. Our NP-hardness proof for 3CONS is by reduction from 3SAT. The central idea of the proof is to build a pedigree with associated genotype information from a 3SAT instance in such a way that the structure of the pedigree together with the genotype information mimic the variables and clauses of the input 3SAT instance as closely as possible. The constructed pedigree with genotype information is consistent if, and only if, the 3SAT instance it models is satisfiable.

We recall, for the sake of clarity, that 3SAT is the special case of the satisfiability problem for boolean formulae in which the input formulae are in *conjunctive normal form*, and all of their clauses (i.e., disjunctions of literals) have exactly three literals – where a literal is either a variable or a negated variable. Our aim, in the remainder of this section, is to offer a polynomial time reduction from 3SAT to 3CONS. In fact, it is not too hard to see that, without loss of generality, we can restrict ourselves to considering boolean formulae in conjunctive normal form whose clauses have the form $x \vee y$, $\overline{x} \vee \overline{y}$, $x \vee y \vee z$, or $\overline{x} \vee \overline{y} \vee \overline{z}$, for some distinct variables x, y, z. Indeed, any 3SAT instance can be brought into that form in the following four steps:

1. Remove all clauses containing complementary literals (as they evaluate to true). If all clauses are removed in this step, then the original formula is satisfiable.
2. Replace multiple occurrences of the same literal within a single clause with a single occurrence of the same literal (as $l \vee l = l$, for every literal l).

3. If a clause consists of a single literal, then
   (a) remove all clauses that contain this literal (as it must be assigned the value true)
       and
   (b) remove all occurrences of its negation in other clauses (as they have to be
       assigned the value false).
   If all clauses are removed in step 3a above, then the original formula is satisfiable.
   If some clause reduces to the empty clause in step 3b, then we know that there is
   no assignment that can satisfy the clause, and the formula is not satisfiable.
4. Finally, we put every clause in the formula into one of the forms $x \vee y$, $\overline{x} \vee \overline{y}$,
   $x \vee y \vee z$, or $\overline{x} \vee \overline{y} \vee \overline{z}$, for some distinct variables x, y, z. This can be done by
   introducing dummy variables. For instance, a clause of the form $\overline{x} \vee y \vee z$ is replaced
   with $(\overline{x} \vee \overline{p}) \wedge (y \vee z \vee p)$, for some fresh variable p. (We use a different variable p
   for each clause.) The complete set of reduction rules used in this step may be found
   in Table 1.

Table 1. The rules for step 4 in the transformation of 3SAT instances.

	2 literals	3 literals
0 negations	$x \vee y$ (no reduction)	$x \vee y \vee z$ (no reduction)
1 negation	$\overline{x} \vee y \rightarrow (\overline{x} \vee \overline{p}) \wedge (y \vee p)$	$\overline{x} \vee y \vee z \rightarrow (\overline{x} \vee \overline{p}) \wedge (y \vee z \vee p)$
2 negations	$\overline{x} \vee \overline{y}$ (no reduction)	$\overline{x} \vee \overline{y} \vee z \rightarrow (\overline{x} \vee \overline{y} \vee \overline{p}) \wedge (z \vee p)$
3 negations		$\overline{x} \vee \overline{y} \vee \overline{z}$ (no reduction)

It is clear that any instance of 3SAT can be rewritten to the form described above in
polynomial time, and that the resulting formula is satisfiable if, and only if, so was the
original one.

We are now ready to present our reduction from 3SAT to 3CONS. Let ϕ be an
instance of 3SAT. In light of the above discussion, we may assume that ϕ is in conjunc-
tive normal form, and that its clauses have one of the forms $x \vee y$, $\overline{x} \vee \overline{y}$, $x \vee y \vee z$,
or $\overline{x} \vee \overline{y} \vee \overline{z}$, for some distinct variables x, y, z. Furthermore, we assume a fixed total
ordering on the variables, and that the variables always appear in clauses in an order
that is compatible with it. The construction of a pedigree P_ϕ with associated genotype
information $\mathcal{G}_\phi$ from a formula ϕ proceeds in the following three steps. First we make
variable gadgets for each of the variables in ϕ. Next, we construct clause gadgets for
each of the clauses in ϕ. Finally, we combine the variable gadgets with the clause gadgets, and output the resulting pedigree.

In the construction outlined below, the genotype information $\mathcal{G}_\phi$ will be explicitly
described in stepwise fashion as we show how P_ϕ is built.

We start by describing the construction of the variable gadgets. In our construction,
we shall make use of three alleles, denoted by **A**, **F** and **T**. The alleles **T** and **F** are
intended to play the role of "true" and "false" in the 3SAT problem. The third allele **A**
is an auxiliary dummy allele used for controlling possible inheritance patterns.

For each variable x that occurs in ϕ we construct the pedigree P_x thus:

$$P_x = \langle V_x, F_x, \mathbf{p}_x, \mathbf{m}_x \rangle \ ,$$

where $V_x = \{f_x, m_x, v_x, s_x\}$, $F_x = \{f_x, m_x, s_x\}$, and the paternal and maternal functions are given by $\mathbf{p}_x(v_x) = f_x$ and $\mathbf{m}_x(v_x) = m_x$. The genotype information $\mathcal{G}_\phi$ assigns genotype $\mathbf{AA}$ to both m_x (the *mother* of v_x) and s_x (the *spouse* of v_x), and genotype $\mathbf{TF}$ to f_x (the *father* of v_x). The genotyped pedigree P_x is depicted in Fig. 3. (In that figure, v_x and her spouse s_x are joined by a "mating line" to indicate that they will mate when the variable gadget is incorporated in the clause gadgets – see Fig. 4.) The pedigree P_x consists of three genotyped members, and one ungenotyped individual v_x. The genotype of v_x can, however, be partly inferred by the Mendelian laws, and has the form $x\mathbf{A}$, where the "allelic variable" x takes either the value $\mathbf{F}$ or $\mathbf{T}$. This is indicated by $x\mathbf{A}$ on the figure. Moreover, the allele x associated with the individual v_x is the only possible origin of a $\mathbf{T}$ or $\mathbf{F}$ allele that can be inherited further from the inheritance point of P_x. We shall refer to individual v_x in Fig. 3, as the *variable individual* for x. The illustration on the left of P_x in Fig. 3 shows how the variable gadgets are depicted in larger pedigrees.

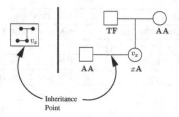

Fig. 3. The variable gadget P_x.

The next step in the reduction is to construct a clause gadget P_γ, for each clause γ in the formula ϕ. As we have already pointed out, there are only four different types of clauses we need to consider, and each leads to a different type of clause gadget. The clause gadgets for clauses γ of the form $x \vee y$ and $\overline{x} \vee \overline{y}$ (respectively, $x \vee y \vee z$ and $\overline{x} \vee \overline{y} \vee \overline{z}$) have the same pedigree structure P_γ, but the genotype information $\mathcal{G}_\phi$ assigns a different genotype to the one individual in P_γ without offspring. In each pedigree P_γ, we shall use c_γ to denote this single "leaf", and f_γ and m_γ to stand for its father and mother, respectively. If the clause γ contains three literals, the pedigree P_γ also contains individuals gf_γ and gm_γ, who are, respectively, the maternal grandfather and grandmother of c_γ. The paternal and maternal functions $\mathbf{p}_\gamma$ and $\mathbf{m}_\gamma$ encode the family structure that we have just described – that is:

$$\mathbf{p}_\gamma(u) = \begin{cases} f_\gamma & \text{if } u = c_\gamma \\ gf_\gamma & \text{if } u = m_\gamma \text{ and } \gamma \text{ contains three literals} \end{cases}$$

$$\mathbf{m}_\gamma(u) = \begin{cases} m_\gamma & \text{if } u = c_\gamma \\ gm_\gamma & \text{if } u = m_\gamma \text{ and } \gamma \text{ contains three literals.} \end{cases}$$

In what follows, we shall write V_γ for the set of individuals of the pedigree P_γ. The only new genotyped individual in P_γ is its leaf c_γ. The genotype $\mathcal{G}_\phi(c_\gamma)$ is **TA** if γ contains only positive literals, and **FA** otherwise.

The four different types of clause gadgets are depicted in Fig. 4, where we also show how the clause gadgets will be linked to the variable gadgets in the construction of the pedigree P_ϕ. The genotype information associated with the leaves of these pedigrees is used to code constraints on the values of the variables in a satisfying assignment for the original clauses. For instance, the leaves of the pedigrees associated with the clauses containing only positive literals have genotype **TA** to represent the fact that one of the variables in that clause must be assigned the truth value true in every satisfying assignment.

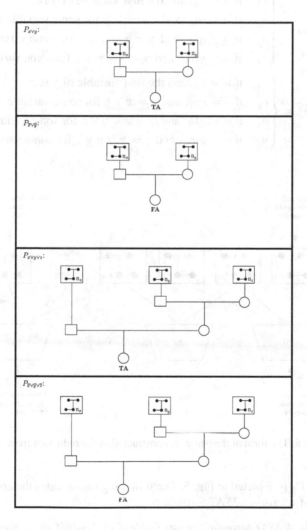

Fig. 4. The pedigrees constructed for the four basic clause types along with their connections with the appropriate variable gadgets.

Having constructed a variable gadget for each variable and a clause gadget for each clause occurring in ϕ, we combine these gadgets, and output the resulting pedigree P_ϕ. The pedigree $P_\phi = \langle V_\phi, F_\phi, \mathbf{p}_\phi, \mathbf{m}_\phi \rangle$ is built thus:

- the set V_ϕ of members of P_ϕ is the union of the V_x's (with x a variable occurring in ϕ) and of the V_γ's (with γ a clause of ϕ);
- the set F_ϕ of founders of P_ϕ is the union of the F_x's (with x a variable occurring in ϕ);
- the functions $\mathbf{p}_\phi : V_\phi \backslash F_\phi \rightarrow V_\phi$ and $\mathbf{m}_\phi : V_\phi \backslash F_\phi \rightarrow V_\phi$ are obtained by extending the paternal and maternal functions for the pedigrees P_x and P_γ thus:

$$
\mathbf{p}_\phi(u) = \begin{cases}
s_x & \text{if } u = f_\gamma, \text{ and the first variable of } \gamma \text{ is } x \\
s_y & \text{if } u = m_\gamma, \text{ and } \gamma = x \vee y \text{ for some variable } x \\
s_y & \text{if } u = gf_\gamma, \text{ and } \gamma = x \vee y \vee z \text{ for some variables } x, z \\
s_z & \text{if } u = gm_\gamma, \text{ and } \gamma = x \vee y \vee z \text{ for some variables } x, y
\end{cases}
$$

$$
\mathbf{m}_\phi(u) = \begin{cases}
v_x & \text{if } u = f_\gamma, \text{ and the first variable of } \gamma \text{ is } x \\
v_y & \text{if } u = m_\gamma, \text{ and } \gamma = x \vee y \text{ for some variable } x \\
v_y & \text{if } u = gf_\gamma, \text{ and } \gamma = x \vee y \vee z \text{ for some variables } x, z \\
v_z & \text{if } u = gm_\gamma, \text{ and } \gamma = x \vee y \vee z \text{ for some variables } x, y.
\end{cases}
$$

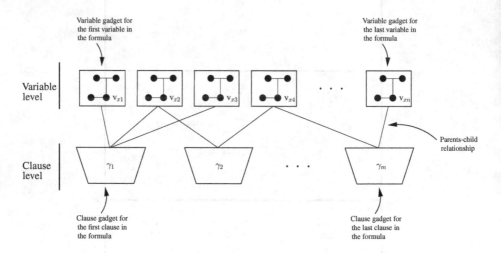

Fig. 5. The form of the pedigree constructed in the reduction from 3SAT.

The pedigree P_ϕ is depicted in Fig. 5. The following result states the correctness of our construction of P_ϕ from a 3SAT formula ϕ.

Proposition 1. *A 3SAT formula ϕ is satisfiable if, and only if, the genotype information $\mathcal{G}_\phi$ is consistent with P_ϕ.*

Since the pedigree P_ϕ can be constructed in polynomial time from the formula ϕ, the proposition above allows us to conclude that 3CONS is NP-hard, and the proof of Thm. 1 is now complete.

As already remarked in Sect. 1, our reduction from 3SAT to 3CONS employs looping pedigrees. The following result, which seems to be folklore in the literature on computational genetics, offers strong evidence that this is most likely necessary.

Theorem 2. *Checking the consistency of non-looping pedigrees can be performed in polynomial time.*

4 Further Results

In this section we discuss briefly three new problems related to CONS motivated by the underlying biology, and study their computational complexity.

Tolerance to Critical Genotypes. A *critical genotype* is genotype information on an individual that, if removed, would make an inconsistent pedigree with genotype information consistent. Assume that it is revealed that some application of pedigrees with genotype information is tolerant to a specific number, say k, of critical genotypes in the genotype information. We denote the problem of deciding whether there are k critical genotypes in a CONS instance as kCRIT. Note that 0CRIT is just the CONS problem.

Theorem 3. *In the presence of at least three alleles, kCRIT is NP-complete for every $k \geq 0$.*

Consistency Checking with Two Alleles. According to [16, p. 274], *single nucleotide polymorphisms* are utilized markers where two alleles exist. Consistency checking of such data amounts to the problem 2CONS. A relevant question is whether 2CONS is also NP-complete or whether it is polynomial time decidable. Three is often a "magic number", when it comes to the structural complexity of a computational problem. For instance, 3COLORING and 3SAT are NP-complete, while 2COLORING and 2SAT are polynomial time decidable (see, e.g., [13, pp. 185 and 198]). The same holds for consistency checking of pedigrees in light of the following result:

Theorem 4. *The problem 2CONS is decidable in polynomial time.*

In light of Thms. 2 and 4, one can argue that 3CONS is indeed the simplest consistency checking problem that is still intractable. In fact, restricting our attention to genes over two alleles or to pedigrees without loops yields algorithmic problems that can be solved in polynomial time.

Phase Known Consistency Checking. In this paper, we have considered consistency checking in a phase unknown setting – that is, when it is not possible, by observing a chromosome pair, to say which component is inherited paternally or maternally. We now briefly turn our focus to the task of consistency checking where the phase of the genotype information is known. The motivation for this type of investigation is that it is sometimes possible to infer the identity of the parent from whom some allele originated (and thereby also the origin of the other allele).

Definition 5. *A phase known genotype information for a pedigree* $P = \langle V, F, \mathbf{p}, \mathbf{m} \rangle$ *is a partial function* $\mathcal{G}^p : V \hookrightarrow \mathcal{A} \times \mathcal{A}$. *The genotype information* $\mathcal{G}^p$ *is complete if* $\mathrm{dom}(\mathcal{G}^p) = V$.

A complete, phase known genotype information $\mathcal{G}^p$ *for a pedigree* P *is consistent with* P *if whenever* $v \in N$ *and* $\mathcal{G}^p(v) = (\mathbf{A}, \mathbf{B})$, *then* $\mathbf{A}$ *is one of the components of* $\mathcal{G}^p(\mathbf{p}(v))$, *and* $\mathbf{B}$ *is one of the components of* $\mathcal{G}^p(\mathbf{m}(v))$.

A phase known genotype information is consistent with P *if it can be extended to a complete and consistent phase known genotype information for* P.

Let PCONS be the problem of checking the consistency of a pedigree with phase known genotype information. We have that:

Theorem 5. *In the presence of at least four alleles, PCONS is NP-complete.*

5   Concluding Remarks

The results in this paper show that certain basic combinatorial problems in pedigree analysis, viz. consistency checking and determining whether a genotyped pedigree has some number of critical genotypes, are NP-complete, even if we focus on a single gene with a fixed, small number of alleles. It follows that these problems are most likely computationally intractable. It would be most interesting, however, to develop heuristic algorithms for these problems, and evaluate their efficiency on real-life and/or randomly generated data. In particular, we plan to develop and evaluate algorithms for consistency checking based upon *Binary Decision Diagrams* [3] and various available SAT-solvers and tautology checkers – see, e.g., the reference [5] for a survey. We believe that the experimental evaluation of these algorithms would be of value, because consistency checking routines, like genotype elimination ones, may be used as pre-processing steps in algorithms for, e.g., linkage analysis and haplotype reconstruction [10].

From a theoretical viewpoint, we conjecture that the problem of computing the number of complete consistent extensions of a genotype information for a pedigree is $\#P$-complete [17] – i.e., it is as hard as counting the number of satisfying assignments of a boolean formula. It would also be interesting to study the complexity of approximation algorithms for computing the number of critical genotypes in a pedigree. We leave an in-depth study of these problems as future work.

Acknowledgments

We thank Mogens Nielsen for the initial inspiration on a possible reduction showing that consistency checking is NP-complete, and Emmanuel Fleury for fruitful discussions on the topic of this paper, and comments on its draft versions. We are most grateful to Dan Gusfield for his comments on the connections between our respective contributions, and for bringing the reference [10] to our attention. Kenneth Lange offered prompt and informative replies to our enquiries related to extant complexity analyses for the Lange-Goradia algorithm from [9]. We are indebted to Tao Jiang for making his paper [10] available to us. Any remaining infelicities are solely our responsibility.

The work reported in this paper was partly carried out while Luca Aceto was an invited professor at Reykjavík University, and Anna Ingólfsdóttir was at Iceland Genomics Corporation. Both authors thank these institutions for their hospitality and the excellent working conditions.

References

1. G. R. ABECASIS, S. S. CHERNY, W. O. COOKSON, AND L. R. CARDON, *Merlin: Rapid analysis of dense genetic maps using sparse gene flow trees*, Nature Genetics, 30 (2002), pp. 97–101.

2. L. ACETO, J. A. HANSEN, A. INGÓLFSDÓTTIR, J. JOHNSEN, AND J. KNUDSEN, *The complexity of checking consistency of pedigree information and related problems*, Research Report RS–03–17, BRICS, 2003. Available from http://www.brics.dk/RS/03/17/.

3. R. BRYANT, *Graph-based algorithms for boolean function manipulation*, IEEE Trans. Comput., C-35 (1986), pp. 677–691.

4. DECODE NEWS CENTER, November 2001. http://www.decode.com/news/releases/.

5. J. GU, P. W. PURDOM, J. FRANCO, AND B. W. WAH, *Algorithms for the satisfiability (SAT) problem: a survey*, in Satisfiability problem: theory and applications (Piscataway, NJ, 1996), vol. 35 of DIMACS Ser. Discrete Math. Theoret. Comput. Sci., Amer. Math. Soc., Providence, RI, 1997, pp. 19–151.

6. D. F. GUDBJARTSSON, K. JONASSON, AND C. A. KONG, *Fast multipoint linkage calculation with Allegro*, Nature Genetics, 20 (2000), pp. 12–13.

7. W. S. KLUG AND M. R. CUMMINGS, *Concepts of Genetics*, Prentice Hall, 5th ed., 1997.

8. L. KRUGLYAK, M. J. DALY, M. P. REEVE-DALY, AND E. S. LANDER, *Parametric and nonparametric linkage analysis: A unified multipoint approach*, American Journal of Human Genetics, 58 (1996), pp. 1347–1363.

9. K. LANGE AND T. M. GORADIA, *An algorithm for automatic genotype elimination*, American Journal of Human Genetics, 40 (1987), pp. 250–256.

10. J. LI AND T. JIANG, *Efficient rule-based haplotyping algorithms for pedigree data [extended abstract]*, in Proceedings of RECOMB'03, April 10–13, 2003, Berlin, Germany, ACM, 2003, pp. 197–206.

11. J. R. O'CONNELL AND D. E. WEEKS, *Pedcheck: A program for identification of genotype incompatibilities in linkage analysis*, American Journal of Human Genetics, 63 (1998), pp. 259–266.

12. ———, *An optimal algorithm for automatic genotype elimination*, American Journal of Human Genetics, 65 (1999), pp. 1733–1740.

13. C. H. PAPADIMITRIOU, *Computational Complexity*, Addison Wesley, 1995.

14. A. PICCOLBONI AND D. GUSFIELD, *On the complexity of fundamental computational problems in pedigree analysis*, Tech. Rep. CSE-99-8, Computer Science Department, University of California, Davis, September 1999. Revised version to appear in the *Journal of Computational Biology*.

15. E. SOBEL, J. C. PAPP, AND K. LANGE, *Detection and integration of genotyping errors in statistical genetics*, American Journal of Human Genetics, 70 (2002), pp. 496–508.

16. T. STRACHAN AND A. P. READ, *Human Molecular Genetics 2*, Wiley-Liss, 1999.

17. L. G. VALIANT, *The complexity of computing the permanent*, Theoret. Comput. Sci., 8 (1979), pp. 189–201.

On Clausal Equivalence and Hull Inclusion

K. Subramani[*]

LCSEE
West Virginia University
Morgantown, WV
ksmani@csee.wvu.edu

Abstract. This paper is concerned with threee closely related problems,
viz., checking boolean equivalence of CNF formulas, deciding hull inclusion (linear and integer) in certain polyhedral families and determining
the satisfiability of CNF formulas. With the exception of linear hull inclusion, these problems are provably "hard" in that there are instances
of these problems that are complete for classes, which are not known
to be tractable. In the case of satisfiability testing, we design a simple
randomized algorithm for the problem of checking whether a Q2CNF
formula has a model.

1 Introduction

This paper is concerned with three related problems, viz., boolean equivalence
checking of CNF formulas, checking hull inclusion in polyhedra specified by
systems of linear inequalities and satisfiability checking in CNF formulas. The
boolean equivalence checking problem is `coNP-complete`, even when problem
instances are restricted to be 3CNF formulas; likewise it is `PSPACE-complete`
in case of Q3CNF formulas (See Section §2.). It follows that the integer hull
inclusion problem is also `coNP-complete`, while the quantified integer hull inclusion problem is `PSPACE-Hard`. We show that for certain clausal families, the
boolean equivalence problem is tractable; the techniques developed therein are
suitably extended to show that integer hull inclusion is also tractable for certain
polyhedral classes. Finally, we develop a randomized algorithm for the Q2SAT
problem.

The primary contributions of this paper are as follows:

1. Demonstrating the existence of polynomial time algorithms for boolean
   equivalence checking in certain clausal families.
2. Designing a polynomial time algorithm for the linear hull inclusion problem.
3. Providing polynomial time algorithms for the integer hull inclusion problem
   and the quantified integer hull inclusion problem in case of 2SAT polyhedra.
4. Designing a randomized algorithm for the problem of checking whether a
   Q2CNF formula has a boolean model.

[*] This research has been supported in part by a CISS Faculty Fellowship, while the
author was at Aalborg Universitet.

C. Blundo and C. Laneve (Eds.): ICTCS 2003, LNCS 2841, pp. 188–201, 2003.

The rest of this paper is organized as follows: Section §2 formally describes each of the problems considered in this paper. A detailed discussion on the motivation for our work as well as related approaches in the literature is available in the journal version of this paper. Algorithms for boolean equivalence are detailed in Section §3, while Section §4 deals with the linear hull inclusion problem. The integer hull inclusion problem and the quantified integer hull inclusion problem are addressed in Section §5. In Section §6 we propose a randomized algorithm for Q2SAT decidability. We conclude in Section §7, by summarizing our work in this paper and identifying avenues for future research.

2   Statement of Problems

Let $\phi_1 = C_1 \wedge C_2 \wedge \ldots C_m$ and $\phi_2 = C'_1 \wedge C'_2 \wedge \ldots C'_{m'}$ denote 2 boolean formulas, where the C_is and C'_js are disjunctions on the literals $\{x_1, \bar{x}_1, x_2, \bar{x}_2, \ldots, x_n, \bar{x}_n\}$.

Definition 1. *The boolean equivalence problem,* $\mathbf{B_{eq}}$*, is defined as follows:* Given 2 CNF formulas ϕ_1 and ϕ_2, is $\phi_1 \Leftrightarrow \phi_2$, i.e., does $\phi_1 \Rightarrow \phi_2$ and $\phi_2 \Rightarrow \phi_1$?

Lemma 1. $\mathbf{B_{eq}}$ *is* coNP-complete.

Proof: Note that $\mathbf{B_{eq}}$ is clearly in coNP, since a nondeterministic Turing machine (NDTM) need merely guess an assignment that satisfies ϕ_1 and falsifies ϕ_2 or vice versa, in order to show that $\phi_1 \not\Leftrightarrow \phi_2$.

Let A_1 denote an algorithm that takes any pair of CNF formulas (ϕ_1, ϕ_2) and decides whether $\phi_1 \Leftrightarrow \phi_2$. We can use A_1 to decide whether an arbitrary 3CNF formula, ϕ, is satisfiable, as follows: Set ϕ_1 to ϕ and ϕ_2 to $\{(x_1)(\bar{x}_1)\}$; now, provide (ϕ_1, ϕ_2) as the input to A_1. If A_1 outputs "yes", we know that ϕ is unsatisfiable; likewise, if it outputs "no", we know that ϕ is satisfiable. In other words, we have a Turing reduction[1] from the 3CNF satisfiability problem, which is NP-complete, to $\mathbf{B_{eq}}$, thereby establishing the coNP-hardness of $\mathbf{B_{eq}}$. $\square$

Observe that the proof of Lemma (1) explicitly uses the hardness of 3CNF satisfiability, in order to prove the hardness of the boolean equivalence checking problem. So the following question arises naturally:
Problem: *Is* $\mathbf{B_{eq}}$ *solvable in polynomial time for clausal families, in which the satisfiability problem can be decided in polynomial time?*

We now discuss the boolean equivalence problem, in case of Quantified Boolean Formulas (QBFs).
Let $\Phi_1 = Q(x, y)\ \phi(x, y)$ and $\Phi_2 = Q(x, y)\ \phi_2(x, y)$ denote two QBFs, where,

1. ϕ_1 and ϕ_2 are CNF formulas on the set of variables
   $V = \{x_1, x_2, \ldots, x_n, y_1, y_2, \ldots, y_n\}$,
2. The x_i variables are existentially quantified, while the y_i variables are universally quantified;

---

[1] In this paper Turing reduction means polynomial time Turing reduction.

3. The quantifier specification, $Q(x, y)$, *which is common to* Φ_1 *and* Φ_2, imposes a linear ordering on the set V.

If a boolean formula ϕ, is simple, i.e., all the quantifiers are existential, a solution to ϕ, is an assignment of {**true, false**} values to its variables, such that ϕ evaluates to **true**. In case of a QBF $\Phi = Q(x, y) \ \phi(x, y)$ though, the concept of a solution satisfying Φ is a lot more involved and better understood through the use of a 2-person game or 2 Non-deterministic machines working in parallel, each basing its decision on the moves made by the other, thus far [6].

Definition 2. *The quantified boolean equivalence problem,* **QB**$_{\mathbf{eq}}$, *is defined as:* Given two CNF formulas $\phi_1(x, y)$ and $\phi_2(x, y)$ and a quantifier specification $Q(x, y)$), is $Q(x, y) \ \phi_1 \Leftrightarrow Q(x) \ \phi_2$?

Lemma 2. **QB**$_{\mathbf{eq}}$ *is* PSPACE-complete, *in general.*

Proof: We first show that **QB**$_{\mathbf{eq}}$ is in PSPACE. Observe that to show that $\Phi_1 = Q(x, y) \ \phi_1(x, y) \not\Leftrightarrow \Phi_2 = Q(x, y)\phi_2(x, y)$, it suffices to find one sequence of moves made by the players **X** and **Y**, so that ϕ_1 evaluates to **true** and ϕ_2 evaluates to **false**, or vice versa. Since there are at most $2^{2 \cdot n}$ distinct assignments to the variables in V, all the assignments can be generated using a $2 \cdot n$ bit counter. For each *valid* assignment (as per $Q(x, y)$), verifying that $\phi_1 \Leftrightarrow \phi_2$ can be carried out in polynomial time and hence polynomial space. If it is the case that for all valid assignments $\phi_1 \Leftrightarrow \phi_2$, it follows that $Q(x, y) \ \phi_1 \Leftrightarrow Q(x) \ \phi_2$.

It has been shown in [8] that the problem of checking whether a Q3CNF formula has a model is PSPACE-complete.
Let $\Phi_1 = Q(x, y) \ \phi(x, y)$ denote an arbitrary Q3CNF formula and let $\Phi_2 = Q(x, y) \ \{(x_1)(\bar{x}_1)\}$. We can now argue, exactly as we did in case of Lemma (1), that the problem of Q3CNF decidability can be Turing reduced to **QB**$_{\mathbf{eq}}$, thereby establishing the PSPACE-hardness of **QB**$_{\mathbf{eq}}$. □

Problem: *Is* **QB**$_{\mathbf{eq}}$ *decidable in polynomial time, when* Φ_1 *and* Φ_2 *belong to a clausal family for which QBF decidability is tractable?*

We proceed to describe the linear hull, integer hull and quantified integer hull inclusion problems. Assume that we are given two polytopes $P_1 : \{\mathbf{A_1} \cdot \vec{\mathbf{x}} \le \vec{\mathbf{b_1}}\}$ and $P_2 : \{\mathbf{A_2} \cdot \vec{\mathbf{x}} \le \vec{\mathbf{b_2}}\}$. The linear hull of P_1 is defined as the set of its extreme points, whereas its integer hull viz., S_{P_1}, is defined as the set of its extreme lattice points [4]; S_{P_2} is defined similarly.

Definition 3. *The linear hull inclusion problem is defined as follows:* Given polyhedra P_1 and P_2, is it the case that $P_1 \subseteq P_2$?

Definition 4. *The lattice point equivalence problem,* **L**$_{\mathbf{eq}}$ *is defined as follows:* Given polyhedra P_1 and P_2, is it the case that $S_{P_1} = S_{P_2}$?

We shall focus our efforts on a related problem.

Definition 5. *The integer hull inclusion problem,* **IHI***, is defined as follows: Given polyhedra P_1 and P_2, is it the case that $S_{P_1} \subseteq S_{P_2}$?*

It is not hard to see that the **IHI** problem is closely related to the lattice point equivalence problem, since $S_{P_1} = S_{P_2}$ if and only if $S_{P_1} \subseteq S_{P_2}$ and $S_{P_2} \subseteq S_{P_1}$.

Lemma 3. **IHI** *is* coNP-complete *in general.*

Proof: Set P_1 to be the polyhedral system representing a 3SAT formula and P_2 to $\{x_1 \geq 1,\ x_1 \leq 0\}$. The Lemma follows, from Lemma (1). $\square$

The natural question is:
Problem: *Are there classes of polytopes, for which* **IHI** *can be decided in polynomial time?*

Definition 6. *Let $x_1, x_2, \ldots x_n$ be a set of n variables with integral ranges. A mathematical program of the form*

$$Q_1\, x_1 \in \{a^1 - b^1\}\ Q_2\, x_2 \in \{a^2 - b^2\}, \ldots$$
$$Q_n\, x_n \in \{a^n - b^n\}\ \mathbf{A} \cdot \vec{x} \leq \vec{b} \tag{1}$$

where each Q_i is either $\exists$ or $\forall$ is called a Quantified Integer Program (QIP).

It is easy to see that Quantified Integer Programs generalize QBFs and that QIP decidability is PSPACE-Hard. Further, the solution to a QIP is a model (i.e., a vector of integer Skolem functions), in exactly the same way as for a QBF.

Definition 7. *Given two Quantified Integer Programs $M_1 = Q(x)\, P_1$ and $M_2 = Q(x)\, P_2$, the Quantified Integer Hull Inclusion problem (**QIHI**) is defined as follows: Is every model $\vec{x}$ for M_1, also a model for M_2?*

It is easily seen that **QIHI** is PSPACE-Hard.

We now define some special classes of polytopes; the structure of these polytopes will be exploited to design polynomial time algorithms for one or more type of hull inclusion.

Definition 8. *A polyhedral system $P_1 : \mathbf{A} \cdot \vec{x} \leq \vec{b}$ is said to be a 2SAT polytope, if all entries of $\mathbf{A}$ belong to the set $\{0, 1, -1\}$ and further, there are at most 2 non-zero entries per row of $\mathbf{A}$.*

Definition 9. *A polyhedral system of the form $P_1 : \{\vec{x} : \mathbf{A} \cdot \vec{x} \geq \vec{b}\}$, where all entries in $\mathbf{A}$ belong to $\{1, 0, -1\}$ and at most one entry in each row is positive, is called a Horn polytope.*

Observe that 2SAT polytopes and Horn polytopes generalize 2CNF clauses and HornCNF clauses respectively.

Definition 10. *A matrix $\mathbf{A}$ is said to be totally unimodular (TUM), if every square submatrix of $\mathbf{A}$ has determinant 0, 1 or -1.*

3   Boolean Equivalence

Harking back to Section §2, we are interested in checking if two given CNF formulas, ϕ_1 and ϕ_2 are equivalent. Observe that the equivalence problem can be broken into 2 subproblems, viz., $\phi_1 \Rightarrow \phi_2$ and $\phi_2 \Rightarrow \phi_1$.

Consider the subproblem $\phi_1 \Rightarrow \phi_2$. As before, we assume that $\phi_1 = C_1 \wedge C_2 \ldots \wedge C_m$ and $\phi_2 = C_1' \wedge C_2' \ldots C_{m'}'$. Now,

$$\phi_1 \Rightarrow \phi_2$$
$$\Leftrightarrow [\phi_1 \Rightarrow C_1' \wedge C_2' \ldots C_{m'}']$$
$$\Leftrightarrow \wedge_{i=1}^{m'}[\phi_1 \Rightarrow C_i']$$

Pick a particular clause $C_i' \in \phi_2$. It is clear that $[\phi_1 \Rightarrow C_i']$ if and only if $[\phi_1 \wedge \bar{C}_i']$ is unsatisfiable. Observe that C_i' is a disjunction of literals, so that $\bar{C}_i'$ is a conjunction of unit literal clauses; hence $\phi_1 \wedge \bar{C}_i'$ is in CNF form. Thus, in order to check whether $\phi_i \Rightarrow \phi_2$, we merely need to confirm that all the CNF formulas in the set $\{\phi_1 \wedge \bar{C}_1', \phi_1 \wedge \bar{C}_2', \ldots, \phi_1 \wedge \bar{C}_{m'}'\}$ are unsatisfiable. In other words, the implication problem for CNF problems has been Turing reduced to the CNF unsatisfiability problem.

It follows that

Theorem 1. *The problem* $\mathbf{B_{eq}}$ *is Turing reducible to the problem of checking whether a CNF formula is unsatisfiable.*

Proof: Given ϕ_1 and ϕ_2, first check whether $\phi_1 \Rightarrow \phi_2$ and then whether $\phi_2 \Rightarrow \phi_1$. □

Corollary 1. $\mathbf{B_{eq}}$ *can be decided in polynomial time for the 2CNF and HornCNF formulas.*

Proof: There exist polynomial time algorithms to decide unsatisfiability in 2CNF and HornCNF formulas [6]. □

We proceed to address the $\mathbf{QB_{eq}}$ problem. We first focus on the subproblem $Q(x, y) \; \phi_1(x, y) \Rightarrow Q(x, y) \; \phi_2(x, y)$. Once again, observe that,

$$Q(x, y) \; \phi_1(x, y) \Rightarrow Q(x, y) \; \phi_2(x, y)$$
$$\Leftrightarrow [Q(x, y) \; \phi_1(x, y) \Rightarrow Q(x, y) \; (C_1' \wedge C_2' \ldots C_{m'}')]$$
$$\Leftrightarrow \wedge_{i=1}^{m'}[Q(x, y) \; (\phi_1(x, y) \Rightarrow Q(x, y) \; C_i')]$$
$$\Leftrightarrow \wedge_{i=1}^{m'}[Q(x, y) \; (\phi_1(x, y) \Rightarrow C_i')]$$

Pick a particular clause $C_i' \in \phi_2$. It is clear that $Q(x, y) \; (\phi_1(x, y) \Rightarrow C_i')$ if and only if $Q(x, y) \; (\phi_1 \wedge \bar{C}_i')$ is unsatisfiable (i.e., does not have a model.) Observe that C_i' is a disjunction of literals, so that $\bar{C}_i'$ is a conjunction of unit literal clauses;

hence $\phi_1 \wedge \bar{C}'_i$ is in CNF form. Thus, in order to check whether $Q(x,y)\ (\phi_i \Rightarrow \phi_2)$, we merely need to confirm that all the QCNF formulas in the set $\{Q(x,y)\ (\phi_1 \wedge \bar{C}'_1),\ Q(x,y)\ (\phi_1 \wedge \bar{C}'_2),\ldots,Q(x,y)\ (\phi_1 \wedge \bar{C}'_{m'})\}$ are unsatisfiable. In other words, the implication problem for QCNF problems has been Turing reduced to the QCNF unsatisfiability problem.

From the above discussion it follows that

Theorem 2. $\mathbf{QB_{eq}}$ *is Turing reducible to the problem of checking whether a QCNF formula has a model.*

and hence,

Corollary 2. $\mathbf{QB_{eq}}$ *is decidable in polynomial time for Q2CNF and QHornCNF formulas.*

Proof: Both Q2CNF [1] and QHornCNF [3] can be checked for unsatisfiability in polynomial time. $\square$

4 Linear Hull Inclusion

In this section, we provide a polynomial time algorithm for the linear hull inclusion problem, which is also referred to as the Polytope Inclusion problem.

Consider 2 polyhedra represented by:

$$\mathbf{A} \cdot \vec{\mathbf{x}} \le \vec{\mathbf{b}},\ \vec{\mathbf{x}} \ge \vec{\mathbf{0}} \tag{2}$$

where,

1. $\mathbf{A}$, is an $m \times n$ rational matrix,
2. $\vec{\mathbf{b}}$ is a rational $m-$vector,
3. $\vec{\mathbf{x}} \in \Re^n_+$

and

$$\mathbf{C} \cdot \vec{\mathbf{x}} \le \vec{\mathbf{d}},\ \vec{\mathbf{x}} \ge \vec{\mathbf{0}} \tag{3}$$

where,

1. $\mathbf{C}$, is an $m' \times n$ rational matrix,
2. $\vec{\mathbf{d}}$ is a rational $m'-$vector,
3. $\vec{\mathbf{x}} \in \Re^n_+$

The goal is to decide the following predicate:

$$(\forall \vec{\mathbf{x}},\ \vec{\mathbf{x}} \ge \vec{\mathbf{0}})(\mathbf{A} \cdot \vec{\mathbf{x}} \le \vec{\mathbf{b}} \Rightarrow \mathbf{C} \cdot \vec{\mathbf{x}} \le \vec{\mathbf{d}})? \tag{4}$$

Algorithm (1) represents our strategy to decide Query (4).

4.1 Analysis

Let $\mathcal{L}(m,n)$ denote the running time of the fastest linear programming algorithm on m constraints and n variables [10]. Since a total of m' calls are made, the running time of Algorithm (1) is $O(m' \cdot \mathcal{L})$, which is a polynomial function, since $\mathcal{L}$ is a polynomial function of m and n.

Algorithm 1 Algorithm for Polytope Inclusion.

Function POLYTOPE-INCLUDE($\mathbf{A}, \vec{b}, \mathbf{C}, \vec{d}$)

1: { Let the ith constraint of $\mathbf{C} \cdot \vec{x} \le \vec{d}$, $\vec{x} \ge \vec{0}$ be represented as: $\vec{c_i} \cdot \vec{x} \le d_i$ }.
2: **for** ($i = 1$ **to** m') **do**
3:     **if** ($\max_{\mathbf{A} \cdot \vec{x} \le \vec{b}} \vec{c_i} \cdot \vec{x} > d_i$) **then**
4:         return(**false**)
5:     **end if**
6: **end for**
7: return(**true**)

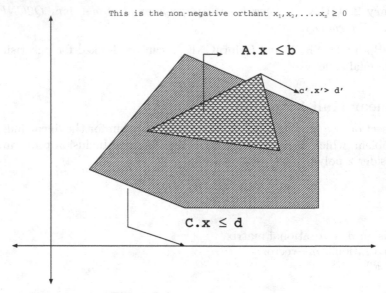

Fig. 1. Polytope non-inclusion.

4.2   Correctness

Lemma 4. *If Algorithm (1) returns* **true**, *then for all* $\vec{x} \in \Re^n_+$,
$\mathbf{A} \cdot \vec{x} \le \vec{b} \Rightarrow \mathbf{C} \cdot \vec{x} \le \vec{d}$.

Proof: Let us assume the contrary, i.e. Algorithm (1) returns **true**, yet there exists a point $\vec{x'}$, such that $\mathbf{A} \cdot \vec{x'} \le \vec{b}$, but $\mathbf{C} \cdot \vec{x'} \not\le \vec{d}$. We note that the notation $\mathbf{C} \cdot \vec{x'} \not\le \vec{d}$, is used to indicate the fact that at least one of the m' constraints defining the polyhedron $\mathbf{C} \cdot \vec{x} \le \vec{d}$ is violated. Let $\vec{c'} \cdot \vec{x} \le d'$ denote a violated constraint, i.e., $\vec{c'} \cdot \vec{x'} > d'$. (See Figure (1).) Clearly, $\max_{\mathbf{A} \cdot \vec{x} \le \vec{b}} \vec{c'} \cdot \vec{x}$ is greater than d', contradicting the hypothesis that **true** was returned by the algorithm. $\square$

Lemma 5. *If Algorithm (1) returns* **false**, *there exists a point* $\vec{x'} \in \mathbf{R}^n_+$ *such that* $\mathbf{A} \cdot \vec{x'} \le \vec{b}$ *and* $\mathbf{C} \cdot \vec{x'} \not\le \vec{d}$.

Proof: See Figure (1). Let $\max_{\mathbf{A} \cdot \vec{x} \le \vec{b}} \vec{c'} \cdot \vec{x}$ exceed d' at point $\vec{x'}$. Clearly $\vec{x'}$ is the required offending point! $\square$

Corollary 3. *Algorithm (1) decides if the polyhedron defined by* $\{\vec{x} \geq \vec{0} : \mathbf{A} \cdot \vec{x} \leq \vec{b}\}$ *is contained in the polyhedron represented by:* $\{\vec{x} \geq \vec{0} : \mathbf{C} \cdot \vec{x} \leq \vec{d}\}$

5 Integer Hull Inclusion

Let us restate the Integer Hull inclusion problem (**IHI**): *Given polyhedra* P_1 : $\mathbf{A_1} \cdot \vec{x} \leq \vec{b_1}$ *and* P_2 : $\mathbf{A_2} \cdot \vec{x} \leq \vec{b_2}$, *is it the case that the integer hull of* P_1, *i.e.,* S_{P_1} *is contained within the integer hull of* P_2, *i.e.,* S_{P_2}?

We note Algorithm (1) shows that the hull inclusion problem (Linear or Integer) is Turing reducible to the problem of finding the maximum (linear or integer) of a linear function over a polyhedron, and it therefore follows that the **IHI** problem can be solved in polynomial time, when $\mathbf{A_1}$, $\mathbf{A_2}$ are TUM. In case of both 2SAT polytopes and Horn polytopes, finding the integer maximum of a linear function is `NP-complete`. Thus a different strategy is needed to decide integer hull inclusion in case of these polytopes.

Assume that $\mathbf{A_1}$ has dimension $m \times n$ and that $\mathbf{A_2}$ has dimensions $m' \times n$; we consider P_1 as being constructed by taking the intersection of the m half-spaces $\vec{a_1^1} \cdot \vec{x} \leq b_1^1$, $\vec{a_1^2} \cdot \vec{x} \leq b_1^2, \ldots \vec{a_1^m} \cdot \vec{x} \leq b_1^m$. Likewise, we consider P_2 as being constructed by the intersection of the m' half-spaces, $\vec{a_2^1} \cdot \vec{x} \leq b_2^1$, $\vec{a_2^2} \cdot \vec{x} \leq b_2^2, \ldots \vec{a_2^{m'}} \cdot \vec{x} \leq b_2^{m'}$.

Observe that $\{\forall \vec{x}, \vec{x} \in S_{P_1} \Rightarrow \vec{x} \in S_{P_2}\}$ if and only if for all lattice points $\vec{x}$, $\vec{x} \in P_1 \Rightarrow \vec{x} \in P_2$. Now, for a lattice point $\vec{x}$

$$\vec{x} \in P_1 \Rightarrow \vec{x} \in P_2$$
$$\Leftrightarrow \vec{x} \in P_1 \Rightarrow \vec{x} \in \wedge_{j=1}^{m'} \vec{a_2^j} \cdot \vec{x} \leq b_2^j,$$
$$\Leftrightarrow \wedge_{j=1}^{m'} [\vec{x} \in P_1 \Rightarrow \vec{a_2^j} \cdot \vec{x} \leq b_2^j]$$

Let us focus on proving $\vec{x} \in P_1 \Rightarrow \vec{a_2^j} \cdot \vec{x} \leq b_2^j$, for a specific constraint of P_2, i.e., the jth half-space defining P_2. As in the case of CNF equivalence, we observe that for lattice points $\vec{x}$, $\vec{x} \in P_1 \Rightarrow \vec{a_2^j} \cdot \vec{x} \leq b_2^j$, if and only if the set $P_1 \wedge [\vec{a_2^j} \cdot \vec{x} \not\leq b_2^j]$ is empty with respect to lattice points. Note that the constraint $\vec{a_2^j} \cdot \vec{x} \not\leq b_2^j$ can be written as: $l_1 : \vec{a_2^j} \cdot \vec{x} > b_2^j$. However, l_1 is an open constraint; in general, the theory of polyhedral combinatorics does not apply to open sets. In particular, no algorithm is known for the problem of checking whether the intersection of open half-spaces is non-empty [2]. But we are only interested in lattice point solutions. Consequently, a lattice point solution will satisfy the constraint l_1 if and only if it satisfies the constraint $\vec{a_2^j} \cdot \vec{x} \geq (b_2^j + 1)$, which is a closed half-space. Thus, we can check whether for lattice points $\vec{x}$, $\vec{x} \in P_1 \Rightarrow \vec{a_2^j} \cdot \vec{x} \leq b_2^j$ by checking whether the polyhedron $P_1 \wedge \vec{a_2^j} \cdot \vec{x} \geq (b_2^j + 1)$ does not have any lattice points. The operation of negating a constraint is referred to as *Constraint Complementation*.

From the above discussion, it follows that

Theorem 3. *Given polyhedra P_1 and P_2, the **IHI** problem Turing reduces to the problem of checking whether a polyhedron does not have any lattice point.*

Corollary 4. *The **IHI** problem can be solved in polynomial time for 2SAT polytopes.*

Proof: 2SAT polytopes are defined by constraints that are closed under Constraint Complementation, insofar as lattice points are concerned. For instance, the complement of the constraint $x_1 - x_2 \leq 4$ is $x_1 - x_2 > 4$, which is equivalent to $x_1 - x_2 \geq 5$, and hence equivalent to $-x_1 + x_2 \leq -5$, if only integral values of x_1 and x_2 are permitted. In other words, the complement of a constraint in a 2SAT polytope is also a 2SAT constraint. The presence (or absence) of lattice points in a 2SAT algorithm can be checked, using the algorithm in [9], which runs in $O(n^3)$ time; the corollary follows. □

Corollary 5. *The Quantified Integer hull inclusion problem (**QIHI**) is decidable in polynomial time, when P_1 and P_2 are defined by 2SAT polytopes.*

Proof: We combine the arguments used in establishing Theorem (2) and Corollary (4). Once again, we note that constraints of 2SAT polytopes are closed under Constraint Complementation and the emptiness of a QIP can be checked in $O(n^3)$ time, if the constraint system is a 2SAT polytope (See [9].). □

6   A Randomized Algorithm for Q2SAT

In [5], an elegant polynomial time Monte Carlo algorithm was presented for the 2SAT problem, i.e., for the problem of checking whether a given 2CNF formula has a satisfying assignment. They show that if the input 2CNF formula ϕ is satisfiable, then their coin-flipping algorithm finds a satisfying assignment with probability greater than one half. Their analysis is based on the following simple, but useful observations:

1. If the current truth value assignment T, to the variables $\{x_1, x_2, \ldots, x_n\}$ of the 2CNF formula ϕ, does not satisfy ϕ, then exists a clause $C \in \phi$, such that both its literals are set to **false** under T. Let us say that ϕ is satisfiable and there exists a unique assignment $\hat{T}$ that satisfies ϕ. Let us also say that the current assignment differs from $\hat{T}$, in exactly k variables. In any truth assignment that satisfies ϕ, at least one of the 2 literals in C must be set to **true**; thus in $\hat{T}$ at least one of the literals of C is set to **true**. It follows that if T is altered by picking one of the 2 literals in C (uniformly and at random) and flipping its value, with probability at least $\frac{1}{2}$, the resulting truth assignment T' is closer to $\hat{T}$ than T is. In fact, with probability $\frac{1}{2}$, T' is one variable closer (than T) to $\hat{T}$ and with probability $\frac{1}{2}$, T' is one variable farther away from a satisfying assignment than T is.

2. Consequently, the strategy of choosing an unsatisfied clause and flipping one of its literals at random, can be modeled as a one-dimensional random walk with a reflecting and absorbing barrier. The random walk is over the integers in the range $[0..n]$, with 0 as the absorbing barrier (indicating that the current assignment T disagrees with $\hat{T}$ on 0 variables and n serving as the reflecting barrier (indicating that T disagrees with $\hat{T}$ on all n variables).

We now present a convergence analysis of the algorithm in [5]; our description is modeled on the analysis in [7].

Lemma 6. *Let X and Y denote two random variables; let $E[X|Y]$ denote that function of the random variable Y, whose value at $Y = y$ is $E[X|Y = y]$. Then,*

$$E[X] = E[E[X|Y]].$$

In other words,

$$E[X] = \sum_y E[X|Y = y] \cdot Pr[Y = y].$$

Proof: See pages $101 - 103$ of [7]. $\square$

Essentially, Lemma (6) allows us to calculate the expectation of a random variable X, by taking the weighted average of the conditional expectation of X, given that $Y = y$, with the conditional expectation being weighted with the probability that $Y = y$.

Assume that ϕ has a satisfying assignment $\hat{T}$. Let $t(i)$ denote the expected number of flips from the current assignment to get to $\hat{T}$, assuming that the current assignment is exactly i values away from $\hat{T}$.

As argued above and using Lemma (6), it is not hard to see that:

$$t(0) = 0$$
$$t(i) = \frac{1}{2} \cdot [(t(i - 1) + 1) + (t(i + 1) + 1)]$$
$$t(n) = 1 + t(n - 1) \tag{5}$$

Note that if we start off with $T = \hat{T}$, i.e., T agrees with $\hat{T}$, on all n variables, then we do not need any flips. Likewise, if the initial assignment T, differs from $\hat{T}$ on all n variables, then flipping any literal must increase the number of variables on which T and $\hat{T}$ agree. Finally, for $i \neq 0, 1$, note that with probability one half, the new assignment will differ from $\hat{T}$, in one more variable than T; likewise, with the same probability, it will differ from $\hat{T}$, in one less variable than T; applying Lemma (6), we get the desired weighted average.

In [6], it is shown that the System (5) can be solved to yield $t(n) = n^2$, i.e., the expected number of literal flips is n^2.

From classical probability, we know that

Theorem 4. *Let X be a random variable that assumes non-negative values only. For any $a > 0$,*

$$Pr[X \geq a \cdot E[X]] \leq \frac{1}{a} \tag{6}$$

Theorem (4) is known as Markov's inequality ([7]) and it can be applied to our flipping algorithm to conclude that if there is a satisfying assignment, the probability that this assignment is not discovered after $2 \cdot n^2$ literal flips times is less than $\frac{1}{2}$.

6.1   A Coin-Flipping Strategy for Q2SAT

There are 2 preconditions that need to be met, for the above analysis to hold for a randomized algorithm for satisfiability testing:

1. $\mathbf{Y_1}$: For a literal to be flipped, it must have exactly 2 assignable values, at the time at which it is assigned.
2. $\mathbf{Y_2}$: Given that the current assignment (model) differs from the satisfying assignment (model) in exactly i variables, flipping a literal should result in exactly one of two events, viz.,
   (a) The resulting assignment differs from the satisfying assignment in $(i-1)$ variables,
   (b) The resulting assignment differs from the satisfying assignment in $(i+1)$ variables,

   Event (2a) should have probability *at least* one half, while event (2b) should have probability *at most* one half.

Note that $\mathbf{Y_1}$ is trivially met by simple CNF formulas, since every variable must be either **true** or **false**, in any satisfying assignment. In case of QBFs though, a solution is a vector of Skolemized boolean functions and hence $\mathbf{Y_1}$ does not hold, in general. Condition $\mathbf{Y_2}$ cannot be met if the clause that is not satisfied by the current assignment has more than 2 literals; indeed, both [6] and [7] provide an instance of a HornCNF formula that takes exponential time to converge, under randomized literal flipping.

We now show that the above 2 conditions can be met in case of Q2CNF decidability. Let $\Phi = Q(x, y) \, \phi(x, y)$ denote a Q2CNF formula, with the existentially quantified variables being drawn from the set $V_1 = \{x_1, x_2, \ldots, x_n\}$ and the universally quantified variables being drawn from the set $V_2 = \{y_1, y_2, \ldots, y_n\}$. $Q(x, y)$ imposes a linear ordering on the set $V_1 \cup V_2$; each clause $C \in \phi(x, y)$ has exactly 2 literals.

We first establish that $\mathbf{Y_1}$ is met. Observe that

1. Satisfiable Q2CNF formulas have simple models, i.e., models in which every existentially quantified variable x_j, is assigned **true**, **false**, y_i or $\bar{y}_i$, where y_i is a universally quantified variable that preceded x_j in $Q(x, y)$; indeed the linear time algorithm in [1], which checks whether a Q2CNF formula Φ has a model, produces a simple model, if the Q2SAT instance is satisfiable. Further, note that that verifying a simple model for a Q2CNF formula is a linear time procedure.
2. Now process the clauses in ϕ sequentially. Let C be an arbitrary clause in $\phi(x, y)$. Note that

(a) If C is of the form (y_i, y_j), i.e., both its literals universally quantified, then Φ does not have a model.

(b) If C is of the form (x_j, y_k), and x_j occurs after y_k in $Q(x, y)$, then $x_j = 1$ or $\bar{y}_k$ in any model that satisfies Φ. Proceed to the next clause.
    However, if y_k succeeds x_j in $Q(x, y)$, or if x_j is also paired with y_p, $p \neq k$, in a clause distinct from C, then x_j *must* be **true** in any model for Φ. (If the existential literal is $\bar{x}_j$, instead of x_j, replace **true** with **false**.) Delete x_j from $Q(x, y)$ and all clauses containing x_j. Likewise, replace all clauses of the form $(\bar{x}_j, u)$, with the unit clause (u). If u is universally quantified, then Φ does not have a model; if it is existentially quantified, it must be set to **true** in any model and the process of altering clauses and $Q(x, y)$ is repeated.

(c) If C is of the form (x_i, x_j), the following cases arise:
    i. Both x_i and x_j have been assigned in Step (2b); in this case, there is nothing to be done;
    ii. x_i is not assigned, but x_j is assigned to **true**. Delete this clause from $\phi(x, y)$, since it has no bearing on the existence of a model.
    iii. x_i is not assigned, but x_j is assigned to **false**. Set x_i to **true**; delete x_i from $Q(x, y)$ and reprocess all clauses, as in the latter half of Step (2b).
    iv. Neither x_i nor x_j has been assigned. Proceed to the next clause.

When Step (2 :) terminates, we will be left with a collection of clauses (say ϕ_{eh}) of the form (x_i, x_k), i.e., both literals will be existential. ϕ_{eh} is called the existential hull of Φ; in any model for Φ, the variables in ϕ_{eh} are assigned either **true** or **false**! This assertion follows immediately from the proof of correctness for Q2CNF decidability in [1]. We have thus established that condition $\mathbf{Y_1}$ is met by Q2CNF formulas.

We proceed to show that condition $\mathbf{Y_2}$ is also met. Assume that Φ has a model $\hat{T}$. Let the current assignment T, differ from $\hat{T}$, in exactly i variables and let C be a clause, that is not satisfied by T. First observe that under our assignment scheme, C cannot be of the form (x_i, y_j); hence C must be of the form (x_i, x_j). Since C is falsified, at least one of the 2 variables is set to a different value in $\hat{T}$. Further, there are only 2 possible values for each of these variables, as per the above discussion. It therefore follows that picking one of the variables at random and flipping it, moves T closer to $\hat{T}$ with probability at least one half.

Algorithm (2) is a formal description of our strategy:

Using an analysis, that is almost identical to the one for 2SAT formulas, we can conclude that

Theorem 5. *Algorithm (2) is a randomized algorithm for the Q2SAT problem. Given a satisfiable Q2CNF formula, the probability that it finds a model in at most $2 \cdot n^2$ literal flips is at least one half.*

7   Conclusion

In this paper, we proved a number of interesting results, regarding clausal equivalence and hull inclusion. In particular, we showed that the clausal equivalence

---

Algorithm 2 Randomized algorithm for the Q2SAT problem.

Function Q2SAT-SOLVE($\Phi = Q(x, y) \, \phi(x, y)$)

1: Process each clause in $\phi(x, y)$ till every existentially quantified variable is set to one of: (a)**true**, (b)**false**, (c)**true**$|\bar{y}_j$, (d) **true**|**false**.

2: {There are a few more symmetric categories, but we ignore them to simplify the exposition. The crucial observation is that each variable has at most 2 valid values.}

3: Let T be the initial truth assignment to the variables $\{x_1, x_2, \ldots, x_n\}$.

4: **if** (T is a model for Φ) **then**

5:    **return**("Φ is satisfiable")

6: **end if**

7: **while** (T is not a model) **do**

8:    Pick a clause C that is falsified in ϕ by T.

9:    Choose a literal at random and flip its value in T, so that C is satisfied.

10:    **if** (T is now a model for ϕ) **then**

11:       **return**("Φ is satisfiable")

12:    **end if**

13: **end while**

14: **return**("Φ is probably unsatisfiable")

---

problem could be solved in polynomial time, if the formulas involved had the forms 2CNF, Q2CNF, Horn or QHorn. We also showed that the integer hull inclusion problem (and the Quantified Integer Hull inclusion problem) could be solved in polynomial time, in case of 2SAT polytopes, whereas the linear hull inclusion problem is polynomial time Turing reducible to the Linear Programming problem.

We are interested in the following 2 open problems have arisen, as a consequence of our work in this paper:

1. Is there a simple approach for the problem of checking feasibility in HornSAT polytopes, i.e., a method that does not use Linear Programming?
2. Can the Random walk strategy discussed in Section §6 for Q2SAT feasibility can be extended to boolean equivalence problems?

Acknowledgements

We are indebted to Samuel R. Buss, R. Chandrasekharan and Klaus Truemper for friendly discussions.

References

1. Bengt Aspvall, Michael F. Plass, and Robert Tarjan. A linear-time algorithm for testing the truth of certain quantified boolean formulas. *Information Processing Letters*, 8(3), 1979.

2. M. S. Bazaraa, H. D. Sherali, and C. M. Shetty. *Nonlinear Programming: Theory and Algorithms*. John Wiley, New York, second edition, 1993.

3. H. Kleine Buning, M. Karpinski, and A.Flogel. Resolution for quantified boolean formulas. *Information and Computation*, 117:12–18, 1995.
4. G. L. Nemhauser and L. A. Wolsey. *Integer and Combinatorial Optimization*. John Wiley & Sons, New York, 1999.
5. C. H. Papadimitriou. On selecting a satisfying truth assignment. In IEEE, editor, *Proceedings: 32nd annual Symposium on Foundations of Computer Science, San Juan, Puerto Rico, October 1–4, 1991*, pages 163–169, 1109 Spring Street, Suite 300, Silver Spring, MD 20910, USA, 1991. IEEE Computer Society Press.
6. Christos H. Papadimitriou. *Computational Complexity*. Addison-Wesley, New York, 1994.
7. Sheldon M. Ross. *Probability Models*. Academic Press, Inc., 7th edition, 2000.
8. T.J. Schaefer. The complexity of satisfiability problems. In Alfred Aho, editor, *Proceedings of the 10th Annual ACM Symposium on Theory of Computing*, pages 216–226, New York City, NY, 1978. ACM Press.
9. K. Subramani. On identifying simple and quantified lattice points in the 2sat polytope. In et. al. Jacques Calmet, editor, *Proceedings of the 5th International Conference on Artificial Intelligence and Symbolic Computation (AISC)*, volume 2385 of *Lecture Notes in Artificial Intelligence*, pages 217–230. Springer-Verlag, July 2002.
10. P. M. Vaidya. An algorithm for linear programming which requires $O(((m+n)n^2 + (m + n)^{1.5}n)L)$ arithmetic operations. In Alfred Aho, editor, *Proceedings of the 19th Annual ACM Symposium on Theory of Computing*, pages 29–38, New York City, NY, May 1987. ACM Press.

Logical Semantics for the First Order ς-Calculus

Steffen van Bakel[1],[*] and Ugo de'Liguoro[2],[**]

[1] Department of Computing
Imperial College
180 Queen's Gate, London SW7 2BZ, UK
svb@doc.ic.ac.uk
[2] Dipartimento di Informatica
Università di Torino
Corso Svizzera 185, 10149 Torino, Italy
deliguoro@di.unito.it

Abstract. We investigate logical semantics of the first order ς-calculus. An assignment system of predicates to first order typed terms of the OB_1 calculus is introduced. We define retraction models for that calculus and an interpretation of terms, types and predicates into such models. The assignment system is then proved to be sound and complete w.r.t. retraction models.

1 Introduction

The essence of logical semantics of a calculus is a system of predicates and a relation of satisfiability, such that the meaning of a term in the calculus can be identified with the set of predicates it satisfies. Examples are intersection types for the type-free λ-calculus [7, 6], pre-locales for typed λ-calculi and domain logic [4], Hennessy-Milner logic for CCS terms [15, 3]. The present work is aimed at defining a logical semantics suitable for typed object calculi.

In [12] it is shown that certain characterizations of reduction properties of pure λ-terms via intersection types (for which see e.g. [10, 16, 6, 11]) are smoothly inherited by the type-free ς-calculus, provided we extend the intersection type discipline to a λ-calculus with records, and interpret ς-terms using the self-application interpretation of [14]. Nonetheless the focus of research in the area of object calculi is on typed systems and typed equational theories. To make our approach applicable to the latter case we have to put on a clear footing the idea of an assignment system of predicates to typed objects: a first investigation is [13].

For monomorphic typed calculi predicates differ from types in that each term has exactly one type, but satisfies (often infinitely) many predicates. This difference is blurred in the polymorphic case (indeed, in the literature, Curry types, intersection types and ML types are considered as forms of polymorphism), but it is still true that, while predicates give partial information about the behavior of single terms, types are concerned

---

[*] Partially supported by EU project IST-1999-20975, SecSafe.

[**] Partially supported by MURST Cofin'01 COMETA Project, IST-2001-33477 DART Project and IST-2001-322222 MIKADO Project. The funding bodies are not responsible for any use that might be made of the results presented here.

C. Blundo and C. Laneve (Eds.): ICTCS 2003, LNCS 2841, pp. 202–215, 2003.

with general properties of the system, like strong normalization for typed λ-calculi, or error-freeness of the reducts of typed terms in object calculi.

The solution we propose is to consider types as languages of predicates, or even better as theories. The denotation of a term is then a set of predicates closed under conjunction and logical implication (technically a filter), but when such a denotation is relativized to a type, which is the counterpart of typing the term, its denotation is restricted to the language associated with that type. This suggests a natural interpretation of features of polymorphic typed systems, as it is the case of subtyping: $A <: B$ if the theory associated to B is "included" into the theory of A, which means that its discriminating power is at most that of A (for a topological interpretation of the same idea, and its relation to realizability models and PER inclusion see [13]).

In the present paper we investigate logical semantics of the first order ς-calculus of [1], called there system OB_1. This is the core of the object calculi studied in that book, even if it is poorly expressive and does not include any form of subtyping. Still it is an interesting case study, as the recursive nature of types is challenging to model (it is the most complex and contrived part of the semantic constructions in [2, 1, 8]). It comes out that the filter model of the typed calculus has the structure of a retraction model, in the sense of [18], where retractions map filters of predicates to their intersection with the language associated to the given type. This leads to a completeness theorem of the assignment system with respect to retraction models of the calculus. We stress that languages, which define the retractions over the filter model, are inductively defined sets of predicates: a concept of lower logical complexity, and much easier to understand, than fixed-points of contractive operators over ideals or over complete uniform PERs.

2   Assignment for the Typed ς-Calculus

In this section we introduce the calculus, its types and typing rules, the syntax of the predicates and an assignment system, to syntactically derive judgements associating predicates to typed terms under the assumption of similar judgements about a finite set of typed variables. Predicates are transparently intersection types for a λ-calculus with records, and come from [12]. The essential difference is that the set of predicates is stratified into languages, in such a way that whenever a predicate can be deduced for a term a^A, it belongs to the language $\mathcal{L}_A$ associated with A.

2.1   The Calculus

Definition 1 (Untyped terms). *Let* $L = \{\ell_i \mid i \in N\}$ *be a denumerable set of labels. The terms of the first order ς-calculus are defined through the following grammar.*

$$a, b ::= x \mid [\ell_i = \varsigma(x_i)b_i{}^{i \in I}] \mid a.\ell \mid a.\ell \Leftarrow \varsigma(x)b$$

In the expression $\varsigma(x^A)b$, the operator $\varsigma(\cdot)$ binds x in b; free and bound variables are defined as usual. Terms are considered equal modulo α-conversion, i.e. up to renaming of bound variables.

Definition 2 (Reduction). *On terms, the* reduction relation *is defined as the contextual, transitive closure of the following reduction rules:*

$$[\ell_i = \varsigma(x_i)b_i{}^{i \in I}].\ell_j \quad \rightarrow \quad b_j\{x_j \hookleftarrow [\ell_i = \varsigma(x_i)b_i{}^{i \in I}]\}$$
$$[\ell_i = \varsigma(x_i)b_i{}^{i \in I}].\ell_j \Leftarrow \varsigma(x)b \quad \rightarrow \quad [\ell_i = \varsigma(x_i)b_i{}^{i \in I \setminus j}, \ell_j = \varsigma(x)b]$$

where $j \in I$ *and* $a\{x \hookleftarrow b\}$ *is the substitution of* x *by* b *in* a, *avoiding variable clashes.*

The reduction relation is confluent (see [1] Ch. 6). Terms do not necessarily have a normal form: e.g. $\Omega \equiv [\ell = \varsigma(x)x.\ell].\ell$ is such that $\Omega \rightarrow \Omega$.

2.2 The Typed System

The following is a presentation of the system OB_1 of [1], with minor changes consisting in writing a^A instead of $a{:}A$, and omitting rules for deriving well formed types and contexts: first order types are indeed defined by a simple inductive definition.

Definition 3 (Types). *Let* $\mathcal{K}$ *be a set of type constants, ranged over by* K. *The set of types is defined by the following grammar:*

$$A, B ::= K \mid [\ell_i : B_i{}^{i \in I}]$$

where I *is a finite set of indexes.*

In the present setting, a *context* for a type judgement is just a finite set E of type decorated variables, of the shape x^A.

Definition 4. *The* type judgements *are defined by the following natural deduction system (where* $A = [\ell_k : B_k{}^{k \in I}]$*):*

$$(\textit{Var}) \ \frac{}{E \vdash x^A} \ (x^A \in E) \qquad (\textit{Val Object}) \ \frac{E, x_i^A \vdash b_i^{B_i}}{E \vdash [\ell_i = \varsigma(x_i^A)b_i^{B_i} {}^{i \in I}]^A} \ (\forall i \in I)$$

$$(\textit{Val Select}) \ \frac{E \vdash a^A}{E \vdash (a^A.\ell_j)^{B_j}} \ (j \in I) \quad (\textit{Val Update}) \ \frac{E \vdash a^A \quad E, x^A \vdash b^{B_j}}{E \vdash (a^A.\ell_j \Leftarrow \varsigma(x^A)b^{B_j})^A} \ (j \in I)$$

Having adopted the notation x^A for a term variable x of type A, the context E becomes redundant. We keep it, however, since this turns out to be useful when introducing bases in the subsequent section.

Reduction among typed terms is defined by adapting Definition 2 in the obvious way. The main result about this system (and all its extensions in [1]) is that types are preserved under reduction: since a term of the form $[\ell_i = \varsigma(x^A)b].\ell_j$ or of the form $[\ell_i = \varsigma(x^A)b].\ell_j \Leftarrow \varsigma(y^A)c$ has no type if $i \neq j$, we may conclude that the reduction of typed terms will never get stuck into not well formed terms (see [1] Ch. 7). Typed terms do not necessarily normalize, however: $\vdash \Omega^A \equiv ([\ell = \varsigma(x^{[\ell:A]})x.\ell].\ell)^A$ is derivable in the empty context for all types A.

2.3 A Predicate System

Much in the style of [7], in this section we will present a notion of *intersection types*, called *predicates* here; using these, we will define a notion of *predicate assignment*, which will consists basically of associating a predicate to a typed term.

Definition 5 (Predicates). *The set $\mathcal{L}$ of* predicates *is inductively defined by:*

$$\sigma, \tau ::= \kappa \mid \omega \mid (\sigma{\to}\tau) \mid (\sigma{\wedge}\tau) \mid \langle \ell_i : \sigma_i^{i \in I} \rangle$$

where κ ranges over a countable set of atoms. On predicates a preorder $\leq$ is inductively defined by:

$$\sigma \leq \sigma$$
$$\sigma \leq \omega$$
$$\omega \leq \omega{\to}\omega$$
$$(\sigma{\to}\tau){\wedge}(\sigma{\to}\rho) \leq \sigma{\to}(\tau{\wedge}\rho)$$
$$\rho{\leq}\sigma \wedge \tau{\leq}\mu \Rightarrow \sigma{\to}\tau \leq \rho{\to}\mu$$
$$\sigma{\wedge}\tau \leq \sigma, \sigma{\wedge}\tau{\leq}\tau$$
$$\sigma{\leq}\tau \wedge \sigma{\leq}\rho \Rightarrow \sigma{\leq}\tau{\wedge}\rho$$
$$\sigma{\leq}\tau \Rightarrow \langle \ell : \sigma \rangle \leq \langle \ell : \tau \rangle$$

$$\langle \ell_i : \sigma_i^{i \in I} \rangle {\wedge} \langle \ell_j : \tau_j^{j \in J} \rangle \leq \langle \ell_k : \rho_k^{(k \in I \cup J)} \rangle, \text{ where } \begin{cases} \rho_k = \sigma_k{\wedge}\tau_k, & \text{if } k \in I{\cap}J, \\ \rho_k = \sigma_k, & \text{if } k \in I{\setminus}J, \\ \rho_k = \tau_k, & \text{if } k \in J{\setminus}I \end{cases}$$

$$\langle \ell_i : \sigma_i^{i \in I} \rangle \leq \langle \ell_j : \sigma_j^{j \in J} \rangle, \text{ if } J \subseteq I$$
$$\sigma{\leq}\tau{\leq}\rho \Rightarrow \sigma{\leq}\rho$$

Finally $\sigma = \tau \Longleftrightarrow \sigma{\leq}\tau{\leq}\sigma$.

Atomic predicates κ are intended to describe elements of atomic type in the domain of interpretation; $\sigma{\to}\tau$ is the property of functions sending elements satisfying σ into elements satisfying τ; $\langle \ell_i : \sigma_i^{i \in I} \rangle$ is the property of records having values that satisfy σ_i associated with the field ℓ_i for all $i \in I$. Predicates ω and $\sigma{\wedge}\tau$ mean truth and conjunction respectively; $\sigma \leq \tau$ reads as 'σ implies τ'.

In the following we consider as 'types' also arrow types $A{\to}B$: functional types are indeed implicit in the interpretation of objects (especially of methods) but do not appear in the syntax of the calculus OB_1 (but they do in the calculi in [1] enriched with lambda abstraction and functional application). Here their use allows for more transparent notations.

Definition 6 (Languages). *The set of all predicates $\mathcal{L}$ is stratified into a family $\{\mathcal{L}_A\}_A$ of sets of predicates called* languages, *indexed over types such that:*

1. *any κ belongs exactly to one $\mathcal{L}_K$, for some $K \in \mathcal{K}$;*
2. *any $\mathcal{L}_A$ is the least set (including atoms if $A \equiv K$) such that:*

$$\frac{}{\omega \subset \mathcal{L}_A} \qquad \frac{\sigma \in \mathcal{L}_A \quad \tau \in \mathcal{L}_A}{\sigma{\wedge}\tau \in \mathcal{L}_A} \qquad \frac{\sigma \in \mathcal{L}_A \quad \tau \in \mathcal{L}_B}{\sigma{\to}\tau \subset \mathcal{L}_{A{\to}B}}$$

$$\frac{\sigma \in \mathcal{L}_{A{\to}B_j}}{\langle \ell_j : \sigma \rangle \in \mathcal{L}_A} (A = [\ell_i{:}B_i^{i \in I}], j \in I) \qquad \frac{\sigma \in \mathcal{L}_A}{\tau \in \mathcal{L}_A} (\sigma \leq \tau)$$

A *statement* is an expression of the shape $a^A : \sigma$, where a is a term, A is a type, such that there exists E with $E \vdash a^A$, and σ is a predicate, and a is called the *subject* of this statement.

A *basis* Γ is a finite set of statements with only (distinct) term variables as subject, of which the predicate is not ω. We say that Γ *preserves languages* if $\sigma \in \mathcal{L}_A$ whenever $x^A : \sigma \in \Gamma$.

If E is a context and Γ a basis, we say that E *fits into* Γ, written $E \lhd \Gamma$, if $x^A : \sigma \in \Gamma$ implies $x^A \in E$. We say that two bases Γ_0, Γ_1 are *compatible* if there exists a context E including all variables occurring in both Γ_0 and Γ_1, fitting into both of them.

Definition 7 (Predicate Assignment). *Let* $A \equiv [\ell_i : B_i{}^{i \in I}]$ *and* B, B_i *be any type, then:*

$$(Var) \frac{}{\Gamma \vdash x^B : \sigma} \ (x^B : \sigma \in \Gamma)$$

$$(Type\ Object) \frac{\Gamma, x_i^A : \sigma_i \vdash b_i^{B_i} : \tau_i}{\Gamma \vdash [\ell_i = \varsigma(x_i^A) b_i{}^{i \in I}]^A : \langle \ell_j : \sigma_j \to \tau_j{}^{j \in J} \rangle} \ (\forall i \in I \ \wedge \ J \subseteq I)$$

$$(Val\ Select) \frac{\Gamma \vdash a^A : \langle \ell_j : \sigma_j \to \tau_j{}^{j \in J} \rangle \quad \Gamma \vdash a^A : \sigma_k}{\Gamma \vdash a.\ell_k^{B_k} : \tau_k} \ (k \in J)$$

$$(Val\ Update) \frac{\Gamma \vdash a^A : \langle \ell_j : \sigma_j{}^{j \in J} \rangle \quad \Gamma, y^A : \sigma \vdash b^{B_k} : \tau}{\Gamma \vdash (a.\ell_k \Leftarrow \varsigma(y^A) b)^A : \langle \ell_j : \sigma_j{}^{j \in J \setminus k}, \ell_k : \sigma \to \tau \rangle} \ (k \in J)$$

plus the following 'logical' rules:

$$(\omega) \frac{E \vdash a^B}{\Gamma \vdash a^B : \omega} \ (E \lhd \Gamma) \quad (\wedge I) \frac{\Gamma \vdash a^B : \sigma \quad \Gamma \vdash a^B : \tau}{\Gamma \vdash a^B : \sigma \wedge \tau} \quad (\leq) \frac{\Gamma \vdash a^B : \sigma \quad \sigma \leq \tau}{\Gamma \vdash a^B : \tau}$$

As a straightforward induction shows, if all bases in the derivation of $\Gamma \vdash a^A : \sigma$ preserve languages, then $\sigma \in \mathcal{L}_A$.

We remark that in rule (*Type Object*) it is not required that the σ_i are equal, not even pairwise consistent (but for the fact that they belong to the same language $\mathcal{L}_A$). This should be compared to rule (*Val Update*), which allows for replacing the subexpression σ_k in the predicate $\langle \ell_j : \sigma_j{}^{j \in J} \rangle$ of the first premise by the completely unrelated predicate $\sigma \to \tau$ in the conclusion. This is sound, however, because of rule (*Val Select*), which checks in the crucial place that the antecedent of the arrow holds of a^A, to which the self variable x_k^A is bound.

These features, which surely sound odd to readers familiar with the literature on object calculi, are indeed essential. Suppose in fact that

$$A \equiv [\ell_0 : \mathsf{Int}, \ell_1 : \mathsf{Int}] \text{ and } a \equiv [\ell_0 = \varsigma(x^A)1, \ell_1 = \varsigma(x^A)x.\ell_0]$$

(using a constant 1 of type Int), so that $\vdash a^A$. Then

$$\frac{x^A : \omega \vdash 1 : \mathsf{Odd} \qquad \frac{x^A : \langle \ell_0 : \omega \to \mathsf{Odd} \rangle \vdash x^A : \langle \ell_0 : \omega \to \mathsf{Odd} \rangle \quad x^A : \langle \ell_0 : \omega \to \mathsf{Odd} \rangle \vdash x^A : \omega}{x^A : \langle \ell_0 : \omega \to \mathsf{Odd} \rangle \vdash (x.\ell_0)^{\mathsf{Int}} : \mathsf{Odd}}}{\vdash a^A : \langle \ell_0 : \omega \to \mathsf{Odd}, \ell_1 : \langle \ell_0 : \omega \to \mathsf{Odd} \rangle \to \mathsf{Odd} \rangle}$$

where ℓ_0 is a field and ℓ_1 is the method $\mathtt{get}\ell_0$. By rule (*Val Update*) one might derive the seemingly incorrect:

$$\frac{\vdash a^A : \langle \ell_0 : \omega \to \mathsf{Odd}, \ell_1 : \langle \ell_0 : \omega \to \mathsf{Odd}\rangle \to \mathsf{Odd}\rangle \quad y^A{:}\omega \vdash 2 : \mathsf{Even}}{\vdash (a.\ell_0 \Leftarrow \varsigma(y^A)2)^A : \langle \ell_0 : \omega \to \mathsf{Even}, \ell_1 : \langle \ell_0 : \omega \to \mathsf{Odd}\rangle \to \mathsf{Odd}\rangle}$$

This makes sense, however, since it simply tells that if the value at ℓ_0 is an odd integer, then the method ℓ_1 will return an odd integer; it also tells that this is vacuously true of the actual object $(a.\ell_0 \Leftarrow \varsigma(y^A)2)^A$, since it has an even integer at ℓ_0. Moreover it is harmless: $(a.\ell_0 \Leftarrow \varsigma(y^A)2).\ell_1 \xrightarrow{*} 2$ and we clearly assume that $\nvdash 2 : \mathsf{Odd}$; nonetheless $\nvdash (a.\ell_0 \Leftarrow \varsigma(y^A)2).\ell_1 : \mathsf{Odd}$, because rule (*Val Select*) does not apply since $\nvdash (a.\ell_0 \Leftarrow \varsigma(y^A)2) : \langle \ell_0 : \omega \to \mathsf{Odd}\rangle$.

On the other hand the following odd-looking assignment is legal as well, this time by rule (*Type Object*):

$$\frac{x^A{:}\omega \vdash 1 : \mathsf{Odd} \qquad \dfrac{x^A{:}\langle \ell_0 : \omega \to \mathsf{Even}\rangle \vdash x^A : \langle \ell_0 : \omega \to \mathsf{Even}\rangle \quad x^A{:}\langle \ell_0 : \omega \to \mathsf{Even}\rangle \vdash x^A : \omega}{x^A{:}\langle \ell_0 : \omega \to \mathsf{Even}\rangle \vdash (x.\ell_0)^{\mathsf{Int}} : \mathsf{Even}}}{\vdash a^A{:}\langle \ell_0 : \omega \to \mathsf{Odd}, \ell_1 : \langle \ell_0 : \omega \to \mathsf{Even}\rangle \to \mathsf{Even}\rangle}$$

In the last case, however, the apparently odd predicate we deduce, is of use to conclude by rule (*Val Update*):

$$\frac{\vdash a^A : \langle \ell_0 : \omega \to \mathsf{Odd}, \ell_1 : \langle \ell_0 : \omega \to \mathsf{Even}\rangle \to \mathsf{Even}\rangle \quad y^A : \omega \vdash 2 : \mathsf{Even}}{\vdash (a.\ell_0 \Leftarrow \varsigma(y^A)2)^A : \langle \ell_0 : \omega \to \mathsf{Even}, \ell_1 : \langle \ell_0 : \omega \to \mathsf{Even}\rangle \to \mathsf{Even}\rangle}$$

which is what we expected.

The next lemma will be of use in the last section. Let $\Gamma \leq \Gamma'$ mean that for all $x^A{:}\tau \in \Gamma'$ there exists $\sigma \leq \tau$ such that $x^A{:}\sigma \in \Gamma$.

Lemma 8. *1. $\Gamma \leq \Gamma'$ and $\Gamma' \vdash a^A{:}\sigma$ implies $\Gamma \vdash a^A{:}\sigma$.*
2. If Γ_0, Γ_1 are compatible bases, then there exists the basis $\Gamma_0 \wedge \Gamma_1$ which is the greatest one such that $\Gamma_0 \wedge \Gamma_1 \leq \Gamma_i$ for $i = 0, 1$.

Proof. The first part is proved by induction over the derivation of $\Gamma' \vdash a^A{:}\sigma$, using $(\leq)$. For the second, let $\Gamma_0 \wedge \Gamma_1$ be the basis including exactly the statements $x^A{:}\sigma$ such that either $x^A{:}\sigma$ is in one of the two basis and not in the other, or $x^A{:}\sigma_0 \in \Gamma_0$, $x^A{:}\sigma_1 \in \Gamma_1$ and $\sigma \equiv \sigma_0 \wedge \sigma_1$. ∎

We end this section by stating, without proof, the main theorem about syntactical properties of the assignment system. It establishes that predicates are invariant under conversion.

Theorem 9 (Subject reduction and expansion).

1. If $\Gamma \vdash a^A{:}\rho$, and $a \to a'$, then $\Gamma \vdash a'^A{:}\rho$.
2. If $\Gamma \vdash a^A{:}\rho$ and $a' \to a$ where $E \vdash a'^A$ for $E \triangleleft \Gamma$, then $\Gamma \vdash a'^A{:}\rho$.

3   Models and Logical Semantics

There is no definite agreement about what should be considered as a model of object calculi. Even [1] does not give a general definition of this concept. Rather it is commonly held, especially after Cardelli's seminal work on records calculi, that it should be a model of the λ-calculus including operators to build, access and modify finite records, often seen as finite functions over a set of labels.

Definition 10. *We call a structure* $\mathcal{D} = \langle D, L, \mathsf{emp}, \mathsf{lcond}, \mathsf{sel} \rangle$ *an untyped ς-model if:*

- *D is a λ-model;*
- *$L = \{ \ell_i \mid i \in N \}$ is a denumerable set of labels;*
- *$\mathsf{emp} \in D$;*
- *$\mathsf{sel} : D \times L \to D$;*
- *$\mathsf{lcond} : D \times L \times D \to D$*

such that (writing lcond and sel in a Curryfied form):

1. *$\mathsf{sel}(\mathsf{lcond}\, x\, \ell_i\, y)\ell_i = y$,*
2. *$i \neq j \Rightarrow \mathsf{sel}(\mathsf{lcond}\, x\, \ell_i\, y)\ell_j = \mathsf{sel}\, x\, \ell_j$,*
3. *$i \neq j \Rightarrow \mathsf{lcond}(\mathsf{lcond}\, x\, \ell_i\, y)\, \ell_j\, z = \mathsf{lcond}(\mathsf{lcond}\, x\, \ell_j\, z)\, \ell_i\, y$.*

emp is the empty record; sel is a selection operator, depending on its second argument for the field to be selected on its first argument; lcond is a conditional update operator, setting to the value of its third argument the field of its first argument at the label which is the second argument. Note that, due to the untyped nature of the structure, nothing prevents from field selection or field update of some non record element of the domain.

An untyped ς-model is a particular case of what is called a λ, record-combinatory structure in [17] ch. 10. Differences are that here $\mathcal{D}$ is a λ-model, instead of a partial combinatory algebra, and the third axiom about lcond which is not in the original definition. The present choices allow for a simpler treatment and are satisfied by the untyped structure in [1] ch. 14, which is the only denotational model of the ς-calculus in the literature.

Since any $\mathcal{D}$ is a λ-model, we shall freely use abstraction notation. Moreover, we use the abbreviations:

$$\langle \cdot \rangle = \mathsf{emp}$$
$$\langle \ell_i = d_i{}^{i \in \{1, \ldots, n\}} \rangle = \mathsf{lcond}(\ldots (\mathsf{lcond}\, \mathsf{emp}\, \ell_1\, d_1) \ldots)\ell_n\, d_n$$
$$d \cdot \ell_i = \mathsf{sel}\, d\, \ell_i$$
$$d \cdot \ell_i := e = \mathsf{lcond}\, d\, \ell_i\, e$$

A structure of this form can be constructed by solving the domain equation:

$$D = At + [L \to D] + [D \to D] \tag{1}$$

where At is a domain interpreting atomic (namely ground) types. This equation appears in [9, 5], and is essentially the same as in [1], where it is used to build a model of the (second order) typed ς-calculus.

Definition 11. *To each predicate σ we associate a subset $[\![\sigma]\!]_\eta^{\mathcal{D}} \subseteq D$ (or simply $[\![\sigma]\!]_\eta$ when $\mathcal{D}$ is clear from the context), where η sends each predicate atom κ to some subset of D, and $\eta(\kappa) \subseteq [\![K]\!]$ when $\kappa \in \mathcal{L}_K$ for some constant type K:*

1. $[\![\omega]\!]_\eta = D$,
2. $[\![\kappa]\!]_\eta = \eta(\kappa)$,
3. $[\![\sigma \wedge \tau]\!]_\eta = [\![\sigma]\!]_\eta \cap [\![\tau]\!]_\eta$,
4. $[\![\sigma \to \tau]\!]_\eta = \{d \in D \mid \forall e \in [\![\sigma]\!]_\eta. \ d e \in [\![\tau]\!]_\eta\}$,
5. $[\![\langle \ell_i : \sigma_i {}^{i \in I}\rangle]\!]_\eta = \{d \in D \mid \forall i \in I. \ d \cdot \ell_i \in [\![\sigma_i]\!]_\eta\}$.

The latter definition formalizes the intended meaning of predicates by defining their extensions; the subsequent proposition states that implication corresponds to set theoretic inclusion of predicate denotations as expected.

Proposition 1. *If $\sigma \leq \tau$ then, for any η, $[\![\sigma]\!]_\eta \subseteq [\![\tau]\!]_\eta$.*

Definition 12. *A type interpretation over $\mathcal{D}$ is a mapping associating with each type A a subset $[\![A]\!]^{\mathcal{D}} \subseteq D$. It is said to be consistent with the predicate interpretation $[\![\cdot]\!]_\eta$ if $\sigma \in \mathcal{L}_A$ implies $[\![\sigma]\!]_\eta \subseteq [\![A]\!]$.*

Previous definitions provide the essentials to give meaning to $a^A : \sigma$ and to judgments $\Gamma \vdash a^A : \sigma$.

Definition 13. *Suppose that $\mathcal{D}$ is an untyped ς-model. Let the type interpretation and the predicate interpretation be consistent, E be a context, Γ a basis and ξ a term environment:*

1. $\xi \models E$ *if* $\xi(x^A) \in [\![A]\!]^{\mathcal{D}}$ *whenever* $x^A \in E$;
2. $E \models a^A$ *if for all* ξ *s.t.* $\xi \models E$, $[\![a^A]\!]_\xi^{\mathcal{D}} \in [\![A]\!]^{\mathcal{D}}$;
3. $\xi \models \Gamma$ *if* $x^A : \sigma \in \Gamma$ *implies* $\xi(x^A) \in [\![\sigma]\!]_\eta \subseteq [\![A]\!]^{\mathcal{D}}$;
4. $\Gamma \models a^A : \sigma$ *if for all* ξ *s.t.* $\xi \models \Gamma$, $[\![a^A]\!]_\xi^{\mathcal{D}} \in [\![\sigma]\!]_\eta \subseteq [\![A]\!]^{\mathcal{D}}$.

3.1   A Model of Retractions

Let D be any domain solving the equation (1). Following [18], a *retraction* over D is a continuous function $\rho : D \to D$ such that $\rho^2 = \rho \circ \rho = \rho$. Types can be interpreted by means of retractions by setting $[\![A]\!] = \{d \in D \mid \rho_A(d) = d\}$, which is the same as the range of ρ_A. For basic types one may choose $\rho_K(d) = d$ if $d \in At$, else $\bot$.

Proposition 2. *Let $A \equiv [\ell_i : B_i {}^{i \in I}]$: if ρ_{B_i} is a retraction for all $i \in I$, then there exists a retraction ρ_A such that*

$$\rho_A(d) = \langle \ell_i = \rho_{A \to B_i}(d \cdot \ell_i) {}^{i \in I}\rangle,$$

where $\rho_{A \to B}(d) = \lambda x.\rho_B(d(\rho_A(x)))$ (indeed $\rho_{A \to B}$ is a retraction, if ρ_A and ρ_B are).

Proof. The function (in Curryfied form)

$$\Upsilon_A f d = \langle \ell_i = \lambda x . \rho_{B_i}((d \cdot \ell_i)(fx))^{\ i \in I} \rangle$$

is continuous, hence it has a fixed-point $\rho_A = Fix(\Upsilon_A) = \bigsqcup_n \Upsilon_A^{(n)}$, where $\Upsilon^{(0)} = \lambda x . \bot$, $\Upsilon_A^{(n+1)} = \Upsilon_A(\Upsilon_A^{(n)})$. By its definition we have

$$\rho_A(d) = \langle \ell_i = \lambda x . \rho_{B_i}((d \cdot \ell_i)(\rho_A(x)))^{\ i \in I} \rangle = \langle \ell_i = \rho_{A \to B_i}(d \cdot \ell_i)^{\ i \in I} \rangle.$$

Observe that this is indeed a retraction:

$$\rho_A^2(d) = \bigsqcup_n \Upsilon_A^{(n)}(\bigsqcup_m \Upsilon_A^{(m)}(d)) = \bigsqcup_{n,m} \Upsilon_A^{(n)}(\Upsilon_A^{(m)}(d)) = \bigsqcup_{n+m} \Upsilon_A^{(n+m)}(d) = \rho_A(d).$$

■

We say that $(\mathcal{D}, \{\rho_A\}_A)$ is a *retraction model* if $\mathcal{D}$ is an untyped ς-model and $\{\rho_A\}_A$ is a family of retractions such that $\rho_A(d) = \langle \ell_i = \rho_{A \to B_i}(d \cdot \ell_i)^{\ i \in I} \rangle$, where $A \equiv [\ell_i : B_i^{\ i \in I}]$.

Definition 14. *Let $(\mathcal{D}, \{\rho_A\}_A)$ be a retraction model. The typed interpretation $[\![a^A]\!]_\xi^{\mathcal{D}}$, where ξ is an environment associating with each term variable an element of D, is inductively defined by:*

$$[\![x^A]\!]_\xi = \xi(x)$$
$$[\![[\ell_i = \varsigma(x_i^A)b_i^{B_i\ i \in I}]]\!]_\xi = \langle \ell_i = \lambda d . [\![b_i^{B_i}]\!]_{\xi[x_i := \rho_A(d)]}^{\ i \in I} \rangle$$
$$[\![(a^A . \ell_i)^{B_i}]\!]_\xi = ([\![a^A]\!]_\xi \cdot \ell_i)[\![a^A]\!]_\xi$$
$$[\![a^A . \ell_i \Leftarrow \varsigma(x^A)b^{B_i}]\!]_\xi = [\![a^A]\!]_\xi \cdot \ell_i := \lambda d . [\![b^{B_i}]\!]_{\xi[x := \rho_A(d)]}.$$

Theorem 15 (Soundness of the type system w.r.t. retraction models).
If $E \vdash a^A$ then $E \models a^A$.

Proof. By induction over the derivation of $E \vdash a^A$ we prove that $\rho_A([\![a^A]\!]_\xi) = [\![a^A]\!]_\xi$ for any environment ξ such that $\xi \models E$.   ■

Lemma 16. *Suppose that the image of $\eta(\kappa)$ under ρ_K is included into $\eta(\kappa)$ when $\kappa \in \mathcal{L}_K$. If $\sigma \in \mathcal{L}_A$ and $d \in [\![\sigma]\!]_\eta$ then $\rho_A(d) \in [\![\sigma]\!]_\eta$.*

Proof. By induction on σ. Cases ω and κ are trivial, by definition and hypothesis respectively. Case $\sigma \wedge \tau \in \mathcal{L}_A$ is immediate by induction, since then $\sigma, \tau \in \mathcal{L}_A$.

Case $\sigma \to \tau \in \mathcal{L}_{A \to B}$: then $\sigma \in \mathcal{L}_A$ and $\tau \in \mathcal{L}_B$; if $d \in [\![\sigma \to \tau]\!]_\eta$ then:

$$\begin{aligned}
e \in [\![\sigma]\!]_\eta &\Rightarrow \rho_A(e) \in [\![\sigma]\!]_\eta && \text{by ind.} \\
&\Rightarrow d(\rho_A(e)) \in [\![\tau]\!]_\eta && \text{by hyp. on } d \\
&\Rightarrow \rho_B(d(\rho_A(e))) \in [\![\tau]\!]_\eta && \text{by ind.}
\end{aligned}$$

and we conclude since $\rho_{A \to B}(d) = \lambda x . \rho_B(d(\rho_A(x)))$.

Case $\langle \ell_j : \sigma_j{}^{j \in J} \rangle \in \mathcal{L}_A$, where $A \equiv [\ell_i : B_i{}^{j \in J}]$ and $J \subseteq I$: then $\sigma_j \in \mathcal{L}_{A \to B_j}$ for all j. This implies that, if $d \in [\![\langle \ell_j : \sigma_j{}^{j \in J} \rangle]\!]_\eta$ then $d \cdot \ell_j \in [\![\sigma_j]\!]_\eta$ and by induction $\rho_{A \to B_j}(d) \in [\![\sigma_j]\!]_\eta$: the thesis follows since $\rho_A(d) = \langle \ell_i = \rho_{A \to B_i}(d)^{i \in I} \rangle$. ∎

Theorem 17 (Soundness of the predicate system w.r.t. retraction models).
If $\Gamma \vdash a^A : \sigma$ then $\Gamma \models a^A : \sigma$.

Proof. By induction on the derivation of $\Gamma \vdash a^A : \sigma$. We show only the interesting cases.

The derivation ends with:

$$(\text{Type Object}) \frac{\Gamma, x_i^A : \sigma_i \vdash b_i^{B_i} : \tau_i}{\Gamma \vdash [\ell_i = \varsigma(x_i^A) b_i{}^{i \in I}]^A : \langle \ell_j : \sigma_j \to \tau_j{}^{j \in J} \rangle} \quad (\forall i \in I \wedge J \subseteq I)$$

By definition $([\![a^A]\!]_\xi \cdot \ell_j)d = [\![b_j^{B_j}]\!]_{\xi[x_j := \rho_A(d)]}$, where $j \in J \subseteq I$: if $d \in [\![\sigma_j]\!]_\eta$ then, by Lemma 16, $\rho_A(d) \in [\![\sigma_j]\!]_\eta$, since $\sigma_j \in \mathcal{L}_A$; therefore $\xi[x_j := \rho_A(d)] \models \Gamma, x_j^A : \sigma_j$ and, consequently, by induction, $[\![b_j^{B_j}]\!]_{\xi[x_j := \rho_A(d)]} \in [\![\tau_j]\!]_\eta$. This implies that $[\![a^A]\!]_\xi \in [\![\langle \ell_j : \sigma_j \to \tau_j{}^{j \in J} \rangle]\!]_\eta$.

The derivation ends with:

$$(\text{Val Select}) \frac{\Gamma \vdash a^A : \langle \ell_j : \sigma_j \to \tau_j{}^{j \in J} \rangle \quad \Gamma \vdash a^A : \sigma_k}{\Gamma \vdash (a.\ell_k)^{B_k} : \tau_k} \quad (k \in J)$$

The thesis follows immediately by induction:
$[\![a^A]\!]_\xi \in [\![\langle \ell_j : \sigma_j \to \tau_j{}^{j \in J} \rangle]\!]_\eta$ and $[\![a^A]\!]_\xi \in [\![\sigma_k]\!]_\eta$ and by the definition $[\![(a.\ell_k)^{B_k}]\!]_\xi = ([\![a^A]\!]_\xi \cdot \ell_k)[\![a^A]\!]_\xi$.

The derivation ends with:

$$(\text{Val Update}) \frac{\Gamma \vdash a^A : \langle \ell_j : \sigma_j{}^{j \in J} \rangle \quad \Gamma, y^A : \sigma \vdash b^{B_k} : \tau}{\Gamma \vdash (a.\ell_k \Leftarrow \varsigma(y^A) b)^A : \langle \ell_j : \sigma_j \to \tau_k{}^{j \in J \setminus k}, \ell_k : \sigma \to \tau \rangle} \quad (k \in J)$$

Define $c^A \equiv (a^A.\ell_k \Leftarrow \varsigma(y^A) b^{B_k})^A$, and recall that

$$[\![c^A]\!]_\xi = [\![a^A]\!]_\xi \cdot \ell_k := \lambda d. [\![b^{B_k}]\!]_{\xi[y := \rho_A(d)]}.$$

Let $d \in [\![\sigma_j]\!]_\eta$ for some $j \in J$: if $j \neq k$ then $([\![c^A]\!]_\xi \cdot \ell_j)d = ([\![a^A]\!]_\xi \cdot \ell_j)d \in [\![\tau_j]\!]_\eta$ by induction. Otherwise $j = k$ and $([\![c^A]\!]_\xi \cdot \ell_j)d = [\![b^{B_k}]\!]_{\xi[y := \rho_A(d)]} \in [\![\tau_k]\!]_\eta$, again by induction. ∎

3.2 The Filter Model

Definition 18. *A* filter *of predicates is a subset $F \subseteq \mathcal{L}$ of predicates such that:*

1. $\omega \in F$,
2. *if $\sigma, \tau \in F$ then $\sigma \wedge \tau \in F$,*
3. *if $\sigma \in F$ and $\sigma \leq \tau$ then $\tau \in F$.*

Let $\mathcal{F}$ be the set of all filters of predicates.

A filter is *principal* if it is of the form $\{\tau \mid \sigma \leq \tau\}$, which we denote by $\uparrow \sigma$ (the upset of σ). As is known from the literature (see e.g. [11]), $\mathcal{F}$ is a λ-model, where continuous functions, that is mappings $f : \mathcal{F} \to \mathcal{F}$ such that $f(F) = \bigcup_{\sigma \in F} f(\uparrow\sigma)$, are representable by the filters

$$\Psi(f) = \{\sigma{\to}\tau \mid \tau \in f(\uparrow\sigma)\}$$

and functional application is defined by:

$$FG = \{\tau \mid \exists \sigma \in G \,.\, \sigma{\to}\tau \in F\}.$$

Moreover, $\mathcal{F}$ is a solution of the domain equation (1), hence it is a model of the type-free ς-calculus. In the next proposition we spell out the details of the definitions of record selection and record update operations over filters.

Proposition 3. *The following operations on filters interpret the record constant and operations, turning $\mathcal{F}$ into an untyped ς-model:*

1. $\mathsf{emp} = \uparrow\langle\cdot\rangle$;
2. $F \cdot \ell_i = \{\sigma \mid \langle \ell_i : \sigma\rangle \in F\}$;
3. $(F \cdot \ell_i := G) = \{\langle \ell_j : \sigma_j{}^{j \in J}\rangle \mid (j \neq i \,\wedge\, \langle \ell_j : \sigma\rangle \in F) \,\vee\, (j = i \,\wedge\, \sigma_i \in G)\}$.

Proof. The equations of Definition 10 are checked by straightforward calculations. ∎

We remark that all the operations above, as well as functional composition, are continuous in their arguments which are filters.

Proposition 4. $[\![\sigma]\!]_\eta = \{F \in \mathcal{F} \mid \sigma \in F\}$ *is a predicate interpretation that satisfies all clauses in Definition 11. Moreover, if $\eta(\kappa) \subseteq [\![K]\!]$ whenever $\kappa \in \mathcal{L}_K$, then $[\![\sigma]\!]_\eta \subseteq [\![A]\!]$ if $\sigma \in \mathcal{L}_A$.* ∎

In the following, if X is a variable ranging over filters and $e[X]$ an expression denoting a filter such that the function $\lambda X.e[X]$ is continuous, then we abuse notation writing $\lambda X.e[X]$ for $\Psi(\lambda X.e[X])$.

Lemma 19. *The family $\{\rho_A\}_A$ where $\rho_A(F) = F \cap \mathcal{L}_A$, is a family of retractions turning $\mathcal{F}$ into a retraction model.*

Proof. We check that $F \cap \mathcal{L}_A = \langle \ell_i = \lambda X.(F \cdot \ell_i)(X \cap \mathcal{L}_A) \cap \mathcal{L}_{B_i}{}^{i \in I}\rangle$. Observe that $\sigma \in \langle \ell_i = \lambda X.(F \cdot \ell_i)(X \cap \mathcal{L}_A) \cap \mathcal{L}_{B_i}{}^{i \in I}\rangle$ if and only if $\sigma = \langle \ell_j : \bigwedge \alpha{\to}\beta{}^{j \in J}\rangle$, where $J \subseteq I$ and $\beta \in (F \cdot \ell_i)(\uparrow\alpha \cap \mathcal{L}_A) \cap \mathcal{L}_{B_j}$ for each $\alpha{\to}\beta$ in $\bigwedge \alpha{\to}\beta$ and $j \in J$. On the other hand $\beta \in (F \cdot \ell_i)(\uparrow\alpha \cap \mathcal{L}_A) \cap \mathcal{L}_{B_j}$ if and only if $\langle \ell_j : \alpha'{\to}\beta\rangle \in F \cap \mathcal{L}_A$ for some $\alpha' \in \uparrow\alpha \cap \mathcal{L}_A$.

Now, if $\sigma \in \langle \ell_i = \lambda X.(F \cdot \ell_i)(X \cap \mathcal{L}_A) \cap \mathcal{L}_{B_i}{}^{i \in I}\rangle$ then $\langle \ell_j : \bigwedge \alpha'{\to}\beta{}^{j \in J}\rangle \in F \cap \mathcal{L}_A$ and $\langle \ell_j : \bigwedge \alpha'{\to}\beta{}^{j \in J}\rangle \leq \langle \ell_j : \bigwedge \alpha{\to}\beta{}^{j \in J}\rangle = \sigma$ which is then in $F \cap \mathcal{L}_A$.

Vice versa, if $\sigma \in F \cap \mathcal{L}_A$ then $\sigma = \langle \ell_j : \bigwedge \gamma{\to}\delta{}^{j \in J}\rangle \geq \langle \ell_j : \bigwedge \alpha{\to}\beta{}^{j \in J}\rangle$ for some $J \subseteq I$, $\alpha \in \mathcal{L}_A$, $\beta \in \mathcal{L}_{B_j}$. This implies that $\bigwedge \alpha{\to}\beta \leq \gamma{\to}\delta$ for each $j \in J$ and $\gamma{\to}\delta$ in $\bigwedge \gamma{\to}\delta$. This is true if and only if $\bigwedge Y \leq \delta$ where $Y = \{\beta \mid \alpha \in X\}$ and $X = \{\alpha \mid \alpha \geq \gamma\}$. It follows that $\bigwedge \alpha{\to}\beta \leq \bigwedge X \to \bigwedge Y \leq \gamma{\to}\delta$; since $X \subseteq \uparrow\gamma \cap \mathcal{L}_A$ and both filters and languages are closed under finite intersections, $\bigwedge X \in \uparrow\gamma \cap \mathcal{L}_A$, which implies $\delta \in (F \cdot \ell_j)(\uparrow\gamma \cap \mathcal{L}_A)$: now $\sigma \in \langle \ell_i = \lambda X.(F \cdot \ell_i)(X \cap \mathcal{L}_A) \cap \mathcal{L}_{B_i}{}^{i \in I}\rangle$ follows. ∎

Theorem 20. *For all a^A such that $E \vdash a^A$, for some E, and all environment ξ such that $\xi \models E$:*

$$[\![a^A]\!]_\xi^{\mathcal{F}} = \{\sigma \mid \exists \Gamma.\ \xi \models \Gamma \ \& \ \Gamma \vdash a^A : \sigma\}.$$

Proof. ($\supseteq$): $(\mathcal{F}, \{\rho_A\}_A)$ is a retraction model by Lemma 19 and therefore, by Theorem 17, if $\xi \models \Gamma$ and $\Gamma \vdash a^A : \sigma$ then $[\![a^A]\!]_\xi \in [\![\sigma]\!]_\eta$, so that $\sigma \in [\![a^A]\!]_\xi$ by definition of $[\![\sigma]\!]_\eta$.

($\subseteq$): by induction over a^A.

Case x^A: if $\sigma \in [\![x^A]\!]_\xi^{\mathcal{F}} = \xi(x^A) \subseteq \mathcal{L}_A$, then $\{x^A : \sigma\}$ is a well formed context, $\xi \models \{x^A : \sigma\}$ and $\{x^A : \sigma\} \vdash x^A : \sigma$ by (*Var*).

Case $a^A \equiv [\ell_i = \varsigma(x^A{}_i)b^{B_i\ i \in I}]^A$: if

$$\sigma \in [\![a^A]\!]_\xi^{\mathcal{F}} = \langle \ell_i = \lambda X. [\![b_i^{B_i}]\!]_{\xi[x_i := X \cap \mathcal{L}_A]}^{\mathcal{F}} \cap \mathcal{L}_{B_i}{}^{\ i \in I} \rangle,$$

then $\sigma = \langle \ell_j : \bigwedge \alpha \to \beta^{\ j \in J} \rangle \in \mathcal{L}_A$ for some $J \subseteq I$, where $\beta \in [\![b_j^{B_j}]\!]_{\xi[x_j := \uparrow \alpha \cap \mathcal{L}_A]}^{\mathcal{F}} \cap \mathcal{L}_{B_j}$. By induction hypothesis for each $j \in J$ there exists Γ_j such that $\xi[x_j := \uparrow \alpha \cap \mathcal{L}_A] \models \Gamma_j$ and $\Gamma_j, \vdash b_j^{B_j} : \beta$: this implies that $x^{A_j} : \alpha' \in \Gamma_j$ for some $\alpha' \in \uparrow \alpha \cap \mathcal{L}_A$. Since this holds for all $j \in J$, while clearly $\Gamma_k \vdash b_k^{B_k} : \omega$ for all $k \in I \setminus J$, we derive $\Gamma' \vdash a^A : \langle \ell_j : \bigwedge \alpha' \to \beta \rangle$ by (*Val Object*), where $\Gamma' = \Gamma \setminus x_j^A : \alpha$ for any $j \in J$. Now $\alpha' \geq \alpha$ which implies $\bigwedge \alpha' \to \beta \leq_A \bigwedge \alpha \to \beta$ and we are done.

Case $(a^A.\ell_i)^{B_i}$: if $\tau \in [\![(a^A.\ell_i)^{B_i}]\!]_\xi^{\mathcal{F}} = ([\![a^A]\!]_\xi^{\mathcal{F}} \cdot \ell_i)[\![a^A]\!]_\xi^{\mathcal{F}}$ then there exist $\sigma \in [\![a^A]\!]_\xi^{\mathcal{F}}$ such that $\langle \ell_i : \sigma \to \tau \rangle \in [\![a^A]\!]_\xi^{\mathcal{F}}$. By induction there are Γ_0, Γ_1 such that $\xi \models \Gamma_i$ for $i = 0, 1$, and $\Gamma_0 \vdash a^A : \langle \ell_i : \sigma \to \tau \rangle$ and $\Gamma_1 \vdash a^A : \sigma$: it follows that $\Gamma = \Gamma_0 \wedge \Gamma_1$ is a well formed context such that $\xi \models \Gamma$, and that $\Gamma \vdash a^A : \langle \ell_i : \sigma \to \tau \rangle$ and $\Gamma \vdash a^A : \sigma$. The thesis follows by (*Val Select*).

Case $(a^A.\ell_i \Leftarrow \varsigma(x^A)b^{B_i})^A$: if

$$\tau \in [\![(a^A.\ell_i \Leftarrow \varsigma(x^A)b^{B_i})^A]\!]_\xi^{\mathcal{F}} = [\![a^A]\!]_\xi^{\mathcal{F}} \cdot \ell_i := \lambda X. [\![b^{B_i}]\!]_{\xi[x := X \cap \mathcal{L}_A]}^{\mathcal{F}} \cap \mathcal{L}_{B_i},$$

then $\tau = \langle \ell_j : \bigwedge \alpha \to \beta^{\ j \in J} \rangle$ for some $J \subseteq I$: if $j \neq i$ then $\langle \ell_j : \bigwedge \alpha \to \beta \rangle \in [\![a^A]\!]_\xi^{\mathcal{F}}$, which by induction implies that $\Gamma_j \vdash a^A : \langle \ell_j : \bigwedge \alpha \to \beta \rangle$ for some Γ_j such that $\xi \models \Gamma_j$; if $j = i$ then $\beta \in [\![b^{B_i}]\!]_{\xi[x := \uparrow \alpha \cap \mathcal{L}_A]}^{\mathcal{F}} \cap \mathcal{L}_{B_i}$, hence by induction there exist Γ_i s.t. $\xi \models \Gamma_i, x^A : \alpha$ and $\Gamma_i, x^A : \alpha \vdash b^{B_i} : \beta$. Take $\Gamma = \bigwedge_{j \in J} \Gamma_j$: then $\xi \models \Gamma$ and $\Gamma \vdash a^A : \langle \ell_j : \bigwedge \alpha \to \beta \rangle$ and $\Gamma, x^A : \alpha \vdash b^{B_i} : \beta$, and we conclude by (*Val Update*). ∎

Corollary 1 (Completeness w.r.t. retraction models). $\Gamma \vdash a^A : \sigma \Longleftrightarrow \Gamma \models a^A : \sigma$.

Proof. The 'only if' part is Theorem 17. For the 'if part' define the term environment $\xi_\Gamma(x^B) = \uparrow \tau$ if $x^B : \tau \in \Gamma$, $\uparrow \omega$ if x does not occur in Γ: then $\xi_\Gamma \models \Gamma$, hence $\sigma \in [\![a^A]\!]_{\xi_\Gamma}^{\mathcal{F}}$. By Theorem 20 there exists Γ' such that $\xi_\Gamma \models \Gamma'$ and $\Gamma' \vdash a^A : \sigma$. Now if $\xi_\Gamma \models \Gamma'$ then $\xi_\Gamma(x^B) \in [\![\tau']\!]_\eta$ (for any η consistent with the type interpretation) when $x^B : \tau' \in \Gamma'$; this implies that $\tau' \in \xi_\Gamma(x^B) = \uparrow \tau$, and $x^B : \tau \in \Gamma$: we conclude that $\Gamma \leq \Gamma'$, hence $\Gamma \vdash a^A : \sigma$ by Lemma 8. ∎

4   Conclusions and Further Work

We have shown that an assignment system of predicates (essentially of intersection types) to typed terms of the object calculus OB_1 induces a sound and complete semantics with respect to a family of models of the ς-calculus using the range of a family of retractions as the interpretation of types. This is a logical semantics, since a retraction model can be constructed in which the denotation of a term coincides with the set (namely the filter) of predicates that can be derived for it in the system.

It remains to be seen how retraction models extend to cope with subtyping and bounded quantification, to model the full ς-calculus. It should be also investigated the relation of retraction models to PER models, which are used in [1] to model the calculus, e.g. along the lines of [13]. This will be the topic of further research.

Acknowledgments

The final version of the paper profited of careful readings and remarks by anonymous referees.

References

1. M. Abadi, L. Cardelli, *A Theory of Objects*, Springer 1996.
2. M. Abadi, G.D. Plotkin, "A Per Model of Polymorphism and Recursive Types", proc. of *IEEE-LICS* 1990, 3355-365.
3. S. Abramsky, "Observation Equivalence and Testing Equivalence", *Theoretical Computer Science* 53, 225–241, 1987.
4. S. Abramsky, "Domain Theory in Logical Form", *APAL* 51, 1991, 1-77.
5. R. Amadio, "Recursion over Realizability Structures", *Info. Comp.* 91, 1991, 55-85. *Theoretical Computer Science*, 102(1):135–163, 1992.
6. S. van Bakel. "Intersection Type Assignment Systems", *Theoretical Computer Science*, 151(2):385–435, 1995.
7. H.P. Barendregt, M. Coppo, M. Dezani, "A Filter Lambda Model and the Completeness of Type Assignment", *JSL* 48, 1983, 931-940.
8. K.B. Bruce, J.C. Mitchell, "PER models of subtyping, recursive types and higher-order polymorphism", proc. of *ACM-POPL* 1992.
9. F. Cardone, "Relational semantics for recursive types and bounded quantification", *LNCS* 372, 1989, 164-178.
10. M. Coppo, M. Dezani, B. Venneri, "Functional characters of solvable terms", *Grund. der Math.*, 27, 1981, 45-58.
11. M. Dezani, E. Giovannetti, U. de' Liguoro, "Intersection types, λ-models and Böhm trees", in [19], 45-97.
12. U. de'Liguoro, "Characterizing convergent terms in object calculi via intersection types", *LNCS* 2044, 2001.
13. U. de'Liguoro, "Subtyping in logical form", in ITRS'02, volume 70.1 of *ENTCS*. Elsevier, 2002.
14. S. Kamin, "Inheritance in Smalltalk-80: a denotational definition", *Proc. of POPL'88*, 1988, 80-87.

15. M. Hennessy, R. Milner, "Algebraic laws for nondeterminism and concurrency", *J. of ACM* 32(1), 137–161, 1985.
16. J.L. Krivine, *Lambda-calcul, types et modèles*, Masson 1990.
17. J.C. Mitchell, *Foundations for Programming Languages*, MIT Press, 1996.
18. D. Scott, "Data types as lattices", *SIAM J. Comput.* 5, n. 3, 1976, 522-587.
19. M. Takahashi, M. Okada, M. Dezani eds., *Theories of Types and Proofs*, Mathematical Society of Japan, vol. 2, 1998.

On the Expressive Power of Light Affine Logic

Ugo Dal Lago

Dipartimento di Scienze dell'Informazione
Università di Bologna
Mura Anteo Zamboni 7, 40127 Bologna, Italy
dallago@cs.unibo.it

Abstract. Light Affine Logic (**LAL**) is a formal system derived from Linear Logic that is claimed to correspond, through the Curry-Howard Isomorphism, to the class **FPTIME** of polytime functions. The completeness of the system with respect to **FPTIME** has been proved by embedding different presentations of this complexity class into **LAL**. The dual property of polytime soundness, on the other hand, has been stated and proved in a more debatable way, depending crucially on the underlying coding scheme. In this paper, we introduce two relevant classes of coding schemes, namely uniform and canonical coding schemes. We then investigate on the equality between **FPTIME** and the classes of functions that are representable in **LAL** using these coding schemes, obtaining a positive and a negative result.

1 Introduction

The logical characterization of computational complexity classes has a long tradition. The most followed path has been to extensionally characterize complexity classes as the models of certain logical theories. Logical systems, however, have a built-in computational mechanism — normalization. The definition of logical systems which could be normalized inside an interesting class, and, at the same time, give extensional characterization of that same class, is a much more recent research direction.

In the last ten years, in particular, many different systems derived from Linear Logic [6] have been proposed and claimed to be the logical counterpart of **FPTIME** (i.e. the class of all functions that are computable in polynomial time). Noticeable examples are Bounded Linear Logic (**BLL**, [5]), Light Linear Logic (**LLL**, [7]) and Soft Linear Logic (**SLL**, [8]). An affine variant of Light Linear Logic, called Light Affine Logic (**LAL**, [2, 1]) has deserved the attention of the research community: its use as a programming language has been investigated [13], while phase, coherent and game semantics for **LAL** have been proposed [14, 3, 12]. Furthermore, strong relations between a slight extension of light affine logic and the complexity class **NPTIME** have been recently discovered [10].

A necessary condition for a logic **L** to be considered the counterpart of **FPTIME** is the equality between **FPTIME** itself and the class $\mathcal{F}_{\mathbf{L}}$ of all functions $f : S \to T$ that are *representable* inside **L** using a reasonable *coding scheme*

C. Blundo and C. Laneve (Eds.): ICTCS 2003, LNCS 2841, pp. 216–227, 2003.
© Springer-Verlag Berlin Heidelberg 2003

for f, S and T. This strong condition can be considered as the conjunction of soundness and completeness, each corresponding to an inclusion between $\mathcal{F}_\mathbf{L}$ and **FPTIME**. Actually, **LAL** has not been proved to enjoy the property we have just described in a satisfactory way. Indeed, while completeness has been proved by showing that each polytime function can be represented inside **LAL** [1, 11], soundness has only been proved restricting to *bounded box-depth* coding schemes. Mairson and Møller [9] have recently shown that, if the used coding scheme is not of this kind, **LAL** becomes complete for the class of functions computable in doubly exponential time.

In this paper, we study polytime soundness for **LAL** restricting to *uniform coding schemes*. In a uniform coding scheme, a function $f : S \to T$ is encoded by a proof π with conclusion $A \vdash B$, (where A and B depend on S, T and f); moreover, all elements of S (respectively, T) are encoded by (cut-free) proofs having conclusion $\vdash A$ (respectively, $\vdash B$). This definition is strongly inspired by the Curry-Howard Correspondence, according to which formulae are interpreted as types and proofs are interpreted as programs. Notice that the coding scheme used by Mairson and Møller [9] is not uniform in this sense.

There are many reasons for being interested in uniform coding schemes. For example, a soundness result on uniform coding schemes would justify research on denotational semantics for **LAL** [3, 12]. A number of authors advocated denotational models for light logics as a way to achieve insights on **FPTIME** [7, 4]. If the underlying logical system is polytime unsound with respect to uniform encodings, however, semantical frameworks such as coherent spaces or game models are not expected to be useful for this purpose.

The rest of this paper is organized as follows. Sections 2 and 3 are devoted to preliminary definitions. In Section 4, we show that a function outside **FPTIME** can be uniformly encoded in **LAL**. In Section 5, we define *canonical coding schemes*, showing that every function that can be represented in **LAL** using these coding schemes has to be polytime. The notion of a canonical encoding is justified by showing that a number of encodings which can be found in the literature are actually canonical.

2   Syntax

Following existing literature, we will use an intuitionistic variant of **LAL**, called **ILAL**, as our reference system. *Formulae* are generated by the grammar

$$A ::= \alpha \mid A \multimap A \mid A \otimes A \mid A \& A \mid A \oplus A \mid !A \mid §A \mid \forall \alpha.A$$

where α ranges over a set $\mathcal{L}$ of *atoms*. A^n is an alternative notation for

$$\overbrace{A \otimes \ldots \otimes A}^{n \text{ times}}.$$

Sequents have the form $A_1, \ldots, A_n \vdash B$, where $A_1, \ldots, A_n, B$ are all formulae. **ILAL** *rules* are reported in Figure 1. An **ILAL** *proof* is simply a tree whose

Identity and Cut.

$$\frac{}{A \vdash A} \; I \qquad \frac{\Gamma \vdash A \quad \Delta, A \vdash B}{\Gamma, \Delta \vdash B} \; U$$

Structural Rules.

$$\frac{\Gamma \vdash A}{\Gamma, B \vdash A} \; W \qquad \frac{\Gamma, !A, !A \vdash B}{\Gamma, !A \vdash B} \; C$$

Multiplicative Logical Rules.

$$\frac{\Gamma, A, B \vdash C}{\Gamma, A \otimes B \vdash C} \; L_\otimes \qquad \frac{\Gamma \vdash A \quad \Delta \vdash B}{\Gamma, \Delta \vdash A \otimes B} \; R_\otimes$$

$$\frac{\Gamma \vdash A \quad \Delta, B \vdash C}{\Gamma, \Delta, A \multimap B \vdash C} \; L_\multimap \qquad \frac{\Gamma, A \vdash B}{\Gamma \vdash A \multimap B} \; R_\multimap$$

Additive Logical Rules.

$$\frac{\Gamma, A \vdash B}{\Gamma, A \& C \vdash B} \; L_\&^1 \qquad \frac{\Gamma, A \vdash B}{\Gamma, C \& A \vdash B} \; L_\&^2$$

$$\frac{\Gamma \vdash A \quad \Gamma \vdash B}{\Gamma \vdash A \& B} \; R_\& \qquad \frac{\Gamma, A \vdash C \quad \Gamma, B \vdash C}{\Gamma, A \oplus B \vdash C} \; L_\oplus$$

$$\frac{\Gamma \vdash A}{\Gamma \vdash A \oplus B} \; R_\oplus^1 \qquad \frac{\Gamma \vdash A}{\Gamma \vdash B \oplus A} \; R_\oplus^2$$

Exponential Logical Rules.

$$\frac{A \vdash B}{!A \vdash !B} \; P_!^1 \qquad \frac{\vdash A}{\vdash !A} \; P_!^2 \qquad \frac{\Gamma, \Delta \vdash A}{!\Gamma, \S\Delta \vdash \S A} \; P_\S$$

Second Order Logical Rules.

$$\frac{\vdash \Gamma, A[C/\alpha] \vdash B}{\Gamma, \forall \alpha . A \vdash B} \; L^\forall \qquad \frac{\Gamma \vdash A \quad \alpha \notin FV(\Gamma)}{\Gamma \vdash \forall \alpha . A} \; R^\forall$$

Fig. 1. Intuitionistic Light Affine Logic, **ILAL**.

nodes are labelled with sequents according to **ILAL** rules. A proof π having conclusion $\Gamma \vdash A$ is sometimes denoted as $\pi : \Gamma \vdash A$.

If π has conclusion $\Gamma, A \vdash B$ and ρ has conclusions $\Delta \vdash A$, $\pi(\rho)$ is the proof:

$$\frac{\rho : \Delta \vdash A \quad \pi : \Gamma, A \vdash B}{\Gamma, \Delta \vdash B}$$

If π has conclusion $\Gamma \vdash A$, $\S(\pi)$ is

$$\frac{\pi : \Gamma \vdash A}{\S\Gamma \vdash \S A}$$

and, provided Γ contains at most one formula, $!(\pi)$ is the proof:

$$\frac{\pi : \Gamma \vdash A}{!\Gamma \vdash !A}$$

In this way, ! and § can be easily given the status of (partial) functions on the space of **ILAL** proofs.

Most results about **ILAL** are traditionally given on proof-nets, which are handy in studying the dynamics of proofs. Nevertheless, we chose to present **ILAL** as a sequent calculus, in order to cut down preliminaries. There is a correspondence between proofs in sequence calculus and proof-nets; however, this correspondence is not bijective, because many sequent calculus proofs differing only in the order of application of rules could correspond to the same proof-net. For our purposes this is not a problem, since we can consider sequent calculus as mere *syntactic sugar* for proof-nets.

Definition 1. *Given an* **ILAL** *proof π, the box-depth $\partial(\pi)$ of π is the maximum integer n such that there is a path in π from a leaf to the root which crosses n instances of rules $P_!^1$, $P_!^2$ and $P_\S$.*

This definition of box-depth can be easily checked to be equivalent to the one traditionally given on **ILAL** proof-nets [1].

In the following, we will work with the multiplicative fragment of **ILAL**, which is enough to represent all the polynomial functions (the weakening rule W being unrestricted).

3   Representing Functions on Free Algebras

We are interested in studying the class $\mathcal{F}_{\textbf{ILAL}}$ of all functions representable inside **ILAL**. The first matter we have to deal with is to define precisely the class $\mathcal{F}_{\textbf{ILAL}}$, facing the following two questions:
- What kind of functions has to be encoded?
- What is an acceptable representation of a function inside **ILAL**?

Possible answers to these two questions will be given in the rest of the present section.

3.1   Free Algebras and ILAL

Without losing generality, we could restrict our attention to functions $f : S \to T$ where S and T are both $\{0, 1\}^*$. This is what has been done in the literature. In the following, we relax this constraint, letting S and T being arbitrary free algebras. A *free algebra* $\mathbb{A}$ is a couple $(\mathcal{C}, \mathcal{R})$ where $\mathcal{C}$ is a finite set of *constructors* and $\mathcal{R} : \mathcal{C} \to \mathbb{N}$ maps every constructor to its *arity*. *Terms* of a free algebra $\mathbb{A} = (\mathcal{C}, \mathcal{R})$ are defined as follows:
- If $c \in \mathcal{C}$ and $\mathcal{R}(c) = 0$, then c is a term of $\mathbb{A}$;
- If $c \in \mathcal{C}$, $\mathcal{R}(c) = n \geq 1$ and $t_1, \ldots, t_n$ are terms of $\mathbb{A}$, then $c(t_1, \ldots, t_n)$ is a term of $\mathbb{A}$.

A *word algebra* $\mathbb{W} = (\{c_1, \ldots, c_k, e\}, \mathcal{R})$ is a free algebra such that $\mathcal{R}(c_i) = 1$ for every $i \in \{1, \ldots, k\}$ and $\mathcal{R}(e) = 0$. $\mathbb{E}$ will be the word algebra $(\{c, e\}, \mathcal{R})$. If

$f : \mathbb{A} \to A$ is an injective function, then its *generalized inverse* is the function $f^* : A \to \mathbb{A} \cup \{*\}$ such that

$$f^*(a) = \begin{cases} t & \text{if } f(t) = a \\ * & \text{if } \forall t. f(t) \neq a \end{cases}$$

There is a natural way to encode free algebras into second order (intuitionistic) propositional logic and this encoding can be easily adapted to **ILAL**. Given a free algebra $\mathbb{A} = (\{c_1, \ldots, c_k\}, \mathcal{R})$, the **ILAL** type $F_\mathbb{A}$ is

$$\forall \alpha. !(\alpha^{\mathcal{R}(c_1)} \multimap \alpha) \multimap \ldots \multimap !(\alpha^{\mathcal{R}(c_k)} \multimap \alpha) \multimap \S\alpha.$$

Clearly, $F_\mathbb{A}$ is univoquely determined once a total order on $\{c_1, \ldots, c_k\}$ is fixed. A term t of a free algebra $\mathbb{A}$ can be represented as an **ILAL** cut-free proof $P_\mathbb{A}(t)$ having conclusion $\vdash F_\mathbb{A}$. For example, if $\mathbb{A} = (\{e, f, g\}, \mathcal{R})$, $\mathcal{R}(e) = 0$, $\mathcal{R}(f) = 2$ and $\mathcal{R}(g) = 1$, the proof $P_\mathbb{A}(f(g(e), f(e, e)))$ is:

$$\cfrac{\cfrac{\cfrac{\alpha \vdash \alpha \quad \alpha \vdash \alpha}{\alpha \multimap \alpha, \alpha \vdash \alpha} \quad \cfrac{\alpha \vdash \alpha \quad \cfrac{\alpha \vdash \alpha \quad \alpha \vdash \alpha}{\alpha, \alpha \vdash \alpha \otimes \alpha}}{\alpha \otimes \alpha \multimap \alpha, \alpha, \alpha \vdash \alpha}}{\cfrac{\alpha \vdash \alpha \quad \alpha \otimes \alpha \multimap \alpha, \alpha \multimap \alpha, \alpha, \alpha, \alpha \vdash \alpha \otimes \alpha}{\cfrac{\alpha \otimes \alpha \multimap \alpha, \alpha \otimes \alpha \multimap \alpha, \alpha \multimap \alpha, \alpha, \alpha, \alpha \vdash \alpha}{\vdash \forall \alpha. !(\alpha \otimes \alpha \multimap \alpha) \multimap !(\alpha \multimap \alpha) \multimap !\alpha \multimap \S\alpha}}}$$

In general, if a term t of $\mathbb{A} = (\mathcal{C}, \mathcal{R})$ contains n occurrences of (not necessarily distinct) constructors in $\mathcal{C}$, then $P_\mathbb{A}(t)$ is the proof

$$\cfrac{\pi_t : \alpha^{\mathcal{R}(c_1)} \multimap \alpha, \ldots, \alpha^{\mathcal{R}(c_n)} \multimap \alpha \vdash \alpha}{\vdash F_\mathbb{A}}$$

where, $c_1, \ldots, c_n$ are the constructors appearing in t and π_t is defined by induction on the structure of t as follows:

- If $t = c$ (where $\mathcal{R}(c) = 0$), then π_t is simply:

$$\overline{\alpha \vdash \alpha}.$$

- Suppose $t = c(t_1, \ldots, t_m)$, then π_t is:

$$\cfrac{\overline{\alpha \vdash \alpha} \quad \cfrac{\pi_{t_1} : \Gamma_1 \vdash \alpha \quad \ldots \quad \pi_{t_m} : \Gamma_m \vdash \alpha}{\Gamma_1, \ldots, \Gamma_m \vdash \alpha^m}}{\alpha^m \multimap \alpha, \Gamma_1, \ldots, \Gamma_m \vdash \alpha}$$

The following lemma can be easily proved.

Lemma 1. *If Ω is obtained from $\S$ and $!$ by composition, then both $(\Omega \circ P_\mathbb{A})$ and $(\Omega \circ \overline{P}_\mathbb{A})$ are injective functions ranging over cut-free **ILAL** proofs not containing instances of rule $L_\forall$. Moreover, $(\Omega \circ P_\mathbb{A})$, $(\Omega \circ \overline{P}_\mathbb{A})$, $(\Omega \circ P_\mathbb{A})^*$ and $(\Omega \circ \overline{P}_\mathbb{A})^*$ are all polytime functions.*

If $\mathbb{W} = (\{c_1, \ldots, c_k, e\}, \mathcal{R})$ is a word algebra, a minor variation $\overline{F}_{\mathbb{W}}$ ($\overline{P}_{\mathbb{W}}$, respectively) on $F_{\mathbb{W}}$ ($P_{\mathbb{W}}$, respectively) is often used. In particular, $\overline{F}_{\mathbb{W}}$ is the formula

$$\forall \alpha. \overbrace{!(\alpha \multimap \alpha) \multimap \ldots \multimap !(\alpha \multimap \alpha)}^{k \ times} \multimap \S(\alpha \multimap \alpha).$$

and $\overline{P}_{\mathbb{W}}$ is defined very similarly to $P_{\mathbb{W}}$. For example, $\overline{P}_{\mathbb{E}}(cce)$ is:

$$\cfrac{\cfrac{\cfrac{\cfrac{\alpha \vdash \alpha \quad \cfrac{\alpha \vdash \alpha \quad \alpha \vdash \alpha}{\alpha \multimap \alpha, \alpha \vdash \alpha}}{\alpha \multimap \alpha, \alpha \multimap \alpha, \alpha \vdash \alpha}}{\alpha \multimap \alpha, \alpha \multimap \alpha \vdash \alpha \multimap \alpha}}{\vdash \forall \alpha. !(\alpha \multimap \alpha) \multimap \S(\alpha \multimap \alpha)}}{}$$

3.2 Encoding Functions

As explained in the introduction, we chose to accept only encodings that respect types. In other words, all elements of the domain of a function must be encoded by **ILAL** proofs having the *same* conclusion, this condition holding on the codomain, too. Following another reasonable assumption, all **ILAL** proofs encoding terms must be cut-free.

We are now able to give the notion of a *uniform encoding* of function f : $\mathbb{A} \to \mathbb{B}$ inside **ILAL**: it is a tuple $(\Pi, \pi, A, B, \Phi, \Psi)$ where:

- Π is a set of **ILAL** cut-free proofs;
- π is an **ILAL** proof whose conclusion is $A \vdash B$;
- $\Phi : \mathbb{A} \to \Pi$ is a polytime injective function mapping every term $t \in \mathbb{A}$ to an **ILAL** proof $\Phi(t) \in \Pi$ whose conclusion is $\vdash A$; $\Phi^* : \Pi \to \mathbb{A} \cup \{*\}$ must be itself polytime;
- $\Psi : \mathbb{B} \to \Pi$ is a polytime injective function mapping every term $t \in \mathbb{B}$ to an **ILAL** proof $\Psi(t) \in \Pi$ whose conclusion is $\vdash B$; $\Psi^* : \Pi \to \mathbb{B} \cup \{*\}$ must be itself polytime;
- For every $t \in \mathbb{A}$, $\pi(\Phi(t))$ normalizes to $\Psi(f(t))$.

A function $f : \mathbb{A} \to \mathbb{B}$ is *uniformly representable* in **ILAL** if there is a uniform encoding of f inside **ILAL**. $\mathcal{F}^U_{\mathbf{ILAL}}$ is the class of all functions that are uniformly representable in **ILAL**. Notice that the notions we have just given can be easily extended to many other (intuitionistic) logical systems enjoying cut-elimination.

As we have already explained, the notion of a uniform encoding is inspired by the Curry-Howard Correspondence. We here claim that it is one of the most natural notions of an encoding which can be given. Nevertheless, as we will show in the next section, **ILAL** is not polytime sound if the full power of uniformity is exploited.

A uniform encoding $(\Pi, \pi, A, B, \Phi, \Psi)$ is said to be *canonical* if every proof in Π does not contain instances of the rule $L^{\forall}$. A function $f : \mathbb{A} \to \mathbb{B}$ is *canonically representable* in **ILAL** if there is a canonical encoding of f inside **ILAL**. $\mathcal{F}^C_{\mathbf{ILAL}}$ is the class of all functions that are canonically representable in **ILAL**. Uniform encodings differ from canonical encodings only on the imposed conditions on Π, which are more restrictive in the latter case. The additional requirements on Π are enough to guarantee polytime soundness and, at the same time, do not rule out most of the encodings used to prove polytime completeness [1], as we will see in Section 5.

4   Uniformly Representable Functions

In this section, we prove that $\mathcal{F}_{\mathbf{ILAL}}^{U} \nsubseteq \mathbf{PTIME}$ by giving a uniform encoding (inside $\mathbf{ILAL}$) of an intrinsically exponential function.

Lemma 2. *For every $n \in \mathbb{N}$, there is a cut-free $\mathbf{ILAL}$ proof ρ_n such that $(\Pi, \rho_n, \overline{F}_{\mathbb{E}}, \S^{n+1}\overline{F}_{\mathbb{E}}, \overline{P}_{\mathbb{E}}, \S^{n+1} \circ \overline{P}_{\mathbb{E}})$ (where Π is the set of all cut-free $\mathbf{ILAL}$ proofs) is a uniform encoding of the polynomial $p^n : \mathbb{E} \to \mathbb{E}$, where $p^n(c^m e) = c^{m^n} e$ for every $m \in \mathbb{N}$.*

Proof. In this proof, we use a slightly liberal notion of a uniform encoding, which applies to functions in the form $f : \mathbb{E}^m \to \mathbb{E}^p$ and to proofs having conclusions such as $A_1, \ldots, A_m \vdash B_1 \otimes \ldots \otimes B_p$ or $A_1 \otimes \ldots \otimes A_m \vdash B_1 \otimes \ldots \otimes B_p$. Some results on the representability of basic functions such as successor and addition are here used without an explicit proof, which can be found in the literature [1].

Since the case $n = 0$ is trivial, we can assume $n \geq 1$. For every $m \geq 1$, we can inductively define Γ_m as follows. First of all, $\Gamma_1 = \overline{F}_{\mathbb{E}}$; moreover, $\Gamma_m = \Gamma_{m-1}, \S^{m-1}!\overline{F}_{\mathbb{E}}$ for every $m > 1$. For every $m \geq 1$, A_m denotes the tensor product of all the formulae appearing in Γ_m, taken in the order induced by the definition of Γ_m. We now prove, by induction on m, that there is a proof $\pi_m : A_m \vdash \S^m \overline{F}_{\mathbb{E}}$ encoding m-ary multiplication. If $m = 1$, then σ_m is

$$\cfrac{\cfrac{\pi : \overline{F}_{\mathbb{E}} \vdash \overline{F}_{\mathbb{E}}}{\cfrac{\vdash \overline{F}_{\mathbb{E}} \multimap \overline{F}_{\mathbb{E}}}{\vdash !(\overline{F}_{\mathbb{E}} \multimap \overline{F}_{\mathbb{E}})}} \quad \cfrac{\overline{P}_{\mathbb{E}}(e) : \vdash \overline{F}_{\mathbb{E}} \quad \overline{F}_{\mathbb{E}} \vdash \overline{F}_{\mathbb{E}}}{\cfrac{\overline{F}_{\mathbb{E}} \multimap \overline{F}_{\mathbb{E}} \vdash \overline{F}_{\mathbb{E}}}{\S(\overline{F}_{\mathbb{E}} \multimap \overline{F}_{\mathbb{E}}) \vdash \S\overline{F}_{\mathbb{E}}}}}{\overline{F}_{\mathbb{E}} \vdash \S\overline{F}_{\mathbb{E}}}$$

where π encodes the successor function on $\mathbb{E}$. If $m > 1$, then σ_m is

$$\cfrac{\cfrac{\cfrac{\pi : \overline{F}_{\mathbb{E}}, \overline{F}_{\mathbb{E}} \vdash \overline{F}_{\mathbb{E}}}{\cfrac{\overline{F}_{\mathbb{E}} \vdash \overline{F}_{\mathbb{E}} \multimap \overline{F}_{\mathbb{E}}}{!\overline{F}_{\mathbb{E}} \vdash !(\overline{F}_{\mathbb{E}} \multimap \overline{F}_{\mathbb{E}})}} \quad \cfrac{\overline{P}_{\mathbb{E}}(e) : \vdash \overline{F}_{\mathbb{E}} \quad \sigma_{m-1} : \Gamma_{m-1} \vdash \S^{m-1}\overline{F}_{\mathbb{E}}}{\cfrac{\overline{F}_{\mathbb{E}} \multimap \overline{F}_{\mathbb{E}}, !\overline{F}_{\mathbb{E}}, \ldots, \S^{m-2}!\overline{F}_{\mathbb{E}} \vdash \S^{m-1}\overline{F}_{\mathbb{E}}}{\S(\overline{F}_{\mathbb{E}} \multimap \overline{F}_{\mathbb{E}}), \S!\overline{F}_{\mathbb{E}}, \ldots, \S^{m-1}!\overline{F}_{\mathbb{E}} \vdash \S^m \overline{F}_{\mathbb{E}}}}}{A_m \vdash \S^m \overline{F}_{\mathbb{E}}}$$

where π encodes binary addition on $\mathbb{E}$. We are now able to build ρ_n:

$$\cfrac{\cfrac{\pi : A_n \vdash A_n}{\cfrac{\vdash A_n \multimap A_n}{\vdash !(A_n \multimap A_n)}} \quad \cfrac{\tau : \vdash A_n \quad \cfrac{\sigma_m : \Gamma_n \vdash \S^n \overline{F}_{\mathbb{E}}}{A_n \vdash \S^n \overline{F}_{\mathbb{E}}}}{\cfrac{A_n \multimap A_n \vdash \S^n \overline{F}_{\mathbb{E}}}{\S(A_n \multimap A_n) \vdash \S^{n+1}\overline{F}_{\mathbb{E}}}}}{\overline{F}_{\mathbb{E}} \vdash \S^{n+1}\overline{F}_{\mathbb{E}}}$$

Here, π encodes n-ary successor on $\mathbb{E}$ and τ is obtained from $\overline{P}_{\mathbb{E}}(e), (! \circ \overline{P}_{\mathbb{E}})(e)$, ..., $(\S^{n-1} \circ ! \circ \overline{P}_{\mathbb{E}})(e)$ by repeatedly use $R_{\otimes}$. Notice that ρ_n, as we have defined it, is cut-free. $\square$

We have just proved that, for every $n \in \mathbb{N}$, ρ_n uniformly encodes the polynomial p_n. Now, if all the different ρ_n had the same type, it would be easy to build a proof π such that $\pi(\rho_n)$ reduces to $\rho_n(P_{\mathbb{E}}(cce))$, then normalizing to $(\S^{n+1} \circ P_{\mathbb{E}})(c^{2^n} e)$. Actually, every ρ_n has a conclusion which is different from the conclusion of any other ρ_m. This problem, however, can be circumvented by building another sequence of proofs $\{\sigma_n\}_{n \in \mathbb{N}}$. Every such σ_n behaves similarly to ρ_n, but all the proofs in the sequence have the same conclusion. In this way, we can find a uniform encoding inside **ILAL** of an intrinsically exponential function on the free algebra $\mathbb{E}$:

Proposition 1. *There is a function* $f \in \mathcal{F}_{\mathbf{ILAL}}^U$ *not belonging to the class* **FP-TIME***.*

Proof. $f : \mathbb{E} \to \mathbb{E}$ is the function defined by letting

$$f(c^n e) = c^{2^n} e$$

whenever $n \in \mathbb{N}$. Clearly, f cannot belong to **FPTIME**, because the length of its output is exponential in the length of its input. For every $n \in \mathbb{N}$, the proof σ_n is defined as follows:

$$\frac{\dfrac{\rho_n : \overline{F}_{\mathbb{E}} \vdash \S^{n+1} \overline{F}_{\mathbb{E}} \quad \overline{\alpha \vdash \alpha}}{\overline{F}_{\mathbb{E}}, \S^{n+1} \overline{F}_{\mathbb{E}} \multimap \alpha \vdash \alpha}}{\dfrac{\overline{F}_{\mathbb{E}}, \forall \beta.(\beta \multimap \alpha) \vdash \alpha}{\vdash \overline{F}_{\mathbb{E}} \multimap \forall \beta.(\beta \multimap \alpha) \multimap \alpha}}$$

where ρ_n as in Lemma 2. For every $m \in \mathbb{N}$, the proof τ_m is defined as follows:

$$\frac{\dfrac{\dfrac{\overline{P_{\mathbb{E}}(c^m e) : \vdash \overline{F}_{\mathbb{E}}}}{\vdash \S^{\lceil lgm \rceil+1} \overline{F}_{\mathbb{E}} \quad \overline{\alpha \vdash \alpha}}}{\S^{\lceil lgm \rceil+1} \overline{F}_{\mathbb{E}} \multimap \alpha \vdash \alpha}}{\dfrac{\forall \beta.(\beta \multimap \alpha) \vdash \alpha}{\vdash \forall \beta.(\beta \multimap \alpha) \multimap \alpha}}$$

Let now π be the proof:

$$\frac{\overline{P_{\mathbb{E}}(cce) : \vdash \overline{F}_{\mathbb{E}}} \quad \overline{\forall \beta.(\beta \multimap \alpha) \multimap \alpha \vdash \forall \beta.(\beta \multimap \alpha) \multimap \alpha}}{\overline{F}_{\mathbb{E}} \multimap \forall \beta.(\beta \multimap \alpha) \multimap \alpha \vdash \forall \beta.(\beta \multimap \alpha) \multimap \alpha}$$

$\Phi : \mathbb{E} \to \Pi$ is the function defined by letting $\Phi(c^n e) = \sigma_n$ for every $n \in \mathbb{N}$; Both Φ and its generalized inverse Φ^* can be easily checked to be polytime functions. $\Psi : \mathbb{E} \to \Pi$ is defined by letting $\Psi(c^m e) = \tau_m$; as a consequence of Lemma 1, both Ψ and its generalized inverse Ψ^* are polytime. It is easy to realize that, for every $n \in \mathbb{E}$, $\pi(\sigma_n) = \pi(\Phi(c^n))$ normalizes to $\tau_{2^n} = \Psi(f(c^{2^n}))$, meaning that $(\Pi, \pi, \overline{F}_{\mathbb{E}} \multimap \forall \beta.(\beta \multimap \alpha) \multimap \alpha, \forall \beta.(\beta \multimap \alpha) \multimap \alpha, \Phi, \Psi)$, where Π is the set of all cut-free **ILAL** proofs, is a uniform encoding of f inside **ILAL**. $\square$

5   Canonically Representable Functions

The real issue to guarantee **ILAL** soundness is to force representing inputs and outputs by proofs having bounded box-depth. This, as we have just seen, cannot be achieved by restricting to proofs all having the same conclusion. In this section, we prove that the use of $L_\forall$ in input and output representations is essential to prove a negative result such as Proposition 1. To do this, we show that every function that is canonically representable inside **ILAL** must be polytime.

Given an **ILAL** formula A, the integer $\#(A)$ is defined by induction as follows:

$$\#(\alpha) = 0$$
$$\#(A \otimes B) = \max\{\#(A), \#(B)\}$$
$$\#(A \multimap B) = \max\{\#(A), \#(B)\}$$
$$\#(!A) = \#(A) + 1$$
$$\#(\S A) = \#(A) + 1$$
$$\#(\forall \alpha.A) = \#(A)$$

If $A_1, \ldots, A_n \vdash B$ is an **ILAL** sequent, then $\#(A_1, \ldots, A_n \vdash B)$ is simply $\max\{\#(A_1), \ldots, \#(A_n), \#(B)\}$. $\#(\Gamma \vdash A)$ turns out to be an upper bound on $\partial(\pi)$ whenever π is the representation of a term in a canonical encoding:

Proposition 2. *Let π be a cut-free **ILAL** proof with conclusion $\Gamma \vdash A$. Then, if π does not contain instances of the rule $L^\forall$, $\partial(\pi) \leq \#(\Gamma \vdash A)$.*

Proof. By induction on the structure of π (which cannot contain instances of rules U and $L^\forall$). We can distinguish a number of cases, depending on the last rule used in π:

Case I. By definition, $\partial(\pi) = 0 \leq \#(A)$;

Case W. π must be in the form:

$$\frac{\rho : A_1, \ldots, A_n \vdash C}{A_1, \ldots, A_n, B \vdash C}$$

By inductive hypothesis,

$$\partial(\pi) = \partial(\rho)$$
$$\leq \max\{\#(A_1), \ldots, \#(A_n), \#(C)\}$$
$$\leq \max\{\#(A_1), \ldots, \#(A_n), \#(B), \#(C)\};$$

Case $R_\otimes$. π must be in the form:

$$\frac{\rho : A_1, \ldots, A_n \vdash B \qquad \sigma : C_1, \ldots, C_m \vdash D}{A_1, \ldots, A_n, C_1, \ldots, C_m \vdash B \otimes D}$$

By inductive hypothesis

$$\partial(\pi) = \max\{\partial(\rho), \partial(\sigma)\}$$
$$\leq \max\{\max\{\#(A_1), \ldots, \#(A_n), \#(B)\},$$
$$\max\{\#(C_1), \ldots, \#(C_m), \#(D)\}\}$$
$$= \max\{\#(A_1), \ldots, \#(A_n), \#(B), \#(C_1), \ldots, \#(C_m), \#(D)\}$$
$$= \max\{\#(A_1), \ldots, \#(A_n), \#(C_1), \ldots, \#(C_m), \#(B \otimes D)\}\};$$

Case $L_\otimes$. π must be in the form:

$$\frac{\rho : A_1, \ldots, A_n, B, C \vdash D}{A_1, \ldots, A_n, B \otimes C \vdash D}$$

By inductive hypothesis

$$\partial(\pi) = \partial(\rho)$$
$$\leq \max\{\#(A_1), \ldots, \#(A_n), \#(B), \#(C), \#(D)\}\}$$
$$= \max\{\#(A_1), \ldots, \#(A_n), \#(B \otimes C), \#(D)\}\};$$

Case $P_!^1$. Necessarily, π must be in the form:

$$\frac{\rho : A \vdash B}{!A \vdash !B}$$

By inductive hypothesis

$$\partial(\pi) = \partial(\rho) + 1$$
$$\leq \max\{\#(A), \#(B)\} + 1$$
$$= \max\{\#(A) + 1, \#(B) + 1\}$$
$$= \max\{\#(!A), \#(!B)\};$$

Case $R^\forall$. π is in the form:

$$\frac{\rho : A_1, \ldots, A_n \vdash B}{A_1, \ldots, A_n \vdash \forall \alpha.B}$$

By inductive hypothesis

$$\partial(\pi) = \partial(\rho)$$
$$\leq \max\{\#(A_1), \ldots, \#(A_n), \#(B)\}$$
$$\leq \max\{\#(A_1), \ldots, \#(A_n), \#(\forall \alpha.B)\}.$$

All other cases can be solved similarly   □

We are now able to prove the main result of this section, that is the equality between the class of canonically representable functions and the class of polytime functions.

Theorem 1. $\mathcal{F}_{\mathbf{ILAL}}^C = \mathbf{FPTIME}$.

Proof. By a result in [2, 1], normalization of an **ILAL** proof π takes polynomial time, the exponent of the polynomial depending only on $\partial(\pi)$. Now, if $f : \mathbb{A} \to \mathbb{B}$ is canonically representable, an algorithm that computes $f(t)$, given $t \in \mathbb{A}$ as input, is the following (let $(\Pi, \pi, A, B, \Phi, \Psi)$ be a canonical encoding of f into **ILAL**):

- Compute $\Phi(t)$;
- Normalize $\pi(\Phi(t))$, obtaining ρ;
- Compute $\Psi^*(\rho)$.

By Proposition 2 and by definition of a uniform encoding, this algorithm is polytime. This proves that $\mathcal{F}_{\mathbf{ILAL}}^C \subseteq \mathbf{FPTIME}$.

In the original proof of polytime completeness for **ILAL** [1], inputs and outputs are represented by cut-free proofs not containing instances of $L_\forall$. A set of canonical encodings spanning the entire class **FPTIME** can then be obtained. This, in turn, implies that $\mathbf{FPTIME} \subseteq \mathcal{F}_{\mathbf{ILAL}}^C$. □

All encodings derived from the ones we described in Section 3.1 are, by Lemma 1, canonical encodings. By Theorem 1, it follows that all functions that can be encoded in that way are actually polytime.

6   Conclusions

The main contributions of this paper are a couple of results on the expressiveness of light affine logic. If the full power of second order quantification is exploited, **LAL** becomes polytime unsound and this has many theoretical consequences. For example, the study of denotational models for (second-order) **LAL** is not expected to give any insight on **FPTIME**. On the other hand, a large class of encodings, including the majority of those used in the literature [1, 11], is shown to precisely capture the class of polytime functions. Topics for further research include the study of polytime completeness for the propositional fragment of **LAL**, this fragment being polytime sound in the uniform sense.

Acknowledgements

The author wishes to thank the anonymous referees for numerous helpful suggestions.

References

1. Andrea Asperti and Luca Roversi. Intuitionistic light affine logic. *ACM Transactions on Computational Logic*, 3(1):137–175, 2002.
2. Andrea Asperti. Light affine logic. In *Proceedings of the 13th IEEE Syposium on Logic in Computer Science*, pages 300–308, 1998.

3. Patric Baillot. Stratified coherent spaces: a denotational semantics for light linear logic. Presented at the Second International Workshop on Implicit Computational Complexity, 2000.
4. Vincent Danos and Jean-Baptiste Joinet. Linear logic and elementary time. *Information and Computation*, 183(1):123–137, 2003.
5. Jean-Yves Girard, Andre Scedrov, and Philip J. Scott. Bounded linear logic: A modular approach to polynomial time computability. *Theoretical Computer Science*, 97(1):1–66, 1992.
6. Jean-Yves Girard. Linear logic. *Theoretical Computer Science*, 50:1–102, 1987.
7. Jean-Yves Girard. Light linear logic. *Information and Computation*, 143(2):175–204, 1998.
8. Yves Lafont. Soft linear logic and polynomial time. To appear in Theoretical Computer Science, 2002.
9. Harry Mairson and Peter Møller Neergard. LAL is square: Representation and expressiveness in light affine logic. Presented at the Fourth International Workshop on Implicit Computational Complexity, 2002.
10. Francois Maurel. Nondederministic light logics and NP-time. In *Proceedings of the 6th International Conference on Typed Lambda Calculi and Applications*, pages 241–255, 2003.
11. Andrzej Murawski and Luke Ong. Can safe recursion be interpreted in light logic? Presented at the Second International Workshop on Implicit Computational Complexity, 2000.
12. Andrzej Murawski and Luke Ong. Evolving games and essential nets for affine polymorphism. In *Proceedings of 14th Annual Conference of the European Association of Computer Science Logic*, pages 360–375, 2000.
13. Luca Roversi. Light affine logic as a programming language: a first contribution. *International Journal of Foundations of Computer Science*, 11(1):113 – 152, 2000.
14. Kazushige Terui. *Light logic and polynomial time computation*. PhD thesis, Keio University, 2002.

Reasoning about Self and Others: Communicating Agents in a Modal Action Logic

Matteo Baldoni, Cristina Baroglio, Alberto Martelli, and Viviana Patti

Dipartimento di Informatica
Università degli Studi di Torino
C.so Svizzera 185, I-10149 Torino (Italy)
{baldoni,baroglio,mrt,patti}@di.unito.it

Abstract. We propose an approach to reasoning about conversation protocols within the framework of a logic-based *agent language*. We show how to embed a theory of communicative actions in the framework of a modal logic of action and beliefs, to specify software agents that, situated in a multi-agent environment, can interact with one another by a speech act based communication mechanism. Agents have their own local beliefs on the world and on the other agents mental state. Complex communicative behaviors can be specified as conversation protocols, and agents can reason on the belief dynamics caused by communications, before committing to a given interaction.

1 Introduction and Motivations

In the last few years, great attention has been devoted to the issue of communication and dialogue among agents, in the context of a formal approach to the theory of agency [13]. In particular, the diffusion of open multi-agent systems has led the agent community to focus on the creation of *standardized communication languages* (ACL), that, having an explicit, general and well-defined semantic, could be used by heterogeneous agent programs and give an answer to the interoperability issue [15,17]. In this framework, while a lot of work has been done in defining the semantics of the agent speech acts, those semantics aspects of communication that are related to the conversational context, in which a speech act occurs, started being investigated only recently [20,22]. Moreover, although formal models of speech acts take into account the mental state of other agents, the approaches to communication taken in the practical setting of agent languages [24,12] do not account for this aspect and do not permit to model individual agents that *subjectively* reason about effects of communication on the mental state of their interlocutors.

The capability of reasoning about conversations is useful in many application areas. Let us consider, as an example, a user personal assistant, i.e. a software agent that searches the web to find *web services*, according to a user's specification. The currently available languages for describing web services (e.g. DAML-S [9], WSDL [8]) base descriptions on the lists of inputs/outputs required/returned

C. Blundo and C. Laneve (Eds.): ICTCS 2003, LNCS 2841, pp. 228–241, 2003.
© Springer-Verlag Berlin Heidelberg 2003

by the service. The agent matches the user's request ("book two tickets at a cinema where they show Akira but do not give my credit card number") to the descriptions of the available services and selects one that satisfies all the conditions. Some of these conditions ("do not give my credit card number"), actually concern the way in which the *interaction* between the service provider and the personal assistant should be carried on. Standard description languages do not allow the representation of behavioral information [7] but if a formal specification of the interaction protocol was available, the personal assistant could *reason about* the change caused by a conversation to its own belief state and make rational assumptions on the change caused to the provider beliefs. In the application framework, the agent could, then, either verify if the interaction may be *personalized* by following an execution path that satisfies all the user's requirements, or, when this is not possible, decide to search for another provider.

In this work, we face the problem of describing and reasoning about conversation protocols in an *agent logic programming* setting, by extending the logical framework of the agent language DyLOG [5] so to deal also with *communicative behaviors*. DyLOG is a logic programming language for specifying and reasoning about the behavior of rational agents, based on a modal logic for reasoning about *actions* and *beliefs*, that has successfully been used in the development of adaptive web applications [4]. It permits to define complex actions and sensing actions. Agents programmed in DyLOG choose a course of actions, conditioned by their beliefs about the world, and use sensors for acquiring knowledge. We present an extension of the language, in which a *communication kit*, including both primitive speech acts and conversation protocols, has been integrated. Such an extension is based on an agent theory, in which agents have *local* beliefs about the world and about the mental state of the other agents, and where communications are modelled as actions that transform the interlocutor mental state. Our account of communication aims at coping with two main aspects: the state change caused by a communicative act on an agent local beliefs, and the decision strategy used by the agent for sending suitable answers to a received communication. To these aims, the semantics of primitive speech acts is described in terms of effects on the mental state both in case the agent is the sender and in case it is the recipient. Moreover, in the line of [20], we use conversation protocols as decision procedures that allow agents to suitably respond to communications. Conversation protocols are built upon speech acts, and specify communication patterns for agent conversations. We took a subjective representation of such protocols, by making hypothetical assumptions on the *other*'s answers. They have been easily integrated with the other policies that specify the agent behavior, being both represented as complex actions by DyLOG procedure axioms. We provide a goal-directed proof procedure in order to support agent's reasoning and planning in presence of communication. This procedure allows an agent to reason about the interaction that it is going to enact with another agent, with the aim of proving if there is a possible execution of the *communication protocol*, after which a set of beliefs of interest (goal) will be true in its mental state.

The article is orgnized as follows: Section 2 introduces DyLOG with a particular attention to the tools that it offers for dealing with communication; Section 3 briefly shows the solution to the persistency problem that we adopted; in Section 4 we describe the techniques applied for reasoning in presence of communication; an example application follows, and the article is concluded by a contextualization of the work in the literature and a few considerations.

2   The Agent Language

The agent language accounts both for atomic and complex actions, or procedures. Atomic actions are either world actions, affecting the world, or mental actions, i.e. sensing or communicative actions which only affect the agent beliefs. The set of atomic actions consists of the set $\mathcal{A}$ of the world actions, the set $\mathcal{C}$ of communicative acts, and the set $\mathcal{S}$ of sensing actions. For each atomic action a and agent ag_i we introduce the modalities $[a^{ag_i}]$ and $\langle a^{ag_i} \rangle$. $[a^{ag_i}]\alpha$ means that α holds after every execution of action a by agent ag_i; $\langle a^{ag_i} \rangle \alpha$ means that there is a possible execution of a (by ag_i) after which α holds. For each atomic action a in $\mathcal{A} \cup \mathcal{C}$ we also introduce a modality $Done(a^{ag_i})$ for expressing that a has been executed. $Done(a^{ag_i})\alpha$ is read "a has been executed by ag_i; before its execution, α was true" [1]. The modality $\square$ denotes formulas that hold in all the possible agent mental states. Our formalization of complex actions draws considerably from dynamic logic for the definition of action operators like sequence, test and non-deterministic choice. However, differently than [19], we refer to a *Prolog-like* paradigm: procedures are defined by means of (possibly recursive) Prolog-like clauses. For each procedure p, the language contains also the universal and existential modalities $[p]$ and $\langle p \rangle$. The mental state of an agent is described in terms of a consistent set of *belief formulas*. We enriched the belief state of a DyLOG agent by allowing also nested beliefs, for representing what other agents believe and reasoning on how they can be affected by communicative actions. We use the modal operator $\mathcal{B}^{ag_i}$ to model the beliefs of agent ag_i. The modality $\mathcal{M}^{ag_i}$ is defined as the dual of $\mathcal{B}^{ag_i}$ ($\mathcal{M}^{ag_i}\varphi \equiv \neg\mathcal{B}^{ag_i}\neg\varphi$). Intuitively $\mathcal{M}^{ag_i}\varphi$ means that ag_i consider φ possible.

All the modalities of the language are normal; $\square$ is reflexive and transitive, its interaction with action modalities is ruled by $\square\varphi \supset [a^{ag_i}]\varphi$. The epistemic modality $\mathcal{B}^{ag_i}$ is serial, transitive and euclidean. The interaction of the $Done(a^{ag_i})$ modality with other modalities is ruled by: $\varphi \supset [a^{ag_i}]Done(a^{ag_i})\varphi$ and $Done(a^{ag_j})\varphi \supset \mathcal{B}^{ag_i}Done(a^{ag_j})\varphi$ (awareness), with $ag_i = ag_j$ when $a^{ag_i} \notin \mathcal{C}$.

2.1   The Agent Theory

In the line of [5] the *behavior* of an agent ag_i can be specified by a domain description, which includes, besides a specification of the agent *belief state*: (1)

---

[1] $Done(a^{ag_i})\top$ is read "the action a has been executed by agent ag_i".

action and precondition laws for describing the *atomic world actions* in terms of their preconditions and effects on the executor's mental state; (2) sensing axioms for describing *atomic sensing actions*; (3) procedure axioms for describing *complex behaviors*.

Belief state. Agents are individuals, each having a mental state: its *subjective* point of view on a dynamic domain. Then, we do not model the real world but only the internal dynamics of each agent in relation to the changes caused by actions. A mental state is a set of belief formulas (*belief state*), intuitively it contains what ag_i (dis)believes about the world and about the other agents. A belief state is a complete and consistent set of rank 1 and 2 belief fluents, where a *belief fluent* F is a belief formula $\mathcal{B}^{ag_i}L$ or its negation. L denotes a *belief argument*, i.e. a *fluent literal* (f or $\neg f$), a *done fluent* ($Done(a^{ag_i})\top$ or its negation), or a belief fluent of rank 1 ($\mathcal{B}l$ or $\neg\mathcal{B}l$). We use l for denoting attitude-free fluents: a fluent literal or a done fluent. Consistency is guaranteed by the seriality of the $\mathcal{B}^{ag_i}$ modalities[2]. In essence a belief state provides, for each agent ag_i, a three-valued interpretation of all the possible belief arguments L: each L is either *true*, *false*, or *undefined* when both $\neg\mathcal{B}^{ag_i}L$ and $\neg\mathcal{B}^{ag_i}\neg L$ hold. In the following we use $\mathcal{U}^{ag_i}L$ for expressing the ignorance of ag_i about L.

World actions. are described by their preconditions and effects on the *actor's* mental state; they trigger a revision process on the actor's beliefs. Formally, *action laws* describe the conditional effects on ag_i's belief state of an atomic action $a \in \mathcal{A}$, executed by ag_i itself. They have the form:

$$\Box(\mathcal{B}^{ag_i}L_1 \wedge \ldots \wedge \mathcal{B}^{ag_i}L_n \supset [a^{ag_i}]\mathcal{B}^{ag_i}L_0) \tag{1}$$

$$\Box(\mathcal{M}^{ag_i}L_1 \wedge \ldots \wedge \mathcal{M}^{ag_i}L_n \supset [a^{ag_i}]\mathcal{M}^{ag_i}L_0) \tag{2}$$

Law (1) states that if ag_i believes the preconditions to an action a in a certain epistemic state, after a execution, ag_i will also believe the action's effects. (2) states that when the preconditions of a are unknown to ag_i, after the execution of a, ag_i will consider unknown also its effects[3]. *Precondition laws* specify mental conditions that make an action in $\mathcal{A} \cup \mathcal{C}$ executable in a state. They have form:

$$\Box(\mathcal{B}^{ag_i}L_1 \wedge \ldots \wedge \mathcal{B}^{ag_i}L_n \supset \langle a^{ag_i}\rangle\top) \tag{3}$$

ag_i can execute a when the precondition fluents of a are in ag_i's belief state.

Sensing Actions. produce knowledge about fluents; they are defined as non-deterministic actions, with unpredictable outcome, formally modelled by a set of *sensing axioms*. If we associate to each sensing action s a set $dom(s)$ of literals (domain), when ag_i executes s, it will know which of such literals is true:

$$[s]\varphi \equiv [\bigcup_{l\in dom(s)} s^{\mathcal{B}^{ag_i}l}]\varphi \tag{4}$$

---

[2] A belief state is *not consistent* when it contains: a belief $\mathcal{B}^{ag_i}l$ and its negation, or the belief formulas $\mathcal{B}^{ag_j}\mathcal{B}^{ag_i}l$ and $\mathcal{B}^{ag_j}\mathcal{B}^{ag_i}\neg l$, or the belief formulas $\mathcal{B}^{ag_j}\mathcal{B}^{ag_i}l$ and $\mathcal{B}^{ag_j}\neg\mathcal{B}^{ag_i}l$.

[3] Laws of form (2) allow actions with non-deterministic effects, that may cause a *loss* of knowledge, to be specified.

$\cup$ is the choice operator of dynamic logic and $s^{\mathcal{B}^{ag_i}l}$, for each $l \in dom(s)$, is an *ad hoc* primitive action, that probes one of the possible outcomes of the sensing.

Complex Actions. We specify agent complex behaviors by means of *procedure definitions*, built upon other actions. Formally, a complex action is defined by means of a collection of *inclusion axiom schema* of our modal logic, of form:

$$\langle p_0 \rangle \varphi \subset \langle p_1; p_2; \ldots; p_m \rangle \varphi \tag{5}$$

p_0 is a procedure name and the p_i's ($i = 1, \ldots, m$) are either procedure names, atomic actions, or test actions; the operator ";" is the sequencing operator of dynamic logic. Procedure definitions may be recursive and procedure clauses can be executed in a goal directed way, similarly to standard logic programs.

2.2   Communication

The integration of a *communication theory* in the general agent theory is obtained by adding further axioms and laws to ag_i's domain description. In this section we will introduce a communication kit that allows the specification of communicative behaviors.

Speech Acts. Communication primitives are atomic actions, described in terms of preconditions and effects on the agent mental state. They have the form speech_act(*sender, receiver, l*), where *sender* and *receiver* are agents and l is either a fluent literal or a done fluent. Such actions can be seen as special mental actions, affecting both the sender's and the receiver's mental state. In our model we focused on the *internal representation*, that agents have of each speech act, by specifying ag_i's belief changes both when it is the sender and when it is the receiver. They are modelled by generalizing the action and precondition laws of form (1), (2), and (3), so to allow the representation of the effects of communications performed by other agents on ag_i mental state. Such a representation provides the capability of *reasoning about* conversation effects.

Speech act specification is, then, twofold: one definition holds when the agent is the sender, the other when it is the receiver. In the first case, the precondition laws contain some *sincerity condition* that must hold in the agent mental state. When ag_i is the receiver, the action is *always* executable. Let us consider some primitive speech acts from the standard agent communication language FIPA-ACL, and let us define them and their semantics within our framework:

inform(*sender, receiver, l*)
a) $\Box(\mathcal{B}^{ag_i}l \wedge \mathcal{B}^{ag_i}\mathcal{U}^{ag_j}l \supset \langle \text{inform}(ag_i, ag_j, l) \rangle \top)$
b) $\Box([\text{inform}(ag_i, ag_j, l)]\mathcal{M}^{ag_i}\mathcal{B}^{ag_j}l)$
c) $\Box(\mathcal{B}^{ag_i}\mathcal{B}^{ag_j}authority(ag_i, l) \supset [\text{inform}(ag_i, ag_j, l)]\mathcal{B}^{ag_i}\mathcal{B}^{ag_j}l)$
d) $\Box(\top \supset \langle \text{inform}(ag_j, ag_i, l) \rangle \top)$
e) $\Box([\text{inform}(ag_j, ag_i, l)]\mathcal{B}^{ag_i}\mathcal{B}^{ag_j}l)$
f) $\Box(\mathcal{B}^{ag_i}authority(ag_j, l) \supset [\text{inform}(ag_j, ag_i, l)]\mathcal{B}^{ag_i}l)$
g) $\Box(\mathcal{M}^{ag_i}authority(ag_j, l) \supset [\text{inform}(ag_j, ag_i, l)]\mathcal{M}^{ag_i}l)$

Clause (a) states that an inform act can be executed when the sender believes l and believes that the receiver does not know l. When ag_i is the sender it thinks possible that the receiver will adopt its belief, although it cannot be certain - autonomy assumption (b)-. If it believes that ag_j considers it a trusted *authority* about l, it is confident that the receiver will adopt its belief (c). When ag_i is the receiver, it believes that l is believed by the sender ag_j (e), but it adopts l as an own belief only if it thinks ag_j is a trusted authority (f)-(g).

queryIf($sender, receiver, l$)
a) $\Box(\mathcal{U}^{ag_i}l \wedge \neg\mathcal{B}^{ag_i}\mathcal{U}^{ag_j}l \supset \langle\text{queryIf}(ag_i, ag_j, l)\rangle\top)$
b) $\Box(\top \supset \langle\text{queryIf}(ag_j, ag_i, l)\rangle\top)$
c) $\Box([\text{queryIf}(ag_j, ag_i, l)]\mathcal{B}^{ag_i}\mathcal{U}^{ag_j}l)$

By queryIf ag_i asks ag_j if it believes that l is true. To perform a queryIf act, ag_i must ignore l and it must believe that the receiver does not ignore l (a). After a queryIf act, the receiver will believe that the sender ignores l.

refuseInform($sender, receiver, l$)
a) $\Box(\mathcal{U}^{ag_i}l \wedge \mathcal{B}^{ag_i}Done(\text{queryIf}(ag_j, ag_i, l))\top \supset \langle\text{refuseInform}(ag_i, ag_j, l)\rangle\top)$
b) $\Box(\top \supset \langle\text{refuseInform}(ag_j, ag_i, l)\rangle\top)$
c) $\Box([\text{refuseInform}(ag_j, ag_i, l)]\mathcal{B}^{ag_i}\mathcal{U}^{ag_j}l)$

By refuseInform an agent refuses to give an information it was asked for. The refusal can be executed only if: the sender ignores l and it believes that the receiver previously queried it about l. After a refusal the receiver believes that the sender ignores l.

Get Message Actions. are used for *receiving* messages from other agents. We model them as a special kind of sensing actions, because from the agent perspective they correspond to queries for an external input, whose outcome is unpredictable. The main difference w.r.t. normal sensing actions is that they are defined by means of speech acts performed by the interlocutor. Formally, we use get_message actions defined by an axiom schema of the form:

$$[\text{get\_message}(ag_i, ag_j, l)]\varphi \equiv [\bigcup_{\text{speech\_act}\in\mathcal{C}_{\text{get\_message}}} \text{speech\_act}(ag_j, ag_i, l)]\varphi \qquad (6)$$

Intuitively, $\mathcal{C}_{\text{get\_message}}$ is a finite set of speech acts, which are all the possible communications that ag_i expects from ag_j in the context of a given conversation. We do not associate to a get_message action a domain of mental fluents, but we calculate the information obtained by looking at the effects of the speech acts in $\mathcal{C}_{\text{get\_message}}$ on ag_i's mental state.

Conversation Protocols. We suppose individual speech acts to take place in the context of predefined conversation protocols [20] that specify communication patterns. Each agent has a subjective perception of the communication with other agents, for this reason each protocol has as many procedural representations as the possible roles in the conversation. Let us consider, for instance the yes_no_query protocol reported in Fig. 1, a simplified version of the FIPA

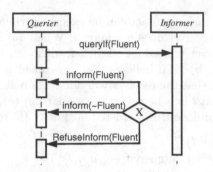

Fig. 1. The AUML graph [21] represents the communicative interactions occurring between the *querier* and the *informer* in the yes_no_query protocol.

Query Interaction Protocol [16]. The protocol has two complementary views, one to be followed for making a query (yes_no_query$_Q$) and one for responding (yes_no_query$_I$). In the following get_answer and get_start definitions are instances of the get_message axiom.

$\langle$yes_no_query$_Q(Self, Other, Fluent)\rangle\varphi \subset$
    $\langle$queryIf$(Self, Other, Fluent)$; get_answer$(Self, Other, Fluent)\rangle\varphi$

[get_answer$(Self, Other, Fluent)]\varphi \equiv$
    [inform$(Other, Self, Fluent)$ $\cup$ inform$(Other, Self, \neg Fluent)$ $\cup$
    refuseInform$(Other, Self, Fluent)]\varphi$

Intuitively, the right hand side of get_answer represents all the possible answers expected by agent *Self* from agent *Other* about *Fluent*, in the context of a conversation ruled by the yes_no_query$_Q$ protocol.

$\langle$yes_no_query$_I(Self, Other, Fluent)\rangle\varphi \subset$
    $\langle$get_start$(Self, Other, Fluent)$;
    $\mathcal{B}^{Self} Fluent?$; inform$(Self, Other, Fluent)\rangle\varphi$
$\langle$yes_no_query$_I(Self, Other, Fluent)\rangle\varphi \subset$
    $\langle$get_start$(Self, Other, Fluent)$;
    $\mathcal{B}^{Self} \neg Fluent?$; inform$(Self, Other, \neg Fluent)\rangle\varphi$
$\langle$yes_no_query$_I(Self, Other, Fluent)\rangle\varphi \subset$
    $\langle$get_start$(Self, Other, Fluent)$;
    $\mathcal{U}^{Self} Fluent?$; refuseInform$(Self, Other, Fluent)\rangle\varphi$

The yes_no_query$_I$ protocol specifies the behavior of the agent *Self*, that waits a query from *Other*; afterwards, it replies according to its beliefs on the query subject. get_start is a get_message action ruled by the following axiom:

[get_start$(Self, Other, Fluent)]\varphi \equiv$ [queryIf$(Other, Self, Fluent)]\varphi$

We can define the *communication kit* of an agent ag_i, CKit^{ag_i}, as the triple $(\Pi_C, \Pi_{CP}, \Pi_{Sget})$, where Π_C is the set of simple action laws defining ag_i's primitive speech acts, Π_{Sget} is a set of axioms for ag_i's get_message actions and Π_{CP}

is the set of procedure axioms specifying the ag_i's conversation protocols. In this extension of the DyLOG language, we define as *Domain Description* for agent ag_i, a triple $(\Pi, \mathsf{CKit}^{ag_i}, S_0)$, where CKit^{ag_i} is ag_i communication kit, S_0 is the initial set of ag_i's belief fluents, and Π is a tuple (Π_A, Π_S, Π_P), where Π_A is the set of ag_i's world action and precondition laws, Π_S is a set of axioms for ag_i's sensing actions, Π_P a set of axioms that define complex actions.

3   Dealing with Persistency

We adopt a non-monotonic solution to the persistency problem, by proposing an abductive semantics for our modal language, in which abductive assumptions are used to model persistency of beliefs fluents, from a state to the following one, when an action is performed. The solution is a generalization of the one in [5], so to deal with nested beliefs and communicative actions, and consists in maximizing persistency assumptions about epistemic fluents after the execution of action sequences. In particular we assume that any belief fluent F which holds in a given state persists through an action, unless it is inconsistent to assume so, i.e. unless $\neg F$ holds after the action execution.

Note that belief states are inconsistent when they contain either a belief $\mathcal{B}^{ag_i}l$ and its negation, or the belief formulas $\mathcal{B}^{ag_j}\mathcal{B}^{ag_i}l$ and $\mathcal{B}^{ag_j}\mathcal{B}^{ag_i}\neg l$, or the belief formulas $\mathcal{B}^{ag_j}\mathcal{B}^{ag_i}l$ and $\mathcal{B}^{ag_j}\neg\mathcal{B}^{ag_i}l$. However, from the seriality of the $\mathcal{B}^{ag_i}$ operators, the general formula schema for the rank 2 beliefs

$$\mathcal{B}^{ag_i}\mathcal{B}^{ag_j}\neg\varphi \supset \neg\mathcal{B}^{ag_i}\mathcal{B}^{ag_j}\varphi \qquad (7)$$

holds in our logic for any two agents ag_i and ag_j [4]. This property guarantees that when an inconsistency arises "locally" in the beliefs ascribed from ag_i to some other agent, the beliefs of ag_i itself will be inconsistent. Therefore, in case of a nested epistemic fluent $\mathcal{B}^{ag_i}\mathcal{B}^{ag_j}l$, the persistency is *correctly blocked* when a locally inconsistent fluent $\mathcal{B}^{ag_i}\mathcal{B}^{ag_j}\neg l$ becomes true after an action execution, because $\neg\mathcal{B}^{ag_i}\mathcal{B}^{ag_j}l$ can be derived from (7). Given these considerations, we can adopt the same approach to the definition of an abductive semantics, that we followed in [5]. In particular, we adopt the same style used by Eshghi and Kowalski in the definition of the abductive semantics for negation as failure [14]. We define as *abducibles* a new set of atomic propositions of the form $\mathbf{M}[a_1]\dots[a_m]F$ [5]. Their meaning is that the fluent expression F can be assumed to hold in the state obtained by the execution of the primitive actions $a_1, \dots, a_m$. Each abducible can be assumed to hold, if it is consistent with the domain description $(\Pi, \mathsf{CKit}^{ag_i}, S_0)$ and with the other assumed abducibles. Then we add to the axiom system, that characterizes the logic defined by the domain description, the *persistency axiom schema*:
$[a_1]\dots[a_{m-1}]F \wedge \mathbf{M}[a_1]\dots[u_{m-1}][u_m]F \supset [a_1]\dots[a_{m-1}][a_m]F$, where $a_1, \quad , a_m$

---

[4] Actually, the general schema for any rank of nesting holds.

[5] Notice that $\mathbf{M}$ is not a modality. $\mathbf{M}\alpha$ denotes a new atomic proposition. $\mathbf{M}\alpha$ means "α is consistent", analogously to default logic.

are primitive actions and F is a belief fluent. It means that if F holds after $a_1, \ldots, a_{m-1}$, and it can be assumed to persist after action a_m (i.e., it is consistent to assume $\mathbf{M}[a_1] \ldots [a_m]F$), then we can conclude that F holds after the sequence of actions $a_1, \ldots, a_m$. The definition of abductive solution is given on the line of [5] and is here omitted.

4 Reasoning in Presence of Communication

Given a domain description, we can reason about it and formalize the *temporal projection* problem and the *planning* problem by existential queries of form:

$$\langle p_1 \rangle \langle p_2 \rangle \ldots \langle p_m \rangle Fs \tag{8}$$

Each p_k, $k = 1, \ldots, m$ in (8) may either be an (atomic or complex) action executed by ag_i or an external speech act, that belongs to CKit^{ag_i} (by the word *external* we denote a speech act in which the agent plays the role of the receiver). By checking if a query of form (8) succeeds we can cope with the planning problem. In fact this corresponds to answering the question "is there an execution trace of p_1, $\ldots$, p_n leading to a state where the conjunction of belief fluents Fs holds for ag_i?". Such an execution trace is a plan to bring about Fs. The procedure definition constrains the search space. Notice that when all the p_k in the query are atomic actions that belong to $\mathcal{A} \cup \mathcal{C}$, by checking if the query succeeds, we cope also with the temporal projection problem: "does Fs hold for ag_i, after the execution of the action sequence $a_1, \ldots, a_m$?".

In presence of communication, the planning and the temporal projection problems turn respectively into the problem of reasoning about *conversation protocols* and reasoning about simple *conversations*, where a conversation is a sequence of speech acts. This allows, for instance, an agent to *investigate* the possible changes to its mental state, produced by a specific conversation, or if a conversation is an instance of some predefined protocol [13]. In the case of temporal projection, the action sequence will contain both actions in which the agent is the sender and actions in which it is the receiver. In the case of conversation protocols, since they represent conversation schemas that guide the communicative behavior of the agent, by answering to the query (8) we find a conversation, which is an instance of the protocol, after which the desired condition Fs holds. In this process we treat get_message actions as sensing actions, whose outcome cannot be known at planning time. Since agents cannot read each other's mind, they cannot know in advance the answers that they will receive. For this reason all of the possible alternatives are to be taken into account; we can foresee them because of the existence of the protocol. Therefore, the extracted plan will be *conditional*, in the sense that for each get_message and for each sensing action it will contain as many branches as possible action outcomes. Each path in the resulting tree is a linear plan that brings about the desired condition Fs. More formally, a conditional plan σ is either:

- an action sequence $a_1; \ldots; a_m$, with $m \geq 0$;
- if $a_1; \ldots; a_m$ $(m \geq 0)$ is an action sequence, $s \in \mathcal{S}$ is a sensing action, and $\sigma_1, \ldots, \sigma_t$ are conditional plans then $a_1; \ldots; a_m; s; ((\mathcal{B}^{ag_i} l_1?); \sigma_1 \cup \ldots \cup (\mathcal{B}^{ag_i} l_t?); \sigma_t)$, where $l_1, \ldots, l_t \in dom(s)$;
- if $a_1; \ldots; a_m$ $(m \geq 0)$ is an action sequence, $g \in \mathcal{S}$ is a get_message action, and $\sigma_1, \ldots, \sigma_t$ are conditional plans then $a_1; \ldots; a_k; g; ((\mathcal{B}^{ag_i} Done(c_1)\top?); \sigma_1 \cup \ldots \cup (\mathcal{B}^{ag_i} Done(c_t)\top?); \sigma_t)$, where $c_1, \ldots, c_t \in \mathcal{C}_g$.

The proof procedure is a natural evolution of the work in [5], it is goal-directed, and based on negation as failure (NAF). NAF is used to deal with the persistency problem to verify that the complement of a mental fluent is not true after an action execution. The proof procedure allows agents to find *linear* and *conditional* plans for achieving a goal from an incompletely specified initial state. The *soundness* w.r.t. the abductive semantics can be proved by imposing domain descriptions to be *e-consistent*, i.e. for any action the set of their effects must be consistent. Moreover, the extracted plans have the following property: they always lead to a state in which the desired condition Fs holds, for all the possible results of the sensing actions.

Figure 2 shows the proof procedure that constructs linear plans, by making assumptions on sensing actions and on external communicative actions. Figure 3 introduces a variant for finding conditional plans. In general, we will need to establish if a goal holds at a given state. Hence, we will write:

$$a_1, \ldots, a_m \vdash \langle p_1; p_2; \ldots; p_n \rangle Fs \text{ with answer (w.a.) } \sigma$$

to mean that the query $\langle p_1; p_2; \ldots; p_n \rangle Fs$ can be proved from the domain description at the state $a_1, \ldots, a_m$ with answer σ. σ is an action sequence which represents the state resulting by the execution of $p_1, \ldots, p_n$ in the current state. We denote by ε the empty action sequence that represents the initial mental state. Rules (1–6) in Fig. 2 deal with the execution of complex, sensing, primitive and test actions. The complex actions in the query are reduced to a sequence of primitive and test actions; the proof procedure verifies if the primitive actions can be executed and if the tests are successful. To do this, it reasons about the execution of the primitive actions and computes the values of fluents at different states. The value of fluents at a state is not explicitly recorded but it is computed when needed in the computation. Rules (7–13), allow the values of mental fluents to be determined and, in particular, to determine if Fs is true after $a_1, \ldots, a_m$. An epistemic fluent F holds in the current state if: either F is an immediate effect of action a_m, whose preconditions hold in the previous state (8a); or a_m is an *ad hoc* primitive action, used in the definition of a sensing action (8b); or F persists from the previous state (8c); or we are in the initial state and F holds (8d). Rule (8c) deals with the *frame problem*: F persists from a state to the next one unless a_m makes $\neg F$ true; *not* represents NAF. Rules (10) and (11) respectively deal with the seriality and the transitivity of the beliefs. Rules (12) and (13) deal with the awareness of action's execution. Fig. 3 reports the two rules that substitute (4) and (5) in Fig. 2 to build conditional plans. The

1)
$$\frac{\overline{a}_{1\cdots m} \vdash \langle p_1'; \ldots; p_{n'}'; \overline{p}_{2\ldots n} \rangle Fs \text{ w. a. } \sigma}{\overline{a}_{1\cdots m} \vdash \langle p; \overline{p}_{2\ldots n} \rangle Fs \text{ w. a. } \sigma}$$

where $p \in \mathcal{P}$ and
$\langle p \rangle \varphi \subset \langle p_1'; \ldots; p_{n'}' \rangle \varphi \in \Pi_{\mathcal{P}} \cup \Pi_{\mathcal{CP}}$

2)
$$\frac{\overline{a}_{1\cdots m} \vdash Fs' \quad \overline{a}_{1\cdots m} \vdash \langle \overline{p}_{2\ldots n} \rangle Fs \text{ w. a. } \sigma}{\overline{a}_{1\cdots m} \vdash \langle (Fs')?; \overline{p}_{2\ldots n} \rangle Fs \text{ w. a. } \sigma}$$

3)
$$\frac{\overline{a}_{1\cdots m} \vdash Fs' \quad \overline{a}_{1\cdots m}, a \vdash \langle \overline{p}_{2\ldots n} \rangle Fs \text{ w. a. } \sigma}{\overline{a}_{1\cdots m} \vdash \langle a; \overline{p}_{2\ldots n} \rangle Fs \text{ w. a. } \sigma}$$

where $a \in \mathcal{A} \cup \mathcal{C}$, and
$\Box(Fs' \supset \langle a \rangle \top) \in \Pi_{\mathcal{A}} \cup \Pi_{\mathcal{C}}$

4)
$$\frac{\overline{a}_{1\cdots m} \vdash \langle s^{\mathcal{B}^{ag_i}l}; \overline{p}_{2\ldots n} \rangle Fs \text{ w. a. } \sigma}{\overline{a}_{1\cdots m} \vdash \langle s; \overline{p}_{2\ldots n} \rangle Fs \text{ w. a. } \sigma}$$

where $s \in \mathcal{S}$ and
$l \in dom(s)$

5)
$$\frac{\overline{a}_{1\cdots m} \vdash \langle c; \overline{p}_{2\ldots n} \rangle Fs \text{ w. a. } \sigma}{\overline{a}_{1\cdots m} \vdash \langle g; \overline{p}_{2\ldots n} \rangle Fs \text{ w. a. } \sigma}$$

where $g \in \mathcal{S}get$ and
$[g]\varphi \equiv [\bigcup_{c \in \mathcal{C}_g} c]\varphi$

6)
$$\frac{\overline{a}_{1\cdots m} \vdash Fs}{\overline{a}_{1\cdots m} \vdash \langle \varepsilon \rangle Fs \text{ w. a. } \sigma}$$

where $\sigma = a_1; \ldots; a_m$

7)
$$\overline{\overline{a}_{1\cdots m} \vdash \top}$$

8a)
$$\frac{\overline{a}_{1\cdots m-1} \vdash Fs'}{\overline{a}_{1\cdots m} \vdash F}$$

where $m > 0$ and
$\Box(Fs' \supset [a_m]F) \in \Pi_{\mathcal{A}}$

8b)
$$\overline{\overline{a}_{1\cdots m} \vdash F}$$

if $a_m = s^F$

8c)
$$\frac{\textbf{not } \overline{a}_{1\cdots m} \vdash \neg F \quad \overline{a}_{1\cdots m-1} \vdash F}{\overline{a}_{1\cdots m} \vdash F}$$

where $m > 0$

8d)
$$\overline{\varepsilon \vdash F}$$

if $F \in S_0$

9)
$$\frac{\overline{a}_{1\cdots m} \vdash Fs' \quad \overline{a}_{1\cdots m} \vdash Fs''}{\overline{a}_{1\cdots m} \vdash Fs' \wedge Fs''}$$

10)
$$\frac{\overline{a}_{1\cdots m} \vdash \mathcal{B}^{ag_i}L}{\overline{a}_{1\cdots m} \vdash \mathcal{M}^{ag_i}L}$$

11)
$$\frac{\overline{a}_{1\cdots m} \vdash \mathcal{B}^{ag_i}l}{\overline{a}_{1\cdots m} \vdash \mathcal{B}^{ag_i}\mathcal{B}^{ag_j}l}$$

12)
$$\frac{\overline{a}_{1\cdots m} \vdash Done(a)\top}{\overline{a}_{1\cdots m} \vdash \mathcal{B}^{ag_i}Done(a)\top}$$

13)
$$\overline{\overline{a}_{1\cdots m} \vdash Done(a_m)\top}$$

Fig. 2. A goal directed proof procedure for DyLOG. Legend: $\overline{a}_{1\cdots m} \equiv a_1, \ldots, a_m$ and $\overline{p}_{2\ldots n} \equiv p_2, \ldots, p_n$.

4-bis)
$$\frac{\forall l_k \in \mathcal{F}, \; \overline{a}_{1\cdots m} \vdash \langle s^{\mathcal{B}^{ag_i}l}; \overline{p}_{2\ldots n} \rangle Fs \text{ w. a. } a_1; \ldots; a_m; s^{\mathcal{B}^{ag_i}l}; \sigma_k'}{\overline{a}_{1\cdots m} \vdash \langle s; \overline{p}_{2\ldots n} \rangle Fs \text{ w. a. } a_1; \ldots; a_m; s; (\bigcup_{k=1\ldots t}(\mathcal{B}^{ag_i}l_k?); \sigma_k')}$$

5-bis)
$$\frac{\forall c_k \in \mathcal{C}_g, \; \overline{a}_{1\cdots m} \vdash \langle c_k; \overline{p}_{2\ldots n} \rangle Fs_i \text{ w. a. } a_1; \ldots; a_m; c_k; \sigma_k'}{\overline{a}_{1\cdots m} \vdash \langle g; \overline{p}_{2\ldots n} \rangle Fs_i \text{ w. a. } a_1; \ldots; a_m; g; (\bigcup_{k=1\ldots t}(\mathcal{B}^{ag_i}Done(c_k)\top?); \sigma_k')}$$

Fig. 3. A variant of the proof procedure for extracting conditional plans. In (4-bis) $s \in \mathcal{S}$ and $\mathcal{F} = \{l_1, \ldots, l_t\} = dom(s)$; in (5-bis) $g \in \mathcal{S}$ and $\{c_1, \ldots, c_t\} = \mathcal{C}_g$.

new rules deal with the execution of sensing and get message actions, respectively. As a difference with the previous proof procedure, when a sensing action is executed, the procedure considers *all the possible outcomes*, thus producing many branches. If all branches lead to success, the main query succeeds. In such a case, the conditional plan will contain the branches as alternative sub-plans. The same holds for the execution of **get_message** actions.

Example 1. Let us consider the protocol **get_ticket_1**$_C$, describing from the *customer* perspective the interaction with a *cinema booking service*:

(a) $\langle$get_ticket_1$_C(Self, WebS, Film)\rangle\varphi \subset$
   $\langle$yes_no_query$_Q(Self, WebS, available(Film))$; $\mathcal{B}^{Self}available(Film)$? ;
   get_info$(Self, WebS, cinema(C))$; yes_no_query$_I(Self, WebS, pay\_by(credit\_card))$;
   $\mathcal{B}^{Self}pay\_by(credit\_card)$? ; inform$(Self, WebS, cc\_number)$;
   get_info$(Self, WebS, booked(Film)))\rangle\varphi$
(b) $\langle$get_ticket_1$_C(Self, WebS, Film)\rangle\varphi \subset$
   $\langle$yes_no_query$_Q(Self, WebS, available(Film))$; $\mathcal{B}^{Self}available(Film)$? ;
   get_info$(Self, WebS, cinema(C))$; yes_no_query$_I(Self, WebS, pay\_by(credit\_card))$;
   $\neg\mathcal{B}^{Self}pay\_by(credit\_card)$? ; get_info$(Self, WebS, pay\_by(cash))$;
   get_info$(Self, WebS, booked(Film)))\rangle\varphi$
(c) $\langle$get_ticket_1$_C(Self, WebS, Film)\rangle\varphi \subset$
   $\langle$yes_no_query$_Q(Self, WebS, available(Film))$; $\neg\mathcal{B}^{Self}available(Film)$?$\rangle\varphi$
(d) [get_info$(Self, WebS, Fluent)]\varphi \equiv$ [inform$(WebS, Self, Fluent)]\varphi$

get_ticket_1$_C$ permits both to book a ticket to be paid later by cash and to buy it by credit card; suppose it is followed by the web service *click_ticket*. Given the query $\langle$get_ticket_1$_C(pa, click\_ticket, akira)\rangle\mathcal{B}^{pa}\neg\mathcal{B}^{click\_ticket}cc\_number$, a *personal assistant pa* could reason on it to determine if there is a conversation between *pa* and *click_ticket* about the movie *akira*, after which the service does *not* know the credit card number of the user. Since such a conversation exists, the agent *pa* finds an execution trace of get_ticket_1$_C$, which corresponds to a *personalized conditional dialogue plan* between itself and the provider *click_ticket*, always leading to satisfy the user goal of not giving the credit card number. For a deeper discussion about personalization of web service fruition see [3].

5   Conclusion and Related Work

Communication among agents has extensively been studied by the AI community. One of the most popular approaches, derived from the work of philosophers and linguists carried on in the sixties [2,23], considers *rationality* as a key concept. In other words, communicative acts are interpreted as rational actions with preconditions and effects on the agent mental state, that can be planned and reasoned about [11,1,10]; this approach lead to the definition of well-known ACLs like FIPA [17]. The semantics of communication can be given at different levels of detail. In many formal approaches [11,10,6,18] the focus is posed at the level of the single speech acts and the task of reasoning about communication and planning is achieved based on their preconditions and desired effects, without considering them in the context of a conversation protocol. Indeed many of these approaches [6,18] have been born for the developement of intelligent human-machine dialogue systems, then they are focussed on techniques where recognizing intentions in communications is fundamental for producing a suitable reply. On the line of [20], we argue that the use of conversation protocols makes the design of software components that must interact easier: the interoperability of the various components (often separately developed) is improved and the verification of compliance to the desired standards is simplified. By working at the level of protocols, agents can more easily be seen as individuals, developed independently, on different platforms and with different approaches, a very attractive view in the applicative field of web applications and web services. For all these reasons we focus on a semantics of communication that supports the specification and reasoning about single speech acts, as well as the specification and reasoning about speech acts in the context of a conversation protocol. In our framework, protocols are intended as tractable decision procedures, that the agent can use for selecting and producing communicative acts, suitable to the agent goals. Since they limit the domain of possible interactions, an advantage is that they reduce the search space.

More specifically, we have presented an approach to reason about conversation protocols within the framework of an agent language based on a modal logic of action and beliefs. The approach extends with communication the proposal to model rational agents in [5]. We used conversation protocols to provide our agents decision procedures for suitably responding to communications. We took a subjective representation of conversation protocols, by making hypothetical assumptions on the other's answers. As a consequence protocols have been easily integrated with other policies defining the agent's behavior, being both represented as procedures specified in DyLOG. Notice that, since we are only interested in reasoning about the local mental state's dynamics, our approach differs from other logic-based approaches to communication in multi-agent systems, as the one taken in [24], where communicative actions affect the global state of a multi-agent system and the target is to prove global properties of the overall multi-agent system's execution. Instead our focus on the internal specification of interaction protocols for planning dialogue's moves is closer to the one taken in [22], where negotiation protocols, expressed by sets of dialogue constraints, are included in the agent program and used for triggering dialogues that achieve goals. However such an approach is not aimed at implementing the kind of reasoning about conversations we focused on: it does not support plan extraction and it cannot exploit the information about the others, that instead we can supply by nested beliefs.

References

1. J. F. Allen. Recognizing intentions from natural language utterances. In M. Brady and R.C. Åqvist, editors, *Computational models of discourse*. MIT Press, Cambridge, MA, 1983.
2. J.A Austin. *How to do things with words*. Harvard University Press, 1962.
3. M. Baldoni, C. Baroglio, A. Martelli, and V. Patti. Reasoning about interaction for personalizing web service fruition. In *Proc. of WOA 2003: dagli Oggetti agli Agenti*, Cagliari, Italy, september 2003. to appear.

4. M. Baldoni, C. Baroglio, V. Patti, and L. Torasso. Using a rational agent in an adaptive web-based tutoring system. In *Proc. of the Workshop on Adaptive Systems for Web-Based Education, AH2002*, Malaga, Spain, 2002.
5. M. Baldoni, L. Giordano, A. Martelli, and V. Patti. Reasoning about Complex Actions with Incomplete Knowledge: A Modal Approach. In *Proc. of ICTCS'2001*, volume 2202 of *LNCS*, pages 405–425. Springer, 2001.
6. P. Bretier and D. Sadek. A rational agent as the kernel of a cooperative spoken dialogue system: implementing a logical theory of interaction. In *Intelligent Agents III, proc. of ECAI-96 Workshop on Agent Theories, Architectures, and Languages (ATAL-96), LNAI* 1193. Springer-Verlag, 1997.
7. J. Bryson, D. Martin, S. McIlraith, and L. A. Stein. Agent-based composite services in DAML-S: The behavior-oriented design of an intelligent semantic web, 2002.
8. R. Chinnici, M. Gudgin, J. J. Moreau, and S. Weerawarana. Web Services Prescription Language (WSDL) version 1.2, 2003. Working Draft.
9. The DAML-S coalition. DAML-S: Web service description for the semantic web. In *the 1st Int. Semantic Web Conference (ISWC)*, Sardinia, Italy, 2002.
10. P.R. Cohen and H. Levesque. Rational interaction as the basis for communication. In P.R Cohen, M.E. Pollack, and J. Morgan, editors, *Intentions in Communication*, pages 221–256, 1990.
11. P.R. Cohen and C.R. Perrault. Elements of a plan-based theory of speech acts. *Cognitive Science*, 3(3):177–212, 1979.
12. M. Dastani, J. van der Ham, and F. Dignum. Communication for goal directed agents. In *Proc. of Workshop on Agent Communication Languages and Conversation Policies, AAMAS'02*, Bologna, Italy, 2002.
13. F. Dignum and M. Greaves. Issues in agent communication. In *Issues in Agent Communication*, volume 1916 of *LNCS*, pages 1–16. Springer, 2000.
14. K. Eshghi and R. Kowalski. Abduction compared with Negation by Failure. In *Proc. of ICLP '89*, Lisbon, 1989. The MIT Press.
15. T. Finin, Y. Labrou, and J. Mayfield. KQML as an Agent Communication Language. In J. Bradshaw, editor, *Software Agents*. MIT Press, 1995.
16. FIPA. FIPA 2000. Technical report, FIPA (Foundation for Intelligent Physical Agents), November 2000.
17. FIPA. FIPA 2002. Technical report, FIPA (Foundation for Intelligent Physical Agents), 2002.
18. A. Herzig and D. Longin. Beliefs dynamics in cooperative dialogues. In *Proc. of AMSTELOGUE 99*, 1999.
19. H. J. Levesque, R. Reiter, Y. Lespérance, F. Lin, and R. B. Scherl. GOLOG: A Logic Programming Language for Dynamic Domains. *J. of Logic Programming*, 31:59–83, 1997.
20. A. Mamdani and J. Pitt. Communication protocols in multi-agent systems: A development method and reference architecture. In *Issues in Agent Communication*, volume 1916 of *LNCS*, pages 160–177. Springer, 2000.
21. J. H. Odell, H. Van Dyke Parunak, and B. Bauer. Representing agent interaction protocols in UML. In *Agent-Oriented Software Engineering*, pages 121–140. Springer, 2001.
22. F. Sadri, F. Toni, and P. Torroni. Dialogues for Negotiation: Agent Varieties and Dialogue Sequences. In *Proc. of ATAL'01*, Seattle, WA, 2001.
23. J.R. Searle. *Speech Acts*. Cambridge University Press, New York, 1969.
24. S. Shapiro, Y. Lespérance, and H. J. Levesque. Specifying communicative multi-agent systems. In *Agents and Multi-Agent Systems - Formalisms, Methodologies, and Applications*, volume 1441 of *LNAI*, pages 1–14. Springer-Verlag, 1998.

Decidability Properties of Recursive Types

Felice Cardone[1] and Mario Coppo[2]

[1] DISCo – Università di Milano-Bicocca
Via Bicocca degli Arcimboldi 8 – 20126 Milano
cardone@disco.unimib.it
[2] Dipartimento di Informatica
Università di Torino
C.so Svizzera 185 – 10149 Torino
coppo@di.unito.it

Abstract. In this paper we study decision problems and invertibility for two notions of equivalence of recursive types. In particular, for recursive types presented by means of a recursion operator μ, we describe an algorithm showing that the natural equivalence generated by finitely many steps of folding and unfolding of μ-types is decidable. For recursive types presented by finite systems of recursive equations, we give a thoroughly coinductive characterization of the equivalence induced by their interpretation as infinite (regular) trees, from which the decidability of this equivalence follows. A formal proof of the former result, to our knowledge, has never appeared in the literature. The latter result, on the contrary, is known but we present here a new proof obtained as an application of general coalgebraic facts to the theory of recursive types. From these results invertibility is easily proved for both equivalences.

1 Introduction

Recursive types are a pervasive notion in programming. This is true both in theoretical investigations, where recursive types appear in the semantics of programming languages of any kind (as witnessed by domain theory and its recent generalizations, or by the use of recursive types in describing fundamental concepts of object-oriented programming [1]), and in programming practice as a unifying notion that is orthogonal to most programming styles. We address in particular those type systems that arise in functional programming and that therefore include a function type constructor $\rightarrow$.

There are basically two ways of concretely presenting recursive types within a type system.

On the one hand, we have μ-types of the form $\mu t.A$, for any type A, whose intended meaning is a canonical solution of a type equation $t = A$, where the type variable t may occur free in type A. Any natural equivalence $\simeq_\mu$ on μ-types, as suggested by the above interpretation, should satisfy

$$\mu t.A \simeq_\mu A[t := \mu t.A], \tag{1}$$

C. Blundo and C. Laneve (Eds.): ICTCS 2003, LNCS 2841, pp. 242–255, 2003.
© Springer-Verlag Berlin Heidelberg 2003

where the latter expression denotes the result of substituting $\mu t.A$ for every (free) occurrence of t in type A. Yet, there is some freedom as to how to describe such an equivalence, and in fact at least two of them have been studied in the literature. One approach (see [2]) consists in taking $\simeq_\mu$ as the smallest congruence $\sim_\mu$ satisfying (1). We shall call this *weak equivalence*. A different view was taken in [3], where μ-types were regarded as finite notations for the infinite (regular) trees that arise from the infinite unwiding of the recursion, according to (1). This suggests a stronger notion of equivalence whereby types A, B (possibly involving μ-types) are equivalent, written $A \approx_\mu B$, whenever the infinite trees associated to A and B are *equal*. The two relations are different, see e. g. example 1 in section 2.3. While the former equivalence admits an inductive characterization, the latter can be described by means of coinductive techniques suggested by the observation that infinite trees are the final coalgebra of a (polynomial) functor over the category of sets ([4,5]).

On the other hand, a recursive type may also be described by a system of equations over a set $\{X_1, \ldots, X_n\}$ of unknowns of the form:

$$\mathcal{R} = \{X_1 = A_1, \ldots, X_n = A_n\} \tag{2}$$

where every A_i is a type possibly containing $X_1, \ldots, X_n$. This view is perhaps closer to what happens in (functional) programming languages, where a typical recursive definition of a data structure may look like the following (Peyton Jones [6]):

```
tree ::= LEAF num | BRANCH tree tree
```

introducing the type of trees of numbers (elements of the type num). Also in this case, there are at least two natural equivalence relations on types induced by a system of recursive type definitions: there is the smallest congruence $\sim_\mathcal{R}$ generated by $\mathcal{R}$, studied in [7,8], and the stronger equivalence relation that identifies types A and B (over the unknowns $X_1, \ldots, X_n$), written $A \approx_\mathcal{R} B$, when $S(A) = S(B)$, where S is the unique substitution $\{X_1, \ldots, X_n\} \to \mathsf{Tr}^\infty$ that solves $\mathcal{R}$ in the set of infinite trees. Also in this case, $\sim_\mathcal{R}$ has an inductive characterization whereas $\approx_\mathcal{R}$ can be described exploiting the coalgebraic nature of systems of equations of the shape (2). The relations between these two equivalences have been studied in [9].

In this paper we discuss some basic properties of type equivalences, namely decidability and invertibility. Invertibility, which roughly means that two types with the same outermost constructor are equivalent only if the corresponding arguments are pairwise equivalent, has been introduced only recently in [7], where it is proved that invertibility of type equivalence is a necessary and sufficient condition to prove the subject reduction theorem for the corresponding typed λ-calculus.

After introducing the basic notations and notions in section 2, we describe in section 3 an algorithm yielding a (constructive) proof that weak equivalence on μ-types is decidable. As far as we know, a direct proof of this fact was part of the folklore of the subject and has never appeared in print. The corresponding problem for $\approx_\mu$ has been solved, among others, by [10]. As a corollary of our proof we easily obtain that $\sim_\mu$ is invertible.

We also give a natural characterization of systems of recursive type equations of a special form (called *simultaneous recursions*, following [7]) as coalgebras (section 2.5); the theory of coalgebras as developed, for example, in [5] yields a simple characterization of the equivalence of two simultaneous recursions, exploited in showing decidability of $\approx_\mathcal{R}$ in section 4 following, for example, the ideas of [11, Remark 3.39].

We should stress that our motivation for studying these problems is their relevance for type systems for λ-terms, which is also the reason for restricting our choice of constructors to $\rightarrow$ and constants. However, the same problems could be studied more generally in the context of a generic first-order signature Σ, and our results could be applied to this more general situation without substantial modifications.

Acknowledgments. The authors would like to thank the referees for their useful suggestions and Wil Dekkers for pointing out a mistake in an earlier proof of Theorem 3.

2   Type Structures and Type Constraints

In this section we define the basic notion of type structure, that we shall use later as one way of describing recursive types. This notion was first motivated by Scott [12] and formally developed in Breazu Tannen and Meyer [13]; more recently, it has been taken up in [7] and [8].

2.1   Type Structures

The main feature of recursive types is that one makes identifications between them. So it is natural to define a type structure as a set of types with a congruence relation.

Definition 1. *Let $\mathbb{T}$ be a set of syntactic objects (types) closed under the $\rightarrow$ type constructor, and possibly including constants $\kappa \in K$ and type variables $t_1, t_2, t_3, \ldots$ from a denumerable set V. A type structure over $\mathbb{T}$ is a pair $\mathcal{T} = \langle \mathbb{T}, \simeq \rangle$ where $\simeq$ is a congruence over $\mathbb{T}$ (i.e. an equivalence relation such that $A \simeq A'$ and $B \simeq B'$ implies $A \rightarrow A' \simeq B \rightarrow B'$).*

The notion of *invertibility* of a type structure has been investigated thoroughly in [7].

Definition 2 (Invertibility). *Let $\langle \mathbb{T}, \simeq \rangle$ be a type structure. Then $\simeq$ is said to be* invertible *if $(A \rightarrow B) \simeq (A' \rightarrow B') \Rightarrow A \simeq A'$ and $B \simeq B'$.*

Invertibility holds, for instance, in the type structure freely generated by $V \cup K$.

2.2   Typed λ-Calculus with Recursive Types

Explicitly typed versions of λ-calculus with recursive types can be defined assuming that types are defined by a type structure. As usual a *type context* Γ is a set of typing assumptions of the shape $x : A$, where x is a variable and A a type.

Definition 3. *Let $\mathcal{T} = \langle \mathbb{T}, \simeq \rangle$ be a type structure and $A, B \in \mathcal{T}$. The well typed terms of the typed λ-calculus over $\mathcal{T}$ are defined by the following term formation rules:*

$$(ax) \quad \Gamma, x : A \vdash_{\mathcal{T}} x : A$$

$$(\to E) \quad \frac{\Gamma \vdash_{\mathcal{T}} M : A \to B \quad \Gamma \vdash_{\mathcal{T}} N : A}{\Gamma \vdash_{\mathcal{T}} MN : B}$$

$$(\to I) \quad \frac{\Gamma, x : A \vdash_{\mathcal{T}} M : B}{\Gamma \vdash_{\mathcal{T}} (\lambda x : A.M) : A \to B}$$

$$(equiv) \quad \frac{\Gamma \vdash_{\mathcal{T}} M : A \quad A \simeq B}{\Gamma \vdash_{\mathcal{T}} M : B}$$

See [3] for a review of the basic properties of typed λ-calculi with recursive types. We shortly mention a couple of them. The first one is that type checking is decidable iff $\simeq$ is decidable.

Proposition 1. *Let Γ be a type context and M a typed λ-terms over a set $\mathbb{T}$ of types. Then it is decidable whether there is a type A such that $\Gamma \vdash_{\langle \mathbb{T}, \simeq \rangle} M : A$ iff $\simeq$ is decidable.*

Moreover we say that a type structure $\mathcal{T}$ has the *subject reduction property* if $\Gamma \vdash_{\mathcal{T}} M : A$ and $M \to_{\beta} N$ imply $\Gamma \vdash_{\mathcal{T}} N : A$. Subject reduction has important consequences like the well known property that "well typed terms cannot go wrong" [14]. The following result has been proved by R. Statman [7].

Theorem 1. *A type structure $\mathcal{T}$ has the subject reduction property iff $\mathcal{T}$ is invertible.*

We introduce below two type structures which are different both in the notion of types and in the nature of the type equivalence.

2.3   μ-Types

Definition 4 (μ-types). *Let $\mathbf{A} = K \cup V$. The set $\mathsf{T}_{\mu} = \mathsf{T}_{\mu}(\mathbf{A})$ is defined by the following abstract syntax:*

$$\mathsf{T}_{\mu} = \mathbf{A} \mid \mathsf{T}_{\mu} \to \mathsf{T}_{\mu} \mid \mu V.\mathsf{T}_{\mu}$$

We assume that $\to$ takes precedence over μ, so that, for example, the type $\mu t.A \to B$ should be parsed as $\mu t.(A \to B)$. The subset of T_μ containing only types without occurrences of the μ operator equations will be identified with the set T of simple types.

In the last clause of this definition, the operator μ binds the variable t, which can therefore be renamed by α-conversion. We will always assume in the sequel that the names of bound and free variables in types are distinct: this can be easily obtained by a renaming of bound variables.

According to the intuitive semantics of recursive types, a type expression of the form $\mu t.A$ should be regarded as the solution for t in the equation $t = A$, and is then equivalent to the type expression $A[t := \mu t.A]$. The notion of type equivalence $\sim_\mu$ is defined by a set of formal rules in which this equality is extended to a congruence on T_μ by adding structural rules and transitivity.

Definition 5. (i) *The equational Theory* (μ) *is defined by the following axioms and rules.*

$$(\mu\text{-}eq) \qquad \vdash \mu t.A = A[t := \mu t.A]$$

$$(ident) \qquad \vdash A = A$$

$$(symm) \qquad \frac{\vdash A = B}{\vdash B = A}$$

$$(\to) \qquad \frac{\vdash A = A' \quad \vdash B = B'}{\vdash A \to B = A' \to B'}$$

$$(\mu) \qquad \frac{\vdash A = A'}{\vdash \mu t.A = \mu t.A'}$$

$$(trans) \qquad \frac{\vdash A = B \quad \vdash B = C}{\vdash A = C}$$

A *is* weakly equivalent *to* B, *notation* $A \sim_\mu B$ *if* $\vdash A = B$ *is provable in* (μ).

(ii) *Let* $\mathcal{T}_\mu$ *denote the type structure* $\langle \mathsf{T}_\mu, \sim_\mu \rangle$.

We call *unfolding* the operation consisting in replacing $\mu t.A$ by $A[t := \mu t.A]$ and *folding* its inverse. Then two types in T_μ are weakly equivalent if they can be transformed one into the other by a finite number of applications of folding and unfolding. Note that the free type structure T can be embedded into $\mathcal{T}_\mu$.

Lemma 1. *If* $A \sim_\mu B$ *then* $A[t := C] \sim_\mu B[t := C]$.

Proof. Routine. □

We will use $\equiv$ to denote definitional equality of types modulo t conversion. For example $\mu t.t \to t \equiv \mu u.u \to u$.

Example 1. Let $T_1 \equiv \mu t.A \to t$. Then we have

$$T_1 \sim_\mu A \to T_1 \sim_\mu A \to A \to T_1 \sim_\mu \cdots$$

Let now $T_2 \equiv \mu t.A \to A \to t$. Notice that

$$T_2 \sim_\mu A \to A \to T_2 \sim_\mu \ldots$$

but it is easy to see that $T_1 \not\sim_\mu T_2$. However, for the stronger notion of equivalence $\approx_\mu$ mentioned in the introduction we have that $T_1 \approx_\mu T_2$

2.4   Type Constraints and Recursive Definitions

A very natural way of generating type structures is to assume a (finite) set of equations between types (called *type constraints*) and to take the congruence generated by it via the rules of equational reasoning. In the definition of recursive types we are particularly interested in the type structures generated by a system of type constraints of the shape $X = C$ where X is a new atomic symbol (an *indeterminate*) and C is a type expression containing possibly X itself. More formally, we consider a set T of types built inductively from constants $\kappa \in K$, type variables $t \in V$ and *indeterminates* $\boldsymbol{X} = X_1, \ldots, X_n$, for some $n \geq 0$, by means of the type constructor $\to$. When we want to highlight the set of indeterminates we write $\mathsf{T}[X_1, \ldots, X_n]$, but often we shall simply write T when the indeterminates are understood from the context. It will be useful to consider types in T as the term algebra generated by the first-order signature Σ containing one binary operation symbol $\to$ and nullary operation symbols $K \cup V \cup \boldsymbol{X}$. The set $K \cup V$ will occasionally be referred to as the set of *atoms*.

Definition 6 (Simultaneous recursion). *A system of equations* $\mathcal{R}$ *over* T *is a simultaneous recursion (s.r. for short) if it has the form* $\mathcal{R} = \{X_i = C_i \mid 1 \leq i \leq n\}$ *where*

1. *for all* $1 \leq i \leq n$, X_i *is an indeterminate and* $C_i \in \mathsf{T}[X_1, \ldots, X_n]$ *is not an indeterminate, for all* $i = 1, \ldots, n$;
2. $X_i \neq X_j$ *for all* $i \neq j$.

The indeterminates $X_1, \ldots, X_n$ *are called in this context the* unknowns *of the simultaneous recursion, and* $\{X_1, \ldots, X_n\}$ *will also be abbreviated as* $Unk(\mathcal{R})$.

Example 2. Let $\mathcal{R}_1 = \{X_1 = A \to X_1\}$ where A is any type be a s.r. defining a type X such that $X_1 =_{\mathcal{R}_1} A \to X_1 =_{\mathcal{R}_1} A \to A \to X_1 \ldots$ and so on. Define now $\mathcal{R}_2 = \{X_2 = A \to A \to X_2\}$. Observe that, in $\mathcal{R}_1 \cup \mathcal{R}_2$, X_1 cannot be proved equal to X_2 by equational reasoning. We will now define an equivalence relation on simultaneous recursions for which X_1 is indeed equivalent to X_2 [1].

2.5   Tree Equivalence of Types

A simultaneous recursion $\mathcal{R}$ can be interpreted as a simultaneous recursive definition of a set of infinite trees $\{\tau_1, \ldots, \tau_n\}$ that satisfy the equations of $\mathcal{R}$, where each τ_i corresponds to the unknown X_i.

---

[1]   Note that X_1, X_2 have the same properties of types T_1, T_2 of Example 1.

Definition 7 (Infinite trees). *(i) Let Σ be the signature $\{\rightarrow\} \cup K \cup V$. A Σ-tree τ is a partial function $\tau : \{1,2\}^* \rightarrow \Sigma$ satisfying the following conditions:*

- *if $uv \in dom(\tau)$, then also $u \in dom(\tau)$;*
- *if $u2 \in dom(\tau)$, then also $u1 \in dom(\tau)$;*
- *if $\tau(u) = \rightarrow$ then $u1, u2 \in dom(\tau)$;*
- *if $\tau(u) \in K \cup V$ then $ui \notin dom(\tau)$, for $i \in \{1,2\}$.*

The set of Σ-trees will be denoted by Tr^∞.
(ii) Given a tree $\tau \in \mathsf{Tr}^\infty$ and a word $w \in dom(\tau)$, let $\tau \upharpoonright w$ (the subtree of τ rooted at w) be the tree defined by:

- *$(\tau \upharpoonright w)(u) = \tau(wu)$, for all $u \in dom(\tau \upharpoonright w)$.*

A solution of a simultaneous recursion $\mathcal{R}$ is just a substitution of infinite trees for the unknowns of $\mathcal{R}$ that satisfies all the equations in $\mathcal{R}$:

Definition 8. *Let $\mathcal{R}$ be a simultaneous recursion, and let $S : Unk(\mathcal{R}) \rightarrow \mathsf{Tr}^\infty$. We say that S solves $\mathcal{R}$ (or that S is a solution of $\mathcal{R}$) if $S(X_i) = S^*(C_i)$, where S^* is the homomorphic extension of S to T.*

The infinite trees that appear as components of solutions of simultaneous recursions are always *regular*, as the number of equations in $\mathcal{R}$ is finite: regular trees are those (finite or) infinite trees that have a finite set of subtrees (Courcelle [15]).

It is easy to see that any simultaneous recursion $\mathcal{R}$ can be transformed into a *flat* simultaneous recursion $\mathcal{R}^\flat$, namely one where every C_i appearing on the right-hand side has the simplest possible form:

Definition 9 (Flat simultaneous recursion). *A s.r. $\mathcal{R}$ is flat if every C_i has one of the following shapes:*

1. *$X_j \rightarrow X_k$, for $X_j, X_k \in Unk(\mathcal{R})$,*
2. *κ, for $\kappa \in K$,*
3. *t, where $t \in V$.*

In order to build $\mathcal{R}^\flat$ from $\mathcal{R}$ it is enough to replace every equation whose right-hand side has not one of the forms listed in the above definition by new equations, in this process adding new unknowns. An algorithm for obtaining $\mathcal{R}^\flat$ is described in [16, §2.3]. The following proposition has a straightforward proof:

Proposition 2. *Let $\mathcal{R}$ be a simultaneous recursion and $S : Unk(\mathcal{R}) \rightarrow \mathsf{Tr}^\infty$ any substitution. For any flat version $\mathcal{R}^\flat$ of $\mathcal{R}$ there is a unique substitution $S^\flat$ such that S solves $\mathcal{R}$ if and only if $S^\flat$ solves $\mathcal{R}^\flat$.*

There is some advantage in adopting a more abstract approach to infinite trees, that exploits the coalgebraic nature of flat simultaneous recursions and of Tr^∞. This will allow us to define an interpretation $(\cdot)^*_\mathcal{R} : \mathsf{T} \rightarrow \mathsf{Tr}^\infty$ and also when two types in T are equivalent modulo a simultaneous recursion $\mathcal{R}$. We first recall the general definition of a coalgebra over the category of sets (see, e. g., [5]).

Definition 10 (Coalgebra). *Let* T : **Set** $\to$ **Set** *be a functor. A* T-*coalgebra is a pair* $\langle A, \alpha : A \to TA \rangle$. *If* $\langle A, \alpha : A \to TA \rangle$ *and* $\langle B, \beta : B \to TB \rangle$ *are* T-*coalgebras, then a* T-*coalgebra homomorphism is is a mapping* $h : A \to B$ *such that the following diagram commutes:*

$$
\begin{array}{ccc}
A & \xrightarrow{\ \alpha\ } & TA \\
h \downarrow & & \downarrow Th \\
B & \xrightarrow{\ \beta\ } & TB
\end{array}
$$

A flat simultaneous recursion $\mathcal{R}$ with unknowns $U =_{\text{def}} \text{Unk}(\mathcal{R})$, may be seen as a T_Σ-coalgebra $\mathcal{R} : U \to T_\Sigma U$, where T_Σ is the polynomial functor defined on objects by the clause:

$$
T_\Sigma A =_{\text{def}} \coprod_{c \in \Sigma} \underbrace{A \times \ldots \times A}_{\text{ar}(c)}
$$

and whose action on maps is defined by the equation:

$$
(T_\Sigma f)(\langle c,\ \langle a_1, \ldots, a_{\text{ar}(c)} \rangle \rangle) =_{\text{def}} \langle c,\ \langle f(a_1), \ldots, f(a_{\text{ar}(c)}) \rangle \rangle, \tag{3}
$$

for any function $f : A \to B$.

Now, given a tree $t \in \text{Tr}^\infty$, the pair

$$
\omega(\tau) =_{\text{def}} \langle \tau(\epsilon),\ \langle \tau \upharpoonright 1, \ldots, \tau \upharpoonright \text{ar}(c) \rangle \rangle \tag{4}
$$

is an element of $\coprod_{c \in \Sigma} \underbrace{\text{Tr}^\infty \times \ldots \times \text{Tr}^\infty}_{\text{ar}(c)}$, therefore

$$
\omega : \text{Tr}^\infty \to T_\Sigma(\text{Tr}^\infty) \tag{5}
$$

is a T_Σ-coalgebra. However, more than this is true and well-known (see, e. g., [4]):

Proposition 3. $\omega : \text{Tr}^\infty \to T_\Sigma(\text{Tr}^\infty)$ *is the final* T_Σ-*coalgebra.*

Note that if $\mathcal{R} : \text{Unk}(\mathcal{R}) \to T_\Sigma(\text{Unk}(\mathcal{R}))$ is a flat simultaneous recursion, then the unique T_Σ-homomorphism $(\cdot)_\mathcal{R} : \text{Unk}(\mathcal{R}) \to \text{Tr}^\infty$ as in the commutative diagram:

$$
\begin{array}{ccc}
\text{Unk}(\mathcal{R}) & \xrightarrow{\ \mathcal{R}\ } & T_\Sigma(\text{Unk}(\mathcal{R})) \\
(\cdot)_\mathcal{R} \downarrow & & \downarrow T_\Sigma(\cdot)_\mathcal{R} \\
\text{Tr}^\infty & \xrightarrow{\ \omega\ } & T_\Sigma(\text{Tr}^\infty)
\end{array}
$$

exists by finality and is precisely the (unique) solution of $\mathcal{R}$.

Corollary 1. *(1) Every (flat) simultaneous recursion* $\mathcal{R}$ *has a unique solution in* Tr^∞.
(2) Let $(X_i)_\mathcal{R} = \tau_i$, *for* $X_i \in \text{Unk}(\mathcal{R})$. *Then* τ_i *is a regular tree.*

Proof. Point (1) follows immediately from the above remark, while for (2) it is enough to observe that every subtree of τ_i is among $\tau_1, \ldots, \tau_n$, hence the number of subtrees of τ_i is bounded by n.

Then, we inductively extend the solution $(\cdot)_\mathcal{R} : \mathrm{Unk}(\mathcal{R}) \to \mathrm{Tr}^\infty$ of $\mathcal{R}$ to the mapping $(\cdot)_\mathcal{R}^* : \mathsf{T}[\mathrm{Unk}(\mathcal{R})] \to \mathrm{Tr}^\infty$ as in definition 8. For types $A, B \in \mathsf{T}[\mathrm{Unk}(\mathcal{R})]$ we can now define when they are equivalent modulo $\mathcal{R}$, written $A \approx_\mathcal{R} B$:

Definition 11. (i) $A \approx_\mathcal{R} B$ *if, and only if,* $(A)_\mathcal{R}^* = (B)_\mathcal{R}^*$.
(ii) $\mathcal{T}_\mathcal{R}$ *denotes the type structure* $\langle \mathsf{T}[\mathit{Unk}(\mathcal{R})], \approx_\mathcal{R} \rangle$.

Observe that the type structure $\mathcal{T}_\mathcal{R}$ is trivially invertible.

Example 3. Take $\mathcal{R}_1$ and $\mathcal{R}_2$ as defined in Example 2. Both X_1 and X_2 have the same interpretation as infinite trees, and so $X_1 \approx_{\mathcal{R}_1 \cup \mathcal{R}_2} X_2$.

3   Decidability of Weak μ-Equivalence

Both invertibility and decidability will be proved by defining a combinatory reduction system (CRS) which generates $\sim_\mu$ as its convertibility relation. For an introduction to term rewriting systems and CRS see e.g. [17] and [18].

Definition 12. *Let* $\Rightarrow_\mu \in \mathsf{T}_\mu \times \mathsf{T}_\mu$ *be the reduction relation defined by:*

1. $\mu t.A \Rightarrow_\mu A[t := \mu t.A]$.
2. *If* $A \Rightarrow_\mu A'$ *then*
   - $A \to B \Rightarrow_\mu A' \to B$
   - $B \to A \Rightarrow_\mu B \to A'$
   - $\mu t.A \Rightarrow_\mu \mu t.A'$.

As usual $\Rightarrow_\mu^n$ *denotes reduction in n steps and* $\Rightarrow_\mu^*$ *is the transitive and reflexive closure of* $\Rightarrow_\mu$.

As usual, a subexpression of a type B of the shape $\mu t.A$ is called a *redex*. The *contraction* of a redex in B is obtained by replacing the redex by the r.h.s. of the corresponding rule. The following lemma can be easily proved by induction on the size of proofs in $\sim_\mu$.

Lemma 2. *The relation* $\sim_\mu$ *is the convertibility relation generated by* $\Rightarrow_\mu$.

It is easy to see that $\langle \mathsf{T}_\mu, \Rightarrow_\mu \rangle$ is an orthogonal Combinatory Rewriting System (see [11]) and then it is Church-Rosser (CR).

Lemma 3. *The reduction relation* $\Rightarrow_\mu$ *is CR, i.e. if* $A \sim_\mu B$ *then there is a type* $C \in \mathsf{T}_\mu$ *such that* $A \Rightarrow_\mu^* C$ *and* $B \Rightarrow_\mu^* C$.

Note however that $\Rightarrow_\mu$ is not normalizing: types can be infinitely unfolded. The CR property however is enough to prove invertibility.

Theorem 2. $\sim_\mu$ is invertible, i.e. $A_1 \to B_1 \sim_\mu A_2 \to B_2$ implies $A_1 \sim_\mu A_2$ and $B_1 \sim_\mu B_2$.

Proof. By Lemma 3 there is a type C such that $A_1 \to B_1 \Rightarrow_\mu^* C$ and $A_2 \to B_2 \Rightarrow_\mu^* C$. But then we must have $C \equiv C_1 \to C_2$ and then $A_i \Rightarrow_\mu^* C_1$ and $B_i \Rightarrow_\mu^* C_2$ for $i = 1, 2$. By Lemma 2 this implies $A_i \sim_\mu B_i$ for $i = 1, 2$.

To prove decidability we need some more properties of reduction systems. An important notion is that of standard reduction. We define this notion in the case of $\Rightarrow_\mu$.

Definition 13. *Let*
$$R : A_1 \Rightarrow_\mu A_2 \Rightarrow_\mu \ldots \Rightarrow_\mu A_n$$
Assume that at each step $A_i \Rightarrow_\mu A_{i+1}$ we mark with $*$ all μ occurring in A_i to the left of the contracted μ and assume that all starred μ remain such through the remaining steps of R. Then R is standard *if only non starred μ are reduced in it.*

In other words, a reduction is standard if reductions are performed from left to right (and from the outside in).

The following standardization theorem for $\Rightarrow_\mu$ can be obtained as a particular case of the standardization theorem for CRS. See [18] for a proof.

Lemma 4. *If $A \Rightarrow_\mu^* B$ then there is standard reduction from A to B.*

Definition 14. *If $A \in \mathsf{T}_\mu$ its subterm closure $SC(A) \subseteq \mathsf{T}_\mu$ is defined by cases in the following way.*

1. $SC(c) = \{c\}$ *if c is a variable or a constant.*
2. $SC(A_1 \to A_2) = \{A_1 \to A_2\} \cup SC(A_1) \cup SC(A_2)$
3. $SC(\mu t.A) = \{\mu t.A\} \cup SC(A[t := \mu t.A])$

The following Lemma is proved in [10, Theorem 2.3].

Lemma 5. *For all types $A \in \mathsf{T}_\mu$ $SC(A)$ is finite.*

Recall that $\vdash A = B$ if $A = B$ can be proved using the rules of system (μ) Definition 5(i). In the following definition we introduce a slightly different (but equivalent) system.

Definition 15. *The system (μ^-) is defined as the system (μ) of Definition 5(i) by replacing $(\mu\text{-eq})$, $(symm)$ and $(trans)$ by the following rules*

$$(\mu\text{-tr-left}) \quad \frac{\vdash A[t := \mu t.A] = B}{\vdash \mu t.A = B}$$

$$(\mu\text{-tr-right}) \quad \frac{\vdash A = B[t := \mu t.B]}{\vdash A = \mu t.B}$$

We write $\vdash^- A = B$ if $A = B$ is provable in (μ^-).

Lemma 6.
$$\vdash A = B \quad (i.e.\ A \sim_\mu B) \quad \Leftrightarrow \quad \vdash^- A = B.$$

Proof. The ($\Leftarrow$) direction is trivial since rules (μ-tr-left), (μ-tr-right) can be derived using (μ-eq) and (trans). As for ($\Rightarrow$), by Lemma 2 we have A and B are convertible under $\Rightarrow_\mu$ and then, by the CR property, there exists a type C such that $A \Rightarrow_\mu^n C$ and $B \Rightarrow_\mu^m C$ for some $n, m \geq 0$. Moreover by the standardization theorem 4 we can assume that both reductions are standard. The proof is now by induction on $n + m$.

If $m = n = 0$ then $A \equiv B$ and we are done.

The induction step is by induction on $|A| + |B|$ where $|T|$ denotes the number of $\to$ and μ operators occurring in T. The base step (A and B atomic) is trivial. In the induction step we distinguish the following cases.

<u>Case 1.</u> Let $A \equiv \mu t.A'$ and let $A \Rightarrow_\mu A'[t := \mu t.A'] \Rightarrow_\mu^{n-1} C$ (i.e. the first step in the reduction of A is an unfolding). By induction hypothesis we have $\vdash^- A'[t := \mu t.A'] = B$ and we can get $\vdash^- \mu t.A' = B$ by rule (μ-tr-left). The symmetric case on B is handled similarly using (μ-tr-right).

<u>Case 2.</u> Let $A \equiv \mu t.A'$, $B \equiv \mu t.B'$ and the first step in the reduction of both A and B is not by unfolding the leftmost μ. In this case, since the reduction is standard, the leftmost μ is never reduced in both A and B. Then we must have $C \equiv \mu t.C'$ and both $A' \Rightarrow_\mu^n C'$ and $B' \Rightarrow_\mu^n C'$. By induction hypothesis on the structure of types then we have $\vdash^- A' = B'$ and we can get $\vdash^- A = B$ by rule (μ).

<u>Case 3.</u> Let $A \equiv A_1 \to A_2$ and $B \equiv B_1 \to B_2$. In this case we must have $C \equiv C_1 \to C_2$ and both $A_1 \Rightarrow_\mu^{n_1} C_1$, $A_2 \Rightarrow_\mu^{n_2} C_2$, $B_1 \Rightarrow_\mu^{m_1} C_1$ and $B_2 \Rightarrow_\mu^{m_2} C_2$ where $n = n_1 + n_2$ and $m = m_1 + m_2$ and then $n_1, n_2 \leq n$, $m_1, m_2 \leq m$. By induction hypothesis on the structure of types then we have $\vdash^- A_1 = B_1$ and $\vdash^- A_2 = B_2$. So we can get $\vdash^- A = B$ by rule ($\to$).

Deductions in $\vdash^-$ are interesting for the following reason.

Lemma 7. (i) *Let $\mathcal{D}$ be a deduction of $\vdash^- A = B$ then all statements $A' = B'$ occurring in it are such that $A' \in \mathcal{SC}(A)$ and $B' \in \mathcal{SC}(B)$.*
   (ii) *It is decidable whether $\vdash^- A = B$.*

Proof. (i) By a straightforward induction on deduction.
(ii) Let $N = |\mathcal{SC}(A)|$ and $M = |\mathcal{SC}(B)|$. Let $\mathcal{D}$ be any deduction in $\vdash^- A = B$. By point (i) there are at most $M \cdot N$ possible distinct statements that can occur in $\mathcal{D}$. So we can assume that $\mathcal{D}$ has no branch of length greater then $M \cdot N$, since otherwise we can reduce the size of $\mathcal{D}$ by replacing the innermost occurrence of a statement $A' = B'$ in a branch of length greater then $M \cdot N$ by the outermost occurrence of the same statement. So there are only a finite number of possible deductions for $\vdash^- A = B$.

By Lemma 6 then we have the decidability of $\sim_\mu$

Theorem 3. *It is decidable whether $A \sim_\mu B$.*

4   Deciding Equivalence of Simultaneous Recursions

In this section we sketch a proof of the decidability of strong equivalence of simultaneous recursions. We are mainly interested in highlighting the coalgebraic characterization of the equivalence of simultaneous recursions $\mathcal{R}$ and $\mathcal{R}'$, in terms of the existence of a bisimulation between $Unk(\mathcal{R})$ and $Unk(\mathcal{R}')$: the definition of the right notion of bisimulation follows from general coalgebraic notions and our characterization of (flat) simultaneous recursions as coalgebras. To our knowledge, this characterization does not seem to have been exploited in the literature on recursive types (for a different application of coinductive techniques to recursive types, see e. g. [19]).

Definition 16. *Given two simultaneous recursions $\mathcal{R}_1, \mathcal{R}_2$, we define a bisimulation between $Unk(\mathcal{R}_1)$ and $Unk(\mathcal{R}_2)$ to be a binary relation $R \subseteq Unk(\mathcal{R}_1) \times Unk(\mathcal{R}_2)$ such that the following conditions hold.*
For all $X \in Unk(\mathcal{R}_1)$ and $Y \in Unk(\mathcal{R}_2)$ such that XRY

- *either $X = X_1 \rightarrow X_2 \in \mathcal{R}_1$ and $Y = Y_1 \rightarrow Y_2 \in \mathcal{R}_2$ and X_1RY_1 and X_2RY_2;*
- *or $X = \xi \in \mathcal{R}_1$ and $Y = \xi \in \mathcal{R}_2$ for some $\xi \in V \cup K$.*

Given two simultaneous recursions $\mathcal{R}_1$ and $\mathcal{R}_2$, they are bisimilar if there is a bisimulation $R \subseteq Unk(\mathcal{R}_1) \times Unk(\mathcal{R}_2)$.

There is a general characterization of bisimulations in categorical terms (see [5], and [4], for example). For the functor $T_\Sigma : \mathbf{Set} \rightarrow \mathbf{Set}$ that we have been using, a (categorical) bisimulation between sets A and B is a relation $R \subseteq A \times B$ for which there is a coalgebra structure $\rho : R \rightarrow T_\Sigma R$ such that the following diagram commutes

$$
\begin{array}{ccccc}
A & \xleftarrow{\;r_1\;} & R & \xrightarrow{\;r_2\;} & B \\
{\scriptstyle\mathcal{R}_1}\downarrow & & \downarrow{\scriptstyle\rho} & & \downarrow{\scriptstyle\mathcal{R}_2} \\
T_\Sigma A & \xleftarrow{T_\Sigma(r_1)} & T_\Sigma R & \xrightarrow{T_\Sigma(r_2)} & T_\Sigma B
\end{array}
\tag{6}
$$

where r_1 and r_2 are respectively the composites $R \hookrightarrow A \times B \xrightarrow{\pi_1} A$ and $R \hookrightarrow A \times B \xrightarrow{\pi_2} B$ and are therefore T_Σ-coalgebra homomorphisms. It is now a straightforward matter to prove the following:

Proposition 4. *For simultaneous recursions $\mathcal{R}$ and $\mathcal{R}'$, a relation $R \subseteq Unk(\mathcal{R}) \times Unk(\mathcal{R}')$ is a bisimulation if and only if the diagram (6) commutes for some $\rho : R \rightarrow T_\Sigma R$.*

Observe also that the following diagram, where S solves $\mathcal{R}$ and S' solves $\mathcal{R}'$,

$$
\begin{array}{ccc}
R & \xrightarrow{\;r_1\;} & Unk(\mathcal{R}) \\
{\scriptstyle r_2}\downarrow & & \downarrow{\scriptstyle S} \\
Unk(\mathcal{R}') & \xrightarrow{\;S'\;} & \mathsf{Tr}^\infty
\end{array}
$$

commutes, by finality of Tr^∞, because all mappings involved are coalgebra homomorphism (see [20]), hence we have the following result, stating that bisimilar unknowns have the same unfolding:

Corollary 2. *For simultaneous recursions $\mathcal{R}$ and $\mathcal{R}'$, if $\langle X, Y \rangle \in R$ for a bisimulation R between $Unk(\mathcal{R})$ and $Unk(\mathcal{R}')$, then $S(X) = S'(Y)$, where S solves $\mathcal{R}$ and S' solves $\mathcal{R}'$.*

Decidability of equivalence for simultaneous recursions has been proved by Courcelle, Kahn and Vuillemin [16] by direct means. Here we use coinduction, but first define precisely what it means for two simultaneous recursions to be equivalent. For a simultaneous recursion $\mathcal{R}$, equation $X_1 = C_1$ is the *principal equation* of $\mathcal{R}$, and X_1 the *principal unknown*.

Definition 17 (Equivalence of simultaneous recursions). *Let $\mathcal{R}_1 \approx \mathcal{R}_2$ be the equivalence relation which holds between simultaneous recursions $\mathcal{R}_1$ and $\mathcal{R}_2$ if and only if $S_1(X_1) = S_2(Y_1)$, where S_i is the solution of $\mathcal{R}_i$ and X_1, Y_1 are the principal unknowns of $\mathcal{R}_1, \mathcal{R}_2$, respectively.*

Now, given two simultaneous recursions $\mathcal{R}_1$ and $\mathcal{R}_2$, the following algorithm can be used to test whether $\mathcal{R}_1 \approx \mathcal{R}_2$ (this is a slight reformulation of the decision procedure described in [11]):

Definition 18. *Define sets of pairs $C^{(n)}, O^{(n)} \subseteq Unk(\mathcal{R}_1) \times Unk(\mathcal{R}_2)$ by the following algorithm:*

- *Let $C^{(0)} = \emptyset$ and $O^{(0)} = \{\langle X_1, Y_1 \rangle\}$;*
- *while $O^{(n)} \neq \emptyset$ build $C^{(n+1)}, O^{(n+1)}$ from $C^{(n)}, O^{(n)}$ in the following way. Take any pair $\langle X, Y \rangle \in O^{(n)}$*
  - *if $X = X_1 \to X_2 \in \mathcal{R}_1$ and $Y = Y_1 \to Y_2 \in \mathcal{R}_2$ set:*
    - *$O^{(n+1)} = O^{(n)} - \{\langle X, Y \rangle\} \cup \{\langle X_i, Y_i \rangle \mid i = 1, 2 \text{ and } \langle X_i, Y_i \rangle \notin C^{(n)}\}$*
    - *$C^{(n+1)} = C^{(n)} \cup \{\langle X, Y \rangle\}$*
  - *if $X = \xi \in \mathcal{R}_1$ and $Y = \xi \in \mathcal{R}_2$ for some $\xi \in V \cup K$ then set:*
    - *$O^{(n+1)} = O^{(n)} - \{\langle X, Y \rangle\}$*
    - *$C^{(n+1)} = C^{(n)} \cup \{\langle X, Y \rangle\}$*
  - *otherwise stop reporting failure.*

It is easy to see that, since the number of equations in each system is finite, either this process stops with failure or eventually $O^{(n)} = \emptyset$ for some n. Furthermore:

Proposition 5. *$\mathcal{R}_1 \approx \mathcal{R}_2$ if and only if the algorithm stops after N steps without reporting failure. In this case the relation $C^{(N)}$ is a bisimulation.*

Finally, given types $A, B \in \mathsf{T}[Unk(\mathcal{R})]$, we can use the above algorithm to decide whether $A \approx_{\mathcal{R}} B$. Let

$$\mathcal{R}_A = \{Z = A\}$$
$$\mathcal{R}_B = \{Z' = B\}$$

where Z, Z' are new unknowns, and take the (flat) simultaneous recursions $\mathcal{R}_A \cup \mathcal{R}$ and $\mathcal{R}_B \cup \mathcal{R}$ with principal unknowns Z and Z' and solutions S_A and S_B, respectively. It is straightforward to prove that $S_A(Z) = (A)^*_{\mathcal{R}}$ and $S_B(Z') = (B)^*_{\mathcal{R}}$, hence $A \approx_{\mathcal{R}} B$ if and only if $\mathcal{R}_A \cup \mathcal{R} \approx \mathcal{R}_B \cup \mathcal{R}$.

References

1. Abadi, M., Cardelli, L.: A Theory of Objects. Springer-Verlag (1996)
2. MacQueen, D., Plotkin, G., Sethi, R.: An ideal model for recursive polymorphic types. Information and Control **71** (1986) 95–130
3. Cardone, F., Coppo, M.: Type inference with recursive types. Syntax and Semantics. Information and Computation **92** (1991) 48–80
4. Fiore, M.: A coinduction principle for recursive data types based on bisimulation. In: Proceedings Eighth Symposium on Logic in Computer Science, IEEE (1993)
5. Rutten, J.: Universal coalgebra: a theory of systems. Theoretical Computer Science **249** (2000) 3–80
6. Jones, S.: The Implementation of Functional Programming Languages. Prentice Hall (1987)
7. Statman, R.: Recursive types and the subject reduction theorem. Technical Report 94–164, Carnegie Mellon University (1994)
8. Marz, M.: An algebraic view on recursive types. Applied Categorical Structures **7(12)** (1999) 147–157
9. Coppo, M.: Type inference with recursive type equations. In Honsell, F., Miculan, M., eds.: FoSSaCS 2001. Volume 2030 of Lecture Notes in Computer Science., Springer (2001) 184–198
10. Brandt, M., Henglein, F.: Coinductive axiomatization of recursive type equality and subtyping. In de Groote, P., Hindley, J.R., eds.: Typed Lambda Calculi and Applications. Volume 1210 of Lecture Notes in Computer Science., Springer-Verlag (1997) 63–81
11. Ariola, Z., Klop, J.: Equational term graph rewriting. Fundamenta Informaticae **26** (1996) 207–240
12. Scott, D.: Some philosophical issues concerning theories of combinators. In Böhm, C., ed.: Lambda calculus and computer science theory. Volume 37 of Lecture Notes in Computer Science., Springer-Verlag (1975) 346–366
13. Breazu-Tannen, V., Meyer, A.: Lambda calculus with constrained types. In Parikh, R., ed.: Logics of Programs. Volume 193 of Lecture Notes in Computer Science., Springer-Verlag (1985) 23–40
14. Milner, R.: A Theory of Type Polymorphism in Programming. Journal of Computer and System Sciences **17** (1978) 348–375
15. Courcelle, B.: Fundamental properties of infinite trees. Theoretical Computer Science **25** (1983) 95–169
16. Courcelle, B., Kahn, G., Vuillemin, J.: Algorithmes d'équivalence et de réduction à des expressions minimales, dans une classe d'équations récursives simples. In: Proceedings of the 2nd International Colloquium on Automata, Languages and Programming. Volume 14 of Lecture Notes in Computer Science., Springer-Verlag (1974) 200–213
17. Klop., J.: Term rewriting systems. In S. Abramsky, D.M.G., Maibaum, T.S.E., eds.: Handbook of Logic in Computer Science. Oxford University Press, New York (1992) 1–116
18. Klop, J.W., van Oostrom, V., van Raamsdonk, F.: Combinatory reduction systems: Introduction and survey. Theoretical Computer Science **121** (1993) 279–308
10. Cardone, F.: A coinductive completeness proof for the equivalence of recursive types. Theoretical Computer Science **275** (2002) 575–587
20. Turi, D., Rutten, J.: On the foundations of final semantics: Non-standard sets, metric spaces, partial orders. Mathematical Structures in Computer Science **8** (1998) 481–540

Algebraic Theories for Contextual Pre-nets*

Roberto Bruni[1], José Meseguer[2], Ugo Montanari[1], and Vladimiro Sassone[3]

[1] Dipartimento di Informatica, Università di Pisa, Italia
{bruni,ugo}@di.unipi.it
[2] University of Illinois at Urbana-Champaign, IL, USA
meseguer@cs.uiuc.edu
[3] COGS, University of Sussex, Brighton, UK
vs@susx.ac.uk

Abstract. The algebraic models of computation for contextual nets that have been proposed in the literature either rely on a non-free monoid of objects, or introduce too many fictitious behaviors that must be somewhat filtered out. In this paper, we exploit partial membership equational logic to define a suitable theory of models, where the meaningful concurrent computations can be selected by means of membership predicates.

1 Introduction

Thanks to their friendly formulation as multiset rewrite systems and to their graphical presentation, Petri nets [25, 26] are an appealing formalism for the specification and study of concurrent and distributed systems: states consist of *token* distributions over the set of *places* and *transitions* can atomically fetch the tokens in their presets and generate new tokens according to their postsets. In particular, several transitions can execute concurrently when they work on mutually disjoint sets of tokens.

Contextual nets [24] (also introduced separately with different names, such as nets with read arcs [30], nets with test arcs [8], and nets with activator arcs [16]) encompass a non-destructive reading operation not present in the basic Petri net model. In fact, read arcs allow multiple concurrent readings of the same resource, an operation whose need arises naturally in many distributed systems, while the naïve encoding of read arcs as self-loops in ordinary Petri nets serializes all the accesses to read tokens with a dramatic loss of concurrency. Nets with read arcs have been used to model a variety of applications and phenomena, such as transaction serializability in databases [11], concurrent constraint programming [23], asynchronous systems [29], and analysis of cryptographic protocols [10].

As a drawback, the presence of read arcs introduces some complication in the mathematical characterization of computations, leading to the development of suitable extensions of well-studied domains and models for Petri nets. Extensions of this kind include: the asymmetric event structures of [2], the match-share categories of [13], and the monoids of places proposed in [17] and fully developed in [7] and in [22].

---

* Research supported by the FET-GC Project IST-2001-32747 AGILE, by the MIUR Project COFIN 2001013518 COMETA. The first author is also supported by an Italian CNR fellowship, and by the CS Department of the University of Illinois at Urbana-Champaign.

C. Blundo and C. Laneve (Eds.): ICTCS 2003, LNCS 2841, pp. 256–270, 2003.

In this paper we extend the so-called "Petri nets are monoids" approach initiated in [19] to find a neat algebraic characterization of the monoidal category of concurrent computations in the presence of read arcs. In particular, we improve upon [13], where such computations were shown to be faithfully embedded in a too large, freely generated category. Our approach is to define a typing discipline – expressed by membership predicates *term* : Sort in partial membership equational logic [18] – that characterizes in that category the valid computations, distinguishing them from "garbage" expressions. Moreover, by considering pre-nets as "implementations" of ordinary Petri nets (in the sense explained in [5] and recalled in Section 2), we are able to give a *functorial* construction, respecting the simulation morphisms between nets, a result not achieved in all previous proposals in the literature [17, 13, 7].

Synopsis. In Section 2 we summarize the techniques used for defining functorial models for Petri nets. Section 3 describes the technical problems arising when extending the approach to nets with read arcs, and Section 4 presents our solution. Section 5 gives our conclusions. Proofs omitted for space limitation can be found in the technical report [6].

We assume the reader has some familiarity with some basic concepts from category theory as, e.g., the notion of natural transformation, adjunction and monoidal category.

2   On the Algebraic Semantics of Petri Nets

Petri nets are one of the most studied models for concurrency, thanks to their natural representation of concurrent and distributed systems based on multiset rewriting. Their flexibility has encouraged many different semantical interpretations. In particular, an overall distinction can be drawn between *collective* and *individual token philosophies* (see, e.g., [14]). According to the collective token philosophy (*CTph*), net semantics should not distinguish between different tokens in the same place, because any such token is *operationally equivalent* to all the others. The individual token philosophy (*ITph*) says that the different origins and histories of tokens must be accounted for, because choosing different tokens can make an event causally dependent on different past events, and causal dependencies may influence the degree of concurrency in the computations. In the classical example below, for instance, after t_0 and t_1 have fired, a firing of t will look as caused by one of them and concurrent to the other, depending on which of two tokens in c is consumed. Also, two instances of t may fire concurrently that only differ in their causal histories.

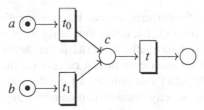

The "Petri nets are monoids" approach [19] is an algebraic approach to the analysis of concurrent semantics based on the observation that the monoidal structure of markings can be lifted to computations, in such a way that the suitably axiomatized terms of the new algebra exactly correspond to the concurrent computations of place/transitions

Petri nets (PT nets), according to the *CTph*. This construction respects the intuitive *simulation morphisms* between nets, when these are seen as graphs with structured nodes. This is expressed as a functor $\mathcal{T}$ from the category **Petri** of PT nets (as objects) and simulation morphisms (as arrows) to the category **CMonCat** of strictly symmetric strict monoidal categories (as objects) and monoidal functors (as arrows). Moreover, $\mathcal{T}$ is the left adjoint to an obvious forgetful functor from the full subcategory of **CMonCat** consisting of categories whose set of objects is a free monoid.

The *functorial* character of the construction is important for at least two reasons: (1) working within categories, we make explicit the associated *morphisms*, which correspond to appropriate notions of "simulation" or "refinement" between nets; (2) functors act on objects and behave consistently on their simulation maps, preserving them. Furthermore, when functors are *adjoints* they preserve limits or colimits, yielding good compositionality properties, since complex models can often be expressed as (co)limits of their simpler constituents [31].

Since the publication of [19], several studies have extended the functorial construction from the *CTph* towards the *ITph* [12, 21, 28]. Building on the notion of *process* presented in [15], the idea has been to take semantic models in the category of *symmetric monoidal categories*. But all the proposed constructions lacked functoriality. The difficulty in dealing with the *ITph* is that net morphisms in **Petri** allow replacing two different tokens a and b in the source net by, say, the same token c in the target net. In this way, an ambiguity about the origin of c is introduced that confuses causal histories in the target net and makes a functorial treatment impossible. A first solution was proposed in [28] based on pseudo functors (see also [21]).

In [5], we introduced *pre-nets*, which are more suitable than PT nets to be given a functorial semantics according to the *ITph*. A pre-net is essentially an implementation of a PT net, where the abstract data structure of multisets is refined into a more concrete *string* structure, and where each transition $t: u \to v$ is simulated by *one*, arbitrarily fixed, linear implementation $t_{\bar{u},\bar{v}}: \bar{u} \to \bar{v}$ for some linearizations $\bar{u}$ and $\bar{v}$ of u and v [1]. Although resorting to pre-nets (instead of PT nets) might at first appear unnatural to net enthusiasts, our formal approach to the *ITph* benefits from several good properties:

- All the pre-net implementations of the same net share the same semantic model, i.e. the semantics is independent of the choice of linearizations.
- Algebraic models of pre-nets are freely generated and, as part of adjunctions, preserve colimit constructions, allowing a form of compositional reasoning.

In [5] it is shown that the construction can be conveniently expressed at the level of algebraic theories of the form (Σ, E), rather than at the level of their categories of models, i.e. of (Σ, E)-algebras. Essentially, if PETRI is the theory of PT nets and CMONCAT is the theory of strictly symmetric monoidal categories, then there is a theory morphism form PETRI to CMONCAT that induces a forgetful functor between the category of CMONCAT-algebras (i.e., strictly symmetric monoidal categories) and the category of

---

[1] We observe, lest confusion arises, that pre-nets differ sharply from phrase-structure grammars, because pre-nets do not distinguish between terminal and non-terminal symbols, and strings can be permuted before performing any step. Grammars only generate monoidal categories, with no symmetries.

PETRI-algebras (i.e., PT nets). The left-adjoint to this forgetful functor is the free construction that associates to each PT net the strictly symmetric monoidal category of its concurrent computations. In such category, objects are the markings of the net, arrows are computations, (arrow) composition models progression in time of a computation, while tensor product accounts for concurrent activities. For instance, in the example above, $t_0;t$ represents the sequential execution of t_0 and t, while $t_0 \otimes t_1$ stands for the concurrent firing of t_0 and t_1. In the individual token philosophy, the strict symmetry – characteristic of the collective token interpretation – must be given up to model the causal flows of tokens in computations. The order of transitions in a parallel composition, say $t_0 \otimes t_1$, determines the order of tokens "in the output" and, consequently, the causal connections to the activities that may follow. For instance, $(t_0 \otimes t_1) ; (t \otimes id_c)$ represents the computation where t depends causally on t_0 (that is, it consumes the instance of c generated by that transitions). We are allowed to exchange t_0 and t_1 in the tensor product only if we keep track of this and maintain the correct order of output tokens, as e.g. in $(t_1 \otimes t_0) ; \gamma; (t \otimes id_c)$, for γ the swap symmetry on $c \otimes c$. (A thorough discussion and the details are given, e.g., in [27], but see also [12, 21].) As explained above, we can relate the theory PRENETS of *pre-nets* (where pre- and post-sets of transitions are taken in the free monoid of places instead than in the free commutative monoid) to the theory SMONCAT of symmetric monoidal categories (details in [5]).

The above-mentioned theories can be conveniently expressed in *partial membership equational logic* (**PMEqtl**, see [18, 20] for self-contained presentations), taking advantage of membership predicates and subsorting to model objects as a special kind of arrows (the identities), and of partiality to model sequential composition, defined only if the codomain of the first arrow coincides with the domain of the second arrow. Moreover, the notion of tensor product of theories allows a more modular presentation of concepts; for example, we can define the theory of monoidal categories as the tensor product of the theory of monoids and that of categories.

3   Atoms, Electrons and Match-Share Categories

The extension of the approach to nets with read arcs has been considered in [7], by relying on non-free monoids of objects, and in [13], exploiting match-share categories in place of symmetric monoidal categories.

Regarding [7], the idea is to model each token a as an *atom* that can emit "negative" particles a^- (*electrons*) while keeping track of their number, i.e., as suggested in [17], we have that for all $k \in \mathbb{N}$, $a = a^k \otimes \bigotimes_{i=1}^k a^-$, where a^k represents an atom that has released exactly k particles to the environment. Then, by replacing context arcs on a with self-loop arcs on a^-, we obtain an axiomatic construction of the monoidal category of concurrent net computations. The approach of [7] deals satisfactorily with both the collective and the individual token philosophy; possibly, a remaining concern is that non-free monoids of objects sit uneasily with the traditional intuition of tokens as atomic pieces of data that one should not be able to decompose. The problem with the construction in [13] is instead that the freely generated model of computations has too many arrows, representing spurious computations that contextual nets cannot perform.

In this paper we improve upon [13] by selecting suitable theories in partial membership equational logic in order to distinguish 'good' arrows – corresponding to computations – from meaningless ones.

```
ops d(_) c(_): Arrow -> Object.     *** domain and codomain
op  _⊗_: Arrow -> Object.           *** monoidal product
op  e : Object.                     *** unit of _⊗_
op  _;_ .                           *** Arrow composition (partial op.)
op  γ(_,_): Object Object -> Arrow. *** symmetric natural transformation
```

Fig. 1. Operators in SMONCAT.

We refer the reader to the appendix of [5] for the essentials of partial membership equational logic. Instead, for the reader's convenience, we summarize in Appendix A the description of the theories of monoids, categories, monoidal categories and symmetric monoidal categories. Here we just remark that SMONCAT includes two sorts called Object and Arrow (with Object a subsort of Arrow, written Object < Arrow), and six operators (see Figure 1) satisfying the axioms of symmetric monoidal categories.

The idea presented in [13] is to model multiple concurrent readings by introducing in the class of net computations suitable transformations that take care of creating as many copies as needed (*sharing* phase) and then reassembling all copies after the reading (*matching* phase). These two transformations are called duplicators and co-duplicators and are denoted by ∇ and Δ respectively. It is worth observing that they are "non-natural", in the technical sense that the naturality axioms $f; \nabla = \nabla; f \otimes f$ and $\Delta; f = f \otimes f; \Delta$ are not enforced.

The theory of match-share categories is summarized in Figure 2. The right-hand side of the figure gives a pictorial representation of the main axioms of the left-hand side. The first group of axioms expresses the coherence of ∇ (defining the domain and codomain of each component of ∇, stating that the unit e is trivially shared and that the component for $a \otimes b$ can be expressed in terms of the components for a and b, the last two axioms roughly establishing that sharing is associative and commutative), and the second group that of Δ. The third group of axioms states how the two transformations interact together. If we look at $\nabla(a)$ as a wiring establishing two connections between the object a in the domain and the occurrences of a in the codomain, and dually for $\Delta(a)$, the last two axioms say that the multiplicity of connections is not important, and that connections are bidirectional, i.e. it is not important how objects are connected but just the fact that they are connected by an undirected path of "wiring."

The theory of match-share categories is a conservative extension of the theory of symmetric monoidal categories and therefore the construction between (pre-)nets and symmetric monoidal categories can be straightforwardly extended to match-share categories. For modeling read arcs, the idea is to first view read arcs as self-loops (i.e. pairs of inbound and outbound arcs), so that a transition $t: u \xrightarrow{w} v$ from u to v in context w is regarded as an ordinary pre-net transition $[t]: u \otimes w \longrightarrow v \otimes w$, and then apply the free construction to the resulting pre-net, building a match-share category of computations. The special role of w – a "context" marking represented as an ordinary one – is dealt with by copying ∇ and matching Δ. This however generates arrows that do not represent admissible computations of the net. The construction is not resource-conscious, and the distinction between read arcs and pre/post-sets is lost, since each token can be matched and shared in all possible ways.

```
fth MSCAT is
  including SMONCAT.
  ops ∇(_) Δ(_) : Object -> Arrow.

  vars a b : Object.

  eq  d(∇(a)) = a.
  eq  c(∇(a)) = a⊗a.
  eq  ∇(e) = e.
  eq  ∇(a⊗b) = (∇(a)⊗∇(b));(a⊗γ(a,b)⊗b).
  eq  ∇(a);(∇(a)⊗a) = ∇(a);(a⊗∇(a)).
  eq  ∇(a);γ(a,a) = ∇(a).
  eq  d(Δ(a)) = a⊗a.
  eq  c(Δ(a)) = a.
  eq  Δ(e) = e.
  eq  Δ(a⊗b) = (a⊗γ(b,a)⊗b);(Δ(a)⊗Δ(b)).
  eq  (Δ(a)⊗a);Δ(a) = (a⊗Δ(a));Δ(a).
  eq  γ(a,a);Δ(a) = Δ(a).

  eq  ∇(a);Δ(a) = a.
  eq  Δ(a);∇(a) = (a⊗∇(a));(Δ(a)⊗a).
endfth
```

Fig. 2. Theory of match-share categories.

On the other hand, once we replace read arcs with self-loops, we can form the free symmetric monoidal category of computations of the pre-net. Such category distinguishes arrows that represent the same concurrent computation, in that the construction enforces sequentialization of all multiple readings of the same resource. For instance, if $t: a \xrightarrow{c} b$, the fact that t can fire two concurrent instances from $a \otimes a \otimes c$ will not be reflected. However, the monoidal and the match-share category can be combined via a mapping from the former to the latter that: (1) identifies all computations that are distinguished because of the order in which multiple readings are performed; and (2) selects only the admissible computations of the net with read arcs.

Notation. Let R be a pre-net with read arcs. We denote by $[R]$ the pre-net with the same places as R and transitions $\{[t]: u \otimes w \longrightarrow v \otimes w \mid t: u \xrightarrow{w} v \in R\}$. Moreover, we let $S([R])$ denote the free symmetric monoidal category generated by $[R]$ and let $\mathbf{MS}([R])$ denote the free match-share category generated by $[R]$.

Definition 1. *The symmetric monoidal functor* $\mathcal{E}: S([R]) \to \mathbf{MS}([R])$ *is defined on generators by:*

$$\mathcal{E}(a) \stackrel{\text{def}}{=} a \qquad \qquad \textit{(for any place } a \in R)$$

$$\mathcal{E}([t]) \stackrel{\text{def}}{=} (u \otimes \nabla_w);([t] \otimes w);(v \otimes \Delta_w) \qquad \textit{(for any transition } t: u \xrightarrow{w} v \in R).$$

```
fth RAUT is including MON.
 sort Rtrans.
 subsort Monoid < Rtrans.
 ops pre(_) post(_) ctx(_) : Rtrans -> Monoid.
 var u : Monoid.
 eq  pre(u) = e.
 eq  post(u) = e.
 eq  ctx(u) = u.
endfth.
```

Fig. 3. Theory of read-automata.

Proposition 1 (cfr. [13]). *The image $\mathcal{E}(\mathbf{S}([R])) \subseteq \mathbf{MS}([R])$ is isomorphic (via a symmetric monoidal functor) to the category of concatenable contextual processes of R.*

The question that then arises is how to tell whether an arrow of $\mathbf{MS}([R])$ belongs to $\mathcal{E}(\mathbf{S}([R]))$. We answer this by reformulating the construction at the level of theories in partial membership equational logic, thus expressing a typing discipline for discarding all meaningless arrows from $\mathbf{MS}([R])$, while keeping all the good ones.

4   Functorial Models for Pre-nets with Read Arcs

The first step is to define the theory of "programs," that is our base category of nets. It is technically convenient to consider a larger class of nets, whose states are elements of a generic, non-free monoid, as expressed in Figure 3. The class of pre-nets with read arcs is then embedded as the full subclass whose states are free monoids (generated from the set of places), and the results can be extended via the obvious embedding.

The theory RAUT has three operations, pre(_), post(_), and ctx(_), that define respectively source, target and (read) context of each read-transition in Rtrans. Idle transitions are included by the subsorting relation Monoid < Rtrans. The sort Monoid comes from the theory MON of monoids, consisting of a total operation $\otimes$ which is associative and has the constant e as unit (see Figure 9 in Appendix A).

The second step is to refine the theory MSCAT into a theory RCOMP by adding sorts and operators that are needed to characterize the class of meaningful arrows. Thus, we add two sorts Rtrans and Rarrow, with Object < Rtrans < Rarrow < Arrow: the sort Rtrans is for embedding basic transitions, and the sort Rarrow is for collecting all correct computations. Among the operators, we add those of RAUT for source, target and context of basic transitions (i.e., pre(_), post(_), and ctx(_)). Note that these operators, unlike those for domain and codomain (i.e., d(_) and c(_)), are not defined for all arrows, but only for the elements of Rtrans. Note also that they are related to the domain and codomain of transitions by the first two equations of the theory. The membership axioms state that the sort Rarrow is closed under monoidal and sequential composition and that it contains all the symmetries. The main novel ingredient is the operator mk(_), which models the embedding $\mathcal{E}$ described above, namely $mk(t) = [t]$, for any transition t, as expressed by the last equation of the theory. The presence of mk(_) is also technically convenient to prove the main correspondence results.

```
fth RCOMP is including MSCAT.
  sorts Rtrans Rarrow.    subsorts Object < Rtrans < Rarrow < Arrow.
  ops pre(_) post(_) ctx(_) : Rtrans -> Object.
  op  mk(_) : Rtrans -> Arrow.
  vars h k : Rarrow.    var t : Rtrans.    var u : Object.
  mb  h⊗k : Rarrow.
  mb  γ(u,v) : Rarrow.
  cmb h;k : Rarrow    if c(h) == d(k).
  eq  pre(t)⊗ctx(t) = d(t).
  eq  post(t)⊗ctx(t) = c(t).
  eq  pre(u) = e.
  eq  post(u) = e.
  eq  ctx(u) = u.
  eq  d(mk(t)) = d(t).
  eq  c(mk(t)) = c(t).
  eq  mk(u) = u.
  eq  (pre(t)⊗∇(ctx(t)));(mk(t)⊗ctx(t));(post(t)⊗Δ(ctx(t))) = t.
endfth.
```

Fig. 4. Theory of read-computations.

```
view RV from RAUT to RCOMP is
  sort Monoid to Object.
endview.
```

Fig. 5. The view RV.

The third step is to express the adjunction between the class of programs and that of models. This task is accomplished by the signature morphism RV in Figure 5, which embeds homonym sorts and operators and maps the sort Monoid of RAUT to the sort Object of RCOMP. It is easy to verify that all axioms in RAUT are respected by RV:

Proposition 2. *The view RV is a theory morphism.*

By Proposition 2 and because of the properties of theory morphisms [18], we know that there is a right-adjoint forgetful functor $\mathcal{U}_{RV}$ from the category of RCOMP-algebras to the category of RAUT-algebras, which includes all pre-nets with read arcs. We denote by $\mathcal{F}_{RV}$ the left-adjoint going in the opposite direction.

Lemma 1. *Given a pre-net with read arcs R, its initial RCOMP-algebra $\mathcal{F}_{RV}(R)$ is a match-share category.*

Proof. The free functor $\mathcal{F}_{RV}$ ensures that the elements of sort Arrow of $\mathcal{F}_{RV}(R)$ are built by composing objects, transitions $t \in R$, symmetries and (co-)duplicators, together with the additional elements $mk(t)$ for any $t \in R$. The axioms of match-share categories are enforced on all the elements of Arrow by inclusion of the theory MSCAT into RCOMP.   □

The fourth and final step is to show that the sort Rarrow can be used to characterize all meaningful computations of R. For the following definition, we recall that a lluf subcategory **A** of a category **C** is just a subcategory having all the objects of **C**.

Definition 2. *Given a pre-net with read arcs R, we let* Rarrow(R) *denote the lluf sub-category of the match-share category* $\mathcal{F}_{RV}(R)$ *whose arrows have sort* Rarrow.

Lemma 2. *For any pre-net with read arcs R, an element t has sort* Rtrans *in* $\mathcal{F}_{RV}(R)$ *if and only if t is a transition of R or t is a string of places.*

Lemma 3. *The category* Rarrow(R) *is symmetric monoidal.*

Theorem 1. *The category* **MS**([R]) *is isomorphic (via a match-share functor* S*) to* $\mathcal{F}_{RV}(R)$*.*

Proof. The match-share category $\mathcal{F}_{RV}(R)$ is generated by composing t and mk(t) (for any transition t) with identities, symmetries and (co-)duplicators in all possible ways. Any expression of sort Arrow can be equivalently expressed as the parallel and sequential composition of just the mk(t)'s with identities, symmetries and (co-)duplicators, because of the equation

eq (pre(t)⊗∇(ctx(t)));(mk(t)⊗ctx(t));(post(t)⊗Δ(ctx(t))) = t.

that allows replacing all occurrences of t. Note that if $t = u$ for some object u, then mk(u) = u. Hence the constructor mk($\_$) cannot be applied to identities for generating new arrows. Moreover, no other axioms involving t : Rtrans are present that could further quotient out the elements of sort Arrow.

Let us consider the match-share functor S: **MS**([R]) → $\mathcal{F}_{RV}(R)$ sending [t] to mk(t) (and being the identity otherwise) which is well-defined by initiality of **MS**([R]). The functor S is full and faithful, it preserves symmetries and (co-)duplicators, and it defines an isomorphism on objects (and thus on arrows).   □

Theorem 2. *The category* $\mathcal{E}(\mathbf{S}([R]))$ *is isomorphic (via a symmetric monoidal functor* $\mathcal{R}$*) to* Rarrow(R)*.*

Proof. The functor $\mathcal{R}$ is S restricted to $\mathcal{E}(\mathbf{S}([R]))$. In fact, suppose that $\alpha \in \mathcal{E}(\mathbf{S}([R]))$, then an arrow $\beta \in \mathbf{S}([R])$ must exist such that $\mathcal{E}(\beta) = \alpha$. Let Q: $\mathbf{S}([R]) \rightarrow$ Rarrow(R) be the symmetric monoidal functor sending [t] to t and preserving identities, symmetries, sequential composition and monoidal composition. Then it is straightforward that $S(\alpha) = Q(\beta)$ and hence $S(\alpha)$ has sort Rarrow. The functor $\mathcal{R}$ is an isomorphism because it is injective on the generators (the transitions of the net) and preserves the operations of symmetric monoidal categories strictly.   □

Note that the categories $\mathcal{E}(\mathbf{S}([R]))$ and Rarrow(R) are not match-share categories, and hence the functor $\mathcal{R}$ is not a match-share functor.

Theorem 2 defines a typing discipline for selecting the admissible computations from the larger class **MS**([R]). Since, under appropriate assumptions [3], membership predicates allow automated verification in languages like Maude [9], then the construction RV answers to the ambiguity of $\mathcal{E}$.

Note that for the arrows in Rarrow(R) only the operations of domain and codomain are defined, not those involved with contexts. However, the properties of the initial model can be exploited to factor out the domain and codomain of arrows in Rarrow(R) into their consumed, read and produced parts. We show this below.

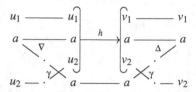

Fig. 6. A read object a for the arrow h.

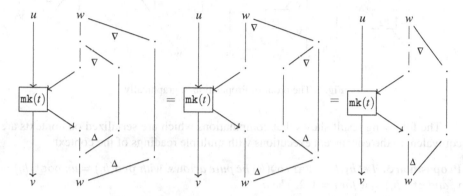

Fig. 7. The proof of Lemma 4, graphically.

Definition 3. *Let $h \in \mathtt{Rarrow}(R)$ and let a be an object with $\mathsf{d}(h) = u_1 \otimes a \otimes u_2$ and $\mathsf{c}(h) = v_1 \otimes a \otimes v_2$ for suitable objects u_1, u_2, v_1, v_2. The object a is said to be read in h if h can be written as (cf. Figure 6):*

$$\bigl(u_1 \otimes \nabla(a) \otimes u_2\bigr); \bigl(u_1 \otimes a \otimes \gamma(a, u_2)\bigr); \bigl(h \otimes a\bigr); \bigl(v_1 \otimes a \otimes \gamma(v_2, a)\bigr); \bigl(v_1 \otimes \Delta(a) \otimes v_2\bigr).$$

Lemma 4. *Let $t : \mathtt{Rtrans}$. Then, $\mathtt{ctx}(t)$ is read in h.*

The proof is graphically illustrated in Figure 7, where for simplicity we let $u = \mathtt{pre}(t)$, $v = \mathtt{post}(t)$ and $w = \mathtt{ctx}(t)$. The marking read – and not consumed – by h is the maximum marking read by h, and it can be characterized as follows.

Definition 4. *Let $h \in \mathtt{Rarrow}(R)$. The arrow h is pure if $\mathsf{d}(h) = u \otimes w$ and $\mathsf{c}(h) = v \otimes w$, with $(u \otimes \nabla(w)); (h \otimes w); (v \otimes \Delta(w)) = h$ and no other object in u and v is read. The object w is called the* context *of h and denoted by $\mathtt{ctx}(h)$, while u and v are denoted respectively by $\mathtt{pre}(h)$ and $\mathtt{post}(h)$.*

For h pure, we denote by $\widehat{h}$ the *twisted* version of h obtained by exchanging the position of the context with that of the pre- and post-set (respectively, in the domain and codomain of h), i.e. $\widehat{h} = \gamma(w, u); h; \gamma(v, w)$.

Corollary 1 (From Lemma 4). *Any arrow $h \in \mathtt{Rtrans}(R)$ is pure.*

Lemma 5. *Let $h \in \mathtt{Rarrow}(R)$ be pure, with $\mathtt{pre}(h) = u$, $\mathtt{post}(h) = v$ and $\mathtt{ctx}(h) = w$. Then $\widehat{h} \in \mathtt{Rarrow}(R)$ and $\widehat{h} = (\nabla(w) \otimes u); (w \otimes \widehat{h}); (\Delta(w) \otimes v)$.*

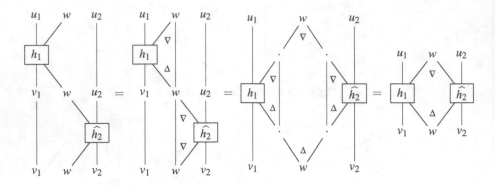

Fig. 8. The proof of Proposition 3, graphically.

The following result shows that computations which are serialized on contexts are equivalent to the concurrent executions with multiple readings of the context.

Proposition 3. *Let* $h_1, h_2 \in \mathtt{Rarrow}(R)$ *be pure arrows, with* $\mathtt{pre}(h_i) = u_i$, $\mathtt{post}(h_i) = v_i$ *and* $\mathtt{ctx}(h_i) = w$ *for* $i = 1, 2$. *Then:*

$$(h_1 \otimes u_2);(v_1 \otimes \widehat{h_2}) = (u_1 \otimes \nabla(w) \otimes u_2);(h_1 \otimes \widehat{h_2});(v_1 \otimes \nabla(w) \otimes v_2)$$
$$= (u_1 \otimes \widehat{h_2});(h_1 \otimes v_2)$$

Proof. The proof exploits Lemmas 4 and 5 and is (partially) illustrated in Figure 8:

- we first make explicit that the arrows h_1 and $\widehat{h_2}$ read the context w by applying the laws (valid for pure arrows):

$$h_1 = (u_1 \otimes \nabla(w));(h_1 \otimes w);(v_1 \otimes \Delta(w))$$
$$\widehat{h_2} = (\nabla(w) \otimes u_1);(w \otimes \widehat{h_2});(\Delta(w) \otimes v_1)$$

- then, we apply the axioms of match-share categories to rearrange the matching and sharing of w to have enough concurrent copies of it available at the same time and use functoriality of the tensor to shift h_1 and $\widehat{h_2}$ in parallel;
- finally, we get rid of additional copies by applying back the laws of pure arrows.

The equality with the expression where $\widehat{h_2}$ precedes h_1 is analogous. $\square$

5   Conclusion

Previous approaches to extending the "Petri nets are monoids" semantics to nets with read arcs have either relied on structured tokens or have defined a too rich category of computations, where it was difficult to filter out meaningless arrows. We have employed theories in partial membership equational logic to solve the latter problem.

Specifically, we have introduced a suitable theory RCOMP that provides us with a typing discipline to select all and only the correct concurrent computations. The theory

RCOMP enucleates the fundamental algebraic principles on which the non-trivial operation of *reading without consuming* is based on. The functorial construction presented in this paper has been reconciled with unfolding semantics in [1]. Moreover, as equational reasoning in **PMEqtl** is supported by the rewriting logic language Maude [9], the theory RCOMP offers a mathematical basis for the analysis and optimization of concurrent computations in systems with many-readers access policies to shared resources (e.g., for the applications of contextual nets in [11, 23, 29, 10]).

We conclude by mentioning that a non-initial match-share category of abstract models for nets with read arcs has been used in [4], based on categories of (co)spans in **Set**. However, the models in [4] do not retain all the information about the concurrent computations of the net: they just keep track of which resources have been read throughout the computation and thus can be concurrently accessed from the environment.

Acknowledgment

We warmfully thank Paolo Baldan for many interesting discussions on the semantics of contextual nets. We thank the anonymous referees for their criticisms and suggestions that helped us in preparing the final version.

References

1. P. Baldan, R. Bruni, and U. Montanari. Pre-nets, read arcs and unfolding: a functorial presentation. *Proc. WADT 2002, LNCS*. Springer, 2003. To appear.
2. P. Baldan, A. Corradini, and U. Montanari. Contextual Petri nets, asymmetric event structures, and processes. *Inform. and Comput.*, 171(1):1–49, 2001.
3. A. Bouhoula, J.-P. Jouannaud, and J. Meseguer. Specification and proof in membership equational logic. *Theoret. Comput. Sci.*, 236:35–132, 2000.
4. R. Bruni and F. Gadducci. Some algebraic laws for spans (and their connections with multirelations). *Proc. RelMiS 2001, ENTCS* 44.3, Elsevier, 2001.
5. R. Bruni, J. Meseguer, U. Montanari, and V. Sassone. Functorial models for petri nets. *Inform. and Comput.*, 170(2):207–236, 2001.
6. R. Bruni, J. Meseguer, U. Montanari, and V. Sassone. Functorial models for contextual pre-nets. Technical Report TR-02-09, Computer Science Department, University of Pisa, 2002.
7. R. Bruni and V. Sassone. Two algebraic process semantics for contextual nets. *Advances in Petri Nets: Unifying Petri Nets, LNCS* 2128, pp. 427–456. Springer, 2001.
8. S. Christensen and N.D. Hansen. Coloured petri nets extended with place capacities, test arcs and inhibitor arcs. *Proc. ICATPN'93, LNCS* 691, pp. 186–205. Springer, 1993.
9. M. Clavel, F. Durán, S. Eker, P. Lincoln, N. Martí-Oliet, J. Meseguer, and J. Quesada. Maude: Specification and programming in rewriting logic. *Th. Comput. Sci.*, 285:187–243, 2002.
10. F. Crazzolara and G. Winskel. Events in security protocols. *Proc. CCS'01*, pp. 96–105. ACM, 2001.
11. N. De Francesco, U. Montanari, and G. Ristori. Modeling concurrent accesses to shared data via Petri nets. *Programming Concepts, Methods and Calculi*, IFIP Transactions A-56, pp. 403–422. North Holland, 1994.
12. P. Degano, J. Meseguer, and U. Montanari. Axiomatizing the algebra of net computations and processes. *Acta Inform.*, 33(7):641–667, 1996.

13. F. Gadducci and U. Montanari. Axioms for contextual net processes. *Proc. ICALP'98, LNCS* 1443, pp. 296–308. Springer, 1996.
14. R.J. van Glabbeek and G.D. Plotkin. Configuration structures. *Proc. LICS'95*, pp. 199–209. IEEE Computer Society Press, 1995.
15. U. Goltz and W. Reisig. The non-sequential behaviour of Petri nets. *Inform. and Comput.*, 57:125–147, 1983.
16. R. Janicki and M. Koutny. Semantics of inhibitor nets. *Inf. and Comput.*, 123(1):1–16, 1995.
17. J. Meseguer. Rewriting logic as a semantic framework for concurrency: A progress report. *Proc. CONCUR'96, LNCS* 1119, pp. 331–372. Springer, 1996.
18. J. Meseguer. Membership algebra as a logical framework for equational specification. *Proc. WADT'97, LNCS* 1376, pp. 18–61. Springer, 1998.
19. J. Meseguer and U. Montanari. Petri nets are monoids. *Inf. and Comp.* 88(2):105–155, 1990.
20. J. Meseguer and U. Montanari. Mapping tile logic into rewriting logic. *Proc. WADT'97, LNCS* 1376, pp. 62–91. Springer, 1998.
21. J. Meseguer, U. Montanari, and V. Sassone. Representation theorems for Petri nets. *Foundations of Computer Science: Potential - Theory - Cognition, to Wilfried Brauer on the occasion of his sixtieth birthday, LNCS* 1337, pp. 239–249. Springer, 1997.
22. J. Meseguer, P.C. Ölveczky, and M.-O. Stehr. Rewriting logic as a unifying framework for Petri nets. *Advances in Petri Nets: Unifying Petri Nets, LNCS* 2128, pp. 250–303. Springer, 2001.
23. U. Montanari and F. Rossi. Contextual occurrence nets and concurrent constraint programming. *Proc. Dagstuhl Seminar on Graph Transformations in Computer Science, LNCS* 776, pp. 280–295. Springer, 1994.
24. U. Montanari and F. Rossi. Contextual nets. *Acta Inform.*, 32:545–596, 1995.
25. C.A. Petri. *Kommunikation mit Automaten*. PhD thesis, Institut für Instrumentelle Mathematik, Bonn, 1962.
26. W. Reisig. *Petri Nets: An Introduction*. EATCS Monographs. Springer, 1985.
27. V. Sassone. An axiomatization of the algebra of Petri net concatenable processes. *Theoret. Comput. Sci.*, 170(1-2):277–296, 1996.
28. V. Sassone. An axiomatization of the category of Petri net computations. *Math. Struct. in Comput. Sci.*, 8(2):117–151, 1998.
29. W. Vogler. Efficiency of asynchronous systems and read arcs in Petri nets. *Proc. ICALP'97, LNCS* 1256, pp. 538–548. Springer, 1997.
30. W. Vogler. Partial order semantics and read arcs. *Proc. MFCS'97, LNCS* 1295, pp. 508–517. Springer, 1997.
31. G. Winskel and M. Nielsen. Models for concurrency. *Handbook of Logic in Computer Science*. Oxford University Press, 1995.

```
fth CAT is                            fth MON is
 sorts Object Arrow.                   sort Monoid.
 subsort Object < Arrow.               op e : -> Monoid.
 ops d(_) c(_) : Arrow -> Object.      op _⊗_ : Monoid Monoid -> Monoid
 op  _;_.                                 [assoc id: e].
 var     a : Object.                  endfth
 vars f g h : Arrow.
 eq  d(a) = a.                         fth MONCAT is
 eq  c(a) = a.                          MON ⊗ CAT renamed by (
 ceq a;f = f                            sort (Monoid,Object) to Object.
    if d(f) == a.                       sort (Monoid,Arrow) to Arrow.
 ceq f;a = f                            op e left to e.
    if c(f) == a.                       op _⊗_ left to _⊗_.
 cmb f;g : Arrow                        op _;_ right to _;_.
    if c(f) == d(g).                    op d(_) right to d(_).
 ceq c(f) = d(g)                        op c(_) right to c(_). ).
    if f;g : Arrow.                    endfth
 ceq d(f;g) = d(f)    if c(f) == d(g).
 ceq c(f;g) = c(g)    if c(f) == d(g).
 ceq (f;g);h = f;(g;h)    if c(f) == d(g) and c(g) == d(h).
endfth
```

Fig. 9. The theories CAT, MON, and MONCAT.

```
fth SMONCAT is including MONCAT.
 op γ(_,_) : Object Object -> Arrow.
 vars a a' b b' c : Object.    vars f f' : Arrow.
 eq   d(γ(a,b)) = a⊗b.
 eq   c(γ(a,b)) = b⊗a.
 eq   γ(a,e) = a.
 eq   γ(e,a) = a.
 eq   γ(a⊗b,c) = (a⊗γ(b,c));(γ(a,c)⊗b).
 cq   γ(a,b);γ(b,a) = a⊗b.
 ceq (f⊗f');γ(b,b') = γ(a,a');(f'⊗f)
     if d(f) == a and d(f') == a' and c(f) == b and c(f') == b'.
endfth
```

Fig. 10. The theory SMONCAT.

A   Theories in Partial Membership Equational Logic

The theory of categories CAT is defined in Figure 9. It has sorts Object and Arrow with Object $<$ Arrow. There are two unary total operations d(_) and c(_), for *domain* and *codomain*, and a binary composition _;_ defined iff the codomain of the first argument is equal to the domain of the second argument. By convention, functions with given domain and codomain are total on that domain and codomain. It is easy to check that a model of CAT is a category (in which objects coincide with identity arrows), and that CAT-homomorphisms are just functors (cf. [20] for the details).

The theory MON of monoids is even simpler (Figure 9). It has a unique sort Monoid and two total operators: the associative tensor $_- \otimes _-$ and the unit element e, which is the identity for $_- \otimes _-$. Then, by exploiting the tensor product of theories $\otimes$ defined in [20], the theory of monoidal categories can be obtained by combining the theories MON and CAT as illustrated in Figure 9. Note that the tensor product construction MON $\otimes$ CAT has the sort poset originated from the product of the two sort posets in MON and CAT and operators "*opM* left" and "*opC* right" for each operator *opM* in MON and *opC* in CAT. The axioms of MON $\otimes$ CAT are generated by combining the axioms of MON and CAT (see the appendix of [5] for details). The theory MONCAT just renames sorts and operators by a more friendly notation.

Finally, the theory of symmetric monoidal categories SMONCAT is defined in Figure 10, by adding the symmetric natural transformation $\gamma(_- , _-)$.

A Coalgebraic Description of Web Interactions*

Daniela Cancila** and Furio Honsell

Dipartimento di Matematica e Informatica
Università di Udine
Via delle Scienze 206, 33100 Udine, Italy
{cancila,honsell}@dimi.uniud.it
Tel. +39 0432 558417, Fax: +39 0432 558499

Abstract. We introduce a *coalgebraic* description of static *web sites*, whereby pages are modeled by their links to other pages together with some extra information. This information can be either related to the *contents* or to the *presentation* or to the *architecture* of the page, *etc.*, and its granularity can vary. This coalgebraic model provides a formal framework for the analysis of the design of single web sites and for the comparison of different sites. We give two alternative coalgebraic accounts of user *visits* to a web site, as they arise by extracting the information contained in the *log file* of the web server. The first one is defined in terms of the notion of injective *simulation*, the latter in terms of an appropriate *lax morphism* in *Rel*. These notions provide formal descriptions of user behaviours and can suggest formal tools for the study of the usability of a site.

Keywords: Web Site, Log File, User-Visit, Coalgebra, Coalgebraic Bisimulation, Simulation, Relators.

Introduction

The social and economic importance of the *World Wide Web* has increased enormously in recent years. Hence *web usability* issues have become essential in site development. Nielsen warns us: The user *"who clicks the mouse gets to decide everything. It is so easy to go elsewhere; all the competitors in the world are but a mouseclick away"* [14]. Therefore the notion of *web interaction* is crucial when dealing with usability. Intuitively, a web interaction occurs when a user *visits* a website.

In spite of the role of the World Wide Web, apart from recent attempts such as the one by J. Goguen on web interfaces, [7,8], no completely satisfactory formal model for dealing rigorously with web-design issues has yet been put forward.

In this paper, we explore the possibility of utilizing *coalgebraic* tools in the description of web sites, and we suggest a basic *coalgebraic* account of web interactions. We feel that this approach can provide a simple, but firm, foundation to a rigorous approach to web design and analysis.

---

* Research partially supported by the MIUR Project COFIN 2001013518 COMETA.
** Corresponding author.

C. Blundo and C. Laneve (Eds.): ICTCS 2003, LNCS 2841, pp. 271–283, 2003.

Coalgebras are algebraic structures *dual* to algebras. They can offer convenient abstract accounts of datastructures, when the focus is on *behaviour, observations, top-down recognition, etc.*, rather than on *compositional generation*. *F-coalgebras*, for F endofunctor on a category $\mathcal{C}$, provide a uniform categorical descritpion of the behaviour of *dynamical systems* and various kinds of *circular* and *infinite* objects [1, 2, 9, 5, 10, 18]. Furthermore, coalgebraic models give natural notions of *behavioural equivalences* between states of a dynamical system, and between dynamical systems themselves. Such equivalences can be *coinductively* characterized as *greatest coalgebraic bisimulations*. Moreover, the unique morphism from the coalgebra representing the system into the *final coalgebra* gives a *canonical model* of the system, where bisimilar states are equated.

In this paper we model *static websites* as coalgebras for the functor $\mathcal{A} \times \mathcal{P}_f(\_)$, where $\mathcal{P}_f$ denotes the finite powerset functor and $\mathcal{A}$ denotes, with varying granularity, page information, which can be either related to the *contents* or to the *presentation*, or to the *architecture* of the page, or *hyperlinks outgoing from the site*.

There is another coalgebraic approach to the *World Wide Web* in the literature due to Lisitsa and Sazonov, [11, 19]. They present an abstract hyperset model of the Web. Coalgebraically, this amounts to modeling the Web as a coalgebra for the (hyper)set functor $\mathcal{P}_f(\mathcal{L} \times \_)$, where $\mathcal{P}_f$ denotes the finite powerset functor and $\mathcal{L}$ is a set of labels for links. This model is link-oriented. Pages are modeled as sets of *"words"*, up to bisimilarity. Words carry a contents and a link component. "Real" links correspond to links to non-empty pages.

The coalgebraic description that we propose takes into account the notions of site and page information, and, unlike Sazonov's model, it is contents-oriented. Hence, we can naturally accomodate many features of web pages and web interactions. First of all, we give a coalgebraic account of *single* web sites, and pages are modeled not only in terms of their links but also of extra non-dynamic information which they can carry. This information can be related to the *contents*, including *hyperlinks outgoing from the site*, or to the *architecture* or *presentation* of the page, according to which aspect of page/site design we wish to focus on. The granularity of this information is not fixed, but in the case of contents, for example, it can range from the entire text to a set of keywords. Page bisimilarity in our abstract representation of web-sites immediately suggests what we feel are correct design principles, which reduce the disorientation in the user w.r.t. contents. We focus on *static* sites; in order to deal with dynamic sites, our model should be enriched with extra information modeling various classes of users. A more detailed comparison of our approach with Sazonov's appears in Section 3. Our coalgebraic model gives a formal framework for the analysis of (static) site design, and for the comparison of different sites in terms of coalgebraic bisimilarity.

In modeling *user visits*, we proceed realistically, namely we utilize only the information which can be extracted from the *log file* of the web server at the site, i.e. the file in which the users' activities concerning that site are registered. We give two alternative (but equivalent) coalgebraic accounts of a *user visit* to a web site. The first one is defined in terms of the notion of *simulation*, the latter in terms of an appropriate *lax coalgebra morphism* in a category of sets and relations between the coalgebra representing the visit and a suitable coalgebra induced by the site. In the latter we use the notion of *relator* [20, 17, 4]. Our coalgebraic account of user visits gives us a formal tool for studying *user behaviour*, and hence for analysing the *usability* of a site, which could fruitfully complement the more standard, but subjective methods of *heuristic evaluation* and *user testing*. In particular, we provide formal descriptions of various web design notions and properties, such as *user behavior*, *locality*, *reachability*. An interesting result of our analysis is that bisimilarity equivalence on sites can be expressed in terms of the *behavioural* equivalence on sites as can be gathered by considering the possible visits to them. This implies that also if we (can) assess the usability of a site in terms of the server-centred information contained in the log file, sites can be taken essentially up-to bisimilarity.

Synopsis. In Section 1, we present an overwiev of the features of the web which are of interest for our purposes. In Section 2, we present our coalgebraic model of web interactions. Comparison with related work and final remarks appear in Section 3. In the Appendix A, some basic notions on coalgebras are recalled.

A preliminary version of this paper was presented at the WADT02 Conference, Frauenchiemsee, Germany.

1 An Overview of Web

1.1 What Is a Website?

A website can be described as a set of web pages together with a link structure, for example a tree, a graph. Recently, Brajnik and Toppano[1] proposed a more analytical definition of a web site, accounting for extra features, which intervene in web design. More precisely, they view a site under three different (independent) perspectives: *contents, architecture*, and *presentation*. Therefore, a site is represented as a triple corresponding to the three aspects above. In particular, the contents part describes the topic of each page. Architectural aspects include the organization of the information, the navigation system, the labeling system [16]. Finally, the presentation part accounts for e.g. font and character size of each page. The main advantage of this approach is a reduction of the complexity in designing and analysing a site.

1.2 How Can We Gather Information on User Behaviour?

In the literature, there are three methods for obtaining information on user behaviour: *Usability Testing* (also known in the literature as *(Discount) User Testing*), *Questionary*, and the *Log File*. The first is a reproduction of the interaction between user and site. Questionaries provide subjective opinions of the

---

[1] private communication.

user on the site. Finally, the Log File is the only *objective* tool available for measuring the workload of a server. In the literature also *Heuristic Evaluation* is considered. This is a usability engineering method for discovering usability problems in a user interface design, so that they can be taken care of through an interactive design process [13]. Heuristic Evaluation does not tell us anything about user behaviour.

1.3   Log File

Broadly speaking, the *log file* is a set of lines. Each of these represents a user's request to a site. More precisely, user's requests are operations on a site, called *hits*. They measure the workload of the server (or rather, the program on the server that manages the interface with the web server).

At a lower level, an interaction between user and site is an interaction between the client of a user and the web server of a site via some protocol. Nowadays the most frequent web protocol is HTTP. In such an interaction, the web server registers the requests of the client on the log file. In the following example, we illustrate a fragment of a log file, where we highlight the first hit.

Example 1 (Fragment of Log File).

#**Software**: Microsoft Internet Information Server 4.0
#**Version**: 1.0
#**Date**: 2000-10-06 00:01:56
#**Fields**: date time c-ip cs-method cs-uri-stem sc-status sc-bytes cs-bytes
cs-version cs(User-Agent) cs(Referer)

$$\text{Hit} = \begin{cases} \text{2000-10-06 00:01:56 193.207.47.2 GET /TimeService.taf 200 174 143} \\ \text{HTTP/1.0 Tango+Application+Server/4.05.020+(WindowsNT/4.0;} \\ \text{+INTEL) -} \end{cases}$$

2000-10-06 00:03:33 209.73.164.40 GET /catalogo.taf 200 27254 284 HTTP/1.0
Scooter/2.0+G.R.A.B.+V1.1.0 -
2000-10-06 00:17:17 212.41.211.28 GET /images/pulsantiera_logo_Alias.gif 200
871 312 HTTP/1.1 Mozilla/4.0+(compatible;+MSIE+4.01;+Windows+98)
http://www.alias.it/
2000-10-06 00:17:18 212.41.211.28 GET /images/pulsantiera_internet.gif 200
1046 310 HTTP/1.1 Mozilla/4.0+(compatible;+MSIE+4.01;+Windows+98)
http://www.alias.it/

A hit represents each individual operation; that is, if a web page has four images, then we have five hits: four for loading the images, and one for loading the web page. Each hit consists of *fields*, such as date, time, and method. More particularly, these fields depend on the format of the log file.

At the beginning of the (fragment) of the log file, we marked by # some notes which help us in reading the hits. The *fields* are only a subset of those available in the Microsoft IIS format. Take for example the first hit. Then 2000-10-06 and 00:01:56 are the date and the GMT time of the request; 193.207.47.2

is the client address; GET is the method used for the client server interaction (called by the acronym cs); /TimeService.taf is the requested resource; the *status* field 200 means that the server satisfied the client request; 174 is the number of bytes sent from the server to the client (called by the acronym sc) whereas 143 is the number of bytes received by the client; HTTP/1.0 and Tango+Application+Server/4.05.020+(WindowsNT/4.0;+INTEL) are respectively the protocol version and the software used by the client in the interaction (note that we have also the information concerning the operating system); finally the *referer* field is the previous requested resource of the client, note that in the first hit the referer is not recordered (in fact we have "-") whereas in the last hit the referer is http://www.alias.it/.

The only information about the user registered in the log file is the IP address of the computer which she is using. Of course, there can be more users on the same computer, or the same user can be on more computers, but these situations are not described in the log file. Several algorithms have been introduced in the literature, in order to understand when several users have the same IP [15], but these algorithms are not normally available. Therefore, we choose to approximate users with IP addresses.

By a *user visit*, we mean the set of *page requests* to a site from the user, registered in the log file. Notice that we consider only *page* requests and not a generic request (e.g. for loading an image). This corresponds to selecting, in the log file, exactly the hits where the method is GET and the file has the extension .html. However, in general, not all pages visited by a user are registered in the log file, due to the mechanisms of *browser caching* and *Internet caching*.

1.4   Browser and Internet Caching

When a page is requested from a client to a server, it is usually loaded in the client's *cache*.
Take for example A= http://www.dimi.uniud.it, and suppose the user visits also a linked page, for example http://www.dimi.uniud.it/people. If the user returns to A, either via a *back link* or via an ordinary link, then the latter operation will not be registered in the server. In fact the user is visiting the copy-cache of A in her client. This gives rise to a GAP in the log file. More properly, we define a GAP as any path of the user on the graph of the site that is unregistered in the log file. In general, the cache memory depends on the architecture of the client. GAPs in the log file can be also due to Internet caching. The mechanism of Internet caching allows to recover a page from the cache memory of a server different from the one which has requested the page. This happens when a client requests a page of a site through another site (typically through a search engine), and the page is resident in the cache of the intermediate site.

Therefore, if we assume an "unlimited" cache memory for the user, which seems to be a good approximation in many concrete cases, then only "first visits" to web pages are registered in the log file. However, *not all* first visits are registered, due to Internet caching. For simplicity, we do not treat Internet caching in this paper.

2   The Coalgebraic Model

In this section, we illustrate our coalgebraic model of web interactions, and we analyse the properties captured by it. First, we give a coalgebraic account of a web site, whereby pages are modelled by their links together with some extra information. This information can be related either to the contents, including hyperlinks outgoing from the site, or to the architecture or to the presentation of the page, according to which aspect of page/site design we wish to focus on. Then, we give a coalgebraic account of user visits, as they can be defined on the basis of the information in the log file.

Rather than using ordinary Set Theory, we prefer we work in the category Set_U^* of *non-wellfounded sets* (or *hypersets*) with *Urelements* (*atoms*), i.e. sets of a universe with atoms satisfying an Antifoundation Axiom [6, 1]. Hypersets provide a very intuitive and convenient way of describing the final coalgebras for the functors involved in this paper, the function being the identity. In ordinary Set Theory this would not be so, and we would need some extra effort to grasp the shape of the final coalgebra. Furthermore, by so doing we make it more easy to compare our approach to Sazonov's.

2.1   Coalgebraic Description of Web Sites

We describe a site w.r.t. three parameters: contents, architecture, presentation. To this end, we define a set $\mathcal{A} \triangleq C \times A \times P$, where C, A, P are sets of atoms encoding contents, architecture, presentation information, respectively.

A web page p can then be represented by a (possibly circular) pair $(a, \{l_1 : p_1, \ldots, l_n : p_n\})$, where $l_i (\in \mathcal{L})$ is a link label in p and p_i is the page linked by l_i, and $a \in \mathcal{A}$ is the encoding of a contents related information on the page p. In this page representation, more than one link from one page to another is allowed. However, link labels are missing in the log file. Therefore, in our model, we assume that there is at most one link from one page to another. This allows us to simplify the above presentation of a web page p with $p = (a, \{p_1, \ldots, p_n\})$. Our assumption is also justified by the fact that it is a design principle to have at most one link from one page to another with the exception of textual links. We emphasize that $\{p_1, \ldots, p_n\}$ are a subset of the pages in the site, since our model is stricly based on the log file. Information of any external link, that is links from an inside page to a outside page can be registered in $\mathcal{A}$.

A (static) web site S, i.e. a set of (link connected) web pages closed under the relation induced by the links, is represented as a *coalgebra* for the functor $F_\mathcal{A}(X) : Set_U^* \rightarrow Set_U^*$ defined by $F_\mathcal{A}(X) \triangleq \mathcal{A} \times \mathcal{P}_f(X)$. For a set of pages S representing a site, the coalgebra structure $f_S : S \rightarrow F_\mathcal{A}(S)$ yields the identifier of the current page (state) and the pages reached via the links from the current page (the next states), i.e. $f_S(p) = (a, \{p_1, \ldots, p_n\})$.

We call *web-site coalgebra* a coalgebra for the functor $F_\mathcal{A}$ above.

Our coalgebraic description of a site induces a notion of *coalgebraic equivalence* on the web-pages of a given site:

Notion	Coalgebraic Description w.r.t. $F_A = A \times P_f(\ )$
Page	$p = (a, \{p_1, \ldots, p_n\})$, where $a \in A$
Site	F_A-coalgebra $f_S : S \to F_A(S)$ defined by $f_S(p) \triangleq \langle a, \{p_1, \ldots p_n\}\rangle$

Definition 1 (Web-page bisimilarity). *Let $f_S : S \to F_A(S)$ be a web-site coalgebra. Two pages $p_1, p_2 \in S$ are* coalgebraically equivalent *if there exists an F_A-bisimulation $R \subseteq S \times S$ relating p_1 and p_2. I.e. there exists a relation R such that $(p_1, p_2) \in R$, and moreover :*

$$(p, p') \in R \implies$$

i) $\pi_1 \circ f_S(p) = \pi_1 \circ f_S(p')$ *and*
ii) $\forall p_1 \in \pi_2 \circ f_S(p) \ \exists p_1' \in \pi_2 \circ f_S(p'). \ (p_1, p_1') \in R$ *and*
iii) $\forall p_1' \in \pi_2 \circ f_S(p') \ \exists p_1 \in \pi_2 \circ f_S(p). \ (p_1, p_1') \in R$.

Similarly, we introduce a *coalgebraic equivalence* between different sites:

Definition 2 (Web-site bisimilarity). *Two web-sites $f_S : S \to F_A(S)$ and $g_T : T \to F_A(T)$ are* coalgebraically equivalent *if there exists an F_A-bisimulation $R \subseteq S \times T$, i.e.*

$$(p, p') \in R \implies$$

i) $\pi_1 \circ f_S(p) = \pi_1 \circ g_T(p')$ *and*
ii) $\forall p_1 \in \pi_2 \circ f_S(p) \ \exists p_1' \in \pi_2 \circ g_T(p'). \ (p_1, p_1') \in R$ *and*
iii) $\forall p_1' \in \pi_2 \circ g_T(p') \ \exists p_1 \in \pi_2 \circ f_S(p). \ (p_1, p_1') \in R$.

According to the coalgebraic paradigm (see Appendix A), the image of the *unique* morphism from the coalgebra representing a site, (S, f_S) say, to the fi-nal F_A *coalgebra* provides the *canonical model* of the site, i.e the minimal (non redundant) web-site equivalent to (S, f_S).

Proposition 1 (Irredundant web-site). *Let (S, f_S) be a web-site coalgebra. Then the image of the* unique *morphism M_S from (S, f_S) into the final F_A-coalgebra* gives the *minimal (non redundant) web site equivalent to S w.r.t. the chosen page representation A, i.e. $M_S(p) = M_S(p')$ iff $p \sim_A p'$, where $\sim_A$ is the largest F_A-bisimulation.*

Clearly, in designing a web-site, one has to have very good reasons not to go for an irredundant web-site, given the contents A.

In our coalgebraic description of web pages, we have not fixed the parameter A, encoding page information. We can choose to model pages with different levels of abstraction, according to the analysis that we want to carry out. E.g., as far as contents, the finest description is obtained by taking the parameter C in $\mathcal{A}$ to encode the entire contents of pages. A coarser description can be obtained when C encodes just the titles of pages. The coarsest possible description is obtained by taking $C \triangleq 1$, where 1 is a one-element set, i.e. the final object in Set_U^*. This corresponds to disregarding contents information completely. Different levels of abstraction in the parameter $\mathcal{A}$ give rise to different functors related by (surjective) natural transformations, $\eta : F_{\mathcal{A}} \dashrightarrow F_{\mathcal{A}'}$; this represents the *abstraction procedure* from one representation to a coarser one. Correspondingly, the coalgebraic representations of a site w.r.t. $F_{\mathcal{A}}$ and $F_{\mathcal{A}'}$ are η-related. I.e. if (S, f_S) is the $F_{\mathcal{A}}$-coalgebra representation of a site, then $(S, \eta_S \circ f_S)$ is the $F_{\mathcal{A}'}$-coalgebra representation of the same site given by $F_{\mathcal{A}'}$. Moreover, as expected, page equivalence is preserved from the finer model to the coarser one.

Our coalgebraic model can be used to study the structure of a given web site. By choosing different levels of granularity for $\mathcal{A}$, we can detect contents (architecture, presentation) related pages or possibly useless page duplications. In particular, the coalgebraic model can capture naturally the property of *coherence* of a site. Informally, a site is *coherent* w.r.t. architecture, respectively presentation, if the corresponding choices are the same for all pages. This can be accounted for in our coalgebraic model, by showing that the site $F_{\mathcal{A}}$-coalgebra is also a site $F_{\mathcal{A}'}$-coalgebra for a suitable $\mathcal{A}'$. Intuitively, the three parameters of $\mathcal{A}$, (that is, contents, architecture and presentation) can be considered as three viewpoints on the site. Take for example the case of architecture of a page. If we abstract both the contents and presentation parameters, then we only see the pages of a site under the architectural feature. As a result, the final coalgebra will exactly give all architectural schemata of the pages.

2.2   Coalgebraic Description of User Visits

We model a user visit to a site (S, f_S), on the basis of the information registered in the log file of S (see Subsection 1.3). We assume first that each client has a personal (unlimited) cache memory. As a consequence, for each user, only the *first visit* to each site page is registered in the log file. Therefore, by abstracting from possible multiple requests of the same page, a visit can be realistically represented as a *tree*, which is a subgraph of the site.

First we need to introduce the notion of $F_{\mathcal{A}}$-simulation, between $F_{\mathcal{A}}$- coalgebras. This is a sort of one-sided bisimulation:

Definition 3. *Let* $f_S : S \to F_{\mathcal{A}}(S)$ *and* $g_T : T \to F_{\mathcal{A}}(T)$ *be* $F_{\mathcal{A}}$-*coalgebras. An* $F_{\mathcal{A}}$-*simulation* $R \subseteq S \times T$, *is a relation such that*

$$(p, p') \in R \implies$$

i) $\pi_1 \circ f_S(p) = \pi_1 \circ g_T(p')$ *and*
ii) $\forall p_1 \in \pi_2 \circ f_S(p) \ \exists p_1' \in \pi_2 \circ g_T(p'). \ (p_1, p_1') \in R.$
An $F_{\mathcal{A}}$-*simulation* R *is* total *if its domain is precisely* S.

Now we are in the position of introducing our first coalgebraic description of user visit:

Definition 4 (User Visit). *A visit to a site $(S, f_S : S \to F_A(S))$ is a total, functional, and injective F_A-simulation between an F_A-coalgebra (V, g_V) and (S, f_S), where (V, g_V) is a tree coalgebra. A tree coalgebra (V, g_V) is a coalgebra such that there exists $p_0 \in V$ representing the entry page and $\forall p \in V$, there exists a unique sequence $(p_0, \ldots, p_n)$ such that $p_n = p$ and, for all $0 \le i < n$, $p_{i+1} \in \pi_2 \circ g_V(p_i)$.*

In the simulation condition above, the injectivity condition guarantees that visits correspond exactly to subgraphs of the site, and not only up-to bisimilarity.

One can notice that user-visits are *not* F_A-subcoalgebras of the original site. A somewhat weaker notion of F_A-coalgebra morphism is necessary to describe user visits, namely that of *lax coalgebra morphisms*. Hence we show that user visits can be alternatively characterized via *lax coalgebra morphisms* in the category Rel_U^* of non-wellfounded sets and relations.

First we need to introduce the notion of *relator*, originally introduced and discussed in the literature by [20, 17, 4]. The notion of relator simulation can be given in any category of relations. For simplicity, we do not give it in its full generality, but we focus on the category Rel_U^*.

Definition 5 (Relator). *i) A strong relator Γ is a functor in the category Rel_U^*.*
ii) A relator is a strong relator which does not necessarily preserve the identity relation.
iii) A F-relator Γ, where $F : Set_U^* \to Set_U^*$ is a functor, is a relator which extends the functor F, i.e.

- *$\Gamma(A) = F(A)$, for every set A*
- *$F(f) \subseteq \Gamma(f)$, for every function f (identified with its graph-relation).*

Relators can be used to provide a purely categorical account of simulations, but we shall not develop this here, see [20] for more details.

We can now define a lax coalgebra morphism between Γ-coalgebras, for a relator Γ:

Definition 6 (Lax Coalgebra Morphism). *Let $\Gamma : Rel_U^* \to Rel_U^*$ be a relator, and let (X, f_X), (Y, f_Y) be Γ-coalgebras. Then $h : (X, f_X) \to (Y, f_Y)$ is a lax coalgebra morphism if $\Gamma(h) \circ f_X \subseteq f_Y \circ h$.*

A direct calculation shows that a user visit can be characterized as follows:

Proposition 2. *A user visit of the site $(S, f_S : S \to F_A(S))$, i.e. a total, functional, injective simulation R between a tree coalgebra (V, g_V) and (S, f_S), is a lax morphism $R : (V, g_V) \to (S, R_{f_S})$ in Rel_U^* w.r.t. the F_A-relator Γ_A defined by: for all $R \subseteq X \times Y$, $\Gamma_A(R) : A \times \mathcal{P}_f(X) \to A \times \mathcal{P}_f(Y)$, $(a, x)\Gamma_A(R)(a, y)$ iff $x \subseteq \widehat{R}(y)$, where $\widehat{R}(y) \triangleq \{z \mid \exists z' \in y . zRz'\}$, and where $R_{f_S} : S \times \Gamma_A(S)$ is defined by $(p, (a, x)) \in R_{f_S}$ iff $a = \pi_1 \circ f_S(p)$ and $x \subseteq \pi_2 \circ f_S(p)$.*

Vice versa any total, functional and injective lax morphism $R : (V, g_V) \to (S, R_{f_S})$ between Γ_A-coalgebras, for Γ_A F_A-relator defined as above, (V, g_V) tree F_A-coalgebra and (S, R_{f_S}), arising from an F_A-coalgebra (S, f_S) as above, is a user visit for (S, f_S).

Various properties concerning user behaviors can now be discussed in our coalgebraic setting.

First of all, the notion of *locality* of a visit R of the site (S, f_S), i.e. the set of pages of the site which have been explored during a visit, can be recovered by taking the image of the user visit R.

In our coalgebraic setting, bisimilarity on visits defines *user behaviours*, in the sense that two users can be taken to have the same behaviour w.r.t. a site, if their visits are bisimilar.

An interesting result that we obtain from our model is that user visits to a site are sufficient to characterize a site up-to bisimilarity, i.e. if we ignore self-references to pages, that is the links from a page to itself. Namely two sites are equivalent (bisimilar) if and only if they admit equivalent (bisimilar) visits.

Proposition 3. *Let (S, f_S), $(S', f_{S'})$ be site F_A-coalgebras, with no self-links. Then S is bisimilar to S', if and only if for any visit V of S there exists a bisimilar visit V' of S' and vice versa.*

Proof. (Sketch) If the sites S, S' are bisimilar then it is immediate that they have bisimilar visits. In order to show the converse, we use coinduction.   □

The problem of self-references arises because in the log file only the first visit to a page is registered. Hence, we cannot "observe" self-links, while any other link connecting different pages is observable. In order to overcome this problem, we could set the life-time of pages in the local cache memory to 0. Under this assumption, all user visits to pages of a site are registered in the log file. As a consequence, a visit can be characterized as a *path* in the graph of the site. In the general case, where we have a bounded cache memory, a visit amounts to a subgraph of the site. Coalgebraically, this can be described as a visit according to Definition 4, where the tree coalgebra hypothesis on the simulation is dropped:

Definition 7 (User Visit, bounded cache). *A user visit of the site $(S, f_S : S \to F_A(S))$ is a total, functional, injective F_A-simulation between a F_A- coalgebra (V, g_V) and (S, f_S).*

Analogous results to those given for user visits under the assumption of unlimited cache memory hold also in this case. In particular, a strenghtening of Proposition 3 holds, whereby bisimilarity equivalence of sites, including pages with self-links, can be exactly characterized in terms of bisimilarity of user visits.

If we (could) assess the usability of a site only in terms of the server-centred information contained in the log file, sites could be taken essentially up-to bisimilarity.

More accurate models for visits can be obtained by exploiting also the time information in the hits of the log file, although we need to be very cautious. The time interval between visits to successive pages could be taken as an approximation of the time spent by the user to "completely understand" each single page, but this is true only up to a first approximation. The functor used in this case would be $F_{A \times \Delta}$, where Δ encodes positive time intervals. A natural notion of

Δ-*enriched visit* can then be defined by taking the domain of the simulation to be (V, g_V), where (V, g_V) is an $F_{A \times \Delta}$-coalgebra, and $(V, \eta_V \circ g_V)$ is a standard visit domain, for $\eta : F_{A \times \Delta} \xrightarrow{\cdot} F_A$ the abstraction natural transformation. The bisimilarity equivalence on this model allows us to study user behaviour on the basis of the time spent for a visit, and hence to judge the usability of pages/sites.

3   Conclusions and Directions for Future Work

In this paper, we have introduced a coalgebraic description of web interactions. In particular, we have defined coalgebraic models of sites and user visits to a site. The latter relies on the information registered in the log file. In our coalgebraic model, we provide formal accounts of some important properties of sites, including coherence of a site, locality of a visit, user behaviour.

Comparison with Sazonov's approach. In the introduction, we have sketched Sazonov's model for the web. He considers the web as a coalgebra for the (hyper)set functor $P_f(\mathcal{L} \times \_)$, where P_f denotes the finite powerset functor and $\mathcal{L}$ is a set of labels for links. His aim was to provide an abstract, "static" set-theoretic view of the web in order to build a query language for Web-like Data Bases. Such a model apparently needs to be link-oriented. Unlike Sazonov, our aim was to give a formal model of the interaction between user and site by exploiting the information in the log file. Ours is a contents-oriented approach. We have chosen therefore the functor $F_A(X) = A \times P(X)$, A denoting the contents, possibly at different levels of abstraction. Moreover, since in the log file the precise nature of links is missing, we did not deal explicitly with them. Hence, unlike in Sazonov's model, we do not have, in general, more than one link from a given page to another page, and similarly two pages, p_1, p_2, whose only difference is in the labels to the same pages, are taken to be equivalent for us but different for Sazonov. In our approach the precise nature of labels can be accounted for in the contents. This is fine unless one wants to access pages using set-theoretic operations acting explicitly on the label as Sazonov does. As a trade-off we do not need to use the "trick" of a label to an empty page to represent contents, which has no hyperlinks. Furthermore, by modifying the nature of A, using natural transformations, we have a more flexible approach which allows for discussing naturally also issues not related to links.

Probably a more complete categorical picture of websites can be achieved by considering as functor $G_A(X) = A \times P(\mathcal{L} \times X)$. However, for the precise purposes of this paper this would have resulted in unnecessary complications.

We end up with a list of open problems issuing from our approach:

- It would to interesting to extend our model, in order to capture possibly *dynamic* sites. To this end it could be interesting to consider the approach by Atzeni and al. [12, 3].
- In this paper we have mainly focussed on possible applications of our coalgebraic model to the analysis of web sites. We are confident that our model can help also in the design of sites. Yet unexplored in the literature are the issues of *site specification* and *site refinement*.

- It would be interesting to study formal (coalgebraic) techniques for reasoning on the correctness of algorithms on web sites. To this end, sites could be formalized as (coinductive) data types, following the approach in this paper.
- The issue of Internet caching would probably lead us to cosider visits as forests. More work needs to be done here.
- There are still a number of other mechanisms which could be better understood, given a formalization of their behaviour, e.g. Forward and Backward moves.

Acknowledgements

We wish to thank Giorgio Brajnik and Marina Lernisa for helpful discussions and the referees for their suggestions and notes.

References

1. P. Aczel. *Non-Well Founded Sets*, volume **14**. CSLI Lecture Notes, Stanford, 1988.
2. P. Aczel and N. Mendler. A Final Coalgebra Theorem. *Category Theory and Computer Science, D.H.Pitt et al. eds., Springer LNCS*, **389**:357–365., 1989.
3. P. Atzeni, G. Mecca, and P. Meraildo. To Weave the Web. In *International Conf. on Very Large Data Bases, VLDB'97*, pages 206–215, 1997.
4. A. Baltag. A Logic for Coalgebraic Simulation. In *Electronic Notes in Theoretical Computer Science*, volume **33**. Elsevier Science Publishers, 2000.
5. J. Barwise and L. Moss. *Vicious Circles*. Number **60** in Lecture Notes. CSLI Publications, 1996.
6. M. Forti and F. Honsell. Set Theory with Free Construction Principles. In *Classe di Scienze*, volume **10**:(4), pages 493–522. Annali Scuola Normale Sup. di Pisa, 1983.
7. J. Goguen. An Introduction to Algebraic Semiotics, with Applications to User Interface Design. *Lecture Notes in Artificial Intelligence*, **1562**:242–291, 1999.
8. J. Goguen. CSE 271 Homepage. User Interface Design: Social and Techinical Issue. http://www-cse.ucsd.edu/users/goguen/courses/271/, Spring 2002.
9. B. Jacobs and J. Rutten. A Tutorial on (Co)Algebras and (Co)Induction. Bulletin, 1997. **62**:222-259.
10. M. Lenisa. *Themes in Final Semantics*. PhD thesis, Dipartimento di Informatica, Università di Pisa, 1998.
11. A. Lisitsa and V. Sazonov. Bounded Hyperset Theory and Web-like data bases. In *Computational Logic and Proof Theory, 5th Kurt Gödel Colloquium, KGC'97*, volume 1289, pages 172–185. LNCS, 1997.
12. G. Mecca, P. Merialdo, P. Atzeni, and V. Crescenzi. The (Short) Araneus Guide to Web-Site Development. Second Intern. Workshop on the Web and Databases (WebDB'99), 1999.
13. J. Nielsen. *Usability Inspection Methods*. John Wiley and Sons, Inc, 1994.
14. J. Nielsen. *Designing Web Usability*. New Riders, 2000.
15. P. Pirolli, J. Pitkow, and R. Rao. Silk from a sow's ear: Extracting esable structures from the web. In *Human Factors in Computing Systems (CHI-96) Conference Proceeding*, Vancouver, British Columbia, Canada, 1996.
16. L. Rosenfeld and P. Morville. *Information Architecture for the World Wide Web*. O'Reilly, 1998.

17. J. Rutten. Relators and metric bisimulations. In CMCS'98 *Conference Proceeding*, volume **11** of *ENTCS*, 1998.
18. J. Rutten. Universal coalgebra: a theory of systems. *TCS*, **249**:3–80, 2000.
19. V. Sazonov. Using Agents for Concurrent Querying of Web-like Databases via a Hyper-Set-Theoretic Approach,. In *PSI'01, Fourth Int. Conf. Perspective of System Informatics*, Novosibirsk, Akademgorodok, Russia, 2001.
20. A. Thijs. *Simulation and Fixpoint Semantics*. PhD thesis, University of Groningen, 1996.

A   Coalgebraic Preliminaries

In this section, we recall the notion of *coalgebra, coalgebra morphism, coalgebraic bisimulation*, and the main result of the coalgebraic paradigm, which characterizes equivalences induced by morphisms into final coalgebras as *coalgebraic bisimilarities*, i.e. *greatest* coalgebraic bisimulations. For more details, see e.g. [9]. We work in the category Set_U^* of *non-wellfounded sets* with *Urelements* (*atoms*), i.e. sets of a universe with atoms satisfying an Antifoundation Axiom, [6, 1].

Definition 8. *Let $F : Set_U^* \to Set_U^*$. A F-coalgebra is a pair (X, f_X), where $f_X : X \to F(X)$ is an arrow in Set_U^*. F-coalgebras can be endowed with the structure of a category by defining F-coalgebra morphisms as follows. $h : (X, f_X) \to (Y, f_Y)$ is a F-coalgebra morphism if $h : X \to Y$ is an arrow of the category Set_U^* such that the following diagram commutes*

$$
\begin{array}{ccc}
X & \xrightarrow{\;\;h\;\;} & Y \\
{\scriptstyle f_X}\downarrow & & \downarrow{\scriptstyle f_Y} \\
F(X) & \xrightarrow[F(h)]{} & F(Y)
\end{array}
$$

Definition 9 (F-bisimulation, [2]). *Let F be an endofunctor on the category Set_U^*. A relation $R \subseteq X \times Y$ is a F-bisimulation on F-coalgebras (X, f_X) and (Y, f_Y), if there exists an arrow of Set_U^*, $\gamma : R \to F(R)$, such that the following diagram commutes*

$$
\begin{array}{ccccc}
X & \xleftarrow{\;\pi_1\;} & R & \xrightarrow{\;\pi_2\;} & Y \\
{\scriptstyle f_X}\downarrow & & \downarrow{\scriptstyle \gamma} & & \downarrow{\scriptstyle f_Y} \\
F(X) & \xleftarrow[F(\pi_1)]{} & F(R) & \xrightarrow[F(\pi_2)]{} & F(Y)
\end{array}
$$

Equivalences induced by *unique* morphisms into *final* coalgebras can be characterized coinductively as the *greatest* F-bisimulations.

Theorem 1. *Suppose that $F : Set_U^* \to Set_U^*$ has a final F-coalgebra (Ω_F, f_{Ω_F}). Let (X, f_X) be a F-coalgebra, and let $\mathcal{M} : (X, f_X) \to (\Omega_F, f_{\Omega_F})$ be the unique final morphism. If F preserves weak pullbacks, then*
i) for all F-bisimulations R on (X, f_X), $\mathcal{M} \circ \pi_1 = \mathcal{M} \circ \pi_2$;
ii) the kernel pair of $\mathcal{M}$ is an F-bisimulation on (X, f_X).

A Calculus for Dynamic Linking*

Davide Ancona, Sonia Fagorzi, and Elena Zucca

DISI - Università di Genova
Via Dodecaneso, 35, 16146 Genova, Italy
{davide,fagorzi,zucca}@disi.unige.it

Abstract. We define a calculus for modeling dynamic linking independently of the details of a particular programming environment.

The calculus distinguishes at the language level the notions of software configuration and execution, by introducing separate syntactic notions of linkset expression and command, respectively.

A reduction step can be either a simplification of a linkset expression, or the execution of a command w.r.t. a specific underlying software configuration denoted by a linkset expression; because of dynamic linking, these two kinds of reductions are interleaved.

The type system of the calculus, which is proved to be sound, relies on an accurate dependency analysis for ensuring type safety without losing the advantages offered by dynamic linking.

1 Introduction

In the early years of programming languages, programs were considered as large self-contained entities. Programming environments offered only primitive facilities for splitting code into single fragments and manipulating these individually. Correspondingly, formal models of type-checking and execution were related to whole programs.

However, the need for mechanisms of modularization has quickly emerged in different phases of the process of software production and execution. At the language level it was soon realized the importance of decomposing software into relatively small pieces, each one corresponding to a single logical unit. This pieces of software are usually called *modules*. In this way it is possible to associate with each module a *specification* of its behavior. Moreover, single modules can be developed and tested independently and then composed by just relying on their specifications. Considerable effort has been invested in studying theoretical foundations and designing advanced forms of module systems [2,13,14,12,5,9,11,1], inspired by the unifying principle of two separate linguistic levels, a *module language* providing operators for combining software components, with their own

---

* Partially supported by Dynamic Assembly, Reconfiguration Type-checking - EC project IST-2001-33477, APPSEM II - Thematic network IST-2001-38957, and Murst NAPOLI - Network Aware Programming: Oggetti, Linguaggi, Implementazioni.

C. Blundo and C. Laneve (Eds.): ICTCS 2003, LNCS 2841, pp. 284–301, 2003.

typing rules, constructed on top of a *core language* for defining module components. The module language should be independent as much as possible from the core language, even more, in principle could be instantiated over different core languages (see, e.g., [12,2] for an effective demonstration of these ideas).

Turning now to consider extra-linguistic aspects, an important feature a programming environment should support in order to achieve modularization is *separate compilation*. This means that modules in the language should correspond to compilation units (actually the necessity of splitting large programs into fragments in order to compile them separately was one of the initial motivations for modularization). Of course, from the compilation of a single source fragment we do not expect in general to get an executable program, since this fragment is open, that is, refers to other fragments on which it specifies some requirements; however, an executable program can be obtained by assembling together in some way a collection of binary fragments obtained by separate compilation, provided that mutual requirements are satisfied. This process, which is, for instance, performed by a (static) linker, is usually underspecified in programming environments, and has not deserved much attention until the recent years. Cardelli's work on foundations of linking [4] can be considered a milestone in this direction and is based on the definition of a simple framework where each module can be separately compiled to a self-contained entity called a *linkset*, which is a collection of named judgments $X_1 \mapsto \Gamma_1 \vdash e_1 : \tau_1, \ldots, X_n \mapsto \Gamma_n \vdash e_n : \tau_n$ where e_i is a code fragment named X_i, τ_i is the type associated to this fragment during separate compilation (here, as in [4], we reduce compilation to type-checking and do not consider issues concerning code generation), and Γ_i is a type environment specifying the requirements on other fragments needed for type-checking e_i. At this point, provided that the linkset *inter-checks* (that is, linkset fragments are consistent with respect to each other), an executable program can be obtained from the linkset by applying a sequence of *linking steps*, where each step consists of resolving (by substitution) the dependencies of all other fragments on a given self-contained fragment X_i (mutual recursion is not considered in [4]), finally leading to a closed piece of code. In addition to Cardelli's paper, it must be pointed out that module calculi such as, e.g., *CMS* introduced in [2], can also be seen as formal models of linking; indeed, in these calculi modules can be viewed both as entities at the language level (hence, operators of the calculus model operators of the module language) and as code fragments. In the latter view, operators of the calculus model operations which can be performed on fragments (such as primitives of a configuration language): for instance, the linking step in [4] corresponds in *CMS* to the application of a *freeze*[1] operator which resolves all dependencies on a given module component X by making a local copy of the current definition of X in such a way that further changes to X will not affect the other components (this allows to also model mutual recursion).

---

[1] This is the name adopted in the original formulation in [2], while in the calculus presented here we will adopt for the analogous operator the more appropriate name *link*.

All these formal frameworks only model *static* linking, that is, the case in which the configuration phase of the software system takes place only before execution and yields a closed piece of code. However, most widely-used modern programming environments such as those of Java and C# provide an even more advanced form of modularization where not only single source fragments can be separately compiled, but the resulting code fragments can be be linked to an already executing program (*dynamic linking*), hence the configuration and execution phases can be interleaved.

To our knowledge, a simple formal model of dynamic linking analogous to that for static linking in [4] is missing; the existing literature on the subject is mainly concerned with the modeling of concrete mechanisms in existing programming environments (see, e.g., the large amount of work of Drossopoulou and others on phases of dynamic linking and verification in Java-like languages [7,6,8]). In this paper, we provide a first step towards an understanding of the dynamic linking mechanism abstracted from the details of a particular programming environment.

To this end, we introduce a simple calculus of *configurations*, which are pairs consisting of a linkset expression and a command. Configurations can evolve in two ways: either by simplifying the linkset expression (that is, performing a configuration step) or by performing a step in the execution of the command. However, configuration and execution are interleaved: an execution step may trigger a configuration step (for instance, when a not linked yet fragment is needed) and modify the execution context (for instance, updating a fragment).

Summary. Section 2 contains the formal definitions and main results together with some simple examples; in Section 3 we draw some conclusion and we discuss possible directions for future work.

2   A Calculus of Linksets

In this section we formally define our calculus. Terms of the calculus, called *configurations*, model snapshots in the lifetime of a software system, and are pairs consisting of a *linkset* and a *command*, corresponding to two different phases called *configuration phase* and *execution phase*, respectively. The configuration phase corresponds to the process of obtaining an executable application by combining in various ways different pieces of software. This phase may be interleaved with the execution phase, even though it typically takes place before execution; for instance, it can correspond to what is performed by a (static) linker. In our calculus, this phase is modeled by the fact that the linkset is, in general, a complex expression, which must be reduced to a normal form for performing some kind of command; after that, it is possible to start reducing the command, in the context provided by the linkset.

Basic linksets are roughly, as in [4], collections of named, interdependent code fragments, and operators for composing linksets correspond to operations one can perform during configuration. In particular, an important operation one can perform on a linkset is what is called in [4] a linking step: we can *link* a fragment, say X, that is, resolve the dependencies on X. *Static linking* (as modeled, e.g., by Cardelli [4]) requires fully linked linksets in order to start the execution of any command, so that all dependencies have been resolved before the execution phase starts.

However, in our model we want to be more flexible by allowing linking to take place at run-time too. Hence, execution can start also when the linkset is not fully linked; during execution of the command, we can find references to other fragments which have not been resolved yet, hence they need to be dynamically linked. We distinguish two forms of run-time linking. In the first form, which we call *(permanent) dynamic* linking or simply dynamic linking, a fragment is permanently linked to the executing program the first time it is needed. This is what dynamic linking means in, e.g., Java and C#. In the second form, which we call *volatile dynamic* linking, or simply volatile linking, a fragment is made available to the executing program when its code is needed, but not permanently linked, so that when a later reference to the same fragment is encountered the linking must be performed again, and in case the fragment's code has been changed thereafter the new version is used. The latter form of linking offers the flexibility necessary for dynamic reconfiguration of systems. Even if this feature is not largely exploited yet in current real-world programming languages, volatile linking can also be seen as an abstraction to manage at the programming language level the new forms of networks (peer-to-peer, ad-hoc, etc.) in which the high-level of mobility requires context-aware programming.

2.1 Syntax

Before defining configurations, we introduce some notations and conventions.

Notations

- $f : A \xrightarrow{fin} B$ means that f is a partial function from A to B with finite domain, written $\mathsf{dom}(f)$; the image of f is written $\mathsf{img}(f)$. We write $a_i : b_i{}^{i \in I}$ for the partial function mapping a_i to b_i for all $i \in I$ (where the a_i must be different, i.e., $a_i = a_j$ implies $i = j$). We use the following operations on partial functions:
  - $\emptyset$ is the everywhere undefined partial function;
  - f and g are *compatible* when $f(x) = g(x)$ for $x \in \mathsf{dom}(f) \cap \mathsf{dom}(g)$;
  - f_1, f_2 denotes the union of two partial functions with disjoint domain;
  - $f_1 \subseteq f_2$ means that the graph of f_1 is included in that of f_2, i.e., $\mathsf{dom}(f_1) \subseteq \mathsf{dom}(f_2)$ and f_1 and f_2 compatible;
  - $f \setminus A$ is defined by $(f \setminus A)(x) \triangleq \begin{cases} f(x) & \text{if } x \notin A \\ \text{undefined} & \text{otherwise;} \end{cases}$
  - $f\{a : b\}$ denotes the update of f in a, that is, $f \setminus \{a\}, a : b$;
- If e is a term, and ρ a finite partial function from a set of variables to a set of terms, then $e\{\rho\}$ denotes the parallel substitution of all variables $x \in \mathsf{dom}(\rho)$ with $\rho(x)$ in e (modulo α-conversion).

$l \in$ Linkset	::=		**linksets**
	$[\iota; o; \rho]$ with		
	$\mathsf{dom}(\iota) \cap \mathsf{dom}(\rho) =$		basic linkset
	$\emptyset \wedge \mathsf{UV}([\iota; o; \rho]) \subseteq (\mathsf{dom}(\iota) \cup \mathsf{dom}(\rho))$		
	|	$l_1 + l_2$	sum
	|	$\mathsf{link}_X(l)$	link
	|	$\mathsf{dlink}_X^{\mathsf{p}}(l)$	(permanent) dynamic link
	|	$\mathsf{dlink}_X^{\mathsf{v}}(l)$	volatile (dynamic) link

$\iota : \mathsf{Var} \overset{fin}{\to} \mathsf{Name}$ **input** assignment

$o : \mathsf{Name} \overset{fin}{\to} \mathsf{Exp}$ **output** assignment

$\rho : \mathsf{Var} \overset{fin}{\to} \mathsf{Exp}$ **local** assignment

$c \in \mathsf{Com}$	::= $e \mid \mathsf{set}(X, e) \mid \mathsf{get}(X) \mid \mathsf{let}\ x = c_1\ \mathsf{in}\ c_2 \mid \ldots$	**commands**
$e \in \mathsf{Exp}$	::= $x \mid * \mid n \mid \ldots$	**(core) expressions**
$\tau \in \mathsf{Type}$	::= $\mathsf{int} \mid \mathsf{void} \mid \ldots$	**(core) types**

$\gamma \in \mathsf{Conf}$	::= (l, c)	**configurations**
	with $\mathsf{FV}(c) \subseteq \mathsf{BV}(l) \wedge \mathsf{FN}(c) \subseteq \mathsf{BN}(l)$	

Fig. 1. Syntax of configurations.

The syntax of the calculus is given in Fig.1. It is parametric in an infinite set Name of (fragment) *names* X, an infinite set Var of *variables* x, and a set Exp of (core) expressions (the expressions of the underlying language used for defining single code fragments). Intuitively, names are used to refer to fragments from outside a linkset, whereas variables are used in code within a linkset (indeed, expressions are assumed to be built on top of variables, see the production for Exp). This distinction between external and internal names of fragments is quite standard now in module and fragment calculi and has motivations both on the methodological side, such as allowing to model name resolution performed by a linker, and on the technical side, such as allowing α-conversion for variables while keeping external interfaces (see, e.g., [2] for an extended discussion of this point).

Linksets are either basic linksets (collections of named code fragments in the underlying expression language) or are constructed by linkset operators corresponding to the operators of a configuration language.

A basic linkset is similar to a basic module in module calculi (see, e.g., [2]), and consists of three components. The ι component is a mapping from variables into names and represents the *input* interface of the linkset; the o component is a mapping from names into expressions and represents the *output* interface of the linkset; the ρ component is a mapping from variables into expressions and represents the local (that is, already linked) fragments. Variables in the domain of ι and ρ are called the *deferred* and the *local* variables of the basic linkset, respectively. Basic linksets must satisfy some well-formedness requirements, that is, the sets of deferred and defined variables must be disjoint, and the set of the *used* variables, that is, free variables in expressions inside the linkset, must be a subset of the deferred and local variables. The set $\mathsf{UV}\,(l)$ of the used variables of a linkset is defined as follows:

- $\mathsf{UV}\,([\iota; o; \rho]) \triangleq \bigcup_{X \in \mathsf{dom}(o)} \mathsf{FV}(o(X)) \cup \bigcup_{x \in \mathsf{dom}(\rho)} \mathsf{FV}(\rho(x));$
- $\mathsf{UV}\,(l_1 + l_2) \triangleq \mathsf{UV}\,(l_1) \cup \mathsf{UV}\,(l_2);$
- $\mathsf{UV}\,(\mathsf{link}_X\,(l)) = \mathsf{UV}\,(\mathsf{dlink}_X^{\mathsf{p}}\,(l)) = \mathsf{UV}\,(\mathsf{dlink}_X^{\mathsf{v}}\,(l)) \triangleq \mathsf{UV}\,(l).$

We consider four operators on linksets: the *sum* operator, which allows merging of two linksets, and three different *link* operators: link for static linking, $\mathsf{dlink}^{\mathsf{p}}$ for permanent dynamic linking and $\mathsf{dlink}^{\mathsf{v}}$ for volatile dynamic linking. We will explain linkset operators in more detail when introducing reduction rules for linksets and configurations.

We will abbreviate $\mathsf{dlink}_{X_1}^{K_1}(\dots(\mathsf{dlink}_{X_n}^{K_n}(l))\dots)$, where $n \geq 0$, $K_i \in \{\mathsf{p}, \mathsf{v}\}$, by $\mathsf{dlink}_{[P;V]}\,(l)$, where $P = \{X_i \mid K_i = \mathsf{p}\}$ and $V = \{X_1, \dots, X_n\} \setminus P$ (so, in the case $n = 0$, $\mathsf{dlink}_{[\emptyset;\emptyset]}\,(l)$ obviously coincides with l).

Note that the above notation is sound since semantics of a linkset expression is invariant w.r.t. to permutations and repetitions in a sequence of application of the dynamic link operators. Moreover, in case of application of both a permanent and a volatile dynamic link operator for the same name, only the permanent one is taken into account (see the reduction rules in Fig.4).

Commands model, intuitively, actions which can be performed in the execution phase, which include standard execution of the underlying core expressions (hence expressions are included into commands) and metaoperations on fragments which can be interleaved with standard execution. In particular, as examples of metaoperations, we consider here a get operation which loadssome fragment's code, and a set operation which updates the code of an existing fragment. Moreover, we use in the examples a standard let-in construct corresponding to a sequence of two commands with value-passing and we abbreviate let $x = c_1$ in c_2 with $c_1; c_2$ when $x \notin \mathsf{FV}(c_2)$.

Expressions of the core language are not specified; we only assume that they contain variables, the constant $*$ which denotes the unique value of type void and, to the aim of writing examples, integer constants n.

A configuration is a pair consisting of a linkset and a command. Configurations must satisfy some well-formedness requirements, that is, the set of the free variables (resp. names) in the command must be a subset of the binding variables (resp. names) of the linkset. Fig.2 contains the definitions of the functions FV, FN, BV and BN.

Note that the command in a configuration may contain both variables (since expressions may contain variables) and names of the current linkset. Indeed, on one hand an execution step can be a standard execution step, that is, an evaluation step of an expression. Code in execution can refer to *internal* names of fragments, either already resolved (local variables in ρ), or still to be resolved (deferred variables in ι); for instance, modeling the execution of a Java appli-

$c \in$ Com	$\mathsf{FV}(\_) \subseteq_{\mathsf{fin}}$ Var
$\mathsf{set}(X, e)$	$\mathsf{FV}(e)$
$\mathsf{get}(X)$	$\emptyset$
let $x = c_1$ in c_2	$\mathsf{FV}(c_1) \cup (\mathsf{FV}(c_2) \setminus \{x\})$

$e \in$ Exp	$\mathsf{FV}(\_) \subseteq_{\mathsf{fin}}$ Var
x	$\{x\}$
$* \mid n$	$\emptyset$

$l \in$ Linkset			$\mathsf{BV}(\_) \subseteq_{\mathsf{fin}}$ Var
$[\iota; o; \rho]$			$\mathrm{dom}(\iota) \cup \mathrm{dom}(\rho)$
$l_1 + l_2$			$\emptyset$
$\mathsf{link}_X(l)$	$\mathsf{dlink}^\rho_X(l)$	$\mathsf{dlink}^v_X(l)$	$\mathsf{BV}(l)$

$\gamma \in$ Conf	$\mathsf{BV}(\_) \subseteq_{\mathsf{fin}}$ Var
(l, c)	$\mathsf{BV}(l)$

$c \in$ Com	$\mathsf{FN}(\_) \subseteq_{\mathsf{fin}}$ Name
$\mathsf{set}(X, e)$	$\{X\}$
$\mathsf{get}(X)$	$\{X\}$
let $x = c_1$ in c_2	$\mathsf{FN}(c_1) \cup \mathsf{FN}(c_2)$

$l \in$ Linkset			$\mathsf{BN}(\_) \subseteq_{\mathsf{fin}}$ Name
$[\iota; o; \rho]$			$\mathrm{dom}(o)$
$l_1 + l_2$			$\mathsf{BN}(l_1) \cup \mathsf{BN}(l_2)$
$\mathsf{link}_X(l)$	$\mathsf{dlink}^\rho_X(l)$	$\mathsf{dlink}^v_X(l)$	$\mathsf{BN}(l)$

Fig. 2. Auxiliary functions.

cation, variables would correspond to class names appearing in Java code, and a class C not loaded yet would be a deferred variable. On the other hand, an execution step can be a metaoperation which manipulates the fragment "from the outside", hence through names. In the Java example above, names would correspond to physical names (in the file system or on the web) of files containing classes, and ρ would model the mechanism used by a loader for associating to a class name C a physical name. A set command would model the fact that the code contained in some file is modified, either by effect of an external agent or even by the application itself.

Free variables are defined as usual. The set of the binding variables of a sum is empty; indeed, in this case it makes no sense to refer to the variables in the linkset, since performing the sum may cause an α-renaming. If the linkset contains no sum operators, hence it is obtained by applying a chain of link operators to a basic linkset, then the set of the binding variables consists of the deferred and local variables of this basic linkset.

The free names of a command are those that appear inside the command as arguments of either a set or a get operation. The binding names of a linkset are those defined inside the linkset, that is, belonging to the domain of its output assignments.

2.2   Semantics

We define two different reduction relations, corresponding to the configuration and execution phase, respectively.

Configuration Phase. The reduction rules for the configuration phase are given in Fig.3. In this phase only the linkset expression in a configuration is reduced.

We assume that the reduction relation $\xrightarrow{l}$ is defined over well-formed linksets, hence we have omitted side conditions ensuring well-formedness of terms, since they are assumed to be implicitly satisfied.

$\mathcal{L}[\ ] \in \mathsf{ECL} ::= \square \mid \mathcal{L}[\ ] + l \mid l + \mathcal{L}[\ ] \mid \mathsf{link}_X (\mathcal{L}[\ ]) \mid \mathsf{dlink}_X^K (\mathcal{L}[\ ])$ **linkset contexts.**

$$(l\text{-ctx}) \ \frac{l \xrightarrow{\iota} l'}{\mathcal{L}[l] \xrightarrow{\iota} \mathcal{L}[l']}$$

$$(\text{sum}) \ \frac{}{\mathsf{dlink}_{[P_1;V_1]} (l_1) + \mathsf{dlink}_{[P_2;V_2]} (l_2) \xrightarrow{\iota} \mathsf{dlink}_{[P;V \setminus P]} ([\iota_1,\iota_2;o_1,o_2;\rho_1,\rho_2])} \quad \begin{array}{l} V = V_1 \cup V_2 \\ P = P_1 \cup P_2 \\ l_i \equiv [\iota_i;o_i;\rho_i], i \in \{1,2\} \end{array}$$

$$(\text{link}) \ \frac{}{\mathsf{link}_X (\mathsf{dlink}_{[P;V]} ([\iota;o;\rho])) \xrightarrow{\iota} \mathsf{dlink}_{[P \setminus \{X\};V \setminus \{X\}]} \left([\iota \setminus L;o;\rho, x : o(X)^{x \in L}]\right)} \quad \begin{array}{l} L = \{x \mid \iota(x) = X\} \\ L \neq \emptyset \Rightarrow X \in \mathsf{dom}(o) \end{array}$$

Fig. 3. Reduction rules for the configuration phase.

Rule (l-ctx) is the usual contextual closure, where one hole evaluation contexs for linksets are also defined in Fig.3.

The reduction rule for the sum is similar to those of module and link calculi (see, e.g.,[2]). This operation has the effect of gluing together two linksets, under some conditions. The binders of one linkset must be disjoint from those of the other, that is, $\mathsf{BV}(l_1) \cap \mathsf{BV}(l_2) = \emptyset$ (implicit side condition). This condition can always be satisfied by an appropriate α-conversion. Moreover, the output fragments of the two linksets must be disjoint, that is, $\mathsf{dom}(o_1) \cap \mathsf{dom}(o_2) = \emptyset$ (implicit side-condition); this conflict cannot be resolved by α-conversion. The set of input fragments of the two arguments can have a non empty intersection and the resulting set of input fragments of the sum is simply the union of them; this means that imported fragments with the same name in the two linksets are shared.

Finally, in the sum the sets of fragment names dynamically linked is obtained by taking the union of the corresponding sets in the two linksets, and taking only the permanent operator into account when both permanent and volatile linking turn out to be applied to the same name.

Note that sum only expresses the possibility of collecting pieces of unrelated code, but does not provide any way for inter-connecting fragments in a linkset (that is, no linking step is performed yet). This inter-connection can take place only at a next stage, after sum has been performed, by means of the link operator, or at an even later stage, after execution has started, by means of the dynamic link operators.

The link operator, as stated above, accomplishes inter-connections of fragments. So, in rule (link), the effect of linking fragment X is that this fragment name is resolved, hence it disappears from the input names and all the variables mapped by ι into it are now linked, that is, they become local. These variables are associated with the definition of X in the output assignment, 'which must exist (side-condition). Moreover, the name X also disappears from those for which a dynamic linking operator is applied.

Note that there are no reduction rules for the dynamic link operators; indeed, the intuition for these operators is that they are not performed during the configuration phase, but they will be performed on demand only after execution is started (see reduction rules for configurations in Fig.4). As a consequence, terms which cannot be further reduced are obtained by a sequence of dynamic linking operators applied to a basic linkset, as formalized below.

Fact 1 *A linkset expression is in normal form w.r.t. the reduction relation* $\xrightarrow{l}$ *iff it has the form* $\mathsf{dlink}_{[P;V]}\left([\iota; o; \rho]\right)$.

In the following, we use ln as metavariable ranging over linksets in normal form.

Execution Phase. The reduction rules for the execution phase are given in Fig.4.

$$\mathcal{C}(\ ) \in \mathsf{ECC} ::= \Box \mid \mathsf{let}\ x = \Box\ \mathsf{in}\ c_2 \mid \ \ldots \ \textbf{command contexts}.$$
$$v \in \mathsf{CVal} \ \ ::= n \mid * \mid \ldots \qquad \textbf{(core) values}$$

(linkset) $\dfrac{l \xrightarrow{l} l'}{(l,\ c)\ \longrightarrow\ (l',\ c)}$
(core) $\dfrac{e \xrightarrow{e} e'}{(l,\ e)\ \longrightarrow\ (l,\ e')}$

(c-ctx) $\dfrac{(l,\ c)\ \longrightarrow\ (l',\ c')}{(l,\ \mathcal{C}(c))\ \longrightarrow\ (l',\ \mathcal{C}(c'))}$

(let) $(l,\ \mathsf{let}\ x = v\ \mathsf{in}\ c)\ \longrightarrow\ (l,\ c\{x : v\})$

(set) $(\mathsf{dlink}_{[P;V]}\left([\iota; o; \rho]\right),\ \mathsf{set}(X, e))\ \longrightarrow\ (\mathsf{dlink}_{[P;V]}\left([\iota; o\{X : e\}; \rho]\right),\ *),\quad X \in \mathsf{dom}(o)$

(get) $(\mathsf{dlink}_{[P;V]}\left([\iota; o; \rho]\right),\ \mathsf{get}(X))\ \longrightarrow\ (\mathsf{dlink}_{[P;V]}\left([\iota; o; \rho]\right),\ o(X)),\quad X \in \mathsf{dom}(o)$

(var) $(\mathsf{dlink}_{[P;V]}\left([\iota; o; \rho]\right),\ x)\ \longrightarrow\ \begin{cases} (\mathsf{dlink}_{[P;V]}\left([\iota; o; \rho]\right),\ \rho(x)) & \text{if } x \in \mathsf{dom}(\rho) \\ (\mathsf{link}_X\left(\mathsf{dlink}_{[P;V]}\left([\iota; o; \rho]\right)\right),\ o(X)) & \text{if } \iota(x) = X \wedge X \in (\mathsf{dom}(o) \cap P) \\ (\mathsf{dlink}_{[P;V]}\left([\iota; o; \rho]\right),\ o(X)) & \text{if } \iota(x) = X \wedge X \in (\mathsf{dom}(o) \cap V) \end{cases}$

Fig. 4. Reduction rules for the execution phase.

The reduction relation $\longrightarrow$ is parametric on the relation $\xrightarrow{e}$ which corresponds to evaluation of core expressions, and on the set CVal of core values which includes at least integer constants and the constant $*$, as shown in Fig.4.

The (linkset) and (core) rules express that an execution step can consist in a configuration step of the linkset or, if the command is a core expression, in an evaluation step at the core level.

The rule (c-ctx) is the usual contextual closure, where one hole evaluation contexts for the particular set of commands we consider are defined at the top of Fig.4.

The (let) rule is the standard call-by-value rule for evaluating a let-in construct.

The subsequent three rules can only be applied when the linkset is in normal form.

The (set) rule expresses that an execution step can consist in updating the definition of an existing output fragment; note that this execution step modifies both the linkset and the command in the current configuration.

The (get) rule expresses that an execution step can consist in obtaining as command to be executed the current definition of an existing fragment.

The (var) rule shows how dynamic and volatile linking work. If a variable x is defined in ρ, then its corresponding code is already available and does not need to be linked; on the other hand, if x is deferred (that is, the corresponding fragment, say X, has not been linked yet), then, in the command, the variable is replaced by the current definition of X. Moreover, if the linking is dynamic, then the corresponding fragment X is permanently linked in the linkset, so that further occurrences of x will always refer to the same definition, while this is not the case if the linking is volatile.

The reduction relations for the configuration and the execution phases enjoy the Church Rosser property.

Proposition 1. *The relations $\xrightarrow{l}$ on linksets and $\longrightarrow$ on configurations are confluent.*

Proof. The reduction rules are left-linear and non-overlapping. □

The following proposition states some properties concerning how names and variables within configurations change during reduction. Here we use the abbreviation $\mathsf{anylink}_{[S;P;V]}(l)$ for

$\mathsf{anylink}_{X_1}(\ldots(\mathsf{anylink}_{X_n}(l))\ldots)$, where $n \geq 0$ and $\mathsf{anylink}_X ::= \mathsf{link}_X \mid \mathsf{dlink}_X^K$.

Proposition 2.

(a) *If $l_1 \xrightarrow{l} l_2$, then $\mathsf{BN}(l_1) = \mathsf{BN}(l_2)$.*

(b) *If $(l_1, c_1) \longrightarrow (l_2, c_2)$, then $\mathsf{BN}(l_1) = \mathsf{BN}(l_2)$, $\mathsf{FN}(c_2) \subseteq \mathsf{FN}(c_1)$, $\mathsf{FV}(c_2) \subseteq \mathsf{FV}(c_1) \cup \mathsf{UV}(l_1)$.*

(c) *If l_i are linksets without any application of the sum operator, that is, $l_i \equiv \mathsf{dlink}_{[S_i;P_i;V_i]}([\iota_i; o_i; \rho_i])$, $i \in \{1, 2\}$, with $l_1 \xrightarrow{*}_l l_2$, then $\iota_2 \subseteq \iota_1$, $\rho_1 \subseteq \rho_2$, $\mathsf{dom}(\iota_1) \cup \mathsf{dom}(\rho_1) = \mathsf{dom}(\iota_2) \cup \mathsf{dom}(\rho_2)$ and $\mathsf{dom}(o_1) = \mathsf{dom}(o_2)$.*

(d) *If $(l_1, c_1) \xrightarrow{*} (l_2, c_2)$, with $l_i \equiv \mathsf{dlink}_{[S_i;P_i;V_i]}([\iota_i; o_i; \rho_i])$, $i \in \{1, 2\}$, then $\iota_2 \subseteq \iota_1$, $\rho_1 \subseteq \rho_2$, $\mathsf{dom}(\iota_1) \cup \mathsf{dom}(\rho_1) = \mathsf{dom}(\iota_2) \cup \mathsf{dom}(\rho_2)$ and $\mathsf{dom}(o_1) = \mathsf{dom}(o_2)$.*

Proof. (a) By case analysis on the reduction rules for the configuration phase; (b) by induction on the reduction rules for the configuration phase and we use the point (a); (c) by case analysis on the reduction rules for the configuration phase; (d) by induction on the reduction rules for the configuration phase and we use the point (c). □

We state now some results concerning the relation between the three different forms of link operators. First of all, if there were no commands affecting the linkset in a configuration, such as the set command, then static, dynamic and volatile linking could not be distinguished, as formally expressed by the following proposition.

Proposition 3. *If in the grammar for commands we do not include the production for the* set *operation, then the three kinds of link operators give the same result, that is, if l is a linkset containing as link operator only the static one, and $(l, c) \xrightarrow{*} (l', v)$, then $(P(l), c) \xrightarrow{*} (l'', v)$ and $(V(l), c) \xrightarrow{*} (l''', v)$, where $P(l)$ and $V(l)$ are the linksets obtained from l by replacing all the static link operators by dynamic and volatile link operators, respectively.*

Proof. By defining a suitable equivalence between linksets and proving that reduction relation preserves the equivalence. □

The difference between the three kinds of linking becomes observable if we allow commands to modify the execution context, for example using the set operation. In this case, it is easy to see that we can obtain different results by using, for example, either dynamic or volatile linking, as illustrated by the following example:

Example 1.

- $(\mathsf{dlink}_Y^{\mathsf{p}}([y:Y;Y:0,X:y;]), \; y; \; \mathsf{set}(Y,3); \; \mathsf{get}(X)) \xrightarrow{(c\text{-}ctx)+(var)}$

  $(\mathsf{link}_Y(\mathsf{dlink}_Y^{\mathsf{p}}([y:Y;Y:0,X:y;])), \; 0; \; \mathsf{set}(Y,3); \; \mathsf{get}(X)) \xrightarrow{(linkset)}$

  $([;Y:0,X:y;y:0], \; 0; \; \mathsf{set}(Y,3); \; \mathsf{get}(X)) \xrightarrow{(let)}$

  $([;Y:0,X:y;y:0], \; \mathsf{set}(Y,3); \; \mathsf{get}(X)) \xrightarrow{(c\text{-}ctx)+(set)} \xrightarrow{(let)}$

  $([;Y:3,X:y;y:0], \; \mathsf{get}(X)) \xrightarrow{(get)} \xrightarrow{(var)} ([;Y:3,X:y;y:0], \; 0)$

- $(\mathsf{dlink}_Y^{\mathsf{v}}([y:Y;Y:0,X:y;]), \; y; \; \mathsf{set}(Y,3); \; \mathsf{get}(X)) \xrightarrow{(c\text{-}ctx)+(var)}$

  $(\mathsf{dlink}_Y^{\mathsf{v}}([y:Y;Y:0,X:y;]), \; 0; \; \mathsf{set}(Y,3); \; \mathsf{get}(X)) \xrightarrow{(let)}$

  $(\mathsf{dlink}_Y^{\mathsf{v}}([y:Y;Y:0,X:y;]), \; \mathsf{set}(Y,3); \; \mathsf{get}(X)) \xrightarrow{(c\text{-}ctx)+(set)} \xrightarrow{(let)}$

  $(\mathsf{dlink}_Y^{\mathsf{v}}([y:Y;Y:3,X:y;]), \; \mathsf{get}(X)) \xrightarrow{(get)} \xrightarrow{(var)}$

  $(\mathsf{dlink}_Y^{\mathsf{v}}([y:Y;Y:3,X:y;]), \; 3)$

Finally, the following proposition states that static, dynamic and volatile linking do not differ w.r.t. dynamic errors. That is, if a configuration containing only the static link operator does not get stuck, then replacing all the static link operators by dynamic and volatile linking operators, respectively, we get a configuration which does not get stuck as well, even though it may evolve in a different way. The only exception is the case in which the configuration can only evolve by performing a (link) step.

Moreover, dynamic link operators strictly increase the expressive power of the language allowing to obtain more results; indeed, if a configuration evaluates to a value, then it still evaluates to the same value even if we apply to the linkset a dynamic link operator. The converse does not hold, as can be easily seen by considering a configuration where the command contains a non local variable.

Proposition 4. *Let* $\xrightarrow{\neg\text{link}}$ *denote a* $\longrightarrow$ *reduction step obtained without applying rule* (link). *If l is a linkset containing as link operator only the static one, then*

1. $(l, c) \xrightarrow{\neg\text{link}}$ *iff* $(P(l), c) \longrightarrow$ *iff* $(V(l), c) \longrightarrow$;
2. $(l, c) \xrightarrow{*} (l', v) \underset{\not\Leftarrow}{\Rightarrow} \left(\text{dlink}_X^K(l), c\right) \xrightarrow{*} (l'', v)$.

Proof. 1. *By induction on the reduction rules for the execution phase;*
2. $\Rightarrow$) *Similar to that of Prop.3.* $\not\Leftarrow$) *A counterexample is the configuration in Example 1 without* dlink *operator.* □

2.3   Type System

We introduce linkset types $[\pi^\iota; \pi^o; \Gamma; R]$, where π^ι, π^o : Name $\xrightarrow{\text{fin}}$ Type are the *input* and *output signature*, respectively, Γ : Var $\xrightarrow{\text{fin}}$ Type is the type environment for variables, and R is a relation on Name $\cup$ Var called a *dependency* relation.

The first two components are standard for module and fragment calculi (see e.g., [2]), while R keeps trace of the variables a name X depends on and is needed in order to type-check configurations which contain a get(X) command (see rule (get) in Fig.7).

Moreover, R and Γ together are used to type-check configurations in which the command contains free variables (hence the current linkset does not contain the sum operator). Indeed, in this case we require that each of these free variables, say x, can be successfully resolved at run-time, that is, x is either local or bound to an input fragment for which there is an application of a dynamic link; moreover, if x depends on another variable y (through R) , then y can be successfully resolved at run-time as well (see the definition of the environment Γ^R in Definition 2).

Well-formedness of linkset types is defined in the following way.

Definition 1 (Well-formed linkset types). *A linkset type $[\pi^\iota; \pi^o; \Gamma; R]$ is well-formed, written $\vdash [\pi^\iota; \pi^o; \Gamma; R] \diamond$, iff the following conditions hold:*

- π^ι *and π^o are compatible;*
- $(X, \_) \in R \Rightarrow X \in \text{dom}(\pi^\iota)$;
- $(\_, X) \in R \Rightarrow X \in \text{dom}(\pi^o)$.

The type system for linksets derives judgments of the form $\vdash_l l : [\pi^\iota; \pi^o; \Gamma; R]$ with meaning "l is a is a well-formed linkset of type $[\pi^\iota; \pi^o; \Gamma; R]$" and is defined in Fig.5. In the type system we use the following conventions:

- given a linkset $l \triangleq [\iota; o; \rho]$, the dependency relation R_l induced by l is the relation on $\text{dom}(\iota) \cup \text{img}(\iota) \cup \text{dom}(o) \cup \text{dom}(\rho)$ defined by

$$R_l \triangleq \begin{array}{l} \{(X, x) \mid X = \iota(x)\} \quad \cup \\ \{(y, X) \mid y \in \text{FV}(o(X))\} \cup \\ \{(y, x) \mid y \in \text{FV}(\rho(x))\} \end{array}$$

– R^* is the transitive closure of R.

Moreover, given Γ and R, we define the type environment Γ^R for the variables which can successfully resolved at run-time as the sub-environment of Γ whose domain is closed w.r.t. R, as shown below.

Definition 2. *Given a linkset type $[\pi^\iota; \pi^o; \Gamma; R]$, we denote by Γ^R the type enviroment s.t. $\Gamma^R \subseteq \Gamma$ and $\mathrm{dom}(\Gamma^R) = \{x \mid \{y \mid (y,x) \in R^*\} \subseteq \mathrm{dom}(\Gamma)\}$.*

(basic)
$$\dfrac{\vdash [\pi^\iota;\ \pi^o;\ \Gamma;\ R_{[\iota;o;\rho]}]\ \diamond \quad \{\Gamma^\iota, \Gamma^\rho \vdash_e o(X) : \pi^o(X) \mid X \in \mathrm{dom}(o)\} \quad \{\Gamma^\iota, \Gamma^\rho \vdash_e \rho(x) : \Gamma^\rho(x) \mid x \in \mathrm{dom}(\rho)\}}{\vdash_l [\iota; o; \rho] : [\pi^\iota;\ \pi^o;\ \Gamma^\rho;\ R_{[\iota;o;\rho]}]}$$
$$\begin{aligned}\mathrm{dom}(\pi^\iota) &= \mathrm{img}(\iota)\\ \mathrm{dom}(\pi^o) &= \mathrm{dom}(o)\\ \Gamma^\iota &= \pi^\iota \circ \iota\\ \mathrm{dom}(\Gamma^\rho) &= \mathrm{dom}(\rho)\end{aligned}$$

(sum)
$$\dfrac{\vdash_l l_1 : [\pi_1^\iota; \pi_1^o; \Gamma_1; R_1] \quad \vdash_l l_2 : [\pi_2^\iota; \pi_2^o; \Gamma_2; R_2]}{\vdash_l l_1 + l_2 : [\pi_1^\iota, \pi_2^\iota; \pi_1^o, \pi_2^o; \emptyset; R_1 \cup R_2]} \qquad \mathrm{dom}(\pi_1^o) \cap \mathrm{dom}(\pi_2^o) = \emptyset$$

(link)
$$\dfrac{\vdash_l l : [\pi^\iota; \pi^o; \Gamma; R]}{\vdash_l \mathrm{link}_X (l) : \left[\pi^\iota \setminus \{X\}; \pi^o; \Gamma, x{:}\pi^o(X)^{x \in L}; R\right]}$$
$$\begin{aligned}X \in \mathrm{dom}(\pi^\iota) &\Rightarrow \pi^\iota(X) = \pi^o(X)\\ L &= \{x \mid (X,x) \in R\}\\ \Gamma' &\triangleq \Gamma, x{:}\pi^o(X)^{x \in L}\end{aligned}$$

(dlink)
$$\dfrac{\vdash_l l : [\pi^\iota; \pi^o; \Gamma; R]}{\vdash_l \mathrm{dlink}_X^K (l) : \left[\pi^\iota; \pi^o; \Gamma, x{:}\pi^o(X)^{x \in L}; R\right]}$$
$$\begin{aligned}X \in \mathrm{dom}(\pi^\iota) &\Rightarrow \pi^\iota(X) = \pi^o(X)\\ L &= \{x \mid (X,x) \in R\}\end{aligned}$$

Fig. 5. Typing rules for for linksets.

In rule (sum) the dependency relation in the result type is obtained gluing together the dependency relations in the types of the arguments. Note that Γ is empty; indeed, as mentioned before, it makes no sense to refer to variables inside a linkset containing a sum operator since performing the sum may cause an α-renaming.

In the result type in rules (link) and (dlink), the type environment Γ is enriched with the variables associated to X.

Moreover, in rule (link) π^ι is updated to keep trace of the linking of the name fact that the input name X is now linked, hence it does no longer appear in the input signature. On the contrary, in rule (dlink) π^ι does not change; this conforms to the intuition that dynamic link operators are not performed during the configuration phase, but they only keep trace of the information that the name X is dynamically linked.

In both (link) and (dlink) rules the dependency relation R is unchanged, since the transformation of a deferred variable into local does not affect the dependencies between variables. The type environment Γ, instead, is updated to keep trace of the variables associated with the linked name.

The type system for linksets depends on that for core expressions, which we assume to derive judgments of the form $\Gamma \vdash_e e : \tau$. In Fig.6 we give the rules for the subset of the core language specified in the syntax.

$$
\text{(C-var)} \quad \frac{}{\Gamma \vdash_e x : \Gamma(x)} \; x \in \mathsf{dom}(\Gamma) \qquad\qquad \text{(C-int)} \quad \frac{}{\Gamma \vdash_e n : \mathsf{int}}
$$

$$
\text{(C-void)} \quad \frac{}{\Gamma \vdash_e * : \mathsf{void}}
$$

Fig. 6. Typing rules for core expressions.

The typing rules for configurations and commands are shown in Fig.7.

$$
\frac{\vdash_l l : [\pi^\iota;\, \pi^o;\, \Gamma;\, R] \quad \pi^o; \Gamma^R; R \vdash_c c : \tau}{\vdash (l,\, c) \diamond}
$$

$$
\text{(core)} \quad \frac{\Gamma \vdash_e e : \tau}{\pi^o; \Gamma; R \vdash_c e : \tau}
$$

$$
\text{(set)} \quad \frac{\Gamma \vdash_e e : \pi^o(X)}{\pi^o; \Gamma; R \vdash_c \mathsf{set}(X, e) : \mathsf{void}} \quad \begin{array}{l} X \in \mathsf{dom}(\pi^o) \\ \mathsf{FV}(e) \subseteq \{y \mid (y, X) \in R^*\} \end{array}
$$

$$
\text{(get)} \quad \frac{}{\pi^o; \Gamma; R \vdash_c \mathsf{get}(X) : \pi^o(X)} \quad \begin{array}{l} X \in \mathsf{dom}(\pi^o) \\ \{y \mid (y, X) \in R^*\} \subseteq \mathsf{dom}(\Gamma) \end{array}
$$

$$
\text{(let)} \quad \frac{\pi^o; \Gamma; R \vdash_c c_1 : \tau_1 \quad \pi^o; \Gamma, x : \tau_1; R \vdash_c c_2 : \tau_2}{\pi^o; \Gamma; R \vdash_c \mathsf{let}\ x = c_1\ \mathsf{in}\ c_2 : \tau_2}
$$

Fig. 7. Typing rules for configurations and commands.

A configuration is well-formed if the linkset is well-formed, and the command is well-formed w.r.t. the linkset, that is, w.r.t. the information π^o, Γ^R and R extracted from the linkset type: π^o is used to check that a command only refers to names defined in the current linkset; Γ^R contains all the variables that can be successfully resolved at run-time; R keeps trace of the dependencies between names and variables in the linkset.

Typing rules for commands derive judgments of the form $\pi^o; \Gamma; R \vdash_c c : \tau$ with meaning "c is a well-formed command of type τ in π^o, Γ and R".

In rule (set), we must check that the new expression which will be associated to X does not introduce new dependencies in R.

In rule (get), we require all the variables on which X depends to be variables that can be successfully resolved at run-time.

Example 2. The configuration $\gamma \triangleq (\mathsf{dlink}_Y^p\,([y : Y, z : Z; Y : 0;]),\ \mathsf{get}(Y))$ is well-formed even though component Y is selected from a linkset that still has an unresolved variable z; indeed, the definition of Y does not depend on z. On the other hand, $(\mathsf{dlink}_Y^p\,([y : Y, z : Z; Y : z;]),\ \mathsf{get}(Y))$ is ill-formed.

2.4   Technical Results

In order to prove the subject reduction and progress properties for the two reduction relations $\xrightarrow{l}$ and $\longrightarrow$ we need to assume that these properties hold for the core language. Formally: if $\Gamma \vdash_e e_1 : \tau$ and $e_1 \xrightarrow{e} e_2$, then $\Gamma \vdash_e e_2 : \tau$; if $\Gamma \vdash_e e : \tau$ and $e \notin \mathsf{CVal}$, then $e \xrightarrow{e}$. Moreover, we need also the assumption: if $e_1 \xrightarrow{e} e_2$, then $\mathsf{FV}(e_2) \subseteq \mathsf{FV}(e_1)$.

We state the following auxiliary lemmas.

Lemma 1. *If $\vdash_l l : [\pi^\iota;\ \pi^o;\ \Gamma;\ R]$, then $[\pi^\iota;\ \pi^o;\ \Gamma;\ R]$ is well-formed.*

Proof. Induction on the typing rules. □

Lemma 2. *If $\vdash_l \mathsf{dlink}_{[P;V]}\,([\iota; o; \rho]) : [\pi^\iota;\ \pi^o;\ \Gamma;\ R]$, then*

1. $X \in \mathsf{dom}(o) \land \{y \mid (y, X) \in R\} \subseteq \mathsf{dom}(\Gamma) \Rightarrow \Gamma \vdash_e o(X) : \pi^o(X)$;
2. $x \in \mathsf{dom}(\rho) \cap \mathsf{dom}(\Gamma) \Rightarrow \Gamma \vdash_e \rho(x) : \Gamma(x)$;
3. $x \in \mathsf{dom}(\iota) \cap \mathsf{dom}(\Gamma) \land \iota(x) \in \mathsf{dom}(o) \cap (P \cup V) \Rightarrow \Gamma(x) = \pi^o(\iota(x))$.

Proof. By case analysis. □

Proposition 5 (Subject Reduction for $\xrightarrow{l}$). *If $\vdash_l l_1 : [\pi_1^\iota;\ \pi_1^o;\ \Gamma_1;\ R_1]$ and $l_1 \xrightarrow{l} l_2$, then $\vdash_l l_2 : [\pi_2^\iota;\ \pi_2^o;\ \Gamma_2;\ R_2]$, with $\pi_2^\iota \subseteq \pi_1^\iota$, $\pi_1^o = \pi_2^o$, $\Gamma_1 \subseteq \Gamma_2$ and $R_1 = R_2$.*

Proof. By case analysis on reduction rules and induction on typing rules. □

Proposition 6 (Progress for $\xrightarrow{l}$). *If $\vdash_l l : [\pi^\iota;\ \pi^o;\ \Gamma;\ R]$ and $l \neq \mathsf{ln}$, then $l \xrightarrow{l}$.*

Proof. By induction on the structure of l. □

Proposition 7. *If $\vdash_l l_1 : [\pi_1^\iota;\ \pi_1^o;\ \Gamma_1;\ R_1]$, $\pi_1^o; \Gamma_1; R_1 \vdash_c c_1 : \tau$ and $(l_1, c_1) \longrightarrow (l_2, c_2)$, then $\vdash_l l_2 : [\pi_2^\iota;\ \pi_2^o;\ \Gamma_2;\ R_2]$, $\pi_2^o; \Gamma_2; R_2 \vdash_c c_2 : \tau$ with $\pi_2^\iota \subseteq \pi_1^\iota$, $\pi_1^o = \pi_2^o$, $\Gamma_1 \subseteq \Gamma_2$ and $R_1 = R_2$.*

Proof. By case analysis on reduction rules and induction on the derivation of the first judgment. We use Lemma 2 and Proposition 5. □

Theorem 2 (Subject Reduction for $\longrightarrow$). *If* $\vdash (l,\ c) \diamond$ *and* $(l,\ c) \longrightarrow (l',\ c')$, *then* $\vdash (l',\ c') \diamond$.

Proof. Follows from Proposition 7.   □

Theorem 3 (Progress for $\longrightarrow$). *If* $\vdash (l,\ c) \diamond$ *and* $(l,\ c) \neq (ln,\ v)$, *then* $(l,\ c) \longrightarrow$.

Proof. By induction on the structure of $(l,\ c)$.   □

3   Conclusion

We have defined a calculus for dynamic linking supporting three different notions of linking:

- the classical notion of *static* linking, whose formalization is inspired by previous pioneering work [4,2,13,14], and where code can be executed only after all variables (that is, references) have been resolved;
- the notion of *dynamic* linking à la Java, where execution can be started even though the code contains an unresolved variable x, whose corresponding code is permanently linked the first time the value of x is really needed;
- the notion of *volatile* linking, which is a more flexible version of dynamic linking, where code for an unresolved variable x is re-linked each time x needs to be evaluated.

For simplicity, the calculus keeps distinct the two phases of code *configuration* and *execution* by distinguishing two different languages: a configuration language whose expressions denote linksets, and a command language, whose terms are evaluated w.r.t. a specific linkset. However, linksets and commands are mutually dependent since not only command execution clearly depends on the configuration specified by the underlying linkset, but also the execution of a command can change its underlying linkset; in fact, evaluations of linksets and commands can be interleaved.

We have defined a reduction semantics for the calculus and shown that, if the language of commands is expressive enough, then the three link‘ operators can be observationally distinguished. Then we have presented a type system for the calculus and proved its soundness; if on one hand dynamic and volatile linking allow more flexible forms of software reconfiguration, on the other hand they make typechecking more challenging, and require a more accurate static analysis for fully exploiting the advantages without losing type safety.

The novelty of our calculus mainly resides in the fact that it is the first attempt we are aware of at providing (1) a theoretic underpinning of dynamic linking, and (2) a formal framework for investigating the behavior of heterogeneous systems where different and hybrid forms of linking may coexist.

Concerning related work, we already cited work on static linking [4,2,13,14] and on concrete linking mechanisms in existing programming environments [7,6,8].

Moreover, the recent [3] presents a simple calculus modeling dynamic software updating, where modules are just records, many versions of the same module may coexist and update is modeled by an external transition which can be enforced by an update primitive in code.

We plan to further study dynamic linking in different directions.

First, we need to test the expressive power of the calculus by showing that it can be effectively used for modeling a variety of programming languages supporting dynamic linking.

Then, since real languages are unlikely to combine different kinds of linking, it would be interesting to define calculi which only support one kind (e.g., either dynamic or volatile linking) and to compare their properties, similarly to distinguishing between call-by-value and call-by-name forms of lambda calculus.

A more challenging issue would be to consider a calculus which would not distinguish between the configuration and the execution phase, so that linksets could be freely manipulated as first class values during execution.

Finally, an aspect which deserves investigation is the relation between our approach and mobile process calculi such as the pi-calculus and the ambient calculus. In particular, the idea of separating the configuration from the execution language reminds of the basics of the so-called coordination approach [10], according to which computation and inter-components interdependencies should be programmed separately.

Acknowledgements

We warmly thank Sophia Drossopoulou, Eugenio Moggi, and the anonymous referees for their useful suggestions and feedback.

References

1. D. Ancona, S. Fagorzi, E. Moggi, and E. Zucca. Mixin Modules and Computational Effects. In *International Colloquium on Automata, Languages and Programming 2003*, 2003. To appear.
2. D. Ancona and E. Zucca. A calculus of module systems. *Journ. of Functional Programming*, 12(2):91–132, 2002.
3. G. Bierman, M. Hicks, P. Sewell, and G. Stoyle. Formalizing dynamic software updating (extended abstract). In *USE'03 - Workshop on Unexpected Software Evolution*, 2003.
4. L. Cardelli. Program fragments, linking, and modularization. In *ACM Symp. on Principles of Programming Languages 1997*, pages 266–277. ACM Press, 1997.
5. K. Crary, R. Harper, and S. Puri. What is a recursive module? In *PLDI'99 - ACM Conf. on Programming Language Design and Implementation*, 1999.
6. S. Drossopoulou. Towards an abstract model of Java dynamic linking and verfication. In R. Harper, editor, *TIC'00 - Third Workshop on Types in Compilation (Selected Papers)*, volume 2071 of *Lecture Notes in Computer Science*, pages 53–84. Springer, 2001.

7. S. Drossopoulou, S. Eisenbach, and D. Wragg. A fragment calculus - towards a model of separate compilation, linking and binary compatibility. In *Proc. 14th Ann. IEEE Symp. on Logic in Computer Science*, July 1999.
8. S. Drossopoulou, G. Lagorio, and S. Eisenbach. Flexible models for dynamic linking. In *European Symposium on Programming 2003*, 2003.
9. R.B. Findler and M. Flatt. Modular object-oriented programming with units and mixins. In *Intl. Conf. on Functional Programming 1998*, September 1998.
10. D. Gelernter and N. Carriero. Coordination languages and their significance. *Comm. ACM*, 35(1):96–107, January 1992.
11. T. Hirschowitz and X. Leroy. Mixin modules in a call-by-value setting. In D. Le Métayer, editor, *European Symposium on Programming 2002*, number 2305 in Lecture Notes in Computer Science, pages 6–20. Springer, 2002.
12. X. Leroy. A modular module system. *Journal of Functional Programming*, 10(3): 269–303, May 2000.
13. E. Machkasova and F.A. Turbak. A calculus for link-time compilation. In *European Symposium on Programming 2000*, number 1782 in Lecture Notes in Computer Science, pages 260–274. Springer, 2000.
14. J.B. Wells and R. Vestergaard. Confluent equational reasoning for linking with first-class primitive modules. In *European Symposium on Programming 2000*, number 1782 in Lecture Notes in Computer Science, pages 412–428. Springer, 2000.

Towards a Smart Compilation Manager for Java*
(Extended Abstract)

Giovanni Lagorio

DISI – Università di Genova
Via Dodecaneso, 35, 16146 Genova, Italy
lagorio@disi.unige.it

Abstract. It is often infeasible to recompile all the sources an application consists of each time a change is made. Yet, a recompilation strategy
which does not guarantee the same outcome of an entire recompilation
is not useful: why wasting time in debugging a program (a set of .class
files in the Java case) which might behave *differently* from the program
obtained recompiling all the sources from scratch?
We say that a compilation strategy is *sound* if it recompiles, besides
the changed sources, all the unchanged sources whose new binary, produced by the overall recompilation, would differ from the existing one
(if any) *and* all the sources for which the recompilation would be undefined: indeed, when the entire compilation fails, so should do the partial
recompilation.
We say that a compilation strategy is *minimal* if it never recompiles an
unchanged source whose new binary would be equal to the existing one.
In this paper we present a compilation strategy for a substantial subset
of Java which is proved to be *sound* and *minimal*.

1   Introduction

When dealing with large applications it is infeasible to recompile all the sources
each time a change is made. Of course, separate compilation is the answer to
such a problem, but a key point has to be considered: in addition to the modified sources, which files have to be recompiled as well? A recompilation strategy
which does not guarantee the same outcome of an entire recompilation is not
useful: why wasting time in debugging a program (a set of .class files in the
Java case) which might behave *differently* from the program obtained recompiling all the sources from scratch? It is known that, using the most common
Java compilers (including the standard one), a program which is the result of a
successful recompilation may throw linking related exceptions at runtime even if
these errors could have been detected at compile time [3]. This is not in contrast

* Partially supported by Dynamic Assembly, Reconfiguration Type-checking – EC
  project IST-2001-33477, APPSEM II – Thematic network IST-2001-38957, and
  Murst NAPOLI – Network Aware Programming: Oggetti, Linguaggi, Implementazioni.

C. Blundo and C. Laneve (Eds.): ICTCS 2003, LNCS 2841, pp. 302–315, 2003.
© Springer-Verlag Berlin Heidelberg 2003

with the soundness for Java investigated by other papers [6, 7] because they did not take separate compilation into account.

Two contrasting requirements have to be considered: on the one hand recompilations can be rather expensive (in time), hence they should be avoided when possible. More precisely, they are useless when the recompilation of an unchanged (with respect to the previous compilation) source fragment S, whose corresponding binary fragment B is already present, would produce a binary equal to B. On the other hand, a recompilation strategy which saves time not recompiling a fragment S, with a corresponding binary fragment B, whose recompilation would produce a new binary B' different from B, could cost a lot of wasted time in debugging an *inconsistent* application, that is, an application that *cannot* be rebuilt by recompiling all the sources.

Albeit some Java IDEs support smart or incremental compilation, to our knowledge there are no publications which explain in detail the inner working of such recompilation strategies. In this paper we chose to analyze Java, a mainstream language, and model its peculiar features, because our final goal is to implement a compilation manager, for a widespread language, whose correctness and minimality (in the sense explained below) can be formally proved.

We say that a compilation strategy is *sound* if it recompiles all the changed sources and the unchanged sources whose new binary, produced by the overall recompilation, would differ from the existing one (if any) *and* all the unchanged sources for which the recompilation would be undefined. This latter requirement is very important: indeed, when the entire recompilation is not defined, so should be the partial recompilation.

Of course, a strategy which recompiles all the sources each time a change is made is trivially sound and, obviously, totally useless in practice. We say that a compilation strategy is *minimal* if it never recompiles an unchanged fragment whose new binary would be equal to the existing one.

In this paper we present a compilation strategy for a substantial subset of Java which is proved to be *sound* and *minimal*.

Section 2 presents the formal framework, Section 3 explains the ideas behind our compilation strategy and Section 4 discusses related and future work.

2 Formalization

2.1 The Language

In this paper we model a substantial subset of Java at both source (Figure 1) and binary (Figure 2) level. Our model of bytecode is rather abstract: it is basically source code enriched with some annotations (discussed below). However, the same source level expression can be compiled to different binary level expressions, as it happens in Java. For instance, a method invocation x.m() can be translated to a virtual method invocation or an interface method invocation depending on the static type of x.

With the exception of arrays and inner-classes we model all the major features of Java: classes (including abstract classes), interfaces, primitive types, ac-

$$
\begin{aligned}
\texttt{S} ::= {} & \texttt{AM CK class C extends } \texttt{C}' \texttt{ implements } \texttt{I}_1 \ldots \texttt{I}_n \texttt{ \{ KDS}^s \texttt{ FDS}^s \texttt{ MDS}^s \texttt{ \}} \mid \\
& \texttt{AM interface I extends } \texttt{I}_1 \ldots \texttt{I}_n \texttt{ \{ FDS}^s \texttt{ MDS}^s \texttt{ \}}
\end{aligned}
$$

$$
\begin{aligned}
\texttt{AM} ::= {} & \texttt{public} \mid \texttt{protected} \mid \epsilon \mid \texttt{private} \\
\texttt{CK} ::= {} & \epsilon \mid \texttt{abstract} \\
\texttt{KDS}^s ::= {} & \texttt{KD}_1^s \ldots \texttt{KD}_n^s \\
\texttt{FDS}^s ::= {} & \texttt{FD}_1^s \ldots \texttt{FD}_n^s \\
\texttt{MDS}^s ::= {} & \texttt{MD}_1^s \ldots \texttt{MD}_n^s \\
\texttt{KD}^s ::= {} & \texttt{AM KH \{ super(}\texttt{E}_1^s, \ldots, \texttt{E}_n^s \texttt{); STMTS}^s \texttt{ \}} \\
\texttt{FD}^s ::= {} & \texttt{AM FINAL FK T f = }\texttt{E}^s \texttt{ ;} \\
\texttt{MD}^s ::= {} & \texttt{AM MK MH \{ STMTS}^s \texttt{ return }\texttt{E}^s\texttt{; \}} \mid \texttt{AM abstract MH ;} \\
\texttt{KH} ::= {} & \texttt{(}\texttt{T}_1 \texttt{ x}_1, \ldots, \texttt{T}_n \texttt{ x}_n\texttt{) throws ES} \\
\texttt{MK} ::= {} & \epsilon \mid \texttt{static} \mid \texttt{abstract} \\
\texttt{MH} ::= {} & \texttt{T m(}\texttt{T}_1 \texttt{ x}_1, \ldots, \texttt{T}_n \texttt{ x}_n\texttt{) throws ES} \\
\texttt{FINAL} ::= {} & \epsilon \mid \texttt{final} \\
\texttt{FK} ::= {} & \epsilon \mid \texttt{static} \\
\texttt{T} ::= {} & \texttt{RT} \mid \texttt{int} \mid \texttt{bool} \\
\texttt{RT} ::= {} & \texttt{C} \mid \texttt{I} \\
\texttt{ES} ::= {} & \texttt{C}_1, \ldots, \texttt{C}_n \\
\texttt{E}^s ::= {} & \texttt{PRIMARY}^s \mid \texttt{ASSIGN}^s \mid \texttt{N} \mid \texttt{true} \mid \texttt{false} \\
\texttt{PRIMARY}^s ::= {} & \texttt{null} \mid \texttt{this} \mid \texttt{NEW}^s \mid \texttt{x} \mid \texttt{INVOKE}^s \mid \texttt{super.f} \mid \texttt{PRIMARY}^s\texttt{.f} \mid \texttt{RT.f} \\
\texttt{ASSIGN}^s ::= {} & \texttt{x = }\texttt{E}^s \mid \texttt{PRIMARY}^s\texttt{.f = }\texttt{E}^s \mid \texttt{super.f = }\texttt{E}^s \mid \texttt{RT.f = }\texttt{E}^s \\
\texttt{NEW}^s ::= {} & \texttt{new C(}\texttt{E}_1^s, \ldots, \texttt{E}_n^s\texttt{)} \\
\texttt{INVOKE}^s ::= {} & \texttt{PRIMARY}^s\texttt{.m(}\texttt{E}_1^s, \ldots, \texttt{E}_n^s\texttt{)} \mid \texttt{super.m(}\texttt{E}_1^s, \ldots, \texttt{E}_n^s\texttt{)} \mid \texttt{RT.m(}\texttt{E}_1^s, \ldots, \texttt{E}_n^s\texttt{)} \\
\texttt{STMTS}^s ::= {} & \texttt{STMT}_1^s \ldots \texttt{STMT}_n^s \\
\texttt{STMT}^s ::= {} & \texttt{\{STMTS}^s\texttt{\}} \mid \texttt{SE}^s \texttt{ ;} \mid \texttt{if (}\texttt{E}^s\texttt{) STMT}_1^s \texttt{ else STMT}_2^s \mid \texttt{while (}\texttt{E}^s\texttt{) STMT}^s \mid \\
& \texttt{try \{STMTS}^s \texttt{ \} CATCHES}^s \texttt{ finally \{ STMTS}_1^s \texttt{ \}} \mid \texttt{throw }\texttt{E}^s \\
\texttt{SE}^s ::= {} & \texttt{ASSIGN}^s \mid \texttt{INVOKE}^s \mid \texttt{NEW}^s \\
\texttt{CATCHES}^s ::= {} & \texttt{CATCH}_1^s \ldots \texttt{CATCH}_n^s \\
\texttt{CATCH}^s ::= {} & \texttt{catch (C x) \{ STMTS}^s \texttt{ \}}
\end{aligned}
$$

Assumptions:

- interface names in S are distinct;
- field names in FDS^s are distinct;
- method/constructor signatures in MDS^s/KDS^s are distinct;
- parameter and exception names in both KH and MH are distinct;
- class names in CATCHES^s are distinct.

Fig. 1. Syntax - Sources.

cess modifiers (including packages, but without the `import` directive), constructors, (instance/static) fields (both in classes and interfaces), (instance/static/abstract) methods, super field accesses and method invocations, exceptions. The treatment of arrays and inner-classes would complicate the model without apparently giving further insights.

Figure 1 gives the syntax of the language. A source fragment S can be a class declaration or an interface declaration. In the former case it consists of: an access modifier AM, a class kind CK (either ϵ or `abstract`), the name of the class, the name of the superclass, the list of the implemented interfaces and the declaration of constructors, fields and methods. Analogously, an interface declaration consists of an access modifier, the name of the interface, the name of the superinterfaces and the declaration of fields and methods.

A constructor declaration KD^s consists of an access modifier AM, a constructor header KH, the invocation of a superclass's constructor[1] and a sequence of statements $STMTS^s$. A constructor header consists of the sequence of parameters and the exception specification ES. In this paper we assume for simplicity that any class can be an exception, that is, we do not model the predefined class Throwable. So, an exception specification is just a sequence of class names.

A field declaration FD^s consists of an access modifier AM, an optional modifier FINAL, a field kind FK, a type T, the name of the field f and the initialization expression E^s.

A method declaration MD^s can be either concrete or abstract. In the former case it consists of an access modifier AM, a method kind MK, a method header MH, a sequence of statements $STMTS^s$ and a return expression E^s. In the latter case it just consists of an access modifier AM, the keyword abstract and a method header. A type T can be a reference type RT or a primitive type (int or bool). We distinguish between class names C and interface names I for clarity only, even though they actually range over the same set of names.

An expression E^s can be: a primary expression, an assignment expression, an integer literal N or a boolean literal. Some expressions, SE^s, can be used as statements; they are: assignment $ASSIGN^s$, method invocation $INVOKE^s$ and instance creation NEW^s.

While Java permits accessing a static member of a class/interface RT via both the type name RT or any expression which has static type RT, here we allow only the former kind of access (because allowing both kinds of access would require additional, uninteresting, typing rules).

Figure 2 gives the syntax of the binary language. As already said, it mostly mimics the source language, except for it is enriched with some annotations enclosed between "≪" and "≫".

For example, the instance creation expression NEW^s is translated to NEW^b, which contains, as annotation, the tuple of types describing the constructor which has been found as most specific at compile time. Analogously, method invocation expressions are annotated with the signature of the most specific method found at compile time and the static type of the receiver. There are four kinds of (binary) method invocation expressions $INVOKE^b$: virtual (instance method invocation), super (invocation via super), static and interface.

2.2 Type Environments

Type environments Γ are defined in Figure 3. A type assignment γ maps a class/interface name to its type.

---

[1] Invocations of a constructor of the same class (using this) are not considered since they are simply syntactic shortcuts (recursive invocations are not allowed - see 8.8.5 of [8]).

$$
\begin{aligned}
\text{B} &::= \text{AM CK class C extends } C' \text{ implements } I_1 \dots I_n \ \{ \ \text{KDS}^b \ \text{FDS}^b \ \text{MDS}^b \ \} \ | \\
&\quad \text{AM interface I extends } I_1 \dots I_n \ \{ \ \text{FDS}^b \ \text{MDS}^b \ \} \\
\text{KDS}^b &::= \text{KD}_1^b \dots \text{KD}_n^b \\
\text{MDS}^b &::= \text{MD}_1^b \dots \text{MD}_n^b \\
\text{FDS}^b &::= \text{FD}_1^b \dots \text{FD}_n^b \\
\text{KD}^b &::= \text{AM KH } \{ \ \text{super}(\text{E}_1^b, \dots, \text{E}_n^b) \ll \bar{\text{T}} \gg_c; \ \text{STMTS}^b \ \} \\
\text{FD}^b &::= \text{AM FINAL FK T f} = \text{E}^b \\
\text{MD}^b &::= \text{AM MK MH } \{ \ \text{STMTS}^b \ \text{return E}^b; \ \} \ | \ \text{AM abstract MH} ; \\
\text{E}^b &::= \text{PRIMARY}^b | \text{ASSIGN}^b | \text{N} | \text{true} | \text{false} \\
\text{PRIMARY}^b &::= \text{null} \ | \ \text{this} \ | \ \text{NEW}^b \ | \ \text{x} \ | \ \text{INVOKE}^b \\
&\quad \text{PRIMARY}^b. \ll \text{C.T} \gg_{\text{if}} \text{f} \ | \ll \text{RT.T} \gg_{\text{sf}} \text{f} \\
\text{ASSIGN}^b &::= \text{x} = \text{E}^b \ | \ \text{PRIMARY}^b. \ll \text{C.T} \gg_{\text{if}} \text{f} = \text{E}^b \ | \ll \text{RT.T} \gg_{\text{sf}} \text{f} = \text{E}^b \\
\text{NEW}^b &::= \text{new C} \ll \bar{\text{T}} \gg_c (\text{E}_1^b, \dots, \text{E}_n^b) \\
\text{INVOKE}^b &::= \text{PRIMARY}^b. \ll \text{C.m}(\bar{\text{T}})\text{T} \gg_{\text{vrt}} \text{m}(\text{E}_1^b, \dots, \text{E}_n^b) \ | \ \text{this.} \ll \text{C.m}(\bar{\text{T}})\text{T} \gg_{\text{spr}} \text{m}(\text{E}_1^b, \dots, \text{E}_n^b) \ | \\
&\quad \text{PRIMARY}^b. \ll \text{C.m}(\bar{\text{T}})\text{T} \gg_{\text{stt}} \text{m}(\text{E}_1^b, \dots, \text{E}_n^b) \ | \ \text{PRIMARY}^b. \ll \text{I.m}(\bar{\text{T}})\text{T} \gg_{\text{int}} \text{m}(\text{E}_1^b, \dots, \text{E}_n^b) \\
\text{STMTS}^b &::= \text{STMT}_1^b \dots \text{STMT}_n^b \\
\text{STMT}^b &::= \{ \text{STMTS}^b \} \ | \ \text{SE}^b \ ; \ | \ \text{if } (\text{E}^b) \ \text{STMT}_1^b \ \text{else STMT}_2^b \ | \ \text{while } (\text{E}^b) \ \text{STMT}^b \\
&\quad \text{try } \{ \text{STMTS}^b \ \} \ \text{CATCHES}^b \ \text{finally } \{ \ \text{STMTS}_1^b \ \} \ | \ \text{throw E}^s \\
\text{SE}^b &::= \text{ASSIGN}^b \ | \ \text{INVOKE}^b \ | \ \text{NEW}^b \\
\text{CATCHES}^b &::= \text{CATCH}_1^b \dots \text{CATCH}_n^b \\
\text{CATCH}^b &::= \text{catch } (\text{C x}) \ \{ \ \text{STMTS}^b \ \}
\end{aligned}
$$

Assumptions:

- interface names in B are distinct;
- field names in FDS^b are distinct;
- method/constructor signatures in MDS^b/KDS^b are distinct;
- class names in CATCHES^b are distinct.

Fig. 2. Syntax - Binaries.

The assignment

$$
\text{C} \mapsto [\text{AM}{=}\text{AM}, \text{CK}{=}\text{CK}, \text{PARENT}{=}C', \text{IS}{=}I_1 \dots I_n, \text{KSS}{=}\text{KSS}, \text{FSS}{=}\text{FSS}, \text{MSS}{=}\text{MSS}]
$$

has the meaning "the class C has access modifier AM and kind CK, extends C', implements $I_1 \dots I_n$ and has constructor signatures KSS, field signatures FSS and method signatures MSS". Analogously, $\text{I} \mapsto [\text{AM}{=}\text{AM}, \text{IS}{=}I_1 \dots I_n, \text{FSS}{=}\text{FSS}, \text{MSS}{=}\text{MSS}]$ has the meaning "the interface I has access modifier AM, extends $I_1 \dots I_n$, and has field signatures FSS and method signatures MSS".

Type assumptions λ, also defined in Figure 3, describe fine-grained requirements; they are:

- $\text{T} \leq \text{T}'$ with the meaning "T is a subtype of T'";
- $\text{RT} <_1 \text{RT}'$ with the meaning "RT *directly* extends RT'";
- $\text{RT} \not\prec \exists \text{T}$ with the meaning "type T exists and is accessible from code contained in type RT"[2];

---

[2] If you think the symbol "$\not\prec$" as an eye, then you can interpret any assumption of the form "RT $\not\prec \dots$" as: "RT *sees* $\dots$" and this is supposed to help ☺.

$$\Gamma ::= \gamma_1 \ldots \gamma_n$$
$$\gamma ::= \text{C} \mapsto [\text{AM=AM}, \text{CK=CK}, \text{PARENT=C}', \text{IS=I}_1 \ldots \text{I}_n, \text{KSS=KSS}, \text{FSS=FSS}, \text{MSS=MSS}] \mid$$
$$\quad \text{I} \mapsto [\text{AM=AM}, \text{IS=I}_1 \ldots \text{I}_n, \text{FSS=FSS}, \text{MSS=MSS}]$$

$$\bar{\text{T}} ::= \text{T}_1 \ldots \text{T}_n$$

$\text{T}^{\perp} ::= \text{T} \mid \perp$	$\bar{\text{T}}^{\perp} ::= \text{T}_1^{\perp} \ldots \text{T}_n^{\perp}$
$\text{KS} ::= \text{AM } \bar{\text{T}} \text{ throws ES}$	$\text{KSS} ::= \text{KS}_1 \ldots \text{KS}_n$
$\text{FS} ::= \text{AM FK T f}$	$\text{FSS} ::= \text{FS}_1 \ldots \text{FS}_n$
$\text{MS} ::= \text{AM MK T m}(\bar{\text{T}}) \text{ throws ES}$	$\text{MSS} ::= \text{MS}_1 \ldots \text{MS}_n$

$$\lambda ::= \text{T} \leq \text{T}' \mid$$
$$\quad \text{RT} <_1 \text{RT}' \mid$$
$$\quad \text{RT} \not< \exists \text{T} \mid$$
$$\quad \text{RT} \not< \exists_{\text{C}} \text{CK}^{\star} \text{ C} \mid$$
$$\quad \text{RT} \not< \exists_{\text{I}} \text{I} \mid$$
$$\quad \text{RT} \not< Cns(\text{C}, \bar{\text{T}}^{\perp}) = [\text{PAR=}\bar{\text{T}}, \text{ES=ES}] \mid$$
$$\quad \text{RT} \not< Fld(\text{RT}', \text{f}) = [\text{FINAL=FINAL}^{\star}, \text{FK=FK}, \text{T=T}] \mid$$
$$\quad \text{RT} \not< Mth(\text{RT}', \text{m}, \bar{\text{T}}^{\perp}) = [\text{MK=MK}^{\star}, \text{RET=T}, \text{PAR=}\bar{\text{T}}, \text{ES=ES}]$$

$$\text{CK}^{\star} ::= \text{CK} \mid \_ \qquad \text{FINAL}^{\star} ::= \text{FINAL} \mid \_ \qquad \text{MK}^{\star} ::= \text{MK} \mid \text{not-static}$$

Fig. 3. Type environments and Type assumptions.

- RT $\not< \exists_{\text{C}}$ CK* C with the meaning "class C, with kind CK*, exists and is accessible from code contained in RT". CK* = $\_$ means "any kind", that is, we do not care whether the class is abstract or not;
- RT $\not< \exists_{\text{I}}$ I with the meaning "interface I exists and is accessible from code contained in RT";
- RT $\not< Cns(\text{C}, \bar{\text{T}}^{\perp})$ = [PAR=$\bar{\text{T}}$, ES=ES] with the meaning "the most specific constructor for class C and parameter types $\bar{\text{T}}^{\perp}$, invoked from code contained in RT, has parameter types $\bar{\text{T}}$ and can throw exceptions which are compatible with the exception specification ES"[3];
- RT $\not< Fld(\text{RT}', \text{f})$ = [FINAL=FINAL, FK=FK, T=T] with the meaning "if code contained in RT looks up a field named f in type RT', then it finds a field with a final modifier FINAL*, kind FK and type T". FINAL* = $\_$ means we do not care whether the field is final or not;
- RT $\not< Mth(\text{RT}', \text{m}, \bar{\text{T}}^{\perp})$ = [MK=MK*, RET=T, PAR=$\bar{\text{T}}$, ES=ES] with the meaning "the most specific method, invoked from code contained in RT, for a method named m, with parameter types $\bar{\text{T}}^{\perp}$ on a receiver with static type RT' is a method which has kind MK*, return type T, parameter types $\bar{\text{T}}$ and can throw exceptions which are compatible with the exception specification ES"[3].

These assumptions can be thought as "the minimal pieces of information" needed to compile a certain source to a certain bytecode, as we will detail in

---

[3] That is, any exception C such that a C's superclass is contained in ES - see 11.2 of [8].

the sequel. The rules defining the judgment $\Gamma \vdash \lambda$ are omitted for lack of space. A forthcoming extended work, containing all the rules, will be available at http://www.disi.unige.it/person/LagorioG/publications.html shortly. Also, the rules for a small subset of Java can be found in [2].

Next subsection shows how and when these assumptions are used in the process of compilation, while Section 3 explain how to exploit type assumptions in order to obtain a recompilation strategy which is both sound and minimal.

2.3   Compilation

Compilation of expressions is expressed by the following judgment:

$$RT; \Pi; ES; \Gamma \vdash E^s \leadsto E^b : T$$

with the meaning "expression E^s has type T and compiles to binary expression E^b when contained in type RT, in a local environment Π, in a context where exceptions ES can be thrown and in a type environment Γ". Type RT is needed to model the access control; for instance, RT's private methods can be invoked only by expressions inside RT. The local environment Π maps parameter names and this to their respective types (this is undefined when typing expressions contained in static cont exts). Figure 4 show some selected rules defining this judgment.

Compilation of statements is expressed by the following judgment:

$$RT; \Pi; ES; \Gamma \vdash STMT^s \leadsto STMT^b$$

with the meaning "statement $STMT^s$ is compiled to $STMT^b$ when contained in type RT, in a local environment Π, in a context where exceptions ES can be thrown and in a type environment Γ". The rules defining this judgment are omitted because of lack of space.

Before describing the compilation of fragments, we need to introduce the notion of *compilation environment*. A compilation environment *ce* maps fragment names to the corresponding fragment.

$$ce : RT \rightharpoonup S \cup B$$

Note that *ce* models a compilation environment from a compiler's point of view; that is, for each fragment name *ce* returns either a source or a binary fragment, but not both. In fact, even if both are present, only one is considered by the compiler, usually the most up-to-date according to the file's attributes. As a consequence, a type environment Γ can be extracted from a compilation environment *ce* by disregarding the code while retaining signatures and information about type hierarchy. Let us assume the function *extractEnv* : *ce* → Γ does this job.

Assume we have a *consistent* compilation environment *ce*, that is, if we compile all the sources in *ce* we obtain, for the sources which have been recompiled, the same binaries already present in *ce*. Assume, then, to change a

$$\frac{\begin{array}{c}\forall i \in 1..n \ RT; \Pi; ES; \Gamma \vdash E_i^s \leadsto E_i^b : T_i \\ \Gamma \vdash RT \not\prec Cns(C, T_1 \ldots T_n) = [\text{PAR}=\bar{T}, \text{ES}=ES] \\ \Gamma \vdash RT \not\prec \exists_c \in C\end{array}}{RT; \Pi; ES; \Gamma \vdash \text{new } C(E_1^s, \ldots E_n^s) \leadsto \text{new } C \ll \bar{T} \gg_c (E_1^b, \ldots, E_n^b) : C}$$

$$\frac{\begin{array}{c}\Gamma \vdash C <_1 C' \\ \Gamma \vdash C \not\prec Fld(C', f) = [\text{FINAL}=\_, \text{FK}=\epsilon, \text{T}=T]\end{array}}{C; \Pi; ES; \Gamma \vdash \text{super.f} \leadsto \text{this.} \ll C'.T \gg_{if} : T} \qquad \text{this} \in Def(\Pi)$$

$$\frac{\begin{array}{c}RT; \Pi; ES; \Gamma \vdash E_1^s \leadsto E_1^b : C \\ \Gamma \vdash RT \not\prec Fld(C, f) = [\text{FINAL}=\epsilon, \text{FK}=\epsilon, \text{T}=T] \\ RT; \Pi; ES; \Gamma \vdash E_2^s \leadsto E_2^b : T_2 \\ \Gamma \vdash T_2 \leq T\end{array}}{\begin{array}{c}RT; \Pi; ES; \Gamma \vdash E_1^s.f = E_2^s \leadsto \\ E_1^b. \ll C.T \gg_{if} = E_2^b : T\end{array}} \qquad \frac{\Gamma \vdash RT \not\prec Fld(RT', f) = [\text{FINAL}=\_, \text{FK}=\textbf{static}, \text{T}=T]}{RT; \Pi; ES; \Gamma \vdash RT'.f \leadsto \ll RT'.T \gg_{sf} : T}$$

$$\frac{\begin{array}{c}RT; \Pi; ES; \Gamma \vdash E^s \leadsto E^b : RT' \\ \Gamma \vdash RT \not\prec \exists_c \_ RT' \\ \Gamma \vdash RT \not\prec Mth(RT', m, T_1 \ldots T_n) = [\text{MK}=\textbf{not-static}, \text{RET}=T, \text{PAR}=\bar{T}, \text{ES}=ES] \\ \forall i \in 1..n \ RT; \Pi; ES; \Gamma \vdash E_i^s \leadsto E_i^b : T_i\end{array}}{RT; \Pi; ES; \Gamma \vdash E^s.m(E_1^s, \ldots, E_n^s) \leadsto E^b. \ll RT'.m(\bar{T}) \gg_{vrt} (E_1^b, \ldots, E_n^b) : T}$$

$$\frac{\begin{array}{c}RT; \Pi; ES; \Gamma \vdash E^s \leadsto E^b : RT' \\ \Gamma \vdash RT \not\prec \exists_I RT' \\ \Gamma \vdash RT \not\prec Mth(RT', m, T_1 \ldots T_n) = [\text{MK}=\textbf{abstract}, \text{RET}=T, \text{PAR}=\bar{T}, \text{ES}=ES] \\ \forall i \in 1..n \ RT; \Pi; ES; \Gamma \vdash E_i^s \leadsto E_i^b : T_i\end{array}}{RT; \Pi; ES; \Gamma \vdash E^s.m(E_1^s, \ldots, E_n^s) \leadsto E^b. \ll RT'.m(\bar{T}) \gg_{int} (E_1^b, \ldots, E_n^b) : T}$$

Fig. 4. Selected expression typing rules.

bunch of sources, say $RT_1, \ldots, RT_n$, obtaining ce_{new} (and a corresponding $\Gamma_{new} = extractEnv(ce_{new})$). What do we have to do in order to obtain a new *consistent* compilation environment?

First of all, we have to check that the environment Γ_{new} is well-formed, for instance, it must not contain a cycle in the type hierarchy. We formally capture this notion with the judgment $\vdash \Gamma_{new}\diamond$. One could argue that we do not want to check the well-formedness of the *whole* Γ_{new} after having changed, say, a *tiny detail* in one source. Right, we do not want to; yet, we need to *unless* we know something more (see Section 3).

After having checked the environment Γ_{new}, we need to decide which fragments to (re)compile. Of course we have to recompile those which have been changed, that is, $RT_1 \ldots RT_n$ but what else? Are you tempted to answer "make clean; make all will do"? A lot of real-world programmers would do just that. When dealing with a small/medium application and a quite powerful computer you can do that. And, it works. It works *fine* actually, but what if you *can not* do that? Next section a ddresses this crucial point. For now, just assume we have to compile $RT_1, \ldots, RT_m$ (obviously $m \geq n$).

When we have a well-formed Γ_{new} and do know which fragments to recompile we can go for it: in our model "running the compilation" on each fragment RT_i amounts to prove the following judgments:

$$RT_i; \Gamma_{new} \vdash ce_{new}(RT_i) \leadsto B_i$$

These metarules assume Γ to be well-formed, that is, $\vdash \Gamma\diamond$.
Anyway, we do *not* want $\vdash \Gamma\diamond$ to be a premise of any of them (see the text for full details).

$$\frac{C;\Gamma \vdash KDS^s \rightsquigarrow KDS^b \quad C;\Gamma \vdash FDS^s \rightsquigarrow FDS^b \quad C;\Gamma \vdash MDS^s \rightsquigarrow MDS^b}{\begin{array}{c}\Gamma \vdash \text{AM CK class C extends } C' \text{ implements } I_1,\ldots,I_m \text{ \{KDS}^s \text{ FDS}^s \text{ MDS}^s\text{\}} \rightsquigarrow \\ \text{AM CK class C extends } C' \text{ implements } I_1,\ldots,I_m \text{ \{KDS}^b \text{ FDS}^b \text{ MDS}^b\text{\}}\end{array}} \quad AM \in \{\epsilon, \text{public}\}$$

$$\frac{I;\Gamma \vdash FDS^s \rightsquigarrow FDS^b \quad I;\Gamma \vdash MDS^s \rightsquigarrow MDS^b}{\begin{array}{c}\Gamma \vdash \text{AM interface I extends } I_1\ldots I_m \text{ \{ FDS}^s \text{ MDS}^s \text{ \}} \rightsquigarrow \\ \text{AM interface I extends } I_1\ldots I_m \text{ \{ FDS}^b \text{ MDS}^b \text{ \}}\end{array}}$$
$$\begin{array}{l} MDS^s = MD_1^s..MD_n^s \\ \forall i \in 1..n \ MD_i^s = \text{public abstract}\ldots \\ FDS^s = FD_1^s..FD_m^s \\ \forall i \in 1..m \ FD_i^s = \text{public static final}\ldots \\ AM \in \{\epsilon, \text{public}\} \end{array}$$

$$\frac{\begin{array}{c}\Gamma \vdash C <_1 C' \\ \forall i \in 1..n \ C;\Pi;ES;\Gamma \vdash E_i^s \rightsquigarrow E_i^b : T_i \\ C;\Pi;ES;\Gamma \vdash STMTS^s \rightsquigarrow STMTS^b \\ \Gamma \vdash C \not\prec Cns(C',T_1\ldots T_n) = [\text{PAR}=\bar{T},\text{ES}=ES]\end{array}}{\begin{array}{c}C;\Gamma \vdash \text{AM } (T_1 \ x_1,\ldots,T_n \ x_n) \text{ throws ES \{ super}(E_1^s,\ldots,E_n^s); \text{ STMTS}^s \text{ \}} \rightsquigarrow \\ \text{AM } (T_1 \ x_1,\ldots,T_n \ x_n) \text{ throws ES \{ super}(E_1^b,\ldots,E_n^b) \ll \bar{T} \gg_c; \text{ STMTS}^b \text{ \}}\end{array}}$$
$$\begin{array}{l} \Pi = \{x_1 \mapsto T_1, \\ \qquad \ldots, \\ x_n \mapsto T_n, \\ \text{this} \mapsto C\} \end{array}$$

$$\frac{\begin{array}{c}RT;\Pi;\emptyset;\Gamma \vdash E^s \rightsquigarrow E^b : T' \\ \Gamma \vdash T' \leq T\end{array}}{RT;\Gamma \vdash \text{AM FINAL FK T } f = E^s ; \ \rightsquigarrow \text{AM FINAL FK T } f = E^b ;} \quad \Pi = This(FK,C)$$

$$\frac{\begin{array}{c}C;\Pi;ES;\Gamma \vdash STMTS^s \rightsquigarrow STMTS^b \\ C;\Pi;ES;\Gamma \vdash E^s \rightsquigarrow E^b : T' \\ \Gamma \vdash T' \leq T\end{array}}{\begin{array}{c}C;\Gamma \vdash \text{AM MK T } m(T_1 \ x_1,\ldots,T_n \ x_n) \text{ throws ES \{ STMTS}^s \text{ return } E^s; \text{ \}} \rightsquigarrow \\ \text{AM MK T } m(T_1 \ x_1,\ldots,T_n \ x_n) \text{ throws ES \{ STMTS}^b \text{ return } E^b; \text{ \}}\end{array}}$$
$$\begin{array}{l} \Pi = \{x_1 \mapsto T_1, \\ \qquad \ldots, \\ x_n \mapsto T_n\} \cup \\ This(MK,C) \\ MK \neq \text{abstract} \end{array}$$

$This(\_,I) = \emptyset$
$This(\text{static},C) = \emptyset;$
$This(\epsilon,C) = \{\text{this} \mapsto C\}$

Fig. 5. Selected compilation rules.

Figure 5 shows some selected rules defining this judgment. In defining the compilation of a set of classes we assume to compile them one by one, that is, we assume that no global optimizations take place. This reflects the fact that in languages with dynamic linking like Java, the concept of "program" is only significant at runtime so it is safer to leave cross class optimizations to virtual machines like HotSpot [9].

3   A Smart Strategy

When dealing with an updated compilation context ce_{new} (in respect to a previous ce_{old}) there are two steps to perform: checking whether the corresponding new type environment Γ_{new} is well-formed and, when it is, decide which (unchanged) source fragments have to be recompiled besides the changed ones. Some information gathered during a previous compilation can be used to speedup both these steps. We first show how we can check only the "updated part" of an environment Γ_{new} when a previous well-formed environment Γ_{old} is known. Then, we show how the type assumptions used to compile a fragment can be used later to decide whether it has to be recompiled.

We define $\texttt{leaves}_\Gamma(\text{RT}) = \{\text{RT}'|\Gamma \vdash \text{RT}' \leq \text{RT} \land \forall \text{RT}''\ \Gamma \vdash \text{RT}'' \leq \text{RT}' \implies \text{RT}'' = \text{RT}'\}$ and the judgment $\Gamma \vdash \texttt{okOvr}\ \text{RT}$ with the meaning "RT correctly extends its parent types (up to Object) in Γ". That is, RT's hierarchy is acyclic and the Java rules on method overriding/hiding are respected. The rules defining such a judgment are omitted for lack of space.

Definition 1. *A type environment Γ_{new} is well-formed w.r.t. another type environment Γ_{old} iff the following conditions hold:*

[add] $\text{RT} \in Def(\Gamma_{new}) \setminus Def(\Gamma_{old}) \implies \begin{cases} \Gamma_{new} \vdash \texttt{okOvr}\ \text{RT} \\ \texttt{used}_{\Gamma_{new}}(\text{RT}) \subseteq Def(\Gamma_{new}) \end{cases}$

[rmv] $Def(\Gamma_{old}) \setminus Def(\Gamma_{new}) \neq \emptyset \implies \forall \text{RT} \in Def(\Gamma_{new})\ \texttt{used}_{\Gamma_{new}}(\text{RT}) \subseteq Def(\Gamma_{new})$

[cng] $\text{RT} \in Def(\Gamma_{old}) \cap Def(\Gamma_{new}), \Gamma_{old}(\text{RT}) \neq \Gamma_{new}(\text{RT}) \implies \begin{cases} \forall \text{RT}' \in \texttt{leaves}_{\Gamma_{new}}(\text{RT})\ \Gamma_{new} \vdash \texttt{okOvr}\ \text{RT}' \\ \texttt{used}_{\Gamma_{new}}(\text{RT}) \subseteq Def(\Gamma_{new}) \end{cases}$

where "used by RT in Γ", $\texttt{used}_\Gamma(\text{RT})$, means all types directly referenced by RT.

Theorem 1. *If $\vdash \Gamma_{old}\diamond$ holds, and Γ_{new} is well-formed w.r.t. Γ_{old} then, $\vdash \Gamma_{new}\diamond$ holds.*

Proof Two requirements have to be met:

- Γ_{new} must be closed, that is, $\texttt{used}_{\Gamma_{new}}(\text{RT}) \subseteq Def(\Gamma_{new})$ for all $\text{RT} \in Def(\Gamma_{new})$;
- overriding rules must be satisfied, that is, for any $\text{RT} \in Def(\Gamma_{new})$ the judgment $\Gamma_{new} \vdash \texttt{okOvr}\ \text{RT}$ must be valid.

The former requirement is met by hypothesis when some type defined in Γ_{old} has been removed from Γ_{new}, see *[rmv]* in Definition 1. When no types have been removed, the unchanged types cannot, trivially, refer to undefined types because, by hypothesis, Γ_{old} is closed. By *[add]* and *[cng]* of Definition 1 new and updated types refer only to types defined in Γ_{new}.

The latter requirement can be proved by case analysis. Consider $Def(\Gamma_{new})$ as the union of three disjoint sets: U, C and N. These sets contain, respectively, the unchanged, changed and new types in Γ_{new} with respect to Γ_{old}. Formally:

$$U = \{\text{RT}|\text{RT} \in Def(\Gamma_{new}) \cap Def(\Gamma_{old}), \Gamma_{new}(\text{RT}) = \Gamma_{old}(\text{RT})\}$$
$$C = \{\text{RT}|\text{RT} \in Def(\Gamma_{new}) \cap Def(\Gamma_{old}), \Gamma_{new}(\text{RT}) \neq \Gamma_{old}(\text{RT})\}$$
$$N = Def(\Gamma_{new}) \setminus Def(\Gamma_{old})$$

Let us consider $N \cup C$ first. For any new type RT, contained in N, the judgment $\Gamma_{new} \vdash \texttt{okOvr}\ \text{RT}$ is valid by the hypothesis, see *[add]* of Definition 1. For any changed type RT, contained in C, the judgment $\Gamma_{new} \vdash \texttt{okOvr}\ \text{RT}$ is valid because of *[cng]* of Definition 1.

It remains to prove that the judgment holds for the unchanged types, contained in U. Since they are unchanged the *direct* supertypes of any type in U are the same in Γ_{old} and Γ_{new}. Furthermore, each direct supertype of RT must be contained in $Def(\Gamma_{\mathrm{old}})$ *and* in $Def(\Gamma_{\mathrm{new}})$ because of, respectively, the fact that $\vdash \Gamma_{\mathrm{old}}\diamond$ holds and the fact that Γ_{new} is closed (which we have proved before). Hence, these direct supertypes must be contained in $Def(\Gamma_{\mathrm{old}}) \cap Def(\Gamma_{\mathrm{new}})$ which, by definition, is equal to: $U \cup C$. If a direct supertype is in U, then the same reasoning can be applied; so, for any $\mathtt{RT} \in U$, only two cases are possible:

- *all* supertypes of RT are in U; then, the hierarchy of RT has not changed and by the hypothesis $\vdash \Gamma_{\mathrm{old}}\diamond$ is valid, so the judgment $\Gamma_{\mathrm{new}} \vdash \mathtt{okOvr\ RT}$ is valid too;
- there exists a supertype $\mathtt{RT}'$ of RT which is in C, whose subtypes till RT are in U. Then, by *[cng]* there exists a type $\mathtt{RT}''$ such that $\mathtt{RT}'' \leq \mathtt{RT}$ and $\Gamma_{\mathrm{new}} \vdash \mathtt{okOvr\ RT}''$ holds. So, $\Gamma_{\mathrm{new}} \vdash \mathtt{okOvr\ RT}$ must be valid too. $\square$

In summary, as long as we keep trace of a previous well-formed environment Γ_{old} we can check for the well-formedness of any new environment Γ_{new} by examining the changes w.r.t. Γ_{old}. The most expensive check must be performed when some classes are removed; this is acceptable because classes are added/changed more often than removed in the usual software development cycle. The requirement of having a previous well-formed environment available may seem restrictive, but it is not, since one can always use the empty environment (which is trivially well-formed) as Γ_{old} when starting to use our strategy from scratch.

Assume we have a compilation environment ce_{old}, a corresponding well-formed type environment $\Gamma_{\mathrm{old}} = extractEnv(ce_{\mathrm{old}})$, and we can prove:

$$\mathtt{RT}; \Gamma_{\mathrm{old}} \vdash ce_{\mathrm{old}}(\mathtt{RT}) \rightsquigarrow \mathtt{B}$$

The proof tree for this judgment can be proved to be unique, and contains a set of assumptions $\Lambda = \lambda_1, \dots, \lambda_n$. We call it the *requirements* for RT in Γ_{old} and write

$$Reqs(\mathtt{RT}, \Gamma_{\mathrm{old}}) = \Lambda$$

Assume to change ce_{old} leaving the fragment for RT untouched. That is, assume to have another compilation environment ce_{new}, with a corresponding well-formed environment Γ_{new}, such that $ce_{\mathrm{new}}(\mathtt{RT}) = ce_{\mathrm{old}}(\mathtt{RT})$.

Does RT compile in ce_{new}? If it does, can we say something about the corresponding binary?

The following theorem states that, if Γ_{new} still satisfy the requirements of RT in Γ_{old}, then we do know that RT compiles in Γ_{new} and it compiles to the *same* binary.

Theorem 2. *If ce_{old} and ce_{new} are two compilation environments which share the same source for RT, that is, $ce_{\mathrm{old}}(RT) = ce_{\mathrm{new}}(RT)$, the corresponding type environments $\Gamma_{\mathrm{old}} = extractEnv(ce_{\mathrm{old}})$ and $\Gamma_{\mathrm{new}} = extractEnv(ce_{\mathrm{new}})$ are well-formed, and the judgment $RT; \Gamma_{\mathrm{old}} \vdash ce_{\mathrm{old}}(RT) \rightsquigarrow B$ can be proved, then:*

$$RT; \Gamma_{\mathrm{new}} \vdash ce_{\mathrm{new}}(RT) \rightsquigarrow B \iff \Gamma_{\mathrm{new}} \vdash Reqs(RT, \Gamma_{\mathrm{old}})$$

Proof (sketch) If $\Gamma_{\text{new}} \vdash Reqs(\text{RT}, \Gamma_{\text{old}})$, that is, $\Gamma_{\text{new}} \vdash \lambda$ holds for all $\lambda \in Reqs(\text{RT}, \Gamma_{\text{old}})$, the proof for $\text{RT}; \Gamma_{\text{old}} \vdash ce_{\text{old}}(\text{RT}) \rightsquigarrow \text{B}$ is a proof for $\text{RT}; \Gamma_{\text{new}} \vdash ce_{\text{new}}(\text{RT}) \rightsquigarrow \text{B}$ too. On the other hand, if $\Gamma_{\text{new}} \nvdash Reqs(\text{RT}, \Gamma_{\text{old}})$, then there exists at least one $\lambda \in Reqs(\text{RT}, \Gamma_{\text{old}})$ such that $\Gamma_{\text{new}} \nvdash \lambda$. Since the proof tree for a compilation judgment is unique, either there is no proof tree for compiling RT in Γ_{new} or the compilation produces another binary B′ which differs from B. $\square$

When the compilation for a fragment RT is undefined, or the binary produced by the compilation differs from the existing one, a sound strategy requires the compilation of RT.

To sum up, our compilation strategy is quite simple: *a fragment has to be recompiled if and only if the new environment does not entail its requirements.* This strategy is both *sound* and *minimal*.

So far so good: if we keep trace of the requirements for a fragment when we compile it we can apply a sound and minimal strategy. However, from a practical point of view there is another point to ponder: the cost of checking whether the requirements of a fragment are entailed by a type environment. If this checking costed more than compiling the source fragment, then all the reasoning so far would be useless. Luckily, this is not the case. In typechecking a source fragment a compiler must necessarily perform all the steps which are necessary to check the validity of the entailment. In addition, a compiler must, of course, parse the source and generate the code. So, checking whether the entailment holds is definitely faster than recompiling, and we expect this to be much faster. Of course, the global cost of using a smart strategy is not easy to determine because it depends on the particular compiler and the compilation context. That is, on the one hand there is the additional cost of checking the entailment, on the other hand there is the saving in not compiling the fragments whose requirements are entailed by the new environment. In a sense, the time used to find that a fragment's requirements are *not* entailed may appear "wasted", because that fragment has to be recompiled. However, if the compilation manager and the compiler are tightly integrated, the compiler's typechecking step can use the results of the previous entailment checking step as a sort of cache and skip many checks when recompiling the fragment. Using this trick, the "wasted" time is extremely small: it just consists in finding that a single requirement λ does not hold.

We can model an *extended* compilation environment as follows:

$$ce_+ : \langle \Gamma, \text{RT} \rightharpoonup \text{S} \cup \text{B} \cup (\text{B} \times \Lambda) \rangle$$

That is, a pair consisting of the previous (well-formed) environment Γ and a function which, for each fragment name, returns either: the source only, the binary only (when the source is not available) or a pair consisting of the binary and the requirements (the idea is that they are the result of a previous compilation).

4   Related and Further Work

This paper, together with [3, 4], can be considered a step towards a better support for separate compilation of Java-like languages.

The solution presented here, which extends the ideas in [2], is similar to attribute recompilation, according to the classification given in [1] - here attributes correspond to assumptions.

An inspiring source of our work has certainly been Dmitriev's paper [5], which describes a make technology, based on smart dependency checking, that aims to keep a project consistent while reducing the number of files to be recompiled. A freely downloadable tool, *Javamake*, is based on such a paper and implements the selective recompilation upon any Java compiler. Unfortunately, as pointed out by the author himself, there is no proof of the correctness of the approach, which is not based on theoretical foundations. So, it might happen that *Javamake* fails to force the recompilation of some classes which is actually needed for ensuring the consistency of the project. Conversely, *Javamake* cannot avoid a considerable amount of unnecessary recompilations. Hence, it is neither sound nor minimal.

The final goal of the work presented in this paper is implementing a smart compilation manager for the whole Java language, à la Javamake, but based on a formal model on which the correctness can be actually proved. To achieve this result, there are some subtle and Java-peculiar features which must be addressed.

- *Unreachable code* is not just a bad idea: it is forbidden (see 14.20 of [8]) - this is the most challenging issue to be tackled.
- *Final methods*: an invocation of a final instance method is compiled to different bytecode w.r.t. an invocation of a non-final instance method (non-virtual invocation vs virtual one, see 15.12.3 of [8]). This issue should not pose major problems.
- *Accessing a final field initialized by a constant expression* is a constant expression (see 15.28 of [8]) and so should be compiled directly to the corresponding value. This issue should not pose problems too, as long as an assumption keeps track that such a constant is really an access to a static final field.

Acknowledgements

We warmly thank Elena Zucca, Davide Ancona and Sophia Drossopoulou for their useful suggestions and feedback.

References

1. Rolf Adams, Walter Tichy, and Annette Weinert. The cost of selective recompilation and environment processing. *ACM Transactions on Software Engineering and Methodology*, 3(1):3–28, January 1994.
2. D. Ancona and G. Lagorio. Stronger Typings for Separate Compilation of Java-like Languages. Technical report, DISI, March 2003.
3. D. Ancona, G. Lagorio, and E. Zucca. A formal framework for Java separate compilation. In B. Magnusson, editor, *ECOOP 2002 - Object-Oriented Programming*, number 2374 in Lecture Notes in Computer Science, pages 609–635. Springer, 2002.

4. D. Ancona, G. Lagorio, and E. Zucca. True separate compilation of Java classes. In *ACM SIGPLAN Conference on Principles and Practice of Declarative Programming (PPDP'02)*, pages 189–200. ACM Press, 2002.

5. M. Dmitriev. Language-specific make technology for the Java programming language. *ACM SIGPLAN Notices*, 37(11):373–385, 2002.

6. S. Drossopoulou and S. Eisenbach. Describing the semantics of Java and proving type soundness. In J. Alves-Foss, editor, *Formal Syntax and Semantics of Java*, number 1523 in Lecture Notes in Computer Science, pages 41–82. Springer, 1999.

7. S. Drossopoulou, T. Valkevych, and S. Eisenbach. Java type soundness revisited. Technical report, Dept. of Computing - Imperial College of Science, Technology and Medicine, September 2000.

8. J. Gosling, B. Joy, G. Steele, and G. Bracha. *The Java™ Language Specification, Second Edition*. Addison-Wesley, 2000.

9. SUN Microsystems. The Java HotSpot Virtual Machine, 2001. Technical White Paper.

Anonymous Group Communication
in Mobile Networks
(Extended Abstract)

Stelvio Cimato, Paolo D'Arco, and Ivan Visconti

Dipartimento di Informatica ed Applicazioni
Università di Salerno, 84081 Baronissi (SA), Italy
{cimato,paodar,visconti}@dia.unisa.it

Abstract. In this paper we propose efficient schemes enabling groups
of users of a mobile network to communicate *anonymously* with respect
to an adversarial party (i.e, other users, network managers, and so on).
Each user can start a group communication, and his identity, as well as
the identities of the other members of the group, are not revealed even
if several other parties of the system collude. We consider two network
settings and, for each of them, we propose an efficient and secure scheme.

Keywords: Mobile Communication, Cryptography, Anonymity, Privacy

1   Introduction

Mobile communication has heavily grown up in the last decade. In order to
provide high-quality services, researches have mainly been focusing on the development of a new mobile network infrastructure, and on the design of enough
powerful and well-equipped mobile devices. Such efforts have given rise to a
scenario where many applications are provided to the users. By means of their
mobile devices, users can have group communication, can receive and exchange
multimedia data, can browse the Internet, as well as can subscribe to certain
information services, offered by public or private agencies. However, as much
as mobile networks, devices and applications are having spread diffusion, so is
user privacy request becoming more and more demanding. In the literature,
many papers examine the security threats involved in mobile communication,
e.g., confidentiality of the conversation, privacy of user location, protection of
user identity.

Our contribution. This paper deals with anonymous group mobile communication. We describe two schemes enabling a user to start anonymously a group
communication with other users, whose identities are hidden to parties who do
not belong to the group. More precisely, only the user starting the conference
knows the identities of the parties involved in the conversation, while neither
the service provider, nor any involved user knows the identities of the others.
Such an anonymous conference system allows discussions on sensitive topics to
be started among participants which do not want to disclose their identities, and

C. Blundo and C. Laneve (Eds.): ICTCS 2003, LNCS 2841, pp. 316–328, 2003.

they have applications in both business and fancy fields (politics boards, chat or dating systems). Each protocol yields a different security degree. Moreover, following a recent trend in cryptographic researches, in designing our scheme, we try to minimize the need for trust in third parties as much as possible.

Related Work. Several papers in the literature have addressed the issue of secure communication in mobile networks. Anonymous communication has been studied in [9]. The issue of anonymous and accountable access to services in mobile communication systems has been instead addressed in [3], where a trusted customer care agency is used, in order to grant and charge accesses to services. An efficient scheme which provides privacy of the conversation (i.e. content protection) in group mobile communication has been recently given in [17]. Another approach for preserving user privacy in mobile communication networks can be found in [12], as well as in [2] a replicated memory service is used in order to preserve user location privacy. Anonymity in wired communication networks has been deeply studied, and it has been source of ideas also for the mobile setting. In [4,15] mix networks have been introduced to achieve several goals in wired networks and later applications to mobile communication have been considered in [8,1].

2   Background

Rabin Cryptosystem. Let Z_n^* be the multiplicative group of the integers x between 1 and $n-1$ such that $gcd(x, n) = 1$. We say that y is a *quadratic residue* modulo an odd integer n iff there exists w such that $w^2 \equiv y \bmod n$. Let Q_n be the set of quadratic residues modulo n. Deciding whether y is a quadratic residue modulo n is easy if n is prime. Indeed, y is a quadratic residue modulo a prime n iff $y^{\frac{n-1}{2}} \equiv 1 \bmod n$ and the two solutions of $w^2 = y \bmod n$ are given by $\pm y^{\frac{n+1}{4}} \bmod n$. On the other hand, if the modulo n is composite, then the quadratic residuosity of y modulo n can be efficiently decided only if the factorization of n is known. In our construction we consider special moduli n called Blum integers. We say that n is a Blum integer if n is the product of two primes p, q of the same length, both congruent to 3 modulo 4. In such a case, the number of solutions of $w^2 = y \bmod n$ is 4. We assume that computing one square root of a quadratic residue modulo a Blum integer is hard if the factorization of the Blum integer is not known. Rabin's cryptosystem works as follows:

- Set-up. A user generates a Blum integer $n = pq$, publishes n and keeps secret its factorization.
- Encryption. A message M is encrypted computing $\hat{M} = M^2 \bmod n$.
- Decryption. An encrypted message $\hat{M}$ is decrypted computing the four square roots modulo n and choosing one of them according to some probabilistic criterion (e.g., the last bits of a message represents the message digest of the other bits).

The encryption operation is very efficient: it just requires a modular multiplication. Hence, several encryptions can be efficiently performed by a smart card. The decryption requires two modular exponentiations.

Chinese Remainder Theorem. An important result from Number Theory, frequently used in Cryptography, is given by the so called Chinese Remainder Theorem (see [18] for details):

Theorem 1. *Let $n_1, \ldots, n_k$ be pairwise relatively prime integers, and let $n = n_1 \cdot n_2 \cdot \ldots \cdot n_k$. Then, for any integers $a_1, a_2, \ldots, a_k$, the set of simultaneous equations $X \equiv a_i \bmod n_i$, for $i = 1, \ldots, k$, has a unique solution modulo n for the unknown X.*

In other words, there exists and can be efficiently computed a single value $0 < X < \prod_{i=1}^{k} n_i$ such that $X \equiv a_i \bmod n_i$, for $i = 1, \ldots, k$.

Secret Sets Constructions. Secret sets where introduced by Molva and Tsudik in [14] as a basic construct for communication with a group of mutually suspicious entities. Loosely speaking, a set is secret if any entity can test its membership in the set but can determine neither the other members nor the cardinality of the set. Secret sets were further studied in [6]. We will use one of the schemes given in [14], based on the Chinese Remainder Theorem, in the design of our first protocol. Basically, the scheme for constructing a secret set will be used at the beginning of the conference to set up a broadcast message for inviting other users to join the conference.

Blind Signatures. Blinding is a well-known cryptographic technique used to allow an entity to sign a message, received from another entity, without knowing the content of the message [5]. In Chaum's blind signature scheme, based on RSA [13], user A is able to obtain B's signature on a message m, releasing no information on m. More precisely, let (n, e) and d be B's public and private key, respectively. Let k be a random integer chosen by A with $0 \le k \le n - 1$ and $gcd(n, k) = 1$. To get the blind signature from B on a message m, A first computes $m^* = h(m)k^e \bmod n$, and sends it to B. B returns to A the message $s^* = (m^*)^d \bmod n$. Finally, A can obtain B's signature on the original message m by computing $s = k^{-1}s^* \bmod n$.

Billing. Anonymous subscription protocols have been proposed in the literature, allowing users to anonymously access an electronic service. Some protocols are based on the use of pseudonyms [4], some others rely on the use of anonymous tokening systems, which make use of blind signatures [19]. The solution we describe here is given by the *bit counting scheme*, which has been recently proposed by Ramzan and Ruhl in [16]. The idea is to give each user, holding a regular subscription to a service, a number of anonymous tokens, encoding the binary representation of the number of allowed accesses. Each time the user wishes to access the service, he sends a subset of the valid tokens to the service provider, such that the validity of the subscription can be checked. The service provider replies by providing the service and by sending back to the user a new set of tokens, encoding the remaining number of allowed accesses.

More precisely, the service provider fixes $V = 2^m - 1$, to be the maximum number of accesses to a service for a valid subscription. Then, it selects $2m$ public/secret key pairs, named $g_1, g_2, \ldots, g_m$ and $f_1, f_2, \ldots, f_m$. Assume that a user buys a subscription for $\ell \leq V$ accesses to the service: he sends to the provider m blinded tokens $t_1, t_2, \ldots, t_m$ (with each $t_i = (m_i, h(m_i)^d)$). The provider returns the tokens signing each t_i with g_i, if the corresponding bit in the binary representation of ℓ is 1, or with f_i, if the corresponding bit in the binary representation of ℓ is 0.

Each time a user wants to access the service, he sends to the provider the subset of tokens $t_1, \ldots, t_i$, such that t_i is the first token signed with g_i, while $t_1, \ldots, t_{i-1}$ are all signed with keys $f_1, \ldots, f_{i-1}$. He also sends i fresh blinded tokens $t_{n_1}, \ldots, t_{n_i}$ to the provider. The provider can check that the tokens $t_1, \ldots, t_i$ are valid and have not been used before. If this is the case, then it provides the user with the requested service, and sends him the i signed fresh tokens $t_{n_1}^*, \ldots, t_{n_i}^*$, where $t_{n_1}, \ldots, t_{n_{i-1}}$ have been signed with keys $g_1, \ldots, g_{i-1}$, while t_{n_i} has been signed with f_i.

Notice that the communication complexity of the above billing scheme is optimal, since the user sends on average only two tokens per item request. If k denotes the security parameter, then communication complexity is $O(k)$ bits. User storage complexity is low as well, since the user is requested to keep $O(k \log \ell)$ bits, where ℓ is usually a small integer. The storage complexity for the service provider is high, since it is requested to store every used token. However, by requiring the $2m$ keys to expire at regular intervals, the provider has to store only $O(kn\ell)$ bits, where n is the number of subscribers.

3   Broadcast-Based Setting

A mobile conference is a synchronous collaboration session, in which conferees communicate through a wireless network. In this section we consider a simple scenario, where users are connected to a service provider. More precisely, the entities involved are the following:

- *Mobile devices*, used by the customers to make or receive a call. Mobile devices are directly connected to the service provider.
- *Service provider* (SP, for short), contacted by the users who wish to setup or participate to a mobile conference. The SP receives messages from conferees, operates on these messages in an appropriate way, and then it broadcasts[1] the results to the other conferees.

We assume that, during an off-line registration phase, users subscribe to the service offered by SP, identify themselves, and pay for the service a certain fee, receiving from SP some tickets that can be spent from time to time to access the service. Moreover, we assume that the following conditions are satisfied:

- *Anonymous channel.* We assume that when the user contacts SP, the channel does not provide the identity of the caller.

---

[1] Broadcast messages directed to a single user can be thought as messages sent along a point-to-point channel between SP and the user.

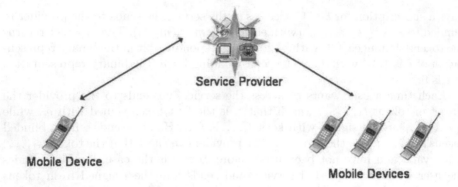

Fig. 1. Broadcast-based Setting.

- *Low Conference Call-Request Rate*: The number of conferences that take place in a certain time-period is low.

The first condition is required because if the channel carries out the identity of the caller, anonymity is impossible. The second condition is required because in our scheme a mobile device has to perform some computation *any* time a new conference call is broadcasted by the SP, in order to find out whether or not the user is part of the conference. Too many calls (i.e., broadcast messages to decrypt) cannot be managed by the low-power mobile device.

3.1 Protocol

Any conference is started by a user, which we refer to as the *Conference Initiator, CI* for short. The structure of a protocol providing anonymous and secure communication is basically divided in four steps:

- ANONYMOUS IDENTIFICATION OF *CI*: The conference initiator *CI* interacts with *SP* in order to be identified as one of the users allowed to access the service. More precisely, *CI* sends a call-request message to *SP* containing anonymous identification information, and tokens for paying the service. At the end of such a phase, the SP sends a randomly chosen conference id, say *cid*, to *CI*.
- CONFERENCE CALL: Once granted the access, the conference initiator *CI*, chooses uniformly at random a session key *k*, embeds *k* in a larger message *M* containing some other information (among which the conference id *cid*), encrypts *M* obtaining *B*, and asks *SP* to broadcast *B* to the users.
- MEMBERSHIP TEST AND KEY RECOVERY: Every user receives *B* and checks in it if he belongs to the conference: If this is the case, then the user succeeds in decrypting the message and in recovering the session key *k*.
- CONFERENCE JOIN AND CONVERSATION: Users belonging to the conference, anonymously identify themselves to the SP and pay for the service. Then, when the conference starts, the SP broadcasts every encrypted message with the prepended conference id *cid*, received by one of the members of the group.

The above general protocol can be instantiated as follows: The conference initiator CI, can anonymously identify himself to the SP as a subscriber, paying the anonymous conference service fee according to the bit counting billing scheme described before, as follows[2]:

Anonymous Identification:
- CI constructs a message $M_I = t_1, \ldots, t_k || tn_1, \ldots, tn_k$ containing a subset of k tokens $t_1, \ldots, t_k$ such that t_k is the first token signed with key g_k, and k fresh blinded tokens $tn_1, \ldots, tn_k$, and sends it to SP.
- SP verifies the validity of the tokens $t_1, \ldots, t_k$ in M_I, signs opportunely the k fresh tokens $tn_1, \ldots, tn_k$, and computes a random number cid. He returns to CI a message $M_R = tn_1^*, \ldots, tn_k^* || cid$ containing the signed tokens $tn_1^*, \ldots, tn_k^*$ and the conference identifier cid.

We assume that every user U_i holds a certified pair of keys (PK_i, SK_i), and he is associated with a public known prime number p_i. Moreover, we denote by $\{M\}_K$ the encryption/decryption of M by using a cryptographic key K. Once CI has been identified by SP as a subscriber of the anonymous conference service, he has paid the fee, and has received the conference identifier cid, then CI proceeds as follows:

Conference Call:
- For each $U_i \in C$, CI constructs a message $M_i = R_i || k || cid || msg$, given by the concatenation of a random string R_i, used for randomization purposes, the session key k, the conference identifier cid, and a message msg establishing membership, and computes $x_i = \{M_i\}_{PK_i}$.
- Then CI, by using the Chinese Remainder Theorem, computes the value X satisfying, for each $U_i \in C$ the congruence $X \bmod p_i = x_i$ and sends it to the SP.
- Finally, SP broadcasts the value X.

Every user of the network, operates as follows:

Membership Test and Key Recovery:
- User U_i, in order to find out whether or not he is part of the conference, computes $x_i = X \bmod p_i$, and then $M_i = \{x_i\}_{SK_i}$.

Finally, each user that is member of the conference, anonymously identify himself to SP, and pays the conference fee. Such a step is basically the same performed by the conference initiator CI. More precisely:

Conference Join and Conversation:
- U_i constructs a message $J_i = t_1, \ldots, t_k || tn_1, \ldots, tn_k || cid$ containing a subset of k tokens $t_1, \ldots, t_k$ such that tokens $t_1, \ldots, t_{k-1}$ are signed with keys $f_1, \ldots, f_{k-1}$ and t_k is signed with key g_k, k fresh blinded tokens $tn_1, \ldots, tn_k$, and the conference identifier cid. Then he sends such a message to SP.
- SP verifies the validity of the tokens $t_1, \ldots, t_k$ in J_i, it signs opportunely the k fresh tokens $tn_1, \ldots, tn_k$, and it returns to U_i the message $J_R = tn_1^*, \ldots, tn_k^*$ containing the signed tokens.

Afterwards, the conversation takes place in a straightforward manner: every user of the group, encrypts the message he wishes to send by using the session

---

[2] Notice that, in order to avoid replay or man-in-the-middle attacks, each message should be encrypted by using a symmetric key established with an asymmetric scheme.

key k, prepends to the message the conference identifier cid, and sends it to SP. Then, SP broadcasts such messages that users in the group receive and decrypt.

The scheme is efficient both from the computational and communication points of view. Indeed, notice that mobile conferences involve usually small groups of users (e.g., $5, 6, \cdots$). It does not make any sense a mobile conference in which $10,000$ people are involved . Conversation would be impossible! In the above scheme, the conference initiator CI only needs to encrypt a message for each member of the conference, and to compute the value X. The first computation is efficient since we are using Rabin's Cryptosystem[3]. The second computation can be easily carried out by means of few multiplications and applications of the Euclidean algorithm. Moreover, the size of the broadcast X is proportional to the number of members of the conference. Finally, every user can check membership by means of a modular division and a single decryption.

In terms of memory storage, the above construction just requires each user to store his own secret key, apart the information needed to anonymously identify himself to the SP. Current smart cards have enough memory storage capability and computational power to support such a scheme[4].

4   Mix-Network Based Setting

The above construction is elegant and efficient but cannot be applied to a large scale network. Indeed, several features of real mobile networks do not match the assumptions we have done before. For example, in the GSM system, the base station to which a mobile device is connected *knows* the identity of the user. Moreover, the idea of a call-for-conference based on an encrypted broadcast message is not feasible in presence of a large number of call-requests. In this section we consider a more feasible scenario resembling widely used mobile communication standards. Mobile users are connected to the network through base stations, which authenticate them and propagate incoming calls. More precisely, the entities we consider are:

- *Mobile devices*: used by the customers to make or receive a call. When making or receiving a call, a radio connection between the mobile device and the nearest radio station is established. The smart card contained in the mobile device allows the user to have the calls charged on his own account, and also to access the services the user has subscribed during the registration phase.
- *Base stations*: consist of transreceivers and controllers who physically manage the communication between the users and the network switching system.

---

[3]   Due to a suitable implementation by means of the Montgomery multiplication algorithm (see [17] for details), we can gain even more efficiency.

[4]   The parameters of the other conferees must be known to the mobile device of the conference initializer as well. Current storage capabilities of mobile devices make it feasible for a few users.

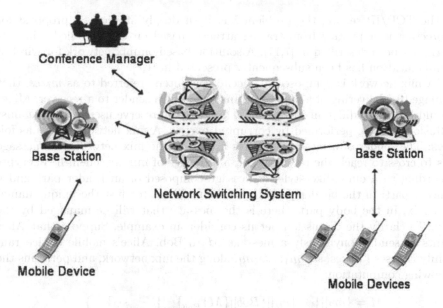

Fig. 2. Mix Network Based Setting.

- *Network switching system*: connects mobile devices to other mobile devices in the same network or in different networks. Mobile switching systems are employed to handle handover, location updating, registration, authentication and call routing. The network switching system usually connects also mobile devices to the fixed (non-mobile) phone networks. The network switching system relies on mix networks (which will be described later on) to redirect messages among mobile users in an anonymous way.
- *Conference manager* (CM, for short): contacted through the network switching system by the users, in order to start a mobile conference. The conference manager receives messages from conferees, operates on these messages in an appropriate way, and then it forwards the results through the network switching system to the conferees.

4.1 Mix Network

In current standard mobile networks the mobile device interacts with a base station, in order to inform the network switching system about the user location. Indeed, the network switching system needs to know the location of a mobile device, in order to redirect a call request to the correct base station. Information about user location is therefore stored in a specific register, called Home Location Register (HLR, for short), and accessed by the network switching system.

Such a mechanism is obviously a strong threat against user privacy, since the information stored by the HLR can be used to trace user movements. A similar threat for user privacy arises in TCP/IP networks for IP addresses. However, in the TCP/IP setting the problem has been deeply studied. A proposal for protecting user privacy from tracing attacks, based on the so called mix network, has been described in [7,11]. A solution based on mix network for wireless communication has been subsequently presented in [1,8].

A mix network is composed of special computers, referred to as *mixes*, that manage the delivering of a message transmitted by a sender to a receiver. Mixes should belong to different institutions, in order to preserve user privacy against collusion attacks, performed by corrupted parties. A mix network works as follows: The sender of a message chooses a path in the mix network the message has to cross to reach the receiver (i.e., a sequence of mixes). Then, he encrypts according to a onion-like style, a message composed of an header part and a content part: in the header part, there is an address (or just the unique name) of a mix. In the body part, there is the message that will be managed by the mix. To clarify the discussion, let us consider an example. Suppose that Alice wants to send anonymously a message M to Bob. Alice's mobile device randomly chooses l mixes, say $m_1, \ldots, m_l$, along the mix network, and performs the following computation:

$$\hat{M} = \{m_2 || \{ \cdots \{m_l || \{Bob || \{M\}_{Bob}\}_{m_l}\}_{m_{l-1}} \cdots \}_{m_2}\}_{m_1}$$

The message M is firstly encrypted with Bob's public key. Then, the resulting message is concatenated to Bob's mobile address and encrypted with m_l's public key. The resulting message is concatenated with the address of m_l and encrypted with m_{l-1}'s public key and so on, until the encryption with m_1's public key is performed. The resulting message $\hat{M}$ is sent by Alice to m_1. The mix m_1 decrypts $\hat{M}$, reads the name m_2 of the next mix in the path, and sends it the remaining message. The mix m_2 proceeds in the same way, and so on until the message reaches m_l. The last mix m_l decrypts the message, reads $Bob's$ address, and sends him the remaining message. The communication between the mixes takes place along a fast communication channel. Finally, Bob receives and decrypts the message. Alice and Bob are unlinkable as long as one of the chosen mix is honest, in the sense that it does not cooperate with the other mixes. In the following, we use the notation $A \Rightarrow_{MIX} B : M$ to say that a message M is sent by A to B by using the MIX network.

Sessions. In order to let a party reply to a caller without knowing his identity we assume that a session is established between the sender and the receiver across the mixes. More precisely, when the first message is sent, the caller chooses a random serial number for the session, and he appends it to the message that is encrypted with the public key of the first mix in the path. The same operation is repeated by all mixes along the path. For example, mix m_i receives for a given message a serial number s_i from m_{i-1} and sends to the next mix m_{i+1} a serial number s_{i+1} with the message. The receiver obtains a serial number s_r and for each message that he sends back to the caller, he uses the same mix that sent him the first message and he appends to the reply message the serial number s_r. The message then can reach the destination using the same path followed by the first message, but in reverse order. Indeed, the mix m_i will receive from mix m_{i+1} a message with serial s_{i+1}. Thus, he knows that the mix he has to forward the received message is m_{i-1} and the serial number he has to append is s_i. Note that the existence of a session does not threat the anonymity of the system.

4.2 Protocol

As before, a conference is started by a certain conferee, referred to as the conference initiator (CI, for short). He contacts through the network switching system a conference manager (CM, for short) in order to start a conference. During this step, a conference identifier (cid, for short) is established, and the initial fee is paid by CI, according to the bit counting billing scheme described in Section 2. The mix network inside the network switching system guarantees the privacy of CI.

Anonymous Identification:

- $CI \Rightarrow_{MIX} CM : \{\texttt{Init}\}_{CM}$. The Init message contains a symmetric session key and the tokens, i.e. $\texttt{Init} = Init||K_{IM}||t_1, \ldots, t_k||tn_1, \ldots, tn_k$.
- $CM \Rightarrow_{MIX} CI : \{\texttt{Start}\}_{K_{IM}}$. $\texttt{Start} = Start||cid||tn_1^*, \ldots, tn_k^*$ where cid is a conference identifier randomly chosen by CM and $tn_1^*, \ldots, tn_k^*$ are the blind signatures of $tn_1, \ldots, tn_k$. This step is performed only if tokens $t_1, \ldots, t_k||tn_1, \ldots, tn_k$ are well computed.

Once CI has been anonymously identified, he invites the other conferees by giving them a randomly chosen session key, the address of the conference manager, and the conference identifier. The conferees then join the conference and pay the required fee. The mix network is used during both invitation and joining since we want to guarantee user privacy also in peer-to-peer communication.

Conference Call

CI generates for conference cid a symmetric key K_{cid}. Let $C_1, \ldots, C_l$ be the conferees of conference cid. For $1 \leq i \leq l$ the following steps are executed:

- $CI \Rightarrow_{MIX} C_i : \{\texttt{Invite}\}_{C_i}$. The Invite message contains the conference identifier cid, the conference key K_{cid}, and the address of the conference manager CM, i.e., $\texttt{Invite} = Invite||cid||K_{cid}||CM$.
- $C_i \Rightarrow_{MIX} CM : \{\texttt{Enrollment}\}_{K_{CM}}$. The Enrollment message contains the conference identifier cid, a symmetric session key K_{iM}, and the tokens for the joining fee, i.e., $\texttt{Enrollment} = Enrollment||cid||K_{iM}||t_1, \ldots, t_k||tn_1, \ldots, tn_k$.
- $CM \Rightarrow_{MIX} C_i : \{\texttt{Join}\}_{K_{iM}}$. The Join message has the following structure: $\texttt{Join} = Join||cid||tn_1^*, \ldots, tn_k^*$, where cid is a conference identifier and $tn_1^*, \ldots, tn_k^*$ are the blind signatures of $tn_1, \ldots, tn_k$. This step is performed only if the tokens sent in the Enrollment message are well computed.

Once a conference has begun and the conferees have joined it, each message of a conferee reaches the conference manager that then forwards it to the other conferees. Moreover each conferee is charged by the conference manager. Notice that our scheme allows an arbitrary charging policy: conferees can pay only at the beginning of the conference a certain fee, as well as they can pay at the end of each fixed time-period a certain fee. The mix network is still used in order to guarantee unlinkability.

Conference Join and Conversation:
Once a conference cid is started the following messages are exchanged between the conference manager and each conferee C_i that has joined cid.

- $C_i \Rightarrow_{MIX} CM$: $\{\text{Pay}\}_{K_{iM}}$. The Pay message contains the conference identifier cid and the tokens corresponding to the amount of money that the conferee C_i must periodically pay established by the charging policy of CM. More precisely, the Pay message has the following structure: $\text{Pay} = Pay||cid||t_1,\ldots,t_k||tn_1,\ldots,tn_k$.
- $CM \Rightarrow_{MIX} C_i$: $\{\text{Ack}\}_{K_{iM}}$. The Ack message is sent in order to give back the signed blind tokens after a Pay message, i.e., $\text{Ack} = Ack||cid||||tn_1^*,\ldots,tn_k^*$.
- $C_i \Rightarrow_{MIX} CM$: $\{\text{Talk}\}_{K_{iM}}$. The Talk message contains the conference identifier cid and the conversation of conferee C_i encrypted with the conference key K_{cid}, i.e., $\text{Talk} = Talk||cid||\{M\}_{K_{cid}}$.
- $CM \Rightarrow_{MIX} C_i$: $\{\text{Conversation}\}_{K_{iM}}$. The Conversation message contains a conference identifier cid and a message that has been previously received by CM from a conferee in a Talk message, i.e., $\text{Conversation} = Conversation||cid||\{M\}_{K_{cid}}$.

4.3   Performance

We briefly discuss now the communication and computation complexities of the mix network based solution. There is a trade-off between the privacy of the system and the communication complexity of our architecture since the work of each mobile device (based essentially on encryptions/decryptions) linearly grows with the number of mixes he wishes to use. Moreover we distinguish between symmetric and asymmetric encryptions/decryptions and between modular multiplications and exponentiations. Indeed, a modular exponentiation corresponds to hundred modular multiplications. We have decided to use Rabin's cryptosystem due to the low computational complexity of its encryptions, that efficiently satisfies the requirements of a mix network. We assume that all encryptions are opportunely randomized.

Mix overhead. If the mix network is composed of mixes belonging to different institutions and each mix in a chosen path belongs to a different institution, a reasonable length for a path has a small constant value. The overhead added by the mix network is thus few modular multiplications that can be reasonably performed also by a smart card.

Symmetric encryption. Almost all messages are encrypted by using a symmetric algorithm like the Advanced Encryption Standard, which is fast and presumed to be secure at the state of current knowledge. The reader is referred to [18] for details.

Conference Initiator. The conference initiator CI performs some extra tasks, compared to the other conferees. Indeed, he has to contact each other conferee in order to invite him to the conference, by giving him the necessary information for joining the conference and encrypting/decrypting the conversation. However, the number of conferees is in general bounded by a small constant as we discussed in Section 3.1.

Conversation. Each conferees that actively attends the conference sends his contribution to the conference by sending to the conference manager his messages. The conference manager then forwards the message to each other conferee. The overhead of the conversation is thus essentially based on a symmetric encryption/decryption for each message.

5   Conclusions

In this extended abstract we have described two protocols providing anonymous group communication in mobile networks. Both schemes satisfy a number of constraints usually presented by mobile devices, such as low computational power and limited memory storage capabilities. Our schemes are based on several cryptographic techniques used in the literature in different (or related to the one we have considered) settings, and provide features like billing and conference management, which are not supported by previous proposed schemes. Due to space limitations, we have not included security analysis and other details, which will be considered in the full version of this paper.

References

1. Askwith, B., Merabti, M., Shi, Q., Whitely, K.: Achieving User Privacy in Mobile Networks. In Proc. of the 13th Annual Computer Security Applications Conference (ACSAC '97), December 08 - 12, 1997, San Diego, CA
2. Birman, K. P., Cooper, D. A.: Preserving Privacy in a Network of Mobile Computers. In Proc. of IEEE Symposium on Security and Privacy, May 8-10, 1995, Oakland, CA
3. Buttyan, L., Hubaux, J.: Accountable Anonymous Access to Services in Mobile Communication Systems. In Proc. of the 18th IEEE Symposium on Reliable Distributed Systems, October 18 - 21, 1999, Lausanne, Switzerland.
4. Chaum, D.: Untraceable Electronic Mail, Return Addresses and Digital Pseudonyms. Communications of the ACM (CACM), Vol. 2, no. 24, 1981
5. Chaum, D.: Security without Identification: Transaction Systems to Make Big Brother Obsolete. Communications of the ACM (CACM), Vol. 10, no. 28, 1985
6. De Santis, A., Masucci, B.: On secret set schemes. Information Processing Letters, Vol. 74, Issues 5-6, June 30, 2000, 243-251
7. Federrath, H., Jerichow, A., Kesdogan, D., Pfitzmann, A.: Security in Public Mobile Communication Networks. In Proc. of the IFIP TC 6 International Workshop on Personal Wireless Communications, Prag, 1995, 105-116
8. Federrath, H., Jerichow, A., Pfitzmann, A.: MIXes in Mobile Communication Systems: Location Management with Privacy. In Proc. of Information Hiding, First International Workshop, Cambridge, U.K., May 30 - June 1, 1996. Lecture Notes in Computer Science, Vol. 1174, 121-135
9. Goldschlag, D. M., Reed, M. G., Syverson, P. F.: Protocols using Anonymous Connections: Mobile Applications. Security Protocols, 5th International Workshop, Paris, France, April 7-9, 1997
10. Goldwasser, S., Micali, S.: Probabilistic Encryption. Journal of Computer and System Sciences (JCSS), Vol. 28, 270-299, April 1984
11. Gulcu, C., Tsudik, G.: Mixing e-mail with Babel. Symposium on Network and Distributed System Security, Feb. 96, 2-16

12. Kesdogan, D., Reichl P., Junghartchen, K.: Distributed Temporary Pseudonyms: A New Approach for Protecting Location Information in Mobile Communication Networks. In Proc. of the 5th European Symposium on Research in Computer Security (ESORICS '98), Louvain-la-Neuve, Belgium, September 1998. Lecture Notes in Computer Science, Vol. 1485, 295-312
13. Menezes, A. J. , Van Oorschot, P. C., Vanstone, S. A.: Handbook of Applied Cryptography. CRC Press, Oct. 1996
14. Molva R., Tsudik, G.: Secret Sets and Applications. Information Processing Letters, Vol. 65, Issue 1, 15 January 1998, 47-55
15. Pfitzmann, A., Pfitzmann, B., Waidner, M.: ISDN-MIXes - Untraceable Communication with very small Bandwidth Overhead. Information Security, in Proc. of IFIP/Sec'91, Mai 1991, Brighton, Amsterdam, Holland. 1991, 245-258
16. Ramzan Z. , Ruhl, M.: Anonymous Subscription Protocols. Available at http://citeseer.nj.nec.com/ramzan00anonymous.html
17. Siew C. K., Tan, C. H., Yi, X.: A Secure and Efficient Conference Scheme for Mobile Communications. IEEE Transactions on Vehicular Technology (to appear)
18. Stinson, D.: Cryptography Theory and Practice, Second Edition. CRC Press. 2002
19. Stubblebine, S. G, Syverson P., GoldSchlag, D.M.: Unlinkable Serial Transactions: Protocols and Applications. ACM Transactions on Information and System Security, Vol. 2, no. 4, Nov. 1999

Aspects of Pseudorandomness
in Nonlinear Generators of Binary Sequences

Amparo Fúster-Sabater

Instituto de Física Aplicada, C.S.I.C.
C/ Serrano 144, 28006 Madrid, SPAIN
amparo@iec.csic.es

Abstract. A method of computing the number of $1's$ and $0's$ as well as
the number of runs of any length in the sequence obtained from a LFSR-
based generator has been developed. The procedure that is based on
the decomposition of the generating function in global minterms allows
one to check balancedness and run distribution goodness in the output
sequence. Simple design rules are also derived.

Keywords: Balancedness, run distribution, minterm, stream cipher,
cryptography.

1 Introduction

Generators based on Linear Feedback Shift Registers (LFSRs) ([1], [12]) are very
common devices to generate keystream sequences in symmetric-key cryptography. Desirable properties for such sequences can be enumerated as follows: 1)
large period, 2) large linear complexity, 3) good statistical properties. There are
well-known proposals ([2], [3], [4], [9], [10], [11]) for which conditions 1) and 2)
above are perfectly satisfied. Nevertheless, how to obtain sequences with good
statistics is a feature that even now remains quite diffuse.

Balancedness and adequate distribution of $1's$ and $0's$ in the output sequence
are necessary (although not sufficient) conditions that every keystream generator
must satisfy. Roughly speaking, a binary sequence is balanced if it has approx-
imately the same number of $1's$ as $0's$. On the other hand, a run of $1's$ ($0's$)
of length k is defined as a succession of k consecutive $1's$ ($0's$) between two $0's$
($1's$). The runs of $1's$ are called *blocks* while the runs of $0's$ are called *gaps*.
It is a well known fact ([1], [13]) that in a pseudorandom binary sequence of
period T there are $T/2$ runs distributed as follows: half the runs have length 1,
one quarter of the runs length 2, one eighth of the runs length 3, and so forth.
Moreover, half the runs of any length are gaps, the other half are blocks. That
is to say, in a pseudorandom binary sequence the number and distribution of
digits is perfectly quantified.

Due to the long period of the keystream sequence, it is unfeasible to produce
an entire cycle of such a sequence and then analyze the number and distribution of $1's$ and $0's$. Therefore, in practice, portions of the output sequence are
chosen randomly and different statistical tests [9](monobit test, run test, poker

C. Blundo and C. Laneve (Eds.): ICTCS 2003, LNCS 2841, pp. 329–341, 2003.
© Springer-Verlag Berlin Heidelberg 2003

test, serial test ...) are applied to all these subsequences. Nevertheless, passing the previous tests merely provides *probabilistic* evidence that the LFSR-based generator produces a sequence with certain characteristics of pseudorandomness.

In this work, a *deterministic* method of computing the degree of balancedness and number of runs of different lengths in one period of the output sequence is proposed. If the computed values are not in the expected range, then the generator must be rejected.

The procedure here presented is based on the expansion of the generating function in global *minterms*. As a straight consequence of this method, simple rules to design generators with good balancedness and run distribution are also derived. Some illustrative examples complete the work.

2   Theoretical Background and Basic Notation

Any L-variable Boolean function can be expressed canonically in terms of its *minterms* [7], that is the logic product of the L variables $(a_1, a_2, ..., a_L)$ where each variable can be in its true or complementary form. Examples of minterms of L variables are:

$$a_1 a_2 ... a_L, \quad \bar{a}_1 a_2 ... \bar{a}_L, \quad \bar{a}_1 \bar{a}_2 ... \bar{a}_L$$

where the superposition of variables represents the logic product. In addition, any L-variable Boolean function can be uniquely expressed in *Algebraic Normal Form* (A.N.F.) or *Muller expansion* [6] by means of the sum exclusive-OR of logic products of different orders in the L variables. A simple example of Boolean function in A.N.F. is:

$$f(a_1, a_2, ..., a_L) = a_1 a_2 \oplus a_2 a_{L-1} \oplus a_L$$

where $\oplus$ represents the exclusive-OR logic operation.

In mathematical terms, a LFSR-based generator is a L-variable nonlinear Boolean function, $F : GF(2)^L - \{0\} \rightarrow GF(2)$, whose L input-variables are the stages of the LFSRs. At each clock pulse the LFSRs generate new stage contents that will be the new input-variables of F. In this way, the generator produces the successive bits of the *output sequence* or *generated sequence*. A LFSR-based generator is a nonlinear Boolean function F given in its A.N.F. Moreover, the LFSRs involved in this kind of generator are *maximal length*-LFSRs [1]. In fact, a LFSR of L stages is a *maximal length*-LFSR whether its characteristic polynomial is primitive. In this case, its output sequence is called a *PN-sequence* of period $T = 2^L - 1$. Balancedness and run distribution of *PN*-sequences have been extensively studied in the literature. See for example [1], [10] and [13].

Let A be an arbitrary *maximal length*-LFSR of length L_A and a_i ($i = 1, ..., L_A$) the binary content of the i-th LFSR stage. A minterm of L_A variables is denoted by $A_{i...j}$ whether such a minterm includes the variables $a_i ... a_j$ in their true form while the other variables are in complementary form. According to the Muller expansion [6], a minterm of L_A variables expressed in A.N.F.

is a nonlinear function with $2^{L_A - j}$ terms ($1 \leq j \leq L_A$, j being the number of variables in true form). Such a function can be easily obtained by expanding out the corresponding minterm.

Let Λ_L denote the set of L-variable Boolean functions in A.N.F. and Φ_F the *minterm function* of F. In fact, $\Phi_F : \Lambda_L \to \Lambda_L$, such that, given F, Φ_F substitutes every term of F by its corresponding minterm. For a nonlinear function in A.N.F., e.g. $F(a_1, a_2, a_3) = a_1 \, a_2 \, a_3 \oplus a_1 \, a_3 \oplus a_2 \, a_3 \oplus a_2 \oplus a_3$, we have:

$$\Phi_F = A_{123} \oplus A_{13} \oplus A_{23} \oplus A_2 \oplus A_3.$$

On the other hand, every minterm considered as a generator applied to the L_A stages of A generates a canonical sequence [10] with an unique 1 and period $T = 2^{L_A} - 1$. Let us see for a simple example the particular form of the minterms and their corresponding canonical sequences. *Example 1:* For a LFSR of $L = 3$ stages, characteristic polynomial $P(D) = D^3 + D + 1$ and initial state $(1, 1, 0)$ we have:

$$
\begin{aligned}
A_{123} &= a_1 \, a_2 \, a_3 & &\longleftrightarrow \{0,0,0,0,0,0,1\} \\
A_{23} &= \overline{a}_1 \, a_2 \, a_3 = a_1 \, a_2 \, a_3 \oplus a_2 \, a_3 & &\longleftrightarrow \{0,0,0,0,0,1,0\} \\
A_{13} &= a_1 \, \overline{a}_2 \, a_3 = a_1 \, a_2 \, a_3 \oplus a_1 \, a_3 & &\longleftrightarrow \{0,0,0,0,1,0,0\} \\
A_2 &= \overline{a}_1 \, a_2 \, \overline{a}_3 = a_1 \, a_2 \, a_3 \oplus a_2 \, a_3 \oplus a_1 \, a_2 \oplus a_2 & &\longleftrightarrow \{0,0,0,1,0,0,0\} \\
A_3 &= \overline{a}_1 \, \overline{a}_2 \, a_3 = a_1 \, a_2 \, a_3 \oplus a_2 \, a_3 \oplus a_1 \, a_3 \oplus a_3 & &\longleftrightarrow \{0,0,1,0,0,0,0\} \\
A_1 &= a_1 \, \overline{a}_2 \, \overline{a}_3 = a_1 \, a_2 \, a_3 \oplus a_1 \, a_2 \oplus a_1 \, a_3 \oplus a_1 & &\longleftrightarrow \{0,1,0,0,0,0,0\} \\
A_{12} &= a_1 \, a_2 \, \overline{a}_3 = a_1 \, a_2 \, a_3 \oplus a_1 \, a_2 & &\longleftrightarrow \{1,0,0,0,0,0,0\}.
\end{aligned}
$$

The left column represents the ordered succession of the corresponding minterms while the right column shows their generated sequences. The cyclic succession of minterms is computed by increasing the previous minterm indexes by 1 and applying the linear recurrence relationship of the LFSR. Indeed, $a_1 \, a_2 \, a_3 \to a_2 \, a_3 \, a_4 = a_2 \, a_3 (a_2 \oplus a_1) = \overline{a}_1 \, a_2 \, a_3$; $\overline{a}_1 \, a_2 \, a_3 \to \overline{a}_2 \, a_3 \, a_4 = \overline{a}_2 \, a_3 \, (a_2 \oplus a_1) = a_1 \overline{a}_2 \, a_3 \ldots$ and so forth. Thus, the ordered minterm succession is:

$$A_{123}, \ A_{23}, \ A_{13}, \ A_2, \ A_3, \ A_1, \ A_{12}.$$

Let us now generalize the previous statements to more than one LFSR. Let $A, B, \ldots, Z$ be N LFSRs whose lengths are respectively $L_A, L_B, \ldots, L_Z$ (supposed $(L_i, L_j) = 1$, $i \neq j$). We denote by a_i ($i = 1, \ldots, L_A$), b_j ($j = 1, \ldots, L_B$), $\ldots$, z_k ($k = 1, \ldots, L_Z$) their corresponding stages. The *global minterms* associated with the generator have now $L_A + L_B + \ldots + L_Z$ variables and are of the form, e.g. $A_{ij} \, B_{pqr} \ldots Z_s$, that is to say the ordered product of the individual minterms of each LFSR. For two ordered successions of individual minterms:

$$A_{12}, \ A_2, \ A_1$$

$$B_{123}, \ B_{23}, \ B_{13}, \ B_2, \ B_3, \ B_1, \ B_{12}$$

the global minterm succession including 3 x 7 elements is:

$$A_{12} B_{123}, \ A_2 B_{23}, \ A_1 B_{13}, \ A_{12} B_2, \ A_2 B_3, \ A_1 B_1, \ \ldots, \ A_2 B_1, \ A_1 B_{12}.$$

As before every global minterm considered as a generator applied to the stages of the LFSRs generates a sequence with an unique 1 and period $T = (2^{L_A} - 1)(2^{L_B} - 1) \ldots (2^{L_Z} - 1)$ [10]. In brief, every LFSR-based generator can be expressed in terms of its global minterms as well as every global minterm provides the output sequence with a unique 1.

Once the nonlinear function F given in its A.N.F. has been converted into its global minterm expansion, the basic ideas of this work can be summarized as follows:

1. The number of global minterms in the representation of F equals the number of $1's$ in the output sequence.
2. The contiguity of such minterms in the ordered global minterm succession determines the run distribution in the generated sequence.

3   Conversion from A.N.F. to Minterm Expansion

Previously to the conversion procedure, the following facts are introduced:

Fact 1: $F = \Phi_F \circ \Phi_F$, where the symbol $\circ$ denotes the composition of functions. Indeed, for the previous example:

$$F(a_1, a_2, a_3) = a_1, \qquad \Phi_F = A_1 = a_1 a_2 a_3 \oplus a_1 a_2 \oplus a_1 a_3 \oplus a_1$$

$$\Phi_F \circ \Phi_F = \Phi_F(a_1 a_2 a_3 \oplus a_1 a_2 \oplus a_1 a_3 \oplus a_1) =$$

$$A_{123} \oplus A_{12} \oplus A_{13} \oplus A_1 = a_1 = F(a_1, a_2, a_3).$$

Fact 2: For every LFSR A, the exclusive-OR of all the possible terms of any order [8] equals 1. In fact,

$$a_{12\ldots L_A} \oplus a_{12\ldots L_A - 1} \oplus \ldots \oplus a_{2\ldots L_A} \oplus \ldots \oplus a_{L_A} \oplus \ldots \oplus a_2 \oplus a_1 =$$
$$A_{12\ldots L_A} \oplus A_{12\ldots L_A - 1} \oplus \ldots \oplus A_{2\ldots L_A} \oplus \ldots \oplus A_{L_A} \oplus \ldots \oplus A_2 \oplus A_1 = 1. \quad (1)$$

The previous equation can be rewritten as:

$$A_1' \oplus A_1 = 1. \tag{2}$$

On the other hand, the total number of terms in (1) is:

$$\sum_{i=1}^{L_A} \binom{L_A}{i} = 2^{L_A} - 1 \tag{3}$$

and, according to the previous section, the number of terms in $A_1 = a_1 \bar{a}_2 \ldots \bar{a}_{L_A}$ is:

$$N_t(A_1) = 2^{L_A - 1}. \tag{4}$$

Thus, the number of terms in A_1' will be:

$$N_t(A_1') = 2^{L_A - 1} - 1. \tag{5}$$

Appropriate notation will be used for the rest of LFSRs.

3.1   Procedure of Conversion

Input: N (number of LFSRs), L_A, L_B, ..., L_Z (lengths of the LFSRs) and a nonlinear function F in A.N.F.

For instance, $N_Z = 2$, $L_A = 2$, $L_B = 3$ and $F(a_1, a_2, b_1, b_2, b_3) = a_1 b_1$.

- *Step 1:* Compute Φ_F

$$\Phi_F = A_1 B_1.$$

- *Step 2:* Substitute every minterm by its corresponding function in A.N.F. and cancel common terms (if there exist)

$$\Phi_F = (a_1 a_2 \oplus a_1)(b_1 b_2 b_3 \oplus b_1 b_2 \oplus b_1 b_3 \oplus b_1) =$$

$$a_1 a_2 b_1 b_2 b_3 \oplus a_1 a_2 b_1 b_2 \oplus a_1 a_2 b_1 b_3 \oplus a_1 a_2 b_1 \oplus$$

$$a_1 b_1 b_2 b_3 \oplus a_1 b_1 b_2 \oplus a_1 b_1 b_3 \oplus a_1 b_1.$$

- *Step 3:* Compute $F(a_i, b_j) = \Phi_F \circ \Phi_F$

$$F(a_i, b_j) = \Phi_F \circ \Phi_F = A_{12} B_{123} \oplus A_{12} B_{12} \oplus A_{12} B_{13} \oplus A_{12} B_1 \oplus$$

$$A_1 B_{123} \oplus A_1 B_{12} \oplus A_1 B_{13} \oplus A_1 B_1.$$

Output: F expressed in terms of its global minterms.

Once the function F has been expressed in terms of its minterms, balancedness and run distribution in the output sequence can be analyzed.

4   Balancedness in the Output Sequence of LFSR-Based Generators

The number of 1's in the generated sequence coincides with the number of global minterms in the expression of F or, equivalently, the number of terms in Φ_F (*Step 2*). Remark that such a number does not depend on the LFSR characteristic polynomials. An illustrative example of application of such a procedure to a well-known generator is presented.

4.1   A Numerical Example

Let A, B, C be three LFSRs of lengths L_A, L_B, L_C respectively. The *combining function* is chosen:

$$F = a_1 b_1 \oplus b_1 c_1 \oplus c_1 \tag{6}$$

that corresponds to the generator of Geffe [12] and the *minterm function* Φ_F is computed:

$$\Phi_F = A_1 D_1 \oplus B_1 C_1 \oplus C_1$$
$$= A_1 B_1 (C_1' \oplus C_1) \oplus (A_1' \oplus A_1) B_1 C_1 \oplus$$
$$\oplus (A_1' \oplus A_1)(B_1' \oplus B_1) C_1$$
$$= A_1 B_1 (C_1' \oplus C_1) \oplus (A_1' \oplus A_1) B_1' C_1.$$

The number of $1's$ in the output sequence can be directly obtained by counting the number of terms in Φ_F via the equations (4) and (5). According to this simple rule, the number of $1's$ in the output sequence obtained from a Geffe's generator is given by:

$$No.\ 1's = 2^{L_A-1}2^{L_B-1}(2^{L_C} - 1) + (2^{L_A} - 1)(2^{L_B-1} - 1)2^{L_C-1}. \qquad (7)$$

Remark that the previous expression is function exclusively of the lengths of the three registers L_A, L_B, L_C. For lengths of the LFSRs in a practical range, we say $L_i \simeq 80$, and keeping in mind that the period is $T = (2^{L_A} - 1)(2^{L_B} - 1)(2^{L_C} - 1)$, the number of $1's$ in the output sequence is: $No.\ 1's \simeq T/2$. Consequently, the generated sequence is balanced.

5   Run Distribution in the Output Sequence of LFSR-Based Generators

The computation of runs in the output sequence is based on the following result.

Proposition 1. *Let us consider the ordered minterm succession of a maximal length-LFSR of length L. If the minterms including an arbitrary index i are replaced by 1 and the minterms not including the index i are replaced by 0, then the resulting binary sequence is the reverse version of the PN-sequence generated by the LFSR.*

The previous result is a straight application of the linear recurrence relationship of the LFSR given by its characteristic polynomial. Thus, a minterm succession can be treated as a PN-sequence but remark that the number of runs of any length of a PN-sequence is perfectly quantified. Indeed, each m-gram (that is every one of the 2^m possible configurations of m bits ($m = 1, ..., L$)) will appear exactly 2^{L-m} times throughout the PN-sequence except for the L-gram $00...0$ that will not appear any time. Moreover, in the global minterm succession each m-gram of any LFSR will coincide once with each one of the m-grams of the other LFSRs. Based on these considerations, the computation of runs in the output sequence can be carried out as it is shown in the following example.

Example 2: For two LFSRs, A and B, of lengths L_A and L_B respectively ($L_A < L_B$) and generating function $F = a_1 b_1$, we proceed:

$$\Phi_F = A_1 B_1 = (a_1 \oplus a_1 a_2 \oplus ... \oplus a_1 a_2 ... a_{L_A})(b_1 \oplus b_1 b_2 \oplus ... \oplus b_1 b_2 ... b_{L_B})$$

$$F = \Phi_F \circ \Phi_F = (A_1 \oplus A_{12} \oplus ... \oplus A_{12...L_A})(B_1 \oplus B_{12} \oplus ... \oplus B_{12...L_B})$$

Notice that the minterm expansion of F will only include products of individual minterms with the index 1. Let us now introduce the following notation:

Y denotes an arbitrary minterm of A or B including the index 1.

N denotes an arbitrary minterm of A or B not including the index 1.

$SecA$ denotes the ordered succession of minterms of A in format Y/N.

SecB denotes the ordered succession of minterms of B in format Y/N.

It is clear that a 1 in the output sequence corresponds to a minterm product YY (for example, A_1B_{12}) while a 0 in the output sequence corresponds to the minterm products YN, NY or NN (for example, A_1B_2, $A_{23}B_{13}$ or A_3B_2). See the formation rule in Table 1.

Table 1. Global minterm formation rule for F in Example 2.

SecB	SecA	Output bit
Y	Y	1
N	Y	0
Y	N	0
N	N	0

Now we can compute the number of runs of different lengths.

5.1 Runs of Length 1

Blocks: They are runs of the form "0 1 0" that come from minterm structures

$$SecB : * \, Y \, *$$
$$SecA : * \, Y \, *$$

The symbol $*$ denotes Y or N. The 3-gram NYN will appear 2^{L_A-3} times in *SecA* and 2^{L_B-3} times in *SecB*, the 2-gram $NY*$ will appear 2^{L_A-2} times in *SecA* and 2^{L_B-2} times in *SecB*, and so forth.

The different configurations of minterms able to generate a block of length 1 are depicted in Table 2 at columns notated "Configurations". The columns notated "No. of config." show the number of times that such configurations will appear on their corresponding minterm sequences.

Table 2. Configurations of minterms producing blocks of length 1.

	Configuration	No. of config.	Configuration	No. of config.
SecB	$* \, Y \, *$	2^{L_B-1}	$* \, Y \, N$	2^{L_B-2}
SecA	$N \, Y \, N$	2^{L_A-3}	$N \, Y \, Y$	2^{L_A-3}
SecB	$N \, Y \, *$	2^{L_B-2}	$N \, Y \, N$	2^{L_B-3}
SecA	$Y \, Y \, N$	2^{L_A-3}	$Y \, Y \, Y$	2^{L_A-3}

Thus, the number of blocks of length 1 will be the sum of all suitable configurations multiplied by the number of times that such configurations appear

$$N_B(1) = (2^{L_B-1} + 2 \cdot 2^{L_B-2} + 2^{L_B-3}) \, 2^{L_A-3} \, . \tag{8}$$

Gaps: They are runs of the form "1 0 1" that come from minterm structures

$$SecB : Y * Y$$
$$SecA : Y * Y$$

The different configurations of minterms able to generate a gap of length 1 are depicted in Table 3.

Table 3. Configurations of minterms producing gaps of length 1.

	Configuration	No. of config.	Configuration	No. of config.
SecB	$Y\,N\,Y$	2^{L_B-3}	$Y * Y$	2^{L_B-2}
SecA	$Y\,Y\,Y$	2^{L_A-3}	$Y\,N\,Y$	2^{L_A-3}

Thus, the number of gaps of length 1 will be the sum of all suitable configurations multiplied by the number of times that such configurations appear

$$N_G(1) = (2^{L_B-3} + 2^{L_B-2})\, 2^{L_A-3} \; . \tag{9}$$

5.2 Runs of Length n

The procedure can be generalized in order to compute the number of runs of length n $(n = 1, ..., L_A - 2)$.

Blocks: They are runs of the form "0 1...1 0" (with n consecutive $1's$) coming out from minterm structures

$$SecB : * Y ... Y *$$
$$SecA : * Y ... Y *$$

with n minterms Y in both sequences. The different configurations able to generate a block of length n and their number are depicted in Table 4.

Table 4. Configurations of minterms producing blocks of length n.

	Configuration	No. of config.	Configuration	No. of config.
SecB	$N\,Y ... Y\,N$	$2^{L_B-(n+2)}$	$*\,Y ... Y\,N$	$2^{L_B-(n+1)}$
SecA	$Y\,Y ... Y\,Y$	$2^{L_A-(n+2)}$	$N\,Y ... Y\,Y$	$2^{L_A-(n+2)}$
SecB	$N\,Y ... Y\,*$	$2^{L_B-(n+1)}$	$*\,Y ... Y\,*$	2^{L_B-n}
SecA	$Y\,Y ... Y\,N$	$2^{L_A-(n+2)}$	$N\,Y ... Y\,N$	$2^{L_A-(n+2)}$

Thus, the number of blocks of length n will be:

$$N_B(n) = (2^{L_B-(n+2)} + 2 \cdot 2^{L_B-(n+1)} + 2^{L_B-n})\, 2^{L_A-(n+2)} \; . \tag{10}$$

Gaps: They are runs of the form "1 0...0 1" (with n consecutive $0's$) coming out from minterm structures

$$SecB : Y * \ldots * Y$$
$$SecA : Y * \ldots * Y$$

with n symbols $*$ in both sequences. Notice that in *SecA* there will be 2^n different configurations able to generate a gap of length n ranging from $Y\ N\ \ldots\ N\ Y$ up to $Y\ Y\ \ldots\ Y\ Y$. Some of such configurations and their number are depicted in Table 5.

Table 5. Configurations of minterms producing gaps of length n.

	Configuration	No. of config.	Configuration	No. of config.
SecB	$Y * \ldots * Y$	$2^{L_B - 2}$	$Y\ N \ldots N\ Y$	$2^{L_B - (n+2)}$
SecA	$Y\ N \ldots N\ Y$	$2^{L_A - (n+2)}$	$Y\ Y\ \ldots\ Y\ Y$	$2^{L_A - (n+2)}$

Thus, the number of gaps of length n will be:

$$N_G(n) = \left(\sum_{i=0}^{n} \binom{n}{i} 2^{L_B - (n+2-i)} \right) \cdot 2^{L_A - (n+2)}. \tag{11}$$

Therefore, the number of runs of any length up to $L_A - 2$ can be easily computed in the proposed example. Equations (10) and (11) give us the exact number of blocks and gaps that can be found in the output sequence. Remark that N_B and N_G depend exclusively on the LFSR's lengths (L_A, L_B) and on the run length (n). There is no dependency on the characteristic polynomials. Consequently, different LFSRs of the same length will produce output sequences with the same number of blocks and gaps.

According to these expressions, it can be seen that the analyzed function F does not match the expected values. Indeed, for a numerical example $L_A = 7, L_B = 8$ the computation of runs is depicted in Table 6. For $n = 1$, $N_B > N_G$. For $n = 2$, both values coincide as equation (10) equals equation (11). For $n \geq 3$, $N_B < N_G$ since in this case the number of terms in (11) is greater than in (10). As expected, there are more gaps than blocks because the formation rule in Table 1 is not balanced.

The upper limit $L_A - 2$, L_A being the length of the shortest LFSR, follows from the fact that blocks and gaps of length n include $n + 2$ bits but we can only guarantee the presence of at most L_A-grams. At any rate, the designer of binary pseudorandom generators is basically interested in the runs of low length (e.g. up to length 15) while in cryptographic applications every LFSR length takes values in the range $L_i \simeq 80$.

Table 6. Numerical example.

n	No. of blocks	No. of gaps
1	4608	1536
2	1152	1152
3	288	864
4	72	648
5	18	486

5.3   Generalization to More Complex Generators

The procedure above developed can be generalized to sequence generators with any number of LFSRs and more complex combining functions. Indeed, general expressions for the number of blocks and gaps of length n can be derived. Next, we present the expressions of N_B and N_G for a LFSR-based generator with three LFSRs of lengths L_A, L_B, L_C and generating function:

$$F = a_1 \oplus b_1 \oplus c_1 \tag{12}$$

that is just the OR-exclusive sum of the three registers. The corresponding *minterm function* Φ_F is:

$$\Phi_F = A_1 B_1 C_1 \oplus A_1 B_1' C_1' \oplus A_1' B_1 C_1' \oplus A_1' B_1' C_1 . \tag{13}$$

Table 7 shows the global minterm formation rule for this linear function. It can be noticed that such a formation rule is balanced. The same procedure developed in subsections 5.1 and 5.2 allows us to get general expressions for the number of runs of length n. Next equation gives us the unified expression of N_B and N_G.

$$N_B(n) = N_G(n) = 2^4 \, 2^{2n} \, 2^{L_A-(n+2)} \, 2^{L_B-(n+2)} \, 2^{L_C-(n+2)}$$
$$-2(2^{n+1} - 1)(\sum_{i,j} 2^{L_i-(n+2)} \, 2^{L_j-(n+2)}) \tag{14}$$
$$- \, 2^{L_i-(n+2)} \, (\sum_j 2^{L_j-(n+2)} - 1)$$

where $i, j \in \{A, B, C\}, \quad i \neq j$.

Table 7. Global minterm formation rule for F defined in (12).

SecC	SecB	SecA	Output bit
Y	Y	Y	1
Y	Y	N	0
Y	N	Y	0
Y	N	N	1
N	Y	Y	0
N	Y	N	1
N	N	Y	1
N	N	N	0

The subtractive terms correspond to configurations with $(n+2)$ consecutive $N's$ in either one of the minterm sequences or in two minterm sequences simultaneously. It can be noticed that in the previous example the run distribution matches the canonical values. Indeed, the number of blocks equals the number of gaps for any run length as well as the following equalities hold:

$$N_B(n+1) = N_B(n)/2 \qquad N_G(n+1) = N_G(n)/2. \qquad (15)$$

Remark that every minterm sequence in Table 7 is compensated too. It means that for every minterm sequence two symbols $Y's$ $(N's)$ correspond to bits 1 in the output sequence while the other two symbols $Y's$ $(N's)$ correspond to bits 0 in the output sequence. Practical results confirm that, for other formation rules balanced although not perfectly compensated, the degree of balancedness and run distribution in the generated sequence is quite satisfactory. See, for example, the run distribution for the Geffe generator (subsection 4.1) whose expressions for $N_B(n)$ and $N_G(n)$ are:

$$N_B(n) = 2^4 \, 2^{2n} \, 2^{L_A - (n+2)} \, 2^{L_B - (n+2)} \, 2^{L_C - (n+2)}$$

$$- \, 3^2 \, 2^{L_A - (n+2)} \, 2^{L_B - (n+2)} \; - \; (2^{n+2} - 1) \, 2^{L_A - (n+2)} \, 2^{L_C - (n+2)} \qquad (16)$$

$$-2^3 \, 2^{L_B - (n+2)} \, 2^{L_C - (n+2)} \; - \; (2^{L_A - (n+2)} + 2^{L_B - (n+2)} - 1) \, 2^{L_C - (n+2)}$$

and

$$N_G(n) = 2^4 \, 2^{2n} \, 2^{L_A - (n+2)} \, 2^{L_B - (n+2)} \, 2^{L_C - (n+2)}$$

$$- \, 3^n \, 2^{L_A - (n+2)} \, 2^{L_B - (n+2)} \; - \; (2^{n+2} - 1) \, 2^{L_A - (n+2)} \, 2^{L_C - (n+2)} \qquad (17)$$

$$-(3^n - 1) \, 2^{L_B - (n+2)} \, 2^{L_C - (n+2)} \; - \; (2^{L_A - (n+2)} + 2^{L_B - (n+2)} - 1) \, 2^{L_C - (n+2)} \, .$$

Its corresponding global minterm formation rule can be seen in Table 8.

Table 8. Global minterm formation rule for F defined in (6).

SecC	SecB	SecA	Output bit
Y	Y	Y	1
Y	Y	N	0
Y	N	Y	1
Y	N	N	1
N	Y	Y	1
N	Y	N	0
N	N	Y	0
N	N	N	0

Notice that the first term in $N_B(n)$ and $N_G(n)$ is the same for every generator with three LFSRs and balanced formation rule. The subtractive terms are function of the output bit distribution in the global minterm formation rule. The more the formation rule is compensated, the better the output sequence matches the standard distribution of runs.

5.4 Simple Design Rules

In the previous subsection, we have seen that a balanced formation rule guarantees good balancedness and run distribution. For a binary sequence generator with N LFSRs there will be 2^{2^N} possible formation rules of which $\binom{2^N}{2^{N-1}}$ will be balanced. So, simple design rules can be enumerated as follows:

– Choose one of the balanced formation rule
– Determine its corresponding minterm function Φ_F
– Compute the combining function F by means of the composition of Φ_F

$$F = \Phi_F \circ \Phi_F.$$

In this way, the output sequence obtained from the LFSR-based generator will exhibit the desired characteristics of pseudorandomness. At the same time and following the same procedure as before, specific expressions for the number of $1's$ and number of runs in the output sequence can be obtained.

6 Conclusions

A method of computing the number of $1's$ and $0's$ as well as the run distribution in the output sequence of LFSR-based generators has been developed. The procedure allows one to reject the generators not satisfying expected values of balancedness and run distribution goodness.

The method here described has been applied exclusively to nonlinear combining functions. Nevertheless, these ideas concerning the analysis of the global minterms seem to be suitable for more general keystream generator. Consider, for instance, the *multiple-speed generators* that can be expressed in terms of a more complex combining function or the *shrinking generator* whose global minterms can be obtained by removing certain individual minterms from the selector register. In both cases, the developed method can be adapted and applied to these schemes in order to evaluate certain aspects of pseudorandomness in the generated sequences.

Acknowledgements

Work supported by Ministerio de Ciencia y Tecnología (Spain) under grant TIC2001-0586.

References

1. S.W. Golomb, Shift Register-Sequences, Aegean Park Press, Laguna Hill, 1982.
2. E.L. Key, An Analysis of the Structure and Complexity of Non-Linear Binary Sequence Generators. IEEE Trans. on Information Theory, 22 (1976), 732-736.

3. A. Klapper, Large Families of Sequences with Near Optimal Correlations and Large Linear Span. IEEE Trans. on Information Theory, 42 (1996), 1241-1248.
4. P.V. Kumar and R.A. Scholtz, Bounds on the Linear Span of Bent Sequences. IEEE Trans. on Information Theory, 29 (1983), 854-862.
5. R. Lidl and H. Niederreiter, Introduction to Finite Fields and Their Applications, Cambridge: Cambridge University Press, 1986.
6. F.J. MacWilliams and N.J. Sloane, The Theory of Error-Correcting Codes, North-Holland Mathematical Library, Elsevier Science Publishers, 1977.
7. D. Mange, Analysis and Synthesis of Logic Systems, Artech House, INC., Norwood 1986.
8. W. Meier and O. Staffelbach, "Nonlinearity Criteria for Cryptographic Functions", EUROCRYPT'89, LNCS Springer-Verlag, Vol. 434, 1990, pp. 549-563.
9. A.J. Menezes *et al.*, Handbook of Applied Cryptography, New York:CRC Press, 1997.
10. R.A. Rueppel, Analysis and Design of Stream Ciphers, New York:Springer-Verlag, 1986.
11. I.E. Shparlinski, On the Linear Complexity of the Power Generator. Design, Codes and Cryptography 23 (2001), 5-10.
12. G.J. Simmons (ed.), Contemporary Cryptology: The Science of Information Integrity, New York:IEEE Press, 1991.
13. H.C. Tilborg, An Introduction to Cryptology, Norwell, Massachusetts:Kluwer Academic Publishers, 1988.

An Information-Theoretic Approach
to the Access Control Problem

Anna Lisa Ferrara and Barbara Masucci

Dipartimento di Informatica ed Applicazioni
Università di Salerno
84081 Baronissi (SA), Italy
{ferrara,masucci}@dia.unisa.it

Abstract. In this paper we propose an information-theoretic approach to the access control problem in a scenario where a group of users is divided into a number of disjoint classes. The set of rules that specify the information flow between different user classes in the system defines an *access control policy*. An access control policy can be implemented by using a *key assignment scheme*, where a trusted central authority (CA) assigns an encryption key and some private information to each class. We consider key assignment schemes which are *unconditionally secure* against attacks carried out by any coalition of classes. We show lower bounds on the size of the private information that each class has to store and on the amount of randomness needed by the CA to set up any key assignment scheme. Finally, we propose an optimal construction for unconditionally secure key assignment schemes.

1 Introduction

The *access control problem* deals with the specification of users' access permission and is a fundamental issue in any system that manages distributed resources, such as e-newspaper, pay-TV subscription services, etc. The access control problem is defined in a scenario where the users of a computer system are organized in a certain number of disjoint classes, called *security classes*. A security class can represent a person, a department, or a user group in an organization. The set of rules that specify the information flow between different user classes in the system defines an *access control policy*. In particular, for any class in the system, the access control policy specifies the set of classes which can be accessed by that class. This set is called the *accessible set* of the class.

Within the scope of cryptography, an access control policy can be implemented by using a *key assignment scheme*, that is, a method to assign a key and some private information to each class. The encryption key will be used by each class to protect its data by means of a symmetric cryptosystem. The private information will be used by each class to compute the keys assigned to all classes in its accessible set. This assignment is carried out by a central authority, the CA, which is active only at the distribution phase.

In a *perfectly secure* key assignment scheme, the key assigned to each class is secure against a coalition of all the classes which are not entitled to access

C. Blundo and C. Laneve (Eds.): ICTCS 2003, LNCS 2841, pp. 342–354, 2003.

its secret data, i.e., even pooling together their private information, they cannot compute anything about that key. The basic and straightforward perfectly secure key assignment scheme requires each class to memorize the encryption keys assigned to all classes in its accessible set. The disadvantage of this solution is that it penalizes users in classes with large accessible sets, since they need to handle more information than users in classes with smaller accessible sets.

Given the high complexity of such a scheme, a natural step is to trade complexity for security. We may still require that the key assigned to each class is unconditionally secure, but only with respect to an adversary controlling a coalition of classes of a limited size. First, we propose an information theoretic approach to key assignment schemes. Afterwards, we show lower bounds on the size of the private information that each class has to store and on the amount of randomness needed by the CA to set up any key assignment scheme. Finally, we propose an optimal construction for unconditionally secure key assignment schemes.

1.1 Related Work

The problem of reducing the inherent complexity of the basic straightforward key assignment scheme was first considered by Akl and Taylor [1], who proposed an elegant solution to solve the access control problem in a system organized as a partially ordered hierarchy (poset). In their scheme, each class is assigned a key that can be used, along with some public parameters generated by a central authority, to compute the key assigned to any class lower down in the hierarchy. Subsequently, many researchers have proposed schemes that either have better performances or allow inserting and deleting classes in the hierarchy (e.g., [2,6,7,8,12,13,14,15,17]). All these schemes can be used to implement only poset-based access control policies.

There are several examples of distributed systems requiring more general access control policies. For example, these access control policies may violate the anti-symmetrical and transitive properties of a poset. The problem of designing cryptographic key assignment schemes for access control policies with transitive and anti-symmetrical exceptions was first considered by Yeh, Chow, and Newman [19]. However, Hwang [9] showed that their scheme was insecure against *collusion attacks* carried out by non-authorized classes. Subsequently, the authors of [4] proposed a general method to construct a cryptographic key assignment scheme for any arbitrary access control policy.

The most used approach to key assignment schemes (different from the one proposed in this paper) is based on unproven specific assumptions (e.g., [1,4,2,6,7,8,12,13,14,15,16,17]). The information theoretic approach differs from the above computational approach since it does not depend on any unproven assumption. Such an approach has been used in [5] to analyze the access control problem in a system organized as a partially ordered hierarchy. In this paper we use the information theoretic approach to analyze key assignment schemes implementing any arbitrary access control policy.

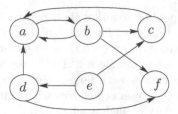

Fig. 1. An arbitrary access control policy.

2   The Model

We consider a scenario where the users of a computer system are divided into a certain number of disjoint classes, called *security classes*. The set of rules that specify the information flow between different user classes in the system defines an *access control policy*. An access control policy can be represented by a directed graph $G = (V, E)$, where the vertex set V corresponds to the set of security classes and there is a directed edge $(u, v) \in E$ if and only if class u can access class v. For each $u \in V$, we define the *accessible set* of u as the set of classes that can be accessed by u, including u itself, i.e., $A_u = \{v \in V : (u, v) \in E\}$. We also define the *forbidden set* of u as the set of classes that cannot access class u, i.e., $F_u = \{v \in V : u \notin A_v\}$. For any subset of classes $X \subseteq V$, we denote by A_X the set $\cup_{v \in X} A_v$.

For example, consider the directed graph of Figure 1, where self-loops are omitted. The accessible and forbidden sets of each class are the following:

$$A_a = \{a, b\} \qquad F_a = \{e, f\}$$
$$A_b = \{a, b, c, f\} \; F_b = \{c, d, e, f\}$$
$$A_c = \{a, c\} \qquad F_c = \{a, d, f\}$$
$$A_d = \{a, d, f\} \qquad F_d = \{a, b, c, f\}$$
$$A_e = \{c, d, e\} \qquad F_e = \{a, b, c, d, f\}$$
$$A_f = \{f\} \qquad F_f = \{a, c, e\}$$

An access control policy represented by a directed graph $G = (V, E)$ can be implemented by using a *key assignment scheme*, where a trusted third party, called the *central authority* (CA), has the task to assign a key and some private information to each class $u \in V$. For any class $u \in V$, we denote by p_u the private information sent by the CA to users in class u and by k_u the key assigned to class u, respectively. Moreover, we denote by P_u and K_u the sets of all possible values that p_u and k_u can assume, respectively. Given a set $X = \{u_1, \cdots, u_\ell\} \subseteq V$, we denote by P_X and K_X the sets $P_{u_1} \times \cdots \times P_{u_\ell}$ and $K_{u_1} \times \cdots \times K_{u_\ell}$, respectively.

In this paper, with a boldface capital letter, say $\mathbf{Y}$, we denote a random variable taking values on a set, denoted by the corresponding capital letter Y, according to some probability distribution $\{Pr_{\mathbf{Y}}(y)\}_{y \in Y}$. The values such a random variable can take are denoted by the corresponding lower case letter. Given a random variable $\mathbf{Y}$, we denote by $H(\mathbf{Y})$ the Shannon entropy of $\{Pr_{\mathbf{Y}}(y)\}_{y \in Y}$ (we refer the reader to [3] for a complete treatment of Information Theory).

We consider key assignment schemes where the key assigned to each class is unconditionally secure with respect to an adversary controlling a coalition of classes of a limited size. Our schemes are characterized by a security parameter r, the size of the adversary coalition. The maximum value that the security parameter r can assume is equal to $\max_{u \in V} |F_u|$, since any adversary coalition for class u can contain at most $|F_u|$ classes. We formally define r-secure key assignment schemes by using the entropy function, mainly because this leads to a compact and simple description of the schemes and because the entropy approach takes into account all probability distributions on the keys assigned to the classes. An r-secure assignment scheme is defined as follows.

Definition 1. *Let $G = (V, E)$ be the directed graph that represents an arbitrary access control policy and let $1 \le r \le \max_{u \in V} |F_u|$. An r-secure key assignment scheme for G is a method to assign a key to each class in such a way that the following two properties are satisfied:*

1. Any class allowed to access another class can compute the key assigned to that class.
   Formally, for any $u \in V$ and any $v \in A_u$, it holds that

$$H(\mathbf{K}_v | \mathbf{P}_u) = 0.$$

2. Any coalition of at most r classes not allowed to access another class have absolutely no information about the key assigned to that class.
   Formally, for any $u \in V$ and any $X \subseteq F_u$ such that $|X| \le r$, it holds that

$$H(\mathbf{K}_u | \mathbf{P}_X) = H(\mathbf{K}_u).$$

3   Lower Bounds

In this section we prove lower bounds on the size of the private information held by each class and on the number of random bits needed by the CA to set up any r-secure key assignment scheme. In order to prove our results we need the next definition.

Definition 2. *Let $G = (V, E)$ be the directed graph that represents an arbitrary access control policy. In any r-secure key assignment scheme for G, a sequence of classes $u_1 \ldots u_m$ is called r-independent if, for any $j = 2, \ldots, m$, there exists a set $X_j \subseteq F_{u_j}$ such that*

1. $|X_j| \le r$,
2. $\{u_1, \ldots, u_{j-1}\} \subseteq A_{X_j}$.

Remark 1. When $r = \max_{u \in V} |F_u|$, any r-independent sequence of classes is called an *independent sequence*.

Consider the graph shown in Figure 1. It is easy to see that cbd and acb are 1-independent sequences, whereas, $acbf$ and $cbde$ are 2-independent sequences. The next lemma will be an useful tool to prove our results.

Lemma 1. *Let $G = (V, E)$ be the directed graph that represents an arbitrary access control policy. In any r-secure key assignment scheme for G, if $u_1 u_2 \ldots u_m$ is an r-independent sequence of classes, then it holds that*

$$H(\mathbf{K}_{u_1} \ldots \mathbf{K}_{u_m}) = \sum_{j=1}^{m} H(\mathbf{K}_{u_j}).$$

Proof. Since $u_1 u_2 \ldots u_m$ is an r-independent sequence, from Definition 2 we have that, for any $j = 2, \ldots, m$, there exists a set $X_j \subseteq F_{u_j}$ such that $|X_j| \leq r$ and $\{u_1, \ldots, u_{j-1}\} \subseteq A_{X_j} = \cup_{v \in X_j} A_v$. Therefore, from 2. of Definition 1 it holds that

$$H(\mathbf{K}_{u_j} | \mathbf{P}_{X_j}) = H(\mathbf{K}_{u_j}). \tag{1}$$

Since $u_i \in A_{X_j}$ for each $i = 1, \ldots, j-1$, it follows that there exists a class $v_i \in X_j$ such that $u_i \in A_{v_i}$. Hence, from 1. of Definition 1 it follows that $H(\mathbf{K}_{u_i} | \mathbf{P}_{v_i}) = 0$ and from (13) of the Appendix we have that

$$H(\mathbf{K}_{u_1} \ldots \mathbf{K}_{u_{j-1}} | \mathbf{P}_{X_j}) \leq \sum_{i=1}^{j-1} H(\mathbf{K}_{u_i} | \mathbf{P}_{X_j}) \leq \sum_{i=1}^{j-1} H(\mathbf{K}_{u_i} | \mathbf{P}_{v_i}) = 0.$$

Hence, from (12) of the Appendix it follows that

$$H(\mathbf{K}_{u_1} \ldots \mathbf{K}_{u_{j-1}} | \mathbf{K}_{u_j} \mathbf{P}_{X_j}) \leq H(\mathbf{K}_{u_1} \ldots \mathbf{K}_{u_{j-1}} | \mathbf{P}_{X_j}) = 0. \tag{2}$$

Consider the mutual information $I(\mathbf{K}_{u_j}; \mathbf{K}_{u_1} \ldots \mathbf{K}_{u_{j-1}} | \mathbf{P}_{X_j})$. From (11) of the Appendix it holds that

$$H(\mathbf{K}_{u_j} | \mathbf{P}_{X_j}) - H(\mathbf{K}_{u_j} | \mathbf{K}_{u_1} \ldots \mathbf{K}_{u_{j-1}} \mathbf{P}_{X_j})$$

$$= H(\mathbf{K}_{u_1} \ldots \mathbf{K}_{u_{j-1}} | \mathbf{P}_{X_j}) - H(\mathbf{K}_{u_1} \ldots \mathbf{K}_{u_{j-1}} | \mathbf{K}_{u_j} \mathbf{P}_{X_j}). \tag{3}$$

Hence, from (2) and (3) it follows that

$$H(\mathbf{K}_{u_j} | \mathbf{K}_{u_1} \ldots \mathbf{K}_{u_{j-1}} \mathbf{P}_{X_j}) = H(\mathbf{K}_{u_j} | \mathbf{P}_{X_j}). \tag{4}$$

Therefore, from (7) and (10) of the Appendix it holds that

$$H(\mathbf{K}_{u_1} \ldots \mathbf{K}_{u_m}) = H(\mathbf{K}_{u_1}) + \sum_{j=2}^{m} H(\mathbf{K}_{u_j} | \mathbf{K}_{u_1} \ldots \mathbf{K}_{u_{j-1}})$$

$$\geq H(\mathbf{K}_{u_1}) + \sum_{j=2}^{m} H(\mathbf{K}_{u_j} | \mathbf{K}_{u_1} \ldots \mathbf{K}_{u_{j-1}} \mathbf{P}_{X_j})$$

$$= H(\mathbf{K}_{u_1}) + \sum_{j=2}^{m} H(\mathbf{K}_{u_j} | \mathbf{P}_{X_j}) \text{ (from (4))}$$

$$= \sum_{j=1}^{m} H(\mathbf{K}_{u_j}) \text{(from (1))}.$$

$\square$

The next theorem shows a lower bound on the size of the private information held by any subset of classes $X \subseteq V$.

Theorem 1. *Let $G = (V, E)$ be the directed graph that represents an arbitrary access control policy. In any r-secure key assignment scheme for G, for any $X \subseteq V$, if there exists an r-independent sequence of classes $u_1 \ldots u_m$ in A_X, then it holds that*

$$H(\mathbf{P}_X) \geq \sum_{j=1}^{m} H(\mathbf{K}_{u_j}).$$

Proof. Let $u_1 \ldots u_m$ be an r-independent sequence of classes in $A_X = \cup_{v \in X} A_v$. Since $u_j \in A_X$ for each $j = 1, \ldots, m$, it follows that there exists a class $v_j \in X$ such that $u_j \in A_{v_j}$. From *1.* of Definition 1 it follows that $H(\mathbf{K}_{u_j} | \mathbf{P}_{v_j}) = 0$ and, from (13) of the Appendix, we have that

$$H(\mathbf{K}_{u_1} \ldots \mathbf{K}_{u_m} | \mathbf{P}_X) \leq \sum_{j=1}^{m} H(\mathbf{K}_{u_j} | \mathbf{P}_X) \leq \sum_{j=1}^{m} H(\mathbf{K}_{u_j} | \mathbf{P}_{v_j}) = 0. \qquad (5)$$

Consider the mutual information $I(\mathbf{P}_X; \mathbf{K}_{u_1} \ldots \mathbf{K}_{u_m})$. From (9) of Appendix it holds that

$$H(\mathbf{P}_X) - H(\mathbf{P}_X | \mathbf{K}_{u_1} \ldots \mathbf{K}_{u_m}) = H(\mathbf{K}_{u_1} \ldots \mathbf{K}_{u_m}) - H(\mathbf{K}_{u_1} \ldots \mathbf{K}_{u_m} | \mathbf{P}_X). \qquad (6)$$

Since $H(\mathbf{P}_X | \mathbf{K}_{u_1} \ldots \mathbf{K}_{u_m}) \geq 0$, from (5) and (6) it follows that

$$H(\mathbf{P}_X) \geq H(\mathbf{K}_{u_1} \ldots \mathbf{K}_{u_m}).$$

Hence, the theorem follows from Lemma 1. □

In Definition 1 we did not make any assumption on the entropies of random variables $\mathbf{K}_u$ and $\mathbf{K}_v$, for different classes u and v. For example, we could have either $H(\mathbf{K}_u) > H(\mathbf{K}_v)$ or $H(\mathbf{K}_u) \leq H(\mathbf{K}_v)$. Our results apply to the general case of arbitrary entropies of keys, but for clarity we state the next result for the simpler case that all entropies of keys are equal, i.e. $H(\mathbf{K}_u) = H(\mathbf{K}_v)$ for all $u, v \in V$. We denote this common entropy by $H(\mathbf{K})$.
The next corollary easily follows from Theorem 1.

Corollary 1. *Let $G = (V, E)$ be the directed graph that represents an arbitrary access control policy. In any r-secure key assignment scheme for G, for any $u \in V$, if there exists an r-independent sequence of length m in A_u, then it holds that*

$$H(\mathbf{P}_u) \geq m \cdot H(\mathbf{K}).$$

In the following we define and analyze a measure for the amount of *randomness* needed by the CA to set up any r-secure key assignment scheme. The measure for the amount of randomness is formally defined using the Shannon entropy of the random variables generating the pieces distributed by the CA to the

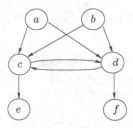

Fig. 2. Example of access control policy.

classes. The entropy is strictly related to the measure of randomness introduced by Knuth and Yao [11]. Let A be an algorithm that generates the probability distribution $\{Pr_{\mathbf{X}}(x)\}_{x \in X}$ using only independent and unbiased random bits in input. Denote by $T(A)$ the average number of random bits used by the algorithm A and let $T(\mathbf{X}) = \min_A T(A)$. Knuth and Yao [11] proved the following inequalities: $H(\mathbf{X}) \leq T(\mathbf{X}) < H(\mathbf{X}) + 2$. Thus, the entropy of a random source is very close to the average number of independent unbiased random bits necessary to simulate the source.

In the following we denote by $H(\mathbf{P}_V)$ the amount of randomness needed by the CA to set up any r-secure key assignment scheme for a directed graph $G = (V, E)$, representing an arbitrary access control policy. The next corollary states a lower bound on the size of the information generated by the CA to set up any r-secure key assignment scheme.

Corollary 2. *Let $G = (V, E)$ be the directed graph that represents an arbitrary access control policy. In any r-secure key assignment scheme for G, if there exists an r-independent sequence of length m in V, then it holds that*

$$H(\mathbf{P}_V) \geq m \cdot H(\mathbf{K}).$$

Proof. Since $A_V = \cup_{v \in V} A_v = V$, the corollary follows from Theorem 1. □

4   Perfectly Secure Key Assignment Schemes

In this section we consider key assignment schemes where each key is secure against any coalition of classes having size at most $r = \max_{u \in V} |F_u|$. These schemes are called *perfectly secure key assignment schemes*.

Let $G = (V, E)$ be the directed graph that represents an arbitrary access control policy. For any $u \in V$, we define the *incoming set* of u as the set of classes that have access to u, i.e., $C_u = \{v \in V : u \in A_v\}$.
For example, consider the graph shown in Figure 2. The incoming sets of the classes are the following:

$$C_a = \{a\} \qquad C_b = \{b\} \quad C_c = \{a, b, c, d\}$$
$$C_d = \{a, b, c, d\} \; C_e = \{c, e\} \; C_f = \{d, f\}.$$

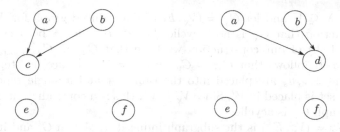

Fig. 3. Two reduced graphs for V.

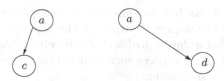

Fig. 4. Two reduced graphs for A_a.

In the following, for any subset of classes $X \subseteq V$, we show how construct an independent sequence in A_X. Our construction works as follows: first, we construct a graph $G_X = (V_X, E_X)$, called the *reduced graph for* X, such that $|V_X| \le |A_X|$ and G_X is acyclic. Afterwards, we execute the topological sort on G_X.

Construction of the Reduced Graph for X.

1. Starting from $G = (V, E)$, we construct a graph $G' = (V', E')$ as follows:
   (a) we partition V in disjoint sets such that, for each $u, v \in V$, u and v are in the same set if and only if $C_u = C_v$. Then, we choose a representative class for each set and we place it in V'.
   Remark 2. Notice that, if $C_u \ne C_v$ for each $u, v \in V$, then $V' = V$.
   (b) $E' = \{(u, v) \in E : u, v \in V', C_u \subseteq C_v \text{ and } u \ne v\}$.
2. $G_X = (V_X, E_X)$ is the subgraph induced by A_X on G'.

Remark 3. Notice that, if $X = V$ then $G_V = G'$.

Remark 4. Notice that we can obtain many reduced graphs for X according to the class chosen to represent a set at step 1.(a). All reduced graphs for X have the same number of classes.

For example, consider the graph shown in Figure 2. Figures 3 and 4 show two reduced graphs for V and two reduced graphs for $A_a = \{a, c, d\}$, respectively.

The next lemma shows that for each $X \subseteq V$, a reduced graph for X is acyclic and such that $|V_X| \le |A_X|$.

Lemma 2. *Let* $G = (V, E)$ *be the directed graph that represents an arbitrary access control policy. For each* $X \subseteq V$ *and for any reduced graph* $G_X = (V_X, E_X)$ *obtained by our construction, it holds that* $|V_X| \le |A_X|$ *and* G_X *is acyclic.*

Proof. Let $X \subseteq V$ and let $G_X = (V_X, E_X)$ be a reduced graph for X. Assume by contradiction that G_X is not acyclic. Let $< u_1 \ldots u_s >$ be a cycle in G_X. From step 1.(b) of our construction we have that $C_{u_j} \subseteq C_{u_{j+1 mod s}}$, for each $j = 1, \ldots, s$. It follows that $C_{u_1} = C_{u_2} = \ldots = C_{u_s}$. Hence, in step 1.(a) the classes $u_1, u_2, \ldots, u_s$ are placed into the same set and a single representative class of the set is placed in V'. Since $V_X \subseteq V'$, this is a contradiction. Hence, the resulting graph G_X is acyclic.

Since $G_X = (V_X, E_X)$ is the subgraph induced by A_X on G' and in step 2 of our construction a single class for any incoming set is placed in V', it follows that $|V_X| \leq |A_X|$.   □

The next lemma shows how to construct an independent sequence in a set $X \subseteq V$ starting from the sequence output by the topological sort on a reduced graph for X. Recall that a *topological sort* of a directed acyclic graph $G = (V, E)$ is a linear ordering of all its vertices such that if E contains an edge (u, v), then u appears before v in the ordering.

Lemma 3. *Let $G = (V, E)$ be the directed graph that represents any arbitrary access control policy. In any perfectly secure key assignment scheme for G, for any $X \subseteq V$ there exists an independent sequence of classes in A_X, whose length is $|V_X|$, where $G_X = (V_X, E_X)$ is a reduced graph for X.*

Proof. We show how to construct an independent sequence of classes in A_X having length $|V_X|$, where $G_X = (V_X, E_X)$ is a reduced graph for X. Since G_X is a directed acyclic graph we can perform the topological sort on it. Let $|V_X| = m$ and let $v_m \cdots v_2 v_1$ be the topologically sorted sequence of classes. We show that the reverse sequence $v_1 v_2 \cdots v_m$ is an independent sequence in A_X. From Definition 2 we need to show that for any $j = 2, \ldots, m$, there exists a set $X_j \subseteq F_{v_j}$ such that $|X_j| \leq r$ and $\{v_1 v_2 \ldots v_{j-1}\} \subseteq A_{X_j}$.

For any $j = 2, \ldots, m$, let $X_j = F_{v_j}$. It follows that $|F_{v_j}| \leq \max_{u \in V} |F_u| = r$. Moreover, if there exists a class $u_i \in F_{v_j}$ such that $v_i \in A_{u_i}$ it follows that $\{v_1, \ldots, v_{j-1}\} \subseteq \cup_{i=1}^{j-1} A_{u_i} \subseteq A_{F_{v_j}} = A_{X_j}$. Hence, in order to show that 2. of Definition 2 holds, we only need to prove that for any $j = 2, \ldots, m$ and for each $i = 1, \ldots, j - 1$, there exists a class $u_i \in F_{v_j}$ such that $v_i \in A_{u_i}$. If $v_i \in F_{v_j}$, it follows that $u_i = v_i$. If $v_i \notin F_{v_j}$, then $v_j \in A_{v_i}$, that is $(v_i, v_j) \in E$. Since in the sequence output by the topological sort on G_X, v_j appears before than v_i, the edge (v_i, v_j) does not belong to E_X. From 1.(b) of our construction, it follows that $C_{v_i} \not\subseteq C_{v_j}$. Hence, there exists a class $u_i \in F_{v_j}$ such that $v_i \in A_{u_i}$ and 2. of Definition 2 holds.   □

For example, consider the reduced graphs shown in Figures 3 and 4. It is easy to see that ca is an independent sequence in A_a and $cbafe$ is an independent sequence in V.

The next lemma shows that the sequence constructed by Lemma 3 is one of the longest independent sequences.

Lemma 4. *Let $G = (V, E)$ be the directed graph that represents an arbitrary access control policy. For each $X \subseteq V$ and any independent sequence S in A_X it holds that $|S| \leq |V_X|$, where $G_X = (V_X, E_X)$ is a reduced graph for X.*

Proof. Let S' be an independent sequence in A_x constructed by Lemma 3, i.e., $|S'| = |V_x|$. Assume by contradiction that there exists an independent sequence S in A_x such that $|S| \geq |S'|$. The sequence S contains at least two classes in the same incoming set. Let u and v be such classes. W.l.o.g, assume that u appears before than v in S. From 2. of Definition 2 there exists a set $X_v \subseteq F_v$ such that $u \in A_{x_v}$. This is a contradiction. Indeed, since $C_u = C_v$, there does not exist any class that has access to u but has no access to v. It follows that there does not exist an independent sequence in A_x whose length is greater than $|V_x|$.   □

4.1   Lower Bounds

The next theorem shows that each class has to store a private information whose size is lower bounded by the sum of the sizes of the keys assigned to all classes in a reduced graph for its accessible set.

Theorem 2. *Let $G = (V, E)$ be the directed graph that represents any arbitrary access control policy. In any perfectly secure key assignment scheme for G, for any $u \in V$ it holds that*

$$H(\mathbf{P}_u) \geq |V_{A_u}| \cdot H(\mathbf{K}),$$

where $G_{A_u} = (V_{A_u}, E_{A_u})$ is a reduced graph for A_u.

Proof. Let $G_{A_u} = (V_{A_u}, E_{A_u})$ be a reduced graph for A_u. From Lemma 3, there exists an independent sequence of classes in A_u, whose length is $|V_{A_u}|$. Thus, the theorem follows from Corollary 1.   □

The next theorem shows that the amount of randomness needed by the CA to setup any perfectly secure key assignment scheme for $G = (V, E)$ is lower bounded by the sum of the sizes of the keys assigned to all classes in a reduced graph for V.

Theorem 3. *Let $G = (V, E)$ be the directed graph that represents any arbitrary access control policy. In any perfectly secure key assignment scheme for G it holds that*

$$H(\mathbf{P}_V) \geq |V'| \cdot H(\mathbf{K}),$$

where $G' = (V', E')$ is a reduced graph for V.

Proof. Let $G' = (V', E')$ be a reduced graph for V. From Lemma 3, there exists an independent sequence of classes in V, whose length is $|V'|$. Thus, the theorem follows from Corollary 2.   □

The bounds of Theorems 2 and 3 are tight. Indeed, in the next section we show a perfectly secure key assignment scheme that meets the bounds.

4.2   An Optimal Construction

In Figure 5 we show an optimal perfectly secure key assignment scheme for any access control policy represented by a directed graph $G = (V, E)$. In our scheme all keys assigned to classes have the same size.

For example, consider the graph of Figure 2. The disjoint sets constructed by the CA during the initialization phase are the following:

Initialization phase

- The CA partitions V into m disjoint sets $S_1, \ldots, S_m$ such that for each $u, v \in V$, u and v are in the same set if and only if their incoming set coincide (i.e., $C_u = C_v$).
- Afterwards, the CA chooses a large prime number $q \geq m$.
- Finally, the CA randomly chooses m integers $x_1, x_2, \ldots, x_m$ in Z_q.

Key generation phase

- For any $i = 1, \ldots, m$ and any $u \in S_i$, let $k_u = x_i$.

Information distribution phase

- The CA sends the value x_i to any class u such that $S_i \subseteq A_u$, over a private channel.

Fig. 5. A perfectly secure key assignment scheme.

$$S_1 = \{a\} \ S_2 = \{b\} \ S_3 = \{c,d\} \ S_4 = \{e\} \ S_5 = \{f\}$$

The key assignment scheme distributes information as follows:

$$a \text{ gets } (x_1, x_3) \quad b \text{ gets } (x_2, x_3) \quad c \text{ gets } (x_3, x_4)$$
$$d \text{ gets } (x_3, x_5) \quad e \text{ gets } (x_4) \quad f \text{ gets } (x_5)$$

It is easy to see that the scheme of Figure 5 satisfies Definition 1. Moreover, our scheme is optimal both with respect to the size of the information kept secret by each class and with respect to the randomness needed by the CA. Indeed, since for any class $u \in V$ there are exactly $|V_{A_u}|$ disjoint sets of classes in A_u, where $G_{A_u} = (V_{A_u}, E_{A_u})$ is a reduced graph for A_u, the users in class u receive exactly $|V_{A_u}|$ keys and the bound of Theorem 2 is met with equality. Moreover, since $m = |V'|$, where $G_V = (V', E')$ is a reduced graph for V, the CA generates exactly $|V'|$ keys and the bound of Theorem 3 is also met with equality.

In the basic and straightforward perfectly secure key assignment scheme each class gets the key assigned to any class in its accessible set. Differently from the scheme of Figure 5, the basic and straightforward perfectly secure key assignment scheme is not optimal in general. For example, consider the graph depicted in Figure 2, corresponding to an organization where users in classes c and d have the same supervisors but are in different classes because they have different access rights. In the basic and straightforward perfectly secure key assignment scheme, classes a and b get three distinct keys, while classes c and d get two distinct keys. On the other hand, in our scheme classes a and b get two different keys, while classes c and d get only one key. Therefore, compared to the basic perfectly secure scheme, our scheme distributes less information to classes.

References

1. S. G. Akl and P. D. Taylor, *Cryptographic Solution to a Problem of Access Control in a Hierarchy*, ACM Trans. Comput. Syst., 1(3), 239–248, 1983.

2. C. C. Chang, R. J. Hwang, and T. C. Wu, *Cryptographic Key Assignment Scheme for Access Control in a Hierarchy*, Information Systems, 17(3), 243–247, 1992.
3. T. M. Cover, J. A. Thomas, *"Elements of Information Theory"*, John Wiley & Sons, 1991.
4. A. De Santis, A. L. Ferrara, and B. Masucci, *Cryptographic Key Assignment Schemes for Any Access Control Policy*, submitted for publication.
5. A. De Santis, A. L. Ferrara, and B. Masucci, *Unconditionally Secure Hierarchical Key Assignment Schemes*, in Proc. of the International Workshop on Coding and Cryptography - WCC 2003, Versailles, France, March 24–28, 2003.
6. L. Harn and H. Y. Lin, *A Cryptographic Key Generation Scheme for Multilevel Data Security*, Computers and Security, 9(6), 539–546, 1990.
7. M. S. Hwang, *A Cryptographic Key Assignment Scheme in a Hierarchy for Access Control*, Math. Comput. Modeling, 26(1), 27–31, 1997.
8. M. S. Hwang, *An Improvement of a Dynamic Cryptographic Key Assignment Scheme in a Tree Hierarchy*, Comput. Math. Appl., 37(3), 19–22, 1999.
9. M. S. Hwang, *Cryptanalysis of YCN Key Assignment Scheme in a Hierarchy*, Information Processing Letters, 73, 97–101, 2000.
10. M. S. Hwang, W. P. Yang, and C. C. Chang, *Modified Chang-Hwang-Wu Access Control Scheme*, Electronic Letters, 29(24), 2095–2096, 1993.
11. D. E. Knuth and A. C. Yao, *"The Complexity of Nonuniform Random Number Generation"*, in *Algorithms and Complexity*, Academic Press, 357–428, 1976.
12. H. T. Liaw, S. J. Wang, and C. L. Lei, *A Dynamic Cryptographic Key Assignment Scheme in a Tree Structure*, Comput. Math. Appl., 25(6), 109–114, 1993.
13. H. T. Liaw and C. L. Lei, *An Optimal Algorithm to Assign Cryptographic Keys in a Tree Structure for Access Control*, BIT, 33, 46–56, 1993.
14. C. H. Lin, *Dynamic Key Management Schemes for Access Control in a Hierarchy*, Computer Communications, 20, 1381–1385, 1997.
15. S. J. MacKinnon, P. D. Taylor, H. Meijer, and S. G. Akl, *An Optimal Algorithm for Assigning Cryptographic Keys to Control Access in a Hierarchy*, IEEE Trans. Comput., C-34(9), 797–802, 1985.
16. I. Ray, I. Ray, and N. Narasimhamurthi, *A Cryptographic Solution to Implement Access Control in a Hierarchy and More*, in Proc. of the Seventh ACM Symposium on Access Models and Technologies, ACM Press, 65–73, 2002.
17. R. S. Sandhu, *Cryptographic Implementation of a Tree Hierarchy for Access Control*, Information Processing Letters, 27, 95–98, 1988.
18. V. R. L. Shen, T. S. Chen, and F. Lai, *Novel Cryptographic Key Assignment Scheme for Dynamic Access Control in a Hierarchy*, IEICE Trans. on Fundamentals, E80-A(10), 2035–2037, 1997.
19. J. H. Yeh, R. Chow, and R. Newman, *A Key Assignment for Enforcing Access Control Policy Exceptions*, in Proc. of the International Symposium on Internet Technology, 54–59, 1998.
20. W.-G. Tzeng, *A Time-Bound Cryptographic Key Assignment Scheme for Access Control in a Hierarchy*, IEEE Trans. on Knowledge and Data Eng., 14, 2002.

Appendix: Information Theory Background

In this Appendix we review the basic concepts of Information Theory used in our definitions and proofs. For a complete treatment of the subject the reader is advised to consult [3].

Given a probability distribution $\{Pr_{\mathbf{X}}(x)\}_{x \in X}$ on a set X, we define the *entropy*[1] of $\mathbf{X}$, $H(\mathbf{X})$, as

$$H(\mathbf{X}) = -\sum_{x \in X} Pr_{\mathbf{X}}(x) \log Pr_{\mathbf{X}}(x).$$

The entropy satisfies the following property: $0 \leq H(\mathbf{X}) \leq \log |X|$, where $H(\mathbf{X}) = 0$ if and only if there exists $x_0 \in X$ such that $Pr_{\mathbf{X}}(x_0) = 1$; whereas, $H(\mathbf{X}) = \log |X|$ if and only if $Pr_{\mathbf{X}}(x) = 1/|X|$, for all $x \in X$.

Given two sets X and Y and a joint probability distribution on their cartesian product, the *conditional entropy* $H(\mathbf{X}|\mathbf{Y})$, is defined as

$$H(\mathbf{X}|\mathbf{Y}) = -\sum_{y \in Y} \sum_{x \in X} Pr_{\mathbf{Y}}(y) Pr(x|y) \log Pr(x|y).$$

From the definition of conditional entropy it is easy to see that $H(\mathbf{X}|\mathbf{Y}) \geq 0$.

Given n sets $X_1, \ldots, X_n$ and a joint probability distribution on their cartesian product, the entropy of $\mathbf{X}_1 \ldots \mathbf{X}_n$ can be expressed as

$$H(\mathbf{X}_1 \ldots \mathbf{X}_n) = H(\mathbf{X}_1) + \sum_{i=2}^{n} H(\mathbf{X}_i | \mathbf{X}_1 \ldots \mathbf{X}_{i-1}). \tag{7}$$

Given $n+1$ sets $X_1, \ldots, X_n, Y$ and a joint probability distribution on their cartesian product, the entropy of $\mathbf{X}_1 \ldots \mathbf{X}_n$ given $\mathbf{Y}$ can be expressed as

$$H(\mathbf{X}_1 \ldots \mathbf{X}_n | \mathbf{Y}) = H(\mathbf{X}_1 | \mathbf{Y}) + \sum_{i=2}^{n} H(\mathbf{X}_i | \mathbf{X}_1 \ldots \mathbf{X}_{i-1} \mathbf{Y}). \tag{8}$$

The *mutual information* $I(\mathbf{X}; \mathbf{Y})$ between $\mathbf{X}$ and $\mathbf{Y}$ is defined by

$$I(\mathbf{X}; \mathbf{Y}) = H(\mathbf{X}) - H(\mathbf{X}|\mathbf{Y}) \tag{9}$$

and satisfies the following properties: $I(\mathbf{X}; \mathbf{Y}) = I(\mathbf{Y}; \mathbf{X})$ and $I(\mathbf{X}; \mathbf{Y}) \geq 0$, from which one gets

$$H(\mathbf{X}) \geq H(\mathbf{X}|\mathbf{Y}). \tag{10}$$

Given three sets X, Y, Z and a joint probability distribution on their cartesian product, the *conditional mutual information* $I(\mathbf{X}; \mathbf{Y}|\mathbf{Z})$ between $\mathbf{X}$ and $\mathbf{Y}$ given $\mathbf{Z}$ is

$$I(\mathbf{X}; \mathbf{Y}|\mathbf{Z}) = H(\mathbf{X}|\mathbf{Z}) - H(\mathbf{X}|\mathbf{Z}\mathbf{Y}) \tag{11}$$

and satisfies the following properties: $I(\mathbf{X}; \mathbf{Y}|\mathbf{Z}) = I(\mathbf{Y}; \mathbf{X}|\mathbf{Z})$ and $I(\mathbf{X}; \mathbf{Y}|\mathbf{Z}) \geq 0$, from which one gets

$$H(\mathbf{X}|\mathbf{Z}) \geq H(\mathbf{X}|\mathbf{Z}\mathbf{Y}). \tag{12}$$

From (8) and (12) one easily gets that for any sets $Y, X_1, \ldots, X_n$ and a joint probability distribution on their cartesian product it holds that

$$\sum_{i=1}^{n} H(\mathbf{X}_i | \mathbf{Y}) \geq H(\mathbf{X}_1 \mathbf{X}_2 \ldots \mathbf{X}_n | \mathbf{Y}). \tag{13}$$

---

[1] All log's in this paper denote basis 2 logarithms.

Security-Aware Program Transformations*

Massimo Bartoletti, Pierpaolo Degano, and Gian Luigi Ferrari

Dipartimento di Informatica
Università di Pisa, Italy
{bartolet,degano,giangi}@di.unipi.it

Abstract. Stack inspection is a basic mechanism for implementing language based security. Stack inspection is time consuming and may prevent from code optimization. A static analysis is presented that safely approximates the access rights granted at run-rime. Stack inspection optimizations are then possible, along with program transformations.

1 Introduction

The growing use of network technologies in current distributed computing has made *security* critical in the design, development and distribution of applications. Indeed, both final users and application designers put special emphasis on security issues. For final users, the *awareness* of security mechanisms is crucial for choosing the best network services that match their requirements. Designers wish to control resource usage and access in order to ensure and maintain adequate security levels.

Designing and implementing security policies at the programming language level help in handling security. Here, we consider an authorization-based model where a security policy is enforced by inserting appropriate checks in a program. Clearly, writing secure applications is difficult: omitting a single check somewhere in the code may compromise the security of the whole application. There is no general mechanism which identifies what kind of security checks have to be inserted in a program, and where.

The Java programming language features constructs and mechanisms for secure execution of mobile code. Java applications run components with different levels of trust, e.g. components originated from different administration domains. In the Java security model, access control decisions are taken by examining the call stack at run-time. A permission is granted, provided that it belongs to *all* principals on the call stack. The so-called *privileged operations* are an exception. These are allowed to execute any code granted to their principal, regardless of the calling sequence. This access control mechanism is known as *stack inspection*. Beyond Java, other run-time environments (e.g. the .NET Common Language Runtime [15]) adopt stack inspection as basic authorization mechanism.

---

* Work partially supported by EU project DEGAS (IST-2001-32072), MIUR project "MEtodi FormalI per la Sicurezza e il TempO" (MEFISTO), and MIUR project "Network Aware Programming: Object, Languages, Implementation" (NAPOLI).

C. Blundo and C. Laneve (Eds.): ICTCS 2003, LNCS 2841, pp. 355–368, 2003.

Stack inspection has some drawbacks. First, the run-time overhead due to the analysis of stack frames may grow very high. Second, stack inspection deeply affects standard program transformations, such as method inlining and tail call elimination. These optimizations may in fact alter the structure of the call stack. Hence, understanding the semantics of program transformations in a setting with stack inspection is a research (and technological) challenge.

Our contribution aims at developing semantic-driven mechanisms as an aid to improve efficiency of architectures for language-based security. We build over control flow analysis [16]. The idea of control flow analysis is to efficiently obtain computable approximations of the set of values that the objects of a program may assume during its execution. These approximations are then used to analyze program properties in a safe way: if a property holds at static time, then it will always hold at run-time. The vice-versa may not be true: the analysis may "err on the safe side".

In Section 2 we consider an idealized object-oriented language with primitive constructs for method invocations, exceptions, and access control. The execution traces of Java code are safely approximated by the traces of their corresponding abstract programs. We represent these programs by *control flow graphs*, a programming model not tied to any particular language. These graphs are equipped with a formal operational semantics.

In Section 3 we introduce a static analysis over control flow graphs, called *Trace Permissions Analysis*. This analysis computes, for each program point and each execution reaching that point, the set of permissions granted at run-time. The analysis is sound and complete with respect to the operational semantics of our idealized language, i.e. it computes all and only the permissions that are granted at run-time.

In Section 4 we show that the Trace Permissions analysis provides us with the basis for some security-aware code optimizations. As a first application, we detect and remove the redundant checks in a program, i.e. the checks which always pass. Dead code elimination is a program optimization which detects and removes the code unused or unreached in executions. Security restrictions may cause more fragments of code to become unreachable, e.g. because a security check protecting it is never passed. Our technique permits to discard such dead code in the linking phase. We also cope with *method inlining*, an optimization that replaces a method invocation with a copy of the called method code. In presence of stack inspection, method inlining may break security, because the protection domain of the inlined method is ignored. The Trace Permissions analysis provides us with the basis to efficiently construct the set of method invocations which can be safely inlined.

In Section 5 we examine the adequacy of our model, and we propose some extensions to make it suitable for real-world applications.

Because of space limitations, here we will provide the overall picture of the technical development of our approach by focusing on the underlying ideas. We refer to the full paper [2] for the proofs, some illustrative examples, and the detailed description of the model.

2   The Program Model

We model programs as *control flow graphs* (CFGs for short) whose nodes represent the activities relevant for stack inspection (i.e. checks, method invocations and returns) and whose arcs represent the flow of control. We do not define how CFGs are extracted from an actual program. This construction is well understood and algorithms and tools exist for it; see for example [10, 16, 20, 21].

By construction, CFGs hide any data flow information, and are therefore approximated; typically, the conditional construct is rendered as non-deterministic choice. This approximation is *safe*, in the sense that any actual execution flow is represented by a path in the CFG. However, the converse may not be true: some paths may exist which do not correspond to any actual execution. For instance, both branches of an "if" statement are represented, even in the cases when always the same branch is taken at run-time.

There is a further source of approximation, especially for object-oriented languages with dynamic resolution of method invocations. In Java, for example, when a program invokes an instance method on an object O, the virtual machine may have to choose among various implementations of that method. The decision is not based on the declared type of O, but on the actual class O belongs to, which is unpredictable at static time. To be safe, CFGs consider a superset of the methods that can be invoked at each program point. This is a main source of approximation for the analyses built over CFGs.

2.1   Syntax

Let $\mathcal{D}$ be a finite set of protection domains, and $\mathcal{P}$ be a finite set of permissions.

Definition 1. *A CFG $\langle N \cup \{n_\varepsilon\}, E, Priv, Dom \rangle$ is an oriented graph, where:*

- *N is the set of nodes. Each node $n \in N$ is associated with a label $\ell(n)$, describing the control flow primitive it represents. Labels partition nodes in three kinds:* `call` *nodes, that stand for method invocation,* `return` *nodes, which represent return from a method, and* `check` *nodes, which enforce the access control policy. For each $P \in \mathcal{P}$, a node labeled* `check`(P) *can be seen as the abstract representation of an* `AccessController.checkPermission(P)` *instruction in the Java language. The distinguished element $n_\varepsilon \notin N$ plays the technical role of a single, isolated entry point.*
- *$E \subseteq (N \cup \{n_\varepsilon\}) \times N$ is the set of edges. Edges are partitioned into four sets: entry edges $\bullet\!\!\longrightarrow n$, that represent the entry points of a program; call edges $n \longrightarrow n'$, which model interprocedural flow; transfer edges $n \dashrightarrow n'$, which correspond to sequencing; and catch edges $n \dashrightarrow_\downarrow n'$, which correspond to exception handling. The last two kinds of edges represent intraprocedural flow. The set of entry edges contains all pairs (n_ε, n) where n is a program entry point. The n_ε element is the source of entry edges, only.*
- *$Priv : N \to Bool$ tells whether a node enables its privileges or not.*
- *$Dom : N \to \mathcal{D}$ is a mapping from nodes to protection domains.*

When unambiguous, we shall write $\langle N, E \rangle$ instead of $\langle N \cup \{n_\varepsilon\}, E, \text{Priv}, \text{Dom} \rangle$.

Each CFG is associated with a *security policy* $\text{Perm} : \mathcal{D} \to 2^{\mathcal{P}}$, which grants a set of permissions to each protection domain. Hereafter, we will always abbreviate $\text{Perm}(\text{Dom}(n))$ with $\text{Perm}(n)$.

Definition 2. *The* methods *of a CFG $\langle N, E \rangle$ are the connected components of the graph $\langle N, E' \rangle$, where E' is the set of intraprocedural edges in E, with no orientation. We call $\mu(n)$ the method to which node n belongs. The entry points of $\mu(n)$ are defined as:*

$$\varepsilon(\mu(n)) \;=\; \{\, n' \in \mu(n) \mid \bullet\!\longrightarrow n' \;\vee\; \exists m \in N.\; m \longrightarrow n' \,\}$$

The set $\rho(n)$ of return nodes associated to a node n is:

$$\rho(n) \;=\; \{\, m \in N \mid \ell(m) = \textbf{\textit{return}} \;\wedge\; n \longrightarrow \varepsilon(\mu(m)) \,\}$$

The set $\xi(n)$ of nodes that may throw an exception catchable by n is defined as the smallest set satisfying:

$$\xi(n) \;=\; \begin{cases} \{n\} & \text{if } \ell(n) = \textbf{\textit{check}}(P) \\ \{\, \xi(n') \mid n \longrightarrow \varepsilon(\mu(n')) \;\wedge\; n' \not\dashrightarrow_{\oint} \,\} & \text{otherwise} \end{cases}$$

The set $\xi_1(n)$ of nodes that may propagate an exception to n is defined as:

$$\xi_1(n) \;=\; \{\, n' \mid n \longrightarrow \varepsilon(\mu(n')) \;\wedge\; n' \not\dashrightarrow_{\oint} \;\wedge\; \xi(n') \neq \emptyset \,\}$$

As discussed in [2], all the CFGs derived from admissible Java programs satisfy the following well-formedness constraints: (1) check nodes have no outgoing call edges; (2) return nodes have no outgoing edges; (3) each method has a single entry point (4) nodes in the same method are in the same protection domain. Moreover, we require that only call nodes can be privileged. In general, security checks can also occur within privileged actions: however, privileged check nodes make little sense, because it is always possible to determine whether a privileged check will succeed or not. Similarly, there is no point in enabling return nodes to be privileged, because a return node will never be on the call stack when stack inspection is performed.

2.2   Semantics

The operational semantics of CFGs is defined by a transition system whose configurations are sequences of nodes, modeling call stacks. Additionally, each state has a boolean tag which tells whether an exception is *active*, i.e. thrown and not caught yet. Formally, we define the set of states as $N^* \times \textit{Bool}$.

If no exception is active, a state is represented as sequence of nodes enclosed in square brackets: for example, $\sigma = [n_0, \ldots, n_k]$ is a state whose top node is n_k. If an exception is active, we append the symbol $\oint$ to the sequence of nodes, i.e.

Table 1. Operational semantics of CFGs.

$$\frac{\bullet \longrightarrow n}{[] \rhd [n]} \qquad \frac{\ell(n) = \mathtt{call} \quad n \longrightarrow n'}{\sigma : n \rhd \sigma : n : n'} \qquad \frac{\ell(m) = \mathtt{return} \quad n \dashrightarrow n'}{\sigma : n : m \rhd \sigma : n'}$$

$$\frac{\ell(n) = \mathtt{check}(P) \quad \sigma : n \vdash P \quad n \dashrightarrow n'}{\sigma : n \rhd \sigma : n'} \qquad \frac{\ell(n) = \mathtt{check}(P) \quad \sigma : n \nvdash P}{\sigma : n \rhd \sigma : n_\xi}$$

$$\frac{n \dashrightarrow_\xi n'}{\sigma : n_\xi \rhd \sigma : n'} \qquad \frac{n \not\dashrightarrow_\xi}{\sigma : n_\xi \rhd \sigma_\xi}$$

$$\frac{}{[] \vdash P} \qquad \frac{P \in \mathrm{Perm}(n) \quad \sigma \vdash P}{\sigma : n \vdash P} \qquad \frac{P \in \mathrm{Perm}(n) \quad \mathrm{Priv}(n)}{\sigma : n \vdash P}$$

σ_ξ abbreviates $\langle \sigma, \mathit{true} \rangle$. Pushing a node n on a stack σ is written as $\sigma : n$ (the infix operator : associates to the left).

The transition relation $\rhd$ between states is the minimal relation induced by the inference rules in Table 1. A *trace* of G leading to $\langle \sigma_k, x_k \rangle$ is a derivation $\langle \sigma_0, x_0 \rangle \rhd \cdots \rhd \langle \sigma_k, x_k \rangle$ where $\sigma_0 = []$ and $x_0 = \mathit{false}$. By overloading the notation, we also denote with $\rhd$ the relation:

$$\frac{}{G \rhd \langle [], \mathit{false} \rangle} \qquad \frac{G \rhd \langle \sigma, x \rangle \quad \langle \sigma, x \rangle \rhd \langle \sigma', x' \rangle}{G \rhd \langle \sigma', x' \rangle}$$

stating when there is a trace of G which can lead to a given state. We say that a node n is reachable iff $\langle \sigma : n, x \rangle$ is a reachable configuration.

In our formalization, we use a slightly simplified version of the full access control algorithm presented in [8]. The simplified algorithm scans the call stack top-down. Each frame in the stack refers to the protection domain containing the class to which the called method belongs. As soon as a frame is found whose protection domain has not the required permission, an `AccessControlException` is raised. The algorithm succeeds when a privileged frame is found that carries the required permission, or when all frames have been visited. We formally specify this behavior by the minimal relation induced by the inference rules for $\vdash$ in Table 1. We say that a permission P is *granted* to a state σ if $\sigma \vdash P$.

3   The Trace Permissions Analysis

In this section we review the static analysis over CFGs called Trace Permissions Analysis (TP). The TP analysis approximates the access rights granted to each reachable state.

Table 2. Flow equations for the TP analysis.

$$TP_{in}(n) = \bigcup_{(m,n)\in E} TP_{out}(m,n)$$

$$TP_{out}(m,n) = \begin{cases} \{\{\mathrm{Dom}(n)\}\} & \text{if } \bullet\!\!\longrightarrow n \\ \{\gamma \cup \{\mathrm{Dom}(n)\} \mid \gamma \in TP_{call}(m)\} & \text{if } m \longrightarrow n \\ TP_{trans}(m) & \text{if } m \dashrightarrow n \\ TP_{catch}(m) & \text{if } m \dashrightarrow_i n \end{cases}$$

$$TP_{call}(n) = \begin{cases} \{\{\mathrm{Dom}(n)\}\} & \text{if } \mathrm{Priv}(n) \text{ and } TP_{in}(n) \neq \emptyset \\ TP_{in}(n) & \text{otherwise} \end{cases}$$

$$TP_{trans}(n) = \begin{cases} \{\gamma \in TP_{in}(n) \mid P \in \Pi(\gamma)\} & \text{if } \ell(n) = \mathtt{check}(P) \\ \{\gamma \in TP_{in}(n) \mid \mathrm{Trans}(n, \{\mathrm{Dom}(n)\})\} & \text{if } \ell(n) = \mathtt{call}, \mathrm{Priv}(n) \\ \{\gamma \in TP_{in}(n) \mid \mathrm{Trans}(n, \gamma)\} & \text{otherwise} \end{cases}$$

$$TP_{catch}(n) = \begin{cases} \{\gamma \in TP_{in}(n) \mid P \notin \Pi(\gamma)\} & \text{if } \ell(n) = \mathtt{check}(P) \\ \{\gamma \in TP_{in}(n) \mid \mathrm{Catch}(n, \{\mathrm{Dom}(n)\})\} & \text{if } \ell(n) = \mathtt{call}, \mathrm{Priv}(n) \\ \{\gamma \in TP_{in}(n) \mid \mathrm{Catch}(n, \gamma)\} & \text{otherwise} \end{cases}$$

$$\mathrm{Trans}(n, \gamma) \stackrel{def}{=} \exists m \in \rho(n). \ \gamma \cup \{\mathrm{Dom}(m)\} \in TP_{in}(m)$$
$$\mathrm{Catch}(n, \gamma) \stackrel{def}{=} \exists m \in \xi_1(n). \ \gamma \cup \{\mathrm{Dom}(m)\} \in TP_{catch}(m)$$

Since the set of permissions granted to a state is just the intersection of the permissions associated to each protection domain traversed after the last privileged frame (if any), we can identify the set $\{P \in \mathcal{P} \mid \sigma \vdash P\}$ with the *security context* $\Gamma(\sigma)$, where $\Gamma : N^* \to 2^{\mathcal{D}}$ is defined as follows:

$$\Gamma([]) = \emptyset \qquad \Gamma(\sigma : n) = \begin{cases} \{\mathrm{Dom}(n)\} & \text{if } \mathrm{Priv}(n) \\ \Gamma(\sigma) \cup \{\mathrm{Dom}(n)\} & \text{otherwise} \end{cases}$$

The set of permissions granted to a security context γ is:

$$\Pi(\gamma) = \bigcap_{D \in \gamma} \mathrm{Perm}(D)$$

The permissions granted to the security context of a state σ are exactly the permissions granted to σ, i.e. $\sigma \vdash P \iff P \in \Pi(\Gamma(\sigma))$ for all $\sigma \in N^*, P \in \mathcal{P}$.

Given a CFG G and a security policy *Perm*, the analysis is specified by the set of equations $TP^=(G, Perm)$ in Table 2. A solution $\tau \models TP^=(G, Perm)$ is a 5-tuple $\tau = \langle \tau_{in}, \tau_{call}, \tau_{trans}, \tau_{catch}, \tau_{out} \rangle$ which satisfies all the equations. The purpose of the analysis is to find, for each node n, the set $\{ \Gamma(\sigma : n) \mid G \rhd \sigma : n \}$.

Technically, TP is a forward, monotone control flow analysis with values in $2^{2^{\mathcal{D}}}$. Since both G and $\mathcal{D}$ are finite, the least solution to the analysis does exist and is finitely computable.

The following theorem states the correctness of the TP analysis. The first equation below states that any solution to the analysis is sound w.r.t. the operational semantics. The second equation states that the least solution to the analysis is also complete. This fact should not seem bizarre: indeed, completeness is only up to the precision of the CFG, which is an approximated model of the analyzed program.

Theorem 1. *Let* $\tau \models TP^{=}(G, Perm)$. *Then:*

$$G \rhd \sigma : n \quad \Longrightarrow \quad \exists \gamma \in \tau_{call}(n).\ \gamma = \Gamma(\sigma : n)$$

Moreover, the minimal solution w.r.t. the inclusion relation on $2^{2^{\mathcal{D}}}$ *is such that:*

$$\gamma \in \tau_{call}(n) \quad \Longrightarrow \quad \exists \sigma.\ G \rhd \sigma : n \ \wedge \ \gamma = \Gamma(\sigma : n)$$

The worklist algorithm which actually computes the (unique) minimal solution to the analysis has computational complexity $\mathcal{O}(c \cdot |N|) = \mathcal{O}(|N|)$. The constant c depends on the number of protection domains occurring in G: in the worst case, $c = 2^{3 \cdot |\mathcal{D}_G|}$, where $\mathcal{D}_G = \bigcup_{n \in N} \mathrm{Dom}(n)$. However, the exponential factor only occurs when the number of protection domains is proportional to the number of nodes. Actually, the number of protection domains can be considered as a constant, because it depends on the security policy, rather than on the size of the program.

Dynamic linking is the mechanism which allows a program to be extended on demand, e.g. with code coming from the network. Although our program model does not directly support this feature, the TP analysis can be computed incrementally. An incremental CFG construction algorithm, e.g. the one presented in [19], can be used in order to correctly perform the dynamic linking of the relevant CFGs. Indeed, this operation cannot be performed by looking at the CFGs alone, because CFGs do not carry enough information to restrict the set of targets of dynamically dispatched method invocations. We now outline how the incremental computation of the analysis is performed. Let $G = \langle N, E \rangle$, and assume that a solution τ to $TP^{=}(G, Perm)$ is available when the CFG $G' = \langle N', E' \rangle$ is loaded. Through the CFG construction algorithm, we single out the set $E_\bowtie$ of *resolved calls* between G and G', i.e. those edges $n \longrightarrow m$ such that n, m do not belong both to the same CFG. Linking G and G' together yields the CFG $G \bowtie G' = \langle N \cup N', E \cup E' \cup E_\bowtie \rangle$. The analysis $\tau' \models TP^{=}(G \bowtie G', Perm)$ is a refinement of τ. To compute it, the worklist algorithm adds to τ all the contexts associated with the new paths created by the resolved calls. It suffices now to restart the algorithm with the worklist containing all nodes n such that, for some node m, $(n, m) \in E_\bowtie$. Moreover, the worklist must include all entry points of G', if any. Although this technique is not fully compositional, note that adding new executable paths to a CFG never affects the analysis of the old ones.

4   Program Transformations

In this section we show that the Trace Permissions analysis provides us with an effective basis for some security-aware code optimizations.

4.1   Redundant Checks Elimination

Our first application of the analysis is a code optimization which detects and removes the redundant checks occurring in a program, i.e. those checks which always pass, regardless of the execution trace.

The following theorem states conditions to recognize redundant checks, so enabling the compiler to safely remove them from the code:

Theorem 2. *Let* $\tau \models TP^=(G, Perm)$. *For each check node* n, *let* $\Pi(n)$ *be the set of permissions (statically) granted to* n:

$$\Pi(n) \;=\; \bigcap \{\, \Pi(\gamma) \mid \gamma \in \tau_{call}(n)\,\}$$

If $\ell(n) = \mathtt{check}(P)$ *and* $P \in \Pi(n)$, *then* n *is redundant, i.e. for each* $\sigma \in N^*$:

$$G \triangleright \sigma : n \quad\Longrightarrow\quad \sigma : n \vdash P$$

Actually, redundant checks can only be *disabled* in presence of dynamic linking, because loading a new method may add new traces where the permission is no longer granted. A similar situation also holds for the other optimizations of stack inspection considered below.

4.2   Dead Code Elimination

Dead code elimination is a program optimization which prevents the compiler from generating bytecode for unreachable or useless pieces of code. Dead code elimination reduces both the size of the generated bytecode and the total application running time (e.g. when code has to be downloaded from the network).

The following theorem allows to detect (and remove) those pieces of code which cannot be reached due to security restrictions:

Theorem 3. *Let* $\tau \models TP^=(G, Perm)$. *Then:*

$$\tau_{call}(n) = \emptyset \quad\Longrightarrow\quad \neg \exists \sigma. \; G \triangleright \sigma : n$$

4.3   Method Inlining

The TP analysis can be exploited to compute the set of method invocations which can be safely inlined. Intuitively, a method invocation may be inlined if the outcome of the security checks is not affected by the the elimination of the protection domain of the inlined method.

We adopt the so-called *original version inlining* approach [11], which always considers the original version of the callee and the current version of the caller when performing inlinings. This can be obtained by duplicating the original code of the inlined method.

Let $\dot{n}$ be the node candidate for inlining, and $\dot{n} \longrightarrow n'$. We assume that the method invocation represented by $\dot{n}$ can be statically dispatched, i.e. it has exactly one callee, represented by $\mu(n')$.

The decision procedure, which tells whether or not the inlining of $\dot{n}$ is safe, is outlined below. We first assign a fresh name to the protection domain of $\mu(n')$, without modifying its granted permissions. Assume that a solution τ to the TP analysis is available. We restart the worklist algorithm from $\dot{n}$, in order to isolate the protection domain of $\mu(n')$ in the computed security contexts. This allows for the definition of a function $Inl_{\dot{n}}$ which simulates the effect of method inlining on security contexts: given a context γ, $Inl_{\dot{n}}(\gamma)$ is obtained by substituting the protection domain of $\mu(n')$ for that of $\mu(\dot{n})$. Each time a check node n is reached, we ensure that for each context $\gamma \in \tau_{in}(n)$, γ and $Inl_{\dot{n}}(\gamma)$ agree on the permission P checked by n, i.e. $P \in \Pi(\gamma) \iff P \in \Pi(Inl_{\dot{n}}(\gamma))$.

The inlining of $\dot{n}$ is safe if this holds for each check node reached during this procedure. Note that it is possible to deal with the general case of virtual calls with many callees: this only requires some more machinery (all the possible callees must be inlined).

We formally define below when a method invocation can be inlined. The condition (1a) guarantees static dispatching of $\dot{n}$, as well as that $\dot{n}$ is not a recursive call (otherwise inlining makes little sense). The condition (1b) rephrases the original version inlining approach. The condition (1c) ensures that the protection domain of $\dot{n}$ is isolated. These conditions, apart from $\dot{n}$ being not recursive, can easily be satisfied, as noted above. The key condition is (1d): it guarantees that the security checks passed after inlining are exactly those passed before inlining.

Definition 3. *We say that $\dot{n}$ is inlineable in G iff:*

$$\exists_1 n' \in N.\ \dot{n} \longrightarrow n' \wedge n' \notin \mu(\dot{n}) \tag{1a}$$

$$\forall m, n' \in N.\ \forall n' \in N.\ \dot{n} \longrightarrow n' \wedge m \longrightarrow n' \implies m = \dot{n} \tag{1b}$$

$$\forall n' \in N.\ \dot{n} \longrightarrow n' \implies \forall m \notin \mu(n').\ Dom(m) \neq Dom(n') \tag{1c}$$

$$\forall n.\ \ell(n) = \mathbf{check}(P), \gamma \in \tau_{in}(n).\ P \in \Pi(\gamma) \iff P \in \Pi(Inl_{\dot{n}}(\gamma)) \tag{1d}$$

Next, we define the effect of the method inlining transformation on CFGs. Instead of substituting $\dot{n}$ for $\mu(n')$ and adjusting the edges accordingly, we equivalently operate on the semantics of the transformed CFG.

The effect of the inlining of $\dot{n}$ on states is simulated by the function $inl_{\dot{n}}$ in Table 3. Given a state σ, $inl_{\dot{n}}(\sigma)$ is obtained by removing all the occurrences of $\dot{n}$ in σ (except when $\dot{n}$ is in top position).

The operational semantics of a CFG after the inlining of $\dot{n}$ is defined by the transition relation $\triangleright^{\dot{n}}$ in Table 3.

We define the $\dot{n}$-*inlined version* of a CFG $G = \langle N \cup \{n_\varepsilon\}, E, \mathrm{Priv}_G, \mathrm{Dom}_G \rangle$ as $\dot{G} = \langle N \cup \{n_\varepsilon\}, E, \mathrm{Priv}_{\dot{G}}, \mathrm{Dom}_{\dot{G}} \rangle$, where:

$$\mathrm{Priv}_{\dot{G}}(n) = \begin{cases} true & \text{if } \mathrm{Priv}_G(\dot{n}) \text{ and } \dot{n} \longrightarrow \mu(n) \\ \mathrm{Priv}_G(n) & \text{otherwise} \end{cases}$$

Table 3. Specification of method inlining.

$$
\frac{}{inl_{\dot{n}}([]) = []} \qquad \frac{inl_{\dot{n}}(\sigma) = \dot{\sigma} \quad top(\sigma) \neq \dot{n}}{inl_{\dot{n}}(\sigma : n') = \dot{\sigma} : n'} \qquad \frac{inl_{\dot{n}}(\sigma) = \dot{\sigma}}{inl_{\dot{n}}(\sigma : \dot{n} : n') = \dot{\sigma} : n'}
$$

$$
\frac{}{Inl_{\dot{n}}(\emptyset) = \emptyset} \qquad \frac{Inl_{\dot{n}}(\gamma) = \dot{\gamma} \quad Inl_{\dot{n}}(\gamma') = \dot{\gamma}'}{Inl_{\dot{n}}(\gamma \cup \gamma') = \dot{\gamma} \cup \dot{\gamma}'}
$$

$$
\frac{\dot{n} \not\longrightarrow \mu(n')}{Inl_{\dot{n}}(\{\mathrm{Dom}(n')\}) = \{\mathrm{Dom}(n')\}} \qquad \frac{\dot{n} \longrightarrow \mu(n')}{Inl_{\dot{n}}(\{\mathrm{Dom}(n')\}) = \{\mathrm{Dom}(\dot{n})\}}
$$

$$
\frac{\ell(n) = \mathtt{call} \quad n \longrightarrow n' \quad n \neq \dot{n}}{\sigma : n \rhd^{\dot{n}}_{inl} \sigma : n : n'} \qquad \frac{\ell(\dot{n}) = \mathtt{call} \quad \dot{n} \longrightarrow n'}{\sigma : \dot{n} \rhd^{\dot{n}}_{inl} \sigma : n'}
$$

$$
\frac{\ell(n') = \mathtt{return} \quad \dot{n} \dashrightarrow m \quad \dot{n} \not\longrightarrow \mu(n')}{\sigma : n : n' \rhd^{\dot{n}}_{inl} \sigma : m} \qquad \frac{\ell(n') = \mathtt{return} \quad \dot{n} \dashrightarrow m \quad \dot{n} \longrightarrow \mu(n')}{\sigma : n' \rhd^{\dot{n}}_{inl} \sigma : m}
$$

$$
\frac{n \not\dashrightarrow \quad \dot{n} \not\longrightarrow \mu(n')}{\sigma : n \zeta \rhd^{\dot{n}}_{inl} \sigma \zeta} \qquad \frac{n \not\dashrightarrow \quad \dot{n} \longrightarrow \mu(n')}{\sigma : n \zeta \rhd^{\dot{n}}_{inl} \sigma : \dot{n} \zeta}
$$

$$
\mathrm{Dom}_{\dot{G}}(n) = \begin{cases} \mathrm{Dom}_G(\dot{n}) & \text{if } \dot{n} \longrightarrow \mu(n) \\ \mathrm{Dom}_G(n) & \text{otherwise} \end{cases}
$$

Note that we may end up with privileged checks and returns, thus violating one of the well-formedness constraints in Section 2. However, this constraint can easily be removed, at the price of a slightly more involved definition of the TP analysis.

The following theorem states the correctness of method inlining: each trace in the original CFG corresponds to a trace in the $\dot{n}$-inlined version of the CFG.

Theorem 4. *If $\dot{n}$ is inlineable in G, and $\dot{G}$ is the $\dot{n}$-inlined version of G, then:*

$$
\langle \sigma_0, x_0 \rangle \rhd \cdots \rhd \langle \sigma_k, x_k \rangle \iff \langle \dot{\sigma}_0, x_0 \rangle \rhd^{\dot{n}}_{inl} \cdots \rhd^{\dot{n}}_{inl} \langle \dot{\sigma}_k, x_k \rangle
$$

where $\sigma_0 = []$, $x_0 = \mathit{false}$, and $\dot{\sigma}_i = inl_{\dot{n}}(\sigma_i)$ for each $i \in 0..k$.

5   Adequacy of the Model

There are some differences between our model and the Java security model [8]:

– our model prevents a permission P to be granted to a state $\sigma : n$ if P does not belong to the permissions granted to $\mathrm{Dom}(n)$. Instead, in the Java security model, P may be *implied* by some permission $P' \in \text{Perm}(n)$. For example, `FilePermission("/-","read")` implies the permission to read any file on the local disk. We can easily extend our program model by introducing a partial order on permissions to encompass permission implications. The inclusion test $P \in \text{Perm}(n)$ in the rules for $\vdash$ should be replaced by $\text{Perm}(n) \Rightarrow P$, which tests if P is implied by some permission $P' \in \text{Perm}(n)$.

- although the Java security model allows for the dynamic instantiation of permissions (e.g. an application that asks the user for a file name and then tries to open that file), we only consider the permissions that can be determined statically. We are currently investigating an extension of our present approach to deal with such *parametric permissions* on the form $P(x)$, where x ranges over the set of possible targets for the permissions of class P.

- in the Java security model, a new thread upon creation inherits the *access control context* (i.e. the set of protection domains for the classes on the call stack) from its parent. When stack inspection is performed, both the context of the current thread and the contexts of all its ancestors are examined. In this way, a child thread cannot obtain a resource access which is not granted to its ancestors. We do not model threads. To consider them, we should first single out the program points where new threads can be created (and started) while constructing the CFG (as done in [12]).

- in our model, we consider a "skeletal" exception handling mechanism, where exceptions are all of the same type, and neither nested `try` blocks nor `finally` clauses are featured. A full treatment of exceptions requires a tailored construction of the CFG, e.g. by the techniques presented in [5, 18], that also suggest how to adjust interprocedural analyses to exceptions.

- the Java Authentication and Authorization Service [13] extends the Java security model by allowing for *user-centric* access control policies, based on the principal who actually runs the code. Permissions can be granted to principals, and the `doAs` method allows a piece of code to be executed on behalf of a given subject. This is done by associating the (authenticated) subject running the code with the current access control context. Stack inspection ensures that subjects are taken into account when access control is performed. Unfortunately, static analysis techniques are weak in detecting the set of principals which can get authenticated at a given program point.

There are some features of the Java security architecture we think difficult to cope with: they are reflection, native methods, some "dangerous" permissions implications (e.g. `AllPermission` may breach the whole security system by replacing the JVM system binaries), and dynamic policies (although some recent works, e.g. [9, 14], have addressed the formal treatment of this issue). Besides deeply affecting security, these features reduce the effectiveness of any static analysis which aims at determining the permissions granted to running code.

6   Conclusions and Related Work

We have developed a technique to perform program transformations in presence of stack inspection. The technique relies on the definition of our Trace Permissions Analysis. It is a control flow analysis, and computes a safe approximation to the set of permissions which are *always* granted to bytecode at run-time. The analysis is sound and complete w.r.t. the control flow graphs derived from the bytecode (however, these graphs only approximate the actual behavior). In this paper, we focused on redundant checks elimination, dead code elimination and method inlining. A similar approach also applies to general tail call elimination (see [2] for details). Although we restricted our attention to Java, the same techniques work with other programming languages whose authorization mechanisms rely on stack inspection (e.g. C♯ [23]).

Many authors advocated the use of static techniques in order to understand and optimize stack inspection.

Besson, Jensen, Le Mètayer and Thorn [4] were among the first to apply static techniques to the verification of global security properties. They formalize classes of security properties through a linear-time temporal logic. They show that a large class of policies (including stack inspection) can be expressed in this formalism, while more sophisticated ones (like the Chinese Wall policy) are not. Model checking is then used to prove that local security checks enforce a given global security policy. Their verification method is based on the translation from linear-time temporal formulae to deterministic finite-state automata, and it can be used to optimize stack inspection. For each node n, the analysis in [4] can compute the set $\{P \in \mathcal{P}_{check} \mid G \triangleright \sigma : n \ \wedge \ \sigma : n \vdash P\}$, where $\mathcal{P}_{check}$ is the set of permissions checked in G. The computational complexity of the method is $\mathcal{O}(c \cdot |N|)$, where the constant c depends on the cardinality of $\mathcal{P}_{check}$ (in the worst case, $c = 2^{|\mathcal{P}_{check}|}$). Therefore, our Trace Permissions analysis performs better when there are few protection domains, while [4] is more efficient when there are few security checks. Note that our analysis is at least as precise as [4], because $\mathcal{P}_{check} \subseteq \mathcal{P}$. Also, the analysis in [4] does not seem to scale up smoothly to handle dynamic linking, because it must be recomputed each time a new permission is discovered.

Wallach, Appel and Felten [22] formalize stack inspection by exploiting the access control logic of [1]. The authors show that their decision procedure is equivalent to Java stack inspection, according to an informal operational semantics. Moreover, they propose an alternative semantics of eager stack inspection, called *security-passing style*. This technique consists of tracking the security state of an execution as an additional parameter of each method invocation. This allows for interprocedural compiler optimizations that do not interfere with stack inspection. The security-passing style allows each security operation to be performed in constant time, but it involves an overhead, because the security state must be computed at each method invocation. Dynamic caching techniques are adopted to reduce this overhead: therefore, in the optimal case, the additional cost of each method invocation is that of a hash lookup. The same technique allows for an implementation of security checks which requires a hash lookup in the optimal case. In [3] we propose an approach to eager stack inspection which allows for security operations that cost as a hash lookup *in the worst case*, while, in the optimal case, they are as cheap as a bitwise operation. A further difference w.r.t. our approach is that [22] assumes that the whole program is available at compilation time, while we can deal with dynamic linking of code.

Pottier, Skalka and Smith [17] address the problem of stack inspection in λ_{sec}, a typed lambda calculus enriched with primitive constructs for enforcing security checks and managing permissions. They have polymorphic types on the form $\tau_1 \rightarrow \varsigma \rightarrow \tau_2$, where τ_1, τ_2 are types and ς is a set of permissions. Intuitively, the type $\tau_1 \rightarrow \varsigma \rightarrow \tau_2$ details the security context necessary to execute a function of type $\tau_1 \rightarrow \tau_2$. Stack inspection never fails on a well typed program, because the set of permissions granted at runtime always includes the security context. These types are very powerful and can deal with several issues (e.g. security policy overriding, dependencies from untrusted code). Moreover, they can be smoothly extended to deal with objects by standard type-theoretic techniques.

The problem of establishing the correctness of program transformations in presence of stack inspection is investigated by Fournet and Gordon in [7]. They present an equational theory, together with a coinductive proof technique, for the λ_{sec} calculus. They study how stack inspection affects program behavior, proving that certain function inlinings and tail-call eliminations are correct. The equational theory is used to reason about the (somewhat limited) security properties actually guaranteed by stack inspection. Some examples are also given of how subtle interaction between trusted and untrusted code may give rise to security breaches. Here, we are more concerned with efficient (semantically-based) optimization procedures, rather than with a general reasoning framework.

Clemens and Felleisen [6] presents a different semantics of (eager) stack inspection on continuation CESK machines, which allows for tail-call optimizing implementations.

Compared with our approach, [6, 7, 17] consider more basic programming primitives (e.g. there is no exception mechanisms). Also, static typing appears to be more difficult than control flow analysis when permissions can be dynamically instantiated. Indeed, we argue that typing and control flow analysis are complementary static techniques. Approaches based on types focus more on defining safe programming disciplines; control flow analysis, instead, seems more accurate in efficiently determining effective program optimizations.

References

1. M. Abadi, M. Burrows, B. Lampson, and G. Plotkin. A calculus for access control in distributed systems. *ACM Transactions on Programming Languages and Systems*, 4(15):706–734, Sept. 1993.
2. M. Bartoletti, P. Degano, and G. Ferrari. Stack inspection and program transformations. http://www.di.unipi.it/~bartolet/static-stack.ps, 2003.
3. M. Bartoletti, P. Degano, and G. Ferrari. Static analysis for eager stack inspection. In *Workshop on Formal Techniques for Java-like Programs (FTfJP'03)*, 2003.

4. F. Besson, T. Jensen, D. Le Métayer, and T. Thorn. Model checking security properties of control flow graphs. *Journal of computer security*, 9:217–250, 2001.
5. J.-D. Choi, D. Grove, M. Hind, and V. Sarkar. Efficient and precise modeling of exceptions for the analysis of Java programs. In *Workshop on Program Analysis For Software Tools and Engineering*, 1999.
6. J. Clemens and M. Felleisen. A tail-recursive semantics for stack inspections. In P. Degano, editor, *Proc. of the 12th European Symposium on Programming (ESOP'03)*, volume 2618 of *LNCS*. Springer-Verlag, 2003.
7. C. Fournet and A. D. Gordon. Stack inspection: theory and variants. *ACM Transactions on Programming Languages and Systems (TOPLAS)*, 25(3):360–399, 2003.
8. L. Gong. *Inside Java 2 platform security: architecture, API design, and implementation*. Addison-Wesley, 1999.
9. D. Gorla and R. Pugliese. Resource access and mobility control with dynamic privileges acquisition. In *Proc. 30th International Colloquium on Automata, Languages and Programming (ICALP'03)*, volume 2719 of *LNCS*. Springer-Verlag, 2003.
10. D. Grove and C. Chambers. A framework for call graph construction algorithms. *ACM Transactions on Programming Languages and Systems (TOPLAS)*, 23(6):685–746, 2001.
11. O. Kaser and C. R. Ramakrishnan. Evaluating inlining techniques. *Computer Languages*, 24(2):55–72, 1998.
12. L. Koved, M. Pistoia, and A. Kershenbaum. Access rights analysis for Java. In *Proc. of the 17th ACM conference on Object-oriented programming, systems, languages, and applications (OOPSLA'02)*. ACM Press, 2002.
13. C. Lai, L. Gong, L. Koved, A. Nadalin, and R. Schemers. User authentication and authorization in the Java platform. In *15th Annual Computer Security Application Reference*. IEEE Computer Society Press, 1999.
14. J. Ligatti, L. Bauer, and D. Walker. Edit automata: enforcement mechanisms for run-time security policies. *International Journal of Information Security*, 2003.
15. Microsoft Corp. *.NET Framework Developer's Guide: Securing Applications*.
16. F. Nielson, H. R. Nielson, and C. L. Hankin. *Principles of Program Analysis*. Springer-Verlag, 1999.
17. F. Pottier, C. Skalka, and S. Smith. A systematic approach to static access control. In D. Sands, editor, *Proc. of the 10th European Symposium on Programming (ESOP'01)*, volume 2028 of *LNCS*. Springer-Verlag, Apr. 2001.
18. S. Sinha and M. J. Harrold. Analysis and testing of programs with exception handling constructs. *Software Engineering*, 26(9):849–871, 2000.
19. A. Souter and L. Pollack. Incremental call graph reanalysis for object-oriented software maintenance. In *IEEE International Conference on Software Maintenance*, Nov. 2001.
20. V. Sundaresan, L. Hendren, C. Razafimahefa, R. Vallée-Rai, P. Lam, E. Gagnon, and C. Godin. Practical virtual method call resolution for Java. In *Proc. of the 2000 ACM SIGPLAN Conference on Object-Oriented Programming Systems, Languages & Applications (OOPSLA'00)*, volume 35(10) of *SIGPLAN Notices*. ACM Press, Oct. 2000.
21. F. Tip and J. Palsberg. Scalable propagation-based call graph construction algorithms. In *Proc. of the 2000 ACM SIGPLAN Conference on Object-Oriented Programming Systems, Languages & Applications (OOPSLA'00)*, 2000.
22. D. S. Wallach, A. W. Appel, and E. W. Felten. SAFKASI: a security mechanism for language-based systems. *ACM TOSEM*, 9(4):341–378, Oct. 2001.
23. C. Wille. *Presenting C♮*. SAMS Publishing, 2000.

Information Flow Security and Recursive Systems[*]

Annalisa Bossi, Damiano Macedonio, Carla Piazza, and Sabina Rossi

Dipartimento di Informatica, Università Ca' Foscari di Venezia
{bossi,mace,piazza,srossi}@dsi.unive.it

Abstract. Information flow security in a multilevel system aims at guaranteeing that no high level information is revealed to low level users, even in the presence of any possible malicious process. *Persistent_BNDC* (*P_BNDC*, for short) is an information-flow security property which is suitable to deal with processes in dynamic contexts. In this work we show that *P_BNDC* is compositional with respect to the replication operator. Then, by exploiting the compositionality properties of the class of *P_BNDC* processes, we define a proof system which provides a very efficient technique for the stepwise development and the verification of recursively defined *P_BNDC* processes.

1 Introduction

The design of large and complex systems that satisfy a given property strongly depends on the ability of dividing the task of the system into subtasks that are solved by system components. It is the classical divide-and-conquer approach, at the basis of any systematic development of complex systems. When security is the property of interest, difficulties can be encountered in applying this approach since secure systems might not be composed by secure components only. Nevertheless it is essential to know how properties of the components behave under composition. General theories of compositionality exist for properties like safety and liveness [25,1] and compositionality results for information-flow based confidentiality properties have also been developed [18,26,15].

The problem of protecting confidential data in a multilevel system is one of the relevant issues in computer security. Information flow security assures confidentiality since it guarantees that no high level (confidential) information is revealed to users running at low levels [12,17,9,22], even in the presence of any possible malicious process. To establish that information does not flow from high to low it is sufficient to establish that high behavior has no effect on what low level users can observe, i.e., the low level view of the system is independent of high behavior. This notion of information flow security, known as Non-Interference,

---

[*] This work has been partially supported by the MURST project "Modelli formali per la sicurezza" and the EU Contract IST-2001-32617 "Models and Types for Security in Mobile Distributed Systems" (MyThS).

C. Blundo and C. Laneve (Eds.): ICTCS 2003, LNCS 2841, pp. 369–382, 2003.

has been introduced in [13], and subsequently developed by many authors in many different settings [9,10,21,23,14].

In this paper we consider the security property *Persistent_BNDC* (*P_BNDC*, for short), proposed in [11], and further studied in [4]. *P_BNDC* is a security property based on Non-Interference suitable to analyze processes in completely dynamic hostile environments. In [11] it is proved that the *P_BNDC* property is equivalent to an already proposed security property called *SBSNNI* and studied in [9]. From the analysis presented in [9] two important problems emerge: how to verify the *P_BNDC* property and how to construct *P_BNDC* processes. The first problem has been considered in [11] and it has been shown to be decidable. The second problem has been analyzed in [4] where we exploit the compositionality properties of *P_BNDC* processes to define a proof system which allows us to *statically prove* that a process is *P_BNDC* by just inspecting its syntax. The proof system consists of two layers, a kernel which deals only with non-recursive processes and a second layer where a rather complex rule, involving many expensive checks, handles recursive processes. The system is correct but not complete, for instance it does not deal with recursive processes involving the parallel operator. The incompleteness and the complexity of the system is due to the lack of a compositionality result for constant definitions, which is the only way recursion is expressed in the SPA language, a variant of Milner's CCS [19].

In this paper we consider another form of recursion expressed using the replication operator (!) instead of constant definitions. The two approaches have the same expressive power in π-calculus [20,24], but as recently proved in [7], replication cannot supplant recursion in CCS. In this paper we show that the class of *P_BNDC* processes is compositional with respect to the replication operator. This allows us to extend the kernel *Core* of the proof system in [4] with a new inference rule for the replication, thus allowing us to deal also with recursive processes involving the parallel operator. Moreover, we prove a partial compositionality of *P_BNDC* with respect to constant definitions, i.e., we identify a class of constant definitions which can be safely added to our language and treated by the extended proof system.

The paper is organized as follows. In Section 2 we introduce the language, and recall the definition of *P_BNDC* process and its properties. In Section 3 we prove that *P_BNDC* is compositional with respect to the replication operator, and then present a proof system which, by exploiting the new compositionality result, extends the kernel presented in [4] by adding recursion through replication in a very simple way. In Section 4 we (re)-introduce constant definitions. Finally, in Section 5 we draw some conclusions. All the proofs can be found in [5].

2   Basic Notions

2.1   The Language

In this section we report the syntax and semantics of the process algebra we consider. It is a variation of Milner's CCS [19], similar to SPA [9], where the set of visible actions is partitioned into high level actions and low level ones in order to specify multilevel systems. Differently from [19], we use the *replication* (!) operator instead of the constant definitions. Intuitively, the process $!E$ (bang E) means $E|E|\ldots$, i.e., the parallel composition of as many copy as needed of the process E. In Section 4 we will reintroduce constant definitions.

The syntax of our process algebra is based on the same elements as CCS that is: a set $\mathcal{L}$ of *visible* actions such that $\mathcal{L} = I \cup O$ where $I = \{a, b, \ldots\}$ is a set of *input* actions and $O = \{\bar{a}, \bar{b}, \ldots\}$ is a set of *output* actions; a special action τ which models internal computations, i.e., not visible outside the system; a complementarily function $\bar{\ } : \mathcal{L} \to \mathcal{L}$, such that $\bar{\bar{a}} = a$, for all $a \in \mathcal{L}$; $Act = \mathcal{L} \cup \{\tau\}$ is the set of all *actions*. The set of visible actions is partitioned into two sets, H and L, of high and low actions such that $\overline{H} = H$ and $\overline{L} = L$. A *process* E is a term built using the following productions:

$$E ::= \mathbf{0} \mid a.E \mid E + E \mid E|E \mid E \setminus v \mid E[f] \mid !E$$

where $a \in Act$, $v \subseteq \mathcal{L}$, $f : Act \to Act$ is such that $f(L) \subseteq L \cup \{\tau\}$, $f(H) \subseteq H \cup \{\tau\}$, $f(\bar{\alpha}) = \overline{f(\alpha)}$ and $f(\tau) = \tau$.

Given a fixed set $\mathcal{L}$ we denote by $\mathcal{E}^!$ the set of all processes, by $\mathcal{E}_H^!$ the set of all high level processes, i.e., those constructed over $H \cup \{\tau\}$, and by $\mathcal{E}_L^!$ the set of all low level processes, i.e., those constructed over $L \cup \{\tau\}$.

The operational semantics of processes is given in terms of a *Labelled Transition System* (LTS). In particular, the operational semantics of our language is the LTS $(\mathcal{E}^!, Act, \to)$, where the states are the terms of the algebra and the transition relation $\to \subseteq \mathcal{E}^! \times Act \times \mathcal{E}^!$ is defined by structural induction as the least relation generated by the inference rules reported in Figure 1.

In the paper we use the following notations. If $t = a_1 \cdots a_n \in Act^*$ and $E \xrightarrow{a_1} \cdots \xrightarrow{a_n} E'$, then we say that E' is reachable from E and write $E \xrightarrow{t} E'$, or simply $E \rightsquigarrow E'$. We also write $E \xRightarrow{t} E'$ if $E(\xrightarrow{\tau})^* \xrightarrow{a_1} (\xrightarrow{\tau})^* \cdots (\xrightarrow{\tau})^* \xrightarrow{a_n} (\xrightarrow{\tau})^* E'$ where $(\xrightarrow{\tau})^*$ denotes a (possibly empty) sequence of τ labelled transitions. If $t \in Act^*$, then $\hat{t} \in \mathcal{L}^*$ is the sequence gained by deleting all occurrences of τ from t. As a consequence, $E \xRightarrow{\hat{a}} E'$ stands for $E \xRightarrow{a} E'$ if $a \in \mathcal{L}$, and for $E(\xrightarrow{\tau})^* E'$ if $a = \tau$ (note that $\xRightarrow{\tau}$ requires at least one τ labelled transition while $\xRightarrow{\hat{\tau}}$ means zero or more τ labelled transitions). Given two processes E, F we write $E \equiv F$ when E and F are syntactically equal.

The concept of *observation equivalence* between two processes is based on the idea that two systems have the same semantics if and only if they cannot be distinguished by an external observer. This is obtained by defining an equivalence relation over $\mathcal{E}^!$. We report the definitions of *weak bisimulation* and *strong bisimulation* [19]. Intuitively, weak bisimulation equates two processes if they mutually simulate their behavior step by step, but it does not care about internal τ actions. So, when P simulates an action of Q, it can also execute some τ actions before or after that action.

Definition 1 (Weak Bisimulation). *A symmetric binary relation* $\mathcal{R} \subseteq \mathcal{E}^! \times \mathcal{E}^!$ *over processes is a weak bisimulation if* $(E, F) \in \mathcal{R}$ *implies, for all* $a \in Act$,

- *if* $E \xrightarrow{a} E'$, *then there exists* F' *such that* $F \xRightarrow{\hat{a}} F'$ *and* $(E', F') \in \mathcal{R}$;

Prefix ─────────────
$$a.E \xrightarrow{a} E$$

Sum
$$\frac{E_1 \xrightarrow{a} E_1'}{E_1 + E_2 \xrightarrow{a} E_1'} \qquad \frac{E_2 \xrightarrow{a} E_2'}{E_1 + E_2 \xrightarrow{a} E_2'}$$

Parallel
$$\frac{E_1 \xrightarrow{a} E_1'}{E_1|E_2 \xrightarrow{a} E_1'|E_2} \qquad \frac{E_2 \xrightarrow{a} E_2'}{E_1|E_2 \xrightarrow{a} E_1|E_2'} \qquad \frac{E_1 \xrightarrow{\ell} E_1' \; E_2 \xrightarrow{\bar{\ell}} E_2'}{E_1|E_2 \xrightarrow{\tau} E_1'|E_2'} \quad \ell \in \mathcal{L}$$

Restriction
$$\frac{E \xrightarrow{a} E'}{E \setminus v \xrightarrow{a} E' \setminus v} \quad \text{if } a \notin v$$

Relabelling
$$\frac{E \xrightarrow{a} E'}{E[f] \xrightarrow{f(a)} E'[f]}$$

Replication
$$\frac{E \xrightarrow{a} E'}{!E \xrightarrow{a} E'|!E} \qquad \frac{E \xrightarrow{\ell} E' \; E \xrightarrow{\bar{\ell}} E''}{!E \xrightarrow{\tau} E'|E''|!E} \quad \ell \in \mathcal{L}$$

Fig. 1. The operational rules.

Two processes $E, F \in \mathcal{E}^!$ are weakly bisimilar, *denoted by $E \approx F$, if there exists a weak bisimulation $\mathcal{R}$ containing the pair (E, F).*

The relation $\approx$ is the largest weak bisimulation and is an equivalence relation [19].

Strong bisimulation is stronger than weak bisimulation, since it consider the τ actions as all the other actions.

Definition 2 (Strong Bisimulation). *A symmetric binary relation $\mathcal{R} \subseteq \mathcal{E}^! \times \mathcal{E}^!$ over processes is a strong bisimulation if $(E, F) \in \mathcal{R}$ implies, for all $a \in Act$,*

- *if $E \xrightarrow{a} E'$, then there exists F' such that $F \xrightarrow{a} F'$ and $(E', F') \in \mathcal{R}$;*

Two processes $E, F \in \mathcal{E}^!$ are strong bisimilar, *denoted by $E \sim F$, if there exists a strong bisimulation $\mathcal{R}$ containing the pair (E, F).*

The relation $\sim$ is the largest weak bisimulation and is an equivalence relation [19]. Moreover, two strongly bisimilar processes are also weakly bisimilar.

2.2 The *P_BNDC* Security Property

In this section we recall the *Persistent Bisimulation-based Non Deducibility on Compositions* (*P_BNDC*, for short) security property (see [11]). We start by introducing an equivalence relation on low actions that is a sort of weak bisimulation which considers only the low actions. Hence, when two processes are weakly bisimilar on low actions they cannot be distinguished by a low level user.

Definition 3 (Weak Bisimulation on Low Actions). *A symmetric binary relation* $\mathcal{R} \subseteq \mathcal{E}^l \times \mathcal{E}^l$ *over processes is a* weak bisimulation on low actions, *if* $(E, F) \in \mathcal{R}$ *implies, for all* $a \in L \cup \{\tau\}$,

- *if* $E \xrightarrow{a} E'$, *then there exists* F' *such that* $F \xrightarrow{\hat{a}} F'$ *and* $(E', F') \in \mathcal{R}$.

Two processes $E, F \in \mathcal{E}^l$ *are* weakly bisimilar on low actions, *denoted by* $E \approx_l F$, *if there exists a weak bisimulation on low actions* $\mathcal{R}$ *containing the pair* (E, F).

The relation $\approx_l$ is the largest weak bisimulation on low actions and it is an equivalence relation [5]. Moreover, it holds $E \approx_l F$ if and only if $E \setminus H \approx F \setminus H$.

Using weak bisimulation on low actions we recall the notion of *Bisimulation-based Non Deducibility on Compositions* (*BNDC*, for short) [9] which is at the basis of *P_BNDC*. The *BNDC* security property aims at guaranteeing that no information flow from the high to the low level is possible, even in the presence of an attacker. A system E is *BNDC* if for every high process Π a low user cannot distinguish E from $(E|\Pi)$, i.e., if Π cannot interfere [13] with the low level execution of E.

Definition 4 (BNDC). *Let* $E \in \mathcal{E}^l$. $E \in BNDC$ *iff* $\forall \ \Pi \in \mathcal{E}_H^l$, $E \approx_l (E|\Pi)$.

In [11] it is shown that *BNDC* is not strong enough for systems in dynamic environments. To deal with these situations, the property *P_BNDC* is introduced. Intuitively, a system E is *P_BNDC* if it never reaches insecure states.

Definition 5 (P_BNDC). *Let* $E \in \mathcal{E}^l$. $E \in P\_BNDC$ *iff* $E \rightsquigarrow E'$ *implies* $E' \in BNDC$.

Although the decidability of *BNDC* is still an open problem, *P_BNDC* is decidable (in polynomial time) as shown in [11]. In [4] another decidable characterization of *P_BNDC* processes has been proposed. It allows us to express *P_BNDC* in terms of a local property of high level actions and it recalls the unwinding conditions proposed in other settings. Also if we are using a variation of the SPA, with replications instead of constant definitions, the characterization presented in [4] holds.

Theorem 1 (Unwinding). *Let* $E \in \mathcal{E}^l$. $E \in P\_BNDC$ *iff if* $E \rightsquigarrow E_i \xrightarrow{h} E_j$, *then* $E_i \xRightarrow{\hat{\tau}} E_k$ *and* $E_j \approx_l E_k$.

The following lemma rephrases the corresponding lemma in [4] and it proves that the class of *P_BNDC* processes enjoys the following compositionality properties.

Lemma 1. *The class of P_BNDC processes contains all the processes in* $\mathcal{E}_L^l \cup \mathcal{E}_H^l$ *and is closed with respect to restriction, renaming, and parallel composition. Moreover, if* $E_i, F_j \in P\_BNDC$, $a_i \in L$ *and* $h_j \in H$, $i \in I$ *and* $j \in J$, *then* $\sum_{i \in I} a_i.E_i + \sum_{j \in J}(h_j.F_j + \tau.F_j) \in P\_BNDC$.

3 *P_BNDC* and Replications

In this section we first extend the compositionality result of Lemma 1 by proving that *P_BNDC* is closed also with respect to the replication operator. Then we present a proof system for *P_BNDC* processes.

3.1 Compositionality of *P_BNDC* wrt!

We start by observing that the processes reachable from $!E$ have the form of a parallel composition of a finite number of processes reachable from E and $!E$.

Lemma 2. *Let $E \in \mathcal{E}^!$ be a process. If $!E \rightsquigarrow E'$, then there exist $n \geq 0$ and $E_1, \ldots, E_n$ such that $E \rightsquigarrow E_i$, for $i = 1, \ldots, n$ and $E' \equiv E_1|E_2|\ldots|E_n|!E$.*

Hence the set $\{E_1, \ldots, E_n\}$ of processes reachable from E characterizes the process $E_1|E_2|\ldots|E_n|!E$ reachable from $!E$.

There is an interesting connection between the processes reachable from E and the processes reachable from $!E$ when E is *P_BNDC*: if the sets $\{F_1, \ldots, F_n\}$ and $\{G_1, \ldots, G_n\}$ of processes reachable from E are pairwise weakly bisimilar on low actions, i.e., $F_i \approx_l G_i$, this relation is preserved also on the processes reachable from $!E$ that they characterize.

Lemma 3. *Let E be a P_BNDC process and $\forall i \in \{1, .., n\}$ F_i, G_i be reachable from E. If $\forall i \in \{1, .., n\}$ $F_i \approx_l G_i$ then $F_1|F_2\ldots|F_n|!E \approx_l G_1|G_2\ldots|G_n|!E$.*

The two previous lemmas, together with the unwinding condition (see Theorem 1), allow us to prove that *P_BNDC* is compositional with respect to the replication operator.

Theorem 2. *Let $E \in \mathcal{E}^!$ be a process. If $E \in P\_BNDC$, then $!E \in P\_BNDC$.*

3.2 A Proof System for Processes with Replications

In [4] it has been presented a proof system which allows us to build *P_BNDC* processes in an incremental way. The proof system is composed by a set of rules whose conclusions are in the form $E \in \mathcal{HP}[A]$, where A is a set of constants. The intended meaning of the judgment is that E is a *P_BNDC* process provided that all the constants in A are *P_BNDC*. The set A plays the role of a set of assumptions: if it is empty then E is *P_BNDC* otherwise we are still working on our construction under open hypothesis. It is immediate to observe that the system described in [4] is correct also using set of processes, instead of set of constants, as assumptions. Hence, in this section the meaning of $E \in \mathcal{HP}[A]$ is that E is a *P_BNDC* process provided that all the processes in A are *P_BNDC*. We show how to exploit Lemma 1 and Theorem 2 in order to extend the system to the case of processes with replication. In particular, let us consider the proof system $System^!$ whose rules are shown in Figure 2 [1].

---

[1] We use $E[F/G]$ to denote the process we obtain by replacing all the occurrences of G in E with F, where G denotes a process whose occurrences in E can be syntactically and unambiguously identified.

$$\frac{\phantom{E \in \mathcal{HP}[\{E\}]}}{E \in \mathcal{HP}[\{E\}]} \quad E \text{ is a process} \quad (Proc)$$

$$\frac{E \in \mathcal{E}_L^!}{E \in \mathcal{HP}[\emptyset]} \quad (Low) \qquad\qquad \frac{E \in \mathcal{E}_H^!}{E \in \mathcal{HP}[\emptyset]} \quad (High)$$

$$\frac{E \in \mathcal{HP}[A]}{E \setminus v \in \mathcal{HP}[A]} \quad (Rest) \qquad\qquad \frac{E \in \mathcal{HP}[A]}{E[f] \in \mathcal{HP}[A]} \quad (Label)$$

$$\frac{E \in \mathcal{HP}[A] \quad F \in \mathcal{HP}[B]}{E|F \in \mathcal{HP}[A \cup B]} \quad (Par)$$

$$\frac{E_i \in \mathcal{HP}[A_i] \quad F_j \in \mathcal{HP}[B_j]}{\sum_{i \in I} a_i.E_i + \sum_{j \in J}(h_j.F_j + \tau.F_j) \in \mathcal{HP}[\cup_I A_i \cup \cup_J B_j]} \quad \substack{a_i \in L \cup \{\tau\}, h_j \in H \\ (Choice)}$$

$$\frac{E \in \mathcal{HP}[A]}{!E \in \mathcal{HP}[A]} \quad (Repl) \qquad\qquad \frac{E[G] \in \mathcal{HP}[A] \quad F \in \mathcal{HP}[B]}{E[F/G] \in \mathcal{HP}[(A \setminus \{F\}) \cup B]} \quad (Subst)$$

Fig. 2. The proof system $System^!$.

Theorem 3 (Correctness). *System$^!$ is correct, i.e., if there exists a proof in System$^!$ which ends with $E \in \mathcal{HP}[A]$, then E is P_BNDC provided that all the processes in A are P_BNDC.*

Corollary 1. *Let $E \in \mathcal{E}^!$. If there exists a proof of $E \in \mathcal{HP}[\emptyset]$, then E is P_BNDC.*

Example 1. Consider the process CH defined as

$$CH \equiv ((in_0.(\overline{out_0}.\overline{\sigma}.0 + \tau.\overline{\sigma}.0) + in_1.(\overline{out_1}.\overline{\sigma}.0 + \tau.\overline{\sigma}.0))|$$
$$!(\sigma.(in_0.(\overline{out_0}.\overline{\sigma}.0 + \tau.\overline{\sigma}.0) + in_1.(\overline{out_1}.\overline{\sigma}.0 + \tau.\overline{\sigma}.0)))) \setminus \{\sigma, \overline{\sigma}\}$$

where $in_0, in_1, \sigma, \overline{\sigma} \in L$ and $\overline{out_0}, \overline{out_1} \in H$. This process CH is a channel which may accept a value 0 (or 1) through the low level input in_0 (or in_1). When it holds a value, it may deliver it through a high level output $\overline{out_0}$ (or $\overline{out_1}$). The channel can transmit values infinitely many times. In fact, when the $\overline{\sigma}$ action is reached the process resets itself and recursively repeats the sequence of actions.

This process is a variation of the channel described in [19]. It is easy to see that we can derive the judgement $CH \in \mathcal{HP}[\emptyset]$ in $System^!$.

This example shows that $System^!$ is more powerful than *Core* of [4], in fact *Core* cannot handle any recursive process. In [4] we introduced a more complex rule to deal with recursion.

4   Adding Constant Definitions

In this section we add some constant definitions to our language. Then, exploiting the compositionality of *P_BNDC* with respect to the replication operator, we prove a compositionality result for *P_BNDC* with respect to the constant definitions we consider. We do not add all constant definitions, since in CCS, differently from π-calculus [24], replication is not expressive enough to represent all constant definitions [7].

4.1   Definitions Using Replications

In standard CCS [19] complex recursive systems are defined parametrically, as $Z \stackrel{\text{def}}{=} E[Z]$, where Z is a process identifier and $E[Z]$ a process expression which may contain "calls" to Z as well as to other parametric processes.

Example 2. Consider the process Z recursively defined as $Z \stackrel{\text{def}}{=} a.Z + b.0$. Intuitively this process can perform either an action a and return in its initial state or an action b and terminate. Similarly it is possible to consider two mutually defined processes X and Y where X performs an action a and then calls Y; while Y performs an action b and calls X. Their definitions are

$$X \stackrel{\text{def}}{=} a.Y \qquad\qquad Y \stackrel{\text{def}}{=} b.X$$

This way of defining recursive processes was taken as basic in [9] and in other previous works on *P_BNDC* (see [4]). In the context of the π-calculus in [20], an encoding is defined which eliminates a finite number of constant definitions using replication. As already noticed in [24], the same encoding applied to full CCS does not work (see also Remark 1). In what follows we identify a fragment of CCS on which the encoding is correct.

Let $Act = \mathcal{L} \cup \{\tau\}$ be a set of actions, with $\mathcal{L}$ partitioned into the two sets H and L, as described in Section 2.1. Let $\mathcal{C}$ be a finite set of constants. Consider all the processes D which can be obtained using the following productions:

$$D ::= 0 \mid a.D \mid D + D \mid D|D \mid Z$$

where $Z \in \mathcal{C}$ is a constant which must be associated to a definition $Z \stackrel{\text{def}}{=} D$. Let $\mathcal{E}^{\text{def}}$ be the set of processes defined with this syntax. Given a process D, $const(D)$ denotes all the constants which occur in D. We say that a process D is *constant-free* if $const(D) = \emptyset$.

In order to define the semantics of the processes in $\mathcal{E}^{\text{def}}$ we add to the rules of Figure 1 the following rule to deal with constant definitions.

$$\text{Constant} \;\frac{\phantom{Z \stackrel{\tau}{\to} D}}{Z \stackrel{\tau}{\to} D} \quad \text{if } Z \stackrel{\text{def}}{=} D$$

This rule tells us that if $Z \stackrel{\text{def}}{=} D$ then Z performs a τ transition and then behaves as D.

Example 3. Let Z be the constant defined in Example 2. By applying once the rule Constant we obtain that $Z \xrightarrow{\tau} a.Z + b.\mathbf{0}$, then either $a.Z + b.\mathbf{0} \xrightarrow{b} \mathbf{0}$ or $a.Z + b.\mathbf{0} \xrightarrow{a} Z$. In the second case we can apply again the rule Constant.

All the processes in $\mathcal{E}^{\mathrm{def}}$ can be translated into an equivalent (bisimilar) process of the language $\mathcal{E}^!$ presented in Section 2.1 (i.e., into a process with restriction and replication and without constant definition).

We briefly recall how the encoding which removes the constant definitions works. Let $Z_1, \ldots, Z_n$ be n constants defined as $Z_i \stackrel{\mathrm{def}}{=} D_i$, where for all $i = 1, \ldots, n$ $const(D_i) \subseteq \{Z_1, \ldots, Z_n\}$. Let $S = \{\sigma_1, \overline{\sigma_1}, \ldots, \sigma_n, \overline{\sigma_n}\}$ be a new set of actions disjoint from Act. We associate to the constant Z_i the actions σ_i and $\overline{\sigma_i}$ and we introduce the notation[2]:

$$\widehat{Z}_i \equiv !(\sigma_i.D_i[\overline{\sigma_1}.\mathbf{0}/Z_1, \ldots, \overline{\sigma_n}.\mathbf{0}/Z_n]),$$

where in D_i each constant Z_j is replaced by the constant-free expression $\overline{\sigma}_j .\mathbf{0}$. Since $const(D_i) \subseteq \{Z_1, \ldots, Z_n\}$, $\widehat{Z}_i$ is a constant-free expression.

Definition 6 (Encoding of $\mathcal{E}^{\mathrm{def}}$). *Let $D \in \mathcal{E}^{\mathrm{def}}$ be a process with $const(D) \subseteq \{Z_1, \ldots, Z_n\}$. Its encoding $[\![D]\!]$ is the constant-free process*

$$[\![D]\!] \equiv (D[\overline{\sigma_1}.\mathbf{0}/Z_1, \ldots, \overline{\sigma_n}.\mathbf{0}/Z_n] | \widehat{Z}_1 | \ldots | \widehat{Z}_n) \setminus S.$$

In particular, when D is one of the Z_i's we obtain

$$[\![Z_i]\!] \equiv (\overline{\sigma_i}.\mathbf{0} | \widehat{Z}_1 | \ldots | \widehat{Z}_n) \setminus S.$$

Example 4. Let Z be the constant defined in Example 2. The encoding of Z is $[\![Z]\!] \equiv (\overline{\sigma}.\mathbf{0}|\widehat{Z})\backslash S$, but $\widehat{Z} \equiv !(\sigma.\mathbf{0}.((a.Z+b.\mathbf{0})[\overline{\sigma}.\mathbf{0}/Z]))) \equiv !(\sigma.\mathbf{0}.(a.\overline{\sigma}.\mathbf{0}+b.\mathbf{0})))$ hence we obtain $[\![Z]\!] \equiv (\overline{\sigma}.\mathbf{0}|!(\sigma.\mathbf{0}.(a.\overline{\sigma}.\mathbf{0}+b.\mathbf{0}))) \setminus S$. Note that $\widehat{Z}$ and $[\![Z]\!]$ are different.

Remark 1. In the encoding, the action $\overline{\sigma}_i$ is used to make a "call to the procedure" Z_i which is represented by $\widehat{Z}_i$. The encoding does not work in the full CCS, since the scope of the restrictions and renamings is not enlarged to the $\widehat{Z}_i$. Consider for instance a constant Z defined as $Z \stackrel{\mathrm{def}}{=} a.Z$ and the process $E \equiv (Z) \setminus \{a\}$. The process E can only perform a τ action, then it terminates. If we apply our encoding we obtain $[\![E]\!] \equiv ((\overline{\sigma}.\mathbf{0}) \setminus \{a\}|!(\sigma.a.\overline{\sigma}.\mathbf{0})) \setminus S$. Differently from E, the process $[\![E]\!]$ performs a τ, and then it is able to perform an action a, since in $\widehat{Z}$ the action a is allowed. Actually, we can overcome this problem and define a correct translation for E (see Definition 7). Another process which cannot be translated is obtained using two mutual recursive constant definitions

$$X \stackrel{\mathrm{def}}{=} (a.X|b.\overline{a}.Y) \setminus \{a, \overline{a}\} \qquad\qquad Y \stackrel{\mathrm{def}}{=} (b.Y|a.\overline{b}.X) \setminus \{b, \overline{b}\}$$

---

[2] We use the notation $D[Z_1, \ldots, Z_n]$ when we want to stress the fact that the constants $Z_1, \ldots, Z_n$ can occur in D.

The process $F \equiv X$ can perform only b and τ actions. Its encoding would be the process $[\![F]\!]$ defined as

$$(\overline{\sigma_X}.0 | !(\sigma_X.((a.\overline{\sigma_X}.0|b.\overline{a}.\overline{\sigma_Y}.0) \setminus \{a,\overline{a}\}))| !(\sigma_Y.((b.\overline{\sigma_Y}.0|a.\overline{b}.\overline{\sigma_X}.0) \setminus \{b,\overline{b}\}))) \setminus S.$$

The process $[\![F]\!]$ can perform also a actions, since the restriction on a is not applied to $\widehat{Y}$. The solution we will apply later to enlarge the encoding cannot be applied to this process.

The following theorem states the observational equivalence between D and $[\![D]\!]$ when D belongs to $\mathcal{E}^{\mathrm{def}}$. Since $D \in \mathcal{E}^{\mathrm{def}}$ and $[\![D]\!] \in \mathcal{E}^!$ the bisimulation we establish is a relation on $\mathcal{E}^{\mathrm{def}} \times \mathcal{E}^!$.

Theorem 4. *For each $D \in \mathcal{E}^{\mathrm{def}}$ it holds $D \sim [\![D]\!]$.*

The actions σ_i's introduced in the encoding are neither high nor low level actions. They are used only in the encoding, in order to obtain constant free-processes, but they are not visible outside because of the outmost restriction. Indeed, they are introduced only to *fire* infinitely many times the actions of the D_i's. Nevertheless, we have to decide how to treat them in the definition of the attackers and in the definition of the low level observational equivalence. We consider this issue in the next section.

Before moving to our security property we show how to apply the encoding to a richer language in which restriction and renaming can be used "outside" the recursive definitions. In particular, consider all the processes E defined by the following productions:

$$E ::= 0 \mid a.E \mid E + E \mid E|E \mid E \setminus v \mid E[f] \mid !E \mid Z$$

where $Z \in \mathcal{C}$ is a constant which must be associated to a definition $Z \stackrel{\mathrm{def}}{=} D$, with $D \in \mathcal{E}^{\mathrm{def}}$. Let $\mathcal{E}^{\mathrm{def}!}$ be the set of processes defined with this syntax.

Since the constants are defined using processes in $\mathcal{E}^{\mathrm{def}}$, by Theorem 4, we have that $Z \sim [\![Z]\!]$. Observing that $\sim$ is a congruence on our language we immediately get that the following encoding can be applied to the processes in $\mathcal{E}^{\mathrm{def}!}$.

Definition 7 (Encoding of $\mathcal{E}^{\mathrm{def}!}$). *Let $E \in \mathcal{E}^{\mathrm{def}!}$ be a process with $const(E) \subseteq \{Z_1, \ldots, Z_n\}$ its encoding $\{\!|E|\!\}$ is the constant-free process*

$$\{\!|E|\!\} \equiv E[[\![Z_1]\!]/Z_1, \ldots, [\![Z_n]\!]/Z_n].$$

Corollary 2. *For each $E \in \mathcal{E}^{\mathrm{def}!}$ it holds $E \sim \{\!|E|\!\}$.*

Example 5. Consider the constant Z and the process E defined in Remark 1. The process E is in $\mathcal{E}^{\mathrm{def}!}$. Its encoding is $\{\!|E|\!\} \equiv ((\overline{\tau}.0|!(\sigma.a.\overline{\tau}.0)) \setminus S) \setminus \{a\}$. Now, we correctly obtain that E performs a τ transitions, then it terminates.

The constants X and Y of Remark 1 do not belong to $\mathcal{E}^{\mathrm{def}!}$. In fact, in order to translate X we would need a correct encoding of Y, and this is not possible without a correct encoding of X, i.e., we enter in a loop. We can conclude that $\mathcal{E}^{\mathrm{def}!}$ is still not expressive as CCS with constant definitions. On the other hand, Corollary 2 says that $\mathcal{E}^{\mathrm{def}!}$ is expressive as $\mathcal{E}^!$. The relation between $\mathcal{E}^{\mathrm{def}!}$ and $\mathcal{E}^{\mathrm{def}}$ is still an open problem; we conjecture that $\mathcal{E}^{\mathrm{def}!}$ is more powerful.

4.2 *P_BNDC* and Definitions

Let $Act = L \cup H \cup \{\tau\}$ as defined in Section 2.1. Let S be a new set of (synchronization) actions such that $S \cap Act = \emptyset$ and $\overline{S} = S$, i.e., S is closed with respect to the complementation operation. In what follows we consider as set of actions $Act' = L \cup H \cup \{\tau\} \cup S$. Moreover, we require that if f is a relabelling function, then $\forall \sigma \in S$, $f(\sigma) = \sigma$. As previously observed the actions of S do not represent 'real' actions, but they are only instrumental for the encoding. The processes we start with have no actions in S, while their encodings do. For this reason it is necessary to decide how to treat S with respect to our security notions. In order to keep the compositionality of *P_BNDC* it is convenient to assimilate them to low level actions. Therefore, the high level attacker cannot perform them and the low level user can observe them. In this way we can treat in a compositional way also processes in which these actions occur. In particular, we extend the concept of weak bisimulation on low actions considering the actions in S as if they were actions in L. With a slight abuse of notation from now on we say that two processes $E, F \in \mathcal{E}^{\text{def!}}$ (built also using actions in S) are *weakly bisimilar on low actions*, denoted by $E \approx_l F$, if there exists a symmetric binary relation $\mathcal{R} \subseteq \mathcal{E}^{\text{def!}} \times \mathcal{E}^{\text{def!}}$ such that if $(E, F) \in \mathcal{R}$, then for all $a \in L \cup S \cup \{\tau\}$,

- if $E \xrightarrow{a} E'$, then there exists F' such that $F \xLongrightarrow{\hat{a}} F'$ and $(E', F') \in \mathcal{R}$.

Clearly $\approx_l$ is still the largest weak bisimulation on low actions and it is an equivalence relation. Moreover it is still true that $E \approx_l F$ iff $E \setminus H \approx F \setminus H$.

Using this definition of $\approx_l$ the notions of *BNDC* and *P_BNDC* can be consistently transposed. Notice that using these extended definitions Theorem 1 and Theorem 2 continue to hold. As far as Lemma 1 is concerned some trivial changes are necessary. In particular, let $\mathcal{E}^{\text{def!}}_{HS}$ ($\mathcal{E}^{\text{def}}_{HS}$) be the set of all processes in $\mathcal{E}^{\text{def!}}$ ($\mathcal{E}^{\text{def}}$) constructed over $H \cup S \cup \{\tau\}$. Similarly, let $\mathcal{E}^{\text{def!}}_{LS}$ ($\mathcal{E}^{\text{def}}_{LS}$) be the set of all processes constructed over $L \cup S \cup \{\tau\}$ and $\mathcal{E}^{\text{def!}}_{HL}$ ($\mathcal{E}^{\text{def}}_{HL}$) be the set of all processes constructed over $L \cup H \cup \{\tau\}$. In the first sentence of Lemma 1 it is necessary to consider constant-free processes in $\mathcal{E}^{\text{def!}}_{LS} \cup \mathcal{E}^{\text{def!}}_{H}$. In the third sentence the actions a_i's can range over $L \cup S \cup \{\tau\}$. Moreover, from Theorem 4 we immediately get the following result.

Corollary 3. *Let* $Z_1, \dots, Z_n$ *be constants defined as* $Z_i \stackrel{\text{def}}{=} D_i$, *with* $D_i \in \mathcal{E}^{\text{def}}_{HL}$ *for* $i = 1, \dots, n$. *If for all* $i = 1, \dots, n$ *it holds* $const(D_i) \subseteq \{Z_1, \dots, Z_n\}$ *and* $[\![Z_i]\!] \in P\_BNDC$, *then all the* Z_i's *are* P_BNDC.

4.3 Extension of the Proof System to Processes with Definitions

In order to deal with the language extended with the actions in S and with the constant definitions we have to modify some of the rules of the proof system described in Section 3.2 and to add new rules to deal with constant definitions. In particular, we change the rules (*Low*) and (*Choice*) by considering $L \cup S$ instead of L and by adding "E is constant-free" to the rules (*Low*) and (*High*).

Then we add the following rules to deal with constant definitions

$$\frac{}{E \setminus S \in \mathcal{HP}[\emptyset]} \quad E \in \mathcal{E}_{HS}^{\text{def}!}, \ E \text{ is constant-free} \quad (High2)$$

$$\frac{[X_i] \in \mathcal{HP}[A]}{X_i \in \mathcal{HP}[A]} \quad (X_i \stackrel{\text{def}}{=} D_i)_{i=1}^n, \ D_i \in \mathcal{E}_{HL}^{\text{def}} \quad (Const)$$

where $[X_i]$ is a constant-free process.

We call $System^{\text{def}!}$ the modified system. Corollary 3 ensures its correctness.

Example 6. Consider the channel C as defined in [3] (see [19]) and its encoding.

$$C = in_0.(\overline{out_0}.C + \tau.C) + in_1.(\overline{out_1}.C + \tau.C)$$
$$[C] \equiv (\overline{\sigma}.0| \ !(\sigma.(in_0.(\overline{out_0}.\overline{\sigma}.0 + \tau.\overline{\sigma}.0) + in_1.(\overline{out_1}.\overline{\sigma}.0 + \tau.\overline{\sigma}.0)))) \setminus S$$

It is easy to see that we can derive $C \in \mathcal{HP}[\emptyset]$ in our extended proof system. Notice that the process CH described in Example 1 is exactly the process we obtain after a τ transition of $[C]$.

Corollary 4. *Let $E \in \mathcal{E}^{\text{def}!}$ be a process. If there exists a proof of $E \in \mathcal{HP}[\emptyset]$ in $System^{\text{def}!}$, then E is P_BNDC.*

By exploiting the result of Corollary 2 we can add the derived rule below, which can be used to shorten derivations involving constant definitions:

$$\frac{\{E\} \in \mathcal{HP}[A]}{E \in \mathcal{HP}[A]} \quad E \in \mathcal{E}_{HL}^{\text{def}!} \quad (Trans)$$

Example 7. Let Z be defined as $Z \stackrel{\text{def}}{=} l.Z + h.l.0 + \tau.l.0$ and consider the process $E \equiv l.Z$, where $l \in L$ and $h \in H$. By applying rule $(Trans)$ we can directly prove that E is P_BNDC without explicitly prove that $[Z]$ is P_BNDC.

Example 8. Consider the two processes X and Y mutually defined as follows

$$X \stackrel{\text{def}}{=} l.X|Y \qquad Y \stackrel{\text{def}}{=} \tau.X + h.X$$

where $l \in L$ and $h \in H$. Their encodings in $\mathcal{E}^!$ are

$$[X] \equiv (\overline{\sigma_X}.0|!(\sigma_X.(l.\overline{\sigma_X}.0|\overline{\sigma_Y}.0))|!(\sigma_Y.(\tau.\overline{\sigma_X}.0 + h.\overline{\sigma_X}.0))) \setminus S$$
$$[Y] \equiv (\overline{\sigma_Y}.0|!(\sigma_X.(l.\overline{\sigma_X}.0|\overline{\sigma_Y}.0))|!(\sigma_Y.(\tau.\overline{\sigma_X}.0 + h.\overline{\sigma_X}.0))) \setminus S$$

It is easy to derive the judgements $[X] \in \mathcal{HP}[\emptyset]$ and $[Y] \in \mathcal{HP}[\emptyset]$ in $System^!$, hence we conclude that X and Y are P_BNDC processes.

It is worth noticing that the system proposed in [4] cannot treat the process of Example 8. In fact, as already observed in the introduction, the system of [4] does not deal with recursive processes involving the parallel operator.

5 Conclusions

In this paper we study the class of P_BNDC processes written in a variant of Security Process Algebra (SPA) where recursive processes are defined by means of replications instead of constant definitions. The modified language is slightly less powerful than the original one, but the loss of expressive power is largely compensated by the compositionality result obtained.

We proved that the class of P_BNDC processes is compositional with respect to replication. This result allows us to define a proof system which provides a very efficient technique for the stepwise development and the verification of recursively defined P_BNDC processes. We also identify a class of constants definitions which can be safely added to our language and treated by an extended proof system.

We are currently working in extending the results on information flow security obtained for SPA to π-calculus, where the two forms of recursion are equivalent. Our feeling is that we could reach the same compositional results reached in SPA language, by choosing a good extension for the P_BNDC class.

As already noticed in [4], there are many other approaches to the verification of information flow properties. In the literature we found only another example of a proof system for security proposed by Martinelli [16] which deals only with finite processes. Other verification techniques for information flow security are based on types (see, e.g., [23,14]) and control flow analysis (see, e.g., [2,6]). However, most of them are concerned with different models, e.g., trace semantics (see, e.g., [8,18]).

References

1. M. Abadi and L. Lamport. Conjoining Specifications. *ACM Transactions on Programming Languages and Systems (TOPLAS)*, 17(3):507–535, May 1995.
2. C. Bodei, P. Degano, F. Nielson, and H. Nielson. Static Analysis for the π-calculus with Applications to Security. *Information and Computation*, 168(1):68–92, 2001.
3. A. Bossi, R. Focardi, C. Piazza, and S. Rossi. Transforming Processes to Ensure and Check Information Flow Security. In H. Kirchner and C. Ringeissen, editors, *Int. Conference on Algebraic Methodology and Software Technology (AMAST'02)*, volume 2422 of *LNCS*, pages 271–286. Springer-Verlag, 2002.
4. A. Bossi, R. Focardi, C. Piazza, and S. Rossi. A Proof System for Information Flow Security. In M. Leuschel, editor, *Logic Based Program Development and Transformation*, volume 2664 of *LNCS*. Springer-Verlag, 2003. To appear.
5. A. Bossi, D. Macedonio, C. Piazza, and S. Rossi. P_BNDC and Replication. Technical Report CS-2003-6, Dipartimento di Informatica, Università Ca' Foscari di Venezia, Italy, 2003. http://www.dsi.unive.it/ricerca/TR/index.htm.
6. C. Braghin, A. Cortesi, and R. Focardi. Control Flow Analysis of Mobile Ambients with Security Boundaries. In *Proc. Int. Conference on Formal Methods for Open Object-Based Distributed Systems (IFIPM'02)*, pages 197–212. Kluwer, 2002.
7. N. Busi, M. Gabbrielli, and G. Zavattaro. Replication vs. Recursive Definitions in Channel Based Calculi. In *Proc. of Int. Colloquium on Automata, Languages and Programming (ICALP'03)*. LNCS, 2003. To appear.

8. McCullough. D. A Hookup Theorem for Multilevel Security. *IEEE Transactions on Software Engineering*, 16(6):563–568, 1990.

9. R. Focardi and R. Gorrieri. Classification of Security Properties (Part I: Information Flow). In R. Focardi and R. Gorrieri, editors, *Foundations of Security Analysis and Design*, volume 2171 of *LNCS*. Springer-Verlag, 2001.

10. R. Focardi, R. Gorrieri, and F. Martinelli. Non Interference for the Analysis of Cryptographic Protocols. In U. Montanari, J. D. P. Rolim, and E. Welzl, editors, *Proc. of Int. Colloquium on Automata, Languages and Programming (ICALP'00)*, volume 1853 of *LNCS*, pages 744–755. Springer-Verlag, 2000.

11. R. Focardi and S. Rossi. Information Flow Security in Dynamic Contexts. In *Proc. of the IEEE Computer Security Foundations Workshop (CSFW'02)*, pages 307–319. IEEE Comp. Soc. Press, 2002.

12. S. N. Foley. A Universal Theory of Information Flow. In *Proc. of the IEEE Symposium on Security and Privacy*, pages 116–122. IEEE Comp. Soc. Press, 1987.

13. J. A. Goguen and J. Meseguer. Security Policies and Security Models. In *Proc. of the IEEE Symposium on Security and Privacy*, pages 11–20. IEEE Comp. Soc. Press, 1982.

14. M. Hennessy and J. Riely. Information Flow vs. Resource Access in the Asynchronous Pi-calculus. *ACM Transactions on Programming Languages and Systems (TOPLAS)*, 24(5):566–591, 2002.

15. H. Mantel. On the Composition of Secure Systems. In *Proc. of the IEEE Symposium on Security and Privacy*, pages 88–101. IEEE Comp. Soc. Press, 2002.

16. F. Martinelli. Partial Model Checking and Theorem Proving for Ensuring Security Properties. In *Proc. of the IEEE Computer Security Foundations Workshop (CSFW'98)*, pages 44–52. IEEE Comp. Soc. Press, 1998.

17. J. McLean. Security Models and Information Flow. In *Proc. of the IEEE Symposium on Security and Privacy*, pages 180–187. IEEE Comp. Soc. Press, 1990.

18. J. McLean. A General Theory of Composition for a Class of "Possibilistic" Security Properties. *IEEE Transactions on Software Engineering*, 22(1):53–67, 1996.

19. R. Milner. *Communication and Concurrency*. Prentice-Hall, 1989.

20. R. Milner. The Polyadic Pi-calculus: a tutorial. In F. L. Bauer, W. Brauer, and H. Schwichtenberg, editors, *Logic and Algebra of Specification*, pages 203–246. Springer-Verlag, 1993.

21. P. Ryan and S. Schneider. Process Algebra and Non-Interference. *Journal of Computer Security*, 9(1/2):75–103, 2001.

22. A. Sabelfeld and A. C. Myers. Language-Based Information-Flow Security. *IEEE Journal on Selected Areas in Communication*, 21(1):5–19, 2003.

23. A. Sabelfeld and D. Sands. Probabilistic Noninterference for Multi-threaded Programs. In *Proc. of the IEEE Computer Security Foundations Workshop (CSFW'00)*, pages 200–215. IEEE Comp. Soc. Press, 2000.

24. D. Sangiorgi and D. Walker. *The π-calculus*. Cambridge University Press, 2001.

25. J. Widom, D. Gries, and F. B. Schneider. Trace-based Network Proof Systems: Expressiveness and Completeness. *ACM Transactions on Programming Languages and Systems (TOPLAS)*, 14(3):396–416, 1992.

26. A. Zakinthinos and E. S. Lee. A General Theory of Security Properties. In *Proc. of the IEEE Symposium on Security and Privacy*, pages 74–102. IEEE Comp. Soc. Press, 1997.

Compositional Verification
of Secure Streamed Data:
A Case Study with EMSS*

Fabio Martinelli, Marinella Petrocchi, and Anna Vaccarelli

Istituto di Informatica e Telematica - C.N.R.
Area della Ricerca di Pisa
Via G. Moruzzi 1, 56124 Pisa, Italy
{fabio.martinelli,marinella.petrocchi,anna.vaccarelli}@iit.cnr.it

Abstract. We consider an instance of the EMSS protocol proposed in
[19], authenticating streamed data in the presence of packet loss. We
formally prove the integrity property of the instance by applying a compositional proof rule that allows us to check a specification with an arbitrary number of parallel processes. We argue that our approach may be
applied to a wider class of stream signature protocols.

Keywords: Security, Compositional Analysis and Verification, Digital
Streams, Integrity.

1 Introduction

Increasing trend to distribute streamed radio and video over the Internet must
provide sufficient security guarantees. In particular, so called stream signature
protocols were born with the intent to efficiently solve the problem to sign digital
streams, i.e. long, possibly infinite, sequence of bits. This class of protocols,
designed for open architectures, makes use of hashing techniques and thrifty use
of standard digital signatures to ensure the integrity of the stream.

Roughly speaking, an intrinsic infinite nature marks the class of stream signature protocols from the standard cryptographic ones, in the sense that a sender
broadcasts a continuous (and possibly unbounded) stream of messages to an arbitrary number of receivers. Further, receivers use information retrieved in earlier
packets to legitimate later packets or vice-versa. In wireless (or semi-wireless)
environments, the mobile receiver may leave a cell without prior negotiation and
reenter any other cell an arbitrary number of times.

Given these peculiarities, the use of formal techniques to analyze stream
signature protocols have recently raised an increasing interest among researchers.
In particular, in [3] it is shown how to build a finite model of the TESLA protocol
[18], despite the possibly unbounded stream of messages (and cryptographic

---

* Work partially supported by MURST Progetto "Metodi Formali per la Sicurezza ed
il Tempo" (MEFISTO); by MIUR project COVER; by Microsoft Research (Cambridge) and by a CSP grant for the project "SeTAPS II".

C. Blundo and C. Laneve (Eds.): ICTCS 2003, LNCS 2841, pp. 383–396, 2003.
© Springer-Verlag Berlin Heidelberg 2003

keys) broadcasted by a sender. This allows the authors of [3] to exploit model checking techniques for the formal verification of TESLA. The work in [1] has previously analyzed the same protocol making use of the theorem prover TAME.

Our approach is quite different and focuses its attention on the verifiability of a system with an arbitrary number of components. In this paper we show how to apply a compositional principle allowing us to compose safely processes, preserving the security properties they enjoy. Broadly speaking, a compositional principle gives sufficient conditions to conclude that the parallel composition of two (or more) processes satisfies a certain property, provided that the single processes by themselves satisfy the same property. Compositional reasoning is often useful. An interesting application field is indeed the analysis of systems with an arbitrary number of components (like the possibly arbitrary number of receivers participating through a stream signature protocol).

The principle we are going to exploit in this paper was first discussed in [11] for the GNDC schema of properties, defined in [4,5]. In turn, the GNDC schema is based on the notion of non-interference, [7]. We aim at applying the principle to stream signature protocols for the verification of the integrity property, where integrity means, informally, that the information accepted by a receiver is exactly what the sender intended.

Digital streams are usually sent over UDP, the User Datagram Protocol, [20]. UDP is considered to be an unreliable transport protocol. When UDP sends packets over a network, it just sends them and forgets about them. This does not mean that UDP is ineffective, only that it does not handle reliability. If a stream is received incomplete, we would still like to be able to prove the integrity of all the packets that were not lost. Stream signature protocols dealing with the problem of packet loss have been recently proposed, [8,16,17,19]. Here, the main target of our analysis will be the EMSS protocol, [19].

The main contribution of this paper is the formal capability to check a stream signature protocol with an arbitrary number of receivers, contrary to previous work in the area, [1,3] (the target of our analysis however being different from the TESLA protocol considered in those papers). To present our methodology, an instance of the EMSS protocol has been formally analyzed with compositional proof rules and the results are reported in the paper. Earlier results in [12] dealt with the protocol in [6], not designed for dealing with packet loss. Finally, this paper is an extended and revised version of [15].

The paper is organized as follows. In Section 2, we present the formal language we use for the description of cryptographic protocols. In Section 3, we describe the EMSS stream signature protocol in more detail. Section 4 recalls a general schema for defining security properties and illustrates a compositional result to establish if a system enjoys security properties defined by means of the general schemes. Sections 5 shows how to apply the compositional results to successfully prove the correctness of an instance of EMSS in terms of packets' integrity. In Section 6 we report some concluding remarks and discuss about related and future work.

2   A Formal Language for the Description of Protocols: Crypto-CCS

A language, a slight modification of CCS process algebra, is adopted for the description of cryptographic protocols. It makes use of cryptographic-modeling constructs and deals with confidential values, hence the name Crypto-CCS [4,5,14]. The Crypto-CCS model consists of a set of sequential agents able to communicate by exchanging messages.

The data handling part of the language consists of messages and inference systems. Messages are the data manipulated by agents, they form a set $Msgs$ of terms possibly containing variables. The set $Msgs$ is defined by the grammar:

$$m ::= x \mid b \mid F^1(m_1, \ldots, m_{k_1}) \mid \ldots \mid F^l(m_1, \ldots, m_{k_l})$$

where F^i (for $1 \leq i \leq l$) are the constructors for messages, $x \in V$, a countable set of variables, $b \in B$, a collection of basic messages, and k_i, for $1 \leq i \leq l$, gives the number of arguments of the constructor F^i. Messages without variables are *closed* messages.

Inference systems model the possible operations on messages. These systems consist of a set of rules r:

$$r = \frac{m_1 \quad \cdots \quad m_n}{m_0}$$

where $m_1, \ldots, m_n$ is a set of premises (possibly empty) and m_0 is the conclusion. An instance of the application of the rule r to closed messages m_i is denoted as $m_1 \quad \cdots \quad m_n \vdash_r m_0$. Given an inference system, we can define a *deduction function* $\mathcal{D}$ s.t. if ϕ is a finite set of closed messages, then $\mathcal{D}(\phi)$ is the set of closed messages that can be deduced starting from ϕ by applying instances of the rules in the system.

The control part of our language consists of compound systems, basically sequential agents running in parallel. The terms of our language are generated by the following grammar:

COMPOUND SYSTEMS: $S ::= (S_1 \mid S_2) \mid S \setminus C \mid A_\phi$
SEQUENTIAL AGENTS: $A ::= \mathbf{0} \mid p.A \mid A + A_1 \mid [m_1 \ldots m_n \vdash_r x]A; A_1$
$\mid [m = m']A; A_1 \mid E(m_1, \ldots, m_n)$
PREFIX CONSTRUCTS: $p ::= c!m \mid c?x$

where $m, m', m_1, \ldots, m_n$ are *closed* messages or variables, $x, x_1, \ldots, x_n$ are message variables, $c \in Ch$, a finite set of channels, ϕ is a finite set of *closed* messages, C is a subset of Ch. Constants are defined as follows: $E(x_1, \ldots, x_n) \doteq A$ where A is a Crypto-CCS agent which may contain no free variables except $x_1, \ldots, x_n$ which must be distinct. The informal semantics of sequential agents and compound systems is as follows:

- $\mathbf{0}$ is the process that does nothing.
- $p.A$ is the process that can perform an action according to the particular prefix construct p and then behaves as A:

- $c!m$ denotes a message m sent on channel c;
- $c?x$ denotes the receiving of a message m on channel c. The received message replaces the variable x.
- $A + A_1$ represents the non deterministic choice between A and A_1.
- $[m_1 \ldots m_n \vdash_r x]A; A_1$ is the inference construct. If, by applying an instance of rule r with premises $m_1 \ldots m_n$, a message m can be inferred then the process behaves as A (where m replaces x), otherwise it behaves as A_1. This is the message-manipulating construct of the language. For instance,

$$[m \quad sk(y) \vdash_{sign} x]A; \mathbf{0}$$

is the process that uses the rule $sign$ to obtain a digitally signed message from plaintext m and private key $sk(y)$ and then behaves like A, or it gets stuck.
- $[m = m']A; A_1$ is the match construct to check message equality: if $m = m'$ then the system behaves as A, otherwise it behaves as A_1.
- $E(m_1, \ldots, m_n)$ is a constant process that behaves like the respective defining term P (see Tab. 1) where all the variables $x_1 \ldots x_n$ are substituted with messages $m_1 \ldots m_n$.
- A compound system $S_1 \,|\, S_2$ denotes the parallel execution of S_1 and S_2. $S_1 \,|\, S_2$ performs an action p if one of its sub-components performs p. A synchronization or internal action, denoted by the symbol τ, may take place whenever S_1 and S_2 are able to perform two complementary actions, i.e. send-receive actions on the same channel.
- A compound system $S \setminus C$ allows only visible actions whose channels are not in C. (Internal action τ being the invisible action).
- The term A_ϕ is a single sequential agent whose knowledge, i.e. the set of messages which occur in its term, is described by ϕ. The agent's knowledge increases either when it receives messages (see rule $(?)$ in Tab. 1) or infers new messages from the messages it knows (see rule $\mathcal{D}$ in Tab. 1). For every sequential agent A_ϕ, we require that all the closed messages that appear in A belong to its knowledge ϕ.

2.1 Operational Semantics and Auxiliary Notions

The agents' activities are described by the actions they can perform. The set Act of actions which may be performed by a compound system ranges over by a and it is defined as: $Act = \{c?m, c!m, \tau \mid c \in C, m \in Msgs, m \text{ closed}\}$. We call $\mathcal{P}$ the set of all the Crypto-CCS $closed$ terms (i.e., with no free variables). We define $sort(P)$ to be the set of all the channels that syntactically occur in the term P.

The operational semantics of a Crypto-CCS term is described by means of the $labeled\ transition\ system$ (lts, for short) $\langle \mathcal{P}, Act, \{\xrightarrow{a}\}_{a \in Act} \rangle$, where $\{\xrightarrow{a}\}_{a \in Act}$ is the least relation between $tCryptoSPA$ processes induced by the axioms and inference rules of Tab. 1

The expression $S \xrightarrow{a} S'$ means that the system can move from the state S to the state S' through the action a. The expression $S \Longrightarrow S'$ denotes that S

Table 1. Operational semantics, where the symmetric rules for $|_1, |_2, \backslash_1, +_2$ are omitted.

$$(!)\frac{}{(c!m.A)_\phi \xrightarrow{c!m} (A)_\phi}$$

$$(?)\frac{m \in Msgs}{(c?x.A)_\phi \xrightarrow{c?m} (A[m/x])_{\phi\cup\{m\}}}$$

$$(\mathcal{D})\frac{m_1 \dots m_n \vdash_r m \quad (A[m/x])_{\phi\cup\{m\}} \xrightarrow{a} (A')_{\phi'}}{([m_1 \dots m_n \vdash_r x]A; A_1)_\phi \xrightarrow{a} (A')_{\phi'}}$$

$$(\mathcal{D}_1)\frac{\nexists m \text{ s.t. } m_1 \dots m_n \vdash_r m \quad (A_1)_\phi \xrightarrow{a} (A'_1)_{\phi'}}{([m_1 \dots m_n \vdash_r x]A; A_1)_\phi \xrightarrow{a} (A'_1)_{\phi'}}$$

$$(=)\frac{m = m' \quad (A)_\phi \xrightarrow{a} (A')_{\phi'}}{([m = m']A; A_1)_\phi \xrightarrow{a} (A')_{\phi'}}$$

$$(=_1)\frac{m \neq m' \quad (A_1)_\phi \xrightarrow{a} (A'_1)_{\phi'}}{([m = m']A; A_1)_\phi \xrightarrow{a} (A'_1)_{\phi'}}$$

$$(Const)\frac{E(x_1, \dots, x_n) =_{def} A \quad A[m_1/x_1, \dots, m_n/x_n] \xrightarrow{a} A_1}{E(m_1, \dots, m_n) \xrightarrow{a} A_1}$$

$$(|_1)\frac{S \xrightarrow{a} S'}{S \,|\, S_1 \xrightarrow{a} S' \,|\, S_1}$$

$$(|_2)\frac{S \xrightarrow{c!m} S' \quad S_1 \xrightarrow{c?m} S'_1}{S \,|\, S_1 \xrightarrow{\tau} S' \,|\, S'_1}$$

$$(\backslash_1)\frac{S \xrightarrow{c!m} S' \quad c \notin L}{S \setminus L \xrightarrow{c!m} S' \setminus L}$$

$$(+_2)\frac{S \xrightarrow{a} S'}{S + S_1 \xrightarrow{a} S'}$$

and S' belong to the reflexive and transitive closure of $\xrightarrow{\tau}$; let $\gamma = \alpha_1 \dots \alpha_n \in (Act\backslash\{\tau\})^*$ be a sequence of actions. Then, $S \xRightarrow{\gamma} S'$ if and only if there exist $S_1, S_2, \dots, S_{n-1} \in \mathcal{P}$ such that $S \xRightarrow{\alpha_1} S_1 \xRightarrow{\alpha_2} S_2 \dots \xRightarrow{\alpha_{n-1}} S_{n-1} \xRightarrow{\alpha_n} S'$.

As behavioral relations among Crypto-CCS terms, in the following we will be mainly interested in trace inclusion (equivalence) and (weak) simulation.

Definition 1. *We say that the traces of P are included in the traces of Q ($P \leq_{trace} Q$) whenever, if $P \xRightarrow{\gamma} P_1$ then $Q \xRightarrow{\gamma} Q_1$. We write that $P =_{trace} Q$ iff $P \leq_{trace} Q$ and $Q \leq_{trace} P$.*

Definition 2. *We say that a relation $\mathcal{R}$ among processes is a weak simulation, if for every $(P, Q) \in \mathcal{R}$ we have:*

- *If $P \xrightarrow{a} P', a \neq \tau$, then there exists Q' s.t. $Q \xRightarrow{a} Q'$ and $(P', Q') \in \mathcal{R}$.*
- *If $P \xrightarrow{\tau} P'$ then there exists Q' s.t. $Q \Rightarrow Q'$ and $(P', Q') \in \mathcal{R}$.*

The union of all weak simulations is a weak simulation and it is denoted by $\prec$. As usual, it holds that if $P \prec Q$ then $P \leq_{trace} Q$.

3   The EMSS Protocol

In [19], Perrig *et al.* presented the Efficient Multi-chained Stream Signature (EMSS) protocol to sign digital streams. EMSS exploits a combination of hash functions and digital signatures and–contrary to previous proposals [6]–achieves (some) robustness against packet loss.

We assume that a sender S wants to send a stream of messages $m_0, m_1, \ldots,$ m_{last} to a set of receivers $\{R_n \mid n \geq 1\}$. The protocol then requires S to divide the stream into packets and send them to the receivers. The basic idea of the construction is the following: a hash of packet P_{i-1} is appended to packet P_i, whose hash is in turn appended to packet P_{i+1} and so on. A signature packet, containing the hash of the final data packet along with a signature, is sent at the end of the stream. To achieve robustness against packet loss (the event of one or more packets loss would break the chain) each packet contains multiple hashes of previous packets and the signature packet signs hashes of multiple packets. [19] uses both deterministic and random distribution of hashes per packet.

Here we focus on a specific instance of the EMSS, viz. the deterministic (1,2) schema, where packet P_i contains hashes of packets $i-1, i-2$ and whose hash is contained in packets $i+1, i+2$. After an initial phase, each packet P_i contains a meaningful payload m_i [1] together with the hashes $h(P_{i-1})$ and $h(P_{i-2})$ of the previous two packets sent. Packets are sent over channels $c_i, 0 \leq i \leq last$. The end of a stream is indicated by a signature packet P_{sign} over channel c_{sign}, containing the hashes of the final two packets, along with a digital signature. The protocol can formally be described as follows.

$$
\begin{aligned}
\text{Packet } P_0 \quad & c_0 \; S \to \{R_n\} : m_0, null, null \\
\text{Packet } P_1 \quad & c_1 \; S \to \{R_n\} : m_1, h(P_0), null \\
\text{Packet } P_i \quad & c_i \; S \to \{R_n\} : m_i, h(P_{i-1}), h(P_{i-2}) \; 2 \leq i \leq last
\end{aligned}
$$

Let P_{last} be the last packet of the stream. Upon sending P_{last} a signature packet is sent:

$$
\text{Sign-Pack} \quad P_{sign} \quad c_{sign} \; S \to \{R_n\} : \{h(P_{last}), h(P_{last-1})\}_{sk(S)}
$$

A packet P_i is said to be verifiable if there exists a path (in terms of hash chains) from P_i to the signature packet. Given a set of verifiable packets, we intend to prove the correctness of the construction in terms of packet integrity, i.e. to assure a receiver that the information he received is exactly what the sender has originally intended.

3.1   Crypto-CCS Specifications of the (1,2) EMSS

We present the Crypto-CCS specifications of the (1,2) scheme of the EMSS protocol. The sender and receiver processes can perform sendings and receptions

---

[1] We assume the sender's private key $sk(S)$ cannot be deduced from the set of messages $\{m_i\}$.

according to the protocol original specifications. Compared with a standard notation like the one in Section 3, the Crypto-CCS representation is more expressive: checks on the received packets are explicitly represented. We remind that the whole formalization, in particular the way a receiver process acts, is based on implementative choices of the authors since some details are not explicitly given in [19].

The sender process is parameterized by variables containing the hashes he should insert in the following packet. With notation x_m we mean "variable x should contain message m".

$$S_0(0,0) \doteq$$

$[m_0 \vdash_{tuple} x_{P_0}]$	*Create tuple*
$[x_{P_0} \vdash_{hash} x_{h(P_0)}]$	*Compute hash of P_0*
$(S_1(x_{h(P_0)}, 0) \mid MB_0(x_{P_0}))$	*Output P_0 and go to next state*

$$S_1(x_{h(P_0)}, 0) \doteq$$

$[m_1 \quad x_{h(P_0)} \vdash_{tuple} x_{P_1}]$	*Create tuple*
$[x_{P_1} \vdash_{hash} x_{h(P_1)}]$	*Compute hash of P_1*
$(S_2(x_{h(P_1)}, x_{h(P_0)}) \mid MB_1(x_{P_1}))$	*Output P_1 and go to next state*

$$S_i(x_{h(P_{i-1})}, x_{h(P_{i-2})}) \doteq$$

$[m_i \quad x_{h(P_{i-1})} \quad x_{h(P_{i-2})} \vdash_{tuple} x_{P_i}]$	*Create tuple*
$[x_{P_i} \vdash_{hash} x_{h(P_i)}]$	*Compute hash of current packet*
$(S_{i+1}(x_{h(P_i)}, x_{h(P_{i-1})}) \mid MB_i(x_{P_i}))$	*Output P_i and go to next state*

$$S_{sign}(x_{h(P_{last})}, x_{h(P_{last-1})}) \doteq$$

$[x_{h(P_{last})} \quad x_{h(P_{last-1})} \vdash_{tuple} x_t]$	*Create tuple of final hashes*
$[x_t \quad sk(S) \vdash_{sign} x_{P_{sign}}]$	*Sign the tuple*
$MB_{sign}(x_{P_{sign}})$	*Output the signature packet*

The special process MB is responsible for potentially sending each packet an unbounded number of times, in order to simulate a one-to-many (one-to-all) sending typical of a multicast/broadcast session. The process is parameterized by the packet the sender is to multicast (or broadcast).

$$MB_i(x_{P_i}) \doteq c_i!x_{P_i}.MB_i(x_{P_i}) \quad 0 \leq i \leq last$$
$$MB_{sign}(x_{P_{sign}}) \doteq c_{sign}!x_{P_{sign}}.MB_{sign}(x_{P_i})$$

Among the set of receivers, each process behaves in the same way. The generic receiver process at step i is parameterized by: 1) the two last packets he received (let them be P_{j_1}, P_{j_2}) - over an ideal channel, without packet loss, we have that $P_{j_1} = P_{i-1}$ and $P_{j_2} = P_{i-2}$; 2) a tuple $tup^{i-1}_{\{m_j\}}$. $tup_{\{m_j\}}$ consists of the ordered sequence of payloads among $\{m_j\}_{j=0,1,\dots last}$ whose corresponding packets' hashes $h(P_j)$ the receiver was able to check[2]. $tup^{i-1}_{\{m_j\}}$ is the tuple updated at step

---

[2] For the sake of readability we assume the receiver may infer the sequence number of a packet by simply observing the packet itself. Otherwise, we should arrange the receiver with more parameters or arrange a "sequence number" field in the packet structure and let the receiver retrieve it. This could introduce a too clumsy notation.

i, by inserting either $x_{m_{i-2}}$ or $x_{m_{i-3}}$. $tup^{i-1}_{\{m_j\}}$ could be either $(x_{m_{i-2}}, tup^{i-1}_{\{m_j\}})$ or $(x_{m_{i-3}}, tup^{i-1}_{\{m_j\}})$ or it may remain unchanged. Similarly, $tup_{\{m_j\}}$ may either be $(x_{m_{last}}, tup^{last}_{\{m_j\}})$ or $(x_{m_{last-1}}, tup^{last}_{\{m_j\}})$ or $tup^{last}_{\{m_j\}}$.

We model the unreliability of the transmission over UDP by considering that process Rec non deterministically chooses whether to receive a packet or not. Finally, we assume that the signature packet P_{sign} is always received (this is likely since in the original protocol multiple copies of the signature packets are sent).

$Rec_0(0,0,0) \doteq$
$\quad Rec_1(0,0,0) +$ *Packet loss : go to next state, otherwise*
$\quad (c_0?x_{P_0}.$ *Receive initial packet*
$\quad\quad Rec_1(x_{P_0}, 0, 0))$ *Go to next state*

$Rec_1(0,0,0) \doteq$
$\quad Rec_2(0,0,0) +$ *Packet loss : go to next state, otherwise*
$\quad (c_1?x_{P_1}.$ *Receive packet P_1*
$\quad\quad Rec_2(x_{P_1}, 0, 0))$ *Go to next state*

$Rec_1(x_{P_0}, 0, 0) \doteq$
$\quad Rec_2(0, x_{P_0}, 0)+$ *Packet loss : go to next state, otherwise*
$\quad (c_1?x_{P_1}.$ *Receive packet P_1*
$\quad\quad [x_{P_1} \vdash_{2-nd} x_{h(P_0)}]$ *Extract hash of previous packet P_0*
$\quad\quad [x_{P_0} \vdash_{hash} x_{h_{MY}(P_0)}]$ *Compute my hash $h_{MY}(P_0)$*
$\quad\quad [x_{h(P_0)} = x_{h_{MY}(P_0)}]$ *Compare the hashes*
$\quad\quad ([x_{P_0} \vdash_{1-st} x_{m_0}]$ *IF equal : extract previous payload*
$\quad\quad\quad Rec_2(x_{P_1}, x_{P_0}, x_{m_0})$ *Update parameters and go to next state*
$\quad\quad);\mathbf{0}$ *ELSE abort*
$\quad)$

$Rec_i(x_{P_{j_1}}, x_{P_{j_2}}, tup^{i-1}_{\{m_j\}}) \doteq$
$\quad Rec_{i+1}(x_{P_{j_1}}, x_{P_{j_2}}, tup^{i-1}_{\{m_j\}}) +$ *Packet loss : go to next state, otherwise*
$\quad (c_i?x_{P_i}.$ *Receive packet P_i*
$\quad\quad ([j_1 = i - 1]$ *Was P_{i-1} received?*
$\quad\quad Rec'_i(x_{P_i}, x_{P_{i-1}}, tup^{i-1}_{\{m_j\}});$ *Go to Rec'_i; otherwise*
$\quad\quad ([j_2 = i - 2]$ *Was P_{i-2} received?*
$\quad\quad Rec''_i(x_{P_i}, x_{P_{i-2}}, tup^{i-1}_{\{m_j\}})$ *Go to Rec''_i; otherwise*
$\quad\quad)$
$\quad); Rec_{i+1}(x_{P_i}, x_{P_{j_1}}, tup^{i-1}_{\{m_j\}})$ *Go to next state :*
$\quad)$ *P_{1-1} and P_{i-2} were not received*
$Rec'_i(x_{P_i}, x_{P_{i-1}}, tup^{i-1}_{\{m_j\}}) \doteq$
$\quad [x_{P_i} \vdash_{2-nd} x_{h(P_{i-1})}]$ *Extract $h(P_{i-1})$ from P_i*
$\quad [x_{P_{i-1}} \vdash_{hash} x_{h_{MY}(P_{i-1})}]$ *Compute my hash $h_{MY}(P_{i-1})$*
$\quad [x_{h_{MY}(P_{i-1})} = x_{h(P_{i-1})}]$ *Compare the hashes*
$\quad ([x_{P_{i-1}} \vdash_{1-st} x_{m_{i-1}}]$ *IF equal : extract m_{i-1} from P_{i-1}*
$\quad Rec_{i+1}(x_{P_i}, x_{P_{j_1}}, (x_{m_{i-1}}, tup^{i-1}_{\{m_j\}}))$ *Update parameters and go to next state*
$\quad);\mathbf{0}$ *ELSE : abort*

$Rec_i''(x_{P_i}, x_{P_{i-2}}, tup_{\{m_j\}}^{i-1}) \doteq$

$\quad [x_{P_i} \vdash_{3-rd} x_{h(P_{i-2})}]$ *Extract $h(P_{i-2})$ from P_i*

$\quad [x_{P_{i-2}} \vdash_{hash} x_{h_{MY}(P_{i-2})}]$ *Compute my hash $h_{MY}(P_{i-2})$*

$\quad [x_{h_{MY}(P_{i-2})} = x_{h(P_{i-2})}]$ *Compare the hashes*

$\quad ([x_{P_{i-2}} \vdash_{1-st} x_{m_{i-2}}]$ *IF equal : extract m_{i-2} from P_{i-2}*

$\quad Rec_{i+1}(x_{P_i}, x_{P_{j_1}}, (x_{m_{i-2}}, tup_{\{m_j\}}^{i-1}))$ *Update parameters and go to next state*

$);\mathbf{0}$ *ELSE : abort*

$Rec_{sign}(x_{P_{j1}}, x_{P_{j2}}, tup_{\{m_j\}}^{last}) \doteq$

$c_{sign}?x_{P_{sign}}.$ *Receive signature packet*

$Rec_{sign}^*(x_{P_{sign}}, x_{P_{j1}}, x_{P_{j2}}, tup_{\{m_j\}}^{last})$ *Go to intermediary state Rec_{sign}^**

$Rec_{sign}^*(x_{P_{sign}}, x_{P_{j1}}, x_{P_{j2}}, tup_{\{m_j\}}^{last}) \doteq$

$\quad [x_{P_{sign}} \quad pk(S) \vdash_{ver} x_{ver}]$ *Verify the signature*

$\quad [j_1 = last]$ *Was P_{last} received?*

$\quad Rec_{sign}'(x_{ver}, x_{P_{last}}, tup_{\{m_j\}}^{last});$ *If so, go to Rec_{sign}'; otherwise*

$\quad ([j_2 = last - 1]$ *Was P_{last-1} received?*

$\quad Rec_{sign}''(x_{ver}, x_{P_{last-1}}, tup_{\{m_j\}}^{last});$ *If so, go to Rec_{sign}''; otherwise*

$\quad (c_{app}!tup_{\{m_j\}}^{last}.\mathbf{0})$ *P_{last} and P_{last-1} were not received.*

$)$ *Send the stream of verifiable payloads*

$\qquad$ *to the application level*

$Rec_{sign}''(x_{ver}, x_{P_{last-1}}, tup_{\{m_j\}}^{last}) \doteq$

$\quad [x_{ver} \vdash_{2-nd} x_{h(P_{last-1})}]$ *Extract $h(P_{last-1})$ from P_{sign}*

$\quad [x_{P_{last-1}} \vdash_{hash} x_{h_{MY}(P_{last-1})}]$ *Compute my hash $h_{MY}(P_{last-1})$*

$\quad [x_{h_{MY}(P_{last-1})} = x_{h(P_{last-1})}]$ *Compare the hashes*

$\quad [x_{P_{last-1}} \vdash_{1-st} x_{m_{last-1}}]$ *IF equal : extract m_{last-1} from P_{last-1}*

$\quad c_{app}!(x_{m_{last-1}}, tup_{\{m_j\}}^{last}).\mathbf{0};$ *Send the stream of verifiable payloads*

$\quad \mathbf{0}$ *to the application level and stop; ELSE*

$\qquad$ *abort*

$Rec_{sign}'(x_{ver}, x_{P_{last}}, tup_{\{m_j\}}^{last}) \doteq$

$\quad [x_{ver} \vdash_{1-st} x_{h(P_{last})}]$ *Extract $h(P_{last})$ from P_{sign}*

$\quad [x_{P_{last}} \vdash_{hash} x_{h_{MY}(P_{last})}]$ *Compute my hash $h_{MY}(P_{last})$*

$\quad [x_{h_{MY}(P_{last})} = x_{h(P_{last})}]$ *Compare the hashes*

$\quad [x_{P_{last}} \vdash_{1-st} x_{m_{last}}]$ *IF equal : extract m_{last} from P_{last}*

$\quad c_{app}!(x_{m_{last}}, tup_{\{m_j\}}^{last}).\mathbf{0};$ *Send the stream of verifiable payloads*

$\quad \mathbf{0}$ *to the application level and stop; ELSE*

$\qquad$ *abort*

In the final state Rec_{sign} (along with intermediary states Rec_{sign}^*, Rec_{sign}', Rec_{sign}'') the receiver aims at verifying the digital signature (we assume he has previously retrieved the public key $pk(S)$ corresponding to the private key of the supposed sender). The correct verification of the signature implies the receiver to have guarantees on the integrity of the verifiable payloads. He can now send the stream to his application level to consume it. In our formalization, this is modeled by a scenario where the receiver sends the content of his parameter tuple (the stream accepted) over channel c_{app}. If the verification of the signature in the final state or the equality tests in the previous states do not succeed the receiver should abort.

4   Compositional Analysis within GNDC

In this section we recall the general schema *Generalized Non Deducibility on Compositions* (GNDC) for the definition of security properties given in [4,5] and a compositional proof rule for such a schema, discussed in [11]. The main idea is the following: a system P satisfies property $GNDC_{\lhd}^{\alpha}$ if the behavior of P, despite the presence of a hostile environment X that can interact with P only through a fixed set of channels C, *appears* to be same (w.r.t. a behavioral relation $\lhd$ of observational equivalence) to the behavior of a modified version $\alpha(P)$ of P that represents the *expected* (correct) behavior of P.

The analysis of cryptographic protocols involves specifying a set of messages known by the adversary at the beginning of the computation. This *static* (initial) knowledge of the hostile environment must be bound to a specific set of messages. This limitation is needed to avoid a too strong hostile environment that would be able to corrupt any secret (as it would know all cryptographic keys, etc.). Given an adversary X, we call $ID(X)$ the set of closed messages that syntactically appear in X. This set, intuitively, contains all the messages that are initially known by X. Let ϕ_X be a set of messages representing the static, initial knowledge that we would like to give to X. We want $ID(X)$ to be consistent with ϕ_X. This can be obtained by requiring that all the messages in $ID(X)$ are *deducible* from ϕ_X by means of the *deduction function* $\mathcal{D}$.

The set $\mathcal{E}_C^{\phi_X}$ of processes that can communicate on a subset of public channels C and have an initial knowledge bound by ϕ_X can be therefore defined as follows:

$$\mathcal{E}_C^{\phi_X} = \{X \in \mathcal{P} \mid sort(X) \subseteq C \text{ and } ID(X) \subseteq \mathcal{D}(\phi_X)\}$$

We consider as hostile processes only the ones belonging to $\mathcal{E}_C^{\phi_X}$.
We define the property $GNDC_{\lhd}^{\alpha}$ as follows:

Definition 3. *A process P is $GNDC_{\lhd}^{\alpha}$ iff $\forall X \in \mathcal{E}_C^{\phi_X} : (P \mid X) \setminus C \lhd \alpha(P)$ where $\lhd$ is a behavioral relation between processes and α is a function between processes.*

For the analysis of safety properties it is enough to consider the trace inclusion relation $\leq_{trace}$ as behavioral relation among the terms of the algebra. When the $\leq_{trace}$ relation is considered, there exists a sufficient criterion for the static characterization (i.e. not involving the universal predicate $\forall$) of $GNDC_{\lhd}^{\alpha}$ properties (for further details see [4,5]). Generally, $GNDC_{\leq_{trace}}$ properties are not compositional. To get a compositional rule we need to strengthen our requirements on the behavior of the processes.

Definition 4. *We say that a process P is stable w.r.t. ϕ_X, whenever for every X with $ID(X) \subseteq \phi_X$, $(P \mid X_{\phi_X}) \setminus C \xRightarrow{\gamma} (P' \mid X'_{\phi'_X}) \setminus C$ then $\mathcal{D}(\phi_X) = \mathcal{D}(\phi'_X)$.*

Basically, a process P is stable when an enemy with a certain knowledge ϕ_X does not increase significantly ϕ_X during the execution of P.

The following compositional rule holds for the $GNDC^{\alpha}_{\leq trace}$ schema (under the assumption that the involved processes are stable).

Proposition 1. *Given ϕ_X and a set of public channels C, assume processes $P_r \in GNDC^{\alpha_r(P_r)}_{\leq trace}$ with $1 \leq r \leq n$ and P_r stable w.r.t. ϕ_X. It follows that $(P_1 | \ldots | P_n)$ is stable w.r.t. ϕ_X and $(P_1 | \ldots | P_n) \in GNDC^{\alpha_1(P_1) | \ldots | \alpha_n(P_n)}_{\leq trace}$.*

5   Compositional Analysis of the (1,2) EMSS Protocol

Our goal is to apply the previous compositional rule for checking that the (1,2) EMSS scheme guarantees integrity of the delivered stream even in presence of an adversary. The specifications of the (1-2) EMSS scheme, namely the sender S_0 and the receiver Rec_0, are given in Subsection 3.1. The general system with n receivers may be considered as $S_0 | \overbrace{Rec_0 | \ldots | Rec_0}^{n}$.

We formally define integrity in the GNDC schema as the ability to accept only the message m_i by a receiver as the $i - th$ message sent by the sender (assuming m_i is not lost). Assume that a receiver signals the acceptance of a stream of messages as a legitimate one, by issuing it, as a unique list of messages, on a special channel c_{app}. Thus, let α_{int} be $Spec_{sign} = \sum_{s \in streams} c_{app}! s.0$, where $streams$ is the set of all the possible ordered sub streams of $m_0 \ldots m_{last}$.

Definition 5. *A system P, consisting of a sender of a stream of messages $\{m_i\}$ and a receiver, enjoys the integrity property whenever $P \in GNDC^{\alpha_{int}}_{\leq trace}$.*

Basically, it means that the receiver accepts exactly a subset of the messages m_i in the correct order even in presence of an adversary. The key point is that the intruder will never acquire the private key of the sender to successfully sign the final packet of the stream. Note that in a multi-receiver environment with one sender, a protocol guarantees integrity whenever each receiver accepts only the stream of messages that the sender wishes to deliver. In our case, the specification for n receivers is simply the parallel composition of α_{int} n-times.

We may prove that S_0, Rec_0 are stable w.r.t. the following initial knowledge ϕ_X:

$$\phi_X = \{P_0\} \cup \{P_1\} \cup \{P_i \mid i = 2, \ldots, last\} \cup \{pk(S), P_{sign}\}$$

Proposition 2. *S_0 and Rec_0 are stable w.r.t. ϕ_X.*

Actually, we include in the initial knowledge ϕ_X the messages an adversary would be able to add to his knowledge by eavesdropping on a run of the protocol. This implies that we arrange for an intruder to have the most powerful means to act since the beginning of the computation. If the protocol satisfies the integrity property in this very hostile environment then it means that it will satisfy this property in a less powerful one (this may be formally justified).

We may prove that S_0 enjoys $GNDC^{\alpha_{int}^0}_{\leq trace}$ and Rec_0 enjoys $GNDC^{\alpha_{int}}_{\leq trace}$, that is to say for all $X \in \mathcal{E}^{\phi_X}_C$ we have $(S_0 | X) \backslash C \leq_{trace} \mathbf{0}$ and $(Rec_0 | X) \backslash C$

$\leq_{trace} \alpha_{int}$. This may be done by finding a suitable weak simulation relation between $(S_0 \mid X)\backslash C$ and $\mathbf{0}$, and between $(Rec_0 \mid X)\backslash C$ and $Spec_{sign}$ ($\forall X \in \mathcal{E}_C^{\phi_X}$), respectively. The set C of channels over which an intruder is able to communicate is $C = \{c_{sign}\} \cup \{c_i \mid 0 \leq i \leq last\}$.

The weak simulation relation we consider for dealing with the sender specifications is the following:

$$\mathcal{R}_{\mathcal{S}} = (((S_i(...)\mid X)\backslash C, \mathbf{0}) \mid X \in \mathcal{E}_C^{\phi_X}, 0 \leq i \leq last)$$
$$\cup(((S_{sign}(...)\mid X)\backslash C, \mathbf{0}) \mid X \in \mathcal{E}_C^{\phi_X})$$

The weak simulation relation we consider for dealing with the receiver specifications is the following:

$$
\begin{aligned}
\mathcal{R}_{\mathcal{R}} = &(((Rec_0(0,0,0)\mid X)\backslash C, Spec_{sign}) \mid X \in \mathcal{E}_C^{\phi_X}) \\
&\cup(((Rec_1(0,0,0)\mid X)\backslash C, Spec_{sign}) \mid X \in \mathcal{E}_C^{\phi_X}) \\
&\cup(((Rec_1(x_{P_0},0,0)\mid X)\backslash C, Spec_{sign}) \mid X \in \mathcal{E}_C^{\phi_X}) \\
&\cup(((Rec_i(x_{P_{j1}},x_{P_{j2}},tup_{\{m_j\}}^{i-1})\mid X)\backslash C, Spec_{sign}) \mid X \in \mathcal{E}_C^{\phi_X}, 2 \leq i \leq last) \\
&\cup(((Rec_i'(x_{P_i},x_{P_{i-1}},tup_{\{m_j\}}^{i-1})\mid X)\backslash C, Spec_{sign}) \mid X \in \mathcal{E}_C^{\phi_X}, 2 \leq i \leq last) \\
&\cup(((Rec_i''(x_{P_i},x_{P_{i-2}},tup_{\{m_j\}}^{i-1})\mid X)\backslash C, Spec_{sign}) \mid X \in \mathcal{E}_C^{\phi_X}, 2 \leq i \leq last) \\
&\cup(((Rec_{sign}(x_{P_{j1}},x_{P_{j2}},tup_{\{m_j\}}^{last})\mid X)\backslash C, Spec_{sign}) \mid X \in \mathcal{E}_C^{\phi_X}) \\
&\cup(((Rec_{sign}^*(x_{P_{sign}},x_{P_{j1}},x_{P_{j2}},tup_{\{m_j\}}^{last})\mid X)\backslash C, Spec_{sign}) \mid X \in \mathcal{E}_C^{\phi_X}) \\
&\cup(((Rec_{sign}'(x_{ver},x_{P_{last}},tup_{\{m_j\}}^{last})\mid X)\backslash C, Spec_{sign}) \mid X \in \mathcal{E}_C^{\phi_X}) \\
&\cup(((Rec_{sign}''(x_{ver},x_{P_{last-1}},tup_{\{m_j\}}^{last})\mid X)\backslash C, Spec_{sign}) \mid X \in \mathcal{E}_C^{\phi_X})
\end{aligned}
$$

$tup_{\{m_j\}}^{i-1}, tup_{\{m_j\}}^{last}$ are lists of meaningful payloads (also updated). By inspection of the possible cases we may show that $\mathcal{R}_{\mathcal{S}}$ and $\mathcal{R}_{\mathcal{R}}$ are weak simulations. We omitted to explicitly put in $\mathcal{R}_{\mathcal{S}}$ and $\mathcal{R}_{\mathcal{R}}$ the pairs in which the first process performs deduction constructs.

Here we give a sketch of the proof dealing with the receiver specifications.

When the first process performs inference (or match) constructs and it gets stuck because an inference rule does not apply, or simply travels to the next state, it can be weakly simulated by whatever process, in particular $Spec_{sign}$. When Rec_0 performs a receiving action, the process on the left may perform a τ action and it can be weakly simulated by whatever process, in particular $Spec_{sign}$. The interesting case is when the first process outputs a tuple of messages $tup_{\{m_j\}}$ over channel $c_{app} \notin C$. In this case, it must be $\{x_{ver}\}_{sk(S)} = P_{sign}$ and, assuming that digital signatures and hash functions cannot be forged, all the messages in $tup_{\{m_j\}}$ must be replaced with one of all the possible ordered sub streams of $m_0 \ldots m_{last}$. This can be weakly simulated by $Spec_{sign}$ that has been defined as the process sending all the possible ordered sub streams of $m_0 \ldots m_{last}$.

Each resulting pair consisting of the derivatives still belong to $\mathcal{R}_{\mathcal{R}}$.

Proposition 3. $S_0 \in GNDC_{\leq trace}^0$ and $Rec_0 \in GNDC_{\leq trace}^{\alpha_{int}}$.

The following proposition follows by Proposition 1, 2, 3.

Proposition 4. $S_0 \mid Rec_0 \in GNDC_{\leq trace}^{\alpha_{int}}$.

Compositional reasoning is powerful: to check a system with an arbitrary number of components we do not consider the whole system but only the components by themselves and the result simply follows by Proposition 1 where index r is not fixed *a priori* and $P_1 = S_0$ and $P_r, 2 \leq r \leq n$ is Rec_0.

Proposition 5. *The (1,2) EMSS Protocol enjoys integrity for whatever number of receivers.*

6   Conclusions

The compositional analysis can be successfully applied to formally verify integrity properties in a multicast/broadcast environment. (We remind that integrity means, from our point of view, assurance that multicast data are not modified *en-route*.) In particular, we considered as a case study EMSS [19] in its deterministic (1,2) scheme variant. We modeled such a scheme considering communication channels with packet loss. We are able to formally check the system with an arbitrary number of receivers.

Prominent works related to streams verification are those in [1], a formal analysis based on theorem proving techniques to analyze a well known stream authentication protocol (the TESLA protocol [18]) and in [3], where the authors verify the same protocol with model checking techniques.

Notable examples of compositional proof techniques for reasoning about cryptographic protocols may be found in [2,13]. In [13] a compositional proof system for an environment-sensitive bisimulation has been developed. One main difference from ours is that we consider a weak notion of observation where the internal actions are not visible. (Actually, the authors of [13] leave as a future work the treatment of such a form of equivalence). In [2] the concept of disjoint encryption has been developed and the authors were able to perform compositional reasoning both for secrecy and authentication properties.

Works in progress are the following: 1) applying our compositional proof rules to erasure codes-based solutions like the ones proposed in [16,17]; 2) extending the analysis to real-time broadcast environments where time synchronization plays an essential role. Compositionality being a fundamental issue in static analysis approaches, we leave as a future work the comparison of our approach with the one proposed in [9,10], based on type systems for checking authenticity/integrity properties.

Acknowledgments

We would like to thank the anonymous referees for their helpful comments.

References

1. M. Archer. Proving Correctness of the Basic TESLA Multicast Stream Authentication Protocol with TAME. In *Proc. of WITS'02*, 2002.

2. M. Boreale and D. Gorla. On Compositional Reasoning in the Spi-Calculus. In *Proc. of FOSSACS'02*, LNCS 2303, 67-81. 2002.
3. P. Broadfoot and G. Lowe. Analysing a Stream Authentication Protocol using Model Checking. In *Proc. of ESORICS'02*, LNCS 2502, 146-161. 2002.
4. R. Focardi, R. Gorrieri, and F. Martinelli. Non Interference for the Analysis of Cryptographic Protocols. In *Proc. of ICALP'00*, LNCS 1853, 354-372. 2000.
5. R. Focardi and F. Martinelli. A uniform approach for the definition of security properties. In *Proc. of FM'99*, LNCS 1708, 794-813. 1999.
6. R. Gennaro and P. Rohatgi. How to Sign Digital Streams. *Information and Computation*, 165(1):100–116, 2001.
7. J. A. Goguen and J. Meseguer. Security Policies and Security Models. In *Proc. of IEEE S&P'82*, pages 11–20, 1982.
8. P. Golle and N. Modadugu. Authenticating Streamed Data in the Presence of Random Packet Loss. In *Proc. of NDSS'01*, 2001.
9. A.D. Gordon and A. Jeffrey. Authenticity by Typing for Security Protocols. In *Proc. of IEEE CSFW'01*, 126-144. 2001.
10. A.D. Gordon and A. Jeffrey. Types and Effects for Asymmetric Cryptographic Protocols. In *Proc. of IEEE CSFW'02*, 77-91. 2002.
11. R. Gorrieri, E. Locatelli, and F. Martinelli. A Simple Language for Real-time Cryptographic Protocol Analysis. In *Proc. of ESOP'03*, LNCS 2618, 114-128. 2003.
12. R. Gorrieri, F. Martinelli, M.Petrocchi, and A.Vaccarelli. Compositional Verification of Integrity for Digital Stream Signature Protocols. In *Proc. of IEEE ACSD'03*, 142-149. 2003.
13. J. Guttman and F.J. Thayer. Protocol Independence through Disjoint Encryption. In *Proc. of IEEE CSFW'00*, 24-34. 2000.
14. F. Martinelli. Analysis of Security Protocols as Open Systems. *Theoretical Computer Science*, 290(1):1057–1106, 2003.
15. F. Martinelli, M.Petrocchi, and A.Vaccarelli. Analysing EMSS with Compositional Proof Rules for Non-Interference. In *Proc. of WITS'03*, 52-61. 2003.
16. A. Pannetrat and R. Molva. Efficient Multicast Packet Authentication. In *Proc. of NDSS'03*, 2003.
17. J. M. Park, E. K. P. Chong, and H. J. Siegel. Efficient Multicast Packet Authentication using Signature Amortization. In *Proc. of IEEE S&P'02*, pages 227–240, 2002.
18. A. Perrig, R. Canetti, D. X. Song, and D. Tygar. Efficient and Secure Source Authentication for Multicast. In *Proc. of NDSS'01*. The Internet Society, 2001.
19. A. Perrig, R. Canetti, J. D. Tygar, and D. X. Song. Efficient Authentication and Signing of Multicast Streams over Lossy Channels. In *Proc. of IEEE S&P'00*, pages 56–73, 2000.
20. J. Postel. The User Datagram Protocol - RFC 768, 1980.

Author Index

Lecture Notes in Computer Science

For information about Vols. 1–2757
please contact your bookseller or Springer-Verlag